MW00379169

Practicing Basic Skills
in Language Arts

Ray Beck, Ed.D., Peggy Anderson, Ph.D.,
and A. Denise Conrad, Ed.D.

 SOPRIS WEST EDUCATIONAL SERVICES
A CAMBIUM LEARNING COMPANY

BOSTON, MA • NEW YORK, NY • LONGMONT, CO

Copyright 2005 by Sopris West Educational Services
All rights reserved.

07 06 05 04   5 4 3 2 1

Permission is granted to the purchasing teacher to reproduce the
worksheets for use in his or her classroom only. No other portion of
this work may be reproduced or transmitted in any form or by any
means, electronic or mechanical, including photocopying or recording, or by any information storage and retrieval system, without the
express written permission of the publisher.

ISBN 1-59318-271-6

Printed in the United States of America
Published and Distributed by

 SOPRIS WEST EDUCATIONAL SERVICES
A CAMBIUM LEARNING COMPANY

BOSTON, MA • NEW YORK, NY • LONGMONT, CO

4093 Specialty Place ■ Longmont, Colorado 80504 ■ (303) 651-2829
www.sopriswest.com

About the Authors

Ray Beck, Ed.D., is currently Senior Consultant for Sopris West Educational Services, where he trains and consults in the development and dissemination of both positive discipline and fluency programs. As a school psychologist and former Director of Special Education in Great Falls, Montana, Beck directed the development of two U.S. Department of Education-validated programs, *Project RIDE* (Responding to Individual Differences in Education) and *Basic Skill Builders*. Beck conducts training and/or workshops on three Sopris West publications: *RIDE, Basic Skill Builders,* and *One-Minute Academic Functional Assessment: Can't Do It … or Won't Do It?*

A. Denise Conrad, Ed.D., is Director of Special Education in Great Falls, Montana. She has past experience as a teacher and administrator in both general and special education. In addition, Conrad has been providing consultation, workshop, and university-level training to educators and other professionals throughout the United States and Canada since 1973. A primary focus of her work has been training educators to provide effective educational programs and services to children and adolescents with various types of disabilities. Conrad has developed numerous classroom curricula and teacher training materials. She is a codeveloper of the *Basic Skill Builders* Program, and she most recently coauthored *Cool Kids: A Proactive Approach to Social Responsibility.*

Peggy Anderson, Ph.D., is the Superintendent of Schools in Frenchtown, Montana. She was an elementary principal for 14 years in Florida and Montana prior to becoming the Superintendent of Schools. An educator for the past 36 years, Anderson has been an elementary classroom teacher, a special education resource room teacher, and the coordinator of the U.S. Department of Education Validated Project "Basic Skill Builders Precision Teaching." She has been a trainer in both *Basic Skill Builders* and *Project RIDE* and is coauthor of the *Basic Skill Builders Handbook*. Anderson brings her experience from both the regular education classroom and her work with special education students to her training with administrators, teachers, parents, and para-educators. She assists districts as they incorporate *Basic Skill Builders* into their current curriculum.

Contents

Introduction I-1

Scoring Guide SG-1

Nouns and Pronouns

Nouns—Fill in the Blanks 3
Nouns in Isolation—Primary 5
Nouns in Isolation 7
Proper Nouns and Common Nouns—Primary 9
Proper Nouns and Common Nouns 11
Change Proper Nouns to Common Nouns 13
Concrete Nouns 15
Abstract Nouns 17
Collective Nouns 19
Concrete Nouns and Abstract Nouns 21
Common Nouns and Proper Nouns 23
Nouns in Sentences—Primary 25
Nouns in Sentences 27
Nouns in Sentences 29
Singular Nouns and Plural Nouns—Primary 31
Singular Nouns 33
Plural Nouns—Primary 35
Plural Nouns 37
Possessive Nouns 39
Subject Pronouns 41
Pronouns After a Verb 43
Pronouns After a Preposition 45

Verbs

Action Verbs in Isolation—Primary 49
Action Verbs in Isolation 51
Action Verbs—Fill in the Blanks 53
Action Verbs in Sentences—Primary 55
Action Verbs in Sentences 57
Verbs in Isolation 59
Verbs in Sentences 61
Verbs in Sentences 63
Helping Verbs in Isolation 65
Helping Verbs in Isolation 67
Helping Verbs in Sentences 69
Helping Verbs—Fill in the Blanks 71
Verb Phrases in Sentences 73

Linking Verbs in Sentences 75
Transitive and Intransitive Verbs—Fill in the Blanks 77
Active and Passive Verbs 79
Principal Parts of a Verb—Fill in the Blanks 81
Verb Tense 83
Irregular Verbs 85
Irregular Verbs 87
Irregular Verbs 89
Irregular Verbs 91
Correct Form of Irregular Verbs in Sentences 93
Correct Form of Irregular Verbs—Fill in the Blanks 95
Correct Form of Rise/Raise in Sentences 97
Correct Form of Lie/Lay in Sentences 99
Correct Form of Sit/Set in Sentences 101
Correct Form of Lie/Lay, Sit/Set, Rise/Raise 103
Subject-Verb Agreement: Was/Were 105
Subject-Verb Agreement: Am/Are/Is 107
Subject-Verb Agreement: Has/Have 109
Subject-Verb Agreement: Has Been/Have Been 111
Correct Verb Form—Usage 113
Participles in Sentences 115
Gerunds in Sentences 117
Infinitives in Sentences 119
Gerunds, Participles, Infinitives in Sentences 121

Adjectives and Adverbs
Articles: A, An, The in Sentences 125
Adjectives In Phrases 127
Adjectives in Sentences 129
Adjectives in Sentences 131
Adjectives in Sentences 133
Limiting and Descriptive Adjectives 135
Limiting and Descriptive Adjectives—Fill in the Blanks 137
Limiting and Descriptive Adjectives—Fill in the Blanks 139
Proper Adjectives in Sentences 141
Common and Proper Adjectives in Sentences 143
Adjectives and the Words They Modify 145
Adjective Phrases and the Words They Modify 147
Predicate Adjectives 149
Comparative and Superlative Adjectives 151
Comparative and Superlative Adjectives (continued) 153
Comparative and Superlative Adjectives—Fill in the Blanks 155
Irregular Adjectives—Comparative and Superlative 157
Irregular Adjectives—Fill in the Blanks 159
Correct Form of Adjectives in Sentences 161
Corrective Form of Adjectives—Fill in the Blanks 163
Adverbs in Phrases 165
Adverbs in Sentences 167
Adverb—Answers Question: Where? When? How? To What Extent? 169
Adverb—Answers Question: Where? When? How? To What Extend? 171
Adverb—Answers Question—Fill in the Blanks 173
Adverb—Answers Question—Fill in the Blanks (continued) 175
Adverb and the Verb It Modifies 177

Adverb and the Verb It Modifies 179
Adverb and the Adjective It Modifies 181
Adverb and the Adjective It Modifies 183
Adverb and the Adverb It Modifies 185
Adverbs Modifying Adverbs or Verbs 187
Adverbs and the Words They Modify 189

Prepositions

Prepositions in Isolation Primary 193
Prepositions in Isolation 195
Prepositions in Sentences Primary 197
Prepositions in Sentences 199
Prepositions and Prepositional Phrases 201
Prepositional Phrases—Preposition and Object 203
Coordinating Conjunctions in Sentence 205
Correlative Conjunctions in Sentences 207
Conjunctions in Sentences 209
Subordinating Conjunctions 211
Subordinating Conjunctions 213
Interjections in Sentences 215

Sentence Structure

Simple Subject and Verb in Sentences 219
Simple Subject and Verb in Sentences 221
Simple Subjects, Verbs, and Helping Verbs in Sentences 223
Subject and Verb in Sentences 225
Compound Subject and Verb in Sentences 227
Direct Objects—Answers Question What or Whom 229
Direct Object in Sentences 231
Subject, Verb, and Direct Object in Sentences 233
Indirect Object—Answers Question to Whom 235
Indirect Object in Sentences 237
Direct Object and Indirect Object in Sentences 239
Predicate Nominative in Sentences 241
Predicate Noun or Pronoun in Sentences 243
Predicate Nouns, Pronouns, and Linking Verbs in Sentences 245
Predicate Adjectives in Sentences 247
Predicate Adjectives and Linking Verbs in Sentences 249
Review Sheet: Direct Objects, Indirect Objects, Predicate Adjectives, and
    Predicate Nominatives in Sentences 251
Six Parts of Sentences 253
Subject-Verb Agreement 255
Subject-Verb Agreement 257
Subject-Verb Agreement 259
Subject-Verb Agreement 261
Subject-Verb Agreement 263
Indefinite Pronouns and Verb Agreement 265
Subjects Joined By Or-Nor, Either-Or, Neither-Nor, and Verb Agreement 267
Compound Subjects and Verb Agreement 269
Compound Subjects and Verb Agreement 271
Plural Subject-Verb Agreement—Fill in the Blank 273
Singular Subject-Verb Agreement—Fill in the Blank 275
Subject-Verb Agreement—Don't/Doesn't 277

Subject-Verb Agreement—Don't/Doesn't 279
Subject-Verb Agreement—Is/Are, Was/Were, Has/Have 281
Noun Clauses. 283
Adjective Clauses. 285
Adverb Clauses 287
Noun, Adjective, and Adverb Clauses. 289
Subordinate Clauses 291
Independent Clauses. 293
Compound Sentences Into Independent Clauses. 295
Form Compound Sentences Using And, But, Or, Nor, So 297
Form Compound Sentences Using And, But, Or, Nor, So 299
Form Complex Sentences 301
Form Complex Sentences 303
Sentence Fragments and Complete Sentences 305
Complete Sentences and Sentence Fragments 307
Review Fragments and Sentences 309
Sentence Fragments and Run-On Sentences. 311
Fragments, Run-Ons, and Complete Sentences 313
Types of Sentences. 315

Capitalization and Punctuation

Capitalize First Word, I, and Proper Nouns in Sentences—Primary. 319
Capitalization of First Word of Sentence and Pronoun I 321
Geographical Locations and Proper Adjectives. 323
Names of Persons and Geographic Names 325
Names of Organizations, Business Firms, Institutions, and Government Bodies 327
Seasons, Clubs, Corporations, Hotels, Churches 329
Special Events, Calendar Items, Historical Events and Periods, Nationalities,
    Races, and Religions. 331
Titles of Books, Magazines, Poems, Stories, Movies, Songs, Works of Art,
    Historical Documents, Historical Events, and Calendar Items. 333
Brand Names, Ships, Planets, Monuments, and Awards 335
Nationalities, Races, Religions, Ships, Planets, and Monuments 337
Proper Adjectives and Names of School Subjects 339
School Subjects, School Names, and Grades. 341
Titles and Relationships 343
Names of Persons, Deities, Relationships, and Titles 345
Capitalization Review 347
Capitalization Review 349
Capitalization Review 351
Ending Punctuation Using . and ?—Primary 353
Ending Punctuation Using . ? and !—Primary 355
Ending Punctuation 357
Ending Punctuation 359
Commas—Items in a Series. 361
Commas to Separate Adjectives 363
Commas After Introductory Words. 365
Commas for Appositives 367
Commas for Parenthetical Expressions. 369
Commas for Nonessential Clauses 371
Commas for Subordinate Clauses 373
Commas for Independent Clauses 375
Commas for Introductory Elements and Nouns of Direct Address 377

Commas for Appositives and Parenthetical Expressions 379
Commas for Appositives, Parenthetical Expressions, Names, and Titles 381
Commas in Dates and Addresses. 383
Commas in Series, Dates, and Addresses. 385
Comma Review 387
Apostrophe to Show Possession 389
Apostrophes to Form Plurals of Letters, Numbers, Signs, and Words 391
Apostrophes to Form Plurals of Letters, Numbers, and Signs. 393
Apostrophe Review 395
Apostrophe Review 397
Apostrophe Review 399
Apostrophe Review 401
Semicolons Between Independent Clauses. 403
Semicolons Between Independent Clauses Joined by Adverbial Connectives. 405
Semicolons in Items in a Series. 407
Semicolon Review 409
Colons for Time and Salutations. 411
Colon Review. 413
Quotation Marks in Conversation 415
Quotation Marks to Enclose Titles 417
Quotation Marks Within a Quotation 419
Quotation Marks and Other Punctuation Marks 421
Quotation Marks and Other Punctuation Marks in Conversation. 423
Hyphens in Numbers and Fractions 425
Hyphens and Dashes. 427
Hyphen Review. 429
Parentheses 431
Underlining Titles of Books, Plays, and Periodicals 433
Underlining Titles of Movies, Works of Art, and Long Musical Compositions 435
Underlining Titles of Ships, Trains, and Airplanes 437
Underlining Review. 439
Punctuation Combinations. 441

Vocabulary Development

Antonyms 445
Antonyms 447
Synonyms and Antonyms. 449
Synonyms and Antonyms. 451
Synonyms and Antonyms. 453
Homonyms: To, Too, or Two. 455
Homonyms: There, Their, They're 457
Homonym Review. 459
Homonym Review. 461
Homonym Review. 463
Homonym Review. 465
Prefixes: Pro, En, Re, Im, Dis 467
Prefixes: Mis, Re, Un, Trans, Dis, Con. 469
Prefixes: De, Super, Im, Sub, Inter. 471
Prefixes: Pre, Manu, Ego, Mono, Sur, Ex 473
Prefixes: Ab, Be, Bi, Co, Com, In, Tri. 475
Prefixes: Circum, Com, Con, Dia, Extra, Out, Post, Trans, Sym, Syn. 477
Prefixes: Mis, Un, Dis, Re, Trans, Con. 479
Prefixes: Pre, Mono, Manu, Sur, Ego, Ex 481

Dictionary Skills

Alphabet: Beginning, Middle, End of Alphabet 485
Alphabet: Beginning, Middle, End of Alphabet 487
Alphabet: Two Letters That Follow a Letter 489
Alphabet: Two Letters That Come Before a Letter 491
Alphabet: Two Letters That Come Before and After a Letter 493
Alphabet: Two Letters That Come Before and After a Letter 495
Alphabetical Order: Before or After Guide Word 497
Alphabetical Order: Before or After Guide Word 499
Alphabetical Order: Before or After Guide Word 501
Alphabetical Order: Before or After Guide Word 503
Alphabetical Order: Before, After, or Between Guide Words 505
Alphabetical Order: Before, After, or Between Guide Words 507
Alphabetical Order: Found on Which Page? 509
Alphabetical Order: Placing 4 Words in Alphabetical Order 511
Alphabetical Order: Placing 4 Words in Alphabetical Order 513
Alphabetical Order : Placing 5 Words in Alphabetical Order 515
Alphabetical Order: Placing 5 Words in Alphabetical Order 517
Alphabetical Order: Placing 5 Words in Alphabetical Order 519
Alphabetical Order: Placing 5 Words in Alphabetical Order 521
Alphabetical Order: Placing 5 Words in Alphabetical Order 523
Alphabetical Order: Placing 5 Words in Alphabetical Order 525
Alphabetical Order: Choose Words Falling Between Two Guide Words 527
Alphabetical Order: Choose Words Falling Between Two Guide Words 529
Alphabetical Order: Choose Words Falling Between Two Guide Words 531
Alphabetical Order: Choose Words Falling Between Two Guide Words 533
Alphabetical Order: Choose Words Falling Between Two Guide Words 535
Alphabetical Order: Choose Words Falling Between Two Guide Words 537
Guide Words: Before Page, Same Page, After Page 539
Guide Words: Before Page, Same Page, After Page 541
Guide Words: Before Page, Same Page, After Page 543
Guide Words: Before Page, Same Page, After Page 545
Guide Words: Find Page in Dictionary for Each Word 547

Appendix

Equal Interval Graph 551
Academic Chart 553

Practicing Basic Skills in Language Arts

Introduction

An individual is considered fluent in a skill, whether it is athletic, musical, artistic, or academic, when he or she is able to demonstrate the skill accurately and perform it quickly. Educators often equate fluency with words like: "automatic," "without thinking," "flows," "can do it quickly," "smooth," and "competent." To become fluent, students need first to be taught the skill and then provided multiple opportunities to practice it.

Becoming fluent means there is a higher probability that the student will retain the skill over time, that the skill can be applied to higher-level tasks, that the student will be less distracted, and that the skill will be generalized across settings. It is important to remember that fluency comes after the student has been "taught" the skill. Without appropriate instruction, including modeling and guided practice, independent practice will have little, if any, impact. Our motto is: TEACH FIRST, then practice.

The full One-Minute Fluency Builders series is a collection of over 1,500 basic skill sheets that focus on math, reading, grammar, spelling, and handwriting, as well as other content areas. These are accompanied by a set of classroom procedures and a monitoring process that, when combined, significantly increase the chances of students in regular and special settings becoming comfortable and competent in everyday skills.

Once a student has been taught a skill, five steps guide the process for fluency building:

I.   Selecting the Skill and Fluency Sheet(s)
II. Providing Practice Opportunities
III. Monitoring and Charting Progress
IV. Making Data-Based Decisions
V.   Refining, Reviewing, and Selecting the Next Skill to Practice

Questions to consider in the process:

- What specific skill will be practiced, and which Fluency Sheet(s) can be used to facilitate the practice activity?
- How will the goal be set, and what is an appropriate goal for each of my students?
- How will practice opportunities be structured during the school day?
- What kind of chart or graph will be used to keep track of the data?
- What are the guidelines for making data-based decisions?
- What is the next step—do we move on, continue, or step back?

The Language Arts Fluency Sheets contain fluency sheets for both primary and intermediate or more advanced skills. In each skill sequence, the Fluency Sheets are organized from easy to more difficult. Keep in mind, it is *not* necessary that a student complete or demonstrate fluency on each sheet in the entire sequence. Part of the process (Step 1) is to select the Fluency Sheet that best fits your language arts curriculum and the needs of your particular student(s).

Step I. Selecting the Skill and Fluency Sheet(s)

When selecting a language arts skill on which to work, first decide the general skill area you want to address: grammar, mechanics, or dictionary skills. Fluency Sheets are available in these and other areas with varying levels of difficulty.

Fluency Sheets can be used to reinforce a skill that the classroom teacher is currently teaching, or they can be used as practice to increase fluency on skills that have been previously taught but with which the student has not yet developed fluency. Recognizing action words or verbs, for example, is a new skill for a first grader. The teacher selects Fluency Sheets that are tied to the classroom curriculum as one way to practice a skill as it is being introduced and taught by the teacher. Identifying action words is not a new skill for a third grader, but rather a review activity. Some student(s) may have developed accuracy, but are not yet fluent in this skill. In other words, the recognition of action words or verbs is not at an automatic level and easily retrieved, nor can they be used for more complex tasks. To assist in building fluency, a teacher would select a Fluency Sheet at a level where the student feels comfortable and confident, and where practice will have a positive impact on helping the student begin to strengthen the skill. Within each of the subdivisions of language arts basic skills, Fluency Sheets range from beginning skills through the more complex applications. Skills that are introduced at primary level become more complex as the student advances and would move, for example, from identifying action words at the primary level to identifying verbs and/or helping verbs, through transitive and intransitive verbs, at the upper intermediate level.

Once you have selected the skill to be practiced, the next step is to ask yourself how the student will be asked to demonstrate knowledge. To answer this question, teachers will need to take learning channels into consideration. Quite simply, learning channels offer a clear way of explaining the modality students use to receive the information (the "input channel") and how we ask the child to respond (the "output channel"). In language arts, most often the input channel is See (see the problem) and the output channel is Write (write the answer), but not always. You might elect to have the student See-Say (see the problem and say the answer) or in some cases See-Mark (see the problem and mark the answer) or even Hear-Write (hear the problem and write the answer).

The following matrix will help you determine the learning channel to use with your student(s).

INPUT (Problem)	OUTPUT (Answer)
See	Write
See	Say
See	Mark
Hear	Write
Hear	Say
Think	Write
Think	Say

Selecting the learning channel may in part depend upon prerequisite skills that the student has demonstrated in the past. In other words, if language arts has typically been presented in a See-Write format, and the student has a sense of comfort and confidence, it follows that subsequent fluency sheets might well be presented in similar fashion. Teachers should also view the use of learning channels as an opportunity to reinforce a skill by practicing using a different combination (e.g., See-Say rather than See-Write). A further explanation will be provided when we talk about practice opportunities. In the beginning select the learning channel that is the most common way students will be responding to the tasks. All tasks selected using See (or reading) as the input channel will need to be at the student's current reading level.

Setting the Fluency Goal

There should be clear expectations defining the level of performance the student must exhibit in order to be considered fluent. After selecting a starting point, it is important to set a goal indicating how accurately and quickly the student must demonstrate the skill before moving on. Remember, a fluent student is one who can perform the skill accurately with little or no hesitation. Accuracy plus speed results in automaticity.

When clear and high expectations are set and are reasonable, students are more likely to engage and attempt to reach the goal. In some cases, however, it might be necessary to establish a short-term aim rather than expect the student to immediately reach a final fluency standard. In this way, teachers can help students celebrate reaching short-term aims, which is reinforcing and demonstrates that skill acquisition is progressing.

With One-Minute Fluency Builders we use "aims" to represent intermediate or short-term goals, and we use "fluency standards" to represent a level of performance that ensures retention over time, ease in transferring the skill to more complex problems, and generalization.

In the area of See-Write words or sentences, the aim is in part dependent upon the student's fine motor skill of writing. An aim for a kindergarten or first grade student will not be the same as for a fourth or fifth grader. The kindergarten student is still working on the tool skill of writing letters or words, while at the fourth grade level and beyond the skill of writing letters and words is automatic—

it takes no thought as to how to form the letters. As a teacher uses the Fluency Sheets, he or she will see that the number of problems and the size and spacing of the numbers have been adjusted to match the developmental level of the student.

There are no suggested fluency standards in language arts. Because the skills are dependent upon the reading ability of the students and the tool skill of writing letters/words, as well as their knowledge of the area being assessed, each group of students may have a different standard based on the grade level and their writing ability. The two procedures commonly used for setting aims or standards are (1) to use either the performance of students who are considered fluent in the class, or (2) to use an adult's fluency in the skill and adjust to the skill level and grade level of the students.

Peer performance is often a fair and effective method for determining aims, particularly if there are no established fluency standards, or little is known about the specific tasks. It is helpful to have three or four peers who are considered fluent take at least three timed practices and average these students' scores for the individual or classwide fluency standard.

The teacher might instead use his or her performance as a beginning standard and, dependent upon the age and grade level of the student, adjust accordingly. Fluency is the smooth, effortless performance of a skill at the student's achievement level. By fifth and sixth grades the students, if fluent readers, should be able to perform the task, when proficient, at close to the same rate as the teacher.

You may want to set fluency ranges, e.g., 70–80, rather than a single specific number. Remember that aims are not set in stone; aims are just short-term goals. For every aim that you set, you will have students who will not only achieve the aim, but will exceed it. As the teacher you need to ensure that students have realistic aims and realize that aims can change as students become more fluent in both the tool skills and the basic skills. Set clear and high expectations for your students.

Step II. Providing Practice Opportunities

Once the skill has been taught, a closely related Fluency Sheet has been selected, and an aim or fluency standard has been established, it is time to start conducting daily practice sessions with the students. Fluency building is guided by timed practice. Pioneers in the movement found that one-minute timed practice provides a sufficient time frame in which students can maximize their performance and that teachers can fit into their busy daily schedules while collecting data on student growth each day.

Managing the Practice Time

Each student has his or her own Fluency Sheet to use, with the answers printed on the back of the page to use in the correction process. To manage the materials, students use a manila folder with a sheet of clear acetate taped inside upon which to write their responses. Acetate is a heavier grade material than a typical sheet of transparency, and it increases the life span of the folder.

NOTE: Student materials such as the acetate and marking pens are sold separately and are available through Sopris West Educational Services.

The Fluency Sheet is placed under the acetate and with a dry erase or water-soluble pen, the student writes the answers on the acetate cover sheet. When the one-minute time sample is complete, the student turns the sheet over, with answers facing up, places it under the acetate, and corrects. It is important to let your students know that they are not expected to complete the entire sheet in one minute, but the expectation is that with each timed practice they will complete more problems.

At the end of each row, you will see a number in parentheses; this number is the number of correct responses for that row.

Timings can be conducted in a couple of different ways.

1. The teacher can start and stop all students at the same time using a stopwatch or the second hand of a clock or watch.
2. An audiotape with music that includes a tone at one-minute intervals can be used. It should have 10–15 minutes of timed music where students can start or stop on their own and don't have to wait for others to be ready. Students should manage their own timed practice, starting/stopping, counting corrects and errors, and self-recording their scores daily.

Many teachers find that starting each math class with the timed practice session sets the tone for the remainder of the class period. Students are ready to work and have practiced a basic skill before moving into the lesson to be taught that day. Another option is to set up the timed practice to occur right after a recess or a break. In this method, materials can be set out before the break; as students file back into the classroom, the music tape begins and students start as they are ready. This also helps to set the stage for the next class and to bring students into the classroom quietly and with a purpose.

Practice Options

Use a different channel to make the skill easier. The See-Write or paper-pencil activity is the easiest channel to manage in a classroom because all of the students can be working at the same time (as a group activity), possibly on different Fluency Sheets. Most teachers elect to use the Fluency Sheets in this manner; however, they can also be used as a See-Say or oral activity if writing is a problem for a student and you want to measure content knowledge when writing is not a fluent skill. For this option the student needs a partner (a peer, a cross-age tutor, volunteer, or teacher) who can listen as the student says the correct responses and mark the errors when they occur.

Use Paired Timings

A teacher might also elect to practice a tool skill sheet before doing the See-Write Fluency Sheet. This strategy is called Paired Timings. A tool skill is the prerequisite skill or building block for the basic skill. For a third grader working on basic sentence structure, the tool skill might be recognizing what is an action word. This skill needs to be at a fluent level, allowing the student to use this information to identify what is a complete sentence. What is a basic skill at one level becomes a tool skill at a more advanced grade level. Identifying the parts of speech in a sentence is a basic skill for middle grade students. The tool skills necessary to perform this basic skill are identifying nouns, verbs, adjectives, adverbs, prepositions, conjunctions, and interjections. If these skills are not at a fluent level, then the basic skill of identifying parts of speech in a sentence is very difficult for the student. If a student is struggling with identifying the basic skill of parts of speech in a sentence because adverbs are still a problem, then the paired

timing Fluency Sheet could be Identify Adverbs prior to the basic skill timing.

Change the Learning Channel to Make the Skill More Challenging

Learning channels might also be used during the practice session as a way to reinforce a basic skill that has been practiced to fluency using another channel. An example would be to use the See-Mark Being Verbs Fluency Sheet, first as a See-Write activity until the students are fluent, and then, using the same Fluency Sheet, change the learning channel to Think-Write to help students strengthen this skill.

Teachers should always start with the largest slice of the curriculum possible to help students move through the curriculum quickly and efficiently. If all students started on Action Verbs, Being Verbs, Helping Verbs and so on, students would fall quickly behind in the curriculum. For most students working on fluency building, it is best to start large and then "slice back" when you see that you have taken too large a slice. One way to determine where to start is to analyze the more complex Fluency Sheets to see where the breakdown is, what problems are giving a student trouble, and use this as either a starting point or provide more teaching or practice in that slice of the skill. Another way to start is to tie the Fluency Sheet to the actual skill being taught in the curriculum that day or week so that practice is *directly* related to instruction.

Step III.   Monitoring and Charting Progress

The most compelling argument for monitoring student performance is in the use of data to make more informed instructional and curricular decisions. By keeping track of performance, you—and more importantly, the students—can see where they have been, where they are now, and where they might be in the future. This continual monitoring allows us to analyze the past, examine the present, and predict the future. As a by-product, the students have the benefit of immediate feedback and a continual visual display of their progress.

Several options exist for tracking students' daily scores. The first is a simple score sheet where the date is posted, the Fluency Sheet is listed, and the correct and error counts are recorded. This procedure allows students to directly view their progress from day to day.

Score Sheet

Date	Fluency Sheet	Correct	Error
10/15	Action Verbs in Isolation	65	5
10/16	Action Verbs in Isolation	70	2
10/17	Action Verbs in Isolation	75	1
10/18	Action Verbs in Sentences	63	2
10/19	Action Verbs in Sentences	68	1
10/22	Action Verbs in Sentences	72	0

Another option is to provide a graphic picture of the scores by using a graph common in most classrooms, which shows both corrects and errors as well as the day. For example, the data recorded in the score sheet would look like this on an Equal Interval Graph:

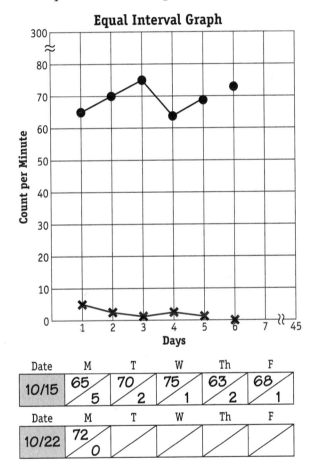

This option allows a student to see his or her progress visually as the lines on the graph show the improvement over time. Students mark the corrects (expressed by a dot •) and errors (expressed by ×) on their graphs as soon as the timed practice is completed. At the end of the week, students connect their dots with a line and connect their ×'s with a line. They do not connect the lines between weeks. Growth can be tracked visually so that student and teacher

can view past performance and present level of fluency.

A third and more accurate tracking option is using a chart that allows student and teacher to see growth proportionally. While this chart, the Academic Chart, may seem somewhat overwhelming at first glance, with practice and use it will become a tool that not only tracks progress, but also allows the teacher to be more precise when making instructional and curricular decisions. Data on this chart can be analyzed and interpreted using proportional growth statements. Because the data is displayed proportionally (the way the learning actually occurs), by extending the learning line, a teacher or student can predict when an aim will be met. On this chart you will see that the day lines have been conveniently divided into separate weeks. This allows the student to connect the number of

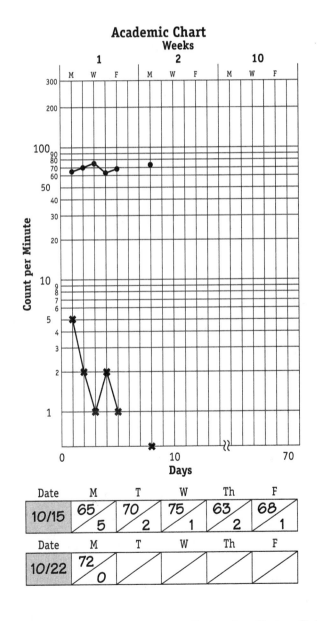

corrects (expressed as dots •) and errors (expressed as ×'s) within the week, but not across the weeks, allowing for more definition to the data.

At first and second grade levels the students can record the number of corrects and errors on the score sheet. By third grade recording of the data on either of the charts/graphs suggested should be a student-managed activity. The recording of data is completed as soon as the timed practice is finished and students have checked for the number of correct digits and errors. Both scores should be recorded; fluency building involves both accuracy and speed. You should be looking for the number of errors to decrease (accuracy) as the number of correct responses increases (speed). A fluent language arts student is one who can respond both quickly and accurately.

See the Appendix for graphs and charts.

Step IV.   Making Data-Based Decisions

To maximize academic achievement, students cannot waste time practicing skills they find too easy, or skills in which they have already become fluent. Nor can they afford the wasted time and frustration that occurs when they "spin their wheels" practicing a skill in a manner that does not result in increased performance or learning. To determine when it is time to move on or time to intervene, the recorded data should be frequently and regularly reviewed, at least once a week. The decision to change is based on three basic rules:

1. **IF at Aim or at Fluency Standard for Two Days, THEN Move to a More Difficult Fluency Sheet**

     If a student's scores are at or above the previously set aim or fluency standard, it is time for a change. To ensure that scores are valid, students are typically expected to demonstrate performance for more than one timed practice.

     When students reach their aim or fluency standard on the first day, teachers may want to check their performance on the second day to ensure that the aim or fluency standard has truly been reached. A teacher might want to have students who are "going for aim" do their second timed practice as a pencil and paper activity rather than using the acetate so that the teacher has a hard copy on the final day to review. Another method is to have a separate

table set up for those students "going for aim" so that the teacher can monitor their timed practice to ensure that the aim is reached.

2. **IF Three Days of Little or No Growth, THEN Change**

     It is possible that students might stop making progress before reaching the set aim or fluency standard. When the data "flattens out" as displayed on the graph or chart, it suggests that the learning has stalled. Once students have three consecutive days of these "flat data," it is unlikely that further increases in performance will occur without some kind of instructional intervention to reactivate learning. Interventions will be discussed in the next section.

3. **IF Less Than 25% Growth Per Week, THEN Change**

     Learning may be occurring, but at such a minimal level that we cannot expect students to reach their aims in any reasonable number of days. Experience and research suggest that we should see at least 25% growth from one week to the next.

Mathematically, a teacher can divide the median (middle score) of the first week into the median score of the second week. For example, if the median score in week one was 30 correct and in week two 35 correct, begin by dividing 35 by 30, which equals 1.16. This is a 16% growth from week one to week two. In this case there was not the minimum of 25% growth.

Another method is to draw a line through the data points for the two weeks that best represent the slope of the data set, and determine if there is at least 25% growth. A template is provided below that can be used in determining whether there is at least a 25% growth pattern.

x 1.25

Perhaps the simplest method to determine growth is to draw a line (free hand) through the data, then place a pencil over the line and judge whether the slope is acceptable. Following is an example:

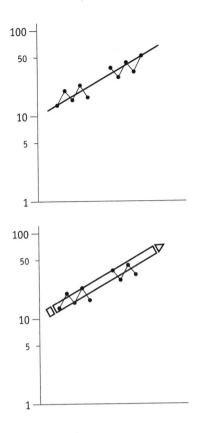

Once a decision has been made that a change is necessary, the next step is: What Change? What Next?

Step V. Refining, Reviewing, and Selecting the Next Skill to Practice

You have reviewed the data. You have looked at the decision rules and see that a change is warranted. How do you decide the next step? This decision will depend on several factors including the level of skill development at which the student is operating with respect to the skill being practiced. When learning a new skill, students typically move through a series of specific skill development levels or stages.

In the **acquisition stage** students are acquiring a new skill. Their scores are usually below 25 correct responses per minute. They are learning how to correctly respond to that skill. Timed practice with Fluency Sheets should not replace teacher instruction, but can be used to monitor the effectiveness of a teaching strategy. If a change is needed and students are performing at the acquisition level, consider:

- Providing more direct instruction on the skill.
- Working on tool skills along with or instead of the current skill.

- Using paired timings with the tool skill or a related easier skill as a warm up activity before the regular skill.
- Slicing the skill to a subset of the skill (e.g., Helping Verbs instead of All Verbs).
- Stepping back to just the tool skill to build fluency and confidence.
- Changing the learning channel to one that is easier for the student.
- Providing more frequent feedback, possibly even reinforcing each response.

In the **fluency building** or **practice stage** students are not yet at their aim but can respond at a rate of more than 25 correct responses per minute. They are refining a skill they have previously acquired. They are becoming more accurate, as well as increasing their frequency. It is at this level that students are working toward mastery of the skill as well as fluency. If a change is necessary when the student is performing at this level, consider:

- Providing instruction specifically addressing the errors made.
- Identifying the errors and hesitations:
  - Encourage student to skip tasks they don't know how to do, or
  - Cross out unknown tasks.
  - Use flash cards to practice before timing with the Fluency Sheets.
  - Use See-Say for a warm-up before doing as a See-Write.
- Providing many short, repeated practice opportunities of 15 seconds, 30 seconds, or one minute in length.
- Practicing identified tasks:
  - See-Say correct responses on the errors and hesitations.
  - See-Copy tasks and correct responses, using the answer sheet for the practice.
- Using paired timings to increase fluency:
  - Warm up with a slice of the total skill.
  - Warm up with a tool skill practice.
  - Warm up timings using different learning channels (e.g., See-Say correct responses).
- Doing multiple timings—do the timing twice and record and chart the best score.
- Keeping the learning channel consistent from day to day, unless a learning channel change is necessary to facilitate growth.

In the **fluency stage** students are strengthening their command of the skill. A fluent learner can demonstrate both accuracy and speed. For example, fluent performance is the difference between knowing how to type accurately but slowly, and being a competent typist. The skill has become automatic and can now be generalized and applied to other, more complex situations. Change is necessary at this level to continue to challenge the student. Consider:

- Continuing the skill past the aim or fluency standard until the chart flattens and there is no growth.
- Raising the aim.
- Having the child establish his or her own aim.
- Changing the task to a more difficult, but related, one (e.g., from Identify Action Verbs to Identify Helping Verbs and Action Verbs).
- Changing the task to another set of skills (e.g., from Identify the Nouns in a Sentence to Identify the Adjectives and the Nouns They Modify).
- Changing the learning channel.
- Doing maintenance timings on the skill periodically to ensure retention.

Whatever the new task, it should add enough curriculum weight that the student's initial scores drop back down to the acquisition or fluency building stage, allowing for continued learning or growth.

Material Management

One of the keys to successful implementation of One-Minute Fluency Builders is establishing a routine for daily practice sessions. Years of practical experience have demonstrated that students must be skilled in participating in timed practice, scoring, and then recording their individual performances. Much like practicing a new academic skill, students should also practice the steps in conducting and scoring one-minute time practices. The following is a typical day:

1. Request that students retrieve their individual folders. Skill folders have been previously constructed by taping a clear piece of acetate to the inside of the folder and an Academic Chart or Equal Interval Graph on the outside of the folder. The folder and the chart are labeled with the student's name. The curriculum area, language arts, is written in the lower right corner of the chart. The Fluency Sheet is placed under the acetate. The folders can be kept at the individual student's desk, or at a central location in the classroom.

2. Once the folders are available and opened, the students should make sure that the appropriate Fluency Sheet is properly placed under the clear acetate. The teacher monitors to ensure that all of the students are ready to begin their timings.

3. Students are reminded to complete as many tasks as possible during the one-minute timed practice.

4. Two options exist when conducting the one-minute timed practice. In the first, the teacher instructs the students to "Please begin," and then in 60 seconds says, "Thank you, stop."

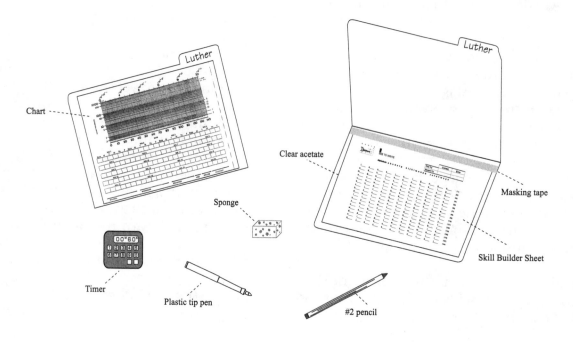

Chart

Sponge

Timer

Plastic tip pen

Clear acetate

Masking tape

Skill Builder Sheet

#2 pencil

Luther

Luther

The second choice involves a music or tone audiotape. In this instance, start a tape player and allow the music to run for 60-second intervals, which are marked by a distinct tone or beep. You can also use a tape with no music, just a tone every 60 seconds. Students score and record the number of corrects and errors from their first trial and prepare for a second try. Give students a second try with the same Fluency Sheet.

5. Scoring is relatively simple. Almost all Fluency Sheets have an answer sheet printed on the reverse side. The answer sheet can be placed under the acetate allowing answers to be quickly scored. More than one timing each day using the same Fluency Sheet is encouraged. Students note their corrects and errors at the top of the page and clean the rest of the acetate using a small sponge or paper towel in preparation for the next timing. The student will record the better of the two trials on their chart/graph.

   NOTE: *Keep sponges collected in a jar with a teaspoon of vinegar and rinse out regularly so that they retain a fresh smell.*

6. The next step is putting the data on the chart/graph. If using the Academic Chart, instruct students how to take the raw scores (corrects and errors) and write them in the appropriate day of the week box on the lower half of the chart. If using an Academic Chart or an Equal Interval Graph, teach the students to plot the corrects and errors on the appropriate day line and frequency line intersection on the chart itself. From third grade on, students should be able to do their own charting. Be sure to use a pencil when charting, because it is difficult if not impossible to erase marks made with an ink or marking pen.

7. At this point, depending on the overall plan, students can either move on to completing additional timed practices on other Fluency Sheets in other curriculum areas, meet with the teacher for further feedback, or store their folders until they use them again. In any case, teachers should review students' performances at least once a week, and more often if students are at aim or seem to be struggling with the task.

Working with students with special needs or in a remedial placement requires essentially the same materials and procedures as working with general classroom students. For example, the difference between managing a group of 25 to 30 general classroom students and 15 students with special needs is that the latter require more individual planning and support. Teaching students who are at risk often means more curriculum slices, tool skill exercises, opportunities to practice, and more time spent in decision making. Additional procedural differences are:

- In these classes there are typically fewer students, but they may have highly complex tasks. The challenge is to individualize, while at the same time managing the timed practice without constant attention. It may be helpful to establish an area or station where students can take their timed practices.
- Establishing a Fluency Sheets "bank" similar to the one found in regular classrooms allows for the storage of reproducible masters, as well as a place for students to store their individual folders.
- Once students are familiar with the location of their individual folders and the timing procedure, they will become their own best managers.

Practicing Basic Skills in Language Arts is a program developed to build basic skills and remediate skill deficits. This program is for educators who believe that in order to be successful in academic settings or the world of work, students need to be fluent in the core skills. The Fluency Sheets and related materials enable teachers to implement a practice program that will improve the students' ability to:

- Learn new skills.
- Maintain newly acquired skills.
- Transfer skills to more complex tasks.
- Apply these skills across the curriculum and to everyday life.

For teachers, One-Minute Fluency Builders provides immediate and positive change in student performance; for students, it provides clear objectives, meaningful feedback, and, most importantly, a dynamic tool for learning.

Suggested materials include acetate, manila folders, and marking pens.
Student materials are available through Sopris West Educational Services.
(800) 547-6747
www.sopriswest.com

References

Beck, R. (1979a). *Report for the Office of Education joint dissemination review panel.* Great Falls, MT: Precision Teaching Project.

Beck, R. (1979b). *Remediation of learning deficits through precision teaching: A follow-up study.* Unpublished doctoral dissertation. University of Montana, Missoula.

Beck, R., & Clement, R. (1991). The Great Falls precision teaching project: An historical review. *Journal of Precision Teaching,* 8(2), 8–12.

Binder, C. (1996). Behavioral fluency: Evolution of a new paradigm. *The Behavior Analyst,* 19(2), 163–197.

Binder, C. (2003). *Doesn't everybody need fluency? Performance Improvement—Special Master's Series Issue.* 42(3), 14–20.

Johnson, K. R., & Layng, T. V. J. (1992). Breaking the structuralist barrier: Literacy and numeracy with fluency. *American Psychologist.* 47, 1475–1490.

Kubina, R. M. Jr., & Morrison, R. S. (2000). Fluency in education. *Behavior and Social Issues,* (10), 83–99.

National Reading Panel. (2000). *Report of the National Reading Panel: Teaching children to read.* Retrieved from http://www.nichd.nih.gov/publications/hrppubskey.cfm.

Torgesen, J. K., Rashotte, C. A., & Alexander, A. W. (2001). Principles of fluency instruction in reading: Relationships with established empirical outcomes. In M. Wolf (Ed.), *Dyslexia, fluency and the brain.* Timonium, MD: York Press.

Williams, J. P. (Ed.) (2001). [Special issue]. *Scientific Studies of Reading,* 5(3), 203–288.

Scoring Guide

Scoring is relatively simple. Each Fluency Sheet has an answer sheet printed on the reverse side. Each student compares his or her answers to those on the answer sheet and determines how many **correct and incorrect** letters, words, phrases, or notations he or she has completed at the end of each timing. As described earlier, with each successive timing a student should be able to increase the number of correct answers (correct letters, words, phrases, or notations).

How to Determine Corrects and Errors

After the students have completed each timing, they determine how many errors (letters, words, phrases, or notations) they completed in the timing. This number is recorded at the top of the page under "Error." They then determine the total number of possible letters, words, phrases, or notations that could have been part of the answer and subtract any errors from the total possible. This is the total and is recorded at the top of the page under "Correct." You may choose to have students graph both their number of errors and corrects or only the number of corrects.

To make it easier to determine the number of possible letters, words, phrases, or notations, the number at the end of each line or column is the total number of letters, words, phrases, or notations (e.g., underlines, arrows, etc.) in that line or column.

Determining number of letters, words, phrases, or notations

Count all letters, words, phrases, or notations that are part of the answer. For instance, some items might ask you to circle the preposition and underline the prepositional phrase. One point is given for correctly circling and another point is given for correctly underlining. Thus, there were 2 points possible.

Additional points and examples

- Some Fluency Sheets do not have answer sheets; for those the cumulative scores appear on the student sheet.
- For some Fluency Sheets there is more than one possible answer for each item. Those Fluency Sheets are marked "Answers May Vary," an example is given, and the teacher should use his or her own knowledge to score.
- An important element in scoring is to remain consistent and score each timing using the same criteria.

Nouns and Pronouns

Nouns—Fill in the Blanks 3
Nouns in Isolation—Primary 5
Nouns in Isolation 7
Proper Nouns and Common Nouns—
    Primary 9
Proper Nouns and Common Nouns 11
Change Proper Nouns to Common
    Nouns 13
Concrete Nouns 15
Abstract Nouns... 17
Collective Nouns... 19
Concrete Nouns and Abstract Nouns 21
Common Nouns and Proper Nouns............. 23

Nouns in Sentences—Primary 25
Nouns in Sentences....................................... 27
Nouns in Sentences....................................... 29
Singular Nouns and Plural Nouns—
    Primary... 31
Singular Nouns... 33
Plural Nouns—Primary 35
Plural Nouns 37
Possessive Nouns.. 39
Subject Pronouns 41
Pronouns After a Verb.................................. 43
Pronouns After a Preposition........................ 45

ONE-MINUTE FLUENCY BUILDER SERIES

	Correct	Error
First Try		
Second Try		

THINK TO WRITE

Nouns—Fill in the Blanks

Directions: Nouns are name words. Nouns say the name of a person, place, or thing.
Example: Fred rode his bike to school. *Fred, bike,* and *school* are nouns. Think of a noun for each blank space below.

_____ ate a _____ yesterday. Tomorrow is _____ birthday. In this room I see a _____ .

Yesterday, _____ found a _____ on her desk. We own a _____ . It is kept in a _____ .

_____ knitted her a _____ . Today I saw a _____ at the _____ . _____ drives a _____ .

red _____ . Please close the _____ . Mary played _____ with her _____ . The kittens played _____ .

with a _____ . Tomorrow _____ is going to _____ . _____ lost her _____ .

order a _____ to go. _____ are pretty to look at. _____ are heavy to carry. Climbing

mountains is a hard _____ . Running away will not solve the _____ . The detective solved the _____ .

was eaten by the _____ . Blue is the color of _____ . Mary is married to _____ .

is his little _____ . _____ is the name of the _____ who led the _____ to

victory. Please, wind the _____ . Put out the _____ . _____ are for climbing. When are we going to _____

? Ling kissed her _____ . Tell me about your _____ . His new _____ was torn.

began to fall when the thunder sounded. The _____ ran across the street and hit the _____ .

Practicing Basic Skills in Language Arts • 3

© 2005 Sopris West Educational Services. All rights reserved. Practicing Basic Skills in Language Arts. Purchaser has permission to photocopy this page for classroom use only.

ONE-MINUTE FLUENCY BUILDER SERIES

THINK TO WRITE

Nouns—Fill in the Blanks

Directions: Nouns are name words. Nouns say the name of a person, place, or thing.
Example: Fred rode his bike to school. *Fred, bike,* and *school* are nouns. Think of a noun for each blank space below.

	Correct	Error
First Try		
Second Try		

_____ ate a _____ yesterday. Tomorrow is _____ birthday. In this room I see a _____. (4)

Yesterday, _____ found a _____ on her desk. We own a _____. It is kept in a _____. (8)

knitted her a _____. Today I saw a _____ at the _____. _____ drives a _____ (13)

red _____. Please close the _____. Mary played _____ with her _____. The kittens played _____ (17)

with a _____. Tomorrow _____ is going to _____. _____ lost her _____ (22)

order a _____ to go. _____ are pretty to look at. _____ are heavy to carry. Climbing (26)

mountains is a hard _____. Running away will not solve the _____. The detective solved the _____. (29)

_____ was eaten by the _____. Blue is the color of _____. Mary is married to _____ (33)

is his little _____. _____ is the name of the _____. _____ who led the _____ to (38)

victory. Please, wind the _____. Put out the _____. _____ are for climbing. When are we going to (41)

_____? Ling kissed her _____. Tell me about your _____. His new _____ was torn. (45)

began to fall when the thunder sounded. The _____ ran across the street and hit the _____. (48)

ANSWER SHEET

Practicing Basic Skills in Language Arts • 4

© 2005 Sopris West Educational Services. All rights reserved. Practicing Basic Skills in Language Arts. Purchaser has permission to photocopy this page for classroom use only.

Nouns in Isolation—Primary

Directions: Underline all of the nouns (person, place, or thing).

ONE-MINUTE FLUENCY BUILDER SERIES

		Correct	Error
First Try			
Second Try			

cat	is	house	the	man	dog	and	ran	is	tree
fish	lake	for	jump	boy	come	boat	not	said	girl
go	new	ball	fast	desk	walk	car	run	sit	sleeping
sing	train	ate	tent	do	like	chair	yes	baby	door
think	mouse	an	old	barn	cup	stop	open	flat	city
teacher	school	no	table	some	of	doctor	then	shut	shirt
child	may	shoes	walk	flower	horse	mother	skip	this	know
sister	as	ant	any	doll	round	wheel	every	book	bird

Practicing Basic Skills in Language Arts • 5

© 2005 Sopris West Educational Services. All rights reserved. Practicing Basic Skills in Language Arts. Purchaser has permission to photocopy this page for classroom use only.

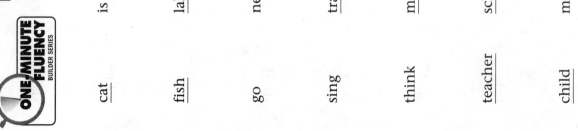

ONE-MINUTE FLUENCY BUILDER SERIES

SEE TO MARK

Nouns in Isolation—Primary
Directions: Underline all of the nouns (person, place, or thing).

	Correct	Error
First Try		
Second Try		

cat	is	house	the	man	dog	and	ran	is	tree	(5)
fish	lake	for	jump	boy	boat	not	said	girl		(11)
go	new	ball	fast	desk	walk	car	run	sit	sleeping	(14)
sing	train	ate	tent	do	like	chair	yes	baby		(19)
think	mouse	an	old	barn	cup	like	do	yes		(23)
teacher	school	no	some	of	doctor	then	shut	shirt		(28)
child	may	shoes	walk	flower	horse	mother	skip	this		(33)
sister	as	ant	any	doll	round	wheel	every	book	bird	(39)

Underlined nouns: cat, house, man, dog, tree; fish, lake, boy, boat, girl; ball, desk, car; train, tent, chair, baby; mouse, barn, cup; teacher, school, doctor, shirt; child, shoes, flower, horse, mother; sister, ant, doll, wheel, book, bird

ANSWER SHEET

Practicing Basic Skills in Language Arts • 6

© 2005 Sopris West Educational Services. All rights reserved. Practicing Basic Skills in Language Arts. Purchaser has permission to photocopy this page for classroom use only.

SEE TO MARK

Nouns in Isolation
Directions: Underline all the nouns.

					Correct	Error
First Try						
Second Try						

keg	skipped	small	whether	school	cabin	silence
nails	climbed	peaches	roses	money	wind	has
came	with	plan	early	playing	parking	store
uncle	burned	trimmed	room	desk	picnic	sang
women	feather	town	adventures	class	holiday	died
seek	duty	time	of	club	may	time
visitors	bravery	mud	coat	settlers	number	to
why	yard	shoes	fire	waiting	delay	before
paper	bought	is	small	captive	opinion	lift
verb	raise	telephone	cat	intermission	hung	horse
blooming	were	talking	school	days	Canada	detective
were	college	friend	run	dream	steps	are
first	teacher	storm	hands	hedge	bandit	children
garden	records	camp	radio	sprang	did	team
hill	ball	flowers	words	match	gas	diver
game	aunt	albums	moved	barn	engine	leader
brother	group	fight	work	Martha	paw	sand
cowboy	four	stone	how	blanket	fingers	girls
face	street	hit	books	neatly	chair	captain
city	wall	often	father	man	meadow	mountain

© 2005 Sopris West Educational Services. All rights reserved. Practicing Basic Skills in Language Arts. Purchaser has permission to photocopy this page for classroom use only.

ONE MINUTE FLUENCY BUILDER SERIES

	Correct	Error
First Try		
Second Try		

SEE TO MARK

Nouns in Isolation

Directions: Underline all the nouns.

keg	strength	skipped	small	whether	school	cabin	silence	(5)
nails	freedom	climbed	peaches	roses	money	wind	has	(11)
came	yacht	with	plan	early	playing	parking	store	(14)
uncle	snow	burned	trimmed	room	desk	picnic	sang	(19)
women	car	feather	town	adventures	class	holiday	died	(26)
seek	doorstep	duty	time	of	club	may	time	(31)
visitors	boys	bravery	mud	coat	settlers	number	to	(38)
why	football	yard	shoes	fire	waiting	delay	before	(43)
paper	box	bought	is	small	captive	opinion	lift	(48)
verb	can	raise	telephone	cat	intermission	hung	horse	(55)
blooming	sentence	were	talking	school	days	Canada	detective	(60)
were	did	college	friend	run	dream	steps	are	(64)
first	subject	teacher	storm	hands	hedge	bandit	children	(71)
garden	section	records	camp	radio	sprang	did	team	(77)
hill	ran	ball	flowers	words	match	gas	diver	(84)
game	pictures	aunt	albums	moved	barn	engine	leader	(91)
brother	medal	group	fight	work	Martha	paw	sand	(99)
cowboy	house	four	stone	how	blanket	fingers	girls	(105)
face	members	street	hit	books	neatly	chair	captain	(112)
city	grass	wall	often	father	man	meadow	mountain	(119)

ANSWER SHEET

© 2005 Sopris West Educational Services. All rights reserved. Practicing Basic Skills in Language Arts. Purchaser has permission to photocopy this page for classroom use only.

ONE-MINUTE FLUENCY
BUILDER SERIES

SEE TO WRITE

Proper Nouns and Common Nouns—Primary

Directions: Mark the common nouns (C) and proper nouns (P).

_____ boy   _____ Susan   _____ table

_____ New York City _____ river   _____ doctor

_____ house   _____ Monroe School   _____ cow

_____ boat   _____ Fish Creek   _____ Paris

_____ Rover   _____ flower   _____ July

_____ dog   _____ Main Street   _____ Mr. Ames

_____ tree   _____ Alaska   _____ shark

Practicing Basic Skills in Language Arts • 9

© 2005 Sopris West Educational Services. All rights reserved. Practicing Basic Skills in Language Arts. Purchaser has permission to photocopy this page for classroom use only.

ONE-MINUTE FLUENCY BUILDER SERIES

	Correct	Error
First Try		
Second Try		

SEE TO WRITE

Proper Nouns and Common Nouns—Primary

Directions: Mark the common nouns (C) and proper nouns (P).

C boy   P Susan   C table (3)

P New York City   C river   C doctor (6)

C house   P Monroe School   C cow (9)

C boat   P Fish Creek   P Paris (12)

P Rover   C flower   P July (15)

C dog   P Main Street   P Mr. Ames (18)

C tree   P Alaska   C shark (21)

ANSWER SHEET

Practicing Basic Skills in Language Arts • 10

© 2005 Sopris West Educational Services. All rights reserved. Practicing Basic Skills in Language Arts. Purchaser has permission to photocopy this page for classroom use only.

	First Try	Second Try
Correct		
Error		

SEE TO WRITE

Proper Nouns and Common Nouns

Directions: Mark the proper nouns (P) and common nouns (C).

tree ___	forest ___	basketball ___	Russia ___	child ___
California ___	Water Avenue ___	Salt Lake City ___	donkey ___	car ___
Utah ___	Spanish ___	English ___	Scotland ___	country ___
Pacific Ocean ___	river ___	Oldsmobile ___	car ___	Pontiac ___
George Smith ___	Gulf of Mexico ___	Abraham Lincoln ___	ocean ___	mother ___
mountain ___	Mount Rainier ___	star ___	Star Wars ___	secretary ___
state ___	Monday ___	September ___	Mexico ___	Thanksgiving ___
library ___	Indian ___	men ___	Robin Hood ___	mouse ___
prairie ___	Texas ___	fog ___	Jordan River ___	hill ___
Lincoln Jr. High ___	school ___	Jefferson School Dist. ___	aunt ___	. uncle ___
Doctor Strangelove ___	kitten ___	book ___	Uncle Remus ___	window ___
dictionary ___	bible ___	Webster's Dictionary ___	Donny Osmond ___	arithmetic ___
encyclopedia ___	New York City ___	Wyoming ___	Tuesday ___	January ___

Practicing Basic Skills in Language Arts • 11

© 2005 Sopris West Educational Services. All rights reserved. Practicing Basic Skills in Language Arts. Purchaser has permission to photocopy this page for classroom use only.

ONE-MINUTE FLUENCY — BUILDER SERIES

SEE TO WRITE

Proper Nouns and Common Nouns

Directions: Mark the proper nouns (P) and common nouns (C).

	First Try	Second Try
Correct		
Error		

tree	C	forest	C	basketball	C	Russia	P	child (5)	C
California	P	Water Avenue	P	Salt Lake City	P	donkey	C	car (10)	C
Utah	P	Spanish	P	English	P	Scotland	P	country (15)	C
Pacific Ocean	P	river	C	Oldsmobile	C	car	C	Pontiac (20)	C
George Smith	P	Gulf of Mexico	P	Abraham Lincoln	P	ocean	C	mother (25)	C
mountain	C	Mount Rainier	P	star	P	Star Wars	P	secretary (30)	C
state	C	Monday	P	September	P	Mexico	P	Thanksgiving (35)	P
library	C	Indian	P	men	P	Robin Hood	C	mouse (40)	C
prairie	C	Texas	P	fog	P	Jordan River	C	hill (45)	C
Lincoln Jr. High	P	school	C	Jefferson School Dist.	C	aunt	P	uncle (50)	C
Doctor Strangelove	P	kitten	P	book	C	Uncle Remus	C	window (55)	C
dictionary	C	bible	C	Webster's Dictionary	C	Donny Osmond	P	arithmetic (60)	C
encyclopedia	C	New York City	P	Wyoming	P	Tuesday	P	January (65)	P

ANSWER SHEET

Practicing Basic Skills in Language Arts • 12

© 2005 Sopris West Educational Services. All rights reserved. Practicing Basic Skills in Language Arts. Purchaser has permission to photocopy this page for classroom use only.

ONE-MINUTE FLUENCY BUILDER SERIES

		First Try	Second Try
Correct			
Error			

Change Proper Nouns to Common Nouns

Directions: Change the following proper nouns into common nouns.

Sahara Desert	Kansas City	Americans	Mississippi
Mrs. Ames	Lincoln High	Helena	Charles Lindbergh
Brazil	The Beatles	San Francisco	Crest
South America	Bill of Rights	Mount Everest	
Bill	Uncle Harry	Yosemite National Park	St. Luke's Church
Fifth Avenue	Ford Mustang	Constitution	Sally
Labor Day	Future Farmers of America	Utah State University	
Venus	December	Thanksgiving	Georgia
Beethoven	Dallas Cowboys	English	Mike
John Travolta	Pacific	McDonald's	Anne
Wednesday	Empire State Building	Dracula	Sprite
Gone With the Wind	General Electric	Safeway	
Queen Elizabeth II	Chevrolet	Russia	New York

Practicing Basic Skills in Language Arts • 13

© 2005 Sopris West Educational Services. All rights reserved. Practicing Basic Skills in Language Arts. Purchaser has permission to photocopy this page for classroom use only.

THINK TO WRITE

Change Proper Nouns to Common Nouns

Directions: Change the following proper nouns into common nouns.

	First Try	Second Try
Correct		
Error		

Proper Noun	Common	Proper Noun	Common	Proper Noun	Common	Proper Noun	Common	
Sahara Desert	desert	Kansas City	town	Americans	people	Mississippi	state	(4)
Mrs. Ames	woman	Lincoln High	school	Helena	town	Charles Lindbergh	pilot	(8)
Brazil	country	The Beatles	rock group	San Francisco	city	Crest	toothpaste	(12)
South America	continent	Bill of Rights	document	Mount Everest	mountain			(15)
Bill	man	Uncle Harry	man	Yosemite National Park	park	St. Luke's Church	church	(19)
Fifth Avenue	street	Ford Mustang	car	Constitution	document	Sally	woman	(23)
Labor Day	holiday	Future Farmers of America	club	Utah State University	school			(26)
Venus	planet	December	month	Thanksgiving	holiday	Georgia	state	(30)
Beethoven	composer	Dallas Cowboys	football team	English	language	Mike	man	(34)
John Travolta	actor	Pacific	ocean	McDonald's	fast food restaurant	Anne	woman	(38)
Wednesday	day	Empire State Building	building	Dracula	vampire	Sprite	drink	(42)
Gone With the Wind	book/movie	General Electric	company	Safeway	store			(45)
Queen Elizabeth II	woman/queen	Chevrolet	car	Russia	country	New York	state/city	(49)

ANSWER SHEET

Practicing Basic Skills in Language Arts • 14

© 2005 Sopris West Educational Services. All rights reserved. Practicing Basic Skills in Language Arts. Purchaser has permission to photocopy this page for classroom use only.

Concrete Nouns

Directions: Mark the nouns that are concrete.

First Try	Second Try
Correct	
Error	

car	eye	jury	gratitude	movie	dollar
club	public	potato	cupboard	team	jury
happiness	herd	thought	admiration	shelf	association
love	banana	money	college	fight	porch
desk	train	bell	ocean	glory	holiness
pen	army	perfection	teacher	army	spite
house	fleet	flock	education	pleasure	mayor
family	store	class	club	avenue	cow
hatred	power	patriotism	misery	jury	month
faculty	assembly	engineer	salt	work	eternity
group	tennis	team	lawyer	newspaper	team
book	socialism	traffic	group	glass	club
curtain	government	public	trust	fleet	football
arm	senate	faith	scientist	coach	flower
audience	leg	sorrow	discussion	audience	committee
freedom	herd	attic	laziness	dedication	sweater
magazine	steak	assembly	faculty	slacks	club
justice	robin	joy	name	heroism	student
committee	watch	airplane	outlaw	farmer	boredom
democracy	sadness	dish	song	flock	assembly
brotherhood	girl	committee	honesty	rocket	equality
shoe	class	chair	example	sympathy	basement
kettle	ring	author	harmony	letter	animal
friendship	rain	family	cat	pencil	janitor

Practicing Basic Skills in Language Arts • 15

© 2005 Sopris West Educational Services. All rights reserved. Practicing Basic Skills in Language Arts. Purchaser has permission to photocopy this page for classroom use only.

ONE-MINUTE FLUENCY BUILDER SERIES

SEE TO MARK

Concrete Nouns

Directions: Mark the nouns that are concrete.

	Correct	Error
First Try		
Second Try		

car	eye	jury	gratitude	movie	dollar (5)
club	public	potato	cupboard	team	jury (10)
happiness	herd	thought	admiration	shelf	association (12)
love	banana	money	college	fight	porch (17)
desk	train	bell	ocean	glory	holiness (21)
pen	army	perfection	teacher	army	spite (25)
house	fleet	flock	education	pleasure	mayor (29)
family	store	class	club	avenue	cow (35)
hatred	power	patriotism	misery	jury	month (36)
faculty	assembly	engineer	salt	work	eternity (39)
group	tennis	team	lawyer	newspaper	team (45)
book	socialism	traffic	group	glass	club (50)
curtain	government	public	trust	fleet	football (53)
arm	senate	faith	scientist	coach	flower (58)
audience	leg	sorrow	discussion	audience	committee (62)
freedom	herd	attic	laziness	dedication	sweater (65)
magazine	steak	assembly	faculty	slacks	club (70)
justice	robin	joy	name	heroism	student (73)
committee	watch	airplane	outlaw	farmer	boredom (78)
democracy	sadness	dish	song	flock	assembly (81)
brotherhood	girl	committee	honesty	rocket	equality (84)
shoe	class	chair	example	sympathy	basement (89)
kettle	ring	author	harmony	letter	animal (94)
friendship	rain	family	cat	pencil	janitor (99)

ANSWER SHEET

© 2005 Sopris West Educational Services. All rights reserved. Practicing Basic Skills in Language Arts. Purchaser has permission to photocopy this page for classroom use only.

Correct | Error
First Try
Second Try

SEE TO MARK

Abstract Nouns

Directions: Mark the nouns that are abstract.

car	eye	jury	gratitude	movie	dollar
club	public	potato	cupboard	team	jury
happiness	herd	thought	admiration	shelf	association
love	banana	money	college	fight	porch
desk	train	bell	ocean	glory	holiness
pen	army	perfection	teacher	army	spite
house	fleet	flock	education	pleasure	mayor
family	store	class	club	avenue	cow
hatred	power	patriotism	misery	jury	month
faculty	assembly	engineer	salt	work	eternity
group	tennis	team	lawyer	newspaper	team
book	socialism	traffic	group	glass	club
curtain	government	public	trust	fleet	football
arm	senate	faith	scientist	coach	flower
audience	leg	sorrow	discussion	audience	committee
freedom	herd	attic	laziness	dedication	sweater
magazine	steak	assembly	faculty	slacks	club
justice	robin	joy	name	heroism	student
committee	watch	airplane	outlaw	farmer	boredom
democracy	sadness	dish	song	flock	assembly
brotherhood	girl	committee	honesty	rocket	equality
shoe	class	chair	example	sympathy	basement
kettle	ring	author	harmony	letter	animal
friendship	rain	family	cat	pencil	janitor

ONE MINUTE FLUENCY BUILDER SERIES

© 2005 Sopris West Educational Services. All rights reserved. Practicing Basic Skills in Language Arts. Purchaser has permission to photocopy this page for classroom use only.

ONE MINUTE FLUENCY BUILDER SERIES

SEE TO MARK

Abstract Nouns

Directions: Mark the nouns that are abstract.

	Correct	Error
First Try		
Second Try		

car	eye	jury	gratitude	movie	dollar	(1)
club	public	potato	cupboard	team	jury	(1)
happiness	herd	thought	admiration	shelf	association	(4)
love	banana	money	college	fight	porch	(5)
desk	train	bell	ocean	glory	holiness	(7)
pen	army	perfection	teacher	army	spite	(8)
house	fleet	flock	education	pleasure	mayor	(10)
family	store	class	club	avenue	cow	(10)
hatred	power	patriotism	misery	jury	month	(15)
faculty	assembly	engineer	salt	work	eternity	(17)
group	tennis	team	lawyer	newspaper	team	(17)
book	socialism	traffic	group	glass	club	(18)
curtain	government	public	trust	fleet	football	(20)
arm	senate	faith	scientist	coach	flower	(21)
audience	leg	sorrow	discussion	audience	committee	(23)
freedom	herd	attic	laziness	dedication	sweater	(26)
magazine	steak	assembly	faculty	slacks	club	(26)
justice	robin	joy	name	heroism	student	(29)
committee	watch	airplane	outlaw	farmer	boredom	(30)
democracy	sadness	dish	song	flock	assembly	(32)
brotherhood	girl	committee	honesty	rocket	equality	(35)
shoe	class	chair	example	sympathy	basement	(36)
kettle	ring	author	harmony	letter	animal	(37)
friendship	rain	family	cat	pencil	janitor	(38)

ANSWER SHEET

Practicing Basic Skills in Language Arts • 18

© 2005 Sopris West Educational Services. All rights reserved. Practicing Basic Skills in Language Arts. Purchaser has permission to photocopy this page for classroom use only.

	Correct	Error
First Try		
Second Try		

SEE TO MARK

Collective Nouns

Directions: Mark the nouns that are collective.

car	eye	jury	gratitude	movie	dollar
club	public	potato	cupboard	team	jury
happiness	herd	thought	admiration	shelf	association
love	banana	money	college	fight	porch
desk	train	bell	ocean	glory	holiness
pen	army	perfection	teacher	army	spite
house	fleet	flock	education	pleasure	mayor
family	store	class	club	avenue	cow
hatred	power	patriotism	misery	jury	month
faculty	assembly	engineer	salt	work	eternity
group	tennis	team	lawyer	newspaper	team
book	socialism	traffic	group	glass	club
curtain	government	public	trust	fleet	football
arm	senate	faith	scientist	coach	flower
audience	leg	sorrow	discussion	audience	committee
freedom	herd	attic	laziness	dedication	sweater
magazine	steak	assembly	faculty	slacks	club
justice	robin	joy	name	heroism	student
committee	watch	airplane	outlaw	farmer	boredom
democracy	sadness	dish	song	flock	assembly
brotherhood	girl	committee	honesty	rocket	equality
shoe	class	chair	example	sympathy	basement
kettle	ring	author	harmony	letter	animal
friendship	rain	family	cat	pencil	janitor

© 2005 Sopris West Educational Services. All rights reserved. Practicing Basic Skills in Language Arts. Purchaser has permission to photocopy this page for classroom use only.

ONE-MINUTE FLUENCY
BUILDER SERIES

SEE TO MARK

	First Try	Second Try
Correct		
Error		

Collective Nouns

Directions: Mark the nouns that are collective.

car	eye	jury	gratitude	movie	dollar (1)
club	public	potato	cupboard	team	jury (5)
happiness	herd	thought	admiration	shelf	association (7)
love	banana	money	college	fight	porch (7)
desk	train	bell	ocean	glory	holiness (7)
pen	army	perfection	teacher	army	spite (9)
house	fleet	flock	education	pleasure	mayor (11)
family	store	class	club	avenue	cow (14)
hatred	power	patriotism	misery	jury	month (15)
faculty	assembly	engineer	salt	work	eternity (17)
group	tennis	team	lawyer	newspaper	team (20)
book	socialism	traffic	group	glass	club (22)
curtain	government	public	trust	fleet	football (24)
arm	senate	faith	scientist	coach	flower (25)
audience	leg	sorrow	discussion	audience	committee (28)
freedom	herd	attic	laziness	dedication	sweater (29)
magazine	steak	assembly	faculty	slacks	club (32)
justice	robin	joy	name	heroism	student (32)
committee	watch	airplane	outlaw	farmer	boredom (33)
democracy	sadness	dish	song	flock	assembly (35)
brotherhood	girl	committee	honesty	rocket	equality (36)
shoe	class	chair	example	sympathy	basement (37)
kettle	ring	author	harmony	letter	animal (37)
friendship	rain	family	cat	pencil	janitor (38)

© 2005 Sopris West Educational Services. All rights reserved. Practicing Basic Skills in Language Arts. Purchaser has permission to photocopy this page for classroom use only.

	First Try	Second Try
Correct		
Error		

SEE TO WRITE

Concrete Nouns and Abstract Nouns

Directions: After each noun, write whether it is concrete or abstract.

apricot	Arizona
hunger	dentist
chipmunk	happiness
truth	honesty
fleet	circus
Salt Lake City	kindness
success	justice
map	college
desk	peacefulness
laughter	committee
island	education
assembly	sickness
courage	people
pilot	stereo
dog	blackboard
freedom	democracy
poverty	beauty
sun	coach
rainbow	car

Practicing Basic Skills in Language Arts • 21

© 2005 Sopris West Educational Services. All rights reserved. Practicing Basic Skills in Language Arts. Purchaser has permission to photocopy this page for classroom use only.

ONE-MINUTE FLUENCY
BUILDER SERIES

SEE TO WRITE

Concrete Nouns and Abstract Nouns

Directions: After each noun, write whether it is concrete or abstract.

	First Try	Second Try
Correct		
Error		

apricot	concrete	Arizona	concrete	(2)
hunger	abstract	dentist	concrete	(4)
chipmunk	concrete	happiness	abstract	(6)
truth	abstract	honesty	abstract	(8)
fleet	concrete	circus	concrete	(10)
Salt Lake City	concrete	kindness	abstract	(12)
success	abstract	justice	abstract	(14)
map	concrete	college	concrete	(16)
desk	concrete	peacefulness	abstract	(18)
laughter	abstract	committee	concrete	(20)
island	concrete	education	abstract	(22)
assembly	concrete	sickness	abstract	(24)
courage	abstract	people	concrete	(26)
pilot	concrete	stereo	concrete	(28)
dog	concrete	blackboard	concrete	(30)
freedom	abstract	democracy	abstract	(32)
poverty	abstract	beauty	abstract	(34)
sun	concrete	coach	concrete	(36)
rainbow	concrete	car	concrete	(38)

ANSWER SHEET

Practicing Basic Skills in Language Arts • 22

© 2005 Sopris West Educational Services. All rights reserved. Practicing Basic Skills in Language Arts. Purchaser has permission to photocopy this page for classroom use only.

ONE-MINUTE FLUENCY
BUILDER SERIES

	Correct	Error
First Try		
Second Try		

Common Nouns and Proper Nouns

Directions: Mark the common nouns with a C and capitalize proper nouns.

boy _____ susan _____ table _____

new york city _____ river _____ doctor _____

house _____ monroe school _____ cow _____

boat _____ fish creek _____ paris _____

rover _____ flower _____ july _____

dog _____ main street _____ mr. ames _____

tree _____ alaska _____ shark _____

Practicing Basic Skills in Language Arts • 23

© 2005 Sopris West Educational Services. All rights reserved. Practicing Basic Skills in Language Arts. Purchaser has permission to photocopy this page for classroom use only.

ONE-MINUTE FLUENCY
BUILDER SERIES

SEE TO WRITE

Common Nouns and Proper Nouns

Directions: Mark the common nouns with a C and capitalize proper nouns.

	First Try	Second Try
Correct		
Error		

C _____ boy	**Susan** _____ susan	C _____ table	(3)
New York City _____ new york city	C _____ river	C _____ doctor	(6)
C _____ house	**Monroe School** _____ monroe school	C _____ cow	(9)
C _____ boat	**Fish Creek** _____ fish creek	**Paris** _____ paris	(12)
Rover _____ rover	C _____ flower	**July** _____ july	(15)
C _____ dog	**Main Street** _____ main street	**Mr. Ames** _____ mr. ames	(18)
C _____ tree	**Alaska** _____ alaska	C _____ shark	(21)

ANSWER SHEET

Practicing Basic Skills in Language Arts • 24

© 2005 Sopris West Educational Services. All rights reserved. Practicing Basic Skills in Language Arts. Purchaser has permission to photocopy this page for classroom use only.

	Correct	Error
First Try		
Second Try		

SEE TO MARK

Nouns in Sentences—Primary

Directions: Underline nouns in the sentences.

1. The man ran into the house.

2. Did you see the dog eat his bone?

3. Put the cup on the table.

4. Pedro is going to school.

5. Can you take the ball to school?

6. It is a very cold night.

7. The cars were going too slow.

8. The baby wanted his bottle.

9. His boat was green and white.

10. Horses are fun to ride.

11. Did the man find his house?

12. Jane rode on the train.

13. He fell asleep in the car.

14. How cold is the water?

15. Books are fun to read.

16. The five cats are all black.

17. The teacher is by the door.

18. The plane is leaving soon.

© 2005 Sopris West Educational Services. All rights reserved. Practicing Basic Skills in Language Arts. Purchaser has permission to photocopy this page for classroom use only.

Nouns in Sentences—Primary

Directions: Underline nouns in the sentences.

	First Try	Second Try
Correct		
Error		

1. The man ran into the house.

2. Did you see the dog eat his bone? (4)

3. Put the cup on the table.

4. Pedro is going to school. (8)

5. Can you take the ball to school?

6. It is a very cold night. (11)

7. The cars were going too slow.

8. The baby wanted his bottle. (14)

9. His boat was green and white.

10. Horses are fun to ride. (16)

11. Did the man find his house?

12. Jane rode on the train. (20)

13. He fell asleep in the car.

14. How cold is the water? (22)

15. Books are fun to read.

16. The five cats are all black. (24)

17. The teacher is by the door.

18. The plane is leaving soon. (27)

ANSWER SHEET

© 2005 Sopris West Educational Services. All rights reserved. Practicing Basic Skills in Language Arts. Purchaser has permission to photocopy this page for classroom use only.

ONE MINUTE FLUENCY BUILDER SERIES

Nouns in Sentences

Directions: Underline all nouns in the following sentences.

	First Try	Second Try
Correct		
Error		

Where should the girls hang their coats? For many years the mariners of Europe had vainly sought a route to India by sea. One

man was carrying a large bundle. Two boys each put down a coin and walked into the place where the show was going on. They

saw many animals. Bob, did Sung help you? Jada found that she had left her bicycle at home. Luis said that the picture was his.

Has your mother called on the new neighbors? The money for your ticket is lying on the table. Which player scored the most

points in the first two games? A funny man came out and made everyone laugh. Then a young person rode around on a beautiful

white animal. Five boys have completed their assignments. The girls served sandwiches and lemonade. The boy with my cousin is

a visitor from my old school. That fly is very annoying. The fire engine raced by at a speed of fifty miles an hour. These tires were

put on our car by the new mechanic. The thirsty boys drank a quart of milk. That man certainly loves his comfort. Mr. Wong

will paper my bedroom. Right is stronger than might. Other countries do not enjoy the freedom that democracy can provide.

The song for our school was written by a student who couldn't read music. The freshmen will hold their picnic soon. A famous

explorer talked to our club about his adventures. For breakfast my dad always wants both cereal and toast. To be a success you

must work hard. The wisdom of studying a foreign language cannot be overlooked. Our dog bit the cat.

© 2005 Sopris West Educational Services. All rights reserved. Practicing Basic Skills in Language Arts. Purchaser has permission to photocopy this page for classroom use only.

SEE TO MARK

Nouns in Sentences

Directions: Underline all nouns in the following sentences.

	Correct	Error
First Try		
Second Try		

Where should the girls hang their coats? For many years the mariners of Europe had vainly sought a route to India by sea. One (8)

man was carrying a large bundle. Two boys each put down a coin and walked into the place where the show was going on. They (14)

saw many animals. Bob, did Sung help you? Jada found that she had left her bicycle at home. Luis said that the picture was his. (22)

Has your mother called on the new neighbors? The money for your ticket is lying on the table. Which player scored the most (28)

points in the first two games? A funny man came out and made everyone laugh. Then a young person rode around on a beautiful (32)

white animal. Five boys have completed their assignments. The girls served sandwiches and lemonade. The boy with my cousin is (40)

a visitor from my old school. That fly is very annoying. The fire engine raced by at a speed of fifty miles an hour. These tires were (48)

put on our car by the new mechanic. The thirsty boys drank a quart of milk. That man certainly loves his comfort. Mr. Wong (56)

will paper my bedroom. Right is stronger than might. Other countries do not enjoy the freedom that democracy can provide. (62)

The song for our school was written by a student who couldn't read music. The freshmen will hold their picnic soon. A famous (68)

explorer talked to our club about his adventures. For breakfast my dad always wants both cereal and toast. To be a success you (76)

must work hard. The wisdom of studying a foreign language cannot be overlooked. Our dog bit the cat. (80)

ANSWER SHEET

Practicing Basic Skills in Language Arts • 28

© 2005 Sopris West Educational Services. All rights reserved. Practicing Basic Skills in Language Arts. Purchaser has permission to photocopy this page for classroom use only.

ONE-MINUTE FLUENCY
BUILDER SERIES

SEE TO MARK

Nouns in Sentences

Directions: Mark all nouns in the following sentences.

In the course of one of his lecture trips, Mark Twain arrived at a small town. Before dinner, he went to a barber shop to be shaved. "You're a stranger?" asked the barber. "Yes," Mark Twain replied, "this is the first time I've been here." "You chose a good time to come," the barber continued. "Mark Twain is going to lecture tonight. You'll go, I suppose?" "Oh, I guess so." "Have you bought your ticket?" "Not yet." "But everything is sold out. You'll have to stand when that fellow lectures." "Stories such as this one do not have with a sigh. "I never heard of such luck! I always have to stand in the wings." "How very annoying!" Mark Twain said, to be long to have a point. A short anecdote that quickly comes to the point is often most effective. Here is another example of this idea: Once Father was picking some of our apples to take to some friends. My little brother Sammy looked at the apples Dad had picked and said, "You tell them that those aren't worm holes, they are just for decoration." When telling an anecdote or joke, keep the point hidden until the last possible word. Don't tell your audience how funny your joke is. Don't try difficult stories unless you are certain that you can remember every detail. There are good humorists and comedians on television today. Watching these comedians can give you some real tips in telling jokes to a live audience. There are few people in the world who have natural ability when it comes to reciting a story; everyone needs practice and help in preparing for the stage. You must try to gain the confidence of your audience. To do this, you need sincerity, honesty, and self-confidence. You must present the facts clearly. Bob Hope was a classic modern comedian who was liked by all age groups because his laughter was contagious. Try talking to small groups first, then work your way up to larger audiences. Have faith in yourself.

Practicing Basic Skills in Language Arts • 29

© 2005 Sopris West Educational Services. All rights reserved. Practicing Basic Skills in Language Arts. Purchaser has permission to photocopy this page for classroom use only.

Nouns in Sentences

Directions: Mark all nouns in the following sentences.

	Correct	Error
First Try		
Second Try		

In the course of one of his lecture trips, Mark Twain arrived at a small town. Before dinner, he went to a barber shop to be shaved. (7)

"You're a stranger?" asked the barber. "Yes," Mark Twain replied, "this is the first time I've been here." "You chose a good time to (12)

come," the barber continued. "Mark Twain is going to lecture tonight. You'll go, I suppose?" "Oh, I guess so." "Have you bought (14)

your ticket?" "Not yet." "But everything is sold out. You'll have to stand in the wings." "How very annoying!" Mark Twain said, (17)

with a sigh. "I never heard of such luck! I always have to stand when that fellow lectures." Stories such as this one do not have (22)

to be long to have a point. A short anecdote that quickly comes to the point is often most effective. Here is another example (26)

of this idea: Once Father was picking some of our apples to take to some friends. My little brother Sammy looked at the apples (33)

Dad had picked and said, "You tell them that those aren't worm holes, they are just for decoration." When telling an anecdote (37)

or joke, keep the point hidden until the last possible word. Don't tell your audience how funny your joke is. Don't try difficult (42)

stories unless you are certain that you can remember every detail. There are good humorists and comedians on television today. (47)

Watching these comedians can give you some real tips in telling jokes to a live audience. There are few people in the world who (53)

have natural ability when it comes to reciting a story; everyone needs practice and help in preparing for the stage. You must try (58)

to gain the confidence of your audience. To do this, you need sincerity, honesty, and self-confidence. You must present the facts (64)

clearly. Bob Hope was a classic modern comedian who was liked by all age groups because his laughter was contagious. Try talking (68)

to small groups first, then work your way up to larger audiences. Have faith in yourself. (72)

Practicing Basic Skills in Language Arts • 30

© 2005 Sopris West Educational Services. All rights reserved. Practicing Basic Skills in Language Arts. Purchaser has permission to photocopy this page for classroom use only.

ONE-MINUTE FLUENCY BUILDER SERIES

Singular Nouns and Plural Nouns—Primary

Directions: Mark the singular nouns with an S and plural nouns with a P.

	First Try	Second Try
Correct		
Error		

house   cats _____ fence

boats _____ man _____ girls

duck _____ mice _____ barn

boy _____ cups _____ shoe

rings _____ men _____ car

apple _____ songs _____ birds

tables _____ street _____ horse

© 2005 Sopris West Educational Services. All rights reserved. Practicing Basic Skills in Language Arts. Purchaser has permission to photocopy this page for classroom use only.

Practicing Basic Skills in Language Arts • 31

ONE-MINUTE FLUENCY
BUILDER SERIES

Singular Nouns and Plural Nouns—Primary

Directions: Mark the singular nouns with an S and plural nouns with a P.

Correct	Error
First Try	
Second Try	

S house	**P** cats	**S** fence	(3)
P boats	**S** man	**P** girls	(6)
S duck	**P** mice	**S** barn	(9)
S boy	**P** cups	**S** shoe	(12)
P rings	**P** men	**S** car	(15)
S apple	**P** songs	**P** birds	(18)
P tables	**S** street	**S** horse	(21)

© 2005 Sopris West Educational Services. All rights reserved. Practicing Basic Skills in Language Arts. Purchaser has permission to photocopy this page for classroom use only.

SEE TO MARK

Singular Nouns
Directions: Circle all the singular nouns.

boy	commander-in-chief	tooth	memos
skies	monkey	calf	plurals
girl	wishes	firemen	formula
hero	potato	army	mathematics
ladies	miss	scissors	Chinese
potatoes	commanders-in-chief	babies	ox
sky	knives	children	copies
heroes	sheep	journey	mice
girls	handful	lilies	speeches
cameo	policemen	inches	dollar
radio	man	bush	guess
monkeys	deer	taxes	tongues
valley	mouse	oxen	quantities
boxes	lice	lives	ally
misses	teeth	halves	person
benches	foot	mother-in-law	medals
radios	solo	pailful	flies
son-in-law	teaspoonfuls	enemies	clock
box	axes	supper	glass

© 2005 Sopris West Educational Services. All rights reserved. Practicing Basic Skills in Language Arts. Purchaser has permission to photocopy this page for classroom use only.

ONE-MINUTE FLUENCY BUILDER SERIES

SEE TO MARK

Singular Nouns

Directions: Circle all the singular nouns.

Correct	Error
First Try	
Second Try	

boy	commander-in-chief	tooth	nickel	memos (4)
skies	monkey	calf	dishes	plurals (6)
girl	wishes	firemen	stories	formula (8)
hero	potato	army	keys	mathematics (12)
ladies	miss	scissors	wife	Chinese (16)
potatoes	commanders-in-chief	babies	belief	ox (18)
sky	knives	children	child	copies (20)
heroes	sheep	journey	sisters-in-law	mice (22)
girls	handful	lilies	notary	speeches (24)
cameo	policemen	inches	vetoes	dollar (26)
radio	man	bush	soprano	guess (31)
monkeys	deer	taxes	shampoo	tongues (33)
valley	mouse	oxen	men-of-war	quantities (35)
boxes	lice	lives	trout	ally (37)
misses	teeth	halves	mouse	person (39)
benches	foot	mother-in-law	deer	medals (42)
radios	solo	pailful	woman	flies (45)
son-in-law	teaspoonfuls	enemies	cars	clock (47)
box	axes	supper	drapery	glass (51)

ANSWER SHEET

Practicing Basic Skills in Language Arts • 34

© 2005 Sopris West Educational Services. All rights reserved. Practicing Basic Skills in Language Arts. Purchaser has permission to photocopy this page for classroom use only.

ONE MINUTE FLUENCY
BUILDER SERIES

SEE TO WRITE

Plural Nouns—Primary

Directions: Write the plural noun for each of these singular nouns.

First Try	Correct	Error
Second Try		

cat _____ house _____ man _____

boat _____ shirt _____ ant _____

wheel _____ dog _____ book _____

mouse _____ fence _____ teacher _____

brother _____ table _____ cup _____

leg _____ tulip _____ horse _____

street _____ tent _____ car _____

Practicing Basic Skills in Language Arts • 35

© 2005 Sopris West Educational Services. All rights reserved. Practicing Basic Skills in Language Arts. Purchaser has permission to photocopy this page for classroom use only.

	First Try	Second Try
Correct		
Error		

SEE TO WRITE

Plural Nouns—Primary
Directions: Write the plural noun for each of these singular nouns.

cat	**cats**	house	**houses**	man	**men**	(3)
boat	**boats**	shirt	**shirts**	ant	**ants**	(6)
wheel	**wheels**	dog	**dogs**	book	**books**	(9)
mouse	**mice**	fence	**fences**	teacher	**teachers**	(12)
brother	**brothers**	table	**tables**	cup	**cups**	(15)
leg	**legs**	tulip	**tulips**	horse	**horses**	(18)
street	**streets**	tent	**tents**	car	**cars**	(21)

ANSWER SHEET

Practicing Basic Skills in Language Arts • 36

© 2005 Sopris West Educational Services. All rights reserved. Practicing Basic Skills in Language Arts. Purchaser has permission to photocopy this page for classroom use only.

	First Try	Second Try
Correct		
Error		

SEE TO WRITE

Plural Nouns

Directions: Write the plural form of each word in the blanks that follow.

army	_____	fox	_____
monkey	_____	cat	_____
life	_____	mess	_____
leaf	_____	church	_____
day	_____	wish	_____
wife	_____	sandwich	_____
sissy	_____	switch	_____
gravy	_____	bush	_____
turkey	_____	brush	_____
key	_____	box	_____
boy	_____	lunch	_____
candy	_____	dish	_____
puppy	_____	top	_____
donkey	_____	carton	_____
jelly	_____	dress	_____
family	_____	boss	_____
scarf	_____	glass	_____
elf	_____	six	_____
shelf	_____	lesson	_____

Practicing Basic Skills in Language Arts • 37

© 2005 Sopris West Educational Services. All rights reserved. Practicing Basic Skills in Language Arts. Purchaser has permission to photocopy this page for classroom use only.

SEE TO WRITE

Plural Nouns

Directions: Write the plural form of each word in the blanks that follow.

First Try	Second Try
Correct	**Error**

army	**armies**		fox	**foxes**	(2)
monkey	**monkeys**		cat	**cats**	(4)
life	**lives**		mess	**messes**	(6)
leaf	**leaves**		church	**churches**	(8)
day	**days**		wish	**wishes**	(10)
wife	**wives**		sandwich	**sandwiches**	(12)
sissy	**sissies**		switch	**switches**	(14)
gravy	**gravies**		bush	**bushes**	(16)
turkey	**turkeys**		brush	**brushes**	(18)
key	**keys**		box	**boxes**	(20)
boy	**boys**		lunch	**lunches**	(22)
candy	**candies**		dish	**dishes**	(24)
puppy	**puppies**		top	**tops**	(26)
donkey	**donkeys**		carton	**cartons**	(28)
jelly	**jellies**		dress	**dresses**	(30)
family	**families**		boss	**bosses**	(32)
scarf	**scarves**		glass	**glasses**	(34)
elf	**elves**		six	**sixes**	(36)
shelf	**shelves**		lesson	**lessons**	(38)

© 2005 Sopris West Educational Services. All rights reserved. Practicing Basic Skills in Language Arts. Purchaser has permission to photocopy this page for classroom use only.

	First Try	Second Try
Correct		
Error		

SEE TO WRITE

Possessive Nouns

Directions: Rewrite each of the following expressions in the possessive case. (For example, the book belonging to Jane = Jane's book.)

a ball belonging to a boy _____

desk belonging to the teacher _____

waiting for an hour _____

the mother of James _____

the garden of Grandmother _____

a vacation for a week _____

a rest for a night _____

the bushy tail of a squirrel _____

the paper of today _____

a creation by Shellie _____

the ranch of my uncle _____

the eggs of chickens _____

the football belonging to Tom _____

the wings of the geese _____

shoes belonging to ladies _____

the costumes of Indians _____

the locker room of the team _____

the game that was yesterday _____

the guitar belonging to me _____

the house belonging to him _____

a report by the secretary _____

the hooves of a horse _____

hair of a baby _____

the nest of a bird _____

a knife belonging to my dad _____

the work of a farmer _____

dresses belonging to girls _____

a world of a man _____

the assignments for tomorrow _____

the venom of a spider _____

the house I live in _____

a club belonging to men _____

the tracks of two deer _____

the nest of mice _____

the children of the Smiths _____

the party of my friend _____

the bristles on brushes _____

a boat belonging to Kip _____

Practicing Basic Skills in Language Arts • 39

© 2005 Sopris West Educational Services. All rights reserved. Practicing Basic Skills in Language Arts. Purchaser has permission to photocopy this page for classroom use only.

SEE TO WRITE

Possessive Nouns

Directions: Rewrite each of the following expressions in the possessive case. (For example, the book belonging to Jane = Jane's book.)

a ball belonging to a boy	**a boy's ball**		the house belonging to him	**his house**	(5)
desk belonging to the teacher	**the teacher's desk**		a report by the secretary	**the secretary's report**	(11)
waiting for an hour	**an hour's wait**		the hooves of a horse	**the horse's hooves**	(17)
the mother of James	**James's mother**		hair of a baby	**baby's hair**	(21)
the garden of Grandmother	**Grandmother's garden**		the nest of a bird	**the bird's nest**	(26)
a vacation for a week	**a week's vacation**		a knife belonging to my dad	**my dad's knife**	(32)
a rest for a night	**a night's rest**		the work of a farmer	**the farmer's work**	(38)
the bushy tail of a squirrel	**the squirrel's bushy tail**		dresses belonging to girls	**the girls' dresses**	(45)
the paper of today	**today's paper**		a world of a man	**a man's world**	(50)
a creation by Shellie	**Shellie's creation**		the assignments for tomorrow	**tomorrow's assignments**	(54)
the ranch of my uncle	**my uncle's ranch**		the venom of a spider	**the spider's venom**	(60)
the eggs of chickens	**the chickens' eggs**		the house I live in	**my house**	(65)
the football belonging to Tom	**Tom's football**		a club belonging to men	**a men's club**	(70)
the wings of the geese	**the geese's wings**		the tracks of two deer	**two deer's tracks**	(76)
shoes belonging to ladies	**ladies' shoes**		the nest of mice	**the mice's nest**	(81)
the costumes of Indians	**the Indians' costumes**		the children of the Smiths	**the Smiths' children**	(87)
the locker room of the team	**the team's locker room**		the party of my friend	**my friend's party**	(94)
the game that was yesterday	**yesterday's game**		the bristles on brushes	**the brushes' bristles**	(99)
the guitar belonging to me	**my guitar**		a boat belonging to Kip	**Kip's boat**	(103)

	Correct	Error
First Try		
Second Try		

ANSWER SHEET

Practicing Basic Skills in Language Arts • 40

© 2005 Sopris West Educational Services. All rights reserved. Practicing Basic Skills in Language Arts. Purchaser has permission to photocopy this page for classroom use only.

ONE-MINUTE FLUENCY BUILDER SERIES

	First Try	Second Try
Correct		
Error		

SEE TO MARK

Subject Pronouns
Directions: Mark the correct pronoun.

1. My dog and (I, me) take long walks.

2. Did (him, he) and his brother leave?

3. Did Carlos and (she, her) help you?

4. (We, Us) girls are ready.

5. May (we, us) boys have a party?

6. (Her, She) and Gay are cousins.

7. May Tyrone and (me, I) count them?

8. Wilfred and (him, he) are partners.

9. At the door stood (he, him) and his wife.

10. Did (she, her) and her sister come?

11. (We, Us) boys are partners.

12. Alvaro and (me, I) are captains.

13. (Her, She) and Sasha wrote the play.

14. (Us, We) editors are very busy.

15. Spot and (he, him) are terriers.

16. (They, Them) and (we, us) are coming.

17. (He, Him) and (me, I) are drawing the comic strips.

18. We and (they, them) are typing the story.

19. (She, Her) and I have been friends.

20. (Us, We) girls will plan the play.

21. Ling and (I, me) went to the pool.

22. Jamar and (they, them) rode to the ranch.

23. Margo and (her, she) dashed to the store.

24. (He, Him) and Tony are close friends.

25. Mother and (her, she) went to the fair.

26. How did Clark and (they, them) escape?

27. What time will Bart and (him, he) return?

28. Shall you or (us, we) collect the paper?

29. Mr. Bennet and (I, me) are coming for lunch.

30. Alicia and (we, us) have decided to stay.

31. Maria and (I, me) went to the library.

32. Dennis and (him, he) visited the museum.

33. How can Adela and (they, them) help?

34. Tran and (they, them) are rehearsing for a play.

Practicing Basic Skills in Language Arts • 41

© 2005 Sopris West Educational Services. All rights reserved. Practicing Basic Skills in Language Arts. Purchaser has permission to photocopy this page for classroom use only.

ONE-MINUTE FLUENCY
BUILDER SERIES

SEE TO MARK

Subject Pronouns
Directions: Mark the correct pronoun.

1. My dog and (I, me) take long walks.
2. Did (him, he) and his brother leave?
3. Did Carlos and (she, her) help you?
4. (We, Us) girls are ready.
5. May (we, us) boys have a party?
6. (Her, She) and Gay are cousins.
7. May Tyrone and (me, I) count them?
8. Wilfred and (him, he) are partners.
9. At the door stood (he, him) and his wife.
10. Did (she, her) and her sister come?
11. (We, Us) boys are partners.
12. Alvaro and (me, I) are captains.
13. (Her, She) and Sasha wrote the play.
14. (Us, We) editors are very busy.
15. Spot and (he, him) are terriers.
16. (They, Them) and (we, us) are coming.
17. (He, Him) and (me, I) are drawing the comic strips.

18. We and (they, them) are typing the story.
19. (She, Her) and I have been friends.
20. (Us, We) girls will plan the play.
21. Ling and (I, me) went to the pool.
22. Jamar and (they, them) rode to the ranch.
23. Margo and (her, she) dashed to the store.
24. (He, Him) and Tony are close friends.
25. Mother and (her, she) went to the fair.
26. How did Clark and (they, them) escape?
27. What time will Bart and (him, he) return?
28. Shall you or (us, we) collect the paper?
29. Mr. Bennet and (I, me) are coming for lunch.
30. Alicia and (we, us) have decided to stay.
31. Maria and (I, me) went to the library.
32. Dennis and (him, he) visited the museum.
33. How can Adela and (they, them) help?
34. Tran and (they, them) are rehearsing for a play.

	First Try	Second Try
Correct		
Error		

(1)
(2)
(3)
(4)
(5)
(6)
(7)
(8)
(9)
(10)
(11)
(12)
(13)
(14)
(15)
(17)
(19)

(20)
(21)
(22)
(23)
(24)
(25)
(26)
(27)
(28)
(29)
(30)
(31)
(32)
(33)
(34)
(35)
(36)

ANSWER SHEET

Practicing Basic Skills in Language Arts • 42

© 2005 Sopris West Educational Services. All rights reserved. Practicing Basic Skills in Language Arts. Purchaser has permission to photocopy this page for classroom use only.

ONE-MINUTE FLUENCY
BUILDER SERIES

Pronouns After a Verb

Directions: Mark the correct pronoun.

1. The lost hikers were (they, them).

2. They invited Lily and (I, me).

3. Tony will drive (we, us) to the lake.

4. Those drivers weren't (they, them).

5. It was Mother and (I, me) who were on time.

6. Were the coach and (he, him) on time?

7. He called our parents and (we, us) then.

8. Will the man direct Father and (she, her)?

9. It was Ned and (I, me).

10. That was (we, us) who locked the cabin.

11. Our part surprised Louis and (she, her).

12. Ann couldn't find the dog and (they, them).

13. The actors were Luke and (me, I).

14. Miss Lee wants you and (we, us) now.

15. The boys in the photograph are (us, we).

16. The detectives followed (they, them).

17. I saw Tam and (he, him) in the cave.

18. The typists were Ted and (I, me).

19. Rosa and we sent (they, them) ahead.

20. Did Tyra invite (her, she) and (I, me)?

21. He asked Jacob and (I, me) to be there.

22. The girl in the blue coat is (she, her).

23. The losers were (they, them).

24. The elevator brought Kim and (me, I) up.

25. It was (she, her) who found the dog.

26. The lucky ones are (we, us).

27. Joshua called Rachel and (she, her).

28. The singers are Boyd and (her, she).

29. Were you and they teasing (him, he)?

30. The boy who won was (him, he).

31. I saw Malik and (he, him) in the cave.

32. Father and she surprised (he, him).

33. Toby and I told (she, her) about it.

34. The champion is (he, him).

© 2005 Sopris West Educational Services. All rights reserved. Practicing Basic Skills in Language Arts. Purchaser has permission to photocopy this page for classroom use only.

ONE-MINUTE FLUENCY
BUILDER SERIES

SEE TO MARK

Pronouns After a Verb

Directions: Mark the correct pronoun.

	First Try	Second Try
Correct		
Error		

1. The lost hikers were (they, them).   (1)

2. They invited Lily and (I, me).   (2)

3. Tony will drive (we, us) to the lake.   (3)

4. Those drivers weren't (they, them).   (4)

5. It was Mother and (I, me) who were on time.   (5)

6. Were the coach and (he, him) on time?   (6)

7. He called our parents and (we, us) then.   (7)

8. Will the man direct Father and (she, her)?   (8)

9. It was Ned and (I, me).   (9)

10. That was (we, us) who locked the cabin.   (10)

11. Our part surprised Louis and (she, her).   (11)

12. Ann couldn't find the dog and (they, them).   (12)

13. The actors were Luke and (me, I).   (13)

14. Miss Lee wants you and (we, us) now.   (14)

15. The boys in the photograph are (us, we).   (15)

16. The detectives followed (they, them).   (16)

17. I saw Tam and (he, him) in the cave.   (17)

18. The typists were Ted and (I, me).   (18)

19. Rosa and we sent (they, them) ahead.   (19)

20. Did Tyra invite (her, she) and (I, me)?   (21)

21. He asked Jacob and (I, me) to be there.   (22)

22. The girl in the blue coat is (she, her).   (23)

23. The losers were (they, them).   (24)

24. The elevator brought Kim and (me, I) up.   (25)

25. It was (she, her) who found the dog.   (26)

26. The lucky ones are (we, us).   (27)

27. Joshua called Rachel and (she, her).   (28)

28. The singers are Boyd and (her, she).   (29)

29. Were you and they teasing (him, he)?   (30)

30. The boy who won was (him, he).   (31)

31. I saw Malik and (he, him) in the cave.   (32)

32. Father and she surprised (he, him).   (33)

33. Toby and I told (she, her) about it.   (34)

34. The champion is (he, him).   (35)

ANSWER SHEET

Practicing Basic Skills in Language Arts • 44

© 2005 Sopris West Educational Services. All rights reserved. Practicing Basic Skills in Language Arts. Purchaser has permission to photocopy this page for classroom use only.

	Correct	Error
First Try		
Second Try		

ONE-MINUTE FLUENCY
BUILDER SERIES

Pronouns After a Preposition

Directions: Mark the correct pronoun.

1. Will Anne be traveling with (they, them)?

2. Our club was started by Ty and (he, him).

3. Please leave the cookies for Doty and (we, us).

4. These costumes belong to you and (she, her).

5. Our coach called for Li and (him, he).

6. Come to the movies with Mother and (I, me).

7. The photographer left his camera with (they, them).

8. A man sent a message to Roger and (us, we).

9. Open the garage for Mrs. Owens and (she, her).

10. José is singing his song for (I, me).

11. Grandma planned a surprise for (they, them).

12. The checker game was a draw between Nick and (he, him).

13. The book was written by Kang and (I, me).

14. Please wait for (us, we).

15. Did you speak to Henry and (her, she)?

16. They took the keys with (them, they).

17. The fire was found by Maria and (I, me).

18. I wrote a letter of thanks to (her, she).

19. We received a letter from (he, him).

20. The reporter wrote about (they, them).

21. The magazines are from (we, us).

22. Jim gave the tickets to Jamar and (we, us).

23. Will you wait for Gene and (she, her)?

24. Walk to the gate with Joan and (I, me).

25. Jorge threw the ball to (her, she).

26. The present is for Mother and (he, him).

27. The stranger looked at (them, they).

28. The posters were made by (he, him).

29. The music was enjoyed by (we, us).

30. He hid Don and him from (us, we).

31. Elena and she played their flutes for (we, us).

Practicing Basic Skills in Language Arts • 45

© 2005 Sopris West Educational Services. All rights reserved. Practicing Basic Skills in Language Arts. Purchaser has permission to photocopy this page for classroom use only.

SEE TO MARK

Pronouns After a Preposition

Directions: Mark the correct pronoun.

	First Try	Second Try
Correct		
Error		

1. Will Anne be traveling with (they, <u>them</u>)?

2. Our club was started by Ty and (he, <u>him</u>).

3. Please leave the cookies for Doty and (we, <u>us</u>).

4. These costumes belong to you and (she, <u>her</u>).

5. Our coach called for Li and (<u>him</u>, he).

6. Come to the movies with Mother and (I, <u>me</u>).

7. The photographer left his camera with (they, <u>them</u>).

8. A man sent a message to Roger and (<u>us</u>, we).

9. Open the garage for Mrs. Owens and (she, <u>her</u>).

10. José is singing his song for (I, <u>me</u>).

11. Grandma planned a surprise for (they, <u>them</u>).

12. The checker game was a draw between Nick and (he, <u>him</u>).

13. The book was written by Kang and (I, <u>me</u>).

14. Please wait for (<u>us</u>, we).

15. Did you speak to Henry and (<u>her</u>, she)?

16. They took the keys with (<u>them</u>, they).

17. The fire was found by Maria and (I, <u>me</u>).

18. I wrote a letter of thanks to (<u>her</u>, she).

19. We received a letter from (he, <u>him</u>).

20. The reporter wrote about (they, <u>them</u>).

21. The magazines are from (we, <u>us</u>).

22. Jim gave the tickets to Jamar and (we, <u>us</u>).

23. Will you wait for Gene and (she, <u>her</u>)?

24. Walk to the gate with Joan and (I, <u>me</u>).

25. Jorge threw the ball to (<u>her</u>, she).

26. The present is for Mother and (he, <u>him</u>).

27. The stranger looked at (<u>them</u>, they).

28. The posters were made by (he, <u>him</u>).

29. The music was enjoyed by (we, <u>us</u>).

30. He hid Don and him from (<u>us</u>, we).

31. Elena and she played their flutes for (we, <u>us</u>).

ANSWER SHEET

Practicing Basic Skills in Language Arts • 46

© 2005 Sopris West Educational Services. All rights reserved. Practicing Basic Skills in Language Arts. Purchaser has permission to photocopy this page for classroom use only.

Verbs

Action Verbs in Isolation—Primary 49
Action Verbs in Isolation 51
Action Verbs—Fill in the Blanks 53
Action Verbs in Sentences—Primary 55
Action Verbs in Sentences 57
Verbs in Isolation 59
Verbs in Sentences 61
Verbs in Sentences 63
Helping Verbs in Isolation 65
Helping Verbs in Isolation 67
Helping Verbs in Sentences 69
Helping Verbs—Fill in the Blanks 71
Verb Phrases in Sentences 73
Linking Verbs in Sentences 75
Transitive and Intransitive Verbs—
     Fill in the Blanks 77
Active and Passive Verbs 79
Principal Parts of a Verb—
     Fill in the Blanks 81
Verb Tense 83
Irregular Verbs 85
Irregular Verbs 87

Irregular Verbs 89
Irregular Verbs 91
Correct Form of Irregular Verbs in
     Sentences 93
Correct Form of Irregular Verbs—
     Fill in the Blanks 95
Correct Form of Rise/Raise in Sentences 97
Correct Form of Lie/Lay in Sentences 99
Correct Form of Sit/Set in Sentences 101
Correct Form of Lie/Lay, Sit/Set, Rise/Raise . 103
Subject-Verb Agreement: Was/Were 105
Subject-Verb Agreement: Am/Are/Is 107
Subject-Verb Agreement: Has/Have 109
Subject-Verb Agreement: Has Been/
     Have Been 111
Correct Verb Form—Usage 113
Participles in Sentences 115
Gerunds in Sentences 117
Infinitives in Sentences 119
Gerunds, Participles, Infinitives in
     Sentences 121

SEE TO MARK

First Try	Correct	Error
Second Try	

Action Verbs in Isolation—Primary
Directions: Underline all of the action verbs.

run	boy	house	sit	street	man	talk	cry	ball
box	hide	cat	mother	skip	barn	eat	tree	sleep
see	cow	fight	snake	touch	read	green	say	apple
train	listen	hat	jump	girl	tent	walk	door	shut
cut	table	finger	hide	Jane	catch	child	river	throw
bird	pick	push	flower	stand	dog	share	plate	fence
give	car	take	pen	grass	hear	dirt	feed	book

© 2005 Sopris West Educational Services. All rights reserved. Practicing Basic Skills in Language Arts. Purchaser has permission to photocopy this page for classroom use only.

ONE-MINUTE FLUENCY BUILDER SERIES

SEE TO MARK

Action Verbs in Isolation—Primary
Directions: Underline all of the action verbs.

	Correct	Error
First Try		
Second Try		

<u>run</u>	boy	house	<u>sit</u>	street	man	<u>talk</u>	<u>cry</u>	ball	(4)
box	<u>hide</u>	cat	mother	<u>skip</u>	barn	<u>eat</u>	tree	<u>sleep</u>	(8)
<u>see</u>	cow	<u>fight</u>	snake	<u>touch</u>	<u>read</u>	green	<u>say</u>	apple	(13)
train	<u>listen</u>	hat	<u>jump</u>	girl	tent	<u>walk</u>	door	<u>shut</u>	(17)
<u>cut</u>	table	finger	<u>hide</u>	Jane	<u>catch</u>	child	river	<u>throw</u>	(21)
bird	<u>pick</u>	<u>push</u>	flower	<u>stand</u>	dog	<u>share</u>	plate	fence	(25)
<u>give</u>	car	<u>take</u>	pen	grass	<u>hear</u>	dirt	<u>feed</u>	book	(29)

ANSWER SHEET

Practicing Basic Skills in Language Arts • 50

© 2005 Sopris West Educational Services. All rights reserved. Practicing Basic Skills in Language Arts. Purchaser has permission to photocopy this page for classroom use only.

Correct	Error
First Try	
Second Try	

ONE-MINUTE FLUENCY BUILDER SERIES

SEE TO MARK

Action Verbs in Isolation
Directions: Circle all action verbs.

jog	discuss	feel	was	shushed	should be
be	seem	puzzled	become	taste	scolded
chattered	whistled	turn	noticed	memorize	stay
appear	being	is	do	shall be	missed
practice	tackled	select	grow	bought	become
barked	taste	shall	directed	galloped	cleaned
has been	seize	found	has	seem	would
escape	am	would be	deliver	may	will be
have	must	told	were	darted	established
remain	stay	sound	baked	will have been	watched
gathered	honked	signed	can	drive	smell
could	locate	appear	compare	should	can be
stirred	have been	offered	shall have been	apologize	quoted
could have been	laugh	return	shot	remain	feel
might	boarded	look	should have been	wait	shouted
shone	would have been	recognize	volleyed	did	paddled
honk	twists	had been	swung	read	caught
beat	had	recall	will	could be	turn

© 2005 Sopris West Educational Services. All rights reserved. Practicing Basic Skills in Language Arts. Purchaser has permission to photocopy this page for classroom use only.

SEE TO MARK

Action Verbs in Isolation

Directions: Circle all action verbs.

First Try	Second Try
Correct	
Error	

jog	discuss	feel	was	shushed	should be (4)
be	seem	puzzled	become	taste	scolded (7)
chattered	whistled	turn	noticed	memorize	stay (12)
appear	being	is	do	shall be	missed (13)
practice	tackled	select	grow	bought	become (18)
barked	taste	shall	directed	galloped	cleaned (23)
has been	seize	found	has	seem	would (25)
escape	am	would be	deliver	may	will be (27)
have	must	told	were	darted	established (30)
remain	stay	sound	baked	will have been	watched (34)
gathered	honked	signed	can	drive	smell (39)
could	locate	appear	compare	should	can be (42)
stirred	have been	offered	shall have been	apologize	quoted (46)
could have been	laugh	return	shot	remain	feel (51)
might	boarded	look	should have been	wait	shouted (55)
shone	would have been	recognize	volleyed	did	paddled (59)
honk	twists	had been	swung	read	caught (64)
beat	had	recall	will	could be	turn (67)

ANSWER SHEET

Practicing Basic Skills in Language Arts • 52

© 2005 Sopris West Educational Services. All rights reserved. Practicing Basic Skills in Language Arts. Purchaser has permission to photocopy this page for classroom use only.

	Correct	Error
First Try		
Second Try		

THINK TO WRITE

Action Verbs—Fill in the Blanks

Directions: Write an appropriate action verb of your choice in each sentence.

Jack _____ twenty laps of the pool every afternoon. Manuel _____ a joke and we all _____ .

That paper will _____ if you put it too close to the flame. The catcher _____ the ball and saved the

game. You must _____ a well-balanced diet for good nutrition. The wild geese _____ over our field each

year. Did you _____ that new book? Corn _____ well in this climate. The boy _____ from the

tree and _____ his arm. This shot will _____ a bit. Did you _____ the milk on the floor? Our

team was disappointed when they _____ by three points. You may _____ for your purchases here. Please

_____ carefully to my instructions. The jogger _____ through the park. Did you _____ this letter?

I will _____ my brother to play handball. My dog won't _____ anyone. The choir will _____ in

the concert. On my birthday, Paul _____ me a fantastic gift. The sun was _____ brightly. The leaky faucet

_____ all the time. The artist _____ portraits for a living. Will you _____ this pencil for me? The

horse _____ across the meadow. I _____ the candy bowl and broke it. I _____ to set my alarm

clock and did not awaken until 10:30. My uncle _____ two books a week. The phone _____ and I answered

it. One of my chores is to _____ the dinner dishes. I was so exhausted that I _____ during my favorite

television show. _____ down and be quiet. When I am sixteen, I will be able to _____ our family car. Li

_____ down the hill in the snow. Rosa _____ behind the beautiful power boat. Will you _____

this machine for me?

Practicing Basic Skills in Language Arts • 53

© 2005 Sopris West Educational Services. All rights reserved. Practicing Basic Skills in Language Arts. Purchaser has permission to photocopy this page for classroom use only.

ONE-MINUTE FLUENCY
BUILDER SERIES

THINK TO WRITE

Action Verbs—Fill in the Blanks

Directions: Write an appropriate action verb of your choice in each sentence.

	First Try	Second Try
Correct		
Error		

Jack _____ twenty laps of the pool every afternoon. Manuel _____ a joke and we all _____. (3)

That paper will _____ if you put it too close to the flame. The catcher _____ the ball and saved the (5)

game. You must _____ a well-balanced diet for good nutrition. The wild geese _____ over our field each (7)

year. Did you _____ that new book? Corn _____ well in this climate. The boy _____ from the (10)

tree and _____ his arm. This shot will _____ a bit. Did you _____ the milk on the floor? Our (13)

team was disappointed when they _____ by three points. You may _____ for your purchases here. Please (15)

_____ carefully to my instructions. The jogger _____ through the park. Did you _____ this letter? (18)

I will _____ my brother to play handball. My dog won't _____ anyone. The choir will _____ in (21)

the concert. On my birthday, Paul _____ me a fantastic gift. The sun was _____ brightly. The leaky faucet (23)

_____ all the time. The artist _____ portraits for a living. Will you _____ this pencil for me? The (26)

horse _____ across the meadow. I _____ the candy bowl and broke it. I _____ to set my alarm (29)

clock and did not awaken until 10:30. My uncle _____ two books a week. The phone _____ and I answered (31)

it. One of my chores is to _____ the dinner dishes. I was so exhausted that I _____ during my favorite (33)

television show. _____ down and be quiet. When I am sixteen, I will be able to _____ our family car. Li (35)

_____ down the hill in the snow. Rosa _____ behind the beautiful power boat. Will you _____ (38)

this machine for me?

ANSWER SHEET

Practicing Basic Skills in Language Arts • 54

© 2005 Sopris West Educational Services. All rights reserved. Practicing Basic Skills in Language Arts. Purchaser has permission to photocopy this page for classroom use only.

ONE MINUTE FLUENCY BUILDER SERIES

	Correct	Error
First Try		
Second Try		

Action Verbs in Sentences—Primary

Directions: Underline the action verbs in the sentences.

The girl ran all the way home.

Find the book in your desk.

Can you hear the wind?

Did you ride on the train?

He threw the ball to the catcher.

Sing a song for the baby.

Lucia read all of the books.

Jim always comes to class.

We will all walk to school.

See the cat up in the tree?

He jumped over the stick.

The baby fell down.

She cried all night long.

She skipped down the sidewalk.

Look down the road for the car.

Don't fight in class.

The cats climbed up the tree.

The birds fly south for the winter.

Practicing Basic Skills in Language Arts • 55

© 2005 Sopris West Educational Services. All rights reserved. Practicing Basic Skills in Language Arts. Purchaser has permission to photocopy this page for classroom use only.

ONE MINUTE FLUENCY
BUILDER SERIES

Action Verbs in Sentences—Primary

Directions: Underline the action verbs in the sentences.

		First Try	Second Try
Correct			
Error			

(1) The girl ran all the way home.

(2) Find the book in your desk.

(3) Can you hear the wind?

(4) Did you ride on the train?

(5) He threw the ball to the catcher.

(6) Sing a song for the baby.

(7) Lucia read all of the books.

(8) Jim always comes to class.

(9) We will all walk to school.

(10) See the cat up in the tree?

(11) He jumped over the stick.

(12) The baby fell down.

(13) She cried all night long.

(14) She skipped down the sidewalk.

(15) Look down the road for the car.

(16) Don't fight in class.

(17) The cats climbed up the tree.

(18) The birds fly south for the winter.

ANSWER SHEET

Practicing Basic Skills in Language Arts • 56

© 2005 Sopris West Educational Services. All rights reserved. Practicing Basic Skills in Language Arts. Purchaser has permission to photocopy this page for classroom use only.

SEE TO MARK

Action Verbs in Sentences

Directions: Mark action verbs in the following sentences.

	First Try	Second Try
Correct		
Error		

We ran to the lake and back. You worry too much about your grades. The quarterback passed for a touchdown. I hope our team wins next weekend. Mrs. Lee saw you at the theater. My family always eats at 6:00. Give your donations to Mr. Hancock, who serves as temporary chairman. Freddie paid five dollars for that mitt. Maria would have won the race, but she fell. Do you think it will freeze tonight? Please lend me some money so I can buy this sweater. The bell rang and the class rushed out of the room. The outfielder caught the ball and relayed it to third base. Sir Edmund Hillary climbed to the top of Mt. Everest, gaining international fame. The soldiers crept from trench to trench. The movie was so funny that we laughed until we cried. Do not bend this computer card, or it will stick in the machine. If you choose, you may attend college. As he bit into the crisp apple, Paul suddenly worried about worms. The concert began as soon as all the members of the audience were seated. The army attacked the enemy camp. Ebony's little brother cried when his balloon burst. Can you come to my party? The sun always sets in the west. Angie swam to victory in the butterfly. Take this money and buy yourself a gift. The ship sank very rapidly. Jamel drank his fruit juice before he left for school. I hung my new coat on the hanger. I saw the car as it sped down the road. Janie gave you the money yesterday. I dropped the antique vase and broke it. Aunt Ling went to the post office. Who tore this picture? We drove three miles on the first day of our trip. Have you written that letter yet? Are you wearing your new suit tonight? They all dived into the water. Show Joe those snapshots from the picnic he planned. I heard some good news yesterday. Manuel has eaten too much pie. My sister sews every evening. The scout threw water on the fire.

© 2005 Sopris West Educational Services. All rights reserved. Practicing Basic Skills in Language Arts. Purchaser has permission to photocopy this page for classroom use only.

ONE-MINUTE FLUENCY
BUILDER SERIES

SEE TO MARK

Action Verbs in Sentences

Directions: Mark action verbs in the following sentences.

	First Try	Second Try
Correct		
Error		

We ran to the lake and back. You worry too much about your grades. The quarterback passed for a touchdown. I hope our (4)

team wins next weekend. Mrs. Lee saw you at the theater. My family always eats at 6:00. Give your donations to Mr. Hancock, (8)

who serves as temporary chairman. Freddie paid five dollars for that mitt. Maria would have won the race, but she fell. Do (12)

you think it will freeze tonight? Please lend me some money so I can buy this sweater. The bell rang and the class rushed out (18)

of the room. The outfielder caught the ball and relayed it to third base. Sir Edmund Hillary climbed to the top of Mt. Everest, (21)

gaining international fame. The soldiers crept from trench to trench. The movie was so funny that we laughed until we cried. (25)

Do not bend this computer card, or it will stick in the machine. If you choose, you may attend college. As he bit into the crisp (30)

apple, Paul suddenly worried about worms. The concert began as soon as all the members of the audience were seated. The (33)

army attacked the enemy camp. Ebony's little brother cried when his balloon burst. Can you come to my party? The sun always (37)

sets in the west. Angie swam to victory in the butterfly. Take this money and buy yourself a gift. The ship sank very rapidly. (42)

Jamel drank his fruit juice before he left for school. I hung my new coat on the hanger. I saw the car as it sped down the road. (47)

Janie gave you the money yesterday. I dropped the antique vase and broke it. Aunt Ling went to the post office. Who tore (52)

this picture? We drove three miles on the first day of our trip. Have you written that letter yet? Are you wearing your new suit (55)

tonight? They all dived into the water. Show Joe those snapshots from the picnic he planned. I heard some good news yesterday. (59)

Manuel has eaten too much pie. My sister sews every evening. The scout threw water on the fire. (62)

ANSWER SHEET

© 2005 Sopris West Educational Services. All rights reserved. Practicing Basic Skills in Language Arts. Purchaser has permission to photocopy this page for classroom use only.

SEE TO MARK

Verbs in Isolation
Directions: Mark all the verbs.

First Try	
Second Try	
Correct	Error

car	honk	and	can	become	found
be	beat	will have	blue	pencil	would be
chattered	books	should be	stapler	teaches	television
carnival	taste	drive	caught	twice	handsome
escape	window	smell	mathematics	almost	may
want	the	beautiful	boxes	also	swung
may be	am	does	had	rush	treehouse
day	twists	turn	praised	baked	seem
remain	asked	English	purpose	did	now
typewriter	is	floor	catalog	too	when
must	wood	parked	discuss	not	shouted
desk	key	apologize	whistled	can	diamond
late	puzzled	room	being	return	moth
stay	told	schoolhouse	special	twenty	do
have been	clock	tacked	building	notebook	today
volleyball	an	recall	missed	movie	

Practicing Basic Skills in Language Arts • 59

© 2005 Sopris West Educational Services. All rights reserved. Practicing Basic Skills in Language Arts. Purchaser has permission to photocopy this page for classroom use only.

ONE MINUTE FLUENCY BUILDER SERIES

SEE TO MARK

First Try		Correct	Error
Second Try			

Verbs in Isolation

Directions: Mark all the verbs.

car	honk	and	can	become	found	(4)
be	beat	will have	blue	pencil	would be	(8)
chattered	books	should be	stapler	teaches	television	(11)
carnival	taste	drive	caught	twice	handsome	(14)
escape	window	smell	mathematics	almost	may	(17)
want	the	beautiful	boxes	also	swung	(19)
may be	am	does	had	rush	treehouse	(24)
day	twists	turn	praised	baked	seem	(29)
remain	asked	English	purpose	did	now	(32)
typewriter	is	floor	catalog	too	when	(33)
must	wood	parked	discuss	not	shouted	(37)
desk	key	apologize	whistled	can	diamond	(40)
late	puzzled	room	being	return	moth	(43)
stay	told	schoolhouse	special	twenty	do	(46)
have been	clock	tacked	building	notebook	today	(48)
volleyball	an	recall	missed	movie		(50)

© 2005 Sopris West Educational Services. All rights reserved. Practicing Basic Skills in Language Arts. Purchaser has permission to photocopy this page for classroom use only.

ONE-MINUTE FLUENCY
BUILDER SERIES

Verbs in Sentences

Directions: Underline each verb in the following sentences.

	First Try	Second Try
Correct		
Error		

The baby cried. The car sped away. The boy parked his bike. John is in the room. We are on a bus. We remained in the room.

We snapped our fingers to the music. The bridge collapsed. A guard sounded the alarm. The rock smashed the window. The

girl combed her hair. A cat jumped. Bears hibernate. The rain continued. A doubt remained. The country surrounds the city.

Pedro has a headache. Mark ran the race. Isaac slowly ate the apple. The cat softly purred. A bell rang. The signal was a flash of

light. Lindbergh crossed the Atlantic. The moon circles the earth. The train left on time. Jim sprained his ankle. Luis practiced

yesterday. Time flies quickly. Roses smell nice. Coral is my favorite color. Turquoise is a popular stone. Iola is a small town.

Roberto is very handsome. Cris came yesterday. John is my cousin. The hospital serves the town. Plants like tender, loving care.

Stephen went home. Ty lived in Colorado. The lamp dangles above a chair. Schools participate in sporting events. Sung sends

people cards. Joyce works hard. Mike is shy. Time heals all wounds. Carol called Rosa to the phone. Pineapples grow in Hawaii.

The boys planned the picnic. Ralph wrote ten letters. Randolph answered his letter. Grandma has a cat. Marcia lives down the

street. I polished the silver. Jade read a book. Bread smells good. The clock was wrong. His answer was right. Linda borrowed

Martin's car. Theresa types practice sheets. George limped after the game. The ball flew through the air. Pedro isn't here. Tables

rest on the floor. The star twinkled brightly. Her rings cost a lot of money. The watermelons grew very large. The students very

slowly erased the board. Andre ran fast yesterday.

© 2005 Sopris West Educational Services. All rights reserved. Practicing Basic Skills in Language Arts. Purchaser has permission to photocopy this page for classroom use only.

ONE-MINUTE FLUENCY BUILDER SERIES

SEE TO MARK

Verbs in Sentences

Directions: Underline each verb in the following sentences.

	First Try	Second Try
Correct		
Error		

The baby cried. The car sped away. The boy parked his bike. John is in the room. We are on a bus. We remained in the room. (6)

We snapped our fingers to the music. The bridge collapsed. A guard sounded the alarm. The rock smashed the window. The (10)

girl combed her hair. A cat jumped. Bears hibernate. The rain continued. A doubt remained. The country surrounds the city. (16)

Pedro has a headache. Mark ran the race. Isaac slowly ate the apple. The cat softly purred. A bell rang. The signal was a flash of (22)

light. Lindbergh crossed the Atlantic. The moon circles the earth. The train left on time. Jim sprained his ankle. Luis practiced (27)

yesterday. Time flies quickly. Roses smell nice. Coral is my favorite color. Turquoise is a popular stone. Iola is a small town. (32)

Roberto is very handsome. Cris came yesterday. John is my cousin. The hospital serves the town. Plants like tender, loving care. (37)

Stephen went home. Ty lived in Colorado. The lamp dangles above a chair. Schools participate in sporting events. Sung sends (42)

people cards. Joyce works hard. Mike is shy. Time heals all wounds. Carol called Rosa to the phone. Pineapples grow in Hawaii. (47)

The boys planned the picnic. Ralph wrote ten letters. Randolph answered his letter. Grandma has a cat. Marcia lives down the (52)

street. I polished the silver. Jade read a book. Bread smells good. The clock was wrong. His answer was right. Linda borrowed (58)

Martin's car. Theresa types practice sheets. George limped after the game. The ball flew through the air. Pedro isn't here. Tables (62)

rest on the floor. The star twinkled brightly. Her rings cost a lot of money. The watermelons grew very large. The students very (66)

slowly erased the board. Andre ran fast yesterday. (68)

ANSWER SHEET

© 2005 Sopris West Educational Services. All rights reserved. Practicing Basic Skills in Language Arts. Purchaser has permission to photocopy this page for classroom use only.

First Try	Correct	Error
Second Try		

SEE TO MARK

Verbs in Sentences

Directions: Mark each verb in the following sentences.

The little child crossed the street. The boys rode their bicycles to the playground. The sun was hot. The girls played baseball for

a while. Then they swam in the pool. It was time for lunch. Many of the boys brought lunch from home. Are the other girls

coming to the playground? Always be polite. Listen to that noise. The storm continued for an hour. My father encouraged me to

continue. We punished him for his acts. We searched everywhere for the lost book. I question his sincerity. That wind feels cold.

The game ended at five o'clock. After dinner the boys watched television. My brother is the leader. The food tasted good. The

sheep ate the green grass. Our cat caught a mouse. Thunder frightened the horses. It was he on the telephone. In the morning

three children appeared at the library door. Does that large red book belong to you, Jenette? We packed the tents an hour ago.

Yesterday Terry swam the length of the pool. He is the first person to arrive. Are Charles and José upstairs? Those skates aren't

mine. The flowers looked beautiful on the piano. Dad tasted the pie while you were out. The girls play hockey in their league.

The boys weren't at the skating rink. The mayor, with several of his assistants, was across the street for lunch. They know that Bill

walked in the marathon. Doesn't Lu live near Andy? Lucia looked unhappy in the halls today. We climbed to the top of the hill.

Damon brought his binoculars to the game. The boys returned in time for supper. The pupils quietly opened their books. Brian

pointed to the Big Dipper. Franco looks tired today. Last night we found the missing book. The president signed the bill. Nobody

remembered the meeting tonight. Was Carmen singing the song solo? Lamar is a reporter on the school paper. The highway runs

through the middle of town. Janice repaired the car. Come tomorrow if you want more information. The dog ran fast.

© 2005 Sopris West Educational Services. All rights reserved. Practicing Basic Skills in Language Arts. Purchaser has permission to photocopy this page for classroom use only.

SEE TO MARK

Verbs in Sentences

Directions: Mark each verb in the following sentences.

	Correct	Error
First Try		
Second Try		

The little child crossed the street. The boys rode their bicycles to the playground. The sun was hot. The girls played baseball for (4)

a while. Then they swam in the pool. It was time for lunch. Many of the boys brought lunch from home. Are the other girls (7)

coming to the playground? Always be polite. Listen to that noise. The storm continued for an hour. My father encouraged me to (12)

continue. We punished him for his acts. We searched everywhere for the lost book. I question his sincerity. That wind feels cold. (16)

The game ended at five o'clock. After dinner the boys watched television. My brother is the leader. The food tasted good. The (20)

sheep ate the green grass. Our cat caught a mouse. Thunder frightened the horses. It was he on the telephone. In the morning (24)

three children appeared at the library door. Does that large red book belong to you, Jenette? We packed the tents an hour ago. (28)

Yesterday Terry swam the length of the pool. He is the first person to arrive. Are Charles and José upstairs? Those skates aren't (33)

mine. The flowers looked beautiful on the piano. Dad tasted the pie while you were out. The girls play hockey in their league. (37)

The boys weren't at the skating rink. The mayor, with several of his assistants, was across the street for lunch. They know that Bill (39)

walked in the marathon. Doesn't Lu live near Andy? Lucia looked unhappy in the halls today. We climbed to the top of the hill. (44)

Damon brought his binoculars to the game. The boys returned in time for supper. The pupils quietly opened their books. Brian (47)

pointed to the Big Dipper. Franco looks tired today. Last night we found the missing book. The president signed the bill. Nobody (51)

remembered the meeting tonight. Was Carmen singing the song solo? Lamar is a reporter on the school paper. The highway runs (56)

through the middle of town. Janice repaired the car. Come tomorrow if you want more information. The dog ran fast. (60)

© 2005 Sopris West Educational Services. All rights reserved. Practicing Basic Skills in Language Arts. Purchaser has permission to photocopy this page for classroom use only.

ONE MINUTE FLUENCY BUILDER SERIES

SEE TO MARK

Helping Verbs in Isolation

Directions: Mark each of the following helping verbs: has, shall, could, may, do, have, should, will, might, does, had, can, would, must, did, does.

	First Try	Second Try
Correct		
Error		

jog	discuss	feel	was	shushed	could	be	should
puzzled	become	taste	scolded	chattered	whistled	have	noticed
memorize	stay	appear	has	is	do	can	missed
practice	tackled	select	grow	bought	become	taste	shall
directed	galloped	cleaned	shall	seize	foul	has	seem
would	escape	am	would	deliver	may	might	have
must	told	were	darted	established	remain	sound	baked
do	watched	stay	gathered	honked	should	can	dive
smell	could	locate	appear	compare	should	will	stirred
would	offered	had	apologize	quoted	does	laugh	return
shot	remain	feel	might	board	have	may	wait

Practicing Basic Skills in Language Arts • 65

© 2005 Sopris West Educational Services. All rights reserved. Practicing Basic Skills in Language Arts. Purchaser has permission to photocopy this page for classroom use only.

ONE-MINUTE FLUENCY BUILDER SERIES

SEE TO MARK

Helping Verbs in Isolation

Directions: Mark each of the following helping verbs: has, shall, could, may, do, have, should, will, might, does, had, can, would, must, did, does.

	Correct	Error
First Try		
Second Try		

jog	discuss	feel	was	shushed	**could**	be	**should**	(2)
puzzled	become	taste	scolded	chattered	whistled	**have**	noticed	(3)
memorize	stay	appear	**has**	is	**do**	**can**	missed	(6)
practice	tackled	select	grow	bought	become	taste	**shall**	(7)
directed	galloped	cleaned	**shall**	seize	foul	seem		(9)
would	escape	am	**would**	deliver	**may**	**might**	**have**	(14)
must	told	were	darted	established	remain	sound	baked	(15)
do	watched	stay	gathered	honked	**should**	**can**	dive	(18)
smell	locate	appear	compare	**should**	will	stirred		(21)
would	offered	**had**	apologize	quoted	**does**	laugh	return	(24)
shot	remain	feel	**might**	board	**have**	**may**	wait	(27)

ANSWER SHEET

© 2005 Sopris West Educational Services. All rights reserved. Practicing Basic Skills in Language Arts. Purchaser has permission to photocopy this page for classroom use only.

Helping Verbs in Isolation

Directions: Mark each of the following helping verbs: can, are, did, be, being, should, could, were, been, is, must, will, may, have, might, am, does, would, do, shall, had, was.

	Correct	Error
First Try		
Second Try		

been	have	with	will	I	you	may
at	off	were	doll	been	being	house
the	might	will	boy	did	black	six
did	ball	was	may	school	shall	is
can	at	can	from	be	five	did
shall	up	should	toy	be	be	from
could	does	am	could	an	red	man
would	them	could	a	does	am	dog
have	might	can	be	must	would	it
him	do	after	should	were	should	am
may	being	can	down	picture	the	woman
are	could	may	shall	white	has	horse
friend	must	do	have	had	blue	should
would	must	would	does	an	might	donkey
might	girl	have	has	does	would	a

Practicing Basic Skills in Language Arts • 67

© 2005 Sopris West Educational Services. All rights reserved. Practicing Basic Skills in Language Arts. Purchaser has permission to photocopy this page for classroom use only.

SEE TO MARK

Helping Verbs in Isolation

Directions: Mark each of the following helping verbs: can, are, did, be, being, should, could, were, been, is, must, will, may, have, might, am, does, would, do, shall, had, was.

				First Try	Second Try	
				Correct		
				Error		

been	have	with	will	you	I	may	(4)
at	off	were	doll	being	been	house	(7)
the	might	will	boy	black	did	six	(10)
did	ball	was	may	school	may	is	(15)
can	at	can	from	be	be	did	(19)
shall	up	should	toy	an	from	from	(22)
could	does	am	could	red	does	man	(27)
would	them	could	a	car	am	dog	(30)
have	might	can	be	must	would	it	(36)
him	do	after	should	be	must	am	(41)
may	being	can	down	the	were	woman	(44)
are	could	may	shall	has	should	horse	(49)
friend	must	do	have	had	the	should	(54)
would	must	would	does	an	had	donkey	(59)
might	girl	have	has	does	might	a	(64)

© 2005 Sopris West Educational Services. All rights reserved. Practicing Basic Skills in Language Arts. Purchaser has permission to photocopy this page for classroom use only.

ONE-MINUTE FLUENCY
BUILDER SERIES

SEE TO MARK

Helping Verbs in Sentences

Directions: Mark the following helping verbs: is, were, has, does, should, must, am, be, have, did, would, can, are, being, had, shall, may, could, was, been, do, will, might.

	First Try	Second Try
Correct		
Error		

The settlers had brought their families along. The sun has not shone all day. Our neighbors are having company. The boys have

surely watched that bonfire carefully. Joe might agree with you. That soldier may soon see his home again. My brother could

have come sooner. A visit to the mill can probably be arranged. The letter may have arrived early. Carlos is just beginning a new

book. Those poor people do need our help. Joe must always have been reading about ventriloquists. Your brother must be told

about our plans. The bell had already rung. The new plans should have been explained to us. The curtain will then be lowered.

Sho was polishing the car. Ana isn't really living here now. The men were working in the garden. This muscle has evidently

been strained before. The work is being rapidly completed. The speaker's voice is not being clearly heard. Yes, Helen does make

her own clothes. Our plans are almost always made at the last minute. Father will be leaving very early. Why has Joe come

with you? Our house can be seen from this corner. What is Father bringing tonight? Tim has changed his mind again. In what

year did Texas become a state? Marco did not go to the game after all. By what nickname was Andrew Jackson known? Jane is

planning a trip for next summer. Could Rosa have come with us? No mail will be delivered tomorrow. Where was Lincoln born?

Most boys would like my Uncle Jack. When will the game begin? These men shall be carefully instructed. Julie was polishing the

furniture. Tyra will agree with you.

© 2005 Sopris West Educational Services. All rights reserved. Practicing Basic Skills in Language Arts. Purchaser has permission to photocopy this page for classroom use only.

Helping Verbs in Sentences

Directions: Mark the following helping verbs: is, were, has, does, should, must, am, be, have, did, would, can, are, being, had, shall, may, could, was, been, do, will, might.

The settlers had brought their families along. The sun has not shone all day. Our neighbors are having company. The boys have (4)

surely watched that bonfire carefully. Joe might agree with you. That soldier may soon see his home again. My brother could (7)

have come sooner. A visit to the mill can probably be arranged. The letter may have arrived early. Carlos is just beginning a new (13)

book. Those poor people do need our help. Joe must always have been reading about ventriloquists. Your brother must be told (18)

about our plans. The bell had already rung. The new plans should have been explained to us. The curtain will then be lowered. (24)

Sho was polishing the car. Ana isn't really living here now. The men were working in the garden. This muscle has evidently (28)

been strained before. The work is being rapidly completed. The speaker's voice is not being clearly heard. Yes, Helen does make (34)

her own clothes. Our plans are almost always made at the last minute. Father will be leaving very early. Why has Joe come (38)

with you? Our house can be seen from this corner. What is Father bringing tonight? Tim has changed his mind again. In what (42)

year did Texas become a state? Marco did not go to the game after all. By what nickname was Andrew Jackson known? Jane is (46)

planning a trip for next summer. Could Rosa have come with us? No mail will be delivered tomorrow. Where was Lincoln born? (51)

Most boys would like my Uncle Jack. When will the game begin? These men shall be carefully instructed. Julie was polishing the (56)

furniture. Tyra will agree with you. (57)

© 2005 Sopris West Educational Services. All rights reserved. Practicing Basic Skills in Language Arts. Purchaser has permission to photocopy this page for classroom use only.

ONE-MINUTE FLUENCY
BUILDER SERIES

SEE TO WRITE

	Correct	Error
First Try		
Second Try		

Helping Verbs—Fill in the Blanks

Directions: Write the helping verbs of your choice to complete the sentences.

Helping Verbs: be   am   is   was   have   had   has   were
will   would   shall   can   could   may   might   are

He _____ specialize in medicine. Jamal _____ gone home. Maria _____ get angry. The witness _____ testify in the afternoon. One fool _____ spoil a party. The principal _____ come with us.

Carlos _____ testing the engine. The tenants _____ barricaded their doors. Her father _____ circulating a petition. The times _____ changing. He _____ learn the poem by tomorrow. Lois _____ called John. The test _____ been here if the mail had come. The lamp _____ dangling from the ceiling. Harry _____ going to the movies. Juan _____ run on the track team. She _____ be the fastest one there. If we go on a picnic, the weather _____ be nice. We _____ have a good time. He _____ be home soon. I want to _____ fun. The class _____ elect Alicia for president. The train _____ roaring loudly. Marco _____ drive carefully. I _____ like to take her with me. My teacher _____ tired. He _____ go if he wants. It _____ terrible. The mail _____ left here. He _____ a good student. She _____ my best friend. We _____ going too. Tomorrow _____ going to be too late. Mary _____ already left. The girls _____ go with us. Their stories _____ interesting.

Pam _____ be the spelling champion. I _____ a member of the club. Li _____ talking to David.

He _____ be the first one there. I _____ want to go with them. It _____ be too late. Math _____ my favorite subject. The leaves _____ falling. Winter _____ soon be here. The water _____ feel very warm. Soon it _____ be solid ice. She _____ bigger than Sue. Mei _____ good friends. We _____ company. We _____ know the answer.

you go with me? I like to

Practicing Basic Skills in Language Arts • 71

© 2005 Sopris West Educational Services. All rights reserved. Practicing Basic Skills in Language Arts. Purchaser has permission to photocopy this page for classroom use only.

ONE-MINUTE FLUENCY BUILDER SERIES

	Correct	Error
First Try		
Second Try		

Helping Verbs—Fill in the Blanks

Directions: Write the helping verbs of your choice to complete the sentences.

Helping Verbs: be   am   is   was   have   had   has   were
will   would   shall   can   could   may   might   are

He _____ specialize in medicine. Jamal _____ gone home. Maria _____ get angry. The witness _____ (3)

_____ testify in the afternoon. One fool _____ spoil a party. The principal _____ come with us. (6)

Carlos _____ testing the engine. The tenants _____ barricaded their doors. Her father (9)

circulating a petition. The times _____ changing. He _____ learn the poem by tomorrow. Lois (11)

_____ called John. The test _____ been here if the mail had come. The lamp _____ dangling (14)

from the ceiling. Harry _____ going to the movies. Juan _____ run on the track team. She (17)

be the fastest one there. If we go on a picnic, the weather _____ be nice. We _____ have a good time. He (19)

_____ be home soon. I want to _____ fun. The class _____ elect Alicia for president. The train (22)

_____ roaring loudly. Marco _____ drive carefully. I _____ like to take her with me. My teacher (25)

_____ tired. He _____ go if he wants. It _____ terrible. The mail _____ left here. He (29)

_____ a good student. She _____ my best friend. We _____ going too. Tomorrow (33)

be too late. Mary _____ already left. The girls _____ go with us. Their stories _____ interesting. (36)

Pam _____ be the spelling champion. I _____ a member of the club. Li _____ talking to David. (39)

He _____ be the first one there. I _____ want to go with them. It _____ be too late. Math (42)

_____ my favorite subject. The leaves _____ falling. Winter _____ soon be here. The water (45)

_____ feel very warm. Soon it _____ be solid ice. She _____ bigger than Sue. Mei (49)

_____ know the answer. _____ you go with me? I like to _____ company. We _____ good friends. (52)

ANSWER SHEET

© 2005 Sopris West Educational Services. All rights reserved. Practicing Basic Skills in Language Arts. Purchaser has permission to photocopy this page for classroom use only.

SEE TO MARK

Verb Phrases in Sentences

Directions: Underline the complete verb phrases in the following sentences.

	Correct	Error
First Try		
Second Try		

Carmen is busily building a weather station. When are you leaving for Toronto? She and I have always been good friends. By this time tomorrow I shall have completed four lessons. Chien has lost his wallet. I should not have eaten that salty popcorn.

Mr. Wong has just gone home. The telephone hasn't rung once today. The car had apparently run out of fuel. The captain is being transferred next month. Have you brought a friend with you? The boys were all wearing ski boots. Hasn't Jed been invited? The extent of his injuries has not yet been determined. For the best results, you should preheat the oven. You should have been at the game. Where will you be this evening? I would have attended if I had known the location of the meeting.

Only one of the plants had not frozen. Committee members will be chosen tomorrow. May I sit down? I am writing a book. Lucia might be playing outside. Did you ever hear about the fight? All students must report to their first period classes. Martin could have been a fine singer if he would have practiced. Have you finished your homework? Who is supervising that activity? Priscilla is beginning karate lessons. I will fly to Seattle later this evening. The rain had not quite stopped. You will have been seen by absolutely no one. The office workers have become used to the traffic noise. Did anybody see my keys? Mai was driving in the car pool. The seeds of the plant were widely scattered by the wind. I have never been arrested by a policeman. Where are you going? Katrina will never understand my views on religion. Haven't you heard the latest news?

Practicing Basic Skills in Language Arts • 73

© 2005 Sopris West Educational Services. All rights reserved. Practicing Basic Skills in Language Arts. Purchaser has permission to photocopy this page for classroom use only.

ONE-MINUTE FLUENCY BUILDER SERIES

SEE TO MARK

Verb Phrases in Sentences

Directions: Underline the complete verb phrases in the following sentences.

	First Try		Second Try	
	Correct	Error		

Carmen is busily building a weather station. When are you leaving for Toronto? She and I have always been good friends. By (6)

this time tomorrow I shall have completed four lessons. Chien has lost his wallet. I should not have eaten that salty popcorn. (14)

Mr. Wong has just gone home. The telephone hasn't rung once today. The car had apparently run out of fuel. The captain (20)

is being transferred next month. Have you brought a friend with you? The boys were all wearing ski boots. Hasn't Jed been (29)

invited? The extent of his injuries has not yet been determined. For the best results, you should preheat the oven. You should (36)

have been at the game. Where will you be this evening? I would have attended if I had known the location of the meeting. (45)

Only one of the plants had not frozen. Committee members will be chosen tomorrow. May I sit down? I am writing a book. (54)

Lucia might be playing outside. Did you ever hear about the fight? All students must report to their first period classes. Martin (61)

could have been a fine singer if he would have practiced. Have you finished your homework? Who is supervising that activity? (71)

Priscilla is beginning karate lessons. I will fly to Seattle later this evening. The rain had not quite stopped. You will have been (80)

seen by absolutely no one. The office workers have become used to the traffic noise. Did anybody see my keys? Mai was driving (87)

in the car pool. The seeds of the plant were widely scattered by the wind. I have never been arrested by a policeman. Where are (93)

you going? Katrina will never understand my views on religion. Haven't you heard the latest news? (98)

ANSWER SHEET

© 2005 Sopris West Educational Services. All rights reserved. Practicing Basic Skills in Language Arts. Purchaser has permission to photocopy this page for classroom use only.

Linking Verbs in Sentences

Directions: Underline the linking verbs in the following sentences.

I am a student. My father is my friend. Our dog looks happy now. His favorite pets were rabbits. Her sugar cookies always

taste good. His story sounds suspicious. The man looks very angry. We should be good friends. You seem sad this evening. The

building had been a warehouse. The champion sprinter was a great athlete. The children remained sleepy after their naps. This

perfume smells heavenly. Their party became a disaster. I am a great cook. Dan stays slim by jogging. We are members of the

safety club. Marco was being silly last night. You must feel great after your success. The children grew restless in the warm room.

The pilot must have been a fool. We were students at that school. Lung cancer is a dreadful disease. You appear content after

that big meal. Mom's apple pie smells delicious. The taste of chocolate cake is wonderful. The old man had been their chief

suspect. Their conversation sounded silly. That kindly old lady could be your grandmother. The problem seems impossible to

solve. His speech was a great success. This material feels velvety. The students stayed quiet throughout the film. I am being

cheerful rather than grouchy. Will you be a teacher next year? Tony and Elena are my neighbors. Mr. Stevens had been ill for

several months. Don't become conceited because of your victory. We felt better after our football team finally won a game. Mark

remained quiet after the bad news. The clouds in the eastern sky appear stormy. You sound hoarse; are you catching a cold?

Yoko's condition remained critical for several days after the accident. This water tastes salty; are you sure it's fresh? Who will be

our next president? I hope he is a responsible man.

© 2005 Sopris West Educational Services. All rights reserved. Practicing Basic Skills in Language Arts. Purchaser has permission to photocopy this page for classroom use only.

ONE-MINUTE FLUENCY
BUILDER SERIES

SEE TO MARK

Linking Verbs in Sentences

Directions: Underline the linking verbs in the following sentences.

	Correct	Error
First Try		
Second Try		

I am a student. My father is my friend. Our dog looks happy now. His favorite pets were rabbits. Her sugar cookies always (4)

taste good. His story sounds suspicious. The man looks very angry. We should be good friends. You seem sad this evening. The (9)

building had been a warehouse. The champion sprinter was a great athlete. The children remained sleepy after their naps. This (12)

perfume smells heavenly. Their party became a disaster. I am a great cook. Dan stays slim by jogging. We are members of the (17)

safety club. Marco was being silly last night. You must feel great after your success. The children grew restless in the warm room. (20)

The pilot must have been a fool. We were students at that school. Lung cancer is a dreadful disease. You appear content after (24)

that big meal. Mom's apple pie smells delicious. The taste of chocolate cake is wonderful. The old man had been their chief (27)

suspect. Their conversation sounded silly. That kindly old lady could be your grandmother. The problem seems impossible to (30)

solve. His speech was a great success. This material feels velvety. The students stayed quiet throughout the film. I am being (34)

cheerful rather than grouchy. Will you be a teacher next year? Tony and Elena are my neighbors. Mr. Stevens had been ill for (37)

several months. Don't become conceited because of your victory. We felt better after our football team finally won a game. Mark (39)

remained quiet after the bad news. The clouds in the eastern sky appear stormy. You sound hoarse; are you catching a cold? (43)

Yoko's condition remained critical for several days after the accident. This water tastes salty; are you sure it's fresh? Who will be (47)

our next president? I hope he is a responsible man. (48)

ANSWER SHEET

© 2005 Sopris West Educational Services. All rights reserved. Practicing Basic Skills in Language Arts. Purchaser has permission to photocopy this page for classroom use only.

ONE-MINUTE FLUENCY BUILDER SERIES

	Correct	Error
First Try		
Second Try		

Transitive and Intransitive Verbs—Fill in the Blanks

Directions: Mark the verbs in the following sentences as being either transitive (T) or intransitive (I).

He opened ___ the package. We left ___ the door open. He cheered ___ enthusiastically. Jim seconded ___ the motion. I could not

hear ___. Finally she left ___ in a fit of anger. The team won ___ easily. Did you accept ___ the invitation? We memorized ___ the

rules. I could not study ___ at all in the noisy study hall. Our team won ___ the championship trophy. I could not learn ___ that

algebraic equation. The band uniforms finally arrived ___ just before the winter holiday. The trainer stepped ___ into the cage of

the wounded leopard. The sophomore class has ___ a very good attendance record. Jane walked ___ unsteadily to the stage and

swallowed ___ hard. Helen enjoys ___ responsibility. In a large city, many people walk ___ their dogs daily. That man appears ___

in the second act. Once, a circus horse literally stuck ___ its foot into its mouth. My grandmother tells ___ such wonderful stories.

The author tells ___ of his childhood in Wyoming. All new cars have ___ safety belts as standard equipment. Maggie always

combs ___ her hair in class. After the storm, the ice melted ___ off the sidewalks. We drove ___ to the beach last Tuesday. Mother

is preparing ___ dinner. It has not rained ___ for days. The teacher read ___ us a very interesting story. The skaters skimmed ___

across the pond. I like ___ orange juice for breakfast. These shrubs will grow ___ quickly. Last night we went ___ to the movies.

Do you like ___ poetry? We sailed ___ our sailboat in the lake. We shall drive ___ to Denver for a day or two. She ate ___ hastily

and left ___. The dogs followed ___ the trail. A radio wave travels ___ around the world with the speed of light.

© 2005 Sopris West Educational Services. All rights reserved. Practicing Basic Skills in Language Arts. Purchaser has permission to photocopy this page for classroom use only.

ONE-MINUTE FLUENCY BUILDER SERIES

	First Try	Second Try
Correct		
Error		

Transitive and Intransitive Verbs—Fill in the Blanks

Directions: Mark the verbs in the following sentences as being either transitive (T) or intransitive (I).

He opened **T** the package. We left **T** the door open. He cheered **I** enthusiastically. Jim seconded **T** the motion. I could not (4)

hear **I** . Finally she left **I** in a fit of anger. The team won **I** easily. Did you accept **T** the invitation? We memorized **T** the (9)

rules. I could not study **I** at all in the noisy study hall. Our team won **T** the championship trophy. I could not learn **T** that (12)

algebraic equation. The band uniforms finally arrived **I** just before the winter holiday. The trainer stepped **I** into the cage of (14)

the wounded leopard. The sophomore class has **T** a very good attendance record. Jane walked **I** unsteadily to the stage and (16)

swallowed **I** hard. Helen enjoys **T** responsibility. In a large city, many people walk **T** their dogs daily. That man appears **I** (20)

in the second act. Once, a circus horse literally stuck **T** its foot into its mouth. My grandmother tells **T** such wonderful stories. (22)

The author tells **I** of his childhood in Wyoming. All new cars have **T** safety belts as standard equipment. Maggie always (24)

combs **T** her hair in class. After the storm, the ice melted **I** off the sidewalks. We drove **I** to the beach last Tuesday. Mother (27)

is preparing **T** dinner. It has not rained **I** for days. The teacher read **T** us a very interesting story. The skaters skimmed **I** (31)

across the pond. I like **T** orange juice for breakfast. These shrubs will grow **I** quickly. Last night we went **I** to the movies. (34)

Do you like **T** poetry? We sailed **T** our sailboat in the lake. We shall drive **I** to Denver for a day or two. She ate **I** hastily (38)

and left **I** . The dogs followed **T** the trail. A radio wave travels **I** around the world with the speed of light. (41)

ANSWER SHEET

© 2005 Sopris West Educational Services. All rights reserved. Practicing Basic Skills in Language Arts. Purchaser has permission to photocopy this page for classroom use only.

ONE-MINUTE FLUENCY BUILDER SERIES

	First Try	Second Try
Correct		
Error		

Active and Passive Verbs

Directions: Mark the verbs in the following sentences as being either active (A) or passive (P).

The lights had been turned down. ___ My brother has already picked a career. ___ We have been invited to the symphony

concert. ___ The next batter was hit by a pitched ball. ___ Many New York school children do not understand English. ___

Several of the games were played at night. ___ A new school will be constructed here. ___ The speaker told of his adventures in

Africa. ___ More than one hundred elements have been discovered. ___ Jack has bought a new book about sports cars. ___ The

class president introduced the speaker. ___ Our record has been challenged by East High. ___ The freshman boys decorated the

gym. ___ The influenza shots were given by the school doctor. ___ The game was ruined by the rain. ___ The officer warned

Pedro to drive more slowly. ___ A flat tire delayed the team bus. ___ The citrus fruit was destroyed by frost. ___ The door was

closed quietly. ___ The boys were building a clubhouse. ___ The plane was ditched at sea by the pilot. ___ Mao took a deep

breath. ___ Every spring, Mother plants a large garden. ___ "Silent Night" was sung by a new quartet. ___ Our corn was ruined

by that awful hailstorm. ___ Maria needs a shovel for that job. ___ At the age of 21, Dick will receive a large sum of money. ___

___ Christopher Columbus sailed to America in 1492. ___ Billions of dollars are spent by the federal government every year. ___

___ Penny ate the last two bananas for lunch. ___ This letter was opened by mistake. ___ Olga must read four books by next

Thursday. ___ Our family prefers hot cereal for breakfast. ___ Eric found a dollar on his way to a movie. ___ Mr. Jameson was

introduced by his daughter-in-law, our principal. ___ I have seen her before. ___ The car was driven by a chauffeur. ___ The

town was destroyed. ___

© 2005 Sopris West Educational Services. All rights reserved. Practicing Basic Skills in Language Arts. Purchaser has permission to photocopy this page for classroom use only.

SEE TO MARK

ONE-MINUTE FLUENCY BUILDER SERIES

Active and Passive Verbs

Directions: Mark the verbs in the following sentences as being either active (A) or passive (P).

	Correct	Error
First Try		
Second Try		

(2) The lights had been turned down. **P** My brother has already picked a career. **A** We have been invited to the symphony

(5) concert. **P** The next batter was hit by a pitched ball. **P** Many New York school children do not understand English. **A**

(7) Several of the games were played at night. **P** A new school will be constructed here. **P** The speaker told of his adventures in

(10) Africa. **A** More than one hundred elements have been discovered. **P** Jack has bought a new book about sports cars. **A** The

(12) class president introduced the speaker. **A** Our record has been challenged by East High. **P** The freshman boys decorated the

(15) gym. **A** The influenza shots were given by the school doctor. **P** The game was ruined by the rain. **P** The officer warned

(18) Pedro to drive more slowly. **A** A flat tire delayed the team bus. **A** The citrus fruit was destroyed by frost. **P** The door was

(21) closed quietly. **P** The boys were building a clubhouse. **A** The plane was ditched at sea by the pilot. **P** Mao took a deep

(24) breath. **A** Every spring, Mother plants a large garden. **A** "Silent Night" was sung by a new quartet. **P** Our corn was ruined

(26) by that awful hailstorm. **P** Maria needs a shovel for that job. **A** At the age of 21, Dick will receive a large sum of money.

(28) **A** Christopher Columbus sailed to America in 1492. **A** Billions of dollars are spent by the federal government every year.

(31) **P** Penny ate the last two bananas for lunch. **A** This letter was opened by mistake. **P** Olga must read four books by next

(34) Thursday. **A** Our family prefers hot cereal for breakfast. **A** Eric found a dollar on his way to a movie. **A** Mr. Jameson was

(37) introduced by his daughter-in-law, our principal. **P** I have seen her before. **A** The car was driven by a chauffeur. **P** The

(38) town was destroyed. **P**

ANSWER SHEET

© 2005 Sopris West Educational Services. All rights reserved. Practicing Basic Skills in Language Arts. Purchaser has permission to photocopy this page for classroom use only.

ONE-MINUTE FLUENCY
BUILDER SERIES

SEE TO SAY OR SEE TO WRITE

Principal Parts of a Verb—Fill in the Blanks

Directions: Write the correct form (past or past participle) of the verb at the beginning of each sentence.

swim   Avery had _____ in deep water before.

run   Everyone _____ as fast as they could.

eat   Has Bernard _____ breakfast?

bring   Anna _____ a raincoat yesterday.

give   After I explained, he _____ me another chance.

drink   Emma sat down and _____ her tea.

use   When I was a child, I _____ to dig tunnels.

know   We have _____ about the test for some time.

risk   The policeman _____ his life in the chase.

break   The champion has _____ the record.

drive   Have you _____ one of the new cars?

fall   You might have _____ over the edge.

speak   The principal has _____ to me about it.

begin   It has _____ to clear in the north.

come   I noticed that he _____ in late this morning.

see   Last night I _____ him at the drugstore.

take   Since I had _____ my rifle, we looked for deer.

go   I was sure Sue Ellen had _____ riding.

freeze   Many of the trees have _____ during the storm.

break   The windshield was _____.

attack   Grasshoppers have _____ the crops.

write   Have you _____ to your grandmother?

steal   A bear had _____ into our tent.

burst   The pile of brush _____ into flames.

do   She _____ her best yesterday.

give   Father has _____ us some suggestions.

ring   The bell _____ an hour ago.

run   Last year Mr. Evans _____ for mayor.

speak   Has anyone _____ to you about me?

choose   Have they _____ a leader?

go   He has _____ after groceries.

ride   Francis has never _____ a horse.

ring   Has the bell _____?

happen   Has this _____ before?

fall   A child has _____ from the ledge.

climb   Has he _____ the ladder of fame?

throw   I _____ his letters away when he left.

throw   I _____ to second base.

© 2005 Sopris West Educational Services. All rights reserved. Practicing Basic Skills in Language Arts. Purchaser has permission to photocopy this page for classroom use only.

ONE-MINUTE FLUENCY BUILDER SERIES

Principal Parts of a Verb—Fill in the Blanks

Directions: Write the correct form (past or past participle) of the verb at the beginning of each sentence.

		Correct	Error
First Try			
Second Try			

swim — Avery had **swum** in deep water before.

run — Everyone **ran** as fast as they could.

eat — Has Bernard **eaten** breakfast?

bring — Anna **brought** a raincoat yesterday.

give — After I explained, he **gave** me another chance.

drink — Emma sat down and **drank** her tea.

use — When I was a child, I **used** to dig tunnels.

know — We have **known** about the test for some time.

risk — The policeman **risked** his life in the chase.

break — The champion has **broken** the record.

drive — Have you **driven** one of the new cars?

fall — You might have **fallen** over the edge.

speak — The principal has **spoken** to me about it.

begin — It has **begun** to clear in the north.

come — I noticed that he **came** in late this morning.

see — Last night I **saw** him at the drugstore.

take — Since I had **taken** my rifle, we looked for deer.

go — I was sure Sue Ellen had **gone** riding.

freeze — Many of the trees have **frozen** during the storm.

break — (2) The windshield was **broken** .

attack — (4) Grasshoppers have **attacked** the crops.

write — (6) Have you **written** to your grandmother?

steal — (8) A bear had **stolen** into our tent.

burst — (10) The pile of brush **burst** into flames.

do — (12) She **did** her best yesterday.

give — (14) Father has **given** us some suggestions.

ring — (16) The bell **rang** an hour ago.

run — (18) Last year Mr. Evans **ran** for mayor.

speak — (20) Has anyone **spoken** to you about me?

choose — (22) Have they **chosen** a leader?

go — (24) He has **gone** after groceries.

ride — (26) Francis has never **ridden** a horse.

ring — (28) Has the bell **rung** ?

happen — (30) Has this **happened** before?

fall — (32) A child has **fallen** from the ledge.

climb — (34) Has he **climbed** the ladder of fame?

throw — (36) I **threw** his letters away when he left.

throw — (38) I **threw** to second base.

ANSWER SHEET

© 2005 Sopris West Educational Services. All rights reserved. Practicing Basic Skills in Language Arts. Purchaser has permission to photocopy this page for classroom use only.

THINK TO WRITE

Verb Tense

Directions: Determine the tense of each verb and write 1 for an infinitive, 2 for a present participle, 3 for past tense, and 4 for a past participle.

	First Try	Second Try
Correct		
Error		

believe	freezing	find
asked	whistling	going
laughing	swim	(had) liked
climb	selling	teaching
digging	(had) called	pulled
dragged	printed	fly
freeze	using	(had) criticized
returning	visit	leaving
(had) traveled	(had) mended	realized
arrive	tricked	discussing
tried	returning	memorized
call	looked	justify
finishing	(had) feasted	reading
helped	sing	(had) cleaned
(had) chased	drinking	fighting
ended	(had) attacked	terrified
working	waiting	shake
sell	invited	(had) reached
traced	playing	following
(had) believed	learn	paint

Practicing Basic Skills in Language Arts • 83

© 2005 Sopris West Educational Services. All rights reserved. Practicing Basic Skills in Language Arts. Purchaser has permission to photocopy this page for classroom use only.

THINK TO WRITE

Verb Tense

Directions: Determine the tense of each verb and write 1 for an infinitive, 2 for a present participle, 3 for past tense, and 4 for a past participle.

First Try		
Second Try	Correct	Error

believe	1	freezing	2	find	1 (3)
asked	3	whistling	2	going	2 (6)
laughing	2	swim	1	(had) liked	4 (9)
climb	1	selling	2	teaching	2 (12)
digging	2	(had) called	4	pulled	3 (15)
dragged	3	printed	3	fly	1 (18)
freeze	1	using	2	(had) criticized	4 (21)
returning	2	visit	1	leaving	2 (24)
(had) traveled	4	(had) mended	4	realized	3 (27)
arrive	1	tricked	3	discussing	2 (30)
tried	3	returning	2	memorized	3 (33)
call	1	looked	3	justify	1 (36)
finishing	2	(had) feasted	4	reading	2 (39)
helped	3	sing	1	(had) cleaned	4 (42)
(had) chased	4	drinking	2	fighting	2 (45)
ended	3	(had) attacked	4	terrified	3 (48)
working	2	waiting	2	shake	1 (51)
sell	1	invited	3	(had) reached	4 (54)
traced	3	playing	2	following	2 (57)
(had) believed	4	learn	1	paint	1 (60)

© 2005 Sopris West Educational Services. All rights reserved. Practicing Basic Skills in Language Arts. Purchaser has permission to photocopy this page for classroom use only.

ONE MINUTE FLUENCY
BUILDER SERIES

THINK TO SAY

Irregular Verbs

Directions: Say the present participle, past tense, and past participle forms of the given verb.

	First Try	Second Try
Correct		
Error		

					steal
					speak
					swim
					take
					throw
					write
					set

	ride
	ring
	rise
	eat
	shrink
	sing
	sit

	see
	fall
	freeze
	give
	go
	know
	lie

begin

blow

break

bring

burst

choose

come

do

© 2005 Sopris West Educational Services. All rights reserved. Practicing Basic Skills in Language Arts. Purchaser has permission to photocopy this page for classroom use only.

ONE-MINUTE FLUENCY BUILDER SERIES

	Correct	Error
First Try		
Second Try		

Irregular Verbs

Directions: Say the present participle, past tense, and past participle forms of the given verb.

begin	beginning	began	begun
blow	blowing	blew	blown
break	breaking	broke	broken
bring	bringing	brought	brought
burst	bursting	burst	burst
choose	choosing	chose	chosen
come	coming	came	come
do	doing	did	done

(24)

see	seeing	saw	seen
fall	falling	fell	fallen
freeze	freezing	froze	frozen
give	giving	gave	given
go	going	went	gone
know	knowing	knew	known
lie	lying	lay	lain

(45)

ride	riding	rode	ridden
ring	ringing	rang	rung
rise	rising	rose	risen
eat	eating	ate	eaten
shrink	shrinking	shrank	shrunk
sing	singing	sang	sung
sit	sitting	sat	sat

(66)

steal	stealing	stole	stolen
speak	speaking	spoke	spoken
swim	swimming	swam	swum
take	taking	took	taken
throw	throwing	threw	thrown
write	writing	wrote	written
set	setting	set	set

(87)

ANSWER SHEET

© 2005 Sopris West Educational Services. All rights reserved. Practicing Basic Skills in Language Arts. Purchaser has permission to photocopy this page for classroom use only.

THINK TO WRITE

	First Try	Second Try
Correct		
Error		

Irregular Verbs

Directions: Write the present participle, past tense, and past participle forms of the given word.

Infinitive	Present Participle	Past Tense	Past Participle
set			
shrink			
sing			
sit			
speak			
steal			
swim			
take			
throw			
write			

Practicing Basic Skills in Language Arts • 87

© 2005 Sopris West Educational Services. All rights reserved. Practicing Basic Skills in Language Arts. Purchaser has permission to photocopy this page for classroom use only.

ONE-MINUTE FLUENCY BUILDER SERIES

THINK TO WRITE

Irregular Verbs

Directions: Write the present participle, past tense, and past participle forms of the given word.

	Correct	Error
First Try		
Second Try		

Infinitive	Present Participle	Past Tense	Past Participle	
set	**setting**	**set**	**set**	(3)
shrink	**shrinking**	**shrank**	**shrunk**	(6)
sing	**singing**	**sang**	**sung**	(9)
sit	**sitting**	**sat**	**sat**	(12)
speak	**speaking**	**spoke**	**spoken**	(15)
steal	**stealing**	**stole**	**stolen**	(18)
swim	**swimming**	**swam**	**swum**	(21)
take	**taking**	**took**	**taken**	(24)
throw	**throwing**	**threw**	**thrown**	(27)
write	**writing**	**wrote**	**written**	(30)

ANSWER SHEET

© 2005 Sopris West Educational Services. All rights reserved. Practicing Basic Skills in Language Arts. Purchaser has permission to photocopy this page for classroom use only.

ONE-MINUTE
FLUENCY
BUILDER SERIES

THINK TO WRITE

	First Try	Second Try
Correct		
Error		

Irregular Verbs

Directions: Write the present participle, past tense, and past participle forms of the given word.

Infinitive	Present Participle	Past Tense	Past Participle
fall			
freeze			
give			
go			
know			
lie			
ride			
ring			
rise			
run			
see			

© 2005 Sopris West Educational Services. All rights reserved. Practicing Basic Skills in Language Arts. Purchaser has permission to photocopy this page for classroom use only.

ONE-MINUTE FLUENCY BUILDER SERIES

	Correct	Error
First Try		
Second Try		

Irregular Verbs

Directions: Write the present participle, past tense, and past participle forms of the given word.

Infinitive	Present Participle	Past Tense	Past Participle	
fall	falling	fell	fallen	(3)
freeze	freezing	froze	frozen	(6)
give	giving	gave	given	(9)
go	going	went	gone	(12)
know	knowing	knew	known	(15)
lie	lying	lay	lain	(18)
ride	riding	rode	ridden	(21)
ring	ringing	rang	rung	(24)
rise	rising	rose	risen	(27)
run	running	ran	run	(30)
see	seeing	saw	seen	(33)

ANSWER SHEET

Practicing Basic Skills in Language Arts • 90

© 2005 Sopris West Educational Services. All rights reserved. Practicing Basic Skills in Language Arts. Purchaser has permission to photocopy this page for classroom use only.

THINK TO WRITE

Irregular Verbs

Directions: Write the present participle, past tense, and past participle forms of the given word.

	First Try	Second Try
Correct		
Error		

Infinitive	Present Participle	Past Tense	Past Participle
begin			
blow			
break			
bring			
burst			
choose			
come			
do			
drink			
drive			
eat			

© 2005 Sopris West Educational Services. All rights reserved. Practicing Basic Skills in Language Arts. Purchaser has permission to photocopy this page for classroom use only.

THINK TO WRITE

	Correct	Error
First Try		
Second Try		

Irregular Verbs

Directions: Write the present participle, past tense, and past participle forms of the given word.

Infinitive	Present Participle	Past Tense	Past Participle	
begin	beginning	began	begun	(3)
blow	blowing	blew	blown	(6)
break	breaking	broke	broken	(9)
bring	bringing	brought	brought	(12)
burst	bursting	burst	burst	(15)
choose	choosing	chose	chosen	(18)
come	coming	came	come	(21)
do	doing	did	done	(24)
drink	drinking	drank	drunk	(27)
drive	driving	drove	driven	(30)
eat	eating	ate	eaten	(33)

© 2005 Sopris West Educational Services. All rights reserved. Practicing Basic Skills in Language Arts. Purchaser has permission to photocopy this page for classroom use only.

SEE TO MARK

Correct Form of Irregular Verbs in Sentences

Directions: Mark the correct form of the verb in the sentences below.

	First Try	Second Try
Correct		
Error		

The party (began, begun) at seven o'clock. The handle had been (broke, broken) long ago. No one had (brung, brought) a

can opener. Has everyone (chose, chosen) a partner? A strange message (came, come) over the radio. Haying was the hardest

work Bob had ever (did, done). At camp, we (drunk, drank) a quart of milk every day. Someone had already (ate, eaten) half

the gumdrops. Have you ever (froze, frozen) your ears? The boss (give, gave) a good report of our work. Everything had (gone,

went) wrong all day. Diego has (grew, grown) two inches this summer. The Indians had never (known, knew) horses before the

Spaniards came. The old scout (lay, lain, laid) his hand on the boy's shoulder. The conductor should have (let, left) us off the train. When

The diamonds had (lay, lain, laid) on the desk all day. Revere had (rode, ridden) only part of the way when he was halted. When

Washington died, the church bells (rang, rung) all day long. The doctor had (rose, risen) early. In 1811, the first steamboat

(run, ran) down the Mississippi. The pilot said he (saw, seen) a strange flying object. The audience (sang, sung) the chorus. The

president has (spoke, spoken) to the people. The relief party had (took, taken) the wrong road. Pitchers have (threw, throwed,

thrown) a baseball 90 miles an hour. Henry has (wrote, written) a good short story. Chien has (went, gone) to see his brother. Mr.

Olsen, have you (came, come) to see my father? Have you (saw, seen) the beautiful flowers? I believe Nancy has (drew, drawn)

the best designs. The wind (blew, blown) down our birdhouse. Has she (wrote, written) her grocery list? Did you (choose, chose)

the pictures you want yet? Have you (did, done) the dishes yet? I (saw, seen) her at the game yesterday. The boys accidentally

(broke, broken) the vase. We were (gave, given) permission to go to the movie. The boy (threw, throwed) the ball at the catcher.

The warning bell has not (rang, rung). Wasn't Jamal (threw, thrown) from his horse? Have you had your picture (took, taken)

lately? Linda (came, come) an hour ago. I have (knew, known) the answers for a week. He (don't, doesn't) come anymore.

© 2005 Sopris West Educational Services. All rights reserved. Practicing Basic Skills in Language Arts. Purchaser has permission to photocopy this page for classroom use only.

ONE-MINUTE FLUENCY BUILDER SERIES

SEE TO MARK

	Correct	Error
First Try		
Second Try		

Correct Form of Irregular Verbs in Sentences

Directions: Mark the correct form of the verb in the sentences below.

The party (began, begun) at seven o'clock. The handle had been (broke, broken) long ago. No one had (brung, brought) a (3)

can opener. Has everyone (chose, chosen) a partner? A strange message (came, come) over the radio. Haying was the hardest (5)

work Bob had ever (did, done). At camp, we (drunk, drank) a quart of milk every day. Someone had already (ate, eaten) half (8)

the gumdrops. Have you ever (froze, frozen) your ears? The boss (give, gave) a good report of our work. Everything had (gone, (11)

went) wrong all day. Diego has (grew, grown) two inches this summer. The Indians had never (known, knew) horses before the (13)

Spaniards came. The old scout (lay, laid) his hand on the boy's shoulder. The conductor should have (let, left) us off the train. (15)

The diamonds had (lay, lain, laid) on the desk all day. Revere had (rode, ridden) only part of the way when he was halted. When (17)

Washington died, the church bells (rang, rung) all day long. The doctor had (rose, risen) early. In 1811, the first steamboat (19)

(run, ran) down the Mississippi. The pilot said he (saw, seen) a strange flying object. The audience (sang, sung) the chorus. The (22)

president has (spoke, spoken) to the people. The relief party had (took, taken) the wrong road. Pitchers have (threw, throwed, (24)

thrown) a baseball 90 miles an hour. Henry has (wrote, written) a good short story. Chien has (went, gone) to see his brother. Mr. (27)

Olsen, have you (came, come) to see my father? Have you (saw, seen) the beautiful flowers? I believe Nancy has (drew, drawn) (30)

the best designs. The wind (blew, blown) down our birdhouse. Has she (wrote, written) her grocery list? Did you (choose, chose) (33)

the pictures you want yet? Have you (did, done) the dishes yet? I (saw, seen) her at the game yesterday. The boys accidentally (35)

(broke, broken) the vase. We were (gave, given) permission to go to the movie. The boy (threw, throwed) the ball at the catcher. (38)

The warning bell has not (rang, rung). Wasn't Jamal (threw, thrown) from his horse? Have you had your picture (took, taken) (41)

lately? Linda (came, come) an hour ago. I have (knew, known) the answers for a week. He (don't, doesn't) come anymore. (44)

ANSWER SHEET

Practicing Basic Skills in Language Arts • 94

© 2005 Sopris West Educational Services. All rights reserved. Practicing Basic Skills in Language Arts. Purchaser has permission to photocopy this page for classroom use only.

ONE MINUTE FLUENCY
BUILDER SERIES

	Correct	Error
First Try		
Second Try		

THINK TO WRITE

Correct Form of Irregular Verbs—Fill in the Blanks

Directions: Write the correct form of the given verb in the blanks provided.

He (drink) _____ his fruit juice yesterday morning. I (see) _____ a car as it drove down the road. I (give) _____ him the money yesterday. The men had (ride) _____ over the same road for years. I am sure he (do) _____ the best he could do. I nearly (freeze) _____ while waiting for you. The book has (fall) _____ into the water. The boys (sing) _____ all the old songs last night. I (see) _____ it myself last Thursday. Maria has (drink) _____ it all herself. The dish is (break) _____ . Was your picture (take) _____ ? Helen (bring) _____ me the letter yesterday. The boys had (steal) _____ the apples. John (write) _____ the lesson too rapidly last night. Last Tuesday Malik (give) _____ me a gift. Has he (eat) _____ all his lunch? Aunt Ann has (go) _____ to her office. He said he had (swim) _____ in the river before. He (throw) _____ the ball into the water and watched it disappear. The boys (choose) _____ Fred to be their new captain at their last meeting. If I had (know) _____ this, I would have passed. We have (drive) _____ fifty miles. The students (begin) _____ to grow restless when the projector broke. The child (blow) _____ his bubble gum until it popped. The bubble had (burst) _____ in his face. We had (come) _____ a long distance to see the fair. The child had (fall) _____ from the pony. My head hurt so badly I (lie) _____ down for a rest. Mai (ride) _____ her bicycle five miles yesterday. The bell (ring) _____ and the students rushed to class.

Practicing Basic Skills in Language Arts • 95

© 2005 Sopris West Educational Services. All rights reserved. Practicing Basic Skills in Language Arts. Purchaser has permission to photocopy this page for classroom use only.

Correct Form of Irregular Verbs—Fill in the Blanks

Directions: Write the correct form of the given verb in the blanks provided.

He (drink) **drank** his fruit juice yesterday morning. I (see) **saw** a car as it drove down the road. I (give) (2) _____

gave him the money yesterday. The men had (ride) **ridden** over the same road for years. I am sure he (do) (4) _____

did the best he could do. I nearly (freeze) **froze** while waiting for you. The book has (fall) **fallen** (7) _____

into the water. The boys (sing) **sang** all the old songs last night. I (see) **saw** it myself last Thursday. Maria (9) _____

has (drink) **drunk** it all herself. The dish is (break) **broken** . Was your picture (take) **taken** ? Helen (12) _____

(bring) **brought** me the letter yesterday. The boys had (steal) **stolen** the apples. John (write) **wrote** (15) _____

the lesson too rapidly last night. Last Tuesday Malik (give) **gave** me a gift. Has he (eat) **eaten** all his (17) _____

lunch? Aunt Ann has (go) **gone** to her office. He said he had (swim) **swum** in the river before. He (throw) (19) _____

threw the ball into the water and watched it disappear. The boys (choose) **chose** Fred to be their new captain (21) _____

at their last meeting. If I had (know) **known** this, I would have passed. We have (drive) **driven** fifty miles. The (23) _____

students (begin) **began** to grow restless when the projector broke. The child (blow) **blew** his bubble gum (25) _____

until it popped. The bubble had (burst) **burst** in his face. We had (come) **come** a long distance to see the (27) _____

fair. The child had (fall) **fallen** from the pony. My head hurt so badly I (lie) **lay** down for a rest. Mai (ride) (29) _____

rode her bicycle five miles yesterday. The bell (ring) **rang** and the students rushed to class. (31) _____

© 2005 Sopris West Educational Services. All rights reserved. Practicing Basic Skills in Language Arts. Purchaser has permission to photocopy this page for classroom use only.

THINK TO WRITE

Correct Form of Rise/Raise in Sentences

Directions: Write the correct form of *rise* or *raise* in the blanks provided.

	Correct	Error
First Try		
Second Try		

As one person, the crowd _____ from their seats. His job each morning is to _____ the flag. I expect him

to _____ early. Baking powder causes cakes to _____ . I wanted to see if the sun had _____ . The

teacher _____ his voice above the noise. Our class in English has been _____ money for a poor family.

Joe _____ and sang a song. I had just _____ the window when the storm broke. The forest ranger had

_____ early. The men _____ the ladder and began to work. The _____ river caused great alarm.

Having at last _____ to her feet, she was too frightened to speak. Mother had just _____ the window when

the blast came. _____ the curtain and see who is at the door. I thought that I was _____ very early, but

everyone else was already up. When at camp last summer, we always _____ very early for a swim before breakfast. At

last the principal _____ to speak to us. The temperature _____ twenty degrees before noon. The sun had

hardly _____ when we got up. Tom _____ and spoke. Will you _____ the bucket for me? If you

_____ early, you will enjoy it. Don has _____ the window. He _____ the flag and started the race.

The crowd _____ to its feet and cheered. The cake _____ high on one side. Will you please _____

the window for me? He is accustomed to _____ early. Will you _____ the box to the upper shelf? If you

_____ early, you may go too.

Practicing Basic Skills in Language Arts • 97

© 2005 Sopris West Educational Services. All rights reserved. Practicing Basic Skills in Language Arts. Purchaser has permission to photocopy this page for classroom use only.

THINK TO WRITE

	Correct	Error
First Try		
Second Try		

Correct Form of Rise/Raise in Sentences

Directions: Write the correct form of *rise* or *raise* in the blanks provided.

As one person, the crowd __rose__ from their seats. His job each morning is to __raise__ the flag. I expect him (2)

to __rise__ early. Baking powder causes cakes to __rise__ . I wanted to see if the sun had __risen__ . The (5)

teacher __raised__ his voice above the noise. Our class in English has been __raising__ money for a poor family. (7)

Joe __rose__ and sang a song. I had just __raised__ the window when the storm broke. The forest ranger had (9)

__risen__ early. The men __raised__ the ladder and began to work. The __rising__ river caused great alarm. (12)

Having at last __risen__ to her feet, she was too frightened to speak. Mother had just __raised__ the window when (14)

the blast came. __Raise__ the curtain and see who is at the door. I thought that I was __rising__ very early, but (16)

everyone else was already up. When at camp last summer, we always __rose__ very early for a swim before breakfast. At (17)

last the principal __rose__ to speak to us. The temperature __rose__ twenty degrees before noon. The sun had (19)

hardly __risen__ when we got up. Tom __rose__ and spoke. Will you __raise__ the bucket for me? If you (22)

__rise__ early, you will enjoy it. Don has __raised__ the window. He __raised__ the flag and started the race. (25)

The crowd __rose__ to its feet and cheered. The cake __rose__ high on one side. Will you please __raise__ (28)

the window for me? He is accustomed to __rising__ early. Will you __raise__ the box to the upper shelf? If you (30)

__rise__ early, you may go too. (31)

ANSWER SHEET

© 2005 Sopris West Educational Services. All rights reserved. Practicing Basic Skills in Language Arts. Purchaser has permission to photocopy this page for classroom use only.

ONE-MINUTE FLUENCY BUILDER SERIES

THINK TO WRITE

Correct Form of Lie/Lay in Sentences

Directions: Write the correct form of *lie* or *lay* in the blanks provided.

	First Try	Second Try
Correct		
Error		

Where did you _____ the book? I _____ down and slept for two hours. My dog _____ before the fireplace and slept. Your book has been _____ there all day. Who _____ it there? Did the book _____ on the porch all night? Mom _____ down for a nap each afternoon this week. It seemed as though the whole summer _____ before us. The cat had been _____ in the chair. I am _____ on the ground. The old ship had _____ on the harbor bottom for many years. I had _____ awake all night. I shall _____ down until you come. The cat is _____ on a rug before the fire. The company has _____ there and never down a new pavement on the street. I had _____ there since you left. The woman _____ there and never stirred. Don't _____ your coat on that chair. Under a tree the little bear was _____ before us. When will the concrete be _____ ? " _____ down and rest," said the doctor. The pirates were surprised to see what _____ in the hold of the ship. _____ the silverware in the chest. She _____ down each day at three. The sidewalk was _____ in a week. The teacher _____ down the book and looked at me. The men _____ away their tools and sat down. _____ down and rest for ten minutes. She has _____ there all morning. Mother _____ her sewing away and answered the phone.

© 2005 Sopris West Educational Services. All rights reserved. Practicing Basic Skills in Language Arts. Purchaser has permission to photocopy this page for classroom use only.

ONE-MINUTE FLUENCY BUILDER SERIES

THINK TO WRITE

Correct Form of Lie/Lay in Sentences

Directions: Write the correct form of *lie* or *lay* in the blanks provided.

	First Try	Second Try
Correct		
Error		

Where did you **lay** the book? I **lay** down and slept for two hours. My dog **lay** before (3)

the fireplace and slept. Your book has been **lying** there all day. Who **laid** it there? Did the book (5)

lie on the porch all night? Mom **lay** down for a nap each afternoon this week. It seemed as though (7)

the whole summer **lay** before us. The cat had been **lying** in the chair. I am **lying** on the (10)

ground. The old ship had **lain** on the harbor bottom for many years. I had **lain** awake all night. I shall (12)

lie down until you come. The cat is **lying** on a rug before the fire. The company has **laid** (15)

down a new pavement on the street. I had **lain** there since you left. The woman **lay** there and never (17)

stirred. Don't **lay** your coat on that chair. Under a tree the little bear was **lying** . The beautiful country (19)

lay before us. When will the concrete be **laid** ? " **Lie** down and rest," said the doctor. (22)

The pirates were surprised to see what **lay** in the hold of the ship. **Lay** the silverware in the chest. (24)

She **lies** down each day at three. The sidewalk was **laid** in a week. The teacher **laid** down (27)

the book and looked at me. The men **laid** away their tools and sat down. **Lie** down and rest for ten (29)

minutes. She has **lain** there all morning. Mother **laid** her sewing away and answered the phone. (31)

ANSWER SHEET

Practicing Basic Skills in Language Arts • 100

© 2005 Sopris West Educational Services. All rights reserved. Practicing Basic Skills in Language Arts. Purchaser has permission to photocopy this page for classroom use only.

ONE-MINUTE FLUENCY BUILDER SERIES

THINK TO WRITE

Correct Form of Sit/Set in Sentences

Directions: Write the correct form of *sit* or *set* in the blanks provided.

	First Try	Second Try
Correct		
Error		

The teacher _____ the time when we should return. When we returned home, we found the dog _____ traps in

where we had left her. She always _____ there and waits for us. In the North they often _____

the winter. Shall we _____ here for a while? All day yesterday she _____ on the porch of her cottage.

The fishermen _____ their nets. Did you _____ your watch correctly? Mr. and Mrs. Brown have always _____ at the

_____ in the front row. The children _____ up the ping pong table. I shall _____

speaker's table. We had _____ the candy on the shelf to cool. _____ the chairs on the lawn. The maid

_____ the pitcher of lemonade on the table. We often just _____ and looked at the beautiful flowers. Do

you intend to _____ there all afternoon? The girls did not _____ the table very attractively. She would

often _____ up all night reading. We have been _____ here for hours. The girls _____ in the

sun all day today. Please _____ the salad in the refrigerator. Shall we _____ the books on the table? They

have always _____ near the third aisle. We _____ the table before we went to bed. He was

up pins at the bowling alley. Father is _____ in the shade. _____ the fruit in the refrigerator. Dad has

always _____ at the head of the table. The pupils were _____ in their seats when I arrived. I always

_____ my clock with the radio. I _____ in this seat last year. Is she still _____ the table?

_____ your knitting on the porch. We _____ the pail of water on the floor.

Practicing Basic Skills in Language Arts • 101

© 2005 Sopris West Educational Services. All rights reserved. Practicing Basic Skills in Language Arts. Purchaser has permission to photocopy this page for classroom use only.

ONE-MINUTE FLUENCY BUILDER SERIES

THINK TO WRITE

Correct Form of Sit/Set in Sentences

Directions: Write the correct form of *sit* or *set* in the blanks provided.

	First Try	Second Try
Correct		
Error		

The teacher **set** ___ the time when we should return. When we returned home, we found the dog **sitting** ___ (2)

where we had left her. She always **sits** ___ there and waits for us. In the North they often **set** ___ traps in (4)

the winter. Shall we **sit** ___ here for a while? All day yesterday she **sat** ___ on the porch of her cottage. (6)

The fishermen **set** ___ their nets. Did you **set** ___ your watch correctly? Mr. and Mrs. Brown have always (8)

sat ___ in the front row. The children **set** ___ up the ping pong table. I shall **sit** ___ at the (11)

speaker's table. We had **set** ___ the candy on the shelf to cool. **Set** ___ the chairs on the lawn. The maid (13)

set ___ the pitcher of lemonade on the table. We often just **sat** ___ and looked at the beautiful flowers. Do (15)

you intend to **sit** ___ there all afternoon? The girls did not **set** ___ the table very attractively. She would (17)

often **sit** ___ up all night reading. We have been **sitting** ___ here for hours. The girls **sat** ___ in the (20)

sun all day today. Please **set** ___ the salad in the refrigerator. Shall we **set** ___ the books on the table? They (22)

have always **sat** ___ near the third aisle. We **set** ___ the table before we went to bed. He was **setting** ___ (25)

up pins at the bowling alley. Father is **sitting** ___ in the shade. **Set** ___ the fruit in the refrigerator. Dad has (27)

always **sat** ___ at the head of the table. The pupils were **sitting** ___ in their seats when I arrived. I always (29)

set ___ my clock with the radio. I **sat** ___ in this seat last year. Is she still **setting** ___ the table? (32)

Set ___ your knitting on the porch. We **set** ___ the pail of water on the floor. (34)

© 2005 Sopris West Educational Services. All rights reserved. Practicing Basic Skills in Language Arts. Purchaser has permission to photocopy this page for classroom use only.

Correct Form of Lie/Lay, Sit/Set, Rise/Raise

Directions: Use the proper form of *lie, lay, sit, set, or rise, raise* in the following sentences. The first letter is given as a clue.

	First Try	Second Try
Correct		
Error		

The teacher (s) _____ the hour of our appointment. After much thought, he (r) _____ and made his

plea. They all (s) _____ on the bench. The boys watched her (r) _____ the cover of the box and (s) _____

the trap. The balloon had (r) _____ only a few feet when it exploded. (L) _____ on your

back for ten weeks is surely not my idea of a vacation. The dog (l) _____ on the lawn and wants to be petted. After I

had (r) _____ to speak, I found that I had entirely forgotten my speech. Please (r) _____ the window and

(s) _____ the pies on the ledge. After the sun had (r) _____, we (l) _____ down under a large

tree. The glider (r) _____ quickly and vanished among the clouds. (L) _____ the boxes on the floor and

(s) _____ in this chair for a few minutes. The course of the ship had been (s) _____ by the captain. We (r) _____

funds for the Red Cross. The man (r) _____ the fallen wreath and put it into position. The trout were

(l) _____ in pools of water. We (s) _____ the table for breakfast before the others had (r) _____ .

She opened the door and (s) _____ the bottle on the steps. The plans were carefully (l) _____ . Mother

had (r) _____ early to get the children ready. As one person the crowd (r) _____ from their seats. I like to

(s) _____ and dream. "(L) _____ down and rest," the doctor said. The temperature (r) _____

twenty degrees before noon. After we had (s) _____ the table, we (s) _____ down to eat. The officer (l) _____

_____ his hand on the weeping child's shoulder. His job is to (r) _____ the flag. We (s) _____ the

pail of water on the floor. Where did you (l) _____ my papers? The girls (s) _____ in the sun all day. I had

just (r) _____ the window when the storm broke. (S) _____ down!

© 2005 Sopris West Educational Services. All rights reserved. Practicing Basic Skills in Language Arts. Purchaser has permission to photocopy this page for classroom use only.

THINK TO WRITE

Correct Form of Lie/Lay, Sit/Set, Rise/Raise

Directions: Use the proper form of *lie, lay, sit, set,* or *rise, raise* in the following sentences. The first letter is given as a clue.

	Correct	Error
First Try		
Second Try		

The teacher (s) **set** the hour of our appointment. After much thought, he (r) **rose** and made his

(2)

plea. They all (s) **sat** on the bench. The boys watched her (r) **raise** the cover of the box and (s)

(4)

set the trap. The balloon had (r) **risen** only a few feet when it exploded. (L) **Lying** on your

(7)

back for ten weeks is surely not my idea of a vacation. The dog (l) **lies** on the lawn and wants to be petted. After I

(8)

had (r) **risen** to speak, I found that I had entirely forgotten my speech. Please (r) **raise** the window and

(10)

(s) **set** the pies on the ledge. After the sun had (r) **risen** , we (l) **lay** down under a large

(13)

tree. The glider (r) **rose** quickly and vanished among the clouds. (L) **Lay** the boxes on the floor and

(15)

(s) **sit** in this chair for a few minutes. The course of the ship had been (s) **set** by the captain. We (r)

(17)

raised funds for the Red Cross. The man (r) **raised** the fallen wreath and put it into position. The trout were

(19)

(l) **lying** in pools of water. We (s) **set** the table for breakfast before the others had (r) **risen** .

(22)

She opened the door and (s) **set** the bottle on the steps. The plans were carefully (l) **laid** . Mother

(24)

had (r) **risen** early to get the children ready. As one person the crowd (r) **rose** from their seats. I like to

(26)

(s) **sit** and dream. "(L) **Lie** down and rest," the doctor said. The temperature (r) **rose**

(29)

twenty degrees before noon. After we had (s) **set** the table, we (s) **sat** down to eat. The officer (l)

(31)

laid his hand on the weeping child's shoulder. His job is to (r) **raise** the flag. We (s) **set**

(34)

pail of water on the floor. Where did you (l) **lay** my papers? The girls (s) **sat** in the sun all day. I had

(36)

just (r) **raised** the window when the storm broke. (S) **Sit** down!

(38)

Practicing Basic Skills in Language Arts • 104

ANSWER SHEET

© 2005 Sopris West Educational Services. All rights reserved. Practicing Basic Skills in Language Arts. Purchaser has permission to photocopy this page for classroom use only.

Subject-Verb Agreement: Was/Were

Directions: Use the proper form of either *was* or *were* in the following sentences.

	Correct	Error
First Try		
Second Try		

They _____ a couple of nuts. It _____ a good movie. I

_____ good cookies. She _____ a good friend. He _____ not a big help. They

dressed for the occasion. They _____ in need of a ride home. She _____ a friend in need. You

_____ a piano student. You _____ lost for a while. She _____ an excellent teacher. I

told not to do that again. They _____ available when I needed them. She _____ clean and neat. He

called. He _____ the star quarterback. I _____ tired of the whole thing. He _____ at the dentist when you

Dallas, Texas. They _____ not sorry to see him go. They _____ expensive earrings. You _____ a resident of

asked to help with the dishes. She _____ laughing when I fell down. It _____ a funny story. He dropped

by to see her. He _____ a professional wrestler. It _____ a snowy day today. You _____ a teacher

I'll always remember. I _____ a television fanatic. She _____ scared to death. He _____ a friendly

dog. She _____ the mail girl. They _____ charged with theft. I _____ down at the river. It

_____ a beautiful work of art. He _____ asked to speak at the meeting. I _____ a dancer in the

show. She _____ the school secretary. They _____ on the track team. He _____ an elementary

school principal. It _____ a beautiful plant. It _____ a hot day for a run. She _____ a mountain

climber. They _____ the main characters in the story. You _____ hungry for ice cream. I

hungry for chocolate. They _____ on the way to the party. It _____ sad. She _____ glad that

you dropped by to see her. You _____ a great help to us. They _____ lost. He _____ an excellent

driver. You _____ not a big help. It _____ a good steak. They _____ gone.

© 2005 Sopris West Educational Services. All rights reserved. Practicing Basic Skills in Language Arts. Purchaser has permission to photocopy this page for classroom use only.

ONE-MINUTE FLUENCY
BUILDER SERIES

ONE-MINUTE FLUENCY BUILDER SERIES

	Correct	Error
First Try		
Second Try		

SEE TO WRITE OR SEE TO SAY

Subject-Verb Agreement: Was/Were

Directions: Use the proper form of either *was* or *were* in the following sentences.

They __were__ a couple of nuts. It __was__ a good movie. I __was__ not a big help. They (3)

__were__ good cookies. She __was__ a good friend. He __was__ a friend in need. You __were__ (7)

dressed for the occasion. They __were__ in need of a ride home. She __was__ an excellent teacher. I (9)

__was__ a piano student. You __were__ lost for a while. She __was__ clean and neat. He __was__ (13)

told not to do that again. They __were__ available when I needed them. She __was__ at the dentist when you (15)

called. He __was__ the star quarterback. I __was__ tired of the whole thing. He __was__ a resident of (18)

Dallas, Texas. They __were__ not sorry to see him go. They __were__ expensive earrings. You __were__ (21)

asked to help with the dishes. She __was__ laughing when I fell down. It __was__ a funny story. He dropped (23)

by to see her. He __was__ a professional wrestler. It __was__ a snowy day today. You __were__ a teacher (26)

I'll always remember. I __was__ a television fanatic. She __was__ scared to death. He __was__ a friendly (29)

dog. She __was__ the mail girl. They __were__ charged with theft. I __was__ down at the river. It (32)

__was__ a beautiful work of art. He __was__ asked to speak at the meeting. I __was__ a dancer in the (35)

show. She __was__ the school secretary. They __were__ on the track team. He __was__ an elementary (38)

school principal. It __was__ a beautiful plant. It __was__ a hot day for a run. She __was__ a mountain (41)

climber. They __were__ the main characters in the story. You __were__ hungry for ice cream. I __was__ (44)

hungry for chocolate. They __were__ on the way to the party. It __was__ sad. She __was__ glad that (47)

you dropped by to see her. You __were__ a great help to us. They __were__ lost. He __was__ an excellent (50)

driver. You __were__ not a big help. It __was__ a good steak. They __were__ gone. (53)

ANSWER SHEET

Practicing Basic Skills in Language Arts • 106

© 2005 Sopris West Educational Services. All rights reserved. Practicing Basic Skills in Language Arts. Purchaser has permission to photocopy this page for classroom use only.

Subject-Verb Agreement: Am/Are/Is

Directions: Use *am*, *are*, or *is* in the following sentences.

	Correct	Error
First Try		
Second Try		

They _____ students in this school. It _____ a very good book. He _____ the bus driver. They

_____ ready for the assignment. He _____ hungry. You _____ thirsty. She _____

a pretty girl. He _____ a doctor. It _____ too bad that you are ill. I _____ sure you will be

welcome. It _____ a beautiful day. It _____ time to go home now. She _____ a nice person.

It _____ the Bicentennial year. I _____ in love. They _____ very good friends of mine. It _____ happy. I

good to be nice to animals. They _____ ready for a water fight. They _____ happy. I

_____ a silly person. You _____ out of gas. She _____ here with me. They _____ not

happy with the plan. He _____ a friendly dog. He _____ out of school today. You _____ not

the first in line. I _____ delighted to see you. She _____ a student of the violin. It _____ fun to

dance. She _____ not a good typist. It _____ not a good day for skating. He _____ happy with

his new car. She _____ a happy person to know. They _____ right in what they do. He _____

sick with a cold. You _____ not a giggling teenager. She _____ not home now. I _____ lost. They

_____ too warm. She _____ a model. They _____ on the way home. He _____ a shoe

salesman. I _____ a girl. We _____ a family. I _____ a human being. You _____ my

best friend. He _____ a student of biology. She _____ around here someplace. I _____ a blonde.

© 2005 Sopris West Educational Services. All rights reserved. Practicing Basic Skills in Language Arts. Purchaser has permission to photocopy this page for classroom use only.

ONE-MINUTE FLUENCY BUILDER SERIES

SEE TO WRITE OR SEE TO SAY

Subject-Verb Agreement: Am/Are/Is

Directions: Use *am*, *are*, or *is* in the following sentences.

	Correct	Error
First Try		
Second Try		

They **are** students in this school. It **is** a very good book. He **is** the bus driver. They (3)

are ready for the assignment. He **is** hungry. You **are** thirsty. She **is** (7)

a pretty girl. He **is** a doctor. It **is** too bad that you are ill. I **am** sure you will be (10)

welcome. It **is** a beautiful day. It **is** time to go home now. She **is** a nice person. (13)

It **is** the Bicentennial year. I **am** in love. They **are** very good friends of mine. It (16)

is good to be nice to animals. They **are** ready for a water fight. They **are** happy. I (19)

am a silly person. You **are** out of gas. She **is** here with me. They **are** not (23)

happy with the plan. He **is** a friendly dog. He **is** out of school today. You **are** not (26)

the first in line. I **am** delighted to see you. She **is** a student of the violin. It **is** fun to (29)

dance. She **is** not a good typist. It **is** not a good day for skating. He **is** happy with (32)

his new car. She **is** a happy person to know. They **are** right in what they do. He **is** (35)

sick with a cold. You **are** not a giggling teenager. She **is** not home now. I **am** lost. They (38)

too warm. She **is** a model. They **are** on the way home. He **is** a shoe (42)

salesman. I **am** a girl. We **are** a family. I **am** a human being. You **are** my (46)

best friend. He **is** a student of biology. She **is** around here someplace. I **am** a blonde. (49)

ANSWER SHEET

© 2005 Sopris West Educational Services. All rights reserved. Practicing Basic Skills in Language Arts. Purchaser has permission to photocopy this page for classroom use only.

THINK TO WRITE

Subject-Verb Agreement: Has/Have

Directions: Use either *has* or *have* in the following sentences.

Mary _____ three dolls. Kwan _____ a cold. Dave and Maria _____ lots of fun. Maria _____

four dresses. Nisha _____ a new coat. Tom and Lamar _____ gone to school. _____

_____ you seen the new school? The school _____ many windows. My house _____ just a few

windows. David _____ two bicycles. Tom and Rosa _____ only one bicycle each. Do you _____

a bicycle? I would like to _____ a blue one. The bike I _____ is very old. I wonder what kind of bike

Ben _____. Don't we _____ time to eat dinner? Lucia _____ enough work for two people.

Do you _____ a new CD? We _____ decided to work late tomorrow. She _____ a lot of work

to do. She _____ a new dress for the dance. It _____ already become dark. Jill _____ three

dolls. _____ you ever gone to the zoo? I _____ two dimes. I _____ been there three times.

Danny _____ a new cat and hat. Luis _____ a new cat too. A tiger _____ a long tail. What

_____ you been doing? Do you _____ to go home now? Mother _____ made us some punch. Kim

_____ a dog for a pet. My pet _____ black stripes. Do you _____ a pet? Susan _____

an apple in her pocket. We _____ to buy a new car. Our car _____ a flat tire. We _____ an apple

tree. Pierre _____ an apple tree too. Do you _____ an apple tree? Sam _____ an airplane. Do you

_____ any toys? I _____ a new book to read. David _____ a new hat. I _____ a red suit. Do you

Tyrone's mother _____ a blue car. Mary _____ red socks. We _____ twins in our family. Do you

_____ twins in your family? Elena _____ a twin sister.

Practicing Basic Skills in Language Arts • 109

© 2005 Sopris West Educational Services. All rights reserved. Practicing Basic Skills in Language Arts. Purchaser has permission to photocopy this page for classroom use only.

	Correct	Error
First Try		
Second Try		

Subject-Verb Agreement: Has/Have

Directions: Use either *has* or *have* in the following sentences.

Mary __has__ three dolls. Kwan __has__ a cold. Dave and Maria __have__ lots of fun. Maria (3)

__has__ four dresses. Nisha __has__ a new coat. Tom and Lamar __have__ gone to school. (6)

__Have__ you seen the new school? The school __has__ many windows. My house __has__ just a few (9)

windows. David __has__ two bicycles. Tom and Rosa __have__ only one bicycle each. Do you __have__ (12)

a bicycle? I would like to __have__ a blue one. The bike I __have__ is very old. I wonder what kind of bike (14)

Ben __has__. Don't we __have__ time to eat dinner? Lucia __has__ enough work for two people. (17)

Do you __have__ a new CD? We __have__ decided to work late tomorrow. She __has__ a lot of work (20)

to do. She __has__ a new dress for the dance. It __has__ already become dark. Jill __has__ three (23)

dolls. __Have__ you ever gone to the zoo? I __have__ two dimes. I __have__ been there three times. (26)

Danny __has__ a new cat and hat. Luis __has__ a new cat too. A tiger __has__ a long tail. What (29)

__have__ you been doing? Do you __have__ to go home now? Mother __has__ made us some punch. Kim (32)

__has__ a dog for a pet. My pet __has__ black stripes. Do you __have__ a pet? Susan __has__ (36)

an apple in her pocket. We __have__ to buy a new car. Our car __has__ a flat tire. We __have__ an apple (39)

tree. Pierre __has__ an apple tree too. Do you __have__ an apple tree? Sam __has__ an airplane. Do you (42)

__have__ any toys? I __have__ a new book to read. David __has__ a new hat. I __have__ a red suit. (46)

Tyrone's mother __has__ red socks. We __have__ twins in our family. Do you (49)

__have__ twins in your family? Elena __has__ a twin sister. (51)

© 2005 Sopris West Educational Services. All rights reserved. Practicing Basic Skills in Language Arts. Purchaser has permission to photocopy this page for classroom use only.

Subject-Verb Agreement: Has Been/Have Been

Directions: Use either *has been* or *have been* in the following sentences.

	Correct	Error
First Try		
Second Try		

ONE MINUTE FLUENCY BUILDER SERIES

They _____ to the movies. I _____ at school. She _____ on vacation. He _____ to

the doctor. We _____ interested in your discussion. You _____ a good student. I _____ in the

kitchen cooking. They _____ to the football game. She _____ a big help to her mother. He

a science student. You _____ gone a long time. She _____ in the hospital. I _____ at the tennis

courts. You _____ on a vacation for a week. They _____ to the zoo. He _____ an interesting

man. It _____ a dangerous journey. She _____ at work for an hour. It _____ a cold day. He

a good dog. You _____ a good friend. She _____ to her guitar lesson. We _____

friends for a long time. They _____ in a good mood. He _____ in bed with a bad cold. She

lonely since you left. We _____ in school for months. It _____ a beautiful day for a picnic. They

at the grocery store. She _____ in the family room watching TV. You _____ a good teacher.

We _____ on the phone for an hour. He _____ eating in the lunchroom. You previously _____ at

my house. She _____ at the shopping center. I _____ in the office of the principal. He _____ my

boss. They _____ on a long trip. She _____ in bed for an hour. You _____ very helpful with your

suggestions. It _____ a long, hard day.

© 2005 Sopris West Educational Services. All rights reserved. Practicing Basic Skills in Language Arts. Purchaser has permission to photocopy this page for classroom use only.

SEE TO SAY OR SEE TO WRITE

Subject-Verb Agreement: Has Been/Have Been

Directions: Use either *has been* or *have been* in the following sentences.

	Correct	Error
First Try		
Second Try		

(4) They __have been__ to the movies. I __have been__ at school. She __has been__ to

(7) the doctor. We __have been__ interested in your discussion. You __have been__ in the

(10) kitchen cooking. They __have been__ to the football game. She __has been__ a big help to her mother. He __has been__

(13) a science student. You __have been__ gone a long time. She __has been__ in the hospital. I __have been__ at the tennis

(16) courts. You __have been__ on a vacation for a week. They __have been__ to the zoo. He __has been__ an interesting

(19) man. It __has been__ a dangerous journey. She __has been__ at work for an hour. It __has been__ a cold day. He

(23) __has been__ a good dog. You __have been__ a good friend. She __has been__ to her guitar lesson. We __have been__

(26) friends for a long time. They __have been__ in a good mood. He __has been__ in bed with a bad cold. She __has been__

(28) lonely since you left. We __have been__ in school for months. It __has been__ a beautiful day for a picnic. They

(31) __have been__ at the grocery store. She __has been__ in the family room watching TV. You __have been__ a good teacher.

(34) We __have been__ on the phone for an hour. He __has been__ eating in the lunchroom. You previously __have been__ at

(37) my house. She __has been__ at the shopping center. I __have been__ in the office of the principal. He __has been__ my

(40) boss. They __have been__ on a long trip. She __has been__ in bed for an hour. You __have been__ very helpful with your

(41) suggestions. It __has been__ a long, hard day.

ANSWER SHEET

Practicing Basic Skills in Language Arts • 112

© 2005 Sopris West Educational Services. All rights reserved. Practicing Basic Skills in Language Arts. Purchaser has permission to photocopy this page for classroom use only.

	Correct	Error
First Try		
Second Try		

SEE TO MARK

Correct Verb Form—Usage

Directions: Underline the correct verb form.

ONE-MINUTE FLUENCY BUILDER SERIES

have ate/eaten
Mike doesn't/don't
has begun/began
have broke/broken
has broken/broke
has come/came
she give/gave
I drank/drunk
I saw/seen
my pencil is busted/broken
the bell has rung/rang
he run/ran
we were/was
it's/its late
they seen/saw
there're/there's two stories
he done/did it
one of the lights are/is out
have wrote/written
her hair are/is long
he don't/doesn't
one of the books is/are lost

they saw/seen it
they're/there's a bike
loan/borrow me a pencil
teach/learn us
she doesn't/don't
the bell has rung/rang
athletics are/is
Sheila and I are/is going
Dave don't/doesn't
she swum/swam
did you see/saw her and me
they sung/sang
he gots/has it
he has sang/sung
I seen/saw
we was/were
she don't/doesn't
they were/was frozen
she has come/came
John and I are/is
he began/begun
we've saw/seen it

had written/wrote
he has swum/swam
its/it's foot
she drank/drunk it
she run/ran
she doesn't/don't
has wrote/written
have sprung/sprang
Susan don't/doesn't
she has/gots it
they was/were
she drank/drunk it
it's/its late
I've got/have a key
phonics are/is
they was/were late
borrow/lend me your bike
I saw/seen it
we've saw/seen it
she rung/rang it
it's/its fur
John seen/saw

I saw/seen her
she run/ran
she has swum/swam
he don't/doesn't
has chose/chosen
has begun/began
he came/come
has drew/drawn
has sunk/sank
has rose/risen
we seen/saw
had worn/wore
had become/became
she don't/doesn't
has sprung/sprang
have wore/worn
had risen/rose
its/it's eyes
has chosen/chose
have began/begun

© 2005 Sopris West Educational Services. All rights reserved. Practicing Basic Skills in Language Arts. Purchaser has permission to photocopy this page for classroom use only.

ONE-MINUTE FLUENCY BUILDER SERIES

SEE TO MARK

Correct Verb Form—Usage

Directions: Underline the correct verb form.

	Correct	Error
First Try		
Second Try		

have ate/eaten

Mike doesn't/don't

has begun/began

have broke/broken

has broken/broke

has come/came

she give/gave

I <u>drank</u>/drunk

I <u>saw</u>/seen

my pencil is busted/broken

the bell has rung/rang

he run/<u>ran</u>

we were/was

<u>it's</u>/its late

they seen/saw

there're/there's two stories

he done/did it

one of the lights are/<u>is</u> out

have wrote/written

her hair are/<u>is</u> long

he don't/doesn't

one of the books <u>is</u>/are lost

they saw/seen it

they're/there's a bike

<u>loan</u>/borrow me a pencil

<u>teach</u>/learn us

she doesn't/don't

the bell has rung/<u>rang</u>

athletics are/<u>is</u>

Sheila and I <u>are</u>/is going

Dave don't/<u>doesn't</u>

she swum/<u>swam</u>

did you <u>see</u>/saw her and me

they sung/<u>sang</u>

he gots/has it

he has sang/<u>sung</u>

I seen/<u>saw</u>

we was/were

she don't/<u>doesn't</u>

they were/was frozen

she has come/<u>came</u>

John and I <u>are</u>/is

he <u>began</u>/begun

we've saw/<u>seen</u> it

had written/wrote

he has swum/swam

its/<u>it's</u> foot

she <u>drank</u>/drunk it

she run/ran

she <u>doesn't</u>/don't

has wrote/<u>written</u>

have sprung/sprang

Susan don't/<u>doesn't</u>

she <u>has</u>/gots it

they was/were

she <u>drank</u>/drunk it

<u>it's</u>/its late

I've <u>got</u>/have a key

phonics are/<u>is</u>

they was/were late

borrow/<u>lend</u> me your bike

I <u>saw</u>/seen it

we've saw/<u>seen</u> it

she rung/<u>rang</u> it

it's/<u>its</u> fur

John seen/<u>saw</u>

I <u>saw</u>/seen her

she run/<u>ran</u>

she has <u>swum</u>/swam

he don't/<u>doesn't</u>

has chose/<u>chosen</u>

has <u>begun</u>/began

he came/come

has drew/<u>drawn</u>

has sunk/sank

has rose/risen

we seen/<u>saw</u>

had worn/wore

had become/<u>became</u>

she don't/<u>doesn't</u>

has sprung/sprang

have wore/<u>worn</u>

had risen/rose

<u>its</u>/it's eyes

has chosen/chose

have began/<u>begun</u>

(4)
(8)
(12)
(16)
(20)
(24)
(28)
(32)
(36)
(40)
(44)
(48)
(52)
(56)
(60)
(64)
(68)
(72)
(76)
(80)
(83)
(86)

ANSWER SHEET

© 2005 Sopris West Educational Services. All rights reserved. Practicing Basic Skills in Language Arts. Purchaser has permission to photocopy this page for classroom use only.

ONE-MINUTE FLUENCY BUILDER SERIES

SEE TO MARK

Participles in Sentences

Directions: A **participle** is a verb form used as an adjective. In the following sentences, underline and identify the participles.

	Correct	Error
First Try		
Second Try		

Leaping the fence, the cat surprised me. Defeated teams should congratulate the winners. Moving quickly, he intercepted the

pass. The crying baby hid under the table. Pointing at me, the teacher snapped a question. The frightened and embarrassed

actor missed his cue. The survivor, shaken by his long ordeal, was frightened. He had finished the assignment by that time. I

was warned that the movie was extremely dull. The baby was crying. The teacher had been pointing at me. The prancing horses

were applauded by the delighted audience. The colorful flags, waving in the breeze, brightened the gloomy day. Swaggering and

boasting, he made us extremely angry. The game scheduled for tonight has been postponed because of rain. Leaving the field,

the happy player rushed to his parents sitting in the bleachers. Rain pattering on the roof made an eerie sound. We thought the

banging shutter upstairs was someone walking in the attic. Painfully sunburned, I vowed never to be so careless again. Terrified

by the big dog, Fluffy yowled and hissed. The platoon of soldiers, marching in step, crossed the field to the stirring music of the

military band. We saw Leon eating watermelon. Smiling happily, Mildred accepted the Citizenship Award.

© 2005 Sopris West Educational Services. All rights reserved. Practicing Basic Skills in Language Arts. Purchaser has permission to photocopy this page for classroom use only.

SEE TO MARK

	First Try	Second Try
Correct		
Error		

Participles in Sentences

Directions: A **participle** is a verb form used as an adjective. In the following sentences, underline and identify the participles.

ONE MINUTE FLUENCY BUILDER SERIES

Leaping the fence, the cat surprised me. Defeated teams should congratulate the winners. Moving quickly, he intercepted the (3) pass. The crying baby hid under the table. Pointing at me, the teacher snapped a question. The frightened and embarrassed (7) actor missed his cue. The survivor, shaken by his long ordeal, was frightened. He had finished the assignment by that time. I (9) was warned that the movie was extremely dull. The baby was crying. The teacher had been pointing at me. The prancing horses (11) were applauded by the delighted audience. The colorful flags, waving in the breeze, brightened the gloomy day. Swaggering and (14) boasting, he made us extremely angry. The game scheduled for tonight has been postponed because of rain. Leaving the field, (17) the happy player rushed to his parents sitting in the bleachers. Rain pattering on the roof made an eerie sound. We thought the (19) banging shutter upstairs was someone walking in the attic. Painfully sunburned, I vowed never to be so careless again. Terrified (23) by the big dog, Fluffy yowled and hissed. The platoon of soldiers, marching in step, crossed the field to the stirring music of the (25) military band. We saw Leon eating watermelon. Smiling happily, Mildred accepted the Citizenship Award. (27)

ANSWER SHEET

© 2005 Sopris West Educational Services. All rights reserved. Practicing Basic Skills in Language Arts. Purchaser has permission to photocopy this page for classroom use only.

ONE-MINUTE FLUENCY
BUILDER SERIES

Gerunds in Sentences

Directions: A gerund is a verb form used as a noun. Gerunds are part verb and part noun. They are formed by adding "ing" to the plain verb form. Like nouns, gerunds are used as subjects, predicate nominatives, direct objects, or objects of prepositions. Using the following symbols, underline and identify the gerunds and how they are used in the sentences below: S.—subject; P.N.—predicate nominative; D.O.—direct object; and O.P.—object of the preposition.

	First Try	Second Try
Correct		
Error		

Walking is a pleasant exercise. My hobby is reading. Marcy enjoys dancing. That is used for writing. His whistling attracted

my attention. By practicing, you can improve your backhand. One requirement is singing. The crying upset her terribly. Dad

discouraged our shouting. Abner's favorite sport is fishing. After snoring loudly, he woke up. In writing, one should strive to

be concise. One of his bad habits is lying. Sewing can be fun. My favorite pastime is painting. Lucy likes skiing. Fishing is a

fun sport. Timings are helpful. His lesson was a ten-minute timing. In hunting, one must practice caution. His choice was to

continue reading. Lying does not really solve problems. Roger disliked skiing. George gave a reading for my mother's club. He

wants to go riding. Murphy gave up skating. Silversmithing is a lucrative pastime. She is not fond of waiting. Buying clothes

can be an experience! Sylvester doesn't enjoy shopping. Dad discouraged our shouting. In writing, one should strive to be

concise. After snoring loudly, he woke up. By practicing, you can improve your backhand. That is used for writing. Marcy enjoys

dancing. My hobby is reading. The crying upset her terribly. My favorite pastime is painting. Lucy likes skiing. Fishing is a fun

sport. Murphy gave up skating.

© 2005 Sopris West Educational Services. All rights reserved. Practicing Basic Skills in Language Arts. Purchaser has permission to photocopy this page for classroom use only.

ONE-MINUTE FLUENCY BUILDER SERIES

SEE TO MARK

Gerunds in Sentences

Directions: A gerund is a verb form used as a noun. Gerunds are part verb and part noun. They are formed by adding "ing" to the plain verb form. Like nouns, gerunds are used as subjects, predicate nominatives, direct objects, or objects of prepositions. Using the following symbols, underline and identify the gerunds and how they are used in the sentences below: S.—subject; P.N.—predicate nominative; D.O.—direct object; and O.P.—object of the preposition.

	First Try	Second Try
Correct		
Error		

[S] **Walking** is a pleasant exercise. My hobby is [PN] **reading**. Marcy enjoys [DO] **dancing**. That is used for [OP] **writing**. His [S] **whistling** attracted (5)

my attention. By [OP] **practicing**, you can improve your backhand. One requirement is [PN] **singing**. The [S] **crying** upset her terribly. Dad (8)

discouraged our [DO] **shouting**. Abner's favorite sport is [PN] **fishing**. After [S] **snoring** loudly, he woke up. In [OP] **writing**, one should strive to (12)

be concise. One of his bad habits is [PN] **lying**. [S] **Sewing** can be fun. My favorite pastime is [PN] **painting**. Lucy likes [DO] **skiing**. [S] **Fishing** is a (17)

fun sport. [S] **Timings** are helpful. His lesson was a ten-minute timing. In [OP] **hunting**, one must practice caution. His choice was to (20)

continue [DO] **reading**. [S] **Lying** does not really solve problems. Roger disliked [DO] **skiing**. George gave a [DO] **reading** for my mother's club. He (24)

wants to go [DO] **riding**. Murphy gave up [DO] **skating**. [S] **Silversmithing** is a lucrative pastime. She is not fond of [OP] **waiting**. [S] **Buying** clothes (29)

can be an experience! Sylvester doesn't enjoy [DO] **shopping**. Dad discouraged our [DO] **shouting**. In [OP] **writing**, one should strive to be (32)

concise. After [OP] **snoring** loudly, he woke up. By [OP] **practicing**, you can improve your backhand. That is used for [PN] **writing**. Marcy enjoys (35)

[DO] **dancing**. My hobby is [PN] **reading**. The [S] **crying** upset her terribly. My favorite pastime is painting. Lucy likes skiing. Fishing is a fun (41)

sport. Murphy gave up [DO] **skating**. (42)

ANSWER SHEET

Practicing Basic Skills in Language Arts • 118

© 2005 Sopris West Educational Services. All rights reserved. Practicing Basic Skills in Language Arts. Purchaser has permission to photocopy this page for classroom use only.

	Correct	Error
First Try		
Second Try		

SEE TO MARK

Infinitives in Sentences

Directions: An infinitive is a verb form, usually preceded by *to*, that is used as a noun, adjective, or adverb. Using the following abbreviations, underline and identify the infinitives and how they are used in the sentences below: S.—subject; P.N.—predicate nominative; D.O.—direct object; O.P.—object of preposition; ADV.—adverb; ADJ.—adjective.

He wanted to go to the store. The boys asked Herbie to play. To think is to be. The man to watch is the catcher. That was a

moment to forget. The author rose to protest. Eager to please, the maid curtsied. To be wise is to give. The one to listen for is the

whistler. There was a fire we weren't soon to forget. The dog ran to greet us. To interrupt a speaker is impolite. We had hoped

to leave at noon. He is the person to see about the job. They were glad to hear an answer. To give advice is easy. We had hoped

to solve the problem. Nelson plans to go. I went to the gym to find him. The door is not easy to open. It is John's turn to write

the play. I want her to think about the problem. Dave wants to play with his friends. We hope to be leaving after school.

To enlist in the Marines is his plan. My dad helped me to wash the car. We are going to see the parade. Maria asked him to walk

her home from school. To keep quiet is hard for some people. We ran to see mother when she got home. That was a day

to remember. To forget is to forgive. The senator rose to speak. Eager to please, my dog obeyed my command. We went to town

to shop. He walked home from the movies. The man to watch is the quarterback. I want him to help me wash the car.

© 2005 Sopris West Educational Services. All rights reserved. Practicing Basic Skills in Language Arts. Purchaser has permission to photocopy this page for classroom use only.

ONE-MINUTE FLUENCY BUILDER SERIES

	Correct	Error
First Try		
Second Try		

Infinitives in Sentences

Directions: An infinitive is a verb form, usually preceded by *to*, that is used as a noun, adjective, or adverb. Using the following abbreviations, underline and identify the infinitives and how they are used in the sentences below: S.—subject; P.N.—predicate nominative; D.O.—direct object; O.P.—object of preposition; ADV.—adverb; ADJ.—adjective.

DO
He wanted to go to the store. The boys asked Herbie to play. To think is to be. The man to watch is the catcher. That was a
(ADJ) (ADJ, S, PN)   (5)

ADJ
moment to forget. The author rose to protest. Eager to please, the maid curtsied. To be wise is to give. The one to listen for is the
(ADV) (ADV) (S, PN) (ADJ)   (11)

whistler. There was a fire we weren't soon to forget. The dog ran to greet us. To interrupt a speaker is impolite. We had hoped
(ADV) (ADV) (S)   (14)

DO
to leave at noon. He is the person to see about the job. They were glad to hear an answer. To give advice is easy. We had hoped
(ADJ) (ADV) (S)   (18)

DO
to solve the problem. Nelson plans to go. I went to the gym to find him. The door is not easy to open. It is John's turn to write
(DO) (ADV) (ADV) (ADJ)   (23)

ADJ
the play. I want her to think about the problem. Dave wants to play with his friends. We hope to be leaving after school.
(DO) (DO) (DO)   (26)

S
To enlist in the Marines is his plan. My dad helped me to wash the car. We are going to see the parade. Maria asked him to walk
(ADV) (ADV) (ADV)   (30)

S
her home from school. To keep quiet is hard for some people. We ran to see mother when she got home. That was a day
(S) (ADV)   (32)

ADJ
to remember. To forget is to forgive. The senator rose to speak. Eager to please, my dog obeyed my command. We went to town
(S, PN) (ADV) (ADV)   (37)

ADV
to shop. He walked home from the movies. The man to watch is the quarterback. I want him to help me wash the car.
(ADJ) (ADJ)   (40)

ANSWER SHEET

© 2005 Sopris West Educational Services. All rights reserved. Practicing Basic Skills in Language Arts. Purchaser has permission to photocopy this page for classroom use only.

ONE MINUTE FLUENCY
BUILDER SERIES

SEE TO MARK

Gerunds, Participles, Infinitives in Sentences

Directions: Using the following abbreviations, underline and identify the gerunds, infinitives, and participles and how they are used: S.—subject; P.N.—predicate nominative; D.O.—direct object; O.P.—object of the preposition; ADV.—adverb; ADJ.—adjective.

Left alone in the dark, Mary was frightened. Walking is a pleasant exercise. My hobby is reading. The boys asked Herbie to play.

Terrified by the big dog, Fluffy howled and hissed. My hobby is reading. He wanted to go to the store. The man to watch is the

catcher. Ann's favorite sport is tennis. He wants to go riding. The colorful flags, waving in the breeze, brightened the gloomy

day. I was warned that the movie was extremely dull. The baby was crying. In writing, one should strive to be concise. Lying

does not really solve problems. To interrupt a speaker is impolite. I went to the gym to find him. Buying clothes can be an

experience. That is used for writing. The teacher had been pointing at me. He had finished the assignment by that time. Murphy

gave up skating. I want her to think about the problem. We weren't happy to hear him talk. We ran to see mother when she got

home. After snoring loudly, he woke up. The prancing horses were applauded by the delighted audience. He is the person to see

about the job. To laugh loudly is rude. We thought the banging shutter upstairs was someone walking in the attic. They were

glad to hear an answer. That is used for writing. His choice was to continue reading. Nelson plans to go. Tackled on the one-yard

line, he fumbled the ball. Wildly cheering for the team, we celebrated the victory.

© 2005 Sopris West Educational Services. All rights reserved. Practicing Basic Skills in Language Arts. Purchaser has permission to photocopy this page for classroom use only.

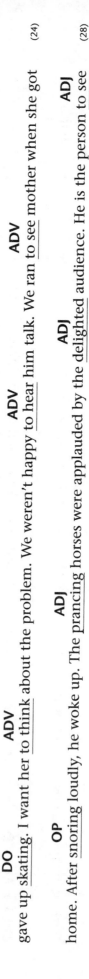

Gerunds, Participles, Infinitives in Sentences

Directions: Using the following abbreviations, underline and identify the gerunds, infinitives, and participles and how they are used: S.—subject; P.N.—predicate nominative; D.O.—direct object; O.P.—object of the preposition; ADV.—adverb; ADJ.—adjective.

ADJ   **ADJ**   **S**   **PN**   **ADV**
Left alone in the dark, Mary was frightened. Walking is a pleasant exercise. My hobby is reading. The boys asked Herbie to play. (5)

ADJ   **PN**   **DO**   **ADJ**
Terrified by the big dog, Fluffy howled and hissed. My hobby is reading. He wanted to go to the store. The man to watch is the (9)

    PN   **DO**   **ADV**   **ADJ**
catcher. Ann's favorite sport is tennis. He wants to go riding. The colorful flags, waving in the breeze, brightened the gloomy (11)

PN   **ADJ**   **OP**   **DO**   **S**
day. I was warned that the movie was extremely dull. The baby was crying. In writing, one should strive to be concise. Lying (16)

    S   **ADV**   **S**
does not really solve problems. To interrupt a speaker is impolite. I went to the gym to find him. Buying clothes can be an (19)

    OP   **ADV**
experience. That is used for writing. The teacher had been pointing at me. He had finished the assignment by that time. Murphy (20)

DO   **ADV**   **ADV**   **ADV**
gave up skating. I want her to think about the problem. We weren't happy to hear him talk. We ran to see mother when she got (24)

    OP   **ADJ**   **ADJ**
home. After snoring loudly, he woke up. The prancing horses were applauded by the delighted audience. He is the person to see (28)

    S   **ADJ**   **ADJ**
about the job. To laugh loudly is rude. We thought the banging shutter upstairs was someone walking in the attic. They were (31)

ADV   **OP**   **DO**   **DO**   **ADJ**
glad to hear an answer. That is used for writing. His choice was to continue reading. Nelson plans to go. Tackled on the one-yard (37)

    ADJ
line, he fumbled the ball. Wildly cheering for the team, we celebrated the victory. (38)

Practicing Basic Skills in Language Arts • 122

	Correct	Error
First Try		
Second Try		

© 2005 Sopris West Educational Services. All rights reserved. Practicing Basic Skills in Language Arts. Purchaser has permission to photocopy this page for classroom use only.

Adjectives and Adverbs

Articles: A, An, The in Sentences 125
Adjectives In Phrases 127
Adjectives in Sentences 129
Adjectives in Sentences 131
Adjectives in Sentences 133
Limiting and Descriptive Adjectives 135
Limiting and Descriptive Adjectives—
    Fill in the Blanks 137
Limiting and Descriptive Adjectives—
    Fill in the Blanks 139
Proper Adjectives in Sentences 141
Common and Proper Adjectives in
    Sentences 143
Adjectives and the Words They Modify 145
Adjective Phrases and the Words They
    Modify 147
Predicate Adjectives 149
Comparative and Superlative Adjectives 151
Comparative and Superlative Adjectives
    (continued) 153
Comparative and Superlative Adjectives—
    Fill in the Blanks 155
Irregular Adjectives—Comparative and
    Superlative 157

Irregular Adjectives—Fill in the Blanks 159
Correct Form of Adjectives in Sentences 161
Corrective Form of Adjectives—
    Fill in the Blanks 163
Adverbs in Phrases 165
Adverbs in Sentences 167
Adverb—Answers Question: Where?
    When? How? To What Extent? 169
Adverb—Answers Question: Where?
    When? How? To What Extend? 171
Adverb—Answers Question—
    Fill in the Blanks 173
Adverb—Answers Question—
    Fill in the Blanks (continued) 175
Adverb and the Verb It Modifies 177
Adverb and the Verb It Modifies 179
Adverb and the Adjective It Modifies 181
Adverb and the Adjective It Modifies 183
Adverb and the Adverb It Modifies 185
Adverbs Modifying Adverbs or Verbs 187
Adverbs and the Words They Modify 189

ONE-MINUTE FLUENCY BUILDER SERIES

SEE TO MARK

Articles: A, An, The in Sentences

Directions: Mark all the articles in the sentences: *a, an, the.*

A violent storm uprooted a large tree in the front yard. The hot sun beat down on the thirsty animals. The kangaroo has short

forelegs and a large, thick tail. The official guide at the United Nations can speak a number of different languages. Lisa bought

a balloon for her sister. The door opened, and a woman was standing there by an old painting. A big, black car pulled up to the

curb. A tall man in the back seat held a mysterious package wrapped in an olive-colored wrapping. It was a cold, grey morning

when the French ambassador arrived. The boy walked a greater distance than necessary. He wore an old, weather-beaten hat.

The late students reported to the office for a pass. The boys who came late had to stay after school. The loudest complainers

have no real cause for a complaint. A slow trickle of blood showed where the pin had stuck him. She used a sharp pair of scissors

to cut an angel from the material. My dog is the most playful of the three. Is George a better player than the other boy? I got a

better grade on that test than the smartest girl in the class. A fur collar feels soft against the rough part of my hand. Sometimes

a dark horse will win the race. You lose the petals when you pick a full-blown rose. A rusty nail may cause an infection if you do

not care for it immediately. An elephant has a long memory. The best book I know is *Treasure Island*. He is an honorable man. I

read the Constitution of the United States of America as an assignment for my history class. This is the best dinner I ever tasted.

I found the dictionary more helpful than the almanac. It was the worst storm since the storms of the early 1900s.

Practicing Basic Skills in Language Arts • 125

© 2005 Sopris West Educational Services. All rights reserved. Practicing Basic Skills in Language Arts. Purchaser has permission to photocopy this page for classroom use only.

ONE-MINUTE FLUENCY BUILDER SERIES

SEE TO MARK

Articles: A, An, The in Sentences
Directions: Mark all the articles in the sentences: *a, an, the.*

	Correct	Error
First Try		
Second Try		

A violent storm uprooted a large tree in the front yard. The hot sun beat down on the thirsty animals. The kangaroo has short (6)

forelegs and a large, thick tail. The official guide at the United Nations can speak a number of different languages. Lisa bought (10)

a balloon for her sister. The door opened, and a woman was standing there by an old painting. A big, black car pulled up to the (16)

curb. A tall man in the back seat held a mysterious package wrapped in an olive-colored wrapping. It was a cold, grey morning (21)

when the French ambassador arrived. The boy walked a greater distance than necessary. He wore an old, weather-beaten hat. (25)

The late students reported to the office for a pass. The boys who came late had to stay after school. The loudest complainers (30)

have no real cause for a complaint. A slow trickle of blood showed where the pin had stuck him. She used a sharp pair of scissors (34)

to cut an angel from the material. My dog is the most playful of the three. Is George a better player than the other boy? I got a (41)

better grade on that test than the smartest girl in the class. A fur collar feels soft against the rough part of my hand. Sometimes (45)

a dark horse will win the race. You lose the petals when you pick a full-blown rose. A rusty nail may cause an infection if you do (51)

not care for it immediately. An elephant has a long memory. The best book I know is *Treasure Island.* He is an honorable man. I (55)

read the Constitution of the United States of America as an assignment for my history class. This is the best dinner I ever tasted. (59)

I found the dictionary more helpful than the almanac. It was the worst storm since the storms of the early 1900s. (64)

ANSWER SHEET

Practicing Basic Skills in Language Arts • 126

© 2005 Sopris West Educational Services. All rights reserved. Practicing Basic Skills in Language Arts. Purchaser has permission to photocopy this page for classroom use only.

Correct Error
First Try
Second Try

ONE-MINUTE FLUENCY
BUILDER SERIES

SEE TO MARK

Adjectives In Phrases
Directions: Mark the adjectives.

three blind mice	a nice boy	a grocery store
on paper plates	balmy summer air	my faithful friend
the white dryer	a terrible time	both reckless drivers
one red rose	the blinding flash	good fortune was expected
he looks tough	the restful quiet	that large bulldog
people have become friendly	soft green sides	each new student
air smells nice	roaring wind	selfish child was disliked
the graceful dancer	of deafening thunder	our only brother
head felt terrible	a slender girl	thoughtful people spoke
neighbors are busy	short and fat puppy	only brother is spoiled
dog became noisy	an alert detective	any unripe apples
house looked deserted	a splendid performance	my oldest aunt
I am tired	muddy, swirling water	her horrible nightmare
the American flag	prompt and tidy worker	wagged its busy tail
the great play	reads many books	every club member
a tall player	both are busy and happy	both library books
a bad hailstorm	four carnival tickets	their electric guitars
an English person	old but strong	your winter jacket is torn
the battered car	speech was long and dull	any metal pan

Practicing Basic Skills in Language Arts • 127

© 2005 Sopris West Educational Services. All rights reserved. Practicing Basic Skills in Language Arts. Purchaser has permission to photocopy this page for classroom use only.

ONE-MINUTE FLUENCY
BUILDER SERIES

	Correct	Error
First Try		
Second Try		

Adjectives In Phrases
Directions: Mark the adjectives.

three blind mice
(2) on paper plates
(3) the white dryer
(4) one red rose
(6) he looks tough
(7) people have become friendly
(8) air smells nice
(9) the graceful dancer
(10) head felt terrible
(11) neighbors are busy
(12) dog became noisy
(13) house looked deserted
(14) I am tired
(15) the American flag
(16) the great play
(17) a tall player
(18) a bad hailstorm
(19) an English person
(20) the battered car
(21)

a nice boy
(22) balmy summer air
(24) a terrible time
(25) the blinding flash
(26) the restful quiet
(27) soft green sides
(29) roaring wind
(30) of deafening thunder
(31) a slender girl
(32) short and fat puppy
(34) an alert detective
(35) a splendid performance
(36) muddy, swirling water
(38) prompt and tidy worker
(40) reads many books
(41) both are busy and happy
(43) four carnival tickets
(45) old but strong
(47) speech was long and dull
(49)

a grocery store
(50) my faithful friend
(52) both reckless drivers
(54) good fortune was expected
(55) that large bulldog
(57) each new student
(59) selfish child was disliked
(61) our only brother
(63) thoughtful people spoke
(64) only brother is spoiled
(66) any unripe apples
(68) my oldest aunt
(70) her horrible nightmare
(72) wagged its busy tail
(73) every club member
(75) both library books
(77) their electric guitars
(79) your winter jacket is torn
(82) any metal pan
(84)

ANSWER SHEET

Practicing Basic Skills in Language Arts • 128

© 2005 Sopris West Educational Services. All rights reserved. Practicing Basic Skills in Language Arts. Purchaser has permission to photocopy this page for classroom use only.

SEE TO MARK

Adjectives in Sentences

Directions: Mark all the adjectives in the following sentences.

The black bear growled at the old woodsman. A scary noise rang through the empty house. A dead tree fell with a loud crash.

The large man drove a small car. A running cowboy roped a wild horse. The weary children saw a long movie. The nearby

worker put out the grease fire. The costumed actress combed the long wig. Three uniformed men caught the shaggy dog.

Brilliant lightning flashed across the dark sky. A cool breeze was blowing. The shrill siren gave the alarm. The rusty knife would

not cut the wood. Old shaggy goats were eating grass. The blue book belongs to me. Fierce lions attacked the camp. The little

girls were jumping rope. Some brave policemen stopped the robbery. That sleek car belongs to my neighbor. Hungry little

children ate the soup. The hot iron scorched the shirt. Rainy weather ruined the picnic. The red and black birds were building a

nest. Each boy drank hot tea and ate apple pie. The ancient, battered car chugged its way down the dusty road. The large table

was a gift from the old emperor. The jeweled tiara had disappeared just as the wicked witch had said it would. We are all meeting

at the Star Trek convention on the California coast. The blue roses became a symbol of the very rare, if not of the impossible.

The black bear bit the old woodsman. A scary noise rang through the empty house. The shrill siren gave the alarm. The rusty

knife would not cut the wood. Old shaggy goats were eating grass. That sleek car belongs to my neighbor. Hungry little children

ate the soup. Fire devoured the shabby old building. The hot iron scorched the new shirt. Rainy weather ruined the picnic. Each

bell has a special tone.

© 2005 Sopris West Educational Services. All rights reserved. Practicing Basic Skills in Language Arts. Purchaser has permission to photocopy this page for classroom use only.

Adjectives in Sentences

Directions: Mark all the adjectives in the following sentences.

	First Try	Second Try
Correct		
Error		

The black bear growled at the old woodsman. A scary noise rang through the empty house. A dead tree fell with a loud crash. (6)

The large man drove a small car. A running cowboy roped a wild horse. The weary children saw a long movie. The nearby (13)

worker put out the grease fire. The costumed actress combed the long wig. Three uniformed men caught the shaggy dog. (19)

Brilliant lightning flashed across the dark sky. A cool breeze was blowing. The shrill siren gave the alarm. The rusty knife would (24)

not cut the wood. Old shaggy goats were eating grass. The blue book belongs to me. Fierce lions attacked the camp. The little (29)

girls were jumping rope. Some brave policemen stopped the robbery. That sleek car belongs to my neighbor. Hungry little (36)

children ate the soup. The hot iron scorched the shirt. Rainy weather ruined the picnic. The red and black birds were building a (40)

nest. Each boy drank hot tea and ate apple pie. The ancient, battered car chugged its way down the dusty road. The large table (47)

was a gift from the old emperor. The jeweled tiara had disappeared just as the wicked witch had said it would. We are all meeting (50)

at the Star Trek convention on the California coast. The blue roses became a symbol of the very rare, if not of the impossible. (54)

The black bear bit the old woodsman. A scary noise rang through the empty house. The shrill siren gave the alarm. The rusty (60)

knife would not cut the wood. Old shaggy goats were eating grass. That sleek car belongs to my neighbor. Hungry little children (67)

ate the soup. Fire devoured the shabby old building. The hot iron scorched the new shirt. Rainy weather ruined the picnic. Each (73)

bell has a special tone. (74)

© 2005 Sopris West Educational Services. All rights reserved. Practicing Basic Skills in Language Arts. Purchaser has permission to photocopy this page for classroom use only.

ONE-MINUTE FLUENCY
BUILDER SERIES

SEE TO MARK

Adjectives in Sentences

Directions: Mark all the adjectives in the following sentences and count each as 1 point.

	First Try	Second Try
Correct		
Error		

There are twenty-five students in this class. Good citizens vote for the best candidate. Two candidates made short speeches. Registered voters may vote if the best person runs. Several well-qualified candidates are running for the same office. Those voters went to the wrong polling place. Every American citizen should vote. I dislike boastful, arrogant people. Two boys, tired and sleepy, were found in the deep woods. Those two boys had been lost before. A big, black car pulled up to the curb. The driver, hot and tired, stepped out. A tall, turbaned man in the back seat held a mysterious, well-wrapped package. Three armed men lurked in the building shadows. A black, wire-haired terrier came to our door. The dog was tired and hungry. A strong, blustery wind blew down our lightweight tent. We are studying English history this year. My mother raises African violets in our backyard. I brought these six red apples for you. Did you see the French movie last Saturday? Trevor has a new truck, red and shiny. It was a battered, black car. December has thirty-one days. Russell's uncle has an auto-repair shop. An unhappy boy sat in the first row. Pamela had seen several large dogs. Those books, old and battered, were found in the vacant house. This purple sweater belongs to that talkative girl. Have these children ever seen that kind of flower? It was a cold, grey morning when the French ambassador arrived. The eighth customer refused to buy the broken umbrella. Cashmere is a beautiful wool. The Asian continent is the most vastly populated. The bright sunshine warmed the colorful flowers. This is the darkest night we've had in some time. Boyd walked a greater distance than the other boys. A weary traveler walked along the narrow path. He wore an old, weather-beaten hat.

Practicing Basic Skills in Language Arts • 131

© 2005 Sopris West Educational Services. All rights reserved. Practicing Basic Skills in Language Arts. Purchaser has permission to photocopy this page for classroom use only.

ONE-MINUTE FLUENCY
BUILDER SERIES

SEE TO MARK

Adjectives in Sentences

Directions: Mark all the adjectives in the following sentences and count each as 1 point.

	Correct	Error
First Try		
Second Try		

There are twenty-five students in this class. Good citizens vote for the best candidate. Two candidates made short speeches. (6)

Registered voters may vote if the best person runs. Several well-qualified candidates are running for the same office. Those voters (12)

went to the wrong polling place. Every American citizen should vote. I dislike boastful, arrogant people. Two boys, tired and (20)

sleepy, were found in the deep woods. Those two boys had been lost before. A big, black car pulled up to the curb. The driver, (26)

hot and tired, stepped out. A tall, turbaned man in the back seat held a mysterious, well-wrapped package. Three armed men (35)

lurked in the building shadows. A black, wire-haired terrier came to our door. The dog was tired and hungry. A strong, blustery (43)

wind blew down our lightweight tent. We are studying English history this year. My mother raises African violets in our (49)

backyard. I brought these six red apples for you. Did you see the French movie last Saturday? Trevor has a new truck, red and (57)

shiny. It was a battered, black car. December has thirty-one days. Russell's uncle has an auto-repair shop. An unhappy boy sat in (62)

the first row. Pamela had seen several large dogs. Those books, old and battered, were found in the vacant house. This purple (71)

sweater belongs to that talkative girl. Have these children ever seen that kind of flower? It was a cold, grey morning when the (77)

French ambassador arrived. The eighth customer refused to buy the broken umbrella. Cashmere is a beautiful wool. The Asian (82)

continent is the most vastly populated. The bright sunshine warmed the colorful flowers. This is the darkest night we've had in (86)

some time. Boyd walked a greater distance than the other boys. A weary traveler walked along the narrow path. He wore an old, (92)

weather-beaten hat. (93)

ANSWER SHEET

Practicing Basic Skills in Language Arts • 132

© 2005 Sopris West Educational Services. All rights reserved. Practicing Basic Skills in Language Arts. Purchaser has permission to photocopy this page for classroom use only.

ONE-MINUTE FLUENCY
BUILDER SERIES

SEE TO MARK

Adjectives in Sentences

Directions: Mark all the adjectives in the following sentences and count each as 1 point.

	First Try	Second Try
Correct		
Error		

The two men in the other car were policemen. The empty, old house was spooky. Most European students can speak the English

language. The new student had read four classic novels. The heavy black clouds warned us of a rainy afternoon. My sister chose

her two best friends to be her bridal attendants. That small Italian restaurant on the next corner serves delicious food. My father

is tall and thin. Several dirty newspapers had blown against the old iron fence. The eager bark of their little French poodle

greeted the three happy boys. Our first plan met with many strong objections. The house seemed haunted. The alert sentry

heard a strange sound. I am frightened by loud thunder. A lone, leafless, sky-pointing tree stenciled a sharp black pattern on the

setting sun. John is the oldest child. The Canadian trapper was once a famous banker in Toronto. Many young married couples

are building new houses. Falling leaves covered the old stone wall. Two strong boys led each prancing horse. Natalie is tall for

a gymnast. Glittering dewdrops reflected the morning sunlight. The boys were sick with terror in a moment. During the long

afternoon, the village seemed empty and dead. We saw a long, exciting football game. Did your sister wear her new red dress?

The new atomic submarines are spacious and comfortable. The second team played during the last quarter. This little book

contains some big ideas. Tom was gloomy and desperate. The night was cloudy and dark. This tall building is new, although it

appears old. Your blonde hair looks red in the bright sunlight. After that strenuous run, my best friend and I were exhausted.

Practicing Basic Skills in Language Arts • 133

© 2005 Sopris West Educational Services. All rights reserved. Practicing Basic Skills in Language Arts. Purchaser has permission to photocopy this page for classroom use only.

ONE MINUTE FLUENCY
BUILDER SERIES

SEE TO MARK

Adjectives in Sentences

Directions: Mark all the adjectives in the following sentences and count each as 1 point.

	Correct	Error
First Try		
Second Try		

The two men in the other car were policemen. The empty, old house was spooky. Most European students can speak the English (8)

language. The new student had read four classic novels. The heavy black clouds warned us of a rainy afternoon. My sister chose (15)

her two best friends to be her bridal attendants. That small Italian restaurant on the next corner serves delicious food. My father (26)

is tall and thin. Several dirty newspapers had blown against the old iron fence. The eager bark of their little French poodle (36)

greeted the three happy boys. Our first plan met with many strong objections. The house seemed haunted. The alert sentry (44)

heard a strange sound. I am frightened by loud thunder. A lone, leafless, sky-pointing tree stenciled a sharp black pattern on the (52)

setting sun. John is the oldest child. The Canadian trapper was once a famous banker in Toronto. Many young married couples (59)

are building new houses. Falling leaves covered the old stone wall. Two strong boys led each prancing horse. Natalie is tall for (68)

a gymnast. Glittering dewdrops reflected the morning sunlight. The boys were sick with terror in a moment. During the long (72)

afternoon, the village seemed empty and dead. We saw a long, exciting football game. Did your sister wear her new red dress? (81)

The new atomic submarines are spacious and comfortable. The second team played during the last quarter. This little book (89)

contains some big ideas. Tom was gloomy and desperate. The night was cloudy and dark. This tall building is new, although it (98)

appears old. Your blonde hair looks red in the bright sunlight. After that strenuous run, my best friend and I were exhausted. (109)

ANSWER SHEET

Practicing Basic Skills in Language Arts • 134

© 2005 Sopris West Educational Services. All rights reserved. Practicing Basic Skills in Language Arts. Purchaser has permission to photocopy this page for classroom use only.

ONE-MINUTE FLUENCY BUILDER SERIES

Limiting and Descriptive Adjectives

Directions: Mark (L) for limiting adjectives and mark (D) for descriptive adjectives.

First Try	Correct	Error
Second Try		

1. bony mongrel
2. frail girl
3. this boy
4. enormous sign
5. tiny figure
6. these packages
7. these books
8. scratchy beard
9. crooked stick
10. few signs
11. third choice
12. green leaf
13. decrepit rocker
14. high note
15. those men
16. five boys
17. toothless mouth
18. that house

19. blue wool
20. angry man
21. both brothers
22. main highways
23. the friend
24. frightened girl
25. model airplanes
26. icy road
27. merry laughter
28. thin man
29. some boys
30. dangerous game
31. small barn
32. loud explosion
33. paper routes
34. huge boss
35. grey house
36. sweet candy

37. long hikes
38. red apple
39. large books
40. happy woman
41. several students
42. ambitious man
43. this dog
44. narrow line
45. yellow roses
46. each girl
47. unusual prize
48. true friend
49. those people
50. every boy
51. tweed coat
52. shoe box
53. hall table
54. tropical birds

55. green hat
56. sour pickle
57. high winds
58. both teams
59. generous man
60. cold icicles
61. some trees
62. lazy cattle
63. all people
64. short tail
65. big cars
66. small daisy
67. those crayons
68. waffle iron
69. each performer
70. angry people
71. some teachers
72. dripping water

Practicing Basic Skills in Language Arts • 135

© 2005 Sopris West Educational Services. All rights reserved. Practicing Basic Skills in Language Arts. Purchaser has permission to photocopy this page for classroom use only.

ONE-MINUTE FLUENCY BUILDER SERIES

SEE TO MARK

Limiting and Descriptive Adjectives

Directions: Mark (L) for limiting adjectives and mark (D) for descriptive adjectives.

	First Try	Second Try
Correct		
Error		

1. bony mongrel — D
2. frail girl — D
3. this boy — L
4. enormous sign — D
5. tiny figure — D
6. these packages — L
7. these books — L
8. scratchy beard — D
9. crooked stick — D
10. few signs — L
11. third choice — L
12. green leaf — D
13. decrepit rocker — D
14. high note — D
15. those men — L
16. five boys — L
17. toothless mouth — D
18. that house — L

19. blue wool — D
20. angry man — D
21. both brothers — L
22. main highways — D
23. the friend — D
24. frightened girl — L
25. model airplanes — L
26. icy road — D
27. merry laughter — D
28. thin man — L
29. some boys — L
30. dangerous game — D
31. small barn — D
32. loud explosion — D
33. paper routes — L
34. huge boss — L
35. grey house — D
36. sweet candy — L

37. long hikes — D (4)
38. red apple — D (8)
39. large books — L (12)
40. happy woman — D (16)
41. several students — L (20)
42. ambitious man — D (24)
43. this dog — D (28)
44. narrow line — D (32)
45. yellow roses — D (36)
46. each girl — D (40)
47. unusual prize — L (44)
48. true friend — D (48)
49. those people — D (52)
50. every boy — D (56)
51. tweed coat — D (60)
52. shoe box — D (64)
53. hall table — D (68)
54. tropical birds — D (72)

55. green hat — D
56. sour pickle — D
57. high winds — D
58. both teams — L
59. generous man — D
60. cold icicles — L
61. some trees — D
62. lazy cattle — D
63. all people — L
64. short tail — D
65. big cars — L
66. small daisy — D
67. those crayons — D
68. waffle iron — L
69. each performer — D
70. angry people — L
71. some teachers — D
72. dripping water — L

ANSWER SHEET

Practicing Basic Skills in Language Arts • 136

© 2005 Sopris West Educational Services. All rights reserved. Practicing Basic Skills in Language Arts. Purchaser has permission to photocopy this page for classroom use only.

	First Try	Second Try
Correct		
Error		

THINK TO WRITE

Limiting and Descriptive Adjectives—Fill in the Blanks

Directions: Under each of the three categories, write an adjective to complete the phrase. There could be many answers.

What Kind?	Which One?	How Much? Or How Many?
_____ woman	_____ the answer	_____ times
_____ car	_____ job	_____ boys
_____ coat	_____ pen	_____ dollars
_____ ribbons	_____ shoes	_____ animals
_____ kangaroo	_____ doors	_____ sheep
_____ books	_____ the question	_____ dresses
_____ girl	_____ clock	_____ countries
_____ goats	_____ the lesson	_____ men
_____ food	_____ street	_____ bands
_____ the boys	_____ map	_____ highways
_____ and	_____ colors	_____ vegetables

Practicing Basic Skills in Language Arts • 137

© 2005 Sopris West Educational Services. All rights reserved. Practicing Basic Skills in Language Arts. Purchaser has permission to photocopy this page for classroom use only.

ONE-MINUTE FLUENCY
BUILDER SERIES

ONE-MINUTE FLUENCY BUILDER SERIES

THINK TO WRITE

	First Try	Second Try
Correct		
Error		

Limiting and Descriptive Adjectives—Fill in the Blanks

Directions: Under each of the three categories, write an adjective to complete the phrase. There could be many answers.

What Kind?	Which One?	How Much? Or How Many?
_____ woman	_____ the answer	_____ times (3)
_____ car	_____ job	_____ boys (6)
_____ coat	_____ pen	_____ dollars (9)
_____ ribbons	_____ shoes	_____ animals (12)
_____ kangaroo	_____ doors	_____ sheep (15)
_____ books	_____ the question	_____ dresses (18)
_____ girl	_____ clock	_____ countries (21)
_____ goats	_____ the lesson	_____ men (24)
_____ food	_____ street	_____ bands (27)
_____ the boys	_____ map	_____ highways (30)
_____ and	_____ colors	_____ vegetables (33)

ANSWER SHEET

Practicing Basic Skills in Language Arts • 138

© 2005 Sopris West Educational Services. All rights reserved. Practicing Basic Skills in Language Arts. Purchaser has permission to photocopy this page for classroom use only.

	Correct	Error
First Try		
Second Try		

ONE-MINUTE FLUENCY
BUILDER SERIES

THINK TO WRITE

Limiting and Descriptive Adjectives—Fill in the Blanks

Directions: Under each of the three categories, write an adjective to complete the phrase.
There could be many answers.

Which One?	What Kind?	How Many?
box	eagle	rockets
brother	city	tourists
summer	giant	geese
building	clown	men
class	flower	days
meeting	desk	eggs
book	money	parents
snapshots	travelers	touchdowns
neighbors	sister	minutes
driveway	fruit	games
pencils	objects	rows
ring	school	cheers
pizza	pizza	pizza
ice cream	bread	awards
idea	idea	idea
records	coins	uniforms

© 2005 Sopris West Educational Services. All rights reserved. Practicing Basic Skills in Language Arts. Purchaser has permission to photocopy this page for classroom use only.

THINK TO WRITE

Limiting and Descriptive Adjectives—Fill in the Blanks

Directions: Under each of the three categories, write an adjective to complete the phrase. There could be many answers.

		First Try	Second Try
Correct			
Error			

Which One? | **What Kind?** | **How Many?**

Which One?	What Kind?	How Many?	
_____ box	_____ eagle	_____ rockets	(3)
_____ brother	_____ city	_____ tourists	(6)
_____ summer	_____ giant	_____ geese	(9)
_____ building	_____ clown	_____ men	(12)
_____ class	_____ flower	_____ days	(15)
_____ meeting	_____ desk	_____ eggs	(18)
_____ book	_____ money	_____ parents	(21)
_____ snapshots	_____ travelers	_____ touchdowns	(24)
_____ neighbors	_____ sister	_____ minutes	(27)
_____ driveway	_____ fruit	_____ games	(30)
_____ pencils	_____ objects	_____ rows	(33)
_____ ring	_____ school	_____ cheers	(36)
_____ pizza	_____ pizza	_____ pizza	(39)
_____ ice cream	_____ bread	_____ awards	(42)
_____ idea	_____ idea	_____ idea	(45)
_____ records	_____ coins	_____ uniforms	(48)

ANSWERS MAY VARY

ANSWER SHEET

Practicing Basic Skills in Language Arts • 140

© 2005 Sopris West Educational Services. All rights reserved. Practicing Basic Skills in Language Arts. Purchaser has permission to photocopy this page for classroom use only.

ONE-MINUTE FLUENCY BUILDER SERIES

SEE TO MARK

Proper Adjectives in Sentences

Directions: Mark all the proper adjectives in the sentences.

	First Try	Second Try
Correct		
Error		

The president was uncertain about the Congressional reaction to his proposal. Two Italian dishes which Americans enjoy are lasagna and spaghetti. American tourists invade the coastline of Europe each summer. Many French children visit the Eiffel Tower on school field trips. The remains of several Roman roads can be seen in England today. The television program presented an interesting discussion of the new African nations. A Belgian farmer and an English miner, both of who lived in Africa, made the session lively. She thinks Paris is the most beautiful of all European cities. A French architect, Jon Santier, designed a number of buildings in the Detroit area. In our study of American literature, we read many works of the New England poets. Speaking in German, the Lutheran minister gave an interesting sermon. Much of our salmon comes from Alaskan canneries. We hope to see a Miller play this summer. Carmen is learning to play the French horn. The South American llama is a cousin of the Arabian camel. Spanish olives are a tasty addition to any meal. The American flag is a symbol that represents the United States of America. We asked the waiter for some Russian dressing for our salads. In Ireland, the Irish potato has been a large export. Did you see the English movie on Saturday? My mother raises African violets. Every Utah citizen should take part in the national and local elections. A beautiful breed of dog is the Irish wolfhound. The importing of Egyptian cotton has hampered the cotton industry of the South. A Chinese doctor joined the staff of the hospital in Ogden. Did Queen Elizabeth visit the Japanese embassy while in New York City? A Scottish miner collapsed while working in a coal mine. Catholic priests were seen entering the church at dawn.

© 2005 Sopris West Educational Services. All rights reserved. Practicing Basic Skills in Language Arts. Purchaser has permission to photocopy this page for classroom use only.

ONE MINUTE FLUENCY
BUILDER SERIES

Proper Adjectives in Sentences

Directions: Mark all the proper adjectives in the sentences.

	First Try	Second Try
Correct		
Error		

The president was uncertain about the Congressional reaction to his proposal. Two Italian dishes which Americans enjoy are (2)

lasagna and spaghetti. American tourists invade the coastline of Europe each summer. Many French children visit the Eiffel (4)

Tower on school field trips. The remains of several Roman roads can be seen in England today. The television program presented (5)

an interesting discussion of the new African nations. A Belgian farmer and an English miner, both of who lived in Africa, made (8)

the session lively. She thinks Paris is the most beautiful of all European cities. A French architect, Jon Santier, designed a number (10)

of buildings in the Detroit area. In our study of American literature, we read many works of the New England poets. Speaking (13)

in German, the Lutheran minister gave an interesting sermon. Much of our salmon comes from Alaskan canneries. We hope (15)

to see a Miller play this summer. Carmen is learning to play the French horn. The South American llama is a cousin of the (18)

Arabian camel. Spanish olives are a tasty addition to any meal. The American flag is a symbol that represents the United States (21)

of America. We asked the waiter for some Russian dressing for our salads. In Ireland, the Irish potato has been a large export. Did (23)

you see the English movie on Saturday? My mother raises African violets. Every Utah citizen should take part in the national (26)

and local elections. A beautiful breed of dog is the Irish wolfhound. The importing of Egyptian cotton has hampered the cotton (28)

industry of the South. A Chinese doctor joined the staff of the hospital in Ogden. Did Queen Elizabeth visit the Japanese (30)

embassy while in New York City? A Scottish miner collapsed while working in a coal mine. Catholic priests were seen entering (32)

the church at dawn.

ANSWER SHEET

Practicing Basic Skills in Language Arts • 142

© 2005 Sopris West Educational Services. All rights reserved. Practicing Basic Skills in Language Arts. Purchaser has permission to photocopy this page for classroom use only.

ONE MINUTE FLUENCY
BUILDER SERIES

Common and Proper Adjectives in Sentences

Directions: Underline all adjectives. Mark common adjectives with a C and proper adjectives with a P.

Example: The French chef wore a big, white hat.

	Correct	Error
First Try		
Second Try		

Many American soldiers sent back beautiful Japanese fans to their wives. Biblical scholars regard the new scrolls as an important

discovery. The stately Parthenon illustrates the basic principles of Greek architecture. Roman roads can be seen in rural England

today. The Shakespearian actors were dressed in Elizabethan costumes for the afternoon performance. The president was

uncertain about the Congressional reaction to his proposal. In swimming class last week we learned to do the Australian crawl.

Two Italian dishes which many Americans enjoy are spicy ravioli and spaghetti. Many British writers have based stories on the

old Arthurian legend. Who put Marion's new coat in the hall closet? We stuffed a Christmas stocking with fruit candy and shiny

toys for each one of the orphan children. An interesting Indian legend tells how early man gained possession of that useful item

fire. The Chinese lady was washing soiled clothes in the cold river. A Montana sunset is very colorful. The little French poodle

hid behind the Franklin stove. Maine lobsters are said to be the tastiest. The stalwart West team won a thundering victory. The

tiny kitten jumped from its loving master's arms and skittered across the German border. The worried man got out his Montana

driver's license. After a long bout of severe Hong Kong flu, he appeared thinner and quite pale. Broiled hamburgers taste better

than Russian caviar.

Practicing Basic Skills in Language Arts • 143

© 2005 Sopris West Educational Services. All rights reserved. Practicing Basic Skills in Language Arts. Purchaser has permission to photocopy this page for classroom use only.

ONE MINUTE FLUENCY BUILDER SERIES

	Correct	Error
First Try		
Second Try		

SEE TO MARK

Common and Proper Adjectives in Sentences

Directions: Underline all adjectives. Mark common adjectives with a C and proper adjectives with a P.

Example: The French chef wore a big, white hat.

Many American soldiers sent back beautiful Japanese fans to their wives. Biblical scholars regard the new scrolls as an important (8)

discovery. The stately Parthenon illustrates the basic principles of Greek architecture. Roman roads can be seen in rural England (13)

today. The Shakespearian actors were dressed in Elizabethan costumes for the afternoon performance. The president was (16)

uncertain about the Congressional reaction to his proposal. In swimming class last week we learned to do the Australian crawl. (22)

Two Italian dishes which many Americans enjoy are spicy ravioli and spaghetti. Many British writers have based stories on the (28)

old Arthurian legend. Who put Marion's new coat in the hall closet? We stuffed a Christmas stocking with fruit candy and shiny (36)

toys for each one of the orphan children. An interesting Indian legend tells how early man gained possession of that useful item (43)

fire. The Chinese lady was washing soiled clothes in the cold river. A Montana sunset is very colorful. The little French poodle (50)

hid behind the Franklin stove. Maine lobsters are said to be the tastiest. The stalwart West team won a thundering victory. The (55)

tiny kitten jumped from its loving master's arms and skittered across the German border. The worried man got out his Montana (63)

driver's license. After a long bout of severe Hong Kong flu, he appeared thinner and quite pale. Broiled hamburgers taste better (70)

than Russian caviar. (71)

ANSWER SHEET

Practicing Basic Skills in Language Arts • 144

© 2005 Sopris West Educational Services. All rights reserved. Practicing Basic Skills in Language Arts. Purchaser has permission to photocopy this page for classroom use only.

ONE-MINUTE FLUENCY
BUILDER SERIES

SEE TO MARK

First Try | Second Try | Correct | Error

Adjectives and the Words They Modify

Directions: Circle the adjectives in the following sentences and draw arrows to the words they modify.

My red dress is too short. The last song has a beautiful melody. Who is your favorite singer? The second team played during

the last quarter. That ancient manuscript is priceless. Tom was gloomy and desperate. The autumn weather is perfect

for a football game. The determined hikers trudged up the rugged mountain. Have you seen my old notebook?

A woman, kind and wise, helped the young girl. Most young children hate to visit a dentist. For several days, the tourist group

visited famous sites. Your stereo is too loud. The team was eager for their first victory. The Olympic team will compete next year.

A famous author, talented and experienced, will speak at the banquet. My best friend is here. After the horrible accident,

the injured driver was taken to the nearest hospital. I saw my first movie when I was a very small child. American artists

admire his work. Some students feel that the new policy is wrong. John is a fantastic cook! Many songs have sad lyrics.

This assignment, long and difficult, is finally completed.

© 2005 Sopris West Educational Services. All rights reserved. Practicing Basic Skills in Language Arts. Purchaser has permission to photocopy this page for classroom use only.

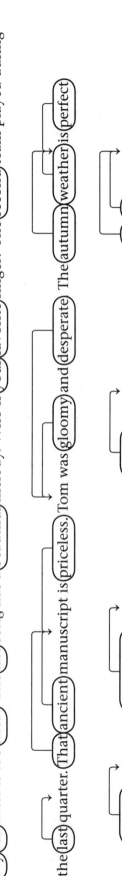
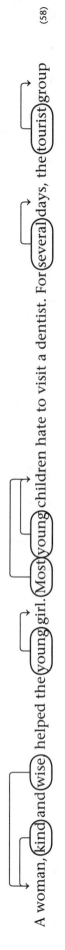

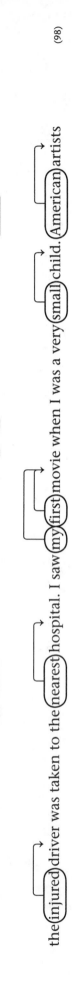
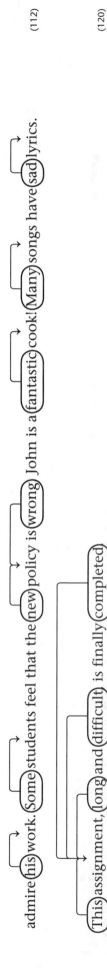

ONE-MINUTE FLUENCY BUILDER SERIES

SEE TO MARK

	First Try	Second Try
Correct		
Error		

Adjectives and the Words They Modify

Directions: Circle the adjectives in the following sentences and draw arrows to the words they modify.

My red dress is too short. The last song has a beautiful melody. Who is your favorite singer? The second team played during (16)

the last quarter. That ancient manuscript is priceless. Tom was gloomy and desperate. The autumn weather is perfect. The (34)

for a football game. The determined hikers trudged up the rugged mountain. Have you seen my old notebook? (44)

A woman, kind and wise, helped the young girl. Most young children hate to visit a dentist. For several days, the tourist group (58)

visited famous sites. Your stereo is too loud. The team was eager for their first victory. The Olympic team will compete next year. (74)

A famous author, talented and experienced, will speak at the banquet. My best friend is here. After the horrible accident, (86)

the injured driver was taken to the nearest hospital. I saw my first movie when I was a very small child. American artists (98)

admire his work. Some students feel that the new policy is wrong. John is a fantastic cook! Many songs have sad lyrics. (112)

This assignment, long and difficult, is finally completed. (120)

ANSWER SHEET

Practicing Basic Skills in Language Arts • 146

© 2005 Sopris West Educational Services. All rights reserved. Practicing Basic Skills in Language Arts. Purchaser has permission to photocopy this page for classroom use only.

SEE TO MARK

Adjective Phrases and the Words They Modify

Directions: Draw a line under the adjective phrase (prepositional phrase), then draw an arrow to the noun it modifies.

	Correct	Error
First Try		
Second Try		

Tom and Paul had enjoyed their walk in the forest preserve. This message to John is signed by me. His decision about the contest

surprised us all. Mr. Bybee had certain fears about the outcome. The outcome of the election was the topic of conversation. Which

is the train to Salt Lake City? Catherine read an article about piano tuning. Paul was talking to the man with the large package. The

building with the green roof is the clubhouse. The boy in the car is the leader. The pile of leaves was very wet. A flock of geese

flew overhead. Do you have the money for our tickets? The squirrels in the yard are eating acorns. The roof of the house

was damaged. We overheard the students from this school talking about the game. He is a boy from Nebraska. The

kids were in the house beside the forest. A notice concerning the meeting will be posted. The newspaper ran an

article on the debate between the two men. She had a box of strawberries in her car. A bird with red wings flew into

the house. The surface of the water was rough. The water from the tub ran over into the basement. The goat ran behind the

house with the white fence. A herd of cows ran through the field.

© 2005 Sopris West Educational Services. All rights reserved. Practicing Basic Skills in Language Arts. Purchaser has permission to photocopy this page for classroom use only.

SEE TO MARK

	Correct	Error
First Try		
Second Try		

Adjective Phrases and the Words They Modify

Directions: Draw a line under the adjective phrase (prepositional phrase), then draw an arrow to the noun it modifies.

Tom and Paul had enjoyed their walk in the forest preserve. This message to John is signed by me. His decision about the contest (6)

surprised us all. Mr. Bybee had certain fears about the outcome. The outcome of the election was the topic of conversation. Which (12)

is the train to Salt Lake City? Catherine read an article about piano tuning. Paul was talking to the man with the large package. The (18)

building with the green roof is the clubhouse. The boy in the car is the leader. The pile of leaves was very wet. A flock of geese (26)

flew overhead. Do you have the money for our tickets? The squirrels in the yard are eating acorns. The roof of the house (32)

was damaged. We overheard the students from this school talking about the game. He is a boy from Nebraska. The (36)

kids were in the house beside the forest. A notice concerning the meeting will be posted. The newspaper ran an (40)

article on the debate between the two men. She had a box of strawberries in her car. A bird with red wings flew into (48)

the house. The surface of the water was rough. The water from the tub ran over into the basement. The goat ran behind the (52)

house with the white fence. A herd of cows ran through the field. (56)

ANSWER SHEET

© 2005 Sopris West Educational Services. All rights reserved. Practicing Basic Skills in Language Arts. Purchaser has permission to photocopy this page for classroom use only.

ONE-MINUTE FLUENCY BUILDER SERIES

Predicate Adjectives
Directions: Mark all the adjectives that follow linking verbs in the sentences.

	Correct	Error
First Try		
Second Try		

The atom bomb is very powerful. The ground looks swampy. My glasses are dirty. The girl seems very happy. The patient felt

heavy to the people who were carrying him. The swimmer felt cold when the water hit her face. Many students are popular in

junior high but find that they need to meet new people in high school. The lights were dim after the blackout. The cave was

cold and damp as we entered it. My shoes looked worn and dusty after the long walk. The boys were tired and sleepy after the

movie. Sunlight is very useful to plants and animals. The sunshine is warm and bright this time of year. The farmers were late in

getting in the crops this year. You seem worried about this test today. That juice tastes better than the other one. These grapes

taste sour. Those colored leaves look beautiful this time of the year. No, I am only thoughtful. Those gloves are too expensive

for me. This book is very interesting. The morning sun was red when we broke camp. The mist over the lake seemed heavy. A

nearby anthill grew feverish with activity. The brightly colored birds were busy and noisy. We were happy as we tramped away.

Our packs felt light. Ahead of us the path was wide and clear. All life appeared good to us that day. The singing sounded good

to us after a long day of working. The other driver was angry after the crash. Karen felt lonesome when everyone left her at the

house. The house appeared empty so we decided to go in. The flowers looked wilted after they had been in the sun. The boys

seemed unhappy. Our new puppy was anxious to prove that he was a part of the family. He is intelligent and nice.

Practicing Basic Skills in Language Arts • 149

© 2005 Sopris West Educational Services. All rights reserved. Practicing Basic Skills in Language Arts. Purchaser has permission to photocopy this page for classroom use only.

SEE TO MARK

Predicate Adjectives

Directions: Mark all the adjectives that follow linking verbs in the sentences.

	First Try	Second Try
Correct		
Error		

(4) The atom bomb is very powerful. The ground looks swampy. My glasses are dirty. The girl seems very happy. The patient felt

(7) heavy to the people who were carrying him. The swimmer felt cold when the water hit her her face. Many students are popular in

(8) junior high but find that they need to meet new people in high school. The lights were dim after the blackout. The cave was

(14) cold and damp as we entered it. My shoes looked worn and dusty after the long walk. The boys were tired and sleepy after the

(18) movie. Sunlight is very useful to plants and animals. The sunshine is warm and bright this time of year. The farmers were late in

(20) getting in the crops this year. You seem worried about this test today. That juice tastes better than the other one. These grapes

(24) taste sour. Those colored leaves look beautiful this time of the year. No, I am only thoughtful. Those gloves are too expensive

(27) for me. This book is very interesting. The morning sun was red when we broke camp. The mist over the lake seemed heavy. A

(31) nearby anthill grew feverish with activity. The brightly colored birds were busy and noisy. We were happy as we tramped away.

(36) Our packs felt light. Ahead of us the path was wide and clear. All life appeared good to us that day. The singing sounded good

(38) to us after a long day of working. The other driver was angry after the crash. Karen felt lonesome when everyone left her at the

(40) house. The house appeared empty so we decided to go in. The flowers looked wilted after they had been in the sun. The boys

(44) seemed unhappy. Our new puppy was anxious to prove that he was a part of the family. He is intelligent and nice.

ANSWER SHEET

Practicing Basic Skills in Language Arts • 150

© 2005 Sopris West Educational Services. All rights reserved. Practicing Basic Skills in Language Arts. Purchaser has permission to photocopy this page for classroom use only.

SEE TO SAY

Comparative and Superlative Adjectives

loud	louder	loudest
happy	happier	happiest
soft	softer	softest
long	longer	longest
pretty	prettier	prettiest
merry	merrier	merriest
graceful	more graceful	most graceful
new	newer	newest
pleasant	more pleasant	most pleasant
old	older	oldest
salty	saltier	saltiest
important	more important	most important
angry	angrier	angriest
little	littler	littlest
cold	colder	coldest
economical	more economical	most economical
small	smaller	smallest
appreciative	more appreciative	most appreciative

Practicing Basic Skills in Language Arts • 151

© 2005 Sopris West Educational Services. All rights reserved. Practicing Basic Skills in Language Arts. Purchaser has permission to photocopy this page for classroom use only.

SEE TO SAY

Comparative and Superlative Adjectives

loud	louder	loudest	(3)
happy	happier	happiest	(6)
soft	softer	softest	(9)
long	longer	longest	(12)
pretty	prettier	prettiest	(15)
merry	merrier	merriest	(18)
graceful	more graceful	most graceful	(21)
new	newer	newest	(24)
pleasant	more pleasant	most pleasant	(27)
old	older	oldest	(30)
salty	saltier	saltiest	(33)
important	more important	most important	(36)
angry	angrier	angriest	(39)
little	littler	littlest	(42)
cold	colder	coldest	(45)
economical	more economical	most economical	(48)
small	smaller	smallest	(51)
appreciative	more appreciative	most appreciative	(54)

ANSWER SHEET

Practicing Basic Skills in Language Arts • 152

© 2005 Sopris West Educational Services. All rights reserved. Practicing Basic Skills in Language Arts. Purchaser has permission to photocopy this page for classroom use only.

	First Try	Second Try
Correct		
Error		

Comparative and Superlative Adjectives (continued)

hopeful	more hopeful	most hopeful
mighty	mightier	mightiest
rough	rougher	roughest
faithful	more faithful	most faithful
loyal	more loyal	most loyal
straight	straighter	straightest
fast	faster	fastest
late	later	latest
modern	more modern	most modern
hard	harder	hardest
serene	more serene	most serene
competent	more competent	most competent
enormous	more enormous	most enormous
friendly	friendlier	friendliest
pale	paler	palest
genuine	more genuine	most genuine
proud	prouder	proudest
scanty	scantier	scantiest

Practicing Basic Skills in Language Arts • 153

© 2005 Sopris West Educational Services. All rights reserved. Practicing Basic Skills in Language Arts. Purchaser has permission to photocopy this page for classroom use only.

	First Try	Second Try
Correct		
Error		

Comparative and Superlative Adjectives (continued)

hopeful	more hopeful	most hopeful	(57)
mighty	mightier	mightiest	(60)
rough	rougher	roughest	(63)
faithful	more faithful	most faithful	(66)
loyal	more loyal	most loyal	(69)
straight	straighter	straightest	(72)
fast	faster	fastest	(75)
late	later	latest	(78)
modern	more modern	most modern	(81)
hard	harder	hardest	(84)
serene	more serene	most serene	(87)
competent	more competent	most competent	(90)
enormous	more enormous	most enormous	(93)
friendly	friendlier	friendliest	(96)
pale	paler	palest	(99)
genuine	more genuine	most genuine	(102)
proud	prouder	proudest	(105)
scanty	scantier	scantiest	(108)

© 2005 Sopris West Educational Services. All rights reserved. Practicing Basic Skills in Language Arts. Purchaser has permission to photocopy this page for classroom use only.

	First Try	
	Correct	Error
	Second Try	

THINK TO WRITE

Comparative and Superlative Adjectives—Fill in the Blanks

ONE-MINUTE FLUENCY
BUILDER SERIES

Positive	Comparative	Superlative
silly		
slim		
glad		
lazy		
dim		
neat		
small		
lonely		
little		
useful		
marvelous		
distinct		
wonderful		
busy		
long		
fine		
lucky		

Positive	Comparative	Superlative
easy		
large		
skillful		
pleasant		
hard		
beautiful		
nice		
careful		
flat		
sad		
funny		
lean		
wet		
happy		
dry		
lovely		
strong		

Practicing Basic Skills in Language Arts • 155

© 2005 Sopris West Educational Services. All rights reserved. Practicing Basic Skills in Language Arts. Purchaser has permission to photocopy this page for classroom use only.

THINK TO WRITE

Comparative and Superlative Adjectives—Fill in the Blanks

	Correct	Error
First Try		
Second Try		

Positive	Comparative	Superlative	
silly	sillier	silliest	(2)
slim	slimmer	slimmest	(4)
glad	gladder	gladdest	(6)
lazy	lazier	laziest	(8)
dim	dimmer	dimmest	(10)
neat	neater	neatest	(12)
small	smaller	smallest	(14)
lonely	lonelier	loneliest	(16)
little	littler	littlest	(18)
useful	more useful	most useful	(20)
marvelous	more marvelous	most marvelous	(22)
distinct	more distinct	most distinct	(24)
wonderful	more wonderful	most wonderful	(26)
busy	busier	busiest	(28)
long	longer	longest	(30)
fine	finer	finest	(32)
lucky	luckier	luckiest	(34)

Positive	Comparative	Superlative	
easy	easier	easiest	(36)
large	larger	largest	(38)
skillful	more skillful	most skillful	(40)
pleasant	more pleasant	most pleasant	(42)
hard	harder	hardest	(44)
beautiful	more beautiful	most beautiful	(46)
nice	nicer	nicest	(48)
careful	more careful	most careful	(50)
flat	flatter	flattest	(52)
sad	sadder	saddest	(54)
funny	funnier	funniest	(56)
lean	leaner	leanest	(58)
wet	wetter	wettest	(60)
happy	happier	happiest	(62)
dry	drier	driest	(64)
lovely	lovelier	loveliest	(66)
strong	stronger	strongest	(68)

ANSWER SHEET

Practicing Basic Skills in Language Arts • 156

© 2005 Sopris West Educational Services. All rights reserved. Practicing Basic Skills in Language Arts. Purchaser has permission to photocopy this page for classroom use only.

	First Try	
	Correct	Error
Second Try		

Irregular Adjectives—Comparative and Superlative

ONE MINUTE FLUENCY
BUILDER SERIES

Adjective	Comparative Form	Superlative Form
ill		
bad		
good		
well		
many		
much		
good		
ill		
much		
bad		
many		
well		
good		
many		
bad		
much		

Practicing Basic Skills in Language Arts • 157

© 2005 Sopris West Educational Services. All rights reserved. Practicing Basic Skills in Language Arts. Purchaser has permission to photocopy this page for classroom use only.

THINK TO WRITE

Irregular Adjectives—Comparative and Superlative

	Correct	Error
First Try		
Second Try		

Adjective	Comparative Form	Superlative Form	
ill	worse	worst	(2)
bad	worse	worst	(4)
good	better	best	(6)
well	better	best	(8)
many	more	most	(10)
much	more	most	(12)
good	better	best	(14)
ill	worse	worst	(16)
much	more	most	(18)
bad	worse	worst	(20)
many	more	most	(22)
well	better	best	(24)
good	better	best	(26)
many	more	most	(28)
bad	worse	worst	(30)
much	more	most	(32)

ANSWER SHEET

Practicing Basic Skills in Language Arts • 158

© 2005 Sopris West Educational Services. All rights reserved. Practicing Basic Skills in Language Arts. Purchaser has permission to photocopy this page for classroom use only.

	Correct	Error
First Try		
Second Try		

THINK TO WRITE

Irregular Adjectives—Fill in the Blanks

Directions: Write the correct form of the irregular comparisons of adjectives in the following sentences.

I feel (bad) _____ today than yesterday. He is the (bad) _____ runner on the team. I feel (ill) _____ today than yesterday. She is a (good) _____ dancer than I am. Marcos is the (good) _____

scholar in the school. I saw (many) _____ birds in South Carolina than in Georgia. The accident was the (bad) _____ in the history of the state. John is (much) _____ intelligent than his younger brother. Uncle

Lee is (ill) _____ today than he was last week. That is the (bad) _____ suit in the store. His writing is (bad) _____ than yours. Joni is the (good) _____ sprinter on the team. Your composition is the (good) _____

of the two. He has the (bad) _____ toothache I've ever seen. George is a good athlete, but Jerome is (good) _____. Max is the (bad) _____ pitcher of the two. This is the (ill) _____ I've ever felt! The

roads here are good, but in Michigan they are (good) _____. You are the (much) _____ intelligent boy in the class. Oregon has the (many) _____ forest land of all the Western states. Are you feeling (well) _____

today than yesterday? Mrs. Wong is the (good) _____ teacher in the school. Mr. Thames is the (bad) _____ lawyer in the area. I feel the (good) _____ I've ever felt! Alan is a (bad) _____ quarterback than Brian. Stan

is the (bad) _____ student I've ever seen. Alana is the (much) _____ beautiful of the twins. Your grammar is the (bad) _____ in the class. This week's assignment is (good) _____ than last week's. Your attitude is the

(much) _____ improved in the class.

Practicing Basic Skills in Language Arts • 159

© 2005 Sopris West Educational Services. All rights reserved. Practicing Basic Skills in Language Arts. Purchaser has permission to photocopy this page for classroom use only.

ONE MINUTE FLUENCY BUILDER SERIES

THINK TO WRITE

	Correct	Error
First Try		
Second Try		

Irregular Adjectives—Fill in the Blanks

Directions: Write the correct form of the irregular comparisons of adjectives in the following sentences.

1. I feel (bad) **worse** today than yesterday.
2. He is the (bad) **worst** runner on the team.
3. I feel (ill) **worse** today than yesterday.
4. She is a (good) **better** dancer than I am.
5. Marcos is the (good) **best** scholar in the school.
6. I saw (many) **more** birds in South Carolina than in Georgia.
7. The accident was the (bad) **worst** in the history of the state.
8. John is (much) **more** intelligent than his younger brother.
9. Uncle Lee is (ill) **worse** today than he was last week.
10. That is the (bad) **worst** suit in the store.
11. His writing is (bad) **worse** than yours.
12. Joni is the (good) **best** sprinter on the team.
13. Your composition is the (good) **better** of the two.
14. He has the (bad) **worst** toothache I've ever seen.
15. George is a good athlete, but Jerome is (good) **better**.
16. Max is the (bad) **worse** pitcher of the two.
17. This is the (ill) **worst** I've ever felt!
18. The (good) **better** . You are the (much) **most** intelligent boy in the class.
19. Roads here are good, but in Michigan they are (good) **better** .
20. Oregon has the (many) **most** forest land of all the Western states.
21. Are you feeling (well) **better** today than yesterday?
22. Mrs. Wong is the (good) **best** teacher in the school.
23. Mr. Thames is the (bad) **worst** teacher in the school.
24. I've ever felt! Alan is a (bad) **worse** quarterback than Brian.
25. Stan is a (good) **best** lawyer in the area.
26. I feel the (good) **best** student I've ever seen.
27. Alana is the (much) **more** beautiful of the twins.
28. Your grammar is the (bad) **worst** in the class.
29. This week's assignment is (good) **better** than last week's.
30. Your attitude is the (much) **most** improved in the class.

ANSWER SHEET

© 2005 Sopris West Educational Services. All rights reserved. Practicing Basic Skills in Language Arts. Purchaser has permission to photocopy this page for classroom use only.

	Correct	Error
First Try		
Second Try		

Correct Form of Adjectives in Sentences

Directions: Mark the correct adjective form in the following sentences.

My dog is the (more, most) playful of the three. Chavez is the (more, most) capable member of the swimming team. Mary is the

(taller, tallest) of the two girls. Jackie is (prettier, more prettier) than her sister. Rex is the (stronger, strongest) of the two. This

flower is the (larger, largest) of the two. Is George a (better, more better) player than Curtis? Mrs. Meng is a (stricter, more stricter)

teacher than Mr. Kapp. This is the (swifter, swiftest) river I have ever seen. Florence is the (more, most) capable student in the

class. Mr. Cyrus is the (most richest, richest) man in town. This one is the (least, less) attractive of the two hats. This piece of candy

is the (sweetest, most sweetest) in the box. My drawing was the (bestest, best) in the school. I got a (more better, better) mark than

Samuel. Anna is the (smartest, smarter) of the two sisters. Of the two teams, I like this one (best, better). Ian's composition was

the (most, more) interesting in the class. Louis is the (less, least) mischievous of the four children. This picture is (more prettier,

prettier) than that one. Whose score is (higher, highest), Donna's or Reuben's? Brahms was a (famous, more famous) composer.

This is the (darker, darkest) color of the two. Kendall and Sylvia are (better, best) readers than Doreena and Roy. Who is the

(funnier, funniest) comedian you know? My problem is (easier, easiest) than yours. How (many, much) money do you have with

you? That is the (wonderfulest, most wonderful) sight I have ever seen. Ruth is a (better, best) speaker than anyone in this class.

Who is the (most famous, more famous) historical person? Thomas Jefferson is (more, most) famous than Abraham Lincoln. This

is the (worse, worst) snowstorm in history. Amos walked a (greater, greatest) distance than any other boy in the school race.

© 2005 Sopris West Educational Services. All rights reserved. Practicing Basic Skills in Language Arts. Purchaser has permission to photocopy this page for classroom use only.

ONE-MINUTE FLUENCY
BUILDER SERIES

SEE TO MARK

Correct Form of Adjectives in Sentences
Directions: Mark the correct adjective form in the following sentences.

	First Try	Second Try
Correct		
Error		

My dog is the (more, most) playful of the three. Chavez is the (more, most) capable member of the swimming team. Mary is the (2)

(taller, tallest) of the two girls. Jackie is (prettier, more prettier) than her sister. Rex is the (stronger, strongest) of the two. This (5)

flower is the (larger, largest) of the two. Is George a (better, more better) player than Curtis? Mrs. Meng is a (stricter, more stricter) (8)

teacher than Mr. Kapp. This is the (swifter, swiftest) river I have ever seen. Florence is the (more, most) capable student in the (10)

class. Mr. Cyrus is the (most richest, richest) man in town. This one is the (least, less) attractive of the two hats. This piece of candy (12)

is the (sweetest, most sweetest) in the box. My drawing was the (bestest, best) in the school. I got a (more better, better) mark than (15)

Samuel. Anna is the (smartest, smarter) of the two sisters. Of the two teams, I like this one (best, better). Ian's composition was (17)

the (most, more) interesting in the class. Louis is the (less, least) mischievous of the four children. This picture is (more prettier, (19)

prettier) than that one. Whose score is (higher, highest), Donna's or Reuben's? Brahms was a (famous, more famous) composer. (22)

This is the (darker, darkest) color of the two. Kendall and Sylvia are (better, best) readers than Doreena and Roy. Who is the (24)

(funnier, funniest) comedian you know? My problem is (easier, easiest) than yours. How (many, much) money do you have with (27)

you? That is the (wonderfulest, most wonderful) sight I have ever seen. Ruth is a (better, best) speaker than anyone in this class. (29)

Who is the (most famous, more famous) historical person? Thomas Jefferson is (more, most) famous than Abraham Lincoln. This (31)

is the (worse, worst) snowstorm in history. Amos walked a (greater, greatest) distance than any other boy in the school race. (33)

ANSWER SHEET

Practicing Basic Skills in Language Arts • 162

© 2005 Sopris West Educational Services. All rights reserved. Practicing Basic Skills in Language Arts. Purchaser has permission to photocopy this page for classroom use only.

THINK TO WRITE

Correct Form of Adjectives—Fill in the Blanks

Directions: Write the correct comparative or superlative adjective in the following sentences.

	First Try	Second Try
Correct		
Error		

Mr. Jones is (intelligent) _____ than Mr. Thomas. The weather is (bad) _____ than it was last

year. This material is (absorbent) _____ than that. Michael is the (weak) _____ boy I know.

English is my (good) _____ subject. There are (many) _____ holidays in July than in June.

Bicycles are (safe) _____ than skateboards. The red package and the blue package are the same price, but

the red one is the (heavy) _____ . Of the three runners, Dick is the (fast) _____ . This hill is much

(steep) _____ than that one. Jack is the (tall) _____ of the two brothers. We looked at both

books, but this one is (good) _____ . The patient looks the (bad) _____ he has for days. We

gave our (good) _____ performance of the week on Friday. These skates are (expensive) _____

than those. This is the (rough) _____ road in the county. Our dog is (loyal) _____ than yours.

My friend is (ill) _____ than you are. That was the (bad) _____ mistake of all. The (large) _____

crowds in history witnessed the World Series. Jack was the (unhappy) _____ boy on the

team. Tokyo is (big) _____ than New York. Marina is the (good) _____ speller of the two. There

are (many) _____ cougars in Wyoming than in Illinois. Where can I find a (complete) _____

dictionary than this one? That man looks (suspicious) _____ than the man on the left. Alissa is the (graceful) _____

_____ ballerina in the company.

Practicing Basic Skills in Language Arts • 163

© 2005 Sopris West Educational Services. All rights reserved. Practicing Basic Skills in Language Arts. Purchaser has permission to photocopy this page for classroom use only.

ONE-MINUTE FLUENCY BUILDER SERIES

THINK TO WRITE

Correct Form of Adjectives—Fill in the Blanks

Directions: Write the correct comparative or superlative adjective in the following sentences.

	First Try	Second Try
Correct		
Error		

Mr. Jones is (intelligent) **more intelligent** than Mr. Thomas. The weather is (bad) **worse** than it was last (2)

year. This material is (absorbent) **more absorbent** than that. Michael is the (weak) **weakest** boy I know. (4)

English is my (good) **best** subject. There are (many) **more** holidays in July than in June. (6)

Bicycles are (safe) **safer** than skateboards. The red package and the blue package are the same price, but (7)

the red one is the (heavy) **heavier** . Of the three runners, Dick is the (fast) **fastest** . This hill is much (9)

(steep) **steeper** than that one. Jack is the (tall) **taller** of the two brothers. We looked at both (11)

books, but this one is (good) **better** . The patient looks the (bad) **worst** he has for days. We (13)

gave our (good) **best** performance of the week on Friday. These skates are (expensive) **more expensive** (15)

than those. This is the (rough) **roughest** road in the county. Our dog is (loyal) **more loyal** than yours. (17)

My friend is (ill) **worse** than you are. That was the (bad) **worst** mistake of all. The (large) (19)

largest crowds in history witnessed the World Series. Jack was the (unhappy) **unhappiest** boy on the (21)

team. Tokyo is (big) **bigger** than New York. Marina is the (good) **better** speller of the two. There (23)

are (many) **more** cougars in Wyoming than in Illinois. Where can I find a (complete) **more complete** (25)

dictionary than this one? That man looks (suspicious) **more suspicious** than the man on the left. Alissa is the (graceful) (26)

most graceful ballerina in the company. (27)

ANSWER SHEET

Practicing Basic Skills in Language Arts • 164

© 2005 Sopris West Educational Services. All rights reserved. Practicing Basic Skills in Language Arts. Purchaser has permission to photocopy this page for classroom use only.

ONE-MINUTE FLUENCY BUILDER SERIES

SEE TO MARK

Adverbs in Phrases
Directions: Mark the adverbs.

	First Try	Second Try
Correct		
Error		

finally was found

eyed the stranger suspiciously

Willie suddenly understood

weatherman gloomily predicted rain

eagerly waved her hand

ate greedily

come home quickly

Paul willingly volunteered

bravely she approached

leave here immediately

casually climbed to the top

infant merrily cooed

arm was severely hurt

he ran fast

he always goes

knows the directions now

you will be there

sleep before the event

now I know

often does not speak

be leaving soon

in its third quarter already

know your mathematics well

never did anything unexpectedly

play now and then

was exhausted so completely

fell asleep instantly

was extremely serious

Bonnie graciously thanked them

she scarcely understood

kitten hardly mewed

children were never late

he responded angrily

drive slowly now

jokes were delightfully funny

an extremely dangerous job

were scattered everywhere

answered quietly

team soundly trounced theirs

are almost too tired to work

near the boat

Gill was intensely interested

wash thoroughly

he was moderately able to do the job

he spoke too sharply

it's readily available

was seriously considering moving

speaks rapidly and clearly

dog ran swiftly

flowers died unusually soon

ducks swam gracefully

has absolutely fine parents

they treat me unfairly

cleaners have nearly finished

© 2005 Sopris West Educational Services. All rights reserved. Practicing Basic Skills in Language Arts. Purchaser has permission to photocopy this page for classroom use only.

SEE TO MARK

Adverbs in Phrases

Directions: Mark the adverbs.

	Correct	Error
First Try		
Second Try		

finally was found	now I know	were scattered everywhere	(3)
eyed the stranger suspiciously	often does not speak	answered quietly	(7)
Willie suddenly understood	be leaving soon	team soundly trounced theirs	(10)
weatherman gloomily predicted rain	in its third quarter already	are almost too tired to work	(14)
eagerly waved her hand	know your mathematics well	near the boat	(17)
ate greedily	never did anything unexpectedly	Gill was intensely interested	(21)
come home quickly	play now and then	wash thoroughly	(25)
Paul willingly volunteered	was exhausted so completely	he was moderately able to do the job	(29)
bravely she approached	fell asleep instantly	he spoke too sharply	(33)
leave here immediately	was extremely serious	it's readily available	(37)
casually climbed to the top	Bonnie graciously thanked them	was seriously considering moving	(40)
infant merrily cooed	she scarcely understood	speaks rapidly and clearly	(44)
arm was severely hurt	kitten hardly mewed	dog ran swiftly	(47)
he ran fast	children were never late	flowers died unusually soon	(51)
he always goes	he responded angrily	ducks swam gracefully	(54)
knows the directions now	drive slowly now	has absolutely fine parents	(58)
you will be there	jokes were delightfully funny	they treat me unfairly	(61)
sleep before the event	an extremely dangerous job	cleaners have nearly finished	(64)

ANSWER SHEET

© 2005 Sopris West Educational Services. All rights reserved. Practicing Basic Skills in Language Arts. Purchaser has permission to photocopy this page for classroom use only.

Adverbs in Sentences

Directions: Underline the adverbs.

He has not come.

I have never been there.

I almost missed the turn.

The boy hit the ball hard.

He hit the ball immediately.

He hit the ball south.

He hit the ball too far.

He speaks loudly and rapidly.

Harold does his work carefully.

The club recently won this banner.

The baby lay there very quietly.

He has called me once or twice.

Haven't they often visited here before?

The new owner should arrive here soon.

Better specimens have never been found.

We usually arrive early.

I am too tired now.

My little sister has just had her sixth birthday.

We work well together.

A really old man came here yesterday.

My brother does not work very rapidly.

I have never taken so many pictures before.

Harry walked away slowly and very unhappily.

Your work is almost always very neat.

Tom is now our captain.

Have you made that trip often?

Soon John will be too busy and will need far more help.

We shall leave early.

Roger answered me nervously but clearly.

They are almost ready. Usually they are rather slow.

I sometimes walk more slowly.

We saw three much larger buildings yesterday.

You shouldn't decide this important matter too quickly.

I really must not stay longer.

Practicing Basic Skills in Language Arts • 167

© 2005 Sopris West Educational Services. All rights reserved. Practicing Basic Skills in Language Arts. Purchaser has permission to photocopy this page for classroom use only.

SEE TO MARK

Adverbs in Sentences

Directions: Underline the adverbs.

He has <u>not</u> come.

I have <u>never</u> been <u>there</u>.

I <u>almost</u> missed the turn.

The boy hit the ball <u>hard</u>.

He hit the ball <u>immediately</u>.

He hit the ball <u>south</u>.

He hit the ball <u>too far</u>.

He speaks <u>loudly</u> and <u>rapidly</u>.

Harold does his work <u>carefully</u>.

The club <u>recently</u> won this banner.

The baby lay <u>there</u> <u>very</u> <u>quietly</u>.

He has called me <u>once</u> or <u>twice</u>.

Haven't they <u>often</u> visited <u>here</u> <u>before</u>?

The new owner should arrive <u>here</u> <u>soon</u>.

Better specimens have <u>never</u> been found.

We <u>usually</u> arrive <u>early</u>.

I am <u>too</u> tired <u>now</u>.

(2) My little sister has <u>just</u> had her sixth birthday.

(5) We work <u>well</u> together.

(9) A <u>really</u> old man came <u>here</u> <u>yesterday</u>.

(13) My brother does <u>not</u> work <u>very</u> <u>rapidly</u>.

(18) I have <u>never</u> taken so many pictures <u>before</u>.

(23) Harry walked <u>away</u> <u>slowly</u> and <u>very</u> <u>unhappily</u>.

(28) Your work is <u>almost</u> <u>always</u> <u>very</u> neat.

(31) Tom is <u>now</u> our captain.

(33) Have you made that trip <u>often</u>?

(38) Soon John will be <u>too</u> busy and will need <u>far</u> <u>more</u> help.

(42) We shall leave <u>early</u>.

(46) Roger answered me <u>nervously</u> but <u>clearly</u>.

(52) They are <u>almost</u> ready. <u>Usually</u> they are <u>rather</u> <u>slow</u>.

(57) I <u>sometimes</u> walk <u>more</u> <u>slowly</u>.

(60) We saw three <u>much</u> larger buildings <u>yesterday</u>.

(65) You shouldn't decide this important matter <u>too</u> <u>quickly</u>.

(70) I <u>really</u> must <u>not</u> stay <u>longer</u>.

ANSWER SHEET

Practicing Basic Skills in Language Arts • 168

© 2005 Sopris West Educational Services. All rights reserved. Practicing Basic Skills in Language Arts. Purchaser has permission to photocopy this page for classroom use only.

ONE-MINUTE FLUENCY BUILDER SERIES

SEE TO WRITE

Adverb—Answers Question: Where? When? How? To What Extent?

Directions: After each sentence, write what the underlined adverb tells: Where? When? How? or To What Extent?

	First Try	
	Correct	Error
	Second Try	

Come <u>here</u>, Fred. _____

Greg makes <u>too</u> many excuses. _____

He is leaving the store <u>now</u>. _____

I will meet you <u>there</u>. _____

We should turn <u>right</u>. _____

He rises <u>early</u>. _____

He receives his paycheck <u>monthly</u>. _____

They ate their lunch <u>quickly</u>. _____

The library will be open <u>tomorrow</u>. _____

The students <u>silently</u> took their places. _____

He reads the paper <u>daily</u>. _____

Haven't you ever wanted to go <u>there</u>? _____

The players left the field <u>quickly</u>. _____

The door banged and <u>in</u> walked the teacher. _____

Mrs. Leatham types <u>fast</u>. _____

The new student is <u>never</u> on time. _____

She reacted <u>very</u> calmly. _____

We'll be home <u>tomorrow</u>. _____

Sometimes Jill plays golf with her dad. _____

She drove <u>carefully</u>. _____

Alice spoke <u>softly</u> but distinctly. _____

Joe was <u>extremely</u> late. _____

Shelley looked <u>around</u>. _____

He was stealing <u>cautiously</u> along the wall. _____

This hat is <u>too</u> big. _____

The principal will be here <u>soon</u>. _____

The students talked <u>quietly</u> for an hour. _____

<u>Tonight</u> I will grade your papers. _____

The building is <u>especially</u> high. _____

<u>Occasionally</u> he forgets his homework. _____

She <u>slowly</u> raised the rifle and fired. _____

The army <u>boldly</u> sent back the enemy. _____

They arrived at the party <u>late</u>. _____

Please put the books <u>down</u>. _____

The stereo was playing <u>softly</u>. _____

The little girl looked <u>sadly</u> at the doll. _____

© 2005 Sopris West Educational Services. All rights reserved. Practicing Basic Skills in Language Arts. Purchaser has permission to photocopy this page for classroom use only.

SEE TO WRITE

Adverb—Answers Question: Where? When? How? To What Extent?

Directions: After each sentence, write what the underlined adverb tells: Where? When? How? or To What Extent?

	First Try		Second Try	
	Correct	Error	Correct	Error

Come <u>here</u>, Fred.   **where**   Sometimes Jill plays golf with her dad.   **when** (2)

Greg makes <u>too</u> many excuses.   **to what extent**   She drove <u>carefully</u>.   **how** (4)

He is leaving the store <u>now</u>.   **when**   Alice spoke softly but <u>distinctly</u>.   **how** (6)

I will meet you <u>there</u>.   **where**   Joe was <u>extremely</u> late.   **to what extent** (8)

We should turn <u>right</u>.   **where**   Shelley looked <u>around</u>.   **where** (10)

He rises <u>early</u>.   **when**   He was stealing <u>cautiously</u> along the wall.   **how** (12)

He receives his paycheck <u>monthly</u>.   **when**   This hat is <u>too</u> big.   **to what extent** (14)

They ate their lunch <u>quickly</u>.   **how**   The principal will be here <u>soon</u>.   **when** (16)

The library will be open <u>tomorrow</u>.   **when**   The students talked <u>quietly</u> for an hour.   **how** (18)

The students <u>silently</u> took their places.   **how**   Tonight I will grade your papers.   **when** (20)

He reads the paper <u>daily</u>.   **when**   The building is <u>especially</u> high.   **to what extent** (22)

Haven't you ever wanted to go <u>there</u>?   **where**   <u>Occasionally</u> he forgets his homework.   **when** (24)

The players left the field <u>quickly</u>.   **how**   She <u>slowly</u> raised the rifle and fired.   **how** (26)

The door banged and in walked the teacher.   **where**   The army <u>boldly</u> sent back the enemy.   **how** (28)

Mrs. Leatham types <u>fast</u>.   **how**   They arrived at the party <u>late</u>.   **when** (30)

The new student is <u>never</u> on time.   **to what extent**   Please put the books <u>down</u>.   **where** (32)

She reacted <u>very</u> calmly.   **to what extent**   The stereo was playing <u>softly</u>.   **how** (34)

We'll be home <u>tomorrow</u>.   **when**   The little girl looked <u>sadly</u> at the doll.   **how** (36)

ANSWER SHEET

Practicing Basic Skills in Language Arts • 170

© 2005 Sopris West Educational Services. All rights reserved. Practicing Basic Skills in Language Arts. Purchaser has permission to photocopy this page for classroom use only.

Adverb—Answers Question: Where? When? How? To What Extend?

Directions: Determine which of the following questions is answered by the underlined adverbs.

WHERE ?   WHEN ?   HOW ?   TO WHAT EXTENT ?

A firefighter ran <u>swiftly</u> past her. _____ Yesterday I saw an awful fire. _____ It <u>completely</u> destroyed the

home of a family on Elm Street. _____ A woman who lives <u>nearby</u> complained about the noise. _____

The fire continued blazing <u>furiously</u> for hours. _____ The fire began <u>early</u> in the morning. _____ I hope

the fire department comes <u>here</u> quickly. _____ Now they must begin the clean-up work. _____ We'll

never be finished with this job. _____ A small boy <u>excitedly</u> reported the fire. _____ I <u>nearly</u> forgot your

address. _____ Tomorrow I have my most important competition. _____ <u>Then</u> begins the real pressure. _____

_____ The fire was <u>quickly</u> extinguished. _____ We <u>often</u> complain about the cooking. _____

The door <u>suddenly</u> flew open. _____ The baby has been crying <u>angrily</u> for hours. _____ You have <u>almost</u>

finished the book report, haven't you? _____ The referee threw the basketball <u>up</u> for a jump ball. _____

Jason passed that test <u>easily</u>. _____ Randy <u>always</u> does a good job. _____ This test is <u>really</u> important. _____

_____ Finally, it has stopped raining. _____ Bring that newspaper <u>here</u>. _____ The fire blazed

<u>dangerously</u>. _____ The damage was <u>very</u> extensive. _____

Practicing Basic Skills in Language Arts • 171

© 2005 Sopris West Educational Services. All rights reserved. Practicing Basic Skills in Language Arts. Purchaser has permission to photocopy this page for classroom use only.

ONE-MINUTE FLUENCY BUILDER SERIES

SEE TO WRITE

Adverb—Answers Question: Where? When? How? To What Extend?

Directions: Determine which of the following questions is answered by the underlined adverbs.

WHERE ?   WHEN ?   HOW ?   TO WHAT EXTENT ?

	First Try	Second Try
Correct		
Error		

__how__ A firefighter ran <u>swiftly</u> past her.

__when__ <u>Yesterday</u> I saw an awful fire.   (2)

__extent__ It <u>completely</u> destroyed the home of a family on Elm Street.

__where__ A woman who lives <u>nearby</u> complained about the noise.   (4)

__how__ The fire continued blazing <u>furiously</u> for hours.

__when__ The fire began <u>early</u> in the morning.   (6)

__where__ I hope the fire department comes <u>here</u> quickly.

__when__ Now they must begin the clean-up work.   (8)

__when__ We'll never be finished with this job.

__how__ I nearly forgot your address.   (10)

__extent__ Tomorrow I have my most important competition.

__when__ Then begins the real pressure.   (12)

__when__ The fire was <u>quickly</u> extinguished.

__how__ We often complain about the cooking.   (15)

__how__ The door <u>suddenly</u> flew open.

__how__ The baby has been crying <u>angrily</u> for hours.   (17)

__how__ You have almost finished the book report, haven't you?

__extent__ The referee threw the basketball <u>up</u> for a jump ball.   (19)

__where__ Jason passed that test <u>easily</u>.

__how__ Randy <u>always</u> does a good job.   (21)

__when__ This test is <u>really</u> important.

__when__ Finally, it has stopped raining.   (24)

__extent__ Bring that newspaper <u>here</u>. The fire blazed dangerously.

__where__ The damage was <u>very</u> extensive.   (26)

__how__ extent

ANSWER SHEET

Practicing Basic Skills in Language Arts • 172

© 2005 Sopris West Educational Services. All rights reserved. Practicing Basic Skills in Language Arts. Purchaser has permission to photocopy this page for classroom use only.

	First Try	Second Try
Correct		
Error		

THINK TO WRITE

Adverb—Answers Question—Fill in the Blanks

Directions: Add an adverb of your choice in the blank for each of the categories.

Where?

Do not sit _____

He put the book _____

Park your car _____

Leave your skates _____

Send the man _____

She ran _____

Place your boots _____

Put the books _____

Move the chair _____

Come _____

The boys ran _____ is my pen.

Pass the papers _____

It is raining _____

Set the packages _____

Look _____

We are moving _____

Put the cat _____

When?

He arrived _____

Dark clouds gathered _____

He's coming _____

John will come _____

She left _____

Carrie wrote _____

They moved _____

He _____ discovered oil.

She _____ explored the cave.

Easter came _____ this year.

Will he be going _____?

A plan was offered _____

The report is due _____

I gave it to him _____

The phone _____ rings.

he's going hunting _____

I was little _____

© 2005 Sopris West Educational Services. All rights reserved. Practicing Basic Skills in Language Arts. Purchaser has permission to photocopy this page for classroom use only.

THINK TO WRITE

	Correct	Error
First Try		
Second Try		

Adverb—Answers Question—Fill in the Blanks

Directions: Add an adverb of your choice in the blank for each of the categories.

Where?

Do not sit _____

He put the book _____

Park your car _____

Leave your skates _____

Send the man _____

She ran _____

Place your boots _____

Put the books _____

Move the chair _____

Come _____

The boys ran _____

_____ is my pen.

Pass the papers _____

It is raining _____

Set the packages _____

Look _____

We are moving _____

Put the cat _____

When?

He arrived _____ (2)

Dark clouds gathered _____ (4)

He's coming _____ (6)

John will come _____ (8)

She left _____ (10)

Carrie wrote _____ (12)

They moved _____ (14)

He _____ discovered oil. (16)

She _____ explored the cave. (18)

Easter came _____ this year. (20)

_____ he saw the danger. (22)

Will he be going _____ ? (24)

A plan was offered _____ (26)

The report is due _____ (28)

_____ I gave it to him. (30)

The phone _____ rings. (32)

_____ he's going hunting. (34)

I was little _____ (36)

© 2005 Sopris West Educational Services. All rights reserved. Practicing Basic Skills in Language Arts. Purchaser has permission to photocopy this page for classroom use only.

First Try	Correct	Error
Second Try		

THINK TO WRITE

Adverb—Answers Question—Fill in the Blanks (continued)

Directions: Add an adverb of your choice in the blank for each of the categories.

How?

He talks _____

The wind blew _____

Lisa reads _____

They listened _____

She dresses _____

Sally spoke _____

Move _____

They came _____

Approach the tiger _____

Barry Gibb sings _____

Speak _____

He raised his hand _____

Come in _____

He _____ became ill.

He gave the orders _____

Write _____

She _____ recovered the ball.

We all chattered _____

To What Extent?

She _____ talked.

Ted _____ arrived.

It _____ rained.

The wind _____ blew.

She _____ can read.

He _____ spoke.

She can _____ write.

He _____ raised his hand.

The fuel was _____ gone.

The field was _____ flooded.

They _____ moved.

She _____ eats.

He can _____ whisper.

It is _____ raining.

The choir was _____ singing.

The students _____ listened.

The dog _____ barked.

He could _____ walk.

Practicing Basic Skills in Language Arts • 175

© 2005 Sopris West Educational Services. All rights reserved. Practicing Basic Skills in Language Arts. Purchaser has permission to photocopy this page for classroom use only.

ONE-MINUTE FLUENCY BUILDER SERIES

Adverb—Answers Question—Fill in the Blanks (continued)

Directions: Add an adverb of your choice in the blank for each of the categories.

	First Try	Second Try
Correct		
Error		

How?

He talks _____

The wind blew _____

Lisa reads _____

They listened _____

She dresses _____

Sally spoke _____

Move _____

They came _____

Approach the tiger _____

Barry Gibb sings _____

Speak _____

He raised his hand _____

Come in _____

He _____ became ill.

He gave the orders _____

Write _____

She _____ recovered the ball.

We all chattered _____

To What Extent?

(38) She _____ talked.

(40) Ted _____ arrived.

(42) It _____ rained.

(44) The wind _____ blew.

(46) She _____ can read.

(48) He _____ spoke.

(50) She can _____ write.

(52) He _____ raised his hand.

(54) The fuel was _____ gone.

(56) The field was _____ flooded.

(58) They _____ moved.

(60) She _____ eats.

(62) He can _____ whisper.

(64) It is _____ raining.

(66) The choir was _____ singing.

(68) The students _____ listened.

(70) The dog _____ barked.

(72) He could _____ walk.

ANSWER SHEET

Practicing Basic Skills in Language Arts • 176

© 2005 Sopris West Educational Services. All rights reserved. Practicing Basic Skills in Language Arts. Purchaser has permission to photocopy this page for classroom use only.

ONE-MINUTE FLUENCY
BUILDER SERIES

	Correct	Error
First Try		
Second Try		

SEE TO WRITE

Adverb and the Verb It Modifies

Directions: Circle the adverb and draw an arrow to the word it modifies.

The sun shone brightly. I often write to John. He left the room immediately. Finally the teacher read the play. Billy

reads slowly but clearly and pleasingly. You are walking rapidly. The phone rang again; this time I quickly answered. Up went

the curtain and down went our spirits. There they go now. The child gazed longingly at the sundae. I often stop here for

lunch. Always walk slowly in the halls. She rocked slowly and sang sweetly to the child. I hardly recognized him. The girl

walked up and down. Dad sometimes plays tennis with us. I have written this twice. I seldom forget my phone number. He has

always done well. Unwillingly, Louise washed the dishes. The girl walked away from him. She surely speaks loudly. Do you

often read at night? Finally I finished my homework and immediately went to my friend's house. Will they build there again?

Do your homework now. I had entirely finished my work. Soon I will be in the ninth grade. I should have returned sooner. It

was warm today.

© 2005 Sopris West Educational Services. All rights reserved. Practicing Basic Skills in Language Arts. Purchaser has permission to photocopy this page for classroom use only.

ONE-MINUTE FLUENCY BUILDER SERIES

SEE TO WRITE

Adverb and the Verb It Modifies

Directions: Circle the adverb and draw an arrow to the word it modifies.

	Correct	Error
First Try		
Second Try		

The sun shone (brightly). I (often) write to John. He left the room (immediately). Finally the teacher read the play. Billy (6)

reads (slowly) but (clearly) and (pleasingly). You are walking (rapidly). The phone rang (again) this time. I (quickly) answered. (Up) went (20)

the curtain and (down) went our spirits. (There) they go (now). The child gazed (longingly) at the sundae. I (often) stop (here) for (32)

lunch. (Always) walk (slowly) in the halls. She rocked (slowly) and sang (sweetly) to the child. I (hardly) recognized him. The girl (42)

walked (up) and (down). Dad (sometimes) plays tennis with us. I have written this (twice). I (seldom) forget my phone number. He has (52)

(always) done (well). (Unwillingly) Louise washed the dishes. The girl walked (away) from him. She (surely) speaks (loudly). Do you (64)

(often) read at night? (Finally) I finished my homework and (immediately) went to my friend's house. Will they build (there) (again)? (74)

Do your homework (now). I had (entirely) finished my work. (Soon) I will be in the ninth grade. I should have returned (sooner). It (80)

was warm (today). (84)

ANSWER SHEET

Practicing Basic Skills in Language Arts • 178

© 2005 Sopris West Educational Services. All rights reserved. Practicing Basic Skills in Language Arts. Purchaser has permission to photocopy this page for classroom use only.

SEE TO MARK

Adverb and the Verb It Modifies

Directions: Circle each adverb and draw an arrow to the verb it modifies.

	Correct	Error
First Try		
Second Try		

Rowena spoke hastily. The attendant told us to park our car here. My sister-in-law from California returned home yesterday.

The frightened child whispered for him to come quickly. The children gathered around. Leave your skates outside.

Send the man away. The entire class worked hard and successfully. The car usually starts easily on cold mornings. The doctor

gave orders quietly and confidently. The young man who graduated from Utah State University went far. The little girl

ran away. The bus almost always arrives late. Polio is sometimes difficult to diagnose. Lately, the summers have been hot.

There goes Dr. Harrison now. Jane wrote for the tickets yesterday. By noon the girls had almost finished the poster. The plane's

fuel supply was now nearly exhausted. Howell raised his hand eagerly. The football field was completely covered. The rocket

ship travels fast. After the second week without snow, several students dropped out. We stood on the balcony watching the

sun go down. The scientists are going deep into the earth's crust. Larry cannot ski. Mark seldom watches TV. He moved slightly

to the left. He cannot run the boat fast on the narrow river. The two cousins quietly renewed acquaintances. The campers

shouted happily. Her old friend squeezed her hand tightly. It had begun suddenly to rain. The sky quickly cleared. The coach

shouted loudly. He exercises daily. She carelessly examined the paper. Shut the door tight. Carefully he drew the plans for his

new energy-saving house. Ms. Alvaro sometimes surprises us with a test. The two boys argued continually and seriously. The

Weber County police soon arrived at the Bank of Utah, which had been robbed. The deserted old car rolled backward. The black

and white spotted dog eats his meals slowly. The young man who sits in the fourth row in the fifth desk reads constantly. The

two small girls bravely opened the huge, tattered, squeaking door. She always studies on the bus. Mrs. Dean carefully explained

how to diagram the sentence.

Practicing Basic Skills in Language Arts • 179

© 2005 Sopris West Educational Services. All rights reserved. Practicing Basic Skills in Language Arts. Purchaser has permission to photocopy this page for classroom use only.

ONE-MINUTE FLUENCY
BUILDER SERIES

SEE TO MARK

	Correct	Error
First Try		
Second Try		

Adverb and the Verb It Modifies

Directions: Circle each adverb and draw an arrow to the verb it modifies.

Rowena spoke (hastily). The attendant told us to park our car (here). My sister-in-law from California returned home (yesterday). (6)

The frightened child whispered for him to come (quickly). The children gathered (around). Leave your skates (outside). (12)

Send the man (away). The entire class worked (hard) and (successfully). The car (usually) starts (easily) on cold mornings. The doctor (22)

gave orders (quietly) and (confidently). The young man who graduated from Utah State University went (far). The little girl (28)

ran (away). The bus almost (always) arrives (late). Polio is (sometimes) difficult to diagnose. (Lately) the summers have been hot. (40)

(There) goes Dr. Harrison (now). Jane wrote for the tickets (yesterday). By noon the girls had (almost) finished the poster. The plane's (48)

fuel supply was (now) (nearly) exhausted. Howell raised his hand (eagerly). The football field was (completely) covered. The rocket (56)

ship travels (fast). After the second week without snow, several students dropped (out). We stood on the balcony watching the (60)

sun go (down). The scientists are going (deep) into the earth's crust. Larry can (not) ski. Mark (seldom) watches TV. He moved (slightly) (70)

to the left. He can (not) run the boat (fast) on the narrow river. The two cousins (quietly) renewed acquaintances. The campers (76)

shouted (happily). Her old friend squeezed her hand (tightly). It had begun (suddenly) to rain. The sky (quickly) cleared. The coach (84)

shouted (loudly). He exercises (daily). She (carelessly) examined the paper. Shut the door (tight). (Carefully) he drew the plans for his (94)

new energy-saving house. Ms. Alvaro (sometimes) surprises us with a test. The two boys argued (continually) and (seriously). The (98)

Weber County police (soon) arrived at the Bank of Utah, which had been robbed. The deserted old car rolled (backward). The black (102)

and white spotted dog eats his meals (slowly). The young man who sits in the fourth row in the fifth desk reads (constantly). The (106)

two small girls (bravely) opened the huge, tattered, squeaking door. She (always) studies on the bus. Mrs. Dean (carefully) explained (112)

how to diagram the sentence.

ANSWER SHEET

Practicing Basic Skills in Language Arts • 180

© 2005 Sopris West Educational Services. All rights reserved. Practicing Basic Skills in Language Arts. Purchaser has permission to photocopy this page for classroom use only.

ONE-MINUTE FLUENCY
BUILDER SERIES

SEE TO MARK

Adverb and the Adjective It Modifies

Directions: Circle the adverbs and draw arrows to the adjectives they modify.

	First Try	Second Try
Correct		
Error		

Sarah is a strikingly beautiful girl. It was a very difficult test. I think it is uncomfortably warm today. The child gazed at the

very tempting sundae. We chose a rather cool day for swimming. This is an uncommonly cool day for June. Helen is an

unusually quiet girl. Wasn't this a very easy lesson? It is going to be slightly cloudy for the next week. I have been very happy

in this school. I have been in almost every national park. Tuft-eared squirrels are the most attractive squirrels. They have

completely white tails. A very strange thing happened to me. I found an almost perfect collection of shells. I heard such awful

noises that I ran for safety. Be extremely careful as you pour that acid. The class was so noisy that the teacher gave them a

terribly difficult assignment. It is rather warm in here. The student was somewhat confused by the teacher's very complicated

instructions. You were completely wrong. The fireman was carrying a very small child out of the house.

© 2005 Sopris West Educational Services. All rights reserved. Practicing Basic Skills in Language Arts. Purchaser has permission to photocopy this page for classroom use only.

Adverb and the Adjective It Modifies

Directions: Circle the adverbs and draw arrows to the adjectives they modify.

	First Try	Second Try
Correct		
Error		

Sarah is a (strikingly) beautiful girl. It was a (very) difficult test. I think it is (uncomfortably) warm today. The child gazed at the (6)

(very) tempting sundae. We chose a (rather) cool day for swimming. This is an (uncommonly) cool day for June. Helen is an (12)

(unusually) quiet girl. Wasn't this a (very) easy lesson? It is going to be (slightly) cloudy for the next week. I have been (very) happy (20)

in this school. I have been in (almost) every national park. Tuft-eared squirrels are the (most) attractive squirrels. They have (24)

(completely) white tails. A (very) strange thing happened to me. I found an (almost) perfect collection of shells. I heard (such) awful (32)

noises that I ran for safety. Be (extremely) careful as you pour that acid. The class was (so) noisy that the teacher gave them a (36)

(terribly) difficult assignment. It is (rather) warm in here. The student was (somewhat) confused by the teacher's (very) complicated (44)

instructions. You were (completely) wrong. The fireman was carrying a (very) small child out of the house. (48)

Practicing Basic Skills in Language Arts • 182

© 2005 Sopris West Educational Services. All rights reserved. Practicing Basic Skills in Language Arts. Purchaser has permission to photocopy this page for classroom use only.

SEE TO MARK

Adverb and the Adjective It Modifies

Directions: Circle the adverbs and draw arrows to the adjectives they modify.

	First Try	Second Try
Correct		
Error		

Your sentence contains too many commas. Seat belts are very necessary. The speaker from the newspaper gave an

extremely informative talk. The day was unbearably hot. The conversation ended quite soon. The streets have become

rather crowded. The heart of nearly every large city is deteriorating. Recently, the winters have been extremely cold. The school

this winter is unusually cold. Too little leisure can affect work. We are so happy you came that we are going to have a party in

your honor. Dawn received a fairly high grade on the test. Who do you think is the most famous tennis player? The troup leader

told us a very sad story. We were greeted with a rather cold stare. The new textbook has extremely good information in it. Dad

is feeling much stronger today. Although the judge had a very fiery temper and an extremely gravelly voice, he had an unfailing

sense of justice. That dress is hardly suitable for the New Year's Eve party. An extremely loud explosion followed the crash. She is

the most careful driver I know. His experiences were most unusual. The new boy was not very friendly. Usually Mr. Ames takes a

much earlier train. Their house is much larger than ours.

© 2005 Sopris West Educational Services. All rights reserved. Practicing Basic Skills in Language Arts. Purchaser has permission to photocopy this page for classroom use only.

ONE MINUTE FLUENCY BUILDER SERIES

	Correct	Error
First Try		
Second Try		

SEE TO MARK

Adverb and the Adjective It Modifies

Directions: Circle the adverbs and draw arrows to the adjectives they modify.

Your sentence contains (too) many commas. Seat belts are (very) necessary. The speaker from the newspaper gave an (4)

(extremely) informative talk. The day was (unbearably) hot. The conversation ended (quite) soon. The streets have become (10)

(rather) crowded. The heart of (nearly) every large city is deteriorating. Recently, the winters have been (extremely) cold. The school (16)

this winter is (unusually) cold. (Too) little leisure can affect work. We are (so) happy you came that we are going to have a party in (22)

your honor. Dawn received a (fairly) high grade on the test. Who do you think is the (most) famous tennis player? The troup leader (26)

told us a (very) sad story. We were greeted with a (rather) cold stare. The new textbook has (extremely) good information in it. Dad (32)

is feeling (much) stronger today. Although the judge had a (very) fiery temper and an (extremely) gravelly voice, he had an unfailing (38)

sense of justice. That dress is (hardly) suitable for the New Year's Eve party. An (extremely) loud explosion followed the crash. She is (42)

the (most) careful driver I know. His experiences were (most) unusual. The new boy was not (very) friendly. Usually Mr. Ames takes a (48)

(much) earlier train. Their house is (much) larger than ours. (52)

ANSWER SHEET

Practicing Basic Skills in Language Arts • 184

© 2005 Sopris West Educational Services. All rights reserved. Practicing Basic Skills in Language Arts. Purchaser has permission to photocopy this page for classroom use only.

ONE-MINUTE FLUENCY BUILDER SERIES

SEE TO MARK

Adverb and the Adverb It Modifies

Directions: Circle the adverbs and draw arrows to the adverbs they modify.

	First Try	Second Try
Correct		
Error		

Bill reads too slowly. The bus almost always arrives late. The golf course was almost completely covered with snow. Miss Mansell

told us not to sing so loud. The huge elephant stood up rather slowly. Very cautiously the cat approached the mouse. We believe

in driving somewhat slowly. John drives too fast for us to be comfortable with him. You should speak more distinctly when

you read aloud. So skillfully did the magician work that I was enthralled. All of them spoke quite rapidly but most interestingly.

The sheriff of Jackson County very quickly arrested the hit and run driver. The driver returned rather soon to the scene of

the accident. Must you play the stereo so loud? The tailor very skillfully mended the tear in my parka. From that day on, she

proofread her work more carefully. Uncle Ralph almost always pays his bills promptly. She can type rather fast for a beginner. I

had never seen appetites so unashamedly voracious. Chris will check the figures more carefully. Does Jim always speak so softly?

Mrs. Casey treated the children very kindly in spite of their bad manners. Karen was afraid to go into the museum because the

guard spoke extremely gruffly. When Carol asked if the plan would work, Tim answered very sadly that he did not think it would.

Practicing Basic Skills in Language Arts • 185

© 2005 Sopris West Educational Services. All rights reserved. Practicing Basic Skills in Language Arts. Purchaser has permission to photocopy this page for classroom use only.

Adverb and the Adverb It Modifies

Directions: Circle the adverbs and draw arrows to the adverbs they modify.

Bill reads (too) slowly. The bus (almost) always arrives late. The golf course was (almost) completely covered with snow. Miss Mansell (8)

told us not to sing (so) loud. The huge elephant stood up (rather) slowly. (Very) cautiously the cat approached the mouse. We believe (14)

in driving (somewhat) slowly. John drives (too) fast for us to be comfortable with him. You should speak (more) distinctly when (20)

you read aloud. (So) skillfully did the magician work that I was enthralled. All of them spoke (quite) rapidly but (most) interestingly. (26)

The sheriff of Jackson County (very) quickly arrested the hit and run driver. The driver returned (rather) soon to the scene of (32)

the accident. Must you play the stereo (so) loud? The tailor (very) skillfully mended the tear in my parka. From that day on, she (36)

proofread her work (more) carefully. Uncle Ralph (almost) always pays his bills promptly. She can type (rather) fast for a beginner. I (44)

had never seen appetites (so) unashamedly voracious. Chris will check the figures (more) carefully. Does Jim always speak (so) softly? (50)

Mrs. Casey treated the children (very) kindly in spite of their bad manners. Karen was afraid to go into the museum because the (52)

guard spoke (extremely) gruffly. When Carol asked if the plan would work, Tim answered (very) sadly that he did not think it would. (56)

Practicing Basic Skills in Language Arts • 186

© 2005 Sopris West Educational Services. All rights reserved. Practicing Basic Skills in Language Arts. Purchaser has permission to photocopy this page for classroom use only.

SEE TO MARK

Adverbs Modifying Adverbs or Verbs

Directions: Circle each adverb and draw an arrow to the adverb or verb it modifies.

	First Try	Second Try
Correct		
Error		

The fire blazed too dangerously for anyone to enter. Jana sang extremely well. She walked very quickly home. He

left the room almost immediately. Erika speaks too rapidly. Janice quietly read her book. Bart and Hal spoke somewhat hesitantly.

You are walking too slowly. He has done very well. Tom almost always rides his bike. You ran too slowly to win the

race. Mark cleaned the room very unwillingly. She screamed very loudly. Stop talking so loudly in the halls. You

finished that assignment rather quickly. He always writes his name neatly. Evan reads so slowly that no one listens to him.

The bus almost always arrives on time. She painted the wall carefully. The doctor approached the sick tiger very carefully.

Try to write more legibly. She sings very well. George ran so quickly that he set a new school record. We are almost there.

The boys were too noisy in class. Mary laughed rather rudely at the speaker. He spoke awfully quietly, however. She

walked quickly and quietly home.

© 2005 Sopris West Educational Services. All rights reserved. Practicing Basic Skills in Language Arts. Purchaser has permission to photocopy this page for classroom use only.

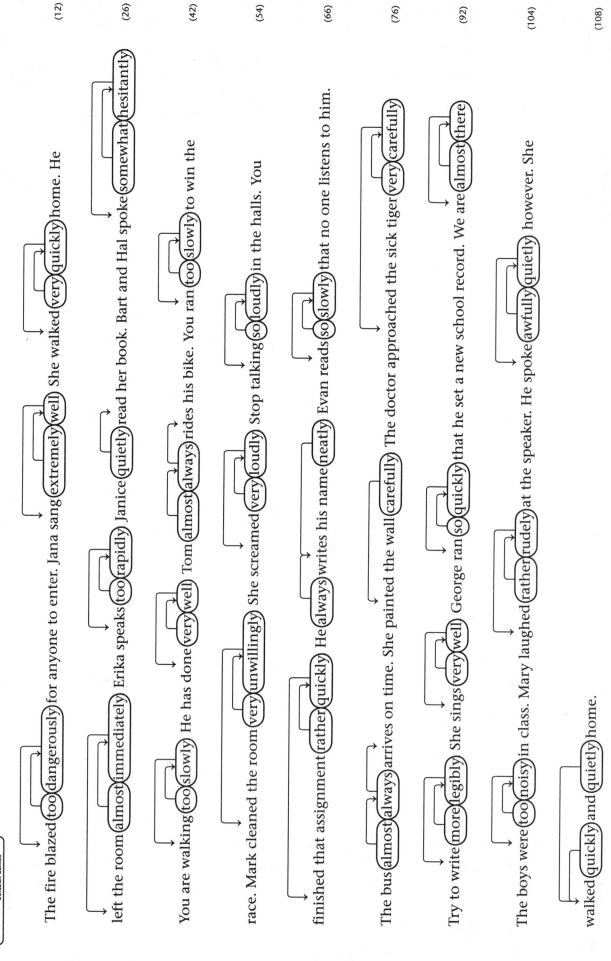

SEE TO MARK

Adverbs Modifying Adverbs or Verbs

Directions: Circle each adverb and draw an arrow to the adverb or verb it modifies.

	Correct	Error
First Try		
Second Try		

The fire blazed (too)(dangerously) for anyone to enter. Jana sang (extremely)(well) She walked (very)(quickly) home. He (12)

left the room (almost)(immediately) Erika speaks (too)(rapidly) Janice (quietly) read her book. Bart and Hal spoke (somewhat)(hesitantly) (26)

You are walking (too)(slowly) He has done (very)(well) Tom (almost)(always) rides his bike. You ran (too)(slowly) to win the (42)

race. Mark cleaned the room (very)(unwillingly) She screamed (very)(loudly) Stop talking (so)(loudly) in the halls. You (54)

finished that assignment (rather)(quickly) He (always) writes his name (neatly) Evan reads (so)(slowly) that no one listens to him. (66)

The bus (almost)(always) arrives on time. She painted the wall (carefully) The doctor approached the sick tiger (very)(carefully) (76)

Try to write (more)(legibly) She sings (very)(well) George ran (so)(quickly) that he set a new school record. We are (almost)(there) (92)

The boys were (too)(noisy) in class. Mary laughed (rather)(rudely) at the speaker. He spoke (awfully)(quietly) however. She (104)

walked (quickly) and (quietly) home. (108)

ANSWER SHEET

© 2005 Sopris West Educational Services. All rights reserved. Practicing Basic Skills in Language Arts. Purchaser has permission to photocopy this page for classroom use only.

ONE-MINUTE FLUENCY
BUILDER SERIES

SEE TO MARK

Adverbs and the Words They Modify

Directions: Circle the adverbs and draw arrows to the words they modify.

	Correct	Error
First Try		
Second Try		

My father spoke impatiently. That unusually tall boy plays center. Joel ran fairly well. I put my bundles down. I was only joking.

James climbed the ladder carefully. This book is really good. We moved very rapidly. The tiger paced back and forth. He

spoke less clearly. The crowd was greatly excited. She spoke most earnestly. The actress walked gracefully to the center of the

stage. The heavyset man rambled around. The men worked swiftly. He never complains. Aren't you being rather foolish? She

speaks German quite well. Tina is seldom absent. She sang beautifully. The experiment was extremely interesting. The object

fell very rapidly through space. Will you be going soon? An extremely large balloon was used. The missile traveled too far. Lower

Michigan has now suffered the most devastating storm of an unusually severe winter. I am somewhat doubtful of his final

success. Yesterday his answers were indirect. Later we went again to the tennis matches. Charles played well against an unusually

skillful opponent. Tomorrow everybody will be out to see the amazingly skillful boxers. Tony has played very consistently

during the entire tennis tournament. There will be four tennis matches tomorrow if the weather is not too cold. They left early.

The extremely cold weather was somewhat unseasonable.

Practicing Basic Skills in Language Arts • 189

© 2005 Sopris West Educational Services. All rights reserved. Practicing Basic Skills in Language Arts. Purchaser has permission to photocopy this page for classroom use only.

Adverbs and the Words They Modify

Directions: Circle the adverbs and draw arrows to the words they modify.

My father spoke (impatiently). That (unusually) tall boy plays center. Joel ran (fairly) (well). I put my bundles (down). I was (only) joking. (12)

James climbed the ladder (carefully). This book is (really) good. We moved (very) (rapidly). The tiger paced (back) and (forth). He (24)

spoke (less) (clearly). The crowd was (greatly) excited. She spoke (most) (earnestly). The actress walked (gracefully) to the center of the (36)

stage. The heavyset man rambled (around). The men worked (swiftly). He (never) complains. Aren't you being (rather) foolish? She (46)

speaks German (quite) (well). Tina is (seldom) absent. She sang (beautifully). The experiment was (extremely) interesting. The object (56)

fell (very) (rapidly) through space. Will you be going (soon)? An (extremely) large balloon was used. The missile traveled (too) (far). Lower (68)

Michigan has (now) suffered the (most) devastating storm of an (unusually) severe winter. I am (somewhat) doubtful of his final success. (76)

(Yesterday) his answers were indirect. (Later) we went (again) to the tennis matches. Charles played (well) against an (unusually) skillful (86)

opponent. (Tomorrow) everybody will be (out) to see the (amazingly) skillful boxers. Tony has played (very) (consistently) during the (96)

entire tennis tournament. There will be four tennis matches (tomorrow) if the weather is (not) (too) cold. They left (early). The (104)

(extremely) cold weather was (somewhat) unseasonable. (108)

© 2005 Sopris West Educational Services. All rights reserved. Practicing Basic Skills in Language Arts. Purchaser has permission to photocopy this page for classroom use only.

Prepositions

Prepositions in Isolation Primary 193
Prepositions in Isolation 195
Prepositions in Sentences Primary.............. 197
Prepositions in Sentences 199
Prepositions and Prepositional Phrases 201
Prepositional Phrases—Preposition and
    Object 203

Coordinating Conjunctions in Sentence..... 205
Correlative Conjunctions in Sentences 207
Conjunctions in Sentences 209
Subordinating Conjunctions 211
Subordinating Conjunctions 213
Interjections in Sentences........................... 215

SEE TO MARK

	Correct	Error
First Try		
Second Try		

Prepositions in Isolation—Primary

Directions: Underline the prepositions: over, under, in, by, behind, at, to, for, up, down, on, from

over	boy	house	sit	for	man	talk	up	ball
to	hide	cat	under	skip	from	eat	tree	over
see	cow	down	on	touch	read	in	say	at
train	by	hat	jump	girl	tent	walk	door	for
cut	table	behind	hide	by	catch	down	river	throw
behind	on	push	flower	stand	in	share	plate	up
give	car	under	at	from	hear	dirt	to	book

Practicing Basic Skills in Language Arts • 193

© 2005 Sopris West Educational Services. All rights reserved. Practicing Basic Skills in Language Arts. Purchaser has permission to photocopy this page for classroom use only.

ONE-MINUTE FLUENCY BUILDER SERIES

ONE-MINUTE FLUENCY BUILDER SERIES

SEE TO MARK

Prepositions in Isolation—Primary

Directions: Underline the prepositions: over, under, in, by, behind, at, to, for, up, down, on, from

	Correct	Error
First Try		
Second Try		

over	boy	house	sit	for	talk	up	ball	(3)
to	hide	cat	under	skip	eat	tree	over	(7)
see	cow	down	on	touch	read	say	at	(11)
train	by	hat	jump	girl	tent	walk	door	for	(13)
cut	table	behind	hide	by	catch	down	throw	(16)
behind	on	push	flower	stand	in	share	plate	up	(20)
give	car	under	at	from	hear	dirt	to	book	(24)

ANSWER SHEET

Practicing Basic Skills in Language Arts • 194

© 2005 Sopris West Educational Services. All rights reserved. Practicing Basic Skills in Language Arts. Purchaser has permission to photocopy this page for classroom use only.

ONE-MINUTE FLUENCY BUILDER SERIES

SEE TO MARK

Prepositions in Isolation
Directions: Circle the prepositions.

First Try		Correct	Error
Second Try			

find	after	may have been	hit	above	in addition to
mine	go	did	about	he	of
to	answer	did	about	art	behind
could not be	work	like	time	into	want
girl	over	their	its	shall	has
up	prior to	middle	in	should	off
finally	team	upon	know	across	fool
spring	speak	join	beside	in front of	train
hot	swiftly	against	aside from	on	toward
aboard	between	able	among	may	below
through	soon	well	hand	along	elect
wash	with	until	under	be	till
around	since	not	wave	could	class
smile	should be	down	instead of	out	had not seen
happily	never	beneath	treat	at	beyond
according to	now	in place of	they	home	may
without	near	often	for	today	might
is	eat	during	besides	because of	underneath

Practicing Basic Skills in Language Arts • 195

© 2005 Sopris West Educational Services. All rights reserved. Practicing Basic Skills in Language Arts. Purchaser has permission to photocopy this page for classroom use only.

ONE-MINUTE FLUENCY
BUILDER SERIES

SEE TO MARK

Prepositions in Isolation

Directions: Circle the prepositions.

First Try		Correct	Error
Second Try			

find	after	may have been	hit	above	in addition to	(3)
mine	go	did	about	he	of	(5)
to	answer	did	about	art	behind	(8)
could not be	work	like	time	into	want	(10)
girl	over	their	its	shall	has	(11)
up	prior to	middle	in	should	off	(15)
finally	team	upon	know	across	fool	(17)
spring	speak	join	beside	in front of	train	(19)
hot	swiftly	against	aside from	on	toward	(23)
aboard	between	able	among	may	below	(27)
through	soon	well	hand	along	elect	(29)
wash	with	until	under	be	till	(33)
around	since	not	wave	could	class	(35)
smile	should be	down	instead of	out	had not seen	(38)
happily	never	beneath	treat	at	beyond	(41)
according to	now	in place of	they	home	may	(43)
without	near	often	for	today	might	(46)
is	eat	during	besides	because of	underneath	(50)

ANSWER SHEET

Practicing Basic Skills in Language Arts • 196

© 2005 Sopris West Educational Services. All rights reserved. Practicing Basic Skills in Language Arts. Purchaser has permission to photocopy this page for classroom use only.

SEE TO MARK

Prepositions in Sentences—Primary

Directions: Underline prepositions in the sentences.

The man ran in the house.

The dog hid his bone under the tree.

Put the cup on the table.

Tom is going to school.

He saved the ball for her.

Look behind the fence.

The bridge is over the water.

The baby crawled up the stairs.

The cat is by the door.

Jack fell down the hill.

The boys looked at the car.

Jane rode on the train.

He fell asleep in the car.

The mouse is under the bed.

The money is for lunch.

Will you go to the store?

They got candy from the man.

Tim walked by the house.

Practicing Basic Skills in Language Arts • 197

© 2005 Sopris West Educational Services. All rights reserved. Practicing Basic Skills in Language Arts. Purchaser has permission to photocopy this page for classroom use only.

ONE-MINUTE FLUENCY
BUILDER SERIES

Prepositions in Sentences—Primary

Directions: Underline prepositions in the sentences.

	First Try	Second Try
Correct		
Error		

The man ran <u>in</u> the house.

The dog hid his bone <u>under</u> the tree. (2)

Put the cup <u>on</u> the table.

Tom is going <u>to</u> school. (4)

He saved the ball <u>for</u> her.

Look <u>behind</u> the fence. (6)

The bridge is <u>over</u> the water.

The baby crawled <u>up</u> the stairs. (8)

The cat is <u>by</u> the door.

Jack fell <u>down</u> the hill. (10)

The boys looked <u>at</u> the car.

Jane rode <u>on</u> the train. (12)

He fell asleep <u>in</u> the car.

The mouse is <u>under</u> the bed. (14)

The money is <u>for</u> lunch.

Will you go <u>to</u> the store? (16)

They got candy <u>from</u> the man.

Tim walked <u>by</u> the house. (18)

ANSWER SHEET

© 2005 Sopris West Educational Services. All rights reserved. Practicing Basic Skills in Language Arts. Purchaser has permission to photocopy this page for classroom use only.

	Correct	Error
First Try		
Second Try		

ONE MINUTE FLUENCY BUILDER SERIES

Prepositions in Sentences

Directions: Underline the words used as prepositions in the following sentences.

The singer wore a hat with a red feather in it. We came for your advice. Look out the window. The children ran through the whirling lawn sprinkler. We cannot go without him. The waitresses are sitting in the kitchen. Behind the ramshackle red barn was an old workhorse. The two girls ran a race around the football field. The man from the water company read the meter. José went reluctantly to the concert. The opening of the new school will be delayed because of the strike. The teachers have their faculty meetings on Wednesday mornings. Dan is the student with the most potential. The town lies on the side of a hill. The energy of an atom is tremendous. We seldom watch television programs in the summer. My dad always pays his bills on time. The treaty between the two nations was signed in Geneva. The workmen were putting a fence around the school playground. Travel rates to Europe are much cheaper during the winter. Hank put the stereo speakers on the bookcase. We will finish the decorations for the dance before dinner. Mike has been the president of the club for almost a year. The hunters rose early in the morning. They arrived at the airport on time. Tyrone knows the way to the station. Robin has become the ringleader of the rebels. Jim stayed a corporal during the entire war. Lu wore flowers in her hair. He was living by the mountains. Cape Horn is at the southernmost tip of South America. There are flies in the soup. In the late afternoon we had our first customer. The books were removed from the shelves. For twenty years the man in the iron mask captured everyone's imagination. The family rented a cottage by the sea. There was a man at the door. The jewels had been hidden in a box of rubbish. There is no answer to that question. During the violent storm, the waves hurled heavy rocks onto the shore. Before the railroads, settlers traveled along the rivers. They went to Yellowstone Park without him. There has been an accident on the highway. A crowd of angry people gather outside the Capital Building. A cloud of smoke appeared on the horizon.

Practicing Basic Skills in Language Arts • 199

© 2005 Sopris West Educational Services. All rights reserved. Practicing Basic Skills in Language Arts. Purchaser has permission to photocopy this page for classroom use only.

SEE TO MARK

Prepositions in Sentences

Directions: Underline the words used as prepositions in the following sentences.

	Correct	Error
First Try		
Second Try		

The singer wore a hat with a red feather in it. We came for your advice. Look out the window. The children ran through the (5)

whirling lawn sprinkler. We cannot go without him. The waitresses are sitting in the kitchen. Behind the ramshackle red barn (8)

was an old workhorse. The two girls ran a race around the football field. The man from the water company read the meter. José (10)

went reluctantly to the concert. The opening of the new school will be delayed because of the strike. The teachers have their (13)

faculty meetings on Wednesday mornings. Dan is the student with the most potential. The town lies on the side of a hill. The (17)

energy of an atom is tremendous. We seldom watch television programs in the summer. My dad always pays his bills on time. (20)

The treaty between the two nations was signed in Geneva. The workmen were putting a fence around the school playground. (23)

Travel rates to Europe are much cheaper during the winter. Hank put the stereo speakers on the bookcase. We will finish the (26)

decorations for the dance before dinner. Mike has been the president of the club for almost a year. The hunters rose early in (31)

the morning. They arrived at the airport on time. Tyrone knows the way to the station. Robin has become the ringleader of the (35)

rebels. Jim stayed a corporal during the entire war. Lu wore flowers in her hair. He was living by the mountains. Cape Horn is at (39)

the southernmost tip of South America. There are flies in the soup. In the late afternoon we had our first customer. The books (42)

were removed from the shelves. For twenty years the man in the iron mask captured everyone's imagination. The family rented (45)

a cottage by the sea. There was a man at the door. The jewels had been hidden in a box of rubbish. There is no answer to that (50)

question. During the violent storm, the waves hurled heavy rocks onto the shore. Before the railroads, settlers traveled along the (54)

rivers. They went to Yellowstone Park without him. There has been an accident on the highway. A crowd of angry people gather (58)

outside the Capital Building. A cloud of smoke appeared on the horizon. (61)

ANSWER SHEET

Practicing Basic Skills in Language Arts • 200

© 2005 Sopris West Educational Services. All rights reserved. Practicing Basic Skills in Language Arts. Purchaser has permission to photocopy this page for classroom use only.

ONE-MINUTE FLUENCY
BUILDER SERIES

SEE TO MARK

Prepositions and Prepositional Phrases

Directions: Circle all prepositions and underline all prepositional phrases.

about across after among around at before behind below beneath beside between by down during for from in inside into near of off on over to under up with

	First Try	Second Try
Correct		
Error		

1. The lodge on the mountain stood unharmed.

2. Bark from a hemlock made red paint.

3. The space between the roads measured five feet.

4. The skin of the white deer was smooth.

5. Voices beneath them spoke loudly.

6. The men of the tribe were there.

7. His love for the girl was real.

8. The girl in the blue jacket is my cousin.

9. He fell into a trap.

10. Some boys fished in the lake.

11. The children waved at the train.

12. The photographs of my friends arrived.

13. Our picnic on the grass included pie.

14. Jane put her model airplane near our planes.

15. The sheriff rode behind the prisoner.

16. The rehearsal will be held at my house.

17. Play the record for Flo and me.

18. Can you swim across the lake?

19. The money inside the envelope is yours.

20. The three doctors in his room left.

21. The nurse put her hand on his forehead.

22. "You are burning with fever," she said.

24. She handed it to the boy.

25. "This drink is good for you," the nurse said.

26. Bobby looked at the glass.

27. "I don't like the taste of medicine," he said.

28. "Don't think about the taste," she advised.

29. In a short time, you'll feel better.

30. Mark ran around the block.

31. The groceries were left on the doorstep.

32. The elm beside the house is very old.

33. We parked our car near yours.

© 2005 Sopris West Educational Services. All rights reserved. Practicing Basic Skills in Language Arts. Purchaser has permission to photocopy this page for classroom use only.

ONE-MINUTE FLUENCY BUILDER SERIES

	Correct	Error
First Try		
Second Try		

SEE TO MARK

Prepositions and Prepositional Phrases

Directions: Circle all prepositions and underline all prepositional phrases.

about across after among around at before behind below beneath beside between
by down during for from in inside into near of off on over to under up with

1. The lodge (on) the mountain stood unharmed. (2)

2. Bark (from) a hemlock made red paint. (4)

3. The space (between) the roads measured five feet. (6)

4. The skin (of) the white deer was smooth. (8)

5. Voices (beneath) them spoke loudly. (10)

6. The men (of) the tribe were there. (12)

7. His love (for) the girl was real. (14)

8. The girl (in) the blue jacket is my cousin. (16)

9. He fell (into) a trap. (18)

10. Some boys fished (in) the lake. (20)

11. The children waved (at) the train. (22)

12. The photographs (of) my friends arrived. (24)

13. Our picnic (on) the grass included pie. (26)

14. Jane put her model airplane (near) our planes. (28)

15. The sheriff rode (behind) the prisoner. (30)

16. The rehearsal will be held (at) my house. (32)

17. Play the record (for) Flo and me. (34)

18. Can you swim (across) the lake? (36)

19. The money (inside) the envelope is yours. (38)

20. The three doctors (in) his room left. (40)

21. The nurse put her hand (on) his forehead. (42)

22. "You are burning (with) fever," she said. (44)

24. She handed it (to) the boy. (46)

25. "This drink is good (for) you," the nurse said. (48)

26. Bobby looked (at) the glass. (50)

27. "I don't like the taste (of) medicine," he said. (52)

28. "Don't think (about) the taste," she advised. (54)

29. (In) a short time, you'll feel better. (56)

30. Mark ran (around) the block. (58)

31. The groceries were left (on) the doorstep. (60)

32. The elm (beside) the house is very old. (62)

33. We parked our car (near) yours. (64)

ANSWER SHEET

Practicing Basic Skills in Language Arts • 202

© 2005 Sopris West Educational Services. All rights reserved. Practicing Basic Skills in Language Arts. Purchaser has permission to photocopy this page for classroom use only.

Prepositional Phrases—Preposition and Object

Directions: Underline the prepositional phrases, label the preposition with the letter P, and label the object of the preposition with the letter O.

He ran to the corner. The young boy ran into that white house. The cow jumped over the moon. The mouse ran up the clock. London Bridge is falling down. They all ran after the farmer's wife. She cut off their tails with a carving knife. They lived happily ever after. Mr. McGregor jumped up. Peter squeezed under the gate. Won't you come over and play? Did you ever see such a sight in your life? Along came a spider and sat down beside her. They are going to town. Give the eraser to him. This message is for you and Lisa. They are giving a party for Scott and Steve. Do not walk across the lawn. Within an hour we were exploring inside the cave. The game with Weber High School was canceled because of rain. After dinner we'll go to the movie. The boy in the car is the captain of our football team. That boat with the broken rudder isn't out of trouble yet. This argument is between the two of you. We'll meet outside the cafeteria after school. Everyone but Jed passed the test in science. Over the fireplace is a picture of the battle at Gettysburg during the Civil War. The woman beside Mr. DeYoung once taught at Bonnevelle High School. The information concerning the dance will be posted on the bulletin board. The batter hit the ball hard. I will arrive next week by train. The bell rang without warning. The bell in the old church tower rang. That bag of empty bottles should be taken to the dump. Your books are on the table in the kitchen. The box of crayons is on your desk. I will meet you in front of the office before we go to the assembly. She fell down. She fell down the stairs. They washed their car in the late afternoon. The children from the elementary school laughed at the clown in the circus. Bill went to the park with his brother and sister. To whom did you give the letter? For dessert you have a choice between cake or pie.

The package on the top shelf is for you.

© 2005 Sopris West Educational Services. All rights reserved. Practicing Basic Skills in Language Arts. Purchaser has permission to photocopy this page for classroom use only.

SEE TO MARK

Prepositional Phrases—Preposition and Object

Directions: Underline the prepositional phrases, label the preposition with the letter P, and label the object of the preposition with the letter O.

	Correct	Error
First Try		
Second Try		

He ran to the corner. The young boy ran into that white house. The cow jumped over the moon. The mouse ran up the clock. (12)

London Bridge is falling down. They all ran after the farmer's wife. She cut off their tails with a carving knife. They lived happily (18)

ever after. Mr. McGregor jumped up. Peter squeezed under the gate. Won't you come over and play? Did you ever see such a (21)

sight in your life? Along came a spider and sat down beside her. They are going to town. Give the eraser to him. This message is (33)

for you and Lisa. They are giving a party for Scott and Steve. Do not walk across the lawn. Within an hour we were exploring (47)

inside the cave. The game with Weber High School was canceled because of rain. After dinner we'll go to the movie. The boy (62)

in the car is the captain of our football team. That boat with the broken rudder isn't out of trouble yet. This argument is (74)

between the two of you. We'll meet outside the cafeteria after school. Everyone but Jed passed the test in science. (92)

Over the fireplace is a picture of the battle at Gettysburg during the Civil War. The woman beside Mr. DeYoung once taught (107)

at Bonneville High School. The information concerning the dance will be posted on the bulletin board. The batter hit the (113)

ball hard. I will arrive next week by train. The bell rang without warning. The bell in the old church tower rang. That bag (122)

of empty bottles should be taken to the dump. Your books are on the table in the kitchen. The box of crayons is on your desk. (140)

I will meet you in front of the office before we go to the assembly. She fell down the stairs. They washed (149)

their car in the late afternoon. The children from the elementary school laughed at the clown in the circus. Bill went (161)

to the park with his brother and sister. To whom did you give the letter? For dessert you have a choice between cake or pie. (178)

The package on the top shelf is for you. (184)

ANSWER SHEET

© 2005 Sopris West Educational Services. All rights reserved. Practicing Basic Skills in Language Arts. Purchaser has permission to photocopy this page for classroom use only.

SEE TO MARK

	First Try	Second Try
Correct		
Error		

Coordinating Conjunctions in Sentence

Directions: Circle the coordinating conjunctions in the sentences.

Homework and sports take most of my spare time, but I still try to read once in a while. Mary is tall, yet she isn't a good

basketball player. Run to the store quickly, for we need milk and eggs. I cannot tolerate this, nor do I intend to! Harry and Carlos

are talented and wealthy. Gene ran fast, but he didn't win the race. Is Lucia or Don next? Your work is neat and accurate. Did

someone knock, or am I imagining things? It rained, yet the picnic was not cancelled. Lisa failed the class, for she never studied.

I like apples and pears, but my brother prefers grapes or bananas. Mother and Father have never seen Boston, nor have they

ever traveled to New York. This souvenir is pretty but useless. The reporter listened to the code and reported it accurately. The

tiny bird could not fly, nor could it feed itself. I am all alone but not bored. These peaches should be used at once, for they are

overripe. I wanted to go, yet I could not afford tickets. Jill and Mei ran for the cross country team. Warren looks happy, yet he

never laughs. Should I write or call? I'd rather be rich or famous than poor and unknown. Rabbits are born blind, but hares can

see at birth. Maria attended junior high school, but never finished high school. The breeze blew lightly and fragrantly into the

room. You should drive up the hill or around the corner. The teacher postponed the test, for the students weren't ready. Mr. and

Mrs. Smith have been married for twenty-five years. He or she will be elected president. Sit down or else! I couldn't see John, nor

could I hear his voice. The boys worked with energy and skill. They painted scenery, and we sold tickets. I cannot swim, nor can

I dive. Is it warm or cool in here? I recognized Jada, yet she did not know me.

© 2005 Sopris West Educational Services. All rights reserved. Practicing Basic Skills in Language Arts. Purchaser has permission to photocopy this page for classroom use only.

Coordinating Conjunctions in Sentence

Directions: Circle the coordinating conjunctions in the sentences.

Homework (and) sports take most of my spare time, (but) I still try to read once in a while. Mary is tall, (yet) she isn't a good (3)

basketball player. Run to the store quickly, (for) we need milk (and) eggs. I cannot tolerate this, (nor) do I intend to! Harry (and) Carlos (7)

are talented (and) wealthy. Gene ran fast, (but) he didn't win the race. Is Lucia (or) Don next? Your work is neat (and) accurate. Did (11)

someone knock, (or) am I imagining things? It rained, (yet) the picnic was not cancelled. Lisa failed the class, (for) she never studied. (14)

I like apples (and) pears, (but) my brother prefers grapes (or) bananas. Mother (and) Father have never seen Boston, (nor) have they (19)

ever traveled to New York. This souvenir is pretty (but) useless. The reporter listened to the code (and) reported it accurately. The (21)

tiny bird could not fly, (nor) could it feed itself. I am all alone (but) not bored. These peaches should be used at once, (for) they are (24)

overripe. I wanted to go, (yet) I could not afford tickets. Jill (and) Mei ran for the cross country team. Warren looks happy, (yet) he (27)

never laughs. Should I write (or) call? I'd rather be rich (or) famous than poor (and) unknown. Rabbits are born blind, (but) hares can (31)

see at birth. Maria attended junior high school, (but) never finished high school. The breeze blew lightly (and) fragrantly into the (33)

room. You should drive up the hill (or) around the corner. The teacher postponed the test, (for) the students weren't ready. Mr. (and) (36)

Mrs. Smith have been married for twenty-five years. He (or) she will be elected president. Sit down (or) else! I couldn't see John, (nor) (39)

could I hear his voice. The boys worked with energy (and) skill. They painted scenery, (and) we sold tickets. I cannot swim, (nor) can (42)

I dive. Is it warm (or) cool in here? I recognized Jada, (yet) she did not know me. (44)

© 2005 Sopris West Educational Services. All rights reserved. Practicing Basic Skills in Language Arts. Purchaser has permission to photocopy this page for classroom use only.

ONE-MINUTE FLUENCY
BUILDER SERIES

	Correct	Error
First Try		
Second Try		

SEE TO MARK

Correlative Conjunctions in Sentences

both . . . and   not only . . . but also   either . . . or   neither . . . nor   whether . . . or

Directions: Circle the correlative conjunctions in the sentences.

Both rain and snow supply moisture. Water is necessary not only for animals but also for plants. Jasmine neither completed her

homework nor wrote a letter. Greg won not only the school speaking contest, but also the city contest. Neither the speeches nor

the music was very exciting. Either Father or Mother will help us. Both the dog and the cat sleep in the house. I could not decide

whether to study or to rest. Neither persuasion nor punishment had any effect. The flowers were not only weather-beaten but also

faded. We must either sell the papers or give up the route. Both the mayor and the councilman opposed the investigation. The

tornado struck not only the house but also the barn. He failed because he was both lazy and dishonest. Our class will furnish

either the punch or the cookies. Neither Chris nor Ana likes science. She was not only a playwright but also an ambassador. We

will play both badminton and volleyball. The class read not only our textbooks but also library books. Whether it rains or not,

we will go hiking. Neither Los Angeles nor San Diego is the capital of California. Either David or Jorge will be a good leader.

Mrs. Ames gives the test whether we are ready or not. Both the seal and the porpoise enjoy showing off for audiences. He was

either a fool or a madman. She was both proud and shy. Neither a borrower nor a lender be. Whether you like it or dislike it,

your homework must be done. I was not only out of money, but also out of gas. Both the coaches and the players were ready for

the game. Either Fred Hopkins or Li Wong will start as quarterback. Wong was not only a good passer, but also a great runner.

Practicing Basic Skills in Language Arts • 207

© 2005 Sopris West Educational Services. All rights reserved. Practicing Basic Skills in Language Arts. Purchaser has permission to photocopy this page for classroom use only.

	Correct	Error
First Try		
Second Try		

SEE TO MARK

Correlative Conjunctions in Sentences

both . . . and   not only . . . but also   either . . . or   neither . . . nor   whether . . . or

Directions: Circle the correlative conjunctions in the sentences.

(Both) rain (and) snow supply moisture. Water is necessary (not only) for animals (but also) for plants. Jasmine (neither) completed her (5)

homework (nor) wrote a letter. Greg won (not only) the school speaking contest, (but also) the city contest. (Neither) the speeches (nor) (10)

the music was very exciting. (Either) Father (or) Mother will help us. (Both) the dog (and) the cat sleep in the house. I could not decide (14)

(whether) to study (or) to rest. (Neither) persuasion (nor) punishment had any effect. The flowers were (not only) weather-beaten (but also) (20)

faded. We must (either) sell the papers (or) give up the route. (Both) the mayor (and) the councilman opposed the investigation. The (24)

tornado struck (not only) the house (but also) the barn. He failed because he was (both) lazy (and) dishonest. Our class will furnish (28)

(either) the punch (or) the cookies. (Neither) Chris (nor) Ana likes science. She was (not only) a playwright (but also) an ambassador. We (34)

will play (both) badminton (and) volleyball. The class read (not only) our textbooks (but also) library books. (Whether) it rains (or) not, (40)

we will go hiking. (Neither) Los Angeles (nor) San Diego is the capital of California. (Either) David (or) Jorge will be a good leader. (44)

Mrs. Ames gives the test (whether) we are ready (or) not. (Both) the seal (and) the porpoise enjoy showing off for audiences. He was (45)

(either) a fool (or) a madman. She was (both) proud (and) shy. (Neither) a borrower (nor) a lender be. (Whether) you like it (or) dislike it, (56)

your homework must be done. I was (not only) out of money, (but also) out of gas. (Both) the coaches (and) the players were ready for (60)

the game. (Either) Fred Hopkins (or) Li Wong will start as quarterback. Wong was (not only) a good passer, (but also) a great runner. (64)

© 2005 Sopris West Educational Services. All rights reserved. Practicing Basic Skills in Language Arts. Purchaser has permission to photocopy this page for classroom use only.

ONE-MINUTE FLUENCY
BUILDER SERIES

SEE TO MARK

	Correct	Error
First Try		
Second Try		

Conjunctions in Sentences

Directions: Circle all the conjunctions in the following sentences.

Homework and sports take most of my spare time. José prefers mashed potatoes, but I like rice. I can come if it doesn't rain. If

you have time, will you visit Miriam while you are in New York? Mother and Father were surprised, but they soon recovered.

He failed because he was both lazy and dishonest. The baby can neither walk nor talk. Grace and Maya will take charge of the

program, but you can't. After the school year had closed, one of my classmates and her sister took a trip through the Black Hills.

I cannot go until the weather changes. Your work is both neat and accurate. Tennis and golf are popular spring sports in our

school. As I have told you, you may have either this one or that one. Did someone knock, or am I imagining things? Is Maria or

Don next? As long as it keeps raining, we will be unable to go on our picnic. Gina ran fast, but she didn't win the race. Whenever

I meet someone for the first time, I try to remember his or her name and face. The tornado struck not only the house but also

the barn. I saw both Tran and his brother while you were away. You may bring either apples or bananas. Though he seems shy,

he is actually very friendly. Marina smiles as if she knows a secret. I ran until I reached the corner. Joey wanted to read, but the

light was too dim. Ling failed because she didn't hand in any assignments. Neither Elena nor Jack had seen the movie. I will

not fight, nor will I protest. Unless I get a raise, I will be bankrupt before I am thirty years old. As soon as we met, I knew where

you were raised. We raised $100, for we knew the trip would be expensive. Sally was a good athlete, yet she was small. Although

Pedro was a good student, he had trouble in chemistry. We ran for our lives when we saw the werewolf. Since Fredrick came to

America, he has enjoyed himself wherever he has gone. Marcella attended medical school so that she could become a doctor.

Practicing Basic Skills in Language Arts • 209

© 2005 Sopris West Educational Services. All rights reserved. Practicing Basic Skills in Language Arts. Purchaser has permission to photocopy this page for classroom use only.

ONE-MINUTE FLUENCY
BUILDER SERIES

SEE TO MARK

Conjunctions in Sentences

Directions: Circle all the conjunctions in the following sentences.

	First Try	Second Try
Correct		
Error		

Homework (and) sports take most of my spare time. José prefers mashed potatoes, (but) I like rice. I can come (if) it doesn't rain. (If) (4)

you have time, will you visit Miriam (while) you are in New York? Mother (and) Father were surprised, (but) they soon recovered. (7)

He failed (because) he was (both) lazy (and) dishonest. The baby can (neither) walk (nor) talk. Grace (and) Maya will take charge of the (13)

program, (but) you can't. (After) the school year had closed, one of my classmates (and) her sister took a trip through the Black Hills. (16)

I cannot go (until) the weather changes. Your work is (both) neat (and) accurate. Tennis (and) golf are popular spring sports in our (20)

school. (As) I have told you, you may have (either) this one (or) that one. Did someone knock, (or) am I imagining things? Is Maria (or) (25)

Don next? (As long as) it keeps raining, we will be unable to go on our picnic. Gina ran fast, (but) she didn't win the race. (Whenever) (28)

I meet someone for the first time, I try to remember his (or) her name (and) face. The tornado struck (not only) the house (but also) (32)

the barn. I saw (both) Tran (and) his brother (while) you were away. You may bring (either) apples (or) bananas. (Though) he seems shy, (38)

he is actually very friendly. Marina smiles (as if) she knows a secret. I ran (until) I reached the corner. Joey wanted to read, (but) the (41)

light was too dim. Ling failed (because) she didn't hand in any assignments. (Neither) Elena (nor) Jack had seen the movie. I will (44)

not fight, (nor) will I protest. (Unless) I get a raise, I will be bankrupt (before) I am thirty years old. (As soon as) we met, I knew where (48)

you were raised. We raised $100, (for) we knew the trip would be expensive. Sally was a good athlete, (yet) she was small. (Although) (51)

Pedro was a good student, he had trouble in chemistry. We ran for our lives (when) we saw the werewolf. (Since) Fredrick came to (53)

America, he has enjoyed himself (wherever) he has gone. Marcella attended medical school (so that) she could become a doctor. (55)

Practicing Basic Skills in Language Arts • 210

ANSWER SHEET

© 2005 Sopris West Educational Services. All rights reserved. Practicing Basic Skills in Language Arts. Purchaser has permission to photocopy this page for classroom use only.

Subordinating Conjunctions

Directions: Copy each conjunction on the line following it.

after	_____	although	_____	as	_____
as if	_____	as long as	_____	because	_____
before	_____	if	_____	in order that	_____
since	_____	so that	_____	than	_____
though	_____	unless	_____	until	_____
when	_____	whenever	_____	where	_____
wherever	_____	while	_____	after	_____
although	_____	as	_____	as if	_____
as long as	_____	as soon as	_____	because	_____
before	_____	if	_____	in order that	_____
since	_____	so that	_____	than	_____
though	_____	unless	_____	until	_____

	First Try	Second Try
Correct		
Error		

Practicing Basic Skills in Language Arts • 211

© 2005 Sopris West Educational Services. All rights reserved. Practicing Basic Skills in Language Arts. Purchaser has permission to photocopy this page for classroom use only.

ONE-MINUTE FLUENCY BUILDER SERIES

SEE TO COPY

Subordinating Conjunctions

Directions: Copy each conjunction on the line following it.

	Correct	Error
First Try		
Second Try		

#			
(3)	after	although	as
(6)	as if	as long as	because
(9)	before	if	in order that
(12)	since	so that	than
(15)	though	unless	until
(18)	when	whenever	where
(21)	wherever	while	after
(24)	although	as	as if
(27)	as long as	as soon as	because
(30)	before	if	in order that
(33)	since	so that	than
(36)	though	unless	until

Practicing Basic Skills in Language Arts • 212

ANSWER SHEET

© 2005 Sopris West Educational Services. All rights reserved. Practicing Basic Skills in Language Arts. Purchaser has permission to photocopy this page for classroom use only.

	Correct	Error
First Try		
Second Try		

Subordinating Conjunctions

Directions: Circle the subordinating conjunctions in the sentences.

As long as you continue studying, your grades will improve. Tonya cannot go unless we are home by 9:00. You will have to

work hard if you are elected. While it snowed outside, we basked in the warmth of a roaring fire. Jared runs wherever he goes.

In order that we get home early, the meeting will be short. I haven't seen you since we were twelve years old. Marion studied

until she was ready for the test. After we left the football game, we went to the drive-in to celebrate. Although we lost, we felt

lucky to have played so well. Alex transferred into Shop II because he had already taken Shop I. We visited the farm where my

grandmother was born. I try to call home whenever I am going to be late. As soon as we moved here, we felt right at home. We

hid behind the furniture so that we could surprise Angie when she came in. We caught Rusty as he was getting ready to leave. I

would rather study now than later. Though she was young, Lu was a fine artist. Tom acts as if he owns the place. Before it gets

too late, we had better go home. Although good weather had been predicted, it rained while we were hiking. Whenever I feel

low, I just act as if nothing were wrong. Since Tyrell has been to college, he talks until he bores everyone. We went swimming

after we had finished our chores. I am taking a tough schedule so that I'll be ready for college. Because Tony is a good athlete, he

will receive a scholarship when he goes to college. Wherever I go, I see people who don't smile unless they have to. As long as

the weather remains nice, you two may play outside.

© 2005 Sopris West Educational Services. All rights reserved. Practicing Basic Skills in Language Arts. Purchaser has permission to photocopy this page for classroom use only.

ONE-MINUTE FLUENCY BUILDER SERIES

SEE TO MARK

Subordinating Conjunctions

Directions: Circle the subordinating conjunctions in the sentences.

(2) (As long as) you continue studying, your grades will improve. Tonya cannot go (unless) we are home by 9:00. You will have to

(5) work hard (if) you are elected. (While) it snowed outside, we basked in the warmth of a roaring fire. Jared runs (wherever) he goes.

(7) (In order that) we get home early, the meeting will be short. I haven't seen you (since) we were twelve years old. Marion studied

(10) (until) she was ready for the test. (After) we left the football game, we went to the drive-in to celebrate. (Although) we lost, we felt

(12) lucky to have played so well. Alex transferred into Shop II (because) he had already taken Shop I. We visited the farm (where) my

(14) grandmother was born. I try to call home (whenever) I am going to be late. (As soon as) we moved here, we felt right at home. We

(17) hid behind the furniture (so that) we could surprise Angie (when) she came in. We caught Rusty (as) he was getting ready to leave. I

(21) would rather study now (than) later. (Though) she was young, Lu was a fine artist. Tom acts (as if) he owns the place. (Before) it gets

(24) too late, we had better go home. (Although) good weather had been predicted, it rained (while) we were hiking. (Whenever) I feel

(27) low, I just act (as if) nothing were wrong. (Since) Tyrell has been to college, he talks (until) he bores everyone. We went swimming

(30) (after) we had finished our chores. I am taking a tough schedule (so that) I'll be ready for college. (Because) Tony is a good athlete, he

(34) will receive a scholarship (when) he goes to college. (Wherever) I go, I see people who don't smile (unless) they have to. (As long as)

the weather remains nice, you two may play outside.

First Try	Correct	Error
Second Try		

ANSWER SHEET

Practicing Basic Skills in Language Arts • 214

© 2005 Sopris West Educational Services. All rights reserved. Practicing Basic Skills in Language Arts. Purchaser has permission to photocopy this page for classroom use only.

ONE-MINUTE FLUENCY BUILDER SERIES

SEE TO MARK

Interjections in Sentences

Directions: Circle the interjections in the sentences below.

Ouch! That hurts! Goodness! What a haircut! Look! The moon is full. Aha! I know the trick. Oops! I dropped the glass. Oh, I

made the same mistake again. The weather here, alas, is worse than I expected. Well, I did my best. Oh! You surprised me! What!

You mean the answer was that simple! Hurrah! We won! Ah! The warm sun feels good! Help! I'm falling! Charge! The time has

come to attack. Oh, I saw that before. My friend, alas, is moving. Look out! The wall is falling! Hey! I know you. Yippee! We

won! Well, I should be leaving. Goodness! I'm ten minutes late. Oh, I think so. Pshaw! My match went out. Well, what do you

know about that? Fire! Sound the alarm! Whew! This is a hot day! Oh, that's all right. Well, I found the key at last. Ouch! That

hurts! Wow! What a hit! Ugh! I hate vegetables. Shoo! Get out of here! We are young and, oh, so glad. Ahem! I would like to

speak now. Nonsense! You can do it. Sh! I can't hear! Hey! I want to go. Hurray! We get to go! Shucks! I missed. But, gosh, what

are we going to do now? Dear me! I can't get it right. Shame! You know better. Aha! I caught you. I was hoping to go, but, alas,

I cannot. Oh, never mind. Hey! Stop that! To you this is nothing, but, ah, what a difference to me. Alas! We shall never see him

again. "Bah! Humbug!" snarled Scrooge. At last! A good meal! Please! I must have your attention. Caution! Blind curve ahead.

Crunch! The two cars collided. Oh boy, what a close call. Hey, look where you're going!

Practicing Basic Skills in Language Arts • 215

© 2005 Sopris West Educational Services. All rights reserved. Practicing Basic Skills in Language Arts. Purchaser has permission to photocopy this page for classroom use only.

	Correct	Error
First Try		
Second Try		

SEE TO MARK

Interjections in Sentences

Directions: Circle the interjections in the sentences below.

(Ouch!) That hurts! (Goodness!) What a haircut! (Look!) The moon is full. (Aha!) I know the trick. (Oops!) I dropped the glass. (Oh!) I (6)

made the same mistake again. The weather here, (alas) is worse than I expected. (Well) I did my best. (Oh!) You surprised me! (What!) (10)

You mean the answer was that simple! (Hurrah!) We won! (Ah!) The warm sun feels good! (Help!) I'm falling! (Charge!) The time has (14)

come to attack. (Oh) I saw that before. My friend, (alas) is moving. (Look out!) The wall is falling! (Hey!) I know you. (Yippee!) We (19)

won! (Well) I should be leaving. (Goodness!) I'm ten minutes late. (Oh) I think so. (Pshaw!) My match went out. (Well) what do you (24)

know about that? (Fire!) Sound the alarm! (Whew!) This is a hot day! (Oh) that's all right. (Well) I found the key at last. (Ouch!) That (29)

hurts! (Wow!) What a hit! (Ugh!) I hate vegetables. (Shoo!) Get out of here! We are young and, (oh) so glad. (Ahem!) I would like to (34)

speak now. (Nonsense!) You can do it. (Sh!) I can't hear! (Hey!) I want to go. (Hurray!) We get to go! (Shucks!) I missed. But, (gosh) what (40)

are we going to do now? (Dear me!) I can't get it right. (Shame!) You know better. (Aha!) I caught you. I was hoping to go, but, (alas) (44)

I cannot. (Oh) never mind. (Hey!) Stop that! To you this is nothing, but, (ah) what a difference to me. (Alas!) We shall never see him (48)

again. "(Bah!) (Humbug!)" snarled Scrooge. (At last!) A good meal! (Please!) I must have your attention. (Caution!) Blind curve ahead. (53)

(Crunch!) The two cars collided. (Oh boy) what a close call. (Hey) look where you're going! (56)

ANSWER SHEET

Practicing Basic Skills in Language Arts • 216

© 2005 Sopris West Educational Services. All rights reserved. Practicing Basic Skills in Language Arts. Purchaser has permission to photocopy this page for classroom use only.

Sentence Structure

Simple Subject and Verb in Sentences.........219
Simple Subject and Verb in Sentences.........221
Simple Subjects, Verbs, and Helping
    Verbs in Sentences.................................223
Subject and Verb in Sentences.....................225
Compound Subject and Verb in
    Sentences..227
Direct Objects—Answers Question
    What or Whom..229
Direct Object in Sentences...........................231
Subject, Verb, and Direct Object in
    Sentences..233
Indirect Object—Answers Question to
    Whom..235
Indirect Object in Sentences........................237
Direct Object and Indirect Object in
    Sentences..239
Predicate Nominative in Sentences.............241
Predicate Noun or Pronoun in Sentences....243
Predicate Nouns, Pronouns, and
    Linking Verbs in Sentences.....................245
Predicate Adjectives in Sentences...............247
Predicate Adjectives and Linking
    Verbs in Sentences.................................249
Review Sheet: Direct Objects, Indirect
    Objects, Predicate Adjectives, and
    Predicate Nominatives in Sentences........251
Six Parts of Sentences.................................253
Subject-Verb Agreement..............................255
Subject-Verb Agreement..............................257
Subject-Verb Agreement..............................259
Subject-Verb Agreement..............................261
Subject-Verb Agreement..............................263
Indefinite Pronouns and Verb
    Agreement...265
Subjects Joined By Or-Nor, Either-Or,
    Neither-Nor, and Verb Agreement..........267

Compound Subjects and Verb
    Agreement...269
Compound Subjects and Verb
    Agreement...271
Plural Subject-Verb Agreement—
    Fill in the Blank....................................273
Singular Subject-Verb Agreement—
    Fill in the Blank....................................275
Subject-Verb Agreement—Don't/Doesn't....277
Subject-Verb Agreement—Don't/Doesn't....279
Subject-Verb Agreement—Is/Are,
    Was/Were, Has/Have..............................281
Noun Clauses..283
Adjective Clauses..285
Adverb Clauses...287
Noun, Adjective, and Adverb Clauses.........289
Subordinate Clauses....................................291
Independent Clauses...................................293
Compound Sentences Into Independent
    Clauses..295
Form Compound Sentences Using
    And, But, Or, Nor, So.............................297
Form Compound Sentences Using
    And, But, Or, Nor, So.............................299
Form Complex Sentences.............................301
Form Complex Sentences.............................303
Sentence Fragments and Complete
    Sentences..305
Complete Sentences and Sentence
    Fragments..307
Review Fragments and Sentences................309
Sentence Fragments and Run-On
    Sentences..311
Fragments, Run-Ons, and Complete
    Sentences..313
Types of Sentences.....................................315

SEE TO MARK

Simple Subject and Verb in Sentences

Directions: Underline the simple subject once; the verb twice.

	First Try	Second Try
Correct		
Error		

1. The band marched down the street.

2. The bright leaves fell on the ground.

3. Sherry jumped happily.

4. The cook cooked the food for the feast.

5. Flour was spilled on the floor.

6. The captain dropped the rope.

7. The librarian typed the letter.

8. Pedro ran and jumped in the snow.

9. The children started to put away their things.

10. The lady bought the hat.

11. The girls laughed and jumped because they were happy.

12. The janitor washed and waxed the floor.

13. My best friend bought a chemistry set.

14. The settlers boiled the sap of maple trees.

15. Some men split logs into boards.

16. The women wove baskets from fibers.

17. The castle stands in that dark forest.

18. A high wall surrounds the castle.

19. A famous nobleman still lives there.

20. A flickering light flashed across the bay.

21. A frog leaped across the path.

22. The scout crept into the woods.

23. My brother stood on the stage.

24. A stranger stood in the hallway.

25. The mighty oak crashed down.

26. In the clearing stood a log cabin.

27. Rosa's school work was completed.

28. David is looking for his mother.

29. Two hungry hawks circled the barnyard.

30. Up and down the hall paced Coach Harris.

31. Three sand crabs were crawling on the beach.

32. The bobcat is smaller than the cougar.

33. The crows are scolding the fox.

34. This little wildcat frightens many people.

35. The steep canyon rose high above the river.

36. Dogs bark.

Practicing Basic Skills in Language Arts • 219

© 2005 Sopris West Educational Services. All rights reserved. Practicing Basic Skills in Language Arts. Purchaser has permission to photocopy this page for classroom use only.

	First Try	Second Try
Correct		
Error		

Simple Subject and Verb in Sentences

Directions: Underline the simple subject once; the verb twice.

1. The band marched down the street. (2)
2. The bright leaves fell on the ground. (4)
3. Sherry jumped happily. (6)
4. The cook cooked the food for the feast. (8)
5. Flour was spilled on the floor. (11)
6. The captain dropped the rope. (13)
7. The librarian typed the letter. (15)
8. Pedro ran and jumped in the snow. (18)
9. The children started to put away their things. (20)
10. The lady bought the hat. (22)
11. The girls laughed and jumped because they were happy. (27)
12. The janitor washed and waxed the floor. (30)
13. My best friend bought a chemistry set. (32)
14. The settlers boiled the sap of maple trees. (34)
15. Some men split logs into boards. (36)
16. The women wove baskets from fibers. (38)
17. The castle stands in that dark forest. (40)
18. A high wall surrounds the castle. (42)

19. A famous nobleman still lives there. (44)
20. A flickering light flashed across the bay. (46)
21. A frog leaped across the path. (48)
22. The scout crept into the woods. (50)
23. My brother stood on the stage. (52)
24. A stranger stood in the hallway. (54)
25. The mighty oak crashed down. (56)
26. In the clearing stood a log cabin. (58)
27. Rosa's school work was completed. (61)
28. David is looking for his mother. (64)
29. Two hungry hawks circled the barnyard. (66)
30. Up and down the hall paced Coach Harris. (69)
31. Three sand crabs were crawling on the beach. (72)
32. The bobcat is smaller than the cougar. (74)
33. The crows are scolding the fox. (77)
34. This little wildcat frightens many people. (79)
35. The steep canyon rose high above the river. (81)
36. Dogs bark. (83)

© 2005 Sopris West Educational Services. All rights reserved. Practicing Basic Skills in Language Arts. Purchaser has permission to photocopy this page for classroom use only.

SEE TO MARK

Simple Subject and Verb in Sentences

Directions: Underline the simple subject once; the verb twice.

	First Try	Second Try
Correct		
Error		

1. My cousins live in Indianapolis.

2. The swimmers waited for the starting whistle.

3. Nancy played the flute in the band.

4. Almost all the beekeepers wear protective masks.

5. Jamal helped with the rink after school.

6. The two boys built a chicken coop.

7. Lucia caught the fly easily.

8. The copilot radioed the tower.

9. Tall elms lined the avenue.

10. The three girls walked home together.

11. The desktop was uneven.

12. The three boys were cousins.

13. The farmer noticed the vacant stall.

14. Their car is a compact.

15. That CD sounds scratchy.

16. The washing machine had stopped.

17. Kathy had been ready for over an hour.

18. The girls have finished their work.

19. The two ducks were huddling near the pond.

20. Chuck does not like chocolate ice cream.

21. I will endorse this candidate.

22. The workers pushed and shoved with their shoulders.

23. Nisha folded the picture and cut it.

24. Everyone swam, played ball, and then ate a good lunch.

25. Marie and her father skate and ski together.

26. High above our heads stretched the Bay Bridge.

27. Over the housetops roared the wind.

28. Please walk the dog after dinner, you

29. Ling ran through the yard.

30. The kittens wandered around the room.

31. Her teacher read the story to the class.

32. Have you seen that movie yet?

33. Their new car was bright red.

34. The children listened to the music.

Practicing Basic Skills in Language Arts • 221

© 2005 Sopris West Educational Services. All rights reserved. Practicing Basic Skills in Language Arts. Purchaser has permission to photocopy this page for classroom use only.

SEE TO MARK

Simple Subject and Verb in Sentences

Directions: Underline the simple subject once; the verb twice.

	First Try	Second Try
Correct		
Error		

1. My cousins live in Indianapolis. (2)

2. The swimmers waited for the starting whistle. (4)

3. Nancy played the flute in the band. (6)

4. Almost all the beekeepers wear protective masks. (8)

5. Jamal helped with the rink after school. (10)

6. The two boys built a chicken coop. (12)

7. Lucia caught the fly easily. (14)

8. The copilot radioed the tower. (16)

9. Tall elms lined the avenue. (18)

10. The three girls walked home together. (20)

11. The desktop was uneven. (22)

12. The three boys were cousins. (24)

13. The farmer noticed the vacant stall. (26)

14. Their car is a compact. (28)

15. That CD sounds scratchy. (30)

16. The washing machine had stopped. (33)

17. Kathy had been ready for over an hour. (36)

18. The girls have finished their work. (39)

19. The two ducks were huddling near the pond. (42)

20. Chuck does not like chocolate ice cream. (45)

21. I will endorse this candidate. (48)

22. The workers pushed and shoved with their shoulders. (51)

23. Nisha folded the picture and cut it. (54)

24. Everyone swam, played ball, and then ate a good lunch. (58)

25. Marie and her father skate and ski together. (62)

26. High above our heads stretched the Bay Bridge. (65)

27. Over the housetops roared the wind. (67)

28. Please walk the dog after dinner, you (69)

29. Ling ran through the yard. (71)

30. The kittens wandered around the room. (73)

31. Her teacher read the story to the class. (75)

32. Have you seen that movie yet? (78)

33. Their new car was bright red. (80)

34. The children listened to the music. (82)

© 2005 Sopris West Educational Services. All rights reserved. Practicing Basic Skills in Language Arts. Purchaser has permission to photocopy this page for classroom use only.

ONE-MINUTE FLUENCY
BUILDER SERIES

SEE TO MARK

Simple Subjects, Verbs, and Helping Verbs in Sentences

Directions: Underline the simple subject once and the verb twice; circle all helping verbs.

Scoring: Give one point for underlining the correct subject, one point for underlining the correct verb, and one point for circling the correct helping verb.

	Correct	Error
First Try		
Second Try		

1. Most fires are caused by carelessness.

2. Will the curtain rise soon?

3. The telephone was invented by Alexander Graham Bell.

4. I shall go to the store.

5. He would have come anyway.

6. The girls did not have a good time at the party.

7. Jack was helping his father.

8. We must answer this letter soon.

9. I am waiting for my family to arrive.

10. I do not know him or his friend.

11. Have you ever seen a redwood tree?

12. Dad could have paid the bill by himself.

13. You must have been waiting for a long time.

14. They did not live happily ever after.

15. Are the robins building their nests yet?

16. Jerry does go to a special school on Saturdays.

17. They were trying too hard to win the race.

18. Who has stolen Joe's bicycle?

19. I have broken my new pencil.

20. Have you given him the money for the football tickets?

21. They have decided not to play in this game.

22. The Wrigley Building is located in Chicago.

23. Marie will be arriving later than the rest of the group.

24. John and Malik were running very fast and won the race.

25. He should have done better on the spelling test this week.

26. Do you understand that math problem on the board?

27. Jane has borrowed a book and has taken it to school.

28. She did not see the cat in the box.

29. We will walk to the store after lunch.

30. How many girls are going to the game?

31. Jerry and Manuel have been there before.

32. Mother will join us at the movie.

33. She should have been here by now.

34. We will be rowing the boat across the lake.

35. Carlos was answering the telephone.

36. He is catching a bad cold.

Practicing Basic Skills in Language Arts • 223

© 2005 Sopris West Educational Services. All rights reserved. Practicing Basic Skills in Language Arts. Purchaser has permission to photocopy this page for classroom use only.

ONE MINUTE FLUENCY
BUILDER SERIES

SEE TO MARK

Simple Subjects, Verbs, and Helping Verbs in Sentences

Directions: Underline the simple subject once and the verb twice; circle all helping verbs.

Scoring: Give one point for underlining the correct subject, one point underlining the correct verb, and one point for circling the correct helping verb.

First Try		
	Correct	Error
First Try		
Second Try		

1. Most fires (are) caused by carelessness. (3)
2. (Will) the curtain rise soon? (6)
3. The telephone (was) invented by Alexander Graham Bell. (9)
4. I (shall) go to the store. (12)
5. He (would have) come anyway. (15)
6. The girls (did) not have a good time at the party. (18)
7. Jack (was) helping his father. (21)
8. We (must) answer this letter soon. (24)
9. I (am) waiting for my family to arrive. (27)
10. I (do) not know him or his friend. (30)
11. (Have) you ever seen a redwood tree? (33)
12. Dad (could have) paid the bill by himself. (36)
13. You (must have been) waiting for a long time. (39)
14. They (did) not live happily ever after. (42)
15. (Are) the robins building their nests yet? (45)
16. Jerry (does) go to a special school on Saturdays. (48)
17. They (were) trying too hard to win the race. (51)
18. Who (has) stolen Joe's bicycle? (54)

19. I (have) broken my new pencil. (57)
20. (Have) you given him the money for the football tickets? (60)
21. They (have) decided not to play in this game. (63)
22. The Wrigley Building (is) located in Chicago. (66)
23. Marie (will be) arriving later than the rest of the group. (69)
24. John and Malik (were) running very fast and won the race. (72)
25. He (should have) done better on the spelling test this week. (75)
26. (Do) you understand that math problem on the board? (78)
27. Jane (has) borrowed a book and (has) taken it to school. (83)
28. She (did) not see the cat in the box. (86)
29. We (will) walk to the store after lunch. (89)
30. How many girls (are) going to the game? (92)
31. Jerry and Manuel (have been) there before. (95)
32. Mother (will) join us at the movie. (98)
33. She (should have been) here by now. (101)
34. We (will be) rowing the boat across the lake. (104)
35. Carlos (was) answering the telephone. (107)
36. He (is) catching a bad cold. (110)

ANSWER SHEET

Practicing Basic Skills in Language Arts • 224

© 2005 Sopris West Educational Services. All rights reserved. Practicing Basic Skills in Language Arts. Purchaser has permission to photocopy this page for classroom use only.

SEE TO MARK

Subject and Verb in Sentences

Directions: Put an S over the subject and a V over the verb in each sentence.

My father, tired and ill, went to bed early. The manager of the team praised his players. Out of the cage flew the bird. Slowly the water dripped from the roof. Have the children dressed? The squirrel ran up the tree. Drink your milk. Very carefully he wrapped the package. Inside the house all was quiet. The old man with his dog was lost in the storm. Marcus, with Jordan, ran to the corner. Will you write me often? Into the puddle fell the child. Lu, Emily, and Nina sang all day. The driver of the bus sounded his horn. May Harry go on the boat ride? At the corner of Main and State Streets we met Luis. The boy, cold and hungry, sat by the fireplace. Father and Mother must have gone to the show. Suddenly we heard a loud cry. Lin and Joe walked home from school. Have you seen Rosa recently? Fortunately, the door was strong. We turned out the light. You should go to the game with us. Franco talked and we listened. In the park we met Clay and Dan. The little girl with the doll is my niece. Suddenly it started to rain. Shall we walk home? Beside the house stood the car. Nervously he opened the letter. The child cried bitterly. About an hour ago, Chien called me. Do you want me to help you? My teacher of English is Mr. Cossen. Onto the couch jumped the dog. That tall girl is captain of the softball team. My French teacher was Ms. Rose. May I go with you? In the meantime, Jane did her lessons. Frequently, I walk to school. I studied hard for that last test. Jim and Latoya had dinner. You should dance more often. The man with the moustache is Joe's father. The captain steered the ship across the ocean. Springtime fills us with new hope. The snow covered the roads overnight. Which of the three men is the owner? The druggist filled the prescription. Some fish swim vertically. The house faces the east. Have the pigeons flown away? Give me the book. I shall be on time today. He was whistling at the umpire.

Correct	Error
First Try	
Second Try	

© 2005 Sopris West Educational Services. All rights reserved. Practicing Basic Skills in Language Arts. Purchaser has permission to photocopy this page for classroom use only.

ONE-MINUTE FLUENCY BUILDER SERIES

SEE TO MARK

Subject and Verb in Sentences

Directions: Put an S over the subject and a V over the verb in each sentence.

	Correct	Error
First Try		
Second Try		

My father, tired and ill, went to bed early. The manager of the team praised his players. Out of the cage flew the bird. Slowly the (6)

water dripped from the roof. Have the children dressed? The squirrel ran up the tree. Drink your milk. Very carefully he wrapped (15)

the package. Inside the house all was quiet. The old man with his dog was lost in the storm. Marcus, with Jordan, ran to the (22)

corner. Will you write me often? Into the puddle fell the child. Lu, Emily, and Nina sang all day. The driver of the bus sounded (33)

his horn. May Harry go on the boat ride? At the corner of Main and State Streets we met Luis. The boy, cold and hungry, sat by (40)

the fireplace. Father and Mother must have gone to the show. Suddenly we heard a loud cry. Lin and Joe walked home from (50)

school. Have you seen Rosa recently? Fortunately, the door was strong. We turned out the light. You should go to the game with (60)

us. Franco talked and we listened. In the park we met Clay and Dan. The little girl with the doll is my niece. Suddenly it started (70)

to rain. Shall we walk home? Beside the house stood the car. Nervously he opened the letter. The child cried bitterly. About an (79)

hour ago, Chien called me. Do you want me to help you? My teacher of English is Mr. Cossen. Onto the couch jumped the dog. (88)

That tall girl is captain of the softball team. My French teacher was Ms. Rose. May I go with you? In the meantime, Jane did (97)

her lessons. Frequently, I walk to school. I studied hard for that last test. Jim and Latoya had dinner. You should dance more (107)

often. The man with the moustache is Joe's father. The captain steered the ship across the ocean. Springtime fills us with new (113)

hope. The snow covered the roads overnight. Which of the three men is the owner? The druggist filled the prescription. Some (119)

fish swim vertically. The house faces the east. Have the pigeons flown away? Give me the book. I shall be on time today. He was (132)

whistling at the umpire. (133)

© 2005 Sopris West Educational Services. All rights reserved. Practicing Basic Skills in Language Arts. Purchaser has permission to photocopy this page for classroom use only.

	Correct	Error
First Try		
Second Try		

SEE TO MARK

Compound Subject and Verb in Sentences
Directions: Circle the compound subjects and underline the verbs.

Ana and her friends are leaving now. The stack of papers on the table can be thrown away. Rick picked the ball up

and threw it. She and her sister drove to Salt Lake City for a day of shopping. Higher and higher soared the balloon.

Kaili, Sherrie, Lindi, and Gaylynn will be on the yearbook staff this year. Lorena went to her mother for help on the long,

difficult assignment. Van and Greg are the boys in the picture. Dad or Pedro will meet you in front of the school at 5 o'clock.

The policeman and the paramedic pried the door open. This box of pencils should not be opened. One of their prize dogs is ill.

Are the players, the band, and the cheerleaders taking this bus to the game? Judy and Lola sat on the floor, listened to records,

and ate popcorn. Thunder and lightning descended on the valley. My mother and my father tell me not to bother them.

Tina and I try not to make any noise. My older brother and his friend often study French together. The squirrel, frightened

by the boy, ran up the tree. Slowly the water dripped from the roof. The old man and his dog were lost in the storm.

Fred and Manuel ran rapidly to the grocery store. Amy, Desiree, and Tanya sang and danced all day. Suddenly we heard a loud cry

coming from the musty basement. You and Mike should have gone to the game with us. Mrs. Ukura, Mrs. Dean, and Ms. Oswald

teach English at different schools. Scott and Lamar walked home from school. In the park we met Mindy and Tammy.

Shaun and Nick will enter the tennis tournament next month. She and her friends will have to explain to their mothers how

the accident happened. The passenger looked suspicious as he approached the pilot. Hal and Pedro can now give first aid to the

injured. My dog and cat have long, tan fur. After the long walk in the park, Vanessa and Cindy stopped for refreshments at the

7-Eleven store.

© 2005 Sopris West Educational Services. All rights reserved. Practicing Basic Skills in Language Arts. Purchaser has permission to photocopy this page for classroom use only.

Compound Subject and Verb in Sentences

Directions: Circle the compound subjects and underline the verbs.

	Correct	Error
First Try		
Second Try		

(Ana and her friends) are leaving now. The stack of papers on the table can be thrown away. Rick picked the ball up (4)

and threw it. (She and her sister) drove to Salt Lake City for a day of shopping. Higher and higher soared the balloon. (8)

(Kaili, Sherrie, Lindi, and Gaylynn) will be on the yearbook staff this year. Lorena went to her mother for help on the long, (11)

difficult assignment. (Van and Greg) are the boys in the picture. (Dad or Pedro) will meet you in front of the school at 5 o'clock. (15)

The (policeman and the paramedic) pried the door open. This box of pencils should not be opened. One of their prize dogs is ill. (19)

Are the (players, the band, and the cheerleaders) taking this bus to the game? (Judy and Lola) sat on the floor, listened to records, (25)

and ate popcorn. (Thunder and lightning) descended on the valley. (My mother and my father) tell me not to bother them. (30)

(Tina and I) try not to make any noise. My older (brother and his friend) often study French together. The squirrel, frightened (34)

by the boy, ran up the tree. Slowly the water dripped from the roof. The old (man and his dog) were lost in the storm. (38)

(Fred and Manuel) ran rapidly to the grocery store. (Amy, Desiree, and Tanya) sang and danced all day. Suddenly we heard a loud cry (44)

coming from the musty basement. (You and Mike) should have gone to the game with us. (Mrs. Ukura, Mrs. Dean, and Ms. Oswald) (47)

teach English at different schools. (Scott and Lamar) walked home from school. In the park we met Mindy and Tammy. (51)

(Shaun and Nick) will enter the tennis tournament next month. (She and her friends) will have to explain to their mothers how (55)

the accident happened. The passenger looked suspicious as he approached the pilot. (Hal and Pedro) can now give first aid to the (59)

injured. (My dog and cat) have long, tan fur. After the long walk in the park, (Vanessa and Cindy) stopped for refreshments at the (63)

7-Eleven store.

ANSWER SHEET

© 2005 Sopris West Educational Services. All rights reserved. Practicing Basic Skills in Language Arts. Purchaser has permission to photocopy this page for classroom use only.

SEE TO WRITE

Direct Objects—Answers Question What or Whom

Directions: Write the word that received the action of the verb or that showed the result of the action. It answers the question "What?" or "Whom?" after an action verb.

	First Try	Second Try
Correct		
Error		

Jane was writing an essay. Was writing what? _____

The sudden whistle surprised me. Surprised whom? _____

Elena cut the material. Cut what? _____

Roy High lost the championship. Lost what? _____

At the top of the hill we saw him. Saw whom? _____

An old elm tree shades our front lawn. Shades what? _____

I have always admired your good manners. Have admired what? _____

Father painted the room. Painted what? _____

Did Mei pick these flowers for the mantel? Did pick what? _____

Tom ate a big breakfast. Ate what? _____

He grabbed his books. Grabbed what? _____

We met them at the theatre. Met whom? _____

Tyra and I took a trip to the museum. Took what? _____

The coach gave the passes to us. Gave what? _____

Freda wrote and directed the one-act play. Wrote and directed what? _____

Shaun planted oats and wheat yesterday. Planted what? _____

Can you tell me where the party will be? Can tell whom? _____

Weber High won the basketball tournament. Won what? _____

The police telephoned them after the accident. Telephoned whom? _____

A heavy snowfall almost buried the old tree stump. Buried what? _____

The store manager greeted her cordially. Greeted whom? _____

Roberto found a billfold but lost his watch today. Found what? _____

Lost what? _____

Each student must read a novel and a biography for English. Read what? _____

Dad drove me to the store to buy the treat. Drove whom? _____

He expressed serious doubt that Ted would play again this season. Expressed what? _____

I can explain the problem. Can explain what? _____

I have lost my keys and my gloves. Have lost what? _____

Rick sent a card from Hawaii. Sent what? _____

© 2005 Sopris West Educational Services. All rights reserved. Practicing Basic Skills in Language Arts. Purchaser has permission to photocopy this page for classroom use only.

SEE TO WRITE

Direct Objects—Answers Question What or Whom

Directions: Write the word that received the action of the verb or that showed the result of the action. It answers the question "What?" or "Whom?" after an action verb.

	First Try	Second Try
Correct		
Error		

Jane was writing an essay. Was writing what? __**essay**__

The sudden whistle surprised me. Surprised whom? __**me**__

Elena cut the material. Cut what? __**material**__

Roy High lost the championship. Lost what? __**championship**__

At the top of the hill we saw him. Saw whom? __**him**__

An old elm tree shades our front lawn. Shades what? __**lawn**__

I have always admired your good manners. Have admired what? __**manners**__

Father painted the room. Painted what? __**room**__

Did Mei pick these flowers for the mantel? Did pick what? __**flowers**__

He grabbed his books. Grabbed what? __**books**__

Tom ate a big breakfast. Ate what? __**breakfast**__

We met them at the theatre. Met whom? __**them**__

Tyra and I took a trip to the museum. Took what? __**trip**__

The coach gave the passes to us. Gave what? __**passes**__

Freda wrote and directed the one-act play. Wrote and directed what? __**play**__

Shaun planted oats and wheat yesterday. Planted what? __**oats and wheat**__

Can you tell me where the party will be? Can tell whom? __**me**__

Weber High won the basketball tournament. Won what? __**tournament**__

The police telephoned them after the accident. Telephoned whom? __**them**__

A heavy snowfall almost buried the old tree stump. Buried what? __**stump**__

The store manager greeted her cordially. Greeted whom? __**her**__

Roberto found a billfold but lost his watch today. Found what? __**billfold**__   Lost what? __**watch**__

Each student must read a novel and a biography for English. Read what? __**novel and biography**__

Dad drove me to the store to buy the treat. Drove whom? __**me**__

I can explain the problem. Can explain what? __**problem**__

He expressed serious doubt that Ted would play again this season. Expressed what? __**doubt**__

I have lost my keys and my gloves. Have lost what? __**keys and gloves**__

Rick sent a card from Hawaii. Sent what? __**card**__

(1)
(3)
(5)
(6)
(8)
(10)
(12)
(13)
(15)
(16)
(18)
(19)
(20)
(22)
(24)
(25)
(26)
(28)
(29)

ANSWER SHEET

Practicing Basic Skills in Language Arts • 230

© 2005 Sopris West Educational Services. All rights reserved. Practicing Basic Skills in Language Arts. Purchaser has permission to photocopy this page for classroom use only.

SEE TO MARK

	First Try	Second Try
Correct		
Error		

Direct Object in Sentences
Directions: Underline the direct objects.

The hunter paddled the canoe swiftly upstream. He then shot a deer. I will investigate the disturbance. The old miner killed

three wildcats near his cabin. They fired the rockets into the air. We saw Linda during the holidays. Several people witnessed

the accident. The boys flew their Jolly Green Giant kites high into the sky. Jack will meet you in the library. The car hit a post.

Wendy cut the material with her new scissors. Salute the flag. Can you help her? Father mixed his own paint to get the right

color. The teacher is still grading our papers. I have lost my keys and gloves. I called him yesterday. Did you ever see such a huge

crowd? Marci was writing a humorous essay for English. Huntsville High School lost the championship yesterday. Stephanie

made a coat in her sewing class this year. Close the door. Mother painted the room. She can speak French, German, Spanish, and

Italian. How much money did you lose? Bring your fishing tackle with you. Mom is washing the car. Sign your name here. He

is reading a magazine while he is waiting. Have you watered the plants lately? Sue brought her pet rabbit and squirrel to school.

Have you ever heard the cry of the loon? Uncle Sam took me to the ball game. The captain shouts quick, sharp orders. Jess took

his brother to the play last night. Where else can you enjoy such beautiful scenery as we have in Utah? The chairman appointed

Huey, Louey, and Dewey to the committee. Who lost his pen? We'll see Dorothy and her at the wrestling meet. Everyone

disliked his grumbling. She threw the ball. Lightning struck the tall pine tree on the hill. The old soldier told many war stories.

The snowfall spoiled the plans for our picnic. I expect to relax and to rest. We enjoyed having you here. I selected what I

wanted. Many people watch boxing in the evening. I want to go with you. He wanted to fly to Disneyland. Her father likes to

fish in any kind of weather. The director of the band dislikes loud playing. We enjoyed going with you.

Practicing Basic Skills in Language Arts • 231

© 2005 Sopris West Educational Services. All rights reserved. Practicing Basic Skills in Language Arts. Purchaser has permission to photocopy this page for classroom use only.

ONE-MINUTE FLUENCY BUILDER SERIES

SEE TO MARK

Direct Object in Sentences
Directions: Underline the direct objects.

	First Try	Second Try
Correct		
Error		

The hunter paddled the canoe swiftly upstream. He then shot a deer. I will investigate the disturbance. The old miner killed (3)

three wildcats near his cabin. They fired the rockets into the air. We saw Linda during the holidays. Several people witnessed (6)

the accident. The boys flew their Jolly Green Giant kites high into the sky. Jack will meet you in the library. The car hit a post. (10)

Wendy cut the material with her new scissors. Salute the flag. Can you help her? Father mixed his own paint to get the right (14)

color. The teacher is still grading our papers. I have lost my keys and gloves. I called him yesterday. Did you ever see such a huge (18)

crowd? Marci was writing a humorous essay for English. Huntsville High School lost the championship yesterday. Stephanie (21)

made a coat in her sewing class this year. Close the door. Mother painted the room. She can speak French, German, Spanish, and (27)

Italian. How much money did you lose? Bring your fishing tackle with you. Mom is washing the car. Sign your name here. He (32)

is reading a magazine while he is waiting. Have you watered the plants lately? Sue brought her pet rabbit and squirrel to school. (36)

Have you ever heard the cry of the loon? Uncle Sam took me to the ball game. The captain shouts quick, sharp orders. Jess took (39)

his brother to the play last night. Where else can you enjoy such beautiful scenery as we have in Utah? The chairman appointed (41)

Huey, Louey, and Dewey to the committee. Who lost his pen? We'll see Dorothy and her at the wrestling meet. Everyone (46)

disliked his grumbling. She threw the ball. Lightning struck the tall pine tree on the hill. The old soldier told many war stories. (50)

The snowfall spoiled the plans for our picnic. I expect to relax and to rest. We enjoyed having you here. I selected what I (55)

wanted. Many people watch boxing in the evening. I want to go with you. He wanted to fly to Disneyland. Her father likes to (59)

fish in any kind of weather. The director of the band dislikes loud playing. We enjoyed going with you. (61)

ANSWER SHEET

Practicing Basic Skills in Language Arts • 232

© 2005 Sopris West Educational Services. All rights reserved. Practicing Basic Skills in Language Arts. Purchaser has permission to photocopy this page for classroom use only.

ONE-MINUTE FLUENCY
BUILDER SERIES

SEE TO MARK

Subject, Verb, and Direct Object in Sentences

Directions: Put an S over each subject, a V over each verb, and a D over each direct object.

	Correct	Error
First Try		
Second Try		

Mike shined Mr. Brown's shoes for him. All the children waved tiny flags. Someone has senselessly destroyed our fence. Who

will inherit his large estate? The new principal read some verses of poetry during the assembly. Have you ever returned those

library books? The first shot of the hunter wounded the lion. She evidently did not understand you. Did you write a letter

to your sister? Last spring we bought a new boat. Father bought new gloves, shoes, and socks yesterday. Elaine's parents took

her to the zoo. The guide at the entrance distributed several pamphlets about the animals. They walked around the building

and studied the giraffes inside. Next they moved away and watched the seals. The Magna Carta gave the people very few new

liberties. Bob must have accidentally dialed the wrong number. Afterwards the children played baseball and ran races. The class

held a picnic in Thatcher Woods. Have you washed and ironed your dress? Every person there enjoyed the hot dogs.

Practicing Basic Skills in Language Arts • 233

© 2005 Sopris West Educational Services. All rights reserved. Practicing Basic Skills in Language Arts. Purchaser has permission to photocopy this page for classroom use only.

ONE-MINUTE FLUENCY BUILDER SERIES

SEE TO MARK

Subject, Verb, and Direct Object in Sentences

Directions: Put an S over each subject, a V over each verb, and a D over each direct object.

	Correct	Error
First Try		
Second Try		

(11) Mike shined Mr. Brown's shoes for him. All the children waved tiny flags. Someone has senselessly destroyed our fence. Who

(20) will inherit his large estate? The new principal read some verses of poetry during the assembly. Have you ever returned those

(32) library books? The first shot of the hunter wounded the lion. She evidently did not understand you. Did you write a letter

(42) to your sister? Last spring we bought a new boat. Father bought new gloves, shoes, and socks yesterday. Elaine's parents took

(48) her to the zoo. The guide at the entrance distributed several pamphlets about the animals. They walked around the building

(56) and studied the giraffes inside. Next they moved away and watched the seals. The Magna Carta gave the people very few new

(67) liberties. Bob must have accidentally dialed the wrong number. Afterwards the children played baseball and ran races. The class

(77) held a picnic in Thatcher Woods. Have you washed and ironed your dress? Every person there enjoyed the hot dogs.

ANSWER SHEET

Practicing Basic Skills in Language Arts • 234

© 2005 Sopris West Educational Services. All rights reserved. Practicing Basic Skills in Language Arts. Purchaser has permission to photocopy this page for classroom use only.

Indirect Object—Answers Question to Whom

Directions: Write the word that answers the question for each sentence.

ONE MINUTE FLUENCY BUILDER SERIES

	First Try	Second Try
Correct		
Error		

Bea mailed Marjorie a letter. Mailed to whom? _____ Nyle bought the child some candy. Bought for whom? _____

_____ The merchant sent the customer some records. Sent to whom? _____ The clerk gave

me the book. Gave to whom? _____ Dad bought my brother a second-hand bicycle. Bought for whom? _____

I wouldn't lend him a penny. Lend to whom? _____ Who sent Kay and Pat those

valentines? Sent to whom? _____ We sold them some raffle tickets. Sold to whom? _____

They gave Joyce the medal. Gave to whom? _____ Did you buy her a present? Did buy for whom? _____

_____ Father bought me a Susan B. Anthony dollar coin. Bought for whom? _____ The speaker

told the class his experiences during the war. Told to whom? _____ The history teacher gave Mr. Nader time for

an illustrated talk. Gave to whom? _____ Her dad bought Teri a Camaro. Bought for whom? _____

The Napoleonic wars taught Europe little about the waste of war. Taught to whom? _____ The World War

brought the American people many new problems. Brought to whom? _____ The lecturer had given us many

problems for further consideration. Had given to whom? _____ Give Colby and him the book. Give to whom? _____

_____ The explanation gave Nick considerable help. Gave to whom? _____ Send my sister that bill

for the groceries. Send to whom? _____ He lent her his assignment sheet. Lent to whom? _____

The lawyer had written his client's opponent a long letter of explanation. Had written to whom? _____ He sent

all the members notices of the meeting. Sent to whom? _____ Mr. Pearson taught us geometry. Taught to whom? _____

_____ The committee has given the basketball team a special trophy. Has given to whom? _____

Will you make mother and me another table? Will make for whom? _____

© 2005 Sopris West Educational Services. All rights reserved. Practicing Basic Skills in Language Arts. Purchaser has permission to photocopy this page for classroom use only.

ONE-MINUTE FLUENCY
BUILDER SERIES

SEE TO WRITE

Indirect Object—Answers Question to Whom

Directions: Write the word that answers the question for each sentence.

	First Try	Second Try
Correct		
Error		

(1) Bea mailed Marjorie a letter. Mailed to whom? **Marjorie** Nyle bought the child some candy. Bought for whom?

(3) **child** The merchant sent the customer some records. Sent to whom? **customer** The clerk gave

(4) me the book. Gave to whom? **me** Dad bought my brother a second-hand bicycle. Bought for whom?

(6) **brother** I wouldn't lend him a penny. Lend to whom? **him** Who sent Kay and Pat those

(8) valentines? Sent to whom? **Kay and Pat** We sold them some raffle tickets. Sold to whom? **them**

(9) They gave Joyce the medal. Gave to whom? **Joyce** Did you buy her a present? Did buy for whom?

(11) **her** Father bought me a Susan B. Anthony dollar coin. Bought for whom? **me** The speaker

(12) told the class his experiences during the war. Told to whom? **class** The history teacher gave Mr. Nader time for

(14) an illustrated talk. Gave to whom? **Mr. Nader** Her dad bought Teri a Camaro. Bought for whom? **Teri**

(15) The Napoleonic wars taught Europe little about the waste of war. Taught to whom? **Europe** The World War

(16) brought the American people many new problems. Brought to whom? **people** The lecturer had given us many

(17) problems for further consideration. Had given to whom? **us** Give Colby and him the book. Give to whom?

(19) **Colby and him** The explanation gave Nick considerable help. Gave to whom? **Nick** Send my sister that bill

(21) for the groceries. Send to whom? **sister** He lent her his assignment sheet. Lent to whom? **her**

(22) The lawyer had written his client's opponent a long letter of explanation. Had written to whom? **opponent** He sent

(23) all the members notices of the meeting. Sent to whom? **members** Mr. Pearson taught us geometry. Taught to whom?

(25) **us** The committee has given the basketball team a special trophy. Has given to whom? **team**

(26) Will you make mother and me another table? Will make for whom? **mother and me**

Practicing Basic Skills in Language Arts • 236

ANSWER SHEET

© 2005 Sopris West Educational Services. All rights reserved. Practicing Basic Skills in Language Arts. Purchaser has permission to photocopy this page for classroom use only.

SEE TO MARK

Indirect Object in Sentences

Directions: Circle the indirect objects in the following sentences.

	First Try	Second Try
Correct		
Error		

The coach granted Jim the request. The boys sent their friend a get-well card. Bring the baby some milk. The tenant paid forty

dollars to Mr. Slocum. Grandfather paid the driver of the cab the fare. The pitcher threw the batter a sharp curve. Aunt Lorraine

bought Mother a novel for Christmas. The judge showed the hardened criminal no mercy. The clerk sold the customer a

damaged lawnmower. Hand me the evening paper. Will that student tell the counselor his problems? For many years he gave

Marcy flowers on her birthday. Dad bought a new suit for Tom. We taught Mark the "Star-Spangled Banner." You surely owe

Alissa an apology. The cowboy taught his horse many useful tricks. The emperor lent the general his bodyguard. The customer

left the waitress a big tip. The company sent a large bouquet of flowers to the sick employee. The old miser gave the salesman a

blank look. Our doctor always gives his patients advice. Mother was always asking the children questions. Young children often

ask their parents difficult questions. Mother gave our old dog a bone. The manager gave his workers a raise. The jeweler showed

the young couple some expensive rings. He often sends funny postcards to his friends. The boys gave their dog a much-needed

bath. The expert magician would not tell anyone his secrets. Our telegram could cause the family some pain. We will send the

customer the bill today. He promised his wife a vacation. Arithmetic always gives me a headache. Defeat may teach you a lesson.

Practicing Basic Skills in Language Arts • 237

© 2005 Sopris West Educational Services. All rights reserved. Practicing Basic Skills in Language Arts. Purchaser has permission to photocopy this page for classroom use only.

ONE MINUTE FLUENCY
BUILDER SERIES

SEE TO MARK

	First Try	Second Try
Correct		
Error		

Indirect Object in Sentences

Directions: Circle the indirect objects in the following sentences.

The coach granted (Jim) the request. The boys sent their (friend) a get-well card. Bring the (baby) some milk. The tenant paid forty (3)

dollars to (Mr. Slocum) Grandfather paid the (driver) of the cab the fare. The pitcher threw the (batter) a sharp curve. Aunt Lorraine (6)

bought (Mother) a novel for Christmas. The judge showed the hardened (criminal) no mercy. The clerk sold the (customer) a (9)

damaged lawnmower. Hand (me) the evening paper. Will that student tell the (counselor) his problems? For many years he gave (11)

(Marcy) flowers on her birthday. Dad bought a new suit for (Tom) We taught (Mark) the "Star-Spangled Banner." You surely owe (14)

(Alissa) an apology. The cowboy taught his (horse) many useful tricks. The emperor lent the (general) his bodyguard. The customer (17)

left the (waitress) a big tip. The company sent a large bouquet of flowers to the sick (employee) The old miser gave the (salesman) a (20)

blank look. Our doctor always gives his (patients) advice. Mother was always asking the (children) questions. Young children often (22)

ask their (parents) difficult questions. Mother gave our old (dog) a bone. The manager gave his (workers) a raise. The jeweler showed (25)

the young (couple) some expensive rings. He often sends funny postcards to his (friends) The boys gave their (dog) a much-needed (28)

bath. The expert magician would not tell (anyone) his secrets. Our telegram could cause the (family) some pain. We will send the (30)

(customer) the bill today. He promised his (wife) a vacation. Arithmetic always gives (me) a headache. Defeat may teach (you) a lesson. (34)

ANSWER SHEET

© 2005 Sopris West Educational Services. All rights reserved. Practicing Basic Skills in Language Arts. Purchaser has permission to photocopy this page for classroom use only.

	Correct	Error
First Try		
Second Try		

SEE TO MARK

Direct Object and Indirect Object in Sentences

Directions: Underline the indirect objects and circle the direct objects.

Jamar wrote the child a poem. The robin brought its baby a worm. Dad handed me his reel. She sent me the recipe for her fruitcake. Mom will make Latoya a new dress for the party. Often our teacher gives us a test on Fridays. Give him the report that is on my desk. Charles sent Sung his compass. Before the game the coach gave the team final instructions. Her parents have given her many privileges. Dan gave Ling a ride in his new car. Can you lend me two dollars? Mrs. Tanner sent her sister a special delivery letter last Wednesday. Mrs. Hartman brought me some flowers for the centerpiece. The stylists gave him several hints about his hair. The quizmaster gave the panel several clues to the answers. Bob sent Bruce and Pedro a card from Hawaii. The principal gave the girls a lecture on manners. The speaker told us his experiences at the South Pole. The committee offered Carlos the job. The new contract guarantees you a month of vacation. A passing motorist offered the boys a lift. The guide showed the visitors several of Jefferson's inventions. Deann sends you her best wishes. The Navy planes brought the party badly needed supplies. The mayor wrote the paramedics a letter of apology. The president awarded the ship a unit citation. The explorers bid the island a happy farewell. Mom made me a birthday cake. The principal wrote the editor a letter. The custodian handed him the broom. I cannot get you a ticket to the Styx concert. I passed Ken the meat and potatoes three times! We paid the treasurer our class dues. The speaker gave Jerome and John a fine compliment. The referee awarded Chad the ball out-of-bounds. The clerk handed Dana the change from the twenty dollar bill. Mom made Shelley and Gaylynn a batch of fudge. Bret has just bought his sister a new camera. Has Kip told Brad and Franco the plans for the New Year's Eve party yet? Give Li the key to your room.

© 2005 Sopris West Educational Services. All rights reserved. Practicing Basic Skills in Language Arts. Purchaser has permission to photocopy this page for classroom use only.

ONE-MINUTE FLUENCY
BUILDER SERIES

SEE TO MARK

	Correct	Error
First Try		
Second Try		

Direct Object and Indirect Object in Sentences

Directions: Underline the indirect objects and circle the direct objects.

Jamar wrote the child a (poem) The robin brought its baby a (worm) Dad handed me his (reel) She sent me the (recipe) for her (8)

fruitcake. Mom will make Latoya a new (dress) for the party. Often our teacher gives us a (test) on Fridays. Give him the (report) (14)

that is on my desk. Charles sent Sung his (compass) Before the game the coach gave the team final (instructions) Her parents (18)

have given her many (privileges) Dan gave Ling a (ride) in his new car. Can you lend me two (dollars?) Mrs. Tanner sent her sister (25)

a special delivery (letter) last Wednesday. Mrs. Hartman brought me some (flowers) for the centerpiece. The stylists gave him (29)

several (hints) about his hair. The quizmaster gave the panel several (clues) to the answers. Bob sent Bruce and Pedro a (card) from (35)

Hawaii. The principal gave the girls a (lecture) on manners. The speaker told us his (experiences) at the South Pole. The committee (39)

offered Carlos the (job) The new contract guarantees you a (month) of vacation. A passing motorist offered the boys a (lift) The (45)

guide showed the visitors (several) of Jefferson's inventions. Deann sends you her best (wishes) The Navy planes brought the party (50)

badly needed (supplies) The mayor wrote the paramedics a (letter) of apology. The president awarded the ship a unit (citation) The (55)

explorers bid the island a happy (farewell) Mom made me a birthday (cake) The principal wrote the editor a (letter) The custodian (61)

handed him the (broom) I cannot get you a (ticket) to the Styx concert. I passed Ken the (meat) and (potatoes) three times! We paid (68)

the treasurer our class (dues) The speaker gave Jerome and John a fine (compliment) The referee awarded Chad the (ball) out-of- (75)

bounds. The clerk handed Dana the (change) from the twenty dollar bill. Mom made Shelley and Gaylynn a (batch) of fudge. Bret (80)

has just bought his sister a new (camera) Has Kip told Brad and Franco the (plans) for the New Year's Eve party yet? Give Li the (key) (87)

to your room.

ANSWER SHEET

Practicing Basic Skills in Language Arts • 240

© 2005 Sopris West Educational Services. All rights reserved. Practicing Basic Skills in Language Arts. Purchaser has permission to photocopy this page for classroom use only.

SEE TO MARK

Predicate Nominative in Sentences

Directions: Draw an arrow from the predicate nominative to the subject.

	Correct	Error
First Try		
Second Try		

The next speaker will be Dr. Delancy. The writer was someone unknown. The man on the dock may be Kyle. Mr. Ardema is

the adviser of our social science club. The most surprised person in the crowd was Elena. Shelly was the editor of the yearbook.

The dog is a hero. Ice cream is my favorite dessert. The girl in the boat is she. You are the chairman. Ricardo is my friend. The

directors for the school play are Ling and Sherrie. Those tests are the ones that I was talking about. For years his father has been

an amateur magician who toured the country. The people in the car are my relatives. The adviser was he. She was the fastest

runner in the race. My colts are rapidly becoming yearlings. The dictionary is probably your most useful reference book. Are

you a good swimmer? Listening is an important skill. That woman is my music teacher. My next car will be a Porsche. My name

is Big Bird. Her watch is either a Timex or a Seiko. This signature is a forgery. Her uncle is a colonel in the Army. The doctor is

the pediatrician for the new clinic. Cindy should have been an astronaut. That dog is part collie and part chow. Dick will be the

chairperson of that committee. Helsinki is the capital of Finland. *Gone With the Wind* is a novel about the Civil War. Phil is the

newest member of the debate team. The American flag is a symbol of freedom. Joyce will be a judge at the livestock show next

month. Rosa is the second girl in the fifth row. Kenji is a student council representative for the ninth grade. Don is a famous

writer. Cathryn may become president someday. Julie Ann was an amateur photographer. Mr. Popkin is the new history teacher.

The gray horse was the winner of the race. My mother has been a plumber for years and my father is a nurse. The house on

Foothill Drive is a mansion. Cathy became a famous doctor.

© 2005 Sopris West Educational Services. All rights reserved. Practicing Basic Skills in Language Arts. Purchaser has permission to photocopy this page for classroom use only.

SEE TO MARK

Predicate Nominative in Sentences

Directions: Draw an arrow from the predicate nominative to the subject.

	Correct	Error
First Try		
Second Try		

The next speaker will be Dr. Delancy. The writer was someone unknown. The man on the dock may be Kyle. Mr. Ardema is (7)

the adviser of our social science club. The most surprised person in the crowd was Elena. Shelly was the editor of the yearbook. (12)

The dog is a hero. Ice cream is my favorite dessert. The girl in the boat is she. You are the chairman. Ricardo is my friend. The (22)

directors for the school play are Ling and Sherrie. Those tests are the ones that I was talking about. For years his father has been (28)

an amateur magician who toured the country. The people in the car are my relatives. The adviser was he. She was the fastest (34)

runner in the race. My colts are rapidly becoming yearlings. The dictionary is probably your most useful reference book. Are (39)

you a good swimmer? Listening is an important skill. That woman is my music teacher. My next car will be a Porsche. My name (48)

is Big Bird. Her watch is either a Timex or a Seiko. This signature is a forgery. Her uncle is a colonel in the Army. The doctor is (57)

the pediatrician for the new clinic. Cindy should have been an astronaut. That dog is part collie and part chow. Dick will be the (64)

chairperson of that committee. Helsinki is the capital of Finland. *Gone With the Wind* is a novel about the Civil War. Phil is the (70)

newest member of the debate team. The American flag is a symbol of freedom. Joyce will be a judge at the livestock show next (75)

month. Rosa is the second girl in the fifth row. Kenji is a student council representative for the ninth grade. Don is a famous (80)

writer. Cathryn may become president someday. Julie Ann was an amateur photographer. Mr. Popkin is the new history teacher. (87)

The gray horse was the winner of the race. My mother has been a plumber for years and my father is a nurse. The house on (94)

Foothill Drive is a mansion. Cathy became a famous doctor. (97)

ANSWER SHEET

© 2005 Sopris West Educational Services. All rights reserved. Practicing Basic Skills in Language Arts. Purchaser has permission to photocopy this page for classroom use only.

ONE-MINUTE FLUENCY BUILDER SERIES

Predicate Noun or Pronoun in Sentences

Directions: Draw an arrow from the predicate noun or pronoun to the subject.

	First Try	Second Try
Correct		
Error		

Mr. Taylor was once a firefighter. In January Bruce will become the captain of our basketball team. My dog is a collie. This park

appears to be a good place for the outing. Mrs. Townly is a plumber. Nick has been president of the National Junior Honors

Society before. The top scorers were you and he. Chicago is a city on Lake Michigan. Her dog, Skooter, is a mongrel. Bozo is a

registered bulldog. The hardest worker on the committee is Ling. It couldn't be you. The main speaker is someone from Utah

Power and Light Company. LeAnn is the first person to complete the long, difficult assignment. Is the owner of this farm your

father or Mr. Gomez? The large boy in the grey plaid shirt is a bully. The money was counterfeit. Suzanne was once my best

friend. An Englishman's home is his castle. Junior is a chip off the old block. Gold is a precious metal. The winner will be Walter

or Kevin. The birds in the area are robins, sparrows, and magpies. Their new car is a Toyota. Our next door neighbor has been

a mailman for twenty years. That gadget is a wire whisk. My watch is a Timex. The father of my best friend may be the next

mayor of Salt Lake City. My favorite desserts are cake and pie.

Practicing Basic Skills in Language Arts • 243

© 2005 Sopris West Educational Services. All rights reserved. Practicing Basic Skills in Language Arts. Purchaser has permission to photocopy this page for classroom use only.

ONE-MINUTE FLUENCY BUILDER SERIES

SEE TO MARK

Predicate Noun or Pronoun in Sentences

Directions: Draw an arrow from the predicate noun or pronoun to the subject.

	First Try	Second Try
Correct		
Error		

Mr. Taylor was once a firefighter. In January Bruce will become the captain of our basketball team. My dog is a collie. This park (7)

appears to be a good place for the outing. Mrs. Townly is a plumber. Nick has been president of the National Junior Honors (12)

Society before. The top scorers were you and he. Chicago is a city on Lake Michigan. Her dog, Skooter, is a mongrel. Bozo is a (20)

registered bulldog. The hardest worker on the committee is Ling. It couldn't be you. The main speaker is someone from Utah (27)

Power and Light Company. LeAnn is the first person to complete the long, difficult assignment. Is the owner of this farm your (30)

father or Mr. Gomez? The large boy in the grey plaid shirt is a bully. The money was counterfeit. Suzanne was once my best (37)

friend. An Englishman's home is his castle. Junior is a chip off the old block. Gold is a precious metal. The winner will be Walter (46)

or Kevin. The birds in the area are robins, sparrows, and magpies. Their new car is a Toyota. Our next door neighbor has been (54)

a mailman for twenty years. That gadget is a wire whisk. My watch is a Timex. The father of my best friend may be the next (59)

mayor of Salt Lake City. My favorite desserts are cake and pie. (64)

Practicing Basic Skills in Language Arts • 244

ANSWER SHEET

© 2005 Sopris West Educational Services. All rights reserved. Practicing Basic Skills in Language Arts. Purchaser has permission to photocopy this page for classroom use only.

SEE TO MARK

Predicate Nouns, Pronouns, and Linking Verbs in Sentences

Directions: Underline the linking verbs, and circle predicate nouns and pronouns.

	Correct	Error
First Try		
Second Try		

Chris is my cousin. The city is now a transportation center. Joe was the boy on the front seat. The captains of the team are you

and he. Ian Savoy is an honest man. Mike is a good cook. Kristy seems a friendly girl. Darby has been a popular president. My

father is a plumber, a bowler, and a White Sox fan. The leader of the band is also our coach. The winner is you. This is it. Nick

has become an Eagle Scout. Mark Twain was a man with many friends. The leader of the group was Mr. Alvara. She is a fine

secretary and treasurer. Doris Sims was the pilot of the plane. He has been a concert pianist for several years. Mr. Prince became a

teacher at the age of twenty-one. Sydney is a very intelligent person. My next vacation will be a trip to Canada. At last our team

has become a real winner. New members of our class are Marcella, Maya, Kathryn, and Tia. This spot seems a good place for a

picnic. Is your uncle the tall man in the brown suit? My pets are a dog, a cat, a rabbit, and two water snakes. My father was an

engineer in the army before he retired. It must be them in the blue car. Miss Mansell is an excellent singer. Mr. Feraro is a friend

of my mother. Pizza is my favorite food. Washington was not the first capital of our country.

© 2005 Sopris West Educational Services. All rights reserved. Practicing Basic Skills in Language Arts. Purchaser has permission to photocopy this page for classroom use only.

ONE MINUTE FLUENCY BUILDER SERIES

SEE TO MARK

	Correct	Error
First Try		
Second Try		

Predicate Nouns, Pronouns, and Linking Verbs in Sentences

Directions: Underline the linking verbs, and circle predicate nouns and pronouns.

(8) Chris is my (cousin) The city is now a transportation (center) Joe was the (boy) on the front seat. The captains of the team are (you)

(17) and (he) Ian Savoy is an honest (man) Mike is a good (cook) Kristy seems a friendly (girl) Darby has been a popular (president) My

(27) father is a plumber a (bowler) and a White Sox (fan) The leader of the band is also our (coach) The winner is (you) This is (it) Nick

(34) has become an (Eagle Scout) Mark Twain was a (man) with many friends. The leader of the group was (Mr. Alvara) She is a fine

(41) (secretary) and (treasurer) Doris Sims was the (pilot) of the plane. He has been a concert (pianist) for several years. Mr. Prince became a

(46) (teacher) at the age of twenty-one. Sydney is a very intelligent (person) My next vacation will be a (trip) to Canada. At last our team

(55) has become a real (winner) New members of our class are (Marcella) (Maya) (Kathryn) and (Tia) This spot seems a good (place) for a

(63) picnic. Is your uncle the tall (man) in the brown suit? My pets are a (dog) a (cat) a (rabbit) and two water (snakes) My father was an

(70) (engineer) in the army before (he) retired. It must be (them) in the blue car. Miss Mansell is an excellent (singer) Mr. Feraro is a (friend)

(74) of my mother. Pizza is my favorite (food) Washington was not the first (capital) of our country.

ANSWER SHEET

Practicing Basic Skills in Language Arts • 246

© 2005 Sopris West Educational Services. All rights reserved. Practicing Basic Skills in Language Arts. Purchaser has permission to photocopy this page for classroom use only.

SEE TO MARK

Predicate Adjectives in Sentences
Directions: Draw an arrow from the predicate adjective to the subject.

	First Try	Second Try
Correct		
Error		

The wind is cold today. The boy became unhappy when the journey ended. This room looks comfortable. The race among the younger horses was thrilling and exciting. Near the finish line, the horse's stirrups became loose. Princess Bug proved superior and demonstrated real stamina in the final race. The shaggy dog seemed lonely. That sweater is too big for you. The little boy looked tired. All this time, Cheryl has been looking very smug. Everyone was happy. The players weren't very happy about the referee's decision. The clear, tropical water felt warm. The watchman seemed uneasy about something. The hot, steaming soup tasted good. Tim appeared very uneasy upon mention of the lost keys. The boy's shoes were muddy. The banner is red, white, and blue. This vase is very old. He looks funny without his toupee. Their cat is black and white. That apple pie smells delicious to me. The defendant appeared nervous. His eyelashes are extremely long. This gravy still tastes too salty. The reports of the affair were very unfair to our friends. The audience became restless. The sky in Barry's picture is too blue. The judge's face turned red. Is that light red or green? The moon is hazy tonight. He is the very pinnacle of politeness. This model is completely automatic. The tropical forests of Brazil are dense and humid. That yellow shirt looks terrific on you. The man on the other end of the line sounded angry when I spoke to him. The lady looks grandmotherly with her shawl and cane. Charles seems very sad these days. Clark's argument sounded very unreasonable to the rest of us. The wind was cold and raw. The new coach seemed pleasant and competent. Some small economy cars are neither small nor economical. His wild adventure looks senseless. Father feels bad today. His letter sounded strange. I am growing taller and thinner.

© 2005 Sopris West Educational Services. All rights reserved. Practicing Basic Skills in Language Arts. Purchaser has permission to photocopy this page for classroom use only.

ONE-MINUTE FLUENCY BUILDER SERIES

SEE TO MARK

	Correct	Error
First Try		
Second Try		

Predicate Adjectives in Sentences

Directions: Draw an arrow from the predicate adjective to the subject.

The wind is cold today. The boy became unhappy when the journey ended. This room looks comfortable. The race among the (8)

younger horses was thrilling and exciting. Near the finish line, the horse's stirrups became loose. Princess Bug proved superior (14)

and demonstrated real stamina in the final race. The shaggy dog seemed lonely. That sweater is too big for you. The little boy (19)

looked tired. All this time, Cheryl has been looking very smug. Everyone was happy. The players weren't very happy about (26)

the referee's decision. The clear, tropical water felt warm. The watchman seemed uneasy about something. The hot, steaming (30)

soup tasted good. Tim appeared very uneasy upon mention of the lost keys. The boy's shoes were muddy. The banner is red, (40)

white, and blue. This vase is very old. He looks funny without his toupee. Their cat is black and white. That apple pie smells (51)

delicious to me. The defendant appeared nervous. His eyelashes are extremely long. This gravy still tastes too salty. The reports (59)

of the affair were very unfair to our friends. The audience became restless. The sky in Barry's picture is too blue. The judge's face (65)

turned red. Is that light red or green? The moon is hazy tonight. He is the very pinnacle of politeness. This model is completely (75)

automatic. The tropical forests of Brazil are dense and humid. That yellow shirt looks terrific on you. The man on the other end (83)

of the line sounded angry when I spoke to him. The lady looks grandmotherly with her shawl and cane. Charles seems very sad (88)

these days. Clark's argument sounded very unreasonable to the rest of us. The wind was cold and raw. The new coach seemed (96)

pleasant and competent. Some small economy cars are neither small nor economical. His wild adventure looks senseless. Father (105)

feels bad today. His letter sounded strange. I am growing taller and thinner. (112)

ANSWER SHEET

Practicing Basic Skills in Language Arts • 248

© 2005 Sopris West Educational Services. All rights reserved. Practicing Basic Skills in Language Arts. Purchaser has permission to photocopy this page for classroom use only.

SEE TO MARK

Predicate Adjectives and Linking Verbs in Sentences

Directions: Underline the linking verbs, and circle the predicate adjectives.

	First Try	Second Try
Correct		
Error		

The music was good. Delores seemed happy today. The vegetable soup on the stove is too salty. That wind is strong. Debbie

must have become bored. This backpack seems extremely heavy. Those lemon pies look marvelous. Our Christmas vacation will

be short. The mud felt good between my toes. The large barn on my uncle's farm is red. The speaker sounded tired. The dark

clouds grew blacker as the day went by. The sky turned cloudy. Greg is growing tall. The test was easy. A baby's skin feels smooth

and soft. Teresa's answers seem clear and sensible. Those ripe pears smell delicious. Your class notes must be neat, clear, and

brief. The basement smelled musty. Ann looks good in glasses. George sounds much older on the phone. The president seemed

unhappy about something this morning. King Henry's costume was too tight across the stomach for Paul. Did Father look angry

or worried? Your plans sound unusual but exciting. His hat was much too big for him. Our car doesn't smell so new anymore.

The milk in the bottle smelled sour. He appeared discouraged when he left the football field. Her newspaper article proved

interesting. The little girl's hand looked dirty.

© 2005 Sopris West Educational Services. All rights reserved. Practicing Basic Skills in Language Arts. Purchaser has permission to photocopy this page for classroom use only.

SEE TO MARK

Predicate Adjectives and Linking Verbs in Sentences

Directions: Underline the linking verbs, and circle the predicate adjectives.

	Correct	Error
First Try		
Second Try		

The music was (good) Delores seemed (happy) today. The vegetable soup on the stove is too (salty) That wind is (strong) Debbie (8)

must have become (bored) This backpack seems extremely (heavy) Those lemon pies look (marvelous) Our Christmas vacation will (15)

be (short) The mud felt (good) between my toes. The large barn on my uncle's farm is (red) The speaker sounded (tired) The dark (22)

clouds grew (blacker) as the day went by. The sky turned (cloudy) Greg is growing (tall) The test was (easy) A baby's skin feels (smooth) (32)

and (soft) Teresa's answers seem (clear) and (sensible) Those ripe pears smell (delicious) Your class notes must be (neat) (clear) and (41)

(brief) The basement smelled (musty) Ann looks (good) in glasses. George sounds much (older) on the phone. The president seemed (49)

(unhappy) about something this morning. King Henry's costume was too (tight) across the stomach for Paul. Did Father look (angry) (55)

or (worried) Your plans sound (unusual) but (exciting) His hat was much too (big) for him. Our car doesn't smell so (new) anymore. (64)

The milk in the bottle smelled (sour) He appeared (discouraged) when he left the football field. Her newspaper article proved (69)

(interesting) The little girl's hand looked (dirty) (72)

ANSWER SHEET

Practicing Basic Skills in Language Arts • 250

© 2005 Sopris West Educational Services. All rights reserved. Practicing Basic Skills in Language Arts. Purchaser has permission to photocopy this page for classroom use only.

SEE TO MARK

Review Sheet: Direct Objects, Indirect Objects, Predicate Adjectives, and Predicate Nominatives in Sentences

Directions: Identify the underlined words, using the following abbreviations: DO for direct objects, IO for indirect objects, PA for predicate adjectives, and PN for predicate nominatives.

	First Try	Second Try
Correct		
Error		

Mrs. Alden was a noted tennis <u>player</u> in college. Dale made two base <u>hits</u> in the game. The coach bought us <u>dinner</u>. Our next

stop on the trip was Salt Lake <u>City</u>. Amherst, an eastern college, is a fine <u>school</u>. After the new snowfall, the weather became

extremely <u>cold</u>. During the past month, Julie read three <u>books</u> and gave <u>reports</u> on them. Denver is the largest <u>city</u> in Colorado.

The green, striped dress is my <u>favorite</u>. The refreshments included <u>sandwiches</u>, <u>cookies</u>, and <u>milk</u>. Will you show your <u>friends</u>

these beautiful <u>cards</u>? Those historic buildings are rather <u>old</u>. Mary Jo is my favorite <u>cousin</u>. Lorraine Hansberry, an American

playwright, wrote A <u>Raisin in the Sun</u>. The train is <u>early</u>. Mr. Bell backed his <u>car</u> into the garage. Did the principal give the <u>girls</u>

two <u>tickets</u>? We gave <u>Dan</u> the <u>picture</u> of the baseball team. The tiny, wet dog appeared <u>neglected</u>. Yeats, an Irish poet, won a

Nobel <u>prize</u>. Ivan the Terrible was the first <u>czar</u> of Russia. An thermometer is a temperature-measuring <u>device</u>. The house was

<u>empty</u> and <u>run-down</u>. The blackberries were thick in both <u>patches</u>. We gave the <u>monkeys</u> two <u>handfuls</u> of nuts. The girls left

their ice <u>skates</u> at the rink. Becky raised <u>potatoes</u> and <u>tomatoes</u> in her garden this year.

© 2005 Sopris West Educational Services. All rights reserved. Practicing Basic Skills in Language Arts. Purchaser has permission to photocopy this page for classroom use only.

SEE TO MARK

Review Sheet: Direct Objects, Indirect Objects, Predicate Adjectives, and Predicate Nominatives in Sentences

Directions: Identify the underlined words, using the following abbreviations: DO for direct objects, IO for indirect objects, PA for predicate adjectives, and PN for predicate nominatives.

	Correct	Error
First Try		
Second Try		

        PN   DO   IO DO
Mrs. Alden was a noted tennis <u>player</u> in college. Dale made two base <u>hits</u> in the game. The coach bought <u>us</u> <u>dinner</u>. Our next (4)

          PN   PN
stop on the trip was <u>Salt Lake City</u>. Amherst, an eastern college, is a fine <u>school</u>. After the new snowfall, the weather became (6)

 PA   DO   DO   PN
extremely <u>cold</u>. During the past month, Julie read three <u>books</u> and gave <u>reports</u> on them. Denver is the largest <u>city</u> in Colorado. (10)

         PA   DO   DO   DO   IO
The green, striped dress is my <u>favorite</u>. The refreshments included <u>sandwiches</u>, <u>cookies</u>, and <u>milk</u>. Will you show your <u>friends</u> (15)

    DO   PA   PN
these beautiful <u>cards</u>? Those historic buildings are rather <u>old</u>. Mary Jo is my favorite <u>cousin</u>. Lorraine Hansberry, an American (18)

PA   DO   PA   DO   IO
playwright, wrote <u>A Raisin in the Sun</u>. The train is <u>early</u>. Mr. Bell backed his <u>car</u> into the garage. Did the principal give the <u>girls</u> (21)

DO   IO   DO   PA
two <u>tickets</u>? We gave <u>Dan</u> the <u>picture</u> of the baseball team. The tiny, wet dog appeared <u>neglected</u>. Yeats, an Irish poet, won a (25)

                            PN   PN
Nobel prize. Ivan the Terrible was the first <u>czar</u> of Russia. An thermometer is a temperature-measuring <u>device</u>. The house was (28)

PA   PA   PA   IO   DO
empty and <u>run-down</u>. The blackberries were <u>thick</u> in both patches. We gave the <u>monkeys</u> two handfuls of <u>nuts</u>. The girls left (33)

DO   DO   DO
their ice <u>skates</u> at the rink. Becky raised <u>potatoes</u> and <u>tomatoes</u> in her garden this year. (36)

ANSWER SHEET

Practicing Basic Skills in Language Arts • 252

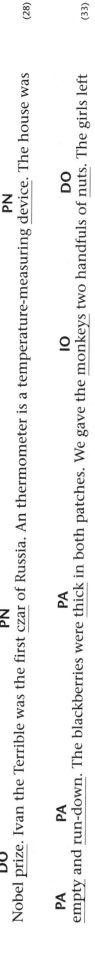

© 2005 Sopris West Educational Services. All rights reserved. Practicing Basic Skills in Language Arts. Purchaser has permission to photocopy this page for classroom use only.

ONE-MINUTE FLUENCY
BUILDER SERIES

SEE TO MARK

Parts of Sentences: Subject, Verb, Direct Object, Indirect Object, Predicate Adjective, Predicate Nomative

Directions: Identify the six parts of sentences indicated below.

Subject (S): The part about which something is being said. **Verb (V):** A word that expresses an action or state of being. **Direct Object (DO):** (Of the verb) A noun or pronoun that receives the action of the verb, or shows result of the action. It answers the question "what" or "whom" after an action verb. **Indirect Object (IO):** (Of the verb) A noun or pronoun that precedes the direct object and usually tells "to whom" or "for whom" (or "to what" or "for what") the action of the verb is done. **Predicate Adjective (PA):** (A subject complement) An adjective that modifies the subject of the sentence. **Predicate Nominative (PN):** (A subject complement) A noun or pronoun that explains the subject of a sentence.

Joel ran. John showed the picture. John showed Nina the picture. Franco will be my partner. Were they lost? The heroine is she.

That building is a school. Cecil had been sick. That dog looks sick. Those roses are sweet. She seemed content. Roadblocks are

often maddening. This is the girl. Does he feel better? Mei mailed several postcards. Mary may kiss Rodney goodbye. He wrote

the book. Pedro mailed Marjorie several postcards. She sang Tyrone a song. Dexter sent Maria miniature mums. Roberta fixes

hair. I leaned against the table and watched Maxine. Many of Ernest Hemingway's novels deal with power and violence. Not all

of his main characters are strong or brave. Mother may broil me a steak. He showed her the new van. The doctor gave Mother

some advice. I bought him a new shirt. My cousin left Damon a basketball. Mary was elected queen. She is foolish. He isn't well.

The cat licked its fur. The flowers were sent away. Rodgers and Hammerstein wrote music. Remy ran. Remy showed the picture.

John showed his picture. Igor will dance. Alma is his sister. Zorro is really Don Diego. Mark is my brother. Mark is also Rick's

brother. Rick is my brother. Rick certainly doesn't look healthy today. Felix is a nice person. Billie is impatient.

Practicing Basic Skills in Language Arts • 253

© 2005 Sopris West Educational Services. All rights reserved. Practicing Basic Skills in Language Arts. Purchaser has permission to photocopy this page for classroom use only.

SEE TO MARK

	Correct	Error
First Try		
Second Try		

Parts of Sentences: Subject, Verb, Direct Object, Indirect Object, Predicate Adjective, Predicate Nominative

Directions: Identify the six parts of sentences indicated below.

Subject (S): The part about which something is being said. **Verb (V):** A word that expresses an action or state of being. **Direct Object (DO):** (Of the verb) A noun or pronoun that receives the action of the verb, or shows result of the action. It answers the question "what" or "whom" after an action verb. **Indirect Object (IO):** (Of the verb) A noun or pronoun that precedes the direct object and usually tells "to whom" or "for whom" (or "to what" or "for what") the action of the verb is done. **Predicate Adjective (PA):** (A subject complement) An adjective that modifies the subject of the sentence. **Predicate Nominative (PN):** (A subject complement) A noun or pronoun that explains the subject of a sentence.

```
  S   V   DO   S    V   IO    DO    S      V      PN      V    S    PA       S    V PN
Joel ran. John showed Nina the picture. John showed the picture. Franco will be my partner. Were they lost? The heroine is she.     (18)

  S    V   PN    S   —V—   PA      S    V   PA       S     V
That building is a school. Cecil had been sick. That dog looks sick. Those roses are sweet. She seemed content. Roadblocks are       (35)

    PA    S   V   PN    V  S  V  PA   S   V        DO    S    —V—   DO       S    V
often maddening. This is the girl. Does he feel better? Mei mailed several postcards. Mary may kiss Rodney goodbye. He wrote        (51)

  DO   S   V  IO      DO    S   V  IO    DO   S    V  IO           DO    S    V
the book. Pedro mailed Marjorie several postcards. She sang Tyrone a song. Dexter sent Maria miniature mums. Roberta fixes           (66)

DO S   V           V   DO   S                                                             S
hair. I leaned against the table and watched Maxine. Many of Ernest Hemingway's novels deal with power and violence. Not all         (74)

            V   PA   PA    S   —V—  IO DO  S   V  IO     DO       S   V    IO
of his main characters are strong or brave. Mother may broil me a steak. He showed her the new van. The doctor gave Mother           (88)

  DO  S  IO     DO       S   V   IO    DO      S    —V—    PN   S  V PA    S   V PA
some advice. I bought him a new shirt. My cousin left Damon a basketball. Mary was elected queen. She is foolish. He isn't well.      (106)

  S   V  DO      S    —V—       S      V   DO   S   V   S     V        DO
The cat licked its fur. The flowers were sent away. Rodgers and Hammerstein wrote music. Remy ran. Remy showed the picture.          (120)

  S    V   DO      S   —V—  S   V   PN        —PN—   S   V       PN   S   V
John showed his picture. Igor will dance. Alma is his sister. Zorro is really Don Diego. Mark is my brother. Mark is also Rick's      (136)

  PN    S    V     S       —V—        PA        S   V   PN    S   V  PA
brother. Rick is my brother. Rick certainly doesn't look healthy today. Felix is a nice person. Billie is impatient.                 (150)
```

© 2005 Sopris West Educational Services. All rights reserved. Practicing Basic Skills in Language Arts. Purchaser has permission to photocopy this page for classroom use only.

	Correct	Error
First Try		
Second Try		

ONE-MINUTE FLUENCY
BUILDER SERIES

SEE TO MARK

Subject-Verb Agreement

Directions: Mark the correct verb.

Joe and I (is, are) going to visit grandmother tomorrow. A dog (was, were) in our trash last night. Do you have enough money for the movies? Neither fruit nor vegetables (grow, grows) well in this area. The team (ran, run) a good race. (Do, Does) either of your friends have a car? Splash (goes, go) the water when the boys jump in the pool. (Has, Have) either of your relatives caused a problem? The football team (travel, travels) to other towns for its games. You (were, was) the first person to arrive at school. I (was, were) gone all day. Discussions about other people (annoy, annoys) my mother. Every one of her patterns (call, calls) for three yards of material. Your blue shoes (look, looks) great with my outfit. Neither of the boys (have, has) been late for dinner. My aunt's children (is, are) traveling with their father. (There's, There are) two more pieces of chicken in the refrigerator. The student congress (has, have) already made its decision. My parents (travel, travels) to visit their relatives all the time. Here (come, comes) the crowd of people for the sale. (Is, Are) the girls going with us tomorrow? Twenty-five students (has, have) decided to attend the play. It (doesn't, don't) seem to make any difference to them. The children (was, were) ready for bed at 8 o'clock. (Do, Does) any of your friends have the latest CDs? The cause of his trouble (was, were) his bad attitude. Most of the people (follow, follows) his advice. Where (was, were) you when I called? I (has, have) all the trouble I want right now. A bunch of cars (surround, surrounds) my house. The television announcers (recommend, recommends) that we watch television. (Doesn't, Don't) it look nice?

Practicing Basic Skills in Language Arts • 255

© 2005 Sopris West Educational Services. All rights reserved. Practicing Basic Skills in Language Arts. Purchaser has permission to photocopy this page for classroom use only.

Subject-Verb Agreement
Directions: Mark the correct verb.

	First Try	Second Try
Correct		
Error		

Joe and I (is, <u>are</u>) going to visit grandmother tomorrow. A dog (was, were) in our trash last night. (Does, <u>Do</u>) you have enough (3)

money for the movies? Neither fruit nor vegetables (<u>grow</u>, grows) well in this area. The team (<u>ran</u>, run) a good race. (Do, <u>Does</u>) (6)

either of your friends have a car? Splash (<u>goes</u>, go) the water when the boys jump in the pool. (<u>Has</u>, Have) either of your relatives (8)

caused a problem? The football team (travel, <u>travels</u>) to other towns for its games. You (<u>were</u>, was) the first person to arrive at (10)

school. I (<u>was</u>, were) gone all day. Discussions about other people (<u>annoy</u>, annoys) my mother. Every one of her patterns (call, (12)

<u>calls</u>) for three yards of material. Your blue shoes (<u>look</u>, looks) great with my outfit. Neither of the boys (have, <u>has</u>) been late for (15)

dinner. My aunt's children (is, <u>are</u>) traveling with their father. (There's, <u>There are</u>) two more pieces of chicken in the refrigerator. (17)

The student congress (<u>has</u>, have) already made its decision. My parents (travel, <u>travels</u>) to visit their relatives all the time. Here (19)

(come, <u>comes</u>) the crowd of people for the sale. (Is, <u>Are</u>) the girls going with us tomorrow? Twenty-five students (has, <u>have</u>) (22)

decided to attend the play. It (doesn't, don't) seem to make any difference to them. The children (was, <u>were</u>) ready for bed at (24)

8 o'clock. (<u>Do</u>, Does) any of your friends have the latest CDs? The cause of his trouble (<u>was</u>, were) his bad attitude. Most of (26)

the people (follow, <u>follows</u>) his advice. Where (was, <u>were</u>) you when I called? I (has, <u>have</u>) all the trouble I want right now. A (29)

bunch of cars (surround, <u>surrounds</u>) my house. The television announcers (recommend, <u>recommends</u>) that we watch television. (31)

(<u>Doesn't</u>, Don't) it look nice? (32)

ANSWER SHEET

© 2005 Sopris West Educational Services. All rights reserved. Practicing Basic Skills in Language Arts. Purchaser has permission to photocopy this page for classroom use only.

SEE TO MARK

	Correct	Error
First Try		
Second Try		

Subject-Verb Agreement

Directions: Mark the correct verb.

The boys (is, are) good ball players. These boats (was, were) used by the Eskimos. (Does, Do) Jim have on a new shirt? Tim (ran, run) all the way home. My aunt (has, have) a problem with her car. Your new coat (look, looks) great with my hat. Most of the people (has, have) paid for the concert. You (were, was) the only one that sent a thank you note. The children (has, have) already left for the movies. My sisters (travel, travels) all over the world. Ugly weeds (surround, surrounds) our house. She (has, have) so many problems. We (are, is) having company for dinner. (Doesn't, Don't) she have on a new dress? The doctor (recommends, recommend) that you get plenty of rest. Here (come, comes) the new neighbors. My brother's dog (is, are) going with him on his trip. Our flowers (grow, grows) until late fall. That person (annoy, annoys) me. The children (were, was) playing in the street. (Does, Do) your sister have any money? Thirty students (has, have) decided to go to the dance. The dogs (follow, follows) the mailman all over the neighborhood. The boys (ran, run) all the way to school. (There's, There are) a five dollar bill on the table for you. I (have, has) three brothers. The CDs (sounds, sound) scratchy. Mrs. Jones (was, were) my teacher last year. (Has, Have) you enough clothes for the long trip? The riders (weren't, was not) able to complete the long journey. (Was, Were) they lost all night?

© 2005 Sopris West Educational Services. All rights reserved. Practicing Basic Skills in Language Arts. Purchaser has permission to photocopy this page for classroom use only.

ONE MINUTE FLUENCY
BUILDER SERIES

Subject-Verb Agreement
Directions: Mark the correct verb.

	Correct	Error
First Try		
Second Try		

The boys (is, are) good ball players. These boats (was, were) used by the Eskimos. (Does, Do) Jim have on a new shirt? Tim (ran, (4)

run) all the way home. My aunt (has, have) a problem with her car. Your new coat (look, looks) great with my hat. Most of (6)

the people (has, have) paid for the concert. You (were, was) the only one that sent a thank you note. The children (has, have) (9)

already left for the movies. My sisters (travel, travels) all over the world. Ugly weeds (surround, surrounds) our house. She (11)

(has, have) so many problems. We (are, is) having company for dinner. (Doesn't, Don't) she have on a new dress? The doctor (14)

(recommends, recommend) that you get plenty of rest. Here (come, comes) the new neighbors. My brother's dog (is, are) going (17)

with him on his trip. Our flowers (grow, grows) until late fall. That person (annoy, annoys) me. The children (were, was) playing (20)

in the street. (Does, Do) your sister have any money? Thirty students (has, have) decided to go to the dance. The dogs (follow, (23)

follows) the mailman all over the neighborhood. The boys (ran, run) all the way to school. (There's, There are) a five dollar bill (25)

on the table for you. I (have, has) three brothers. The CDs (sounds, sound) scratchy. Mrs. Jones (was, were) my teacher last year. (28)

(Has, Have) you enough clothes for the long trip? The riders (weren't, was not) able to complete the long journey. (Was, Were) (31)

they lost all night?

ANSWER SHEET

© 2005 Sopris West Educational Services. All rights reserved. Practicing Basic Skills in Language Arts. Purchaser has permission to photocopy this page for classroom use only.

ONE-MINUTE FLUENCY BUILDER SERIES

SEE TO MARK

First Try

Second Try

Correct	Error

Subject-Verb Agreement

Directions: Mark the correct verb.

Each (was, were) examined by the doctor. Neither (has been, have been) tardy all year. He (is, are) a courageous amateur. (There,

They're, Their) leaving on the six o'clock flight for Los Angeles. The practice of medicine in medieval times (was, were). usually

crude. We (did, done) our planning at the beginning. Take that broken glass over (their, they're, there). The new stores on

Walnut Avenue (has been, have been) completed. All the students (is, are) in favor of your plan. Few apples (is, are) ripe enough

to eat. Both (has been, have been) highly recommended. All the money (has been, have been) spent. Several students (has,

have) lost (they're, their, there) bus tickets. One of (your, you're) sleeves (is, are) torn. Neither of my brothers (have, has) been

to college. Both of his excuses (were, was) poor. The houses on Seventh Street (are, is) large. Every one of his essays (was, were)

too short. Some of the fruit (have, has) spoiled. One of the boxes (has, have) been opened. Both of the boys (look, looks) strong.

Uncle Jody, in his new coat and hat, (look, looks) prosperous. A large group of people (was, were) waiting for the movie to begin.

Mr. Sims, with his son and daughter, (have, has) left. They (wasn't, weren't) ready. A tree and a telephone pole (was lying, were

lying) across the road. Sally and Alicia (is, are) in my class. The engine and one car (was, were) derailed. Steak and French fried

potatoes (is, are) my favorite meal. Room and board (is, are) fifty dollars a week. Hayden or Carl (has, have) your notebook.

Both Brother and Dad (is, are) willing to help us. Neither Mother nor Dad (is, are) willing to help us. Lois and Marco (was, were)

the best players. Neither Kurt nor Tyrone (is, are) going. Bob and Chien (was, were) too confident. Both Lu and Roland (prefer,

prefers) peanut butter sandwiches.

Practicing Basic Skills in Language Arts • 259

© 2005 Sopris West Educational Services. All rights reserved. Practicing Basic Skills in Language Arts. Purchaser has permission to photocopy this page for classroom use only.

SEE TO MARK

	First Try	Second Try
Correct		
Error		

Subject-Verb Agreement
Directions: Mark the correct verb.

Each (was, were) examined by the doctor. Neither (has been, have been) tardy all year. He (is, are) a courageous amateur. (There, (3)

They're, Their) leaving on the six o'clock flight for Los Angeles. The practice of medicine in medieval times (was, were) usually (5)

crude. We (did, done) our planning at the beginning. Take that broken glass over (their, they're, there). The new stores on (7)

Walnut Avenue (has been, have been) completed. All the students (is, are) in favor of your plan. Few apples (is, are) ripe enough (10)

to eat. Both (has been, have been) highly recommended. All the money (has been, have been) spent. Several students (has, (12)

have) lost (they're, their, there) bus tickets. One of (your, you're) sleeves (is, are) torn. Neither of my brothers (have, has) been (17)

to college. Both of his excuses (were, was) poor. The houses on Seventh Street (are, is) large. Every one of his essays (was, were) (20)

too short. Some of the fruit (have, has) spoiled. One of the boxes (has, have) been opened. Both of the boys (look, looks) strong. (23)

Uncle Jody, in his new coat and hat, (look, looks) prosperous. A large group of people (was, were) waiting for the movie to begin. (25)

Mr. Sims, with his son and daughter, (have, has) left. They (wasn't, weren't) ready. A tree and a telephone pole (was lying, were (28)

lying) across the road. Sally and Alicia (is, are) in my class. The engine and one car (was, were) derailed. Steak and French fried (31)

potatoes (is, are) my favorite meal. Room and board (is, are) fifty dollars a week. Hayden or Carl (has, have) your notebook. (34)

Both Brother and Dad (is, are) willing to help us. Neither Mother nor Dad (is, are) willing to help us. Lois and Marco (was, were) (37)

the best players. Neither Kurt nor Tyrone (is, are) going. Bob and Chien (was, were) too confident. Both Lu and Roland (prefer, (40)

prefers) peanut butter sandwiches.

ANSWER SHEET

Practicing Basic Skills in Language Arts • 260

© 2005 Sopris West Educational Services. All rights reserved. Practicing Basic Skills in Language Arts. Purchaser has permission to photocopy this page for classroom use only.

ONE MINUTE FLUENCY
BUILDER SERIES

SEE TO MARK

Subject-Verb Agreement
Directions: Mark the correct verb.

	Correct	Error
First Try		
Second Try		

This deck of cards (has, have) never been used. Yes, the committee (has, have) already turned in its report. Neither Tom nor

the twins (has, have) any right to complain. It just (don't, doesn't) make sense. Each of the stories (ends, end) in a tragedy. A

number of students (has, have) signed up already. Two-thirds of the carpet (was, were) badly faded. Here (comes, come) the

twins. (Doesn't, Don't) that cake smell good? Here (come, comes) my best friend and bitterest rival, Tim Polk. Hidden under the

blotter (was, were) the two photographs. Why (doesn't, don't) someone answer the doorbell? Where (was, were) Andy and Joel?

(Has, Have) Mr. Thiesen or his assistant arrived yet? You (was, were) wrong, and they (was, were) wrong too. "Thirteen Ways to

Improve Your Looks" (is, are) in the Easter issue. Mrs. Penrod, like her husband, (like, likes) peace and quiet. His main problem

(was, were) the constant interruptions. The basketball team (travel, travels) to other schools for one-half of its games. Mr. Neelly

and Mr. Wong (is, are) here to help us. Nobody, not even the students, (wants, want) another tournament. My favorite dessert

(is, are) chocolate parfaits; their favorite (is, are) brownies. Arguments about politics and religion (annoy, annoys) my aunt,

but neither of the guests (was, were) aware of this. Meyers Bell, of Slotkin, (is, are) going to pitch the first baseball game of the

season. A long line (surrounds, surround) the school this morning. (Has, Have) either of your neighbors ever complained about

your parking the car in the alley? The only guide they had on these trips (was, were) the stars. Their survey showed that one out

of every four doctors (recommends, recommend) Slim-slo. (There's, There are) two more sandwiches in the refrigerator. Joanie,

like her brothers, (is, are) a top-notch swimmer.

© 2005 Sopris West Educational Services. All rights reserved. Practicing Basic Skills in Language Arts. Purchaser has permission to photocopy this page for classroom use only.

ONE-MINUTE FLUENCY BUILDER SERIES

SEE TO MARK

	Correct	Error
First Try		
Second Try		

Subject-Verb Agreement

Directions: Mark the correct verb.

This deck of cards (has, have) never been used. Yes, the committee (has, have) already turned in its report. Neither Tom nor (2)

the twins (has, have) any right to complain. It just (don't, doesn't) make sense. Each of the stories (ends, end) in a tragedy. A (5)

number of students (has, have) signed up already. Two-thirds of the carpet (was, were) badly faded. Here (comes, come) the (8)

twins. (Doesn't, Don't) that cake smell good? Here (come, comes) my best friend and bitterest rival, Tim Polk. Hidden under the (10)

blotter (was, were) the two photographs. Why (doesn't, don't) someone answer the doorbell? Where (was, were) Andy and Joel? (13)

(Has, Have) Mr. Thiesen or his assistant arrived yet? You (was, were) wrong, and they (was, were) wrong too. "Thirteen Ways to (16)

Improve Your Looks" (is, are) in the Easter issue. Mrs. Penrod, like her husband, (like, likes) peace and quiet. His main problem (18)

(was, were) the constant interruptions. The basketball team (travel, travels) to other schools for one-half of its games. Mr. Neelly (20)

and Mr. Wong (is, are) here to help us. Nobody, not even the students, (wants, want) another tournament. My favorite dessert (22)

(is, are) chocolate parfaits; their favorite (is, are) brownies. Arguments about politics and religion (annoy, annoys) my aunt, (25)

but neither of the guests (was, were) aware of this. Meyers Bell, of Slotkin, (is, are) going to pitch the first baseball game of the (27)

season. A long line (surrounds, surround) the school this morning. (Has, Have) either of your neighbors ever complained about (29)

your parking the car in the alley? The only guide they had on these trips (was, were) the stars. Their survey showed that one out (30)

of every four doctors (recommends, recommend) Slim-slo. (There's, There are) two more sandwiches in the refrigerator. Joanie, (32)

like her brothers, (is, are) a top-notch swimmer. (33)

ANSWER SHEET

Practicing Basic Skills in Language Arts • 262

© 2005 Sopris West Educational Services. All rights reserved. Practicing Basic Skills in Language Arts. Purchaser has permission to photocopy this page for classroom use only.

ONE MINUTE FLUENCY
BUILDER SERIES

SEE TO MARK

Subject-Verb Agreement
Directions: Mark the correct verb.

	First Try	Second Try
Correct		
Error		

(Doesn't, Don't) we have time to eat dinner? The water (surround, surrounds) the small island. She (recommends, recommend)

that we finish our homework on time. Mary (has, have) enough work for two people. (Was, Were) you home early last night?

His patients (follow, follows) his advice. (Does, Do) you have a new record? We (have, has) decided to work late tomorrow.

(There's, There are) more snow predicted for Thursday. We (travels, travel) all over the country every year. Sue's children (is, are)

staying with Mom. Your hat (look, looks) fantastic with your dress. The recipe (call, calls) for three eggs. My children (annoy,

annoys) me sometimes. The salesmen (travel, travels) to yearly meetings. (Do, Does) your teacher get a vacation? The boys will

(ran, run) in the race. The wind (was, were) blowing trees over. (Is, Are) you going to Texas for the holidays? She (has, have) a lot

of work to do. She (has, have) a new dress for the dance. When (was, were) you going to see my aunt? His bad grades (were, was)

a problem for him. We (is, are) going shopping on Saturday. The boys (grow, grows) faster than the girls. She (calls, call) us all

the time. The stores (recommend, recommends) that everyone buy a lot of presents. The party (wasn't, weren't) long enough.

Practicing Basic Skills in Language Arts • 263

© 2005 Sopris West Educational Services. All rights reserved. Practicing Basic Skills in Language Arts. Purchaser has permission to photocopy this page for classroom use only.

	Correct	Error
First Try		
Second Try		

ONE-MINUTE FLUENCY BUILDER SERIES

SEE TO MARK

Subject-Verb Agreement

Directions: Mark the correct verb.

(Doesn't, Don't) we have time to eat dinner? The water (surround, surrounds) the small island. She (recommends, recommend) (3)

that we finish our homework on time. Mary (has, have) enough work for two people. (Was, Were) you home early last night? (5)

His patients (follow, follows) his advice. (Does, Do) you have a new record? We (have, has) decided to work late tomorrow. (8)

(There's, There are) more snow predicted for Thursday. We (travels, travel) all over the country every year. Sue's children (is, are) (11)

staying with Mom. Your hat (look, looks) fantastic with your dress. The recipe (call, calls) for three eggs. My children (annoy, (14)

annoys) me sometimes. The salesmen (travel, travels) to yearly meetings. (Do, Does) your teacher get a vacation? The boys will (16)

(ran, run) in the race. The wind (was, were) blowing trees over. (Is, Are) you going to Texas for the holidays? She (has, have) a lot (20)

of work to do. She (has, have) a new dress for the dance. When (was, were) you going to see my aunt? His bad grades (were, was) (23)

a problem for him. We (is, are) going shopping on Saturday. The boys (grow, grows) faster than the girls. She (calls, call) us all (26)

the time. The stores (recommend, recommends) that everyone buy a lot of presents. The party (wasn't, weren't) long enough. (28)

ANSWER SHEET

Practicing Basic Skills in Language Arts • 264

© 2005 Sopris West Educational Services. All rights reserved. Practicing Basic Skills in Language Arts. Purchaser has permission to photocopy this page for classroom use only.

ONE-MINUTE FLUENCY BUILDER SERIES

SEE TO MARK

	Correct	Error
First Try		
Second Try		

Indefinite Pronouns and Verb Agreement

Directions: Mark the verb which agrees with the subject in number.

Each of us (do, does) baby-sitting. Everyone on both teams (seem, seems) nervous. Several of those girls (has, have) been working here. Each of the boys (want, wants) a ticket. Anybody in these classes (are, is) eligible for the contest. One of those men (don't, doesn't) live in this town. Everybody in these groups (do, does) careful work. One of the buttons (are, is) missing. (Have, Has) either of the trees lost its leaves? Everything (were, was) in its place. One of the books (were, was) put by itself. Each of the rock collections (have, has) its special shelf. (Does, Do) anyone want his or her dessert now? Each of the members (has, have) offered his or her help. Neither of them (have, has) recovered from his cold. Both of the students (were, was) awarded first place. (Do, Does) everybody understand his or her part of the work? Both of these roads (lead, leads) to the lake. Neither of my brothers (wear, wears) glasses. Several of my friends (are, is) working after school. A few of the boys (was, were) playing touch football. Neither Richard nor his brother (works, work) here. Some of the lights in the room (has, have) gone out. Each of the girls (is, are) displaying her sewing project. (Have, Has) anyone seen either of my two pens? Several of his friends (is, are) giving him a surprise party. Both of the neighbors (have, has) installed an automatic sprinkling system. None of the students (is, are) receiving deficiency letters this term. Neither of the twins (has, have) entered the writing contest this year. Several of the visitors (hope, hopes) to see the Statue of Liberty when they visit New York City. No one in the library (is, are) reading. Somebody (were, was) speaking to the class when the power went off. Neither of them (like, likes) pizza as well as I do. Both of the administrators (were, was) watching you as you ran wildly down the stairs. No one (are, is) ever late to first period class. Everyone (dream, dreams) of growing up to be an adult. Each of the groups (are, is) competing in the district fair. All of the winners (are, is) to receive an award.

Practicing Basic Skills in Language Arts • 265

© 2005 Sopris West Educational Services. All rights reserved. Practicing Basic Skills in Language Arts. Purchaser has permission to photocopy this page for classroom use only.

	First Try	Second Try
Correct		
Error		

Indefinite Pronouns and Verb Agreement

Directions: Mark the verb which agrees with the subject in number.

Each of us (do, <u>does</u>) baby-sitting. Everyone on both teams (seem, <u>seems</u>) nervous. Several of those girls (has, <u>have</u>) been working (3)

here. Each of the boys (want, <u>wants</u>) a ticket. Anybody in these classes (are, <u>is</u>) eligible for the contest. One of those men (<u>don't</u>, (5)

<u>doesn't</u>) live in this town. Everybody in these groups (do, <u>does</u>) careful work. One of the buttons (are, <u>is</u>) missing. (Have, <u>Has</u>) (9)

either of the trees lost its leaves? Everything (were, <u>was</u>) in its place. One of the books (were, <u>was</u>) put by itself. Each of the rock (11)

collections (have, <u>has</u>) its special shelf. (<u>Does</u>, Do) anyone want his or her dessert now? Each of the members (<u>has</u>, have) offered (14)

his or her help. Neither of them (have, <u>has</u>) recovered from his cold. Both of the students (<u>were</u>, was) awarded first place. (Do, (16)

<u>Does</u>) everybody understand his or her part of the work? Both of these roads (<u>lead</u>, leads) to the lake. Neither of my brothers (18)

(wear, <u>wears</u>) glasses. Several of my friends (<u>are</u>, is) working after school. A few of the boys (was, <u>were</u>) playing touch football. (21)

Neither Richard nor his brother (<u>works</u>, work) here. Some of the lights in the room (has, <u>have</u>) gone out. Each of the girls (<u>is</u>, (24)

are) displaying her sewing project. (Have, <u>Has</u>) anyone seen either of my two pens? Several of his friends (is, <u>are</u>) giving him a (26)

surprise party. Both of the neighbors (<u>have</u>, has) installed an automatic sprinkling system. None of the students (is, <u>are</u>) receiving (28)

deficiency letters this term. Neither of the twins (<u>has</u>, have) entered the writing contest this year. Several of the visitors (<u>hope</u>, (30)

hopes) to see the Statue of Liberty when they visit New York City. No one in the library (<u>is</u>, are) reading. Somebody (were, <u>was</u>) (32)

speaking to the class when the power went off. Neither of them (like, <u>likes</u>) pizza as well as I do. Both of the administrators (<u>were</u>, (34)

was) watching you as you ran wildly down the stairs. No one (are, <u>is</u>) ever late to first period class. Everyone (dream, <u>dreams</u>) of (36)

growing up to be an adult. Each of the groups (are, <u>is</u>) competing in the district fair. (38)

© 2005 Sopris West Educational Services. All rights reserved. Practicing Basic Skills in Language Arts. Purchaser has permission to photocopy this page for classroom use only.

ONE MINUTE FLUENCY BUILDER SERIES

	Correct	Error
First Try		
Second Try		

Subjects Joined By Or-Nor, Either-Or, Neither-Nor and Verb Agreement

Directions: Mark the correct verb.

The governor or the mayor (are, is) responsible. Either my friend or my roommate (has, have) borrowed my newest CD. A sweater or a light jacket (were, was) sufficient. Neither my aunt nor my grandmother (live, lives) in Florida. The cheerleaders and the team (has, have) left for the game. An eighth grader and a ninth grader (was, were) elected as representatives from our junior high school. The faculty and the administrators (were, was) planning the activities for field day in the event of rain. Neither spaghetti nor meatballs (is, are) on the school lunch menu this week. A teacher or a principal (avoid, avoids) swear words. Mr. Goodey and a student (was, were) having a discussion about future student activities at our school. Neither Marcia nor Linda (has, have) turned in her overdue books. Either the first contestant or the second one (has, have) the best chance to win the pageant. The kangaroo and the deer (is, are) leaping through the grass at the zoo. Neither she nor her friend (is, are) invited to the party tonight. Either evaporated milk or cream (are, is) used in the recipe. Either Sadowsky or Fisher (is, are) starting as quarterback. The tricycle and the other toys (belong, belongs) on the porch. Neither elephants nor monkeys (was, were) bought for this zoo. (Doesn't, Don't) Mother or her sisters want that old chair? Neither the piano nor the violin (sound, sounds) in tune. The pen and the pencil (was, were) marked with my name. Either John or his brothers (come, comes) here every day. Neither the roses nor the geraniums (has, have) frozen. The man and the women (were, was) strangers to me. Tea or coffee (are, is) his usual drink. Cats and dogs (is, are) plentiful at our house. Either James or Shaun (are, is) the winner. Neither the tables nor the chairs (is, are) new. Neither the chickens nor the mother hen (were, was) nearby. These scissors and shears (is, are) sharp. There (are, is) three children and two dogs playing in the park. (Has, Have) your parents and your brothers returned yet? The package of books and the box of pencils (is, are) still missing.

Practicing Basic Skills in Language Arts • 267

© 2005 Sopris West Educational Services. All rights reserved. Practicing Basic Skills in Language Arts. Purchaser has permission to photocopy this page for classroom use only.

SEE TO MARK

	Correct	Error
First Try		
Second Try		

Subjects Joined By Or-Nor, Either-Or, Neither-Nor and Verb Agreement
Directions: Mark the correct verb.

The governor or the mayor (are, <u>is</u>) responsible. Either my friend or my roommate (<u>has</u>, have) borrowed my newest CD. A (2)

sweater or a light jacket (were, was) sufficient. Neither my aunt nor my grandmother (live, <u>lives</u>) in Florida. The cheerleaders and (4)

the team (has, <u>have</u>) left for the game. An eighth grader and a ninth grader (was, <u>were</u>) elected as representatives from our junior (6)

high school. The faculty and the administrators (<u>were</u>, was) planning the activities for field day in the event of rain. Neither (7)

spaghetti nor meatballs (is, <u>are</u>) on the school lunch menu this week. A teacher or a principal (avoid, <u>avoids</u>) swear words. Mr. (9)

Goodey and a student (was, <u>were</u>) having a discussion about future student activities at our school. Neither Marcia nor Linda (10)

(<u>has</u>, have) turned in her overdue books. Either the first contestant or the second one (<u>has</u>, have) the best chance to win the (12)

pageant. The kangaroo and the deer (is, <u>are</u>) leaping through the grass at the zoo. Neither she nor her friend (<u>is</u>, are) invited (14)

to the party tonight. Either evaporated milk or cream (are, <u>is</u>) used in the recipe. Either Sadowsky or Fisher (<u>is</u>, are) starting as (16)

quarterback. The tricycle and the other toys (<u>belong</u>, belongs) on the porch. Neither elephants nor monkeys (was, <u>were</u>) bought (18)

for this zoo. (<u>Doesn't</u>, Don't) Mother or her sisters want that old chair? Neither the piano nor the violin (sound, <u>sounds</u>) in tune. (20)

The pen and the pencil (was, <u>were</u>) marked with my name. Either John or his brothers (<u>come</u>, comes) here every day. Neither (22)

the roses nor the geraniums (has, <u>have</u>) frozen. The man and the women (<u>were</u>, was) strangers to me. Tea or coffee (are, <u>is</u>) his (25)

usual drink. Cats and dogs (is, <u>are</u>) plentiful at our house. Either James or Shaun (are, <u>is</u>) the winner. Neither the tables nor the (27)

chairs (is, <u>are</u>) new. Neither the chickens nor the mother hen (were, <u>was</u>) nearby. These scissors and shears (is, <u>are</u>) sharp. There (30)

(<u>are</u>, is) three children and two dogs playing in the park. (Has, <u>Have</u>) your parents and your brothers returned yet? The package (32)

of books and the box of pencils (is, <u>are</u>) still missing. (33)

ANSWER SHEET

Practicing Basic Skills in Language Arts • 268

© 2005 Sopris West Educational Services. All rights reserved. Practicing Basic Skills in Language Arts. Purchaser has permission to photocopy this page for classroom use only.

SEE TO MARK

Compound Subjects and Verb Agreement

Directions: Mark the correct verb.

	Correct	Error
First Try		
Second Try		

When (was, were) you and your mother at the doctor's office? The teacher and the principal (were, was) surprised by Betty's report. The captain of the football team and the captain of the basketball team (have, has) many responsibilities. (Is, Are) the book reports and the rough drafts due this week or next? The president and his aides (was, were) studying the latest crisis. The singer and the band members (is, are) on tour for six months. The brain and spinal cord (is, are) part of the central nervous system. A quartet by Haydn and a quintet by Mozart (were, was) played at the concert. Imported pure silks and domestic cottons (are, is) on display at the store. Oranges, grapes, and boxes of candy (is, are) welcome gifts. Streams and rivers (are, is) overflowing and flooding the valley. Unjust punishment and excessive flogging (turn, turns) crews against their captains. Both the coach and his assistant (was, were) injured in the crash. Bells, sirens, and whistles (were, was) screeching a warning. The bus and the semi (was, were) racing at a maddening pace toward a head-on collision. The paramedics and the police (were, was) rushing to the scene of the accident when they found out it was just an April Fool's prank. The girls and their parents (was, were) sentenced to pay expenses caused by their thoughtless deed. Lisa, Ling, and Natalie (have, has) decided to take metal shop this semester. Rambling stories and trivial chatter (is, are) boring to even the best listener. Thoughtless words and rude remarks (are, is) offensive and gain little. Thoughtful boys and girls (is, are) not rude. Courtesy and a pleasing manner (are, is) desirable personality traits. The cast and the stage crew (has, have) spent many long hours preparing the school play. Stan and Pedro (has, have) been friends since the first grade. (Is, Are) Penny and Myra still studying ballet? Alyson and Rosa (has, have) seen all the latest movies at the theatres. The rocks and the minerals (are, is) not difficult to identify once you become familiar with them. Joe and Tyronne (is, are) coming to the party late.

© 2005 Sopris West Educational Services. All rights reserved. Practicing Basic Skills in Language Arts. Purchaser has permission to photocopy this page for classroom use only.

SEE TO MARK

Compound Subjects and Verb Agreement

Directions: Mark the correct verb.

When (was, <u>were</u>) you and your mother at the doctor's office? The teacher and the principal (<u>were</u>, was) surprised by Betty's (2)

report. The captain of the football team and the captain of the basketball team (<u>have</u>, has) many responsibilities. (Is, <u>Are</u>) the (4)

book reports and the rough drafts due this week or next? The president and his aides (was, <u>were</u>) studying the latest crisis. The (5)

singer and the band members (is, <u>are</u>) on tour for six months. The brain and spinal cord (is, <u>are</u>) part of the central nervous (7)

system. A quartet by Haydn and a quintet by Mozart (<u>were</u>, was) played at the concert. Imported pure silks and domestic (8)

cottons (<u>are</u>, is) on display at the store. Oranges, grapes, and boxes of candy (is, <u>are</u>) welcome gifts. Streams and rivers (<u>are</u>, is) (11)

overflowing and flooding the valley. Unjust punishment and excessive flogging (<u>turn</u>, turns) crews against their captains. Both (12)

the coach and his assistant (was, <u>were</u>) injured in the crash. Bells, sirens, and whistles (<u>were</u>, was) screeching a warning. The (14)

bus and the semi (was, <u>were</u>) racing at a maddening pace toward a head-on collision. The paramedics and the police (<u>were</u>, was) (16)

rushing to the scene of the accident when they found out it was just an April Fool's prank. The girls and their parents (was, (16)

<u>were</u>) sentenced to pay expenses caused by their thoughtless deed. Lisa, Ling, and Natalie (<u>have</u>, has) decided to take metal shop (18)

this semester. Rambling stories and trivial chatter (is, <u>are</u>) boring to even the best listener. Thoughtless words and rude remarks (19)

(<u>are</u>, is) offensive and gain little. Thoughtful boys and girls (is, <u>are</u>) not rude. Courtesy and a pleasing manner (<u>are</u>, is) desirable (22)

personality traits. The cast and the stage crew (has, <u>have</u>) spent many long hours preparing the school play. Stan and Pedro (has, (23)

<u>have</u>) been friends since the first grade. (Is, <u>Are</u>) Penny and Myra still studying ballet? Alyson and Rosa (has, <u>have</u>) seen all the (26)

latest movies at the theatres. The rocks and the minerals (<u>are</u>, is) not difficult to identify once you become familiar with them. (27)

Joe and Tyronne (is, <u>are</u>) coming to the party late. (28)

ANSWER SHEET

Practicing Basic Skills in Language Arts • 270

© 2005 Sopris West Educational Services. All rights reserved. Practicing Basic Skills in Language Arts. Purchaser has permission to photocopy this page for classroom use only.

ONE-MINUTE FLUENCY
BUILDER SERIES

Compound Subjects and Verb Agreement

Directions: Mark the correct verb.

Each of the buildings (have, has) a fire escape. Letters and phone calls (pour, pours) in after his speeches. Only a few (know, knows) Nancy's secret. There (is, are) some fresh doughnuts in the kitchen. My brother (don't, doesn't) like hot weather, but I (don't, doesn't) mind it. Several of the roads (are, is) doublelane highways. Neither flattery nor persuasion (change, changes) his mind. The pilot's report (don't, doesn't) mention spotting any survivors. (Here's, Here are) some tomatoes from my garden. Neither low clouds nor fog (prevents, prevent) planes from landing. There (is, are) two students working on each experiment. The cars and buses (was, were) stalled in the traffic jam. Either the switchboard or the telephone (are, is) out of order. All of the farm animals (has, have) to be fed. There (is, are) a big tropical storm moving up the coast. Few of the men on submarines ever (wants, want) to change to shore service. That tomcat and his friends (has, have) serenaded us all night. (Here's, Here are) the flowers we picked for the banquet. The cake looks good but it (don't, doesn't) taste good. There (was, were) two men and three women on the committee. Someone in the group (is, are) missing. It seems that everyone in the school (is, are) coming. My coat and hat (has, have) been stolen. Strawberry pie (don't, doesn't) agree with me. (There's, There are) twelve more days until mid-year vacation. There (was, were) nothing we could do about it. Either an apple or two bananas (is, are) in her lunch sack. The girls and their mother (was, were) baking cookies. Neither the flowers nor the vegetables (has, have) been watered today. There (is, are) a lot of new students in our class now. (Don't, Doesn't) the owner of this car live here? Rhubarb and strawberries (make, makes) a good pie. There (is, are) more than twenty overdue books from the library. The airplanes and trains (is, are) running late because of the heavy snowfall. Why (don't, doesn't) they take the back road?

© 2005 Sopris West Educational Services. All rights reserved. Practicing Basic Skills in Language Arts. Purchaser has permission to photocopy this page for classroom use only.

	Correct	Error
First Try		
Second Try		

Compound Subjects and Verb Agreement

Directions: Mark the correct verb.

Each of the buildings (have, has) a fire escape. Letters and phone calls (pour, pours) in after his speeches. Only a few (know, (3)

knows) Nancy's secret. There (is, are) some fresh doughnuts in the kitchen. My brother (don't, doesn't) like hot weather, but I (5)

(don't, doesn't) mind it. Several of the roads (are, is) doublelane highways. Neither flattery nor persuasion (change, changes) (8)

his mind. The pilot's report (don't, doesn't) mention spotting any survivors. (Here's, Here are) some tomatoes from my garden. (10)

Neither low clouds nor fog (prevents, prevent) planes from landing. There (is, are) two students working on each experiment. (12)

The cars and buses (was, were) stalled in the traffic jam. Either the switchboard or the telephone (are, is) out of order. All of the (14)

farm animals (has, have) to be fed. There (is, are) a big tropical storm moving up the coast. Few of the men on submarines ever (16)

(wants, want) to change to shore service. That tomcat and his friends (has, have) serenaded us all night. (Here's, Here are) the (19)

flowers we picked for the banquet. The cake looks good but it (don't, doesn't) taste good. There (was, were) two men and three (21)

women on the committee. Someone in the group (is, are) missing. It seems that everyone in the school (is, are) coming. My coat (23)

and hat (has, have) been stolen. Strawberry pie (don't, doesn't) agree with me. (There's, There are) twelve more days until mid- (26)

year vacation. There (was, were) nothing we could do about it. Either an apple or two bananas (is, are) in her lunch sack. The (28)

girls and their mother (was, were) baking cookies. Neither the flowers nor the vegetables (has, have) been watered today. There (30)

(is, are) a lot of new students in our class now. (Don't, Doesn't) the owner of this car live here? Rhubarb and strawberries (make, (33)

makes) a good pie. There (is, are) more than twenty overdue books from the library. The airplanes and trains (is, are) running (35)

late because of the heavy snowfall. Why (don't, doesn't) they take the back road? (36)

Practicing Basic Skills in Language Arts • 272

© 2005 Sopris West Educational Services. All rights reserved. Practicing Basic Skills in Language Arts. Purchaser has permission to photocopy this page for classroom use only.

Plural Subject-Verb Agreement—Fill in the Blank

Directions: Write in the correct present tense plural form of the verb in parentheses. (or) Say the sentences aloud using the correct plural form of the verb.

	Correct	Error
First Try		
Second Try		

ONE MINUTE FLUENCY BUILDER SERIES

We (be) _____ going home. They (do) _____ their work after school. They (be) _____ younger than the others. They (want) _____ to go home after the party. The cars (travel) _____ better on dry pavement. My parents (arrive) _____ tomorrow afternoon. The men (run) _____ past our house every evening. We (do) _____ not let people break the rules. All of the people (be) _____ welcome to join the fun. The girls (understand) _____ their duties. Margaret and Mary (be) _____ coming to the party. Perhaps all of them (see) _____ the car. There (be) _____ good people in this city. Both Jan and Burton (look) _____ sad. These hamburgers (taste) _____ dry. These flowers (do) _____ not need to be watered each day. The attorneys (have) _____ closed their cases. Both of the fingers (be) _____ broken. They (talk) _____ faster than they (think) _____. The divisions of the lecture (be) _____ written on the outline. These papers (look) _____ weathered. (be) _____ these books yours? Prices of clothing (jump) _____ a few dollars each year. Mark and Jack (sell) _____ magazines door to door. The Tanabe sisters, as well as Gracie, (be) _____ looking after my house while we (travel) _____ around the country. All (be) _____ invited to the reunion. The girls (ride) _____ motorcycles to work. Both of the toys (have) _____ been thrown away. (be) _____ they waiting for me outside? Here (come) _____ Janet and Raye. Policemen (work) _____ long shifts. The Foleys (live) _____ in that white house. Sheep (be) _____ found in the high country. Missiles (have) _____ replaced many methods of defense. Many countries (seem) _____ unable to protect themselves. My brothers-in-law (be) _____ in my front room. Maxine and Brad (live) _____ close by. The curtains in the bedroom (need) _____ cleaning.

© 2005 Sopris West Educational Services. All rights reserved. Practicing Basic Skills in Language Arts. Purchaser has permission to photocopy this page for classroom use only.

Plural Subject-Verb Agreement—Fill in the Blank

Directions: Write in the correct present tense plural form of the verb in parentheses. (or) Say the sentences aloud using the correct plural form of the verb.

	First Try	Second Try
Correct		
Error		

We (be) **are** going home. They (do) **do** their work after school. They (be) **are** younger (3)

than the others. They (want) **want** to go home after the party. The cars (travel) **travel** better on dry (5)

pavement. My parents (arrive) **arrive** tomorrow afternoon. The men (run) **run** past our house every (7)

evening. We (do) **do** not let people break the rules. All of the people (be) **are** welcome to join (9)

the fun. The girls (understand) **understand** their duties. Margaret and Mary (be) **are** coming to the party. (11)

Perhaps all of them (see) **see** the car. There (be) **are** good people in this city. Both Jan and Burton (13)

(look) **look** sad. These hamburgers (taste) **taste** dry. These flowers (do) **do** not need to be (16)

watered each day. The attorneys (have) **have** closed their cases. Both of the fingers (be) **are** broken. (18)

They (talk) **talk** faster than they (think) **think** . The divisions of the lecture (be) **are** written (21)

on the outline. These papers (look) **look** weathered. (be) **Are** these books yours? Prices of clothing (23)

(jump) **jump** a few dollars each year. Mark and Jack (sell) **sell** magazines door to door. The Tanabe (25)

sisters, as well as Gracie, (be) **are** looking after my house while we (travel) **travel** around the country. (27)

All (be) **are** invited to the reunion. The girls (ride) **ride** motorcycles to work. Both of the toys (have) **have** (29)

been thrown away. (be) **Are** they waiting for me outside? Here (come) **come** Janet (32)

and Raye. Policemen (work) **work** long shifts. The Foleys (live) **live** in that white house. Sheep (be) (34)

are found in the high country. Missiles (have) **have** replaced many methods of defense. Many countries (36)

(seem) **seem** unable to protect themselves. My brothers-in-law (be) **are** in my front room. Maxine and (38)

Brad (live) **live** close by. The curtains in the bedroom (need) **need** cleaning. (40)

Practicing Basic Skills in Language Arts • 274

© 2005 Sopris West Educational Services. All rights reserved. Practicing Basic Skills in Language Arts. Purchaser has permission to photocopy this page for classroom use only.

	First Try	Second Try
Correct		
Error		

SEE TO SAY OR SEE TO WRITE

Singular Subject-Verb Agreement—Fill in the Blank

Directions: Write in the correct present tense singular form of the verb in parentheses to agree with the subject. (or) Say the sentences aloud using the correct singular verb for each sentence.

I (be) _____ going home. He (do) _____ his homework every evening. He (be) _____ older

than John. She (want) _____ my homework turned in. The car (travel) _____ well on the road. My father

(arrive) _____ today on the train. The man (walk) _____ past our house. He (do) _____ not

(see) _____ us. You (be) _____ a careful worker. Each of you (be) _____ a good listener. Anyone

(be) _____ welcome to join us. The girl (understand) _____ the question. Neither John nor Mary (be) _____

ready to go. My brother (do) _____ his work faithfully. The bird (fly) _____ in our window

each day. Mei (live) _____ on this block. Measles (be) _____ bad. Here (come) _____ Harold

or Pedro. Perhaps one of them (see) _____ us. There (be) _____ a good actor in the audience. Sandra (do) _____

not like television. Each of the dogs (come) _____ by here each day. The jury (have) _____

reached its decision. The boy (play) _____ hockey well. The subject of the lectures (be) _____ Latin America.

Jerome (ride) _____ his motorcycle to school. Brenda (plan) _____ to attend college. Either Lucia or Mike

(be) _____ expected at the meeting. She (know) _____ the plan of action. Dylan's job (be) _____

terrific. Chien (look) _____ unhappy. This chow mein (taste) _____ really good. Each of the girls (have) _____

a new bike. The paper (look) _____ rather dirty. Keesha, as well as her sisters, (be) _____

looking for a job. The flower (do) _____ look nice in your hair. (be) _____ she waiting for me? The cost of the

books (have) _____ gone up over the year. There (be) _____ only one reason why you have given up. Zak, as

well as his brother, (be) _____ planning to attend. Meta (come) _____ to school about once per week. Neither

of the girls (plan) _____ to give a gift. Each of the boys (want) _____ to play first base.

Practicing Basic Skills in Language Arts • 275

© 2005 Sopris West Educational Services. All rights reserved. Practicing Basic Skills in Language Arts. Purchaser has permission to photocopy this page for classroom use only.

ONE-MINUTE FLUENCY BUILDER SERIES

SEE TO SAY OR SEE TO WRITE

Singular Subject-Verb Agreement—Fill in the Blank

Directions: Write in the correct present tense singular form of the verb in parentheses to agree with the subject. (or) Say the sentences aloud using the correct singular verb for each sentence.

	Correct	Error
First Try		
Second Try		

I (be) __am__ going home. He (do) __does__ his homework every evening. He (be) __is__ older (3)

than John. She (want) __wants__ my homework turned in. The car (travel) __travels__ well on the road. My father (5)

(arrive) __arrives__ today on the train. The man (walk) __walks__ past our house. He (do) __does__ not (8)

(see) __see__ us. You (be) __are__ a careful worker. Each of you (be) __is__ a good listener. Anyone (11)

(be) __is__ welcome to join us. The girl (understand) __understands__ the question. Neither John nor Mary (be) (13)

__is__ ready to go. My brother (do) __does__ his work faithfully. The bird (fly) __flies__ in our window (16)

each day. Mei (live) __lives__ on this block. Measles (be) __are__ bad. Here (come) __comes__ Harold (19)

or Pedro. Perhaps one of them (see) __sees__ us. There (be) __is__ a good actor in the audience. Sandra (do) (21)

__does__ not like television. Each of the dogs (come) __comes__ by here each day. The jury (have) __has__ (24)

reached its decision. The boy (play) __plays__ hockey well. The subject of the lectures (be) __is__ Latin America. (26)

Jerome (ride) __rides__ his motorcycle to school. Brenda (plan) __plans__ to attend college. Either Lucia or Mike (28)

(be) __is__ expected at the meeting. She (know) __knows__ the plan of action. Dylan's job (be) __is__ (31)

terrific. Chien (look) __looks__ unhappy. This chow mein (taste) __tastes__ really good. Each of the girls (have) (33)

__has__ a new bike. The paper (look) __looks__ rather dirty. Keesha, as well as her sisters, (be) __is__ (36)

looking for a job. The flower (do) __does__ look nice in your hair. (be) __Is__ she waiting for me? The cost of the (38)

books (have) __has__ gone up over the year. There (be) __is__ only one reason why you have given up. Zak, as (40)

well as his brother, (be) __is__ planning to attend. Meta (come) __comes__ to school about once per week. Neither (42)

of the girls (plan) __plans__ to give a gift. Each of the boys (want) __wants__ to play first base. (44)

ANSWER SHEET

Practicing Basic Skills in Language Arts • 276

© 2005 Sopris West Educational Services. All rights reserved. Practicing Basic Skills in Language Arts. Purchaser has permission to photocopy this page for classroom use only.

ONE-MINUTE FLUENCY
BUILDER SERIES

SEE TO WRITE

Subject-Verb Agreement—Don't/Doesn't

Directions: Fill in the blank with either *don't* or *doesn't* to complete the sentence correctly.

He _____ mind if we ask lots of questions. It _____ matter whether the party is held this week or the

next. My little sister _____ believe in Santa Claus. Margaret _____ like skiing. My uncle

work. Jean loves spaghetti, but she _____ like to gain weight. _____ it look like rain? I

like playing soccer in the rain. _____ you think the scenery is beautiful? Nick and Gary _____ want to

study. _____ Tom look happy? The new suit I bought for the Christmas dance _____ need alterations.

_____ you think they will be disappointed if we _____ go to their party? The switch to the basement

light _____ work. Why _____ he try out for the school play? The people who moved in across the street

_____ like our dog. The paint on the bricks _____ come off easily. It _____ seem possible.

Lana says she _____ know how to skate. _____ that pie look good? The Smiths _____ approve

of the new school. My cousin _____ want to go with us to Salt Lake City this weekend. He _____ feel

like shoveling the driveway, and I _____ either. That tie _____ look right with that shirt. The game

start before two. The factory _____ make that model of car anymore. _____ the snow

on the mountains look like marshmallow topping? Our cherry trees _____ need to be sprayed this spring. Wendy

_____ care how much the tour to Mexico costs. The baby likes ice cream, _____ she? I wonder why he

_____ answer the phone. The *Ogden Standard Examiner* _____ come until five o'clock during the week.

Practicing Basic Skills in Language Arts • 277

© 2005 Sopris West Educational Services. All rights reserved. Practicing Basic Skills in Language Arts. Purchaser has permission to photocopy this page for classroom use only.

ONE-MINUTE FLUENCY BUILDER SERIES

SEE TO WRITE

	Correct	Error
First Try		
Second Try		

Subject-Verb Agreement—Don't/Doesn't

Directions: Fill in the blank with either *don't* or *doesn't* to complete the sentence correctly.

He **doesn't** mind if we ask lots of questions. It **doesn't** matter whether the party is held this week or the (2)

next. My little sister **doesn't** believe in Santa Claus. Margaret **doesn't** like skiing. My uncle (5)

work. Jean loves spaghetti, but she **doesn't** like to gain weight. **Doesn't** it look like rain? I (8)

like playing soccer in the rain. **Don't** you think the scenery is beautiful? Nick and Gary **don't** want to (10)

study. **Doesn't** Tom look happy? The new suit I bought for the Christmas dance **doesn't** need alterations. (12)

Don't you think they will be disappointed if we **don't** go to their party? The switch to the basement (14)

light **doesn't** work. Why **doesn't** he try out for the school play? The people who moved in across the street (16)

don't like our dog. The paint on the bricks **doesn't** come off easily. It **doesn't** seem possible. (19)

Lana says she **doesn't** know how to skate. **Doesn't** that pie look good? The Smiths **don't** approve (22)

of the new school. My cousin **doesn't** want to go with us to Salt Lake City this weekend. He **doesn't** feel (24)

like shoveling the driveway, and I **don't** either. That tie **doesn't** look right with that shirt. The game (26)

start before two. The factory **doesn't** make that model of car anymore. **Doesn't** the snow (29)

on the mountains look like marshmallow topping? Our cherry trees **don't** need to be sprayed this spring. Wendy (30)

doesn't care how much the tour to Mexico costs. The baby likes ice cream, **doesn't** she? I wonder why he (32)

doesn't answer the phone. The *Ogden Standard Examiner* **doesn't** come until five o'clock during the week. (34)

© 2005 Sopris West Educational Services. All rights reserved. Practicing Basic Skills in Language Arts. Purchaser has permission to photocopy this page for classroom use only.

ONE-MINUTE FLUENCY BUILDER SERIES

Subject-Verb Agreement—Don't/Doesn't

Directions: Mark the correct verb for the following sentence: *don't/doesn't.*

	Correct	Error
First Try		
Second Try		

(Don't, Doesn't) they know that Frank is your cousin? He (don't, doesn't) want to play catch. Mark and Luis (don't, doesn't) like

to practice for an hour every afternoon. (Don't, Doesn't) he arrive on the five

o'clock flight from Denver? It (don't, doesn't) really matter if you are a little late. (Don't, Doesn't) the new books in the media

center look interesting? I know you, (don't, doesn't) I? A canary, a robin, and a bluejay (don't, doesn't) weigh very much. Mom

(don't, doesn't) get up before noon on Saturdays. The boys and girls (don't, doesn't) take very good care of their new bikes.

My parakeet (don't, doesn't) talk when strangers come to the house. She (don't, doesn't) speak Spanish very well. Gary and

Darnell (don't, doesn't) skate very well. (Don't, Doesn't) you have my assignment graded yet? The leaders of the expeditions

(don't, doesn't) dare to take chances on the roaring river. He (don't, doesn't) have a fishing rod that he can take with him on

the camping trip. (Don't, Doesn't) the bus stop at this corner anymore? I (don't, doesn't) like Chinese food. She (don't, doesn't)

know how to whistle. I (don't, doesn't) understand why she (don't, doesn't) live here anymore. (Don't, Doesn't) he ever drink

milk? Our lawn furniture (don't, doesn't) rust because it is made of aluminum. Our TV (don't, doesn't) work anymore. It (don't,

doesn't) make any difference. The football team (don't, doesn't) practice on weekends. Why (don't, doesn't) they take the back

road? She (don't, doesn't) like spinach, and I (don't, doesn't) either. Male mosquitoes (don't, doesn't) bite. Peggy and Latoya

(don't, doesn't) have their bikes with them today. The fresh air feels good, (don't, doesn't) it? Some people in our math class

(don't, doesn't) do their homework on time. The dining room table and chairs (don't, doesn't) need painting. Marcos tried to fix

the radio, but it still (don't, doesn't) work. Mr. Lee and his wife (don't, doesn't) swim.

Practicing Basic Skills in Language Arts • 279

© 2005 Sopris West Educational Services. All rights reserved. Practicing Basic Skills in Language Arts. Purchaser has permission to photocopy this page for classroom use only.

ONE-MINUTE FLUENCY BUILDER SERIES

SEE TO MARK

Subject-Verb Agreement—Don't/Doesn't

Directions: Mark the correct verb for the following sentence: *don't/doesn't.*

	First Try	Second Try
Correct		
Error		

(Don't, Doesn't) they know that Frank is your cousin? He (don't, doesn't) want to play catch. Mark and Luis (don't, doesn't) like (3)

to practice for an hour every afternoon. (Don't, Doesn't) he arrive on the five (5)

o'clock flight from Denver? It (don't, doesn't) really matter if you are a little late. (Don't, Doesn't) the new books in the media (7)

center look interesting? I know you, (don't, doesn't) I? A canary, a robin, and a bluejay (don't, doesn't) weigh very much. Mom (9)

(don't, doesn't) get up before noon on Saturdays. The boys and girls (don't, doesn't) take very good care of their new bikes. (11)

My parakeet (don't, doesn't) talk when strangers come to the house. She (don't, doesn't) speak Spanish very well. Gary and (13)

Darnell (don't, doesn't) skate very well. (Don't, Doesn't) you have my assignment graded yet? The leaders of the expeditions (15)

(don't, doesn't) dare to take chances on the roaring river. He (don't, doesn't) have a fishing rod that he can take with him on (17)

the camping trip. (Don't, Doesn't) the bus stop at this corner anymore? I (don't, doesn't) like Chinese food. She (don't, doesn't) (20)

know how to whistle. I (don't, doesn't) understand why she (don't, doesn't) live here anymore. (Don't, Doesn't) he ever drink (23)

milk? Our lawn furniture (don't, doesn't) rust because it is made of aluminum. Our TV (don't, doesn't) work anymore. It (don't, (25)

doesn't) make any difference. The football team (don't, doesn't) practice on weekends. Why (don't, doesn't) they take the back (28)

road? She (don't, doesn't) like spinach, and I (don't, doesn't) either. Male mosquitoes (don't, doesn't) bite. Peggy and Latoya (31)

(don't, doesn't) have their bikes with them today. The fresh air feels good, (don't, doesn't) it? Some people in our math class (33)

(don't, doesn't) do their homework on time. The dining room table and chairs (don't, doesn't) need painting. Marcos tried to fix (35)

the radio, but it still (don't, doesn't) work. Mr. Lee and his wife (don't, doesn't) swim. (37)

ANSWER SHEET

Practicing Basic Skills in Language Arts • 280

© 2005 Sopris West Educational Services. All rights reserved. Practicing Basic Skills in Language Arts. Purchaser has permission to photocopy this page for classroom use only.

ONE-MINUTE
FLUENCY
BUILDER SERIES

	Correct	Error
First Try		
Second Try		

SEE TO MARK

Subject-Verb Agreement—Is/Are, Was/Were, Has/Have

Directions: Mark the correct verb for each sentence: *is/are, was/were, has/have.*

There (has, have) been some changes in our plans. Just an hour ago there (was, were) twenty pieces of homemade candy on that plate. Here (is, are) a new idea for you to use in your essay. There (is, are) room for you. There (was, were) swordfish, angelfish, and guppies in my friend's new aquarium. There (was, were) eight puppies in the litter. (There's, There are) some ripe melons on that vine. There (was, were) five homers hit out of the stadium during the first game of the double-header. There (was, were) not a house in sight. There (hasn't, haven't) been many customers today because of the heavy snowfall. (There's, There are) only five shopping days left until Christmas. There (was, were) a fire drill during third period today. There (is, are) three children sliding down the hill on their sleds. Mr. Prince told us that there (is, are) nine planets revolving around the sun. For every contestant there (was, were) a prize. (There's, There are) a man knocking at her front door. The announcer said, "There (is, are) five first prizes, ten second prizes, fifteen third prizes and twenty fourth prizes in the new magazine contest." (Here's, Here are) the skis for Jeff. There (has, have) been a delay. (There's, There are) days when I'd like to wring my little brother's neck. (There's, There are) four letters on the kitchen table that are for you. There (was, were) a better road up this canyon when I was here last summer. Today (there's, there are) shots for whooping cough, chicken pox, measles, and almost every other disease. There (is, are) an additional charge if we deliver the flowers. There (is, are) other visitors in the audience from Arizona. On Saturday mornings (there's, there are) usually four hours of cartoons on television. There (was, were) several answers to the question. There once (was, were) a small cottage in this grove of pine trees. There (was, were) animal tracks all around the camp. There (is, are) good programs on television on Wednesday evenings. There (was, were) a great deal of excitement in the halls during Spirit Week. There (is, are) sounds downstairs.

© 2005 Sopris West Educational Services. All rights reserved. Practicing Basic Skills in Language Arts. Purchaser has permission to photocopy this page for classroom use only.

ONE-MINUTE FLUENCY BUILDER SERIES

SEE TO MARK

Subject-Verb Agreement—Is/Are, Was/Were, Has/Have

Directions: Mark the correct verb for each sentence: *is/are, was/were, has/have.*

	First Try	Second Try
Correct		
Error		

There (has, <u>have</u>) been some changes in our plans. Just an hour ago there (was, <u>were</u>) twenty pieces of homemade candy on that (2)

plate. Here (<u>is</u>, are) a new idea for you to use in your essay. There (<u>is</u>, are) room for you. There (was, <u>were</u>) swordfish, angelfish, (5)

and guppies in my friend's new aquarium. There (was, <u>were</u>) eight puppies in the litter. (There's, <u>There are</u>) some ripe melons (7)

on that vine. There (was, <u>were</u>) five homers hit out of the stadium during the first game of the double-header. There (<u>was</u>, were) (9)

not a house in sight. There (hasn't, <u>haven't</u>) been many customers today because of the heavy snowfall. (There's, <u>There are</u>) only (11)

five shopping days left until Christmas. There (<u>was</u>, were) a fire drill during third period today. There (is, <u>are</u>) three children (13)

sliding down the hill on their sleds. Mr. Prince told us that there (is, <u>are</u>) nine planets revolving around the sun. For every (14)

contestant there (<u>was</u>, were) a prize. (<u>There's</u>, There are) a man knocking at her front door. The announcer said, "There (is, <u>are</u>) (17)

five first prizes, ten second prizes, fifteen third prizes and twenty fourth prizes in the new magazine contest." (Here's, <u>Here are</u>) (18)

the skis for Jeff. There (<u>has</u>, have) been a delay. (There's, <u>There are</u>) days when I'd like to wring my little brother's neck. (There's, (20)

<u>There are</u>) four letters on the kitchen table that are for you. There (was, <u>were</u>) a better road up this canyon when I was here (22)

last summer. Today (there's, <u>there are</u>) shots for whooping cough, chicken pox, measles, and almost every other disease. There (23)

(<u>is</u>, are) an additional charge if we deliver the flowers. There (is, <u>are</u>) other visitors in the audience from Arizona. On Saturday (25)

mornings (there's, <u>there are</u>) usually four hours of cartoons on television. There (was, <u>were</u>) several answers to the question. (27)

There once (<u>was</u>, were) a small cottage in this grove of pine trees. There (was, <u>were</u>) animal tracks all around the camp. There (is, (29)

are) good programs on television on Wednesday evenings. There (<u>was</u>, were) a great deal of excitement in the halls during Spirit (31)

Week. There (is, <u>are</u>) sounds downstairs. (32)

ANSWER SHEET

Practicing Basic Skills in Language Arts • 282

© 2005 Sopris West Educational Services. All rights reserved. Practicing Basic Skills in Language Arts. Purchaser has permission to photocopy this page for classroom use only.

ONE-MINUTE FLUENCY
BUILDER SERIES

SEE TO MARK

Noun Clauses

Directions: Underline each noun clause.

	First Try	Second Try
Correct		
Error		

What effect the oil spill might have was discussed by the concerned citizens. The Bakers moved to where the climate is drier.

Heather could guess whose voice had boomed out. The writer's greatest concern was whether her book would sell. Give this

message to whoever answers. Dr. Ching explained how solar batteries work. Noel is the person who was chosen to represent

the group. The practical joker was embarrassed about what he had done. What you do with your money is your business. Why

you did not get my letter puzzles me. I wonder if she will come to the party. She couldn't see from where she sat. I hope that we

can find it. His strength is not equal to what he has to do. The principal said that he would not need us. You must ask for what

you want. How he can do it so well is really amazing. That he is not guilty is believed by all. Do you think she is sorry for what

she said? He saw too late that he was wrong. He asked if he might leave. That he won surprised everyone. There may be some

truth in what he says. Where he had been for so long puzzled me. The boy regretted what he had done. What they said did not

matter. Does anyone know where he lives? How he escaped is a mystery. My idea is that he had inside help. I wonder where he

is hiding. We have offered whoever finds him a reward. We have no word of where he is. I heard what you said. Whoever told

you is wrong. Whoever finds the ring will be rewarded. His excuse is that his alarm did not ring. This beautiful trophy goes to

whoever wins the match. Do you know why people are cheering?

Practicing Basic Skills in Language Arts • 283

© 2005 Sopris West Educational Services. All rights reserved. Practicing Basic Skills in Language Arts. Purchaser has permission to photocopy this page for classroom use only.

SEE TO MARK

Noun Clauses

Directions: Underline each noun clause.

ONE MINUTE FLUENCY
BUILDER SERIES

	First Try	Second Try
Correct		
Error		

What effect the oil spill might have was discussed by the concerned citizens. The Bakers moved to where the climate is drier. (2)

Heather could guess whose voice had boomed out. The writer's greatest concern was whether her book would sell. Give this (4)

message to whoever answers. Dr. Ching explained how solar batteries work. Noel is the person who was chosen to represent (7)

the group. The practical joker was embarrassed about what he had done. What you do with your money is your business. Why (10)

you did not get my letter puzzles me. I wonder if she will come to the party. She couldn't see from where she sat. I hope that we (13)

can find it. His strength is not equal to what he has to do. The principal said that he would not need us. You must ask for what (16)

you want. How he can do it so well is really amazing. That he is not guilty is believed by all. Do you think she is sorry for what (19)

she said? He saw too late that he was wrong. He asked if he might leave. That he won surprised everyone. There may be some (22)

truth in what he says. Where he had been for so long puzzled me. The boy regretted what he had done. What they said did not (26)

matter. Does anyone know where he lives? How he escaped is a mystery. My idea is that he had inside help. I wonder where he (30)

is hiding. We have offered whoever finds him a reward. We have no word of where he is. I heard what you said. Whoever told (34)

you is wrong. Whoever finds the ring will be rewarded. His excuse is that his alarm did not ring. This beautiful trophy goes to (36)

whoever wins the match. Do you know why people are cheering? (38)

ANSWER SHEET

Practicing Basic Skills in Language Arts • 284

© 2005 Sopris West Educational Services. All rights reserved. Practicing Basic Skills in Language Arts. Purchaser has permission to photocopy this page for classroom use only.

SEE TO MARK

Adjective Clauses
Directions: Underline each adjective clause.

Salamanders that live in caves are usually blind. The Red Cross sheltered the people whose homes had been destroyed. Some

of the fragile glasses that the customer had ordered were broken in shipping. The county supervisor whom I interviewed was

re-elected. Animals that carry babies in a pouch are called marsupials. Only guests whose names appeared on the list were

admitted to the private club. Can you name the scientist who discovered penicillin? The murderers of Julius Caesar were friends

whom he had trusted. The man who bought our house is Mr. Smith. This is the park about which I spoke. Everybody likes a

boy whom they can trust. Carl King, the boy who called you, is my cousin. This book is by an author whose name you know.

Pedro, who is my oldest brother, looks like Father. This is Chien, of whom I have spoken so often. The place where we camped

was well hidden. Have you any idea when Elmer left? The boy who won that race lives near us. We had soon eaten the lunch,

which tasted delicious. Stephen K. Meader is an author whose books young people enjoy. Uncle Bob, whom you saw tonight,

is a Korean veteran. I do not remember the town where I was born. People who always come late may lose their friends. There

were two days recently when I really worked hard. My apartment, which is air-conditioned, is cool in hot weather. He is a coach

whom everyone admires. I remember one time when I was really embarrassed. The coat that Maria is wearing is made of velvet.

© 2005 Sopris West Educational Services. All rights reserved. Practicing Basic Skills in Language Arts. Purchaser has permission to photocopy this page for classroom use only.

SEE TO MARK

Adjective Clauses

Directions: Underline each adjective clause.

First Try | Second Try

Correct | Error

Salamanders that live in caves are usually blind. The Red Cross sheltered the people whose homes had been destroyed. Some (2)

of the fragile glasses that the customer had ordered were broken in shipping. The county supervisor whom I interviewed was (4)

re-elected. Animals that carry babies in a pouch are called marsupials. Only guests whose names appeared on the list were (6)

admitted to the private club. Can you name the scientist who discovered penicillin? The murderers of Julius Caesar were friends (7)

whom he had trusted. The man who bought our house is Mr. Smith. This is the park about which I spoke. Everybody likes a (10)

boy whom they can trust. Carl King, the boy who called you, is my cousin. This book is by an author whose name you know. (13)

Pedro, who is my oldest brother, looks like Father. This is Chien, of whom I have spoken so often. The place where we camped (16)

was well hidden. Have you any idea when Elmer left? The boy who won that race lives near us. We had soon eaten the lunch, (18)

which tasted delicious. Stephen K. Meader is an author whose books young people enjoy. Uncle Bob, whom you saw tonight, (21)

is a Korean veteran. I do not remember the town where I was born. People who always come late may lose their friends. There (23)

were two days recently when I really worked hard. My apartment, which is air-conditioned, is cool in hot weather. He is a coach (25)

whom everyone admires. I remember one time when I was really embarrassed. The coat that Maria is wearing is made of velvet. (28)

ANSWER SHEET

Practicing Basic Skills in Language Arts • 286

© 2005 Sopris West Educational Services. All rights reserved. Practicing Basic Skills in Language Arts. Purchaser has permission to photocopy this page for classroom use only.

SEE TO MARK

Adverb Clauses

Directions: Underline each adverb clause.

	Correct	Error
First Try		
Second Try		

Since Carl isn't home, leave him a message. Public television stations can't operate unless their communities support them.

Minoru measured tea into the pot while the water heated. After Rosa learned the metric system, she preferred it. Although the

price of coffee soared, some people still drank it. Vincent van Gogh had sold only one painting when he died. The mother

raccoon holds her young when she washes them with her tongue. Pluto is usually farther from Earth than any other planet. As

soon as Galileo heard about the first telescope, he made one for himself. When porcupines find a suitable tree, they often stay

aloft for several days. We did not leave until the sun had set. After darkness had fallen, we could see the beacon clearly. When

you see John, give him this ring. Mother, working as she talked, gave directions for our trip. Stevenson wrote and rewrote his

stories before they satisfied him. We kept our neighbors' dog while they toured Canada. I have not traveled since I was a small

child. The tournament will be held if ten teams enter. John, whistling as he went, left school early. We must draw names again,

as there has been a mistake. Wally remained until the others had left. Lyle, looking as if he had a good idea, walked away.

Although I hurried, I arrived after Mr. Akers had begun. If you need me, call me before lunch. While we sit here, I shall tell you

my story. I stayed where I could watch the man. Elsie walked around the campus while she waited for Mother.

© 2005 Sopris West Educational Services. All rights reserved. Practicing Basic Skills in Language Arts. Purchaser has permission to photocopy this page for classroom use only.

SEE TO MARK

Adverb Clauses
Directions: Underline each adverb clause.

	Correct	Error
First Try		
Second Try		

(2) Since Carl isn't home, leave him a message. Public television stations can't operate unless their communities support them.

(5) Minoru measured tea into the pot while the water heated. After Rosa learned the metric system, she preferred it. Although the

(6) price of coffee soared, some people still drank it. Vincent van Gogh had sold only one painting when he died. The mother

(9) raccoon holds her young when she washes them with her tongue. Pluto is usually farther from Earth than any other planet. As

(10) soon as Galileo heard about the first telescope, he made one for himself. When porcupines find a suitable tree, they often stay

(13) aloft for several days. We did not leave until the sun had set. After darkness had fallen, we could see the beacon clearly. When

(14) you see John, give him this ring. Mother, working as she talked, gave directions for our trip. Stevenson wrote and rewrote his

(17) stories before they satisfied him. We kept our neighbors' dog while they toured Canada. I have not traveled since I was a small

(19) child. The tournament will be held if ten teams enter. John, whistling as he went, left school early. We must draw names again,

(22) as there has been a mistake. Wally remained until the others had left. Lyle, looking as if he had a good idea, walked away.

(26) Although I hurried, I arrived after Mr. Akers had begun. If you need me, call me before lunch. While we sit here, I shall tell you

(28) my story. I stayed where I could watch the man. Elsie walked around the campus while she waited for Mother.

ANSWER SHEET

Practicing Basic Skills in Language Arts • 288

© 2005 Sopris West Educational Services. All rights reserved. Practicing Basic Skills in Language Arts. Purchaser has permission to photocopy this page for classroom use only.

SEE TO MARK

First Try / Second Try | Correct | Error

Noun, Adjective, and Adverb Clauses

Directions: Underline the subordinate clause and indicate whether it is a noun clause (N), an adjective clause (J), or an adverb clause (V).

I saw them as they left the house. ____   This house, which has been redecorated, belongs to Uncle John. ____   The principal said

that he would not need us. ____   He asked if he might leave. ____   If you are quiet, you may sit here. ____   When he left, we all

missed him. ____   Here is some candy that you will like. ____   That he had won surprised everyone. ____   She found the book where

she had left it. ____   This is a picture of Robert Frost, the poet who has written many poems about New England. ____   They robbed

the house while we slept. ____   What they said did not matter much. ____   The book that you are reading is mine. ____   They will

not go because it is raining. ____   Last night I dreamed that I had a million dollars. ____   After you have finished, give it to me. ____

We enjoyed all the places we visited. ____   We did not leave until the sun had set. ____   The bulldog growled ferociously at

whomever came close. ____   Dinosaurs had disappeared before humans existed. ____   When I saw John, I gave him your message. ____

Galileo saw that four moons revolved around Jupiter. ____   Since it was Halloween, we told ghost stories. ____   You should be

angry with whoever told you such a lie. ____   The man who bought our house is from Indiana. ____   Because you have been such

a good friend, I would like to give you a gift. ____   Mr. Borda told us that many auto accidents are caused by carelessness. ____

Mother looks as if she had seen a ghost. ____   Tell me where you have put the newspaper. ____   The corsage that you made has won

first prize. ____   This is the place where the first battle of the Revolution was fought. ____   Unless you can prove your point, don't

argue. ____   What he said had nothing to do with my decision. ____   He apologized because he had been rude. ____

© 2005 Sopris West Educational Services. All rights reserved. Practicing Basic Skills in Language Arts. Purchaser has permission to photocopy this page for classroom use only.

ONE-MINUTE FLUENCY BUILDER SERIES

	Correct	Error
First Try		
Second Try		

SEE TO MARK

Noun, Adjective, and Adverb Clauses

Directions: Underline the subordinate clause and indicate whether it is a noun clause (N), an adjective clause (J), or an adverb clause (V).

V   I saw them as they left the house.

J   This house, which has been redecorated, belongs to Uncle John.   The principal said   (4)

N   He asked if he might leave.   that he would not need us.   N   If you are quiet, you may sit here.   N   When he left, we all   (11)

V   Here is some candy that you will like.   J   That he had won surprised everyone.   N   missed him.   V   She found the book where   (16)

V   This is a picture of Robert Frost, the poet who has written many poems about New England.   J   she had left it.   V   They robbed   (20)

V   What they said did not matter much.   N   The book that you are reading is mine.   J   the house while we slept.   V   They will   (26)

V   Last night I dreamed that I had a million dollars.   N   not go because it is raining.   V   After you have finished, give it to me.   J   (31)

V   We enjoyed all the places we visited.   J   We did not leave until the sun had set.   V   The bulldog growled ferociously at   (36)

N   Dinosaurs had disappeared before humans existed.   V   whomever came close.   N   When I saw John, I gave him your message.   V   (41)

V   Galileo saw that four moons revolved around Jupiter.   N   Since it was Halloween, we told ghost stories.   V   You should be   (46)

N   The man who bought our house is from Indiana.   J   angry with whoever told you such a lie.   N   Because you have been such   (50)

V   Mr. Borda told us that many auto accidents are caused by carelessness.   N   a good friend, I would like to give you a gift.   V   (54)

N   The corsage that you made has won   Mother looks as if she had seen a ghost.   J   Tell me where you have put the newspaper.   N   (59)

J   This is the place where the first battle of the Revolution was fought.   J   first prize.   J   Unless you can prove your point, don't   (63)

V   What he said had nothing to do with my decision.   N   argue.   V   He apologized because he had been rude.   V   (68)

ANSWER SHEET

Practicing Basic Skills in Language Arts • 290

© 2005 Sopris West Educational Services. All rights reserved. Practicing Basic Skills in Language Arts. Purchaser has permission to photocopy this page for classroom use only.

ONE-MINUTE FLUENCY BUILDER SERIES

SEE TO MARK

Subordinate Clauses

Directions: Underline each subordinate clause.

	Correct	Error
First Try		
Second Try		

Pat Ryan, who pinch hit for us, hit a home run. After we had eaten dinner, we went to the game. The little girl in the blue

apron that touched her toes wildly beat the candy with a big wooden spoon. Do you remember the day when we first met? We

did not leave until the sun had set. When I saw Rand, I gave him the ring. Mother looks as if she is tired. Mary is a girl whom I

can trust. Bob was not playing when the touchdown was made. He smiled whenever he saw her. Although we listened, we did

not hear you. Nero fiddled while Rome burned. He never forgot Christine, since she was the first girl he had ever loved. Unless

you have patience, you should not become a fisherman. If she is going to the party, I am not. The man who bought our house

is Mr. Souza. I believe that he eats vitamins. You should go with whoever asks you first. Red Parsons, who hadn't had a hit all

day, stepped up to bat. At the end of its snout, the angler fish has a fish pole with fleshy projections that look like worms. If a

starfish is cut into five equal parts, each arm will grow into a new starfish. Mr. Cotter told us that the mirror was twenty-seven

inches thick. Cuckoos are among the few birds that eat hairy caterpillars. A New England poet who had never visited Louisiana

preserved the legend of the Acadians. Dinosaurs had disappeared before humans existed. Everyone was downcast when the

rocket didn't go off. After his supplies were gone, the general agreed to surrender.

Practicing Basic Skills in Language Arts • 291

© 2005 Sopris West Educational Services. All rights reserved. Practicing Basic Skills in Language Arts. Purchaser has permission to photocopy this page for classroom use only.

Subordinate Clauses

Directions: Underline each subordinate clause.

	First Try	Second Try
Correct		
Error		

Pat Ryan, who pinch hit for us, hit a home run. After we had eaten dinner, we went to the game. The little girl in the blue (2)

apron that touched her toes wildly beat the candy with a big wooden spoon. Do you remember the day when we first met? We (4)

did not leave until the sun had set. When I saw Rand, I gave him the ring. Mother looks as if she is tired. Mary is a girl whom I (8)

can trust. Bob was not playing when the touchdown was made. He smiled whenever he saw her. Although we listened, we did (11)

not hear you. Nero fiddled while Rome burned. He never forgot Christine, since she was the first girl he had ever loved. Unless (14)

you have patience, you should not become a fisherman. If she is going to the party, I am not. The man who bought our house (16)

is Mr. Souza. I believe that he eats vitamins. You should go with whoever asks you first. Red Parsons, who hadn't had a hit all (19)

day, stepped up to bat. At the end of its snout, the angler fish has a fish pole with fleshy projections that look like worms. If a (21)

starfish is cut into five equal parts, each arm will grow into a new starfish. Mr. Cotter told us that the mirror was twenty-seven (22)

inches thick. Cuckoos are among the few birds that eat hairy caterpillars. A New England poet who had never visited Louisiana (24)

preserved the legend of the Acadians. Dinosaurs had disappeared before humans existed. Everyone was downcast when the (26)

rocket didn't go off. After his supplies were gone, the general agreed to surrender. (27)

ANSWER SHEET

Practicing Basic Skills in Language Arts • 292

© 2005 Sopris West Educational Services. All rights reserved. Practicing Basic Skills in Language Arts. Purchaser has permission to photocopy this page for classroom use only.

SEE TO MARK

Independent Clauses

Directions: Underline the subject of the independent clause once and the verb twice.

	First Try	Second Try
Correct		
Error		

Pat Ryan, who pinch hit for us, hit a home run. After we had eaten dinner, we went to the game. The little girl in the blue

apron that touched her toes wildly beat the candy with a big wooden spoon. Do you remember the day when we first met? We

did not leave until the sun had set. When I saw Rand, I gave him the ring. Mother looks as if she is tired. Mary is a girl whom I

can trust. Bob was not playing when the touchdown was made. He smiled whenever he saw her. Although we listened, we did

not hear you. Nero fiddled while Rome burned. He never forgot Christine, since she was the first girl he had ever loved. Unless

you have patience, you should not become a fisherman. If she is going to the party, I am not. The man who bought our house

is Mr. Souza. I believe that he eats vitamins. You should go with whoever asks you first. Red Parsons, who hadn't had a hit all

day, stepped up to bat. At the end of its snout, the angler fish has a fish pole with fleshy projections that look like worms. If a

starfish is cut into five equal parts, each arm will grow into a new starfish. Mr. Cotter told us that the mirror was twenty-seven

inches thick. Cuckoos are among the few birds that eat hairy caterpillars. A New England poet who had never visited Louisiana

preserved the legend of the Acadians. Dinosaurs had disappeared before humans existed. Everyone was downcast when the

rocket didn't go off. After his supplies were gone, the general agreed to surrender.

Practicing Basic Skills in Language Arts • 293

© 2005 Sopris West Educational Services. All rights reserved. Practicing Basic Skills in Language Arts. Purchaser has permission to photocopy this page for classroom use only.

ONE-MINUTE FLUENCY BUILDER SERIES

	Correct	Error
First Try		
Second Try		

Independent Clauses

Directions: Underline the subject of the independent clause once and the verb twice.

Pat Ryan, who pinch hit for us, hit a home run. After we had eaten dinner, we went to the game. The little girl in the blue (5)

apron that touched her toes wildly beat the candy with a big wooden spoon. Do you remember the day when we first met? We (10)

did not leave until the sun had set. When I saw Rand, I gave him the ring. Mother looks as if she is tired. Mary is a girl whom I (18)

can trust. Bob was not playing when the touchdown was made. He smiled whenever he saw her. Although we listened, we did (25)

not hear you. Nero fiddled while Rome burned. He never forgot Christine, since she was the first girl he had ever loved. Unless (30)

you have patience, you should not become a fisherman. If she is going to the party, I am not. The man who bought our house (36)

is Mr. Souza. I believe that he eats vitamins. You should go with whoever asks you first. Red Parsons, who hadn't had a hit all (42)

day, stepped up to bat. At the end of its snout, the angler fish has a fish pole with fleshy projections that look like worms. If a (45)

starfish is cut into five equal parts, each arm will grow into a new starfish. Mr. Cotter told us that the mirror was twenty-seven (49)

inches thick. Cuckoos are among the few birds that eat hairy caterpillars. A New England poet who had never visited Louisiana (52)

preserved the legend of the Acadians. Dinosaurs had disappeared before humans existed. Everyone was downcast when the (57)

rocket didn't go off. After his supplies were gone, the general agreed to surrender. (59)

ANSWER SHEET

Practicing Basic Skills in Language Arts • 294

© 2005 Sopris West Educational Services. All rights reserved. Practicing Basic Skills in Language Arts. Purchaser has permission to photocopy this page for classroom use only.

Compound Sentences Into Independent Clauses

Directions: Separate the compound sentences into independent clauses.

	First Try		Second Try	
	Correct	Error		

The whistle blew shrilly, and the game began. I rang the bell, and Sy pounded on the door, but no one came. Nate went to

the game, but Fred could not go. The car sped down the hill and turned the corner. Mother was canning peaches and I

helped her. Last summer we visited Canada, and our neighbors, however, visited Europe. We were very tired but no one had

time for a rest. Marion ran out, jumped into the car, and drove off. You must be our new neighbor, or am I wrong? I must work

harder, or I will not finish in time for supper. My favorite color is red, however, my sister likes blue. The mist rolled away

and the sun shone brightly. Was that a knock at the door, or was it just the wind? Ida, her parents, and her brother took a trip.

This house has its drawbacks, but we like it anyway. Mother must have arrived safely or she would have called us. A summer

on the farm helped Sid, and he is much healthier now. Cold weather came, and the birds flew southward. The fair opened

today, and it will close on Saturday. My coat is new, but Dara's is newer. I can find for you all but one of the necessary books.

Tom won his first match, but I lost mine. Twilight had come after the hot day, and a cool breeze blew. The rain had

stopped, but the sky was still cloudy. Follow these directions, or you will lose your way. I watched the door carefully,

but no one came out. On Friday night our neighbors went out, and I baby-sat for them. Mrs. Mehari had already fed the

children, but I put them to bed.

© 2005 Sopris West Educational Services. All rights reserved. Practicing Basic Skills in Language Arts. Purchaser has permission to photocopy this page for classroom use only.

Compound Sentences Into Independent Clauses

Directions: Separate the compound sentences into independent clauses.

	First Try	Second Try
Correct		
Error		

The whistle blew shrilly, | and the game began. I rang the bell, | and Sy pounded on the door, | but no one came. Nate went to (3)

the game, | but Fred could not go. The car sped down the hill and turned the corner. Mother was canning peaches | and I (5)

helped her. Last summer we visited Canada, | and our neighbors, however visited Europe. We were very tired | but no one had (7)

time for a rest. Marion ran out, jumped into the car, and drove off. You must be our new neighbor, | or am I wrong? I must work (8)

harder, | or I will not finish in time for supper. My favorite color is red, | however, my sister likes blue. The mist rolled away | (11)

and the sun shone brightly. Was that a knock at the door, | or was it just the wind? Ida, her parents, and her brother took a trip. (12)

This house has its drawbacks, | but we like it anyway. Mother must have arrived safely | or she would have called us. A summer (14)

on the farm helped Sid, | and he is much healthier now. Cold weather came, | and the birds flew southward. The fair opened (16)

today, | and it will close on Saturday. My coat is new, | but Dara's is newer. I can find for you all but one of the necessary books. (18)

Tom won his first match, | but I lost mine. Twilight had come after the hot day, | and a cool breeze blew. The rain had (20)

stopped, | but the sky was still cloudy. Follow these directions, | or you will lose your way. I watched the door carefully, | (23)

but no one came out. On Friday night our neighbors went out, | and I baby-sat for them. Mrs. Mehari had already fed the (24)

children, | but I put them to bed. (25)

© 2005 Sopris West Educational Services. All rights reserved. Practicing Basic Skills in Language Arts. Purchaser has permission to photocopy this page for classroom use only.

ANSWER SHEET

ONE-MINUTE FLUENCY BUILDER SERIES

SEE TO WRITE

Form Compound Sentences Using And, But, Or, Nor, So

Directions: Form compound sentences using *and, but, or, nor,* or *so.*

	Correct	Error
First Try		
Second Try		

1. School will be out soon. _____ We will have a long vacation. _____ 2. Linda called Mary yesterday. _____ She was in bed. 3. The waiter brought us the check. _____ Then we left. _____ 4. You must finish your soup. _____ You can't play. 5. Jan can't go with us. _____ Will she stay home. 6. I'll expect you to come home early. _____ Have a good time. 7. The roof blew away. _____ It fell in the neighbor's yard. 8. The book is on the shelf. _____ Don't take it home. 9. Cecil stayed home sick. _____ He did his work anyway. 10. I want to go with you. _____ Mother won't let me. 11. Mary was elected the queen _____ She was happy. 12. We are having company for dinner _____ Come see us anyway. 13. Can you come to my house? _____ Should we come to yours? 14. He got lost yesterday. _____ We found him quickly. 15. Are you going to pick me up? _____ Should I come get you? 16. My favorite hobby is playing tennis. _____ I'm not very good. 17. We went to the zoo. _____ We had a good time. 18. Our team won the tournament. _____ They lost the championship. 19. The snow is starting to fall. _____ It is so pretty. 20. I got dressed as fast as I could. _____ I was still late. 21. It is time to go to school. _____ I'm not quite ready. 22. Will you babysit for me? _____ Should I get someone else? 23. Our class made Christmas decorations. _____ We sold them at the bazaar. 24. Did you paint your house? _____ Did someone else do it? 25. Bill got a new job. _____ It pays a lot more money. 26. Dale put on another shirt and tie. _____ It didn't match. 27. He was telling the truth. _____ We didn't know it. 28. Our team was losing badly. _____ We were upset. 29. The school bus was 30 minutes late. _____ We didn't care. 30. Did the snake scare you? _____ Did you scare him? 31. I just read a new book. _____ It was very interesting.

© 2005 Sopris West Educational Services. All rights reserved. Practicing Basic Skills in Language Arts. Purchaser has permission to photocopy this page for classroom use only.

ONE-MINUTE FLUENCY BUILDER SERIES

SEE TO WRITE

Form Compound Sentences Using And, But, Or, Nor, So

Directions: Form compound sentences using *and, but, or, nor,* or *so.*

	First Try	Second Try
Correct		
Error		

1. School will be out soon. **and** We will have a long vacation.   2. Linda called Mary yesterday.

3. The waiter brought us the check. **and** Then we left.   4. You must finish your soup.

5. Jan can't go with us. **or** You can't play.   6. I'll expect you to come home early. **but** Have a good time.   7. The roof blew away. **nor** Will she stay home.

8. The book is on the shelf. **but** Don't take it home.   It fell in the neighbor's yard.

9. Cecil stayed home sick. **but** He did his work anyway.   10. I want to go with you. **but** Mother won't let me.   11. Mary was elected the queen **and** She was happy.

12. We are having company for dinner **but** Come see us anyway.   13. Can you come to my house? **or** Should we come to yours?

14. He got lost yesterday. **but** We found him quickly.   15. Are you going to pick me up? **or** Should I come get you?

16. My favorite hobby is playing tennis. **but** I'm not very good.   17. We went to the zoo. **and** We had a good time.

18. Our team won the tournament. **but** They lost the championship.   19. The snow is starting to fall. **and** It is so pretty.   20. I got dressed as fast as I could. **but** I was still late.

21. It is time to go to school. **but** I'm not quite ready.   22. Will you babysit for me? **or** Should I get someone else?   23. Our class made Christmas decorations. **and** We sold them at the bazaar.

24. Did you paint your house? **or** Did someone else do it?   25. Bill got a new job. **and** It pays a lot more money.   26. Dale put on another shirt and tie. **but** It didn't match.

27. He was telling the truth. **but** We didn't know it.   28. Our team was losing badly. **and** We were upset.

29. The school bus was 30 minutes late. **but** We didn't care.   30. Did the snake scare you? **and** Did you scare him?   31. I just read a new book. **or** It was very interesting.

(2)
(3)
(5)
(7)
(9)
(11)
(12)
(14)
(16)
(17)
(19)
(21)
(22)
(24)
(26)
(28)
(29)
(31)

Practicing Basic Skills in Language Arts • 298

ANSWER SHEET

© 2005 Sopris West Educational Services. All rights reserved. Practicing Basic Skills in Language Arts. Purchaser has permission to photocopy this page for classroom use only.

ONE-MINUTE FLUENCY BUILDER SERIES

Form Compound Sentences Using And, But, Or, Nor, So

Directions: Form compound sentences using *and, but, or, nor,* or *so.*

	First Try	Second Try
Correct		
Error		

1. I like to have company. _____ It is a lot of work.   2. Joe was talking to Roberto. _____ I couldn't hear

what he said.   3. Mei will be on the track team. _____ She isn't very fast.   4. My teacher was tired. _____

She went home after school.   5. The wind was blowing hard. _____ It didn't bother me.   6. We are going on

a picnic. _____ Jamie is going with us.   7. Our teachers are having a meeting. _____ It will be after

school.   8. She had to help clean house. _____ She couldn't go to the movies with us.   9. The horse ran across the

field. _____ We chased after him.   10. Lamar is my best friend. _____ I still get mad at him.   11. Don't

come to our house so late. _____ Mother will get mad.   12. Math is my favorite subject. _____ so is

science.   13. It takes three hours to get there. _____ I don't mind the drive.   14. All my homework was wrong.

_____ I made the corrections quickly.   15. The children found a frog. _____ They let him go.   16. We ate

a big supper. _____ I was still hungry.   17. I found this hat. _____ It was all dirty.   18. Do you drive a red

car? _____ Do you drive a blue one?   19. I like ice cream. _____ It makes me fat.   20. Let the dog outside.

_____ Then close the door.   21. John fell down the stairs. _____ He wasn't hurt badly.   22. The stoplight

is green. _____ Don't go.   23. We went to the store. _____ We bought a new coat.   24. Thank you for the

new shirt. _____ It doesn't fit.   25. We have a lot of old toys. _____ Most of them are broken.   26. Come

clean your room. _____ I'll tell Mother.   27. The sun is shining right now. _____ It won't be for

long.   28. That is a dangerous animal. _____ I'm not afraid.   29. Hurry home from school. _____ We will

be late for the party.   30. I didn't call you. _____ I didn't call your friend.   31. My cat and dog are always fighting.

_____ They don't hurt each other.   32. The bases were loaded. _____ David hit a home run.

© 2005 Sopris West Educational Services. All rights reserved. Practicing Basic Skills in Language Arts. Purchaser has permission to photocopy this page for classroom use only.

ONE-MINUTE FLUENCY BUILDER SERIES

SEE TO WRITE

Form Compound Sentences Using And, But, Or, Nor, So

Directions: Form compound sentences using *and, but, or, nor,* or *so.*

	Correct	Error
First Try		
Second Try		

1. I like to have company. __but__ It is a lot of work.   2. Joe was talking to Roberto. __but__ I couldn't hear what he said.   3. Mei will be on the track team. __but__ She isn't very fast.   4. My teacher was tired. __so__ She went home after school.   5. The wind was blowing hard. __but__ It didn't bother me.   6. We are going on a picnic. __and__ Jamie is going with us.   7. Our teachers are having a meeting. __and__ It will be after school.   8. She couldn't go to the movies with us. __so__ She had to help clean house.   9. The horse ran across the field. __and__ We chased after him.   10. Lamar is my best friend. __but__ I still get mad at him.   11. Don't come to our house so late. __or__ Mother will get mad.   12. Math is my favorite subject. __and__ so is science.   13. It takes three hours to get there. __but__ I don't mind the drive.   14. All my homework was wrong. __so__ I made the corrections quickly.   15. The children found a frog. __but__ They let him go.   16. We ate a big supper. __but__ I was still hungry.   17. I found this hat. __and__ It was all dirty.   18. Do you drive a red car? __or__ Do you drive a blue one?   19. I like ice cream. __but__ It makes me fat.   20. Let the dog outside. __and__ Then close the door.   21. John fell down the stairs. __but__ He wasn't hurt badly.   22. The stoplight is green. __so__ Don't go.   23. We went to the store. __and__ We bought a new coat.   24. Thank you for the new shirt. __but__ It doesn't fit.   25. We have a lot of old toys. __but__ Most of them are broken.   26. Come clean your room. __or__ I'll tell Mother.   27. The sun is shining right now. __but__ It won't be for long.   28. That is a dangerous animal. __but__ I'm not afraid.   29. Hurry home from school. __or__ We will be late for the party.   30. I didn't call you. __and__ I didn't call your friend.   31. My cat and dog are always fighting. __but__ They don't hurt each other.   32. The bases were loaded. __and__ David hit a home run.

ANSWER SHEET

Practicing Basic Skills in Language Arts • 300

© 2005 Sopris West Educational Services. All rights reserved. Practicing Basic Skills in Language Arts. Purchaser has permission to photocopy this page for classroom use only.

ONE-MINUTE FLUENCY
BUILDER SERIES

SEE TO WRITE

Form Complex Sentences

Directions: Form complex sentences by adding *when, while, after, since, because, as, although, who, whom, which, that, whoever, before, if.*

	First Try	Second Try
Correct		
Error		

1. Some of the people left early. _____ The play was too long. 2. We are going to the movies. _____ She has the money. 3. Joan finished her assignment. _____ We were at her house. 4. He went home. We finished eating dinner. 5. I'll go to the store for you. _____ You ask me nicely. 6. These beads don't match my dress. _____ They are the wrong color. 7. The bike is bright red. _____ Father painted it. 8. He doesn't have a bicycle. _____ He really is careful when he rides one. 9. Where are you going on vacation? You will need warm clothes. 10. John is a good baseball pitcher. _____ His father helps him all the time. 11. Don't come with us to the park. _____ You want to rest. 12. I know you are a good secretary. _____ You never make a mistake. 13. My clothes were full of mud. _____ I fell into a mud puddle. 14. The old man complained all night. _____ The music played. 15. The basketball team got new uniforms. _____ The season started. 16. We want to go with you. _____ It is your birthday. 17. The kids like to play cards. _____ It is a waste of time. 18. We had sandwiches for dinner. _____ She invited us out to eat. 19. Our pond was frozen over this morning. _____ The temperature was so low. 20. The girls bought two new CDs. _____ They have enough already. 21. I was late for school this morning. _____ My alarm clock didn't go off. 22. It will be time to cook supper. _____ The clock chimes six. 23. She is the one. _____ I waited for all day. 24. We'll walk to school. _____ We can't find anyone to give us a ride. 25. The play was a smash hit. _____ The cast worked very hard. 26. The dogs ran away. _____ They chased the cows. 27. Her watch was broken. It was still keeping good time. 28. Her shoes hurt her feet. _____ They were brand new. 29. John plays the guitar. _____ Everyone else sings. 30. The pan will get hot. _____ You're not careful.

Practicing Basic Skills in Language Arts • 301

© 2005 Sopris West Educational Services. All rights reserved. Practicing Basic Skills in Language Arts. Purchaser has permission to photocopy this page for classroom use only.

SEE TO WRITE

Form Complex Sentences

Directions: Form complex sentences by adding *when, while, after, since, because, as, although, who, whom, which, that, whoever, before, if.*

	Correct	Error
First Try		
Second Try		

1. Some of the people left early. **because** The play was too long.   2. We are going to the movies. **if** She has the money. (2)

3. Joan finished her assignment. **while** We were at her house.   4. He went home. **after** We finished eating dinner. (4)

5. I'll go to the store for you. **if** You ask me nicely.   6. These beads don't match my dress. **because** They are the wrong color. (5)

7. The bike is bright red. **because** Father painted it.   8. He doesn't have a bicycle. **although** He really is careful when he rides one. (7)

9. Where are you going on vacation? **that** You will need warm clothes. (9)

10. John is a good baseball pitcher. **because** His father helps him all the time.   11. Don't come with us to the park. **if** You want to rest. (10)

12. I know you are a good secretary. **because** You never make a mistake. (12)

13. My clothes were full of mud. **after** I fell into a mud puddle.   14. The old man complained all night. **while** The music played. (13)

15. The basketball team got new uniforms. **when** The season started. (15)

16. We want to go with you. **since** It is your birthday.   17. The kids like to play cards. **although** It is a waste of time. (17)

18. We had sandwiches for dinner. **although** She invited us out to eat.   19. Our pond was frozen over this morning. **because** The temperature was so low. (18)

20. The girls bought two new CDs. **although** They have enough already. (20)

21. I was late for school this morning. **because** My alarm clock didn't go off.   22. It will be time to cook supper. **when** The clock chimes six. (21)

23. She is the one. **whom** I waited for all day.   24. We'll walk to school. **since** We can't find anyone to give us a ride. (23)

25. The play was a smash hit. **because** The cast worked very hard. (25)

26. The dogs ran away. **after** They chased the cows.   27. Her watch was broken. **although** It was still keeping good time. (26)

28. Her shoes hurt her feet. **since** They were brand new.   29. John plays the guitar. **while** Everyone else sings. (28)

30. The pan will get hot. **if** You're not careful. (30)

© 2005 Sopris West Educational Services. All rights reserved. Practicing Basic Skills in Language Arts. Purchaser has permission to photocopy this page for classroom use only.

SEE TO WRITE

Form Complex Sentences

Directions: Form complex sentences by adding *when, while, after, since, because, as, although, who, whom, which, that, whoever, before, if.*

1. We are going home early. _____ We are going to the play. 2. Rita can come to our house. _____

She doesn't have to work late. 3. The dog barked. _____ We came home. 4. I'll buy you a new dress. _____

_____ You give me the money. 5. I want you to read this. _____ You are waiting for me. 6. We can

go shopping. _____ The stores are open. 7. My shoes don't match my dress. _____ They are the wrong

color. 8. We want to buy a new car. _____ Our old one looks terrible. 9. The little boy cried. _____

He hit his brother. 10. Will you come to school? _____ You go see mother. 11. Mary wants to buy a new

coat. _____ It doesn't cost too much. 12. They have many items on display. _____ I would like to

have. 13. My teacher seems tired. _____ She isn't sick. 14. The mail was left here. _____ The mail

carrier didn't pick it up. 15. She appears calm and relaxed. _____ She is very nervous. 16. The horses ran away.

_____ Someone left the gate open. 17. The new boy watched wistfully. _____ They had fun. 18. We

must find a new player. _____ Bret is hurt in the next game. 19. It will be time for school to start. _____

The bell rings. 20. Our teacher went to the meeting. _____ The principal asked her to go. 21. I want you to come

to my house. _____ You go home. 22. Erin told me a secret. _____ John told her. 23. Carlos is the new

boy in school. _____ You saw yesterday. 24. The team warms up. _____ The game begins. 25. Maria

was talking. _____ I was trying to listen to the speaker. 26. The children will interrupt. _____ They

aren't taught good manners. 27. My car wouldn't start this morning. _____ It was so cold. 28. We are going

to eat dinner. _____ John gets home. 29. The play is going to begin. _____ Soon as the auditorium is

full. 30. I have a new friend. _____ I really like. 31. The sun is shining today. _____ It wasn't shining

yesterday. 32. The plant is turning brown. _____ I forgot to water it.

© 2005 Sopris West Educational Services. All rights reserved. Practicing Basic Skills in Language Arts. Purchaser has permission to photocopy this page for classroom use only.

ONE-MINUTE FLUENCY
BUILDER SERIES

	First Try	Second Try
Correct		
Error		

Form Complex Sentences

Directions: Form complex sentences by adding *when, while, after, since, because, as, although, who, whom, which, that, whoever, before, if.*

1. We are going home early. **because** We are going to the play. 2. Rita can come to our house. **if** She doesn't have to work late. 3. The dog barked. **when** We came home. 4. I'll buy you a new dress. **if** You give me the money. 5. I want you to read this. **while** You are waiting for me. 6. We can go shopping. **when** The stores are open. 7. My shoes don't match my dress. **because** They are the wrong color. 8. We want to buy a new car. **because** Our old one looks terrible. 9. The little boy cried. **after** You go see mother. 10. Will you come to school? **if** It doesn't cost too much. 11. Mary wants to buy a new coat. **if** It doesn't cost too much. 12. They have many items on display. **that** I would like to have. 13. My teacher seems tired. **although** She isn't sick. 14. The mail was left here. **because** The mail carrier didn't pick it up. 15. She appears calm and relaxed. **although** She is very nervous. 16. The horses ran away. **because** Someone left the gate open. 17. The new boy watched wistfully. **while** They had fun. 18. We must find a new player. **before** Bret is hurt in the next game. 19. It will be time for school to start. **when** The bell rings. 20. Our teacher went to the meeting. **because** You go home. 21. I want you to come to my house. **before** You go home. 22. Erin told me a secret. **that** John told her. 23. Carlos is the new boy in school. **whom** You saw yesterday. 24. The team warms up. **before** The game begins. 25. Maria was talking. **while** I was trying to listen to the speaker. 26. The children will interrupt. **if** They aren't taught good manners. 27. My car wouldn't start this morning. **because** It was so cold. 28. We are going to eat dinner. **after** John gets home. 29. The play is going to begin. **as** Soon as the auditorium is full. 30. I have a new friend. **whom** I really like. 31. The sun is shining today. **although** It wasn't shining yesterday. 32. The plant is turning brown. **because** I forgot to water it.

(2) (3) (5) (7) (9) (10) (12) (14) (15) (17) (19) (20) (22) (24) (26) (27) (29) (31) (32)

ANSWER SHEET

© 2005 Sopris West Educational Services. All rights reserved. Practicing Basic Skills in Language Arts. Purchaser has permission to photocopy this page for classroom use only.

SEE TO MARK

Sentence Fragments and Complete Sentences
Directions: Underline the sentence fragments.

	First Try	Second Try
Correct		
Error		

You should not go swimming. After you have eaten. If you want to go to the game. You should buy a ticket. He was tired of work. Lost his way. Was standing in the rain. Our only clue was the old, battered book. On the desk was a book with a green cover. A dog with a brass collar came to our house but did not stay. The father of my best friend. Leigh and the boys could not find the key. Into the backyard. When mother bakes a cake. After the game Amy, Ling, and Sydney went to a party. Hid under the lilac bushes and waited. In five minutes the house was empty. There in the bottom of the bucket. Laughing out loud. One of his favorite songs. Is your name Ricardo? Shut the door and lock it. Waiting for the bus. Your paper is on my desk. Through the door into the hall. Carol plays the guitar. About a boy in school. After the snow had fallen. His father was born in Alaska. Greg will not finish the season. The winner of the race. The dress, the shoes, and the coat fit me and are not too expensive. Called you long distance last night. At the beginning of the second period. Your appointment has been changed. It is not three o'clock. The boy riding the skateboard. Writing a letter to his aunt. That is Jamal's book, but he forgot to take it with him. Under a tree in their yard. Can you type? If I hear first. Promised to help. The man driving the car. Who won? Try the other door. It's her turn now, and then it's yours. The highest mountain in the world. Having a wonderful time. The magazines on the large table. Behind the girl in the third seat. There will be two performances. I am inquiring about a girl in school. The one in the second desk. Here from Arizona. Kenji cut the grass and watered the flowers. To work on it. No more tickets. First place in the Science Fair receives a trophy. Second place a blue ribbon. His brown shirt.

Practicing Basic Skills in Language Arts • 305

© 2005 Sopris West Educational Services. All rights reserved. Practicing Basic Skills in Language Arts. Purchaser has permission to photocopy this page for classroom use only.

ONE MINUTE FLUENCY BUILDER SERIES

SEE TO MARK

	Correct	Error
First Try		
Second Try		

Sentence Fragments and Complete Sentences

Directions: Underline the sentence fragments.

You should not go swimming. After you have eaten. If you want to go to the game. You should buy a ticket. He was tired of (2)

work. Lost his way. Was standing in the rain. Our only clue was the old, battered book. On the desk was a book with a green (4)

cover. A dog with a brass collar came to our house but did not stay. The father of my best friend. Leigh and the boys could not (5)

find the key. Into the backyard. When mother bakes a cake. After the game Amy, Ling, and Sydney went to a party. Hid under (8)

the lilac bushes and waited. In five minutes the house was empty. There in the bottom of the bucket. Laughing out loud. One of (11)

his favorite songs. Is your name Ricardo? Shut the door and lock it. Waiting for the bus. Your paper is on my desk. Through the (13)

door into the hall. Carol plays the guitar. About a boy in school. After the snow had fallen. His father was born in Alaska. Greg (15)

will not finish the season. The winner of the race. The dress, the shoes, and the coat fit me and are not too expensive. Called (17)

you long distance last night. At the beginning of the second period. Your appointment has been changed. It is not three o'clock. (18)

The boy riding the skateboard. Writing a letter to his aunt. That is Jamal's book, but he forgot to take it with him. Under a tree (21)

in their yard. Can you type? If I hear first. Promised to help. The man driving the car. Who won? Try the other door. It's her (24)

turn now, and then it's yours. The highest mountain in the world. Having a wonderful time. The magazines on the large table. (27)

Behind the girl in the third seat. There will be two performances. I am inquiring about a girl in school. The one in the second (29)

desk. Here from Arizona. Kenji cut the grass and watered the flowers. To work on it. No more tickets. First place in the Science (32)

Fair receives a trophy. Second place a blue ribbon. His brown shirt. (34)

ANSWER SHEET

Practicing Basic Skills in Language Arts • 306

© 2005 Sopris West Educational Services. All rights reserved. Practicing Basic Skills in Language Arts. Purchaser has permission to photocopy this page for classroom use only.

	Correct	Error
First Try		
Second Try		

Complete Sentences and Sentence Fragments

Directions: Underline the complete sentences.

You should not go swimming. After you have eaten. If you want to go to the game. You should buy a ticket. He was tired of work. Lost his way. Was standing in the rain. Our only clue was the old, battered book. On the desk was a book with a green cover. A dog with a brass collar came to our house but did not stay. The father of my best friend. Leigh and the boys could not find the key. Into the backyard. When mother bakes a cake. After the game Amy, Ling, and Sydney went to a party. Hid under the lilac bushes and waited. In five minutes the house was empty. There in the bottom of the bucket. Laughing out loud. One of his favorite songs. Is your name Ricardo? Shut the door and lock it. Waiting for the bus. Your paper is on my desk. Through the door into the hall. Carol plays the guitar. About a boy in school. After the snow had fallen. His father was born in Alaska. Greg will not finish the season. The winner of the race. The dress, the shoes, and the coat fit me and are not too expensive. Called you long distance last night. At the beginning of the second period. Your appointment has been changed. It is not three o'clock. The boy riding the skateboard. Writing a letter to his aunt. That is Jamal's book, but he forgot to take it with him. Under a tree in their yard. Can you type? If I hear first. Promised to help. The man driving the car. Who won? Try the other door. It's her turn now, and then it's yours. The highest mountain in the world. Having a wonderful time. The magazines on the large table. Behind the girl in the third seat. There will be two performances. I am inquiring about a girl in school. The one in the second desk. Here from Arizona. Kenji cut the grass and watered the flowers. To work on it. No more tickets. First place in the Science Fair receives a trophy. Second place a blue ribbon. His brown shirt.

© 2005 Sopris West Educational Services. All rights reserved. Practicing Basic Skills in Language Arts. Purchaser has permission to photocopy this page for classroom use only.

SEE TO MARK

Complete Sentences and Sentence Fragments

Directions: Underline the complete sentences.

	First Try	Second Try
Correct		
Error		

You should not go swimming. After you have eaten. If you want to go to the game. You should buy a ticket. He was tired of (3)

work. Lost his way. Was standing in the rain. Our only clue was the old, battered book. On the desk was a book with a green (5)

cover. A dog with a brass collar came to our house but did not stay. The father of my best friend. Leigh and the boys could not (7)

find the key. Into the backyard. When mother bakes a cake. After the game Amy, Ling, and Sydney went to a party. Hid under (8)

the lilac bushes and waited. In five minutes the house was empty. There in the bottom of the bucket. Laughing out loud. One of (9)

his favorite songs. Is your name Ricardo? Shut the door and lock it. Waiting for the bus. Your paper is on my desk. Through the (12)

door into the hall. Carol plays the guitar. About a boy in school. After the snow had fallen. His father was born in Alaska. Greg (15)

will not finish the season. The winner of the race. The dress, the shoes, and the coat fit me and are not too expensive. Called (16)

you long distance last night. At the beginning of the second period. Your appointment has been changed. It is not three o'clock. (18)

The boy riding the skateboard. Writing a letter to his aunt. That is Jamal's book, but he forgot to take it with him. Under a tree (19)

in their yard. Can you type? If I hear first. Promised to help. The man driving the car. Who won? Try the other door. It's her (23)

turn now, and then it's yours. The highest mountain in the world. Having a wonderful time. The magazines on the large table. (23)

Behind the girl in the third seat. There will be two performances. I am inquiring about a girl in school. The one in the second (25)

desk. Here from Arizona. Kenji cut the grass and watered the flowers. To work on it. No more tickets. First place in the Science (27)

Fair receives a trophy. Second place a blue ribbon. His brown shirt. (27)

ANSWER SHEET

Practicing Basic Skills in Language Arts • 308

© 2005 Sopris West Educational Services. All rights reserved. Practicing Basic Skills in Language Arts. Purchaser has permission to photocopy this page for classroom use only.

ONE-MINUTE FLUENCY
BUILDER SERIES

Review Fragments and Sentences

Directions: Mark the fragments with an F and the complete sentences with an S.

	First Try	Second Try
Correct		
Error		

The runner. Mr. Bowcut announced the Economics Fair winners. Will return in an hour. After school. Who won the basketball

game last Friday? Over the loudspeaker. When the bell rang. We have had too much rain this winter. Going up the ski lift. The

pharmacist filled the prescription. The house and the driveway face the busy street. Across the ocean the captain. Seventh,

eighth, and ninth grade students attend junior high school. Covered the roads overnight. This person or thing. When the

lighted fuse. Reached the ammunition dump. There came a loud explosion. When the lighted fuse reached the ammunition

dump, there came a loud explosion. Of the three men. Which of the three men? Which of three men is the owner? John and

I built the wagon. The students wrote letters to their pen pals. To their pen pals. The students. You should save or invest some

of your money. Of the quarterly period. The bank enters. Within the last three days. Within the last three days of the quarterly

period. Within the last three days of the quarterly period the bank enters the interest on your savings account. On your savings

account. As it happens. The important news of the day as it happens. Jeff and

Chad went to the movies. To the movies. At the umpire. Was whistling. He was whistling at the umpire. During the game.

Cheering for the team. Stephanie and Keri were whistling and cheering for the team. Upon hearing cries for help. In a cruising

squad car. As he ran. Of a jewelry store. Upon hearing cries for help, two policemen in a cruising squad car nabbed a robber as

he ran out of a jewelry store. After I packed my bag and put it in the trunk of the car, Dad said we were ready to go. When I

packed my bag and put it in the trunk of the car. To go. With only two minutes left to play. Jumping over the last tackler near

the goal. Can you name the mayor of your town?

Practicing Basic Skills in Language Arts • 309

© 2005 Sopris West Educational Services. All rights reserved. Practicing Basic Skills in Language Arts. Purchaser has permission to photocopy this page for classroom use only.

ONE MINUTE FLUENCY
BUILDER SERIES

SEE TO MARK

	Correct	Error
First Try		
Second Try		

Review Fragments and Sentences

Directions: Mark the fragments with an F and the complete sentences with an S.

[F] The runner. [S] Mr. Bowcut announced the Economics Fair winners. [F] Will return in an hour. [F] After school. [S] Who won the basketball (4)

game last Friday? [F] Over the loudspeaker. [F] When the bell rang. [S] We have had too much rain this winter. [F] Going up the ski lift. The (9)

pharmacist filled the prescription. [S] The house and the driveway face the busy street. [F] Across the ocean the captain. [F] Seventh, (12)

eighth, and ninth grade students attend junior high school. [S] Covered the roads overnight. [F] This person or thing. [S] When the (15)

lighted fuse. [F] Reached the ammunition dump. [S] There came a loud explosion. [F] When the lighted fuse reached the ammunition (18)

dump, there came a loud explosion. [S] Of the three men. [F] Which of three men? [S] Which of the three men is the owner? John and (22)

I built the wagon. [S] The students wrote letters to their pen pals. [F] To their pen pals. [F] The students. [S] You should save or invest some (26)

of your money. [S] Of the quarterly period. [F] The bank enters. [F] Within the last three days. [F] Within the last three days of the quarterly (30)

period. [F] Within the last three days of the quarterly period the bank enters the interest on your savings account. [S] On your savings (32)

account. [F] As it happens. [F] The important news of the day. [S] Television gives the important news of the day as it happens. Jeff and (36)

Chad went to the movies. [S] To the movies. [F] At the umpire. [F] Was whistling. [S] He was whistling at the umpire. During the game. (42)

Cheering for the team. [F] Stephanie and Keri were whistling and cheering for the team. [S] Upon hearing cries for help. [F] In a cruising (45)

squad car. [F] As he ran. [F] Of a jewelry store. [S] Upon hearing cries for help, two policemen in a cruising squad car nabbed a robber as (48)

he ran out of a jewelry store. [S] After I packed my bag and put it in the trunk of the car, Dad said we were ready to go. When I (50)

packed my bag and put it in the trunk of the car. [F] To go. [F] With only two minutes left to play. Jumping over the last tackler near (53)

the goal. [S] Can you name the mayor of your town? (55)

ANSWER SHEET

Practicing Basic Skills in Language Arts • 310

© 2005 Sopris West Educational Services. All rights reserved. Practicing Basic Skills in Language Arts. Purchaser has permission to photocopy this page for classroom use only.

ONE-MINUTE FLUENCY
BUILDER SERIES

SEE TO MARK

Sentence Fragments and Run-On Sentences

Directions: Mark a line to divide the following word groups into sentences.

	First Try	Second Try
Correct		
Error		

We walked to Centerville it is about five miles from here the day was sunny we had been afraid it would rain we had to

make a decision we could go by bus we could go by train we flew to Idaho Falls then we took a bus to the lake it isn't

a new dress I wore it to the holiday party we enjoyed the bus trip nevertheless, the train would have been faster Pat

hasn't called he must be lost you take the general course first then you can specialize Ward is color-blind therefore his

wife always buys his clothes the fog was very heavy no planes left the airport the Krugers have a new car it is a Mazda

Hans is a good walker he also likes to climb mountains last month I visited New York I had a chance to see two

plays I enjoyed it very much in working problems at home, I am always rather weak in classwork I can usually hold

my own it is lucky for me that I can Ted stared at the car it had his father's license plate on it I could not trust him

I have been deceived by him before you have not done very well on this work sometimes you seem not to be trying your

best no one would take Gladys to the play she was too restless I have never seen Europe I have seen much of the United

States I always look for books by Sir Arthur Conan Doyle he is my favorite author Mack Koury won the hundred-yard

dash it was his second victory of the day I swam and swam the tide was against me however, I got ashore my mother

called the television repairman he said he would come as soon as possible where did you put the mustard I can't find it

Asia is the largest continent it reaches over almost one half of the globe from north to south

© 2005 Sopris West Educational Services. All rights reserved. Practicing Basic Skills in Language Arts. Purchaser has permission to photocopy this page for classroom use only.

	Correct	Error
First Try		
Second Try		

Sentence Fragments and Run-On Sentences

Directions: Mark a line to divide the following word groups into sentences.

We walked to Centerville | it is about five miles from here | the day was sunny | we had been afraid it would rain | we had to (4)

make a decision | we could go by bus | we could go by train | we flew to Idaho Falls | then we took a bus to the lake | it isn't (9)

a new dress | I wore it to the holiday party | we enjoyed the bus trip | nevertheless, the train would have been faster | Pat (13)

hasn't called | he must be lost | you take the general course first | then you can specialize | Ward is color-blind | therefore his (18)

wife always buys his clothes | the fog was very heavy | no planes left the airport | the Krugers have a new car | it is a Mazda | (23)

Hans is a good walker | he also likes to climb mountains | last month I visited New York | I had a chance to see two (26)

plays | I enjoyed it very much | in working problems at home, I am always rather weak | in classwork I can usually hold (29)

my own | it is lucky for me that I can | Ted stared at the car | it had his father's license plate on it | I could not trust him | (34)

I have been deceived by him before | you have not done very well on this work | sometimes you seem not to be trying your (36)

best | no one would take Gladys to the play | she was too restless | I have never seen Europe | I have seen much of the United (40)

States | I always look for books by Sir Arthur Conan Doyle | he is my favorite author | Mack Koury won the hundred-yard (43)

dash | it was his second victory of the day | I swam and swam | the tide was against me | however, I got ashore | my mother (48)

called the television repairman | he said he would come as soon as possible | where did you put the mustard | I can't find it | (52)

Asia is the largest continent | it reaches over almost one half of the globe from north to south (53)

ANSWER SHEET

© 2005 Sopris West Educational Services. All rights reserved. Practicing Basic Skills in Language Arts. Purchaser has permission to photocopy this page for classroom use only.

SEE TO MARK

ONE-MINUTE FLUENCY BUILDER SERIES

Fragments, Run-Ons, and Complete Sentences

Directions: After each word group, indicate whether it contains 0 sentences, 1 sentence, or 2 sentences.

	Correct	Error
First Try		
Second Try		

The driver with his hand on the emergency brake ____ At the close of a very exciting day ____ Don't make fun of him, he doesn't know any better ____ Cricket, an English game, is very similar to our baseball ____ I can't help you now you will have to return later ____ Those cold December days having so quickly passed ____ Tired and dirty after our long ride ____ Quickly he responded to the call of his friends ____ Because he felt like it ____ I'll take this one, it attracts me ____ Although I don't really believe you did it ____ In our town is a large vacant field where we played ball all summer ____ The flag flying in the breeze ____ Riding in a fast boat ____ They placed the oars in the boat ____ Steve can come with me I enjoy his company ____ Into the house about midnight ____ Don't wait for me, I may be very late ____ Spending many happy hours at the seashore ____ He was approaching me when the bell rang ____ When I reached their home, the lights were out and I went home ____ The day before Christmas was one of great preparation ____ Into the old deserted house without a flashlight or food ____ At the end of the day ____ Isn't this fine it is just what I need ____ Over the radio came my favorite song ____ Swinging widely around the dangerous corner ____ I went home early I helped get dinner and then I read for a while ____ Sliding down the slippery path ____ They found the child and started home ____ Be quiet I can't hear the program ____ At the close of the most exciting day of my life ____ I returned in September, fully rested and ready for work ____ A boy with large brown eyes ____ At last the letter came ____

© 2005 Sopris West Educational Services. All rights reserved. Practicing Basic Skills in Language Arts. Purchaser has permission to photocopy this page for classroom use only.

ONE MINUTE FLUENCY BUILDER SERIES

SEE TO MARK

Fragments, Run-Ons, and Complete Sentences

Directions: After each word group, indicate whether it contains 0 sentences, 1 sentence, or 2 sentences.

	Correct	Error
First Try		
Second Try		

The driver with his hand on the emergency brake **0** At the close of a very exciting day **0** Don't make fun of him, he doesn't (2)

know any better **2** Cricket, an English game, is very similar to our baseball **1** I can't help you now you will have to return (4)

later **2** Those cold December days having so quickly passed **0** Tired and dirty after our long ride **0** Quickly he responded (7)

to the call of his friends **1** Because he felt like it **0** I'll take this one, it attracts me **2** Although I don't really believe you did (10)

it **0** In our town is a large vacant field where we played ball all summer **1** The flag flying in the breeze **0** Riding in a fast (13)

boat **0** They placed the oars in the boat **1** Steve can come with me I enjoy his company **2** Into the house about midnight (16)

0 Don't wait for me, I may be very late **2** Spending many happy hours at the seashore **0** He was approaching me when (19)

the bell rang **1** When I reached their home, the lights were out and I went home **2** The day before Christmas was one of (21)

great preparation **1** Into the old deserted house without a flashlight or food **0** At the end of the day **0** Isn't this fine it is (24)

just what I need **2** Over the radio came my favorite song **1** Swinging widely around the dangerous corner **0** I went home (27)

early I helped get dinner and then I read for a while **2** Sliding down the slippery path **0** They found the child and started (29)

home **1** Be quiet I can't hear the program **2** At the close of the most exciting day of my life **0** I returned in September, (32)

fully rested and ready for work **1** A boy with large brown eyes **0** At last the letter came **1** (35)

ANSWER SHEET

Practicing Basic Skills in Language Arts • 314

© 2005 Sopris West Educational Services. All rights reserved. Practicing Basic Skills in Language Arts. Purchaser has permission to photocopy this page for classroom use only.

ONE MINUTE FLUENCY
BUILDER SERIES

	First Try	Second Try
Correct		
Error		

Types of Sentences

Directions: Identify the kind of sentence by writing DEC, IMP, INT, or EXC in the blanks provided. Also, put the correct mark of punctuation at the end of each sentence.

DEC—declarative (statement)   INT—interrogative (question)
IMP—imperative (command)   EXC—exclamatory (strong feeling)

_____ Where did you find that dollar bill

_____ The plane was flying low

_____ The catbird built its nest in the plum tree

_____ Next week the strawberries will be ripe

_____ Stand still for a minute

_____ Have you looked in the mirror this morning

_____ How you frightened me

_____ The stars were bright and beautiful

_____ How can we measure the distance to the stars

_____ Look out for the falling rocks

_____ The girls were arguing all afternoon

_____ Can an eagle kill a wolf

_____ Whose tennis shoe is lying here

_____ Much forest land was destroyed by fire

_____ Whom did you call

_____ In the nest were three blue eggs

_____ Here come the fire trucks

_____ Follow this road for a mile

_____ How do you estimate the age of a tree

_____ Please don't play that record again

_____ May I borrow your picture

_____ The tumbleweed scatters its seed over the prairie

_____ What a surprise that was

_____ I have drunk two milk shakes

_____ Are dirty hands a sign of genius

Practicing Basic Skills in Language Arts • 315

© 2005 Sopris West Educational Services. All rights reserved. Practicing Basic Skills in Language Arts. Purchaser has permission to photocopy this page for classroom use only.

ONE-MINUTE FLUENCY
BUILDER SERIES

SEE TO WRITE

Types of Sentences

Directions: Identify the kind of sentence by writing DEC, IMP, INT, or EXC in the blanks provided. Also, put the correct mark of punctuation at the end of each sentence.

DEC—declarative (statement)   INT—interrogative (question)
IMP—imperative (command)   EXC—exclamatory (strong feeling)

	Correct	Error
First Try		
Second Try		

INT (2) Where did you find that dollar bill?

DEC (4) The plane was flying low.

DEC (6) The catbird built its nest in the plum tree.

DEC (8) Next week the strawberries will be ripe.

IMP (10) Stand still for a minute!

INT (12) Have you looked in the mirror this morning?

EXC (14) How you frightened me!

DEC (16) The stars were bright and beautiful.

INT (18) How can we measure the distance to the stars?

EXC (20) Look out for the falling rocks!

DEC (22) The girls were arguing all afternoon.

INT (24) Can an eagle kill a wolf?

INT (26) Whose tennis shoe is lying here?

DEC (28) Much forest land was destroyed by fire.

INT (30) Whom did you call?

DEC (32) In the nest were three blue eggs.

DEC (34) Here come the fire trucks.

IMP (36) Follow this road for a mile.

INT (38) How do you estimate the age of a tree?

IMP (40) Please don't play that record again!

INT (42) May I borrow your picture?

DEC (44) The tumbleweed scatters its seed over the prairie.

EXC (46) What a surprise that was!

DEC (48) I have drunk two milk shakes.

INT (50) Are dirty hands a sign of genius?

© 2005 Sopris West Educational Services. All rights reserved. Practicing Basic Skills in Language Arts. Purchaser has permission to photocopy this page for classroom use only.

Capitalization and Punctuation

Capitalize First Word, I, and Proper
    Nouns in Sentences—Primary 319
Capitalization of First Word of Sentence
    and Pronoun I 321
Geographical Locations and Proper
    Adjectives 323
Names of Persons and Geographic
    Names.. 325
Names of Organizations, Business Firms,
    Institutions, and Government Bodies 327
Seasons, Clubs, Corporations, Hotels,
    Churches 329
Special Events, Calendar Items, Historical
    Events and Periods, Nationalities,
    Races, and Religions............................ 331
Titles of Books, Magazines, Poems, Stories,
    Movies, Songs, Works of Art, Historical
    Documents, Historical Events, and
    Calendar Items 333
Brand Names, Ships, Planets, Monuments,
    and Awards.. 335
Nationalities, Races, Religions, Ships,
    Planets, and Monuments 337
Proper Adjectives and Names of School
    Subjects.. 339
School Subjects, School Names, and
    Grades.. 341
Titles and Relationships............................. 343
Names of Persons, Deities, Relationships,
    and Titles.. 345
Capitalization Review 347
Capitalization Review 349
Capitalization Review 351
Ending Punctuation Using . and ?—
    Primary.. 353
Ending Punctuation Using . ? and !—
    Primary.. 355
Ending Punctuation 357
Ending Punctuation 359

Commas—Items in a Series 361
Commas to Separate Adjectives.................. 363
Commas After Introductory Words 365
Commas for Appositives............................. 367
Commas for Parenthetical Expressions 369
Commas for Nonessential Clauses 371
Commas for Subordinate Clauses............... 373
Commas for Independent Clauses 375
Commas for Introductory Elements and
    Nouns of Direct Address 377
Commas for Appositives and
    Parenthetical Expressions 379
Commas for Appositives, Parenthetical
    Expressions, Names, and Titles 381
Commas in Dates and Addresses................. 383
Commas in Series, Dates, and Addresses..... 385
Comma Review 387
Apostrophe to Show Possession................... 389
Apostrophes to Form Plurals of Letters,
    Numbers, Signs, and Words 391
Apostrophes to Form Plurals of Letters,
    Numbers, and Signs 393
Apostrophe Review 395
Apostrophe Review 397
Apostrophe Review 399
Apostrophe Review 401
Semicolons Between Independent
    Clauses... 403
Semicolons Between Independent Clauses
    Joined by Adverbial Connectives............. 405
Semicolons in Items in a Series................... 407
Semicolon Review 409
Colons for Time and Salutations 411
Colon Review 413
Quotation Marks in Conversation............... 415
Quotation Marks to Enclose Titles.............. 417
Quotation Marks Within a Quotation......... 419
Quotation Marks and Other Punctuation
    Marks... 421

Quotation Marks and Other Punctuation
    Marks in Conversation............................ 423
Hyphens in Numbers and Fractions............ 425
Hyphens and Dashes 427
Hyphen Review 429
Parentheses 431
Underlining Titles of Books, Plays, and
    Periodicals 433

Underlining Titles of Movies, Works of
    Art, and Long Musical Compositions 435
Underlining Titles of Ships, Trains, and
    Airplanes 437
Underlining Review 439
Punctuation Combinations 441

	First Try	Second Try
Correct		
Error		

Capitalize First Word, I, and Proper Nouns in Sentences—Primary

Directions: Capitalize the first word in a sentence, proper nouns, and I.

there is a fence around the field.

i saw jane come in the house.

we walked home alone.

the cat is named tiger.

did you see mary at the party?

my hands were cold.

i like getting letters from friends.

we live on main street.

can i have a cookie?

father and i will be there.

he and sam will be at the party.

did you see my dog?

florida is a beautiful state.

jim and karen will be there.

i will come with you.

the baby is named billy.

we went to mexico on vacation.

the house is new.

she is going to school this year.

my kitten is brown.

did you call his house?

mother is going to sing to us.

if you hurry, i will let you go.

i heard the boat go by.

mrs. may is her name.

summer vacation starts in june.

do you like my name?

Practicing Basic Skills in Language Arts • 319

© 2005 Sopris West Educational Services. All rights reserved. Practicing Basic Skills in Language Arts. Purchaser has permission to photocopy this page for classroom use only.

ONE-MINUTE FLUENCY BUILDER SERIES

Capitalize First Word, I, and Proper Nouns in Sentences—Primary

Directions: Capitalize the first word in a sentence, proper nouns, and I.

	Correct	Error
First Try		
Second Try		

Ⓣhere is a fence around the field.

Ⓦe walked home alone. (4)

Ⓣhe cat is named Ⓣiger.

Ⓜy hands were cold. (9)

Ⓘ like getting letters from friends.

Ⓒan Ⓘ have a cookie? (15)

Ⓕather and Ⓘ will be there.

Ⓓid you see my dog? (20)

Ⓕlorida is a beautiful state.

Ⓘ will come with you. (24)

Ⓣhe baby is named Ⓑilly.

Ⓣhe house is new. (29)

Ⓢhe is going to school this year.

Ⓓid you call his house? (32)

Ⓜother is going to sing to us.

Ⓘ heard the boat go by. (36)

Ⓜrs. Ⓜay is her name.

Ⓓo you like my name? (41)

Ⓘ saw Ⓙane come in the house.

Ⓓid you see Ⓜary at the party?

Ⓦe live on Ⓜain Ⓢtreet.

Ⓗe and Ⓢam will be at the party.

Ⓙim and Ⓚaren will be there.

Ⓦe went to Ⓜexico on vacation.

Ⓜy kitten is brown.

Ⓘf you hurry, Ⓘ will let you go.

Ⓢummer vacation starts in Ⓙune.

ANSWER SHEET

© 2005 Sopris West Educational Services. All rights reserved. Practicing Basic Skills in Language Arts. Purchaser has permission to photocopy this page for classroom use only.

SEE TO MARK

Capitalization of First Word of Sentence and Pronoun I

Directions: Mark the letters that should be capitalized.

if i don't have to work, i'll be there. while driving through the state, i saw hundreds of trailer courts. i am sorry, but i prefer the other book. Caesar's famous report to Rome was, "i came, i saw, i conquered." sally will get lunch, and i shall wash the dishes.

When i have finished my theme, i'll retype it. i forgot my keys. the work is not easy. when i dived in, i found that the water was cold. May i use your pencil, Tony? i do not play the tuba, and i don't wish to learn. where did i put the jacket yesterday?

i've been wondering whose idea that was! he stared at the pretty girl with an i'd-like-to-know-you smile. when the call came i grabbed my coat, hurried out, and ran to the airport. well, Samuel, you may be right, but i wish you would hear my side of the question! i've never seen a larger, busier, more beautiful city. on Sundays i visit my grandmother. it is time for Sasha's music lesson, but she is not home. if you leave the light on, i can find your house more easily. i bought this cheese at the market on the corner. i'm ready for the trip. when i checked, i found i was off by six and three-hundredths degrees. always check your answers carefully. i'm in a good mood today. i practiced my lesson for two hours. the sword in his hands flashed like quicksilver. nothing stirred but the bats overhead. in the summer i spend most of my days at the beach. i have already asked him to notify you. i like the red car best. i'll arrive at 8 P.M. the man behind me turned as i hurried up the stairs. Ouch! i stepped on something! as i've said before, i was absent neither on Thursday nor on Friday. oh, i'll finish my work before i leave. i have not scolded you and him, nor shall i do so. because i didn't take my time, i missed two fair but difficult questions. unless father arrives soon, both Jack and i will have to take the bus. how many pieces of pie shall i cut? no, i've not heard that CD. i help Mother with spring cleaning. either Jan or i will deliver the flowers. Shall i light the candles?

Practicing Basic Skills in Language Arts • 321

© 2005 Sopris West Educational Services. All rights reserved. Practicing Basic Skills in Language Arts. Purchaser has permission to photocopy this page for classroom use only.

Capitalization of First Word of Sentence and Pronoun I

Directions: Mark the letters that should be capitalized.

	First Try	Second Try
Correct		
Error		

(7) if (i) don't have to work, (i)'ll be there. (w)hile driving through the state, (i) saw hundreds of trailer courts. (i)am sorry, but (i)prefer the

(12) other book. Caesar's famous report to Rome was, "(i)came, (i)saw, (i)conquered." (s)ally will get lunch, and (i)shall wash the dishes.

(19) When (i)have finished my theme, (i)'ll retype it. (i)forgot my keys. (t)he work is not easy. (w)hen (i)dived in, (i)found that the water

(24) was cold. May (i)use your pencil, Tony? (i)do not play the tuba, and (i)don't wish to learn. (w)here did (i)put the jacket yesterday?

(29) (i)ve been wondering whose idea that was! (h)e stared at the pretty girl with an (i)d-like-to-know-you smile. (w)hen the call came (i)

(31) grabbed my coat, hurried out, and ran to the airport. (w)ell, Samuel, you may be right, but (i)wish you would hear my side of the

(35) question! (i)ve never seen a larger, busier, more beautiful city. (o)n Sundays (i)visit my grandmother. (i)t is time for Sasha's music

(38) lesson, but she is not home. (i)f you leave the light on, (i)can find your house more easily. (i)bought this cheese at the market on

(44) the corner. (i)m ready for the trip. (w)hen (i)checked, (i)found (i)was off by six and three-hundredths degrees. (a)lways check your

(47) answers carefully. (i)m in a good mood today. (i)practiced my lesson for two hours. (t)he sword in his hands flashed like quicksilver.

(51) (n)othing stirred but the bats overhead. (i)n the summer (i)spend most of my days at the beach. (i)have already asked him to

(56) notify you. (i)like the red car best. (i)ll arrive at 8 P.M. (t)he man behind me turned as (i)hurried up the stairs. Ouch! (i)stepped on

(63) something! (a)s (i)ve said before, (i)was absent neither on Thursday nor on Friday. (o)h, (i)ll finish my work before (i)leave. (i)have not

(68) scolded you and him, nor shall (i)do so. (b)ecause (i)didn't take my time, (i)missed two fair but difficult questions. (u)nless father

(73) arrives soon, both Jack and (i)will have to take the bus. (h)ow many pieces of pie shall (i)cut? no, (i)ve not heard that CD. (i)help

(76) Mother with spring cleaning. (e)ither Jan or (i)will deliver the flowers. Shall (i)light the candles?

ONE-MINUTE FLUENCY BUILDER SERIES

ANSWER SHEET

Practicing Basic Skills in Language Arts • 322

© 2005 Sopris West Educational Services. All rights reserved. Practicing Basic Skills in Language Arts. Purchaser has permission to photocopy this page for classroom use only.

SEE TO MARK

Geographical Locations and Proper Adjectives

Directions: Mark the letters that should be capitalized.

First Try	Correct	Error
Second Try		

victorian poetry

blacktail road

the hawaiian islands

a european country

weber county residents

an australian kangaroo

pleasant view, utah

black rock beach

the weber river

mount whitney

tenth avenue

a new england village

salt lake county

an ogden firm

an ocean beach

the gobi desert

an apache leader

the state of arizona

the capital of utah

the mexican border

the north american continent

willard bay state park

north odgen pass

pine view dam

the red sea

los angeles county, california

san diego freeway

the city of hooper

a japanese village

a lake powell resort

pebble creek

the uintah mountains

wall avenue

the italian people

the pacific ocean

a michigan lake

the great salt lake

washington boulevard

yellowstone national park

a chinese restaurant

a dutch town

lake michigan

an indian legend

u.s. highway 89

the state park

the canadian border

a state in the union

zions national park

oriental cooking

a canadian hockey team

twenty-first street

ethiopian students

american hostages

ben lomond peak

Practicing Basic Skills in Language Arts • 323

© 2005 Sopris West Educational Services. All rights reserved. Practicing Basic Skills in Language Arts. Purchaser has permission to photocopy this page for classroom use only.

SEE TO MARK

Geographical Locations and Proper Adjectives

Directions: Mark the letters that should be capitalized.

	Correct	Error
First Try		
Second Try		

victorian poetry

backtail road

the hawaiian islands

a european country

weber county residents

an australian kangaroo

pleasant view, utah

black rock beach

the weber river

mount whitney

tenth avenue

a new england village

salt lake county

an ogden firm

an ocean beach

the gobi desert

an apache leader

the state of arizona

---

the capital of utah

the mexican border

the north american continent

willard bay state park

north ogden pass

pine view dam

the red sea

los angeles county, california

san diego freeway

the city of hooper

a japanese village

a lake powell resort

pebble creek

the uintah mountains

wall avenue

the italian people

the pacific ocean

a michigan lake

---

the great salt lake (5)

washington boulevard (10)

yellowstone national park (18)

a chinese restaurant (24)

a dutch town (30)

lake michigan (36)

an indian legend (42)

u s highway 89 (52)

the state park (57)

the canadian border (61)

a state in the union (64)

zions national park (71)

oriental cooking (77)

a canadian hockey team (81)

twenty first street (86)

ethiopian students (90)

american hostages (94)

ben lomond peak (99)

ANSWER SHEET

Practicing Basic Skills in Language Arts • 324

© 2005 Sopris West Educational Services. All rights reserved. Practicing Basic Skills in Language Arts. Purchaser has permission to photocopy this page for classroom use only.

SEE TO MARK

Names of Persons and Geographic Names

Directions: Mark the letters that should be capitalized.

	First Try	Second Try
Correct		
Error		

The suez canal is in africa. There is a dam on the colorado river called hoover dam. A program of future plans was developed in

1941 by franklin d. roosevelt and winston churchill. When I went to kansas city last summer, I saw anna josephs. Did you know

that rangoon is the capital and the largest city in burma? samuel clemens, also known as mark twain, lived for several years in

virginia city, nevada. The house is on the corner of park street and jefferson avenue. On their trip, stan johnson and steve bird

visited gettysburg national park in pennsylvania. The republic of ghana lies on the west coast of africa. The explorers skirted the

gulf of mexico until they reached the mississippi river. From manila, dr. james roberts will fly to israel. Is it true that atlanta lies

west of new york? In 1521, cortez conquered mexico, and in 1531, pizarro conquered peru. spain was made wealthy by the gold

and silver from peru and mexico. By 1574, missions could be found from california to chile. Our club elected jana stevens to

represent us at the convention in salt lake city. john fredrick johnson was born in elizabeth city, north carolina. Give the report

to dr. harold j. evans. We listened carefully to sir james brown. Before us we saw mount rainier. The mississippi river and the

ohio river converge at cairo, illinois. I am to meet art wilson on the corner of fairview drive and california street. The beautiful

rocky mountains are in colorado. We are glad to live in the united states of america.

Practicing Basic Skills in Language Arts • 325

© 2005 Sopris West Educational Services. All rights reserved. Practicing Basic Skills in Language Arts. Purchaser has permission to photocopy this page for classroom use only.

SEE TO MARK

	Correct	Error
First Try		
Second Try		

Names of Persons and Geographic Names

Directions: Mark the letters that should be capitalized.

The (s)uez (c)anal is in (a)frica. There is a dam on the (c)olorado (r)iver called (h)oover (d)am. A program of future plans was developed in (7)

1941 by (f)ranklin (d.) (r)oosevelt and (w)inston (c)hurchill. When I went to (k)ansas (c)ity last summer, I saw (a)nna (j)osephs. Did you know (16)

that (r)angoon is the capital and the largest city in (b)urma? (s)amuel (c)lemens, also known as (m)ark (t)wain, lived for several years in (22)

(v)irginia (c)ity, (n)evada. The house is on the corner of (p)ark (s)treet and (j)efferson (a)venue. On their trip, (s)tan (j)ohnson and (s)teve (b)ird (33)

visited (g)ettysburg (n)ational (p)ark in (p)ennsylvania. The (r)epublic of (g)hana lies on the west coast of (a)frica. The explorers skirted the (40)

(g)ulf of (m)exico until they reached the (m)ississippi (r)iver. From (m)anila, (d)r. (j)ames (r)oberts will fly to (i)srael. Is it true that (a)tlanta lies (50)

west of (n)ew (y)ork? In 1521, (c)ortez conquered (m)exico, and in 1531, (p)izarro conquered (p)eru. (s)pain was made wealthy by the gold (57)

and silver from (p)eru and (m)exico. By 1574, missions could be found from (c)alifornia to (c)hile. Our club elected (j)ana (s)tevens to (63)

represent us at the convention in (s)alt (l)ake (c)ity. (j)ohn (f)redrick (j)ohnson was born in (e)lizabeth (c)ity, (n)orth (c)arolina. Give the report (73)

to (d)r. (h)arold (j.) (e)vans. We listened carefully to (s)ir (j)ames (b)rown. Before us we saw (m)ount (r)ainier. The (m)ississippi (r)iver and the (84)

(o)hio (r)iver converge at (c)airo, (i)llinois. I am to meet (a)rt (w)ilson on the corner of (f)airview (d)rive and (c)alifornia (s)treet. The beautiful (94)

(r)ocky (m)ountains are in (c)olorado. We are glad to live in the (u)nited (s)tates of (a)merica. (100)

© 2005 Sopris West Educational Services. All rights reserved. Practicing Basic Skills in Language Arts. Purchaser has permission to photocopy this page for classroom use only.

	First Try	Second Try
Correct		
Error		

Names of Organizations, Business Firms, Institutions, and Government Bodies

Directions: Mark the letters that should be capitalized.

The boston choral society will appear at the university of maine. The lerner string quartet will play at the library of congress.

The new teacher is a leader in the boy scouts of america. Dad knows a vice president at american savings and loan. Allen Dale

is a candidate for the house of representatives! Where are the offices of the american red cross? The new york public library

has a fine collection of books. The utah state legislature met last month. The junior chamber of commerce does fine work in

our community. Ship the books to richmond field junior high school. The jamison company is having a sale. Mr. Jones is a

republican. Will you attend weber state college? All the members attended a rally given by the democratic party. Each afternoon

we swim at the royal palm hotel. Last Wednesday we visited the guggenheim museum. The gulf oil company is not interested

in aluminum. The future teachers of america is the most active organization at viewmont high school. The pentagon sent its

recommendation to congress. My favorite clothing store is ross and company. The weber county athletic club will hold its

annual banquet next month. The league of women voters is active in both the democratic and republican parties. This book

is published by sopris west. anita's hat shop is in the palmolive building. Did you buy that dress at sears? The department of

transportation is working to cut gasoline consumption. The union pacific railroad hires many graduates of utah state university.

© 2005 Sopris West Educational Services. All rights reserved. Practicing Basic Skills in Language Arts. Purchaser has permission to photocopy this page for classroom use only.

	First Try	Second Try
Correct		
Error		

Names of Organizations, Business Firms, Institutions, and Government Bodies

Directions: Mark the letters that should be capitalized.

The (b)oston (c)horal (s)ociety will appear at the (u)niversity of (m)aine. The (l)erner (s)tring (q)uartet will play at the (l)ibrary of (c)ongress. (10)

The new teacher is a leader in the (b)oy (s)couts of (a)merica. Dad knows a vice president at (a)merican (s)avings and (l)oan. Allen Dale (16)

is a candidate for the (h)ouse of (r)epresentatives! Where are the offices of the (a)merican (r)ed (c)ross? The (n)ew (y)ork (p)ublic (l)ibrary (25)

has a fine collection of books. The (u)tah (s)tate (l)egislature met last month. The (j)unior (c)hamber of (c)ommerce does fine work in (31)

our community. Ship the books to (r)ichmond (f)ield (j)unior (h)igh (s)chool. The (j)amison (c)ompany is having a sale. Mr. Jones is a (38)

(r)epublican. Will you attend (w)eber (s)tate (c)ollege? All the members attended a rally given by the (d)emocratic (p)arty. Each afternoon (44)

we swim at the (r)oyal (p)alm (h)otel. Last Wednesday we visited the (g)uggenheim (m)useum. The (g)ulf (o)il (c)ompany is not interested (52)

in aluminum. The (f)uture (t)eachers of (a)merica is the most active organization at (v)ewmont (h)igh (s)chool. The (p)entagon sent its (59)

recommendation to (c)ongress. My favorite clothing store is (r)oss and (c)ompany. The (w)eber (c)ounty (a)thletic (c)lub will hold its (66)

annual banquet next month. The (l)eague of (w)omen (v)oters is active in both the (d)emocratic and (r)epublican parties. This book (71)

is published by (s)opris (w)est. (a)nita's (h)at (s)hop is in the (p)almolive (b)uilding. Did you buy that dress at (s)ears? The (d)epartment of (80)

(t)ransportation is working to cut gasoline consumption. The (u)nion (p)acific (r)ailroad hires many graduates of (u)tah (s)tate (u)niversity. (87)

Practicing Basic Skills in Language Arts • 328

© 2005 Sopris West Educational Services. All rights reserved. Practicing Basic Skills in Language Arts. Purchaser has permission to photocopy this page for classroom use only.

SEE TO MARK

Seasons, Clubs, Corporations, Hotels, Churches

Directions: Mark the letters that should be capitalized.

	First Try	Second Try
Correct		
Error		

Is winter your favorite season? In recent years, the united states air force has been doing a study on unidentified flying objects.

This year, our school is having a winter carnival. Even congress said that studies should be done. Jane hopes to go south this

winter and return to the west next summer. Recently, a show on nbc television described the air force study. Have you ever

visited the northwest? How would it be to have a martian in the united nations? You must travel north to get to canada. In the

meantime, the sigs toy company has made toy flying objects. It's a lovely place to visit in autumn. For several years the small

cars from toyota, datsun, volkswagen, and fiat sold well in the united states. The great american desert lies in the southwest. He

lives on the eastern corner of twenty-third street. Students and faculty members at westlake high and hillview college found that

japanese, german, and italian cars were reliable. ford, general motors, and chrysler have been making small cars to compete. The

midwest contains fertile farm land. Government agencies, such as the department of labor, buy only american cars. California

lies south of oregon. In auto mechanics II, we work on cars from any country. Be sure to visit massachusetts during the spring

festival. Our teacher had lived with a german family while taking special training in the volkswagen factory. Colorado Springs

lies a good distance southeast of ogden. The bus driver said, "This bus does not stop at johnson's hardware store; however, it

does stop at the intersection of walnut street and lowell avenue, which is only two blocks south." Some states in the south

experience lengthy summers.

Practicing Basic Skills in Language Arts • 329

© 2005 Sopris West Educational Services. All rights reserved. Practicing Basic Skills in Language Arts. Purchaser has permission to photocopy this page for classroom use only.

ONE MINUTE FLUENCY BUILDER SERIES

SEE TO MARK

Seasons, Clubs, Corporations, Hotels, Churches

Directions: Mark the letters that should be capitalized.

	Correct	Error
First Try		
Second Try		

Is winter your favorite season? In recent years, the (u)nited (s)tates (a)ir (f)orce has been doing a study on unidentified flying objects. (4)

This year, our school is having a (w)inter (c)arnival. Even (c)ongress said that studies should be done. Jane hopes to go south this (7)

winter and return to the (w)est next summer. Recently, a show on (bbc) television described the (a)ir (f)orce study. Have you ever (13)

visited the (n)orthwest? How would it be to have a (m)artian in the (u)nited (n)ations? You must travel north to get to (c)anada. In the (18)

meantime, the (s)igs (t)oy (c)ompany has made toy flying objects. It's a lovely place to visit in autumn. For several years the small (21)

cars from (t)oyota, (d)atsun, (v)olkswagen, and (f)iat sold well in the (u)nited (s)tates. The (g)reat (a)merican (d)esert lies in the (s)outhwest. He (31)

lives on the eastern corner of (t)wenty-(t)hird (s)treet. Students and faculty members at (w)estlake (h)igh and (h)illview (c)ollege found that (38)

(j)apanese, (g)erman, and (i)talian cars were reliable. (f)ord, (g)eneral (m)otors, and (c)hrysler have been making small cars to compete. The (45)

(m)idwest contains fertile farm land. Government agencies, such as the (d)epartment of (l)abor, buy only (a)merican cars. California (49)

lies south of (o)regon. In (a)uto (m)echanics II, we work on cars from any country. Be sure to visit (m)assachusetts during the (s)pring (54)

festival. Our teacher had lived with a (g)erman family while taking special training in the (v)olkswagen factory. Colorado Springs (57)

lies a good distance southeast of (o)gden. The bus driver said, "This bus does not stop at (j)ohnson's (h)ardware (s)tore; however, it (61)

does stop at the intersection of (w)alnut (s)treet and (l)owell (a)venue, which is only two blocks south." Some states in the (s)outh (66)

experience lengthy summers. (66)

ANSWER SHEET

Practicing Basic Skills in Language Arts • 330

© 2005 Sopris West Educational Services. All rights reserved. Practicing Basic Skills in Language Arts. Purchaser has permission to photocopy this page for classroom use only.

SEE TO MARK

Special Events, Calendar Items, Historical Events and Periods, Nationalities, Races, and Religions

Directions: Mark the letters that should be capitalized.

	Correct	Error
First Try		
Second Try		

The hungarian people have an asiatic background. He is an englishman, but he doesn't belong to the caucasian race. In New

York, columbus day is always a holiday. The prohibition era was a time of confusion. Jane is reading the chapters on the middle

ages. The battle of the bulge was a decisive event in world war II. Members of the local audubon society attend meetings every

tuesday. thanksgiving is always celebrated on thursday. We will celebrate new year's eve by going out to dinner. The american

revolution actually began with the battle of lexington on april 19, 1775. The fourth of july commemorates the signing of the

declaration of independence. Can you read a french newspaper? halloween this year falls on the fifth wednesday in october.

Where were you on sunday, july 10? On july 14, the french celebrate bastille day. Although Tom attended purdue university, his

wife attended duke university. The cambodian people have had many hardships. The swedish language is difficult to learn. Our

library has a fine collection of books on buddhism. The NAACP has done much to improve the civil rights of african americans.

On our trip, we bought some unusual mexican pottery. The bill of rights is a part of the constitution. The use of tools began in

the stone age. My favorite part of american history is the age of jackson. My visitor is a brazilian. The countries in the middle

east have been in the news recently.

© 2005 Sopris West Educational Services. All rights reserved. Practicing Basic Skills in Language Arts. Purchaser has permission to photocopy this page for classroom use only.

SEE TO MARK

Special Events, Calendar Items, Historical Events and Periods, Nationalities, Races, and Religions

Directions: Mark the letters that should be capitalized.

	First Try	Second Try
Correct		
Error		

The hungarian people have an asiatic background. He is an englishman, but he doesn't belong to the caucasian race. In New (4)

York, columbus day is always a holiday. The prohibition era was a time of confusion. Jane is reading the chapters on the middle (9)

ages. The battle of the bulge was a decisive event in world war II. Members of the local audubon society attend meetings every (16)

tuesday. thanksgiving is always celebrated on thursday. We will celebrate new year's eve by going out to dinner. The american (23)

revolution actually began with the battle of lexington on april 19, 1775. The fourth of july commemorates the signing of the (29)

declaration of independence. Can you read a french newspaper? halloween this year falls on the fifth wednesday in october. (35)

Where were you on sunday, july 10? On july 14, the french celebrate bastille day. Although Tom attended purdue university, his (43)

wife attended duke university. The cambodian people have had many hardships. The swedish language is difficult to learn. Our (47)

library has a fine collection of books on buddhism. The NAACP has done much to improve the civil rights of african americans. (50)

On our trip, we bought some unusual mexican pottery. The bill of rights is a part of the constitution. The use of tools began in (54)

the stone age. My favorite part of american history is the age of jackson. My visitor is a brazilian. The countries in the middle (61)

east have been in the news recently. (62)

ANSWER SHEET

© 2005 Sopris West Educational Services. All rights reserved. Practicing Basic Skills in Language Arts. Purchaser has permission to photocopy this page for classroom use only.

ONE-MINUTE FLUENCY BUILDER SERIES

SEE TO MARK

Titles of Books, Magazines, Poems, Stories, Movies, Songs, Works of Art, Historical Documents, Historical Events, and Calendar Items

Directions: Mark the letters that should be capitalized.

	Correct	Error
First Try		
Second Try		

My uncle has acted in both *julius caesar* and *the king and i*. The treaty of paris is an important document in the history of france.

the diary of anne frank will be made into a television program for the the "hallmark hall of fame." This story is set in germany

during world war II. One of my favorite television programs is *jeopardy*. In july of 1776, many famous americans gathered to

sign the declaration of independence. This act led to the revolutionary war. Today, we still celebrate this event with a holiday,

the fourth of july. Last wednesday, the *ogden standard examiner* carried an article on the *mona lisa*, a painting by Leonardo da

Vinci. In 1862, president lincoln issued the emancipation proclamation, officially freeing all slaves on january 1, 1863. Benet's

john brown's body gives a vivid account of the attack on harper's ferry. *the thinker*, a sculpture by rodin, is displayed in the

museum of modern art in new york. We subscribe to several magazines, among them *sports illustrated*, *newsweek*, and *national*

geographic. One of my favorite holidays, mother's day, is always celebrated on a sunday in may. The school choir will sing "frosty

the snowman" in their december concert. Two of my favorite songs are "rudolph the red-nosed reindeer" and "jingle bells."

The first poem to be recited at the district speech festival was "the ghost that jim saw" by bret harte. Ms. Cashmore, head of

the english department, discovered that book reports on such classics as Scott's *ivanhoe* and Dumas' *the count of monte cristo*

were actually based on the classic comics versions sold at country club drug store. One of my favorite short stories is "the most

dangerous game" by richard connell.

© 2005 Sopris West Educational Services. All rights reserved. Practicing Basic Skills in Language Arts. Purchaser has permission to photocopy this page for classroom use only.

ONE-MINUTE FLUENCY BUILDER SERIES

SEE TO MARK

Titles of Books, Magazines, Poems, Stories, Movies, Songs, Works of Art, Historical Documents, Historical Events, and Calendar Items

Directions: Mark the letters that should be capitalized.

	First Try	Second Try
Correct		
Error		

My uncle has acted in both (j)ulius (c)aesar and (t)he (k)ing and (i) The (t)reaty of (p)aris is an important document in the history of (f)rance. (8)

(t)he (d)iary of (a)nne (f)rank will be made into a television program for the the "(h)allmark (h)all of (f)ame." This story is set in (g)ermany (16)

during (w)orld (w)ar II. One of my favorite television programs is (j)eopardy. In (j)uly of 1776, many famous (a)mericans gathered to (21)

sign the (d)eclaration of (i)ndependence. This act led to the (r)evolutionary (w)ar. Today, we still celebrate this event with a holiday, (25)

the (f)ourth of (j)uly. Last (w)ednesday, the (o)gden (s)tandard (e)xaminer carried an article on the (m)ona (l)isa, a painting by Leonardo da (33)

Vinci. In 1862, (p)resident (l)incoln issued the (e)mancipation (p)roclamation, officially freeing all slaves on (j)anuary 1, 1863. Benet's (38)

(j)ohn (b)rown's (b)ody gives a vivid account of the attack on (h)arper's (f)erry. (t)he (t)hinker, a sculpture by (r)odin, is displayed in the (46)

(m)useum of (m)odern (a)rt in (n)ew (y)ork. We subscribe to several magazines, among them (s)ports (i)llustrated, (n)ewsweek, and (n)ational (55)

(g)eographic. One of my favorite holidays, (m)other's (d)ay, is always celebrated on a (s)unday in (m)ay. The school choir will sing "(f)rosty (61)

the (s)nowman" in their (d)ecember concert. Two of my favorite songs are "(r)udolph the (r)ed-(n)osed (r)eindeer" and "(j)ingle (b)ells." (68)

The first poem to be recited at the (d)istrict (s)peech (f)estival was "(t)he (g)host that (j)im (s)aw" by (b)ret (h)arte. Ms. Cashmore, head of (77)

the (e)nglish department, discovered that book reports on such classics as Scott's (i)vanhoe and Dumas' (t)he (c)ount of (m)onte (c)risto (83)

were actually based on the (c)lassic (c)omics versions sold at (c)ountry (c)lub drug store. One of my favorite short stories is "(t)he (m)ost (89)

(d)angerous (g)ame" by (r)ichard (c)onnell. (93)

ANSWER SHEET

Practicing Basic Skills in Language Arts • 334

© 2005 Sopris West Educational Services. All rights reserved. Practicing Basic Skills in Language Arts. Purchaser has permission to photocopy this page for classroom use only.

ONE-MINUTE FLUENCY
BUILDER SERIES

	Correct	Error
First Try		
Second Try		

SEE TO MARK

Brand Names, Ships, Planets, Monuments, and Awards

Directions: Mark the letters that should be capitalized.

dad once saw mercury, venus, mars, jupiter, and saturn close together in the constellation of gemini. I ordered a book of recipes

that use campbell's soups. We went on a riverboat called the *delta queen*. The series *roots* received several emmys, the award of

the television industry. We read a science fiction story about life on mars. We went to visit the soldiers and sailors monument.

My dentist recommended either crest or pepsodent toothpaste. My grandmother arrived yesterday on the *santa fe chief*. charles

white won the heisman award for his excellence in football. I believe saturn is the most beautiful planet. The recipe called

for crisco salad oil. On our trip to south dakota, we visited mount rushmore. The *titanic* was ironically described as being

"unsinkable." I'll never forget seeing the lincoln memorial at night. sally field was nominated for an oscar. Our toro mower is

much easier to use than our old model. Have you ever seen the big dipper? Did that movie receive an academy award? I have

always liked jantzen sportswear. jo wanted to buy adidas running shoes, but they didn't have her size. Do you think there is life

on mars? Did ellen and stan climb to the top of the washington monument? Again loretta lynn was nominated for a grammy,

the award of the music industry. My cousin sandi just bought a ford economy car. Our flight was called the silver eagle. Is pluto

the most distant planet? The tony is the award given for a broadway performance. Is wonder bread enriched?

Practicing Basic Skills in Language Arts • 335

© 2005 Sopris West Educational Services. All rights reserved. Practicing Basic Skills in Language Arts. Purchaser has permission to photocopy this page for classroom use only.

SEE TO MARK

	First Try	Second Try
Correct		
Error		

Brand Names, Ships, Planets, Monuments, and Awards

Directions: Mark the letters that should be capitalized.

(d)ad once saw (m)ercury, (v)enus, (m)ars, (j)upiter, and (s)aturn close together in the constellation of (g)emini. I ordered a book of recipes (7)

that use (C)ampbell's soups. We went on a riverboat called the *(d)elta (q)ueen*. The series (r)oots received several (e)nmys, the award of (12)

the television industry. We read a science fiction story about life on (m)ars. We went to visit the (s)oldiers and (s)ailors (m)onument. (16)

My dentist recommended either (c)rest or (p)epsodent toothpaste. My grandmother arrived yesterday on the *(s)anta (f)e (c)hief*. (c)harles (22)

(w)hite won the (h)eisman (a)ward for his excellence in football. I believe (s)aturn is the most beautiful planet. The recipe called (26)

for (C)isco salad oil. On our trip to (s)outh (d)akota, we visited (m)ount (r)ushmore. The *(t)itanic* was ironically described as being (32)

"unsinkable." I'll never forget seeing the (l)incoln (m)emorial at night. (s)ally (f)ield was nominated for an (o)scar. Our (t)oro mower is (38)

much easier to use than our old model. Have you ever seen the (b)ig (d)ipper? Did that movie receive an (a)cademy (a)ward? I have (42)

always liked (j)antzen (s)portswear. (j)o wanted to buy (a)didas running shoes, but they didn't have her size. Do you think there is life (46)

on (m)ars? Did (e)len and (s)tan climb to the top of the (w)ashington (m)onument? Again (l)oretta (l)ynn was nominated for a (g)rammy, (54)

the award of the music industry. My cousin (s)andi just bought a (f)ord economy car. Our flight was called the (s)ilver (e)agle. Is (p)luto (59)

the most distant planet? The (t)ony is the award given for a (b)roadway performance. Is (w)onder bread enriched? (62)

ANSWER SHEET

Practicing Basic Skills in Language Arts • 336

© 2005 Sopris West Educational Services. All rights reserved. Practicing Basic Skills in Language Arts. Purchaser has permission to photocopy this page for classroom use only.

ONE MINUTE FLUENCY
BUILDER SERIES

SEE TO MARK

Proper Nouns
Directions: Mark the letters that should be capitalized.

	Correct	Error
First Try		
Second Try		

We sailed on the *northlander* to seattle and on the *coastal queen* to sitka, alaska. This spring we shall visit lincoln's tomb in

springfield, illinois. ancient greeks worshipped many gods. The people of ethiopia fear a civil war. Charleston is a large city

named for an english king. The moon was so bright that it illuminated the streets throughout the town. The report of the lewis

and clark expedition is written in all american history books. Mr. Meyer's collections of mexican silverware and german pottery

are on exhibit in the lobby of the pittsfield building. The chinese are members of the mongolian race. They live in the orient.

The *panama limited* is a train that runs between chicago and new orleans. The churches of the middle ages and renaissance are

fine examples of european architecture. Almost everyone is inspired by the great french cathedral, notre dame. The movie, *the*

hunchback of notre dame, takes place in this church. The story for the movie is from a book by victor hugo, a french writer.

In paris we saw the eiffel tower. mars, jupiter, and the milky way are visible on a clear evening. The fifth largest planet of the

solar system is earth. The name of John's airplane is *skyscraper*. Marguerites, a spanish exchange student, attended the museum

opening with me last sunday. i bought this italian cheese at ott's market on branning avenue. The newly elected mayor is a

democrat. I believe that Ruth is jewish. Arlene took her scotch collie with her to portugal. Lindbergh's plane, the *spirit of st. louis*,

took off from roosevelt field, new york, on may 20, 1927. He told us that he would arrive early at the airport.

© 2005 Sopris West Educational Services. All rights reserved. Practicing Basic Skills in Language Arts. Purchaser has permission to photocopy this page for classroom use only.

ONE-MINUTE FLUENCY BUILDER SERIES

SEE TO MARK

	First Try	Second Try
Correct		
Error		

Proper Nouns

Directions: Mark the letters that should be capitalized.

We sailed on the *(n)orthlander* to (s)eattle and on the *(c)oastal (q)ueen* to (s)itka, (a)laska. This spring we shall visit (l)incoln's (t)omb in (8)

(s)pringfield, (i)llinois. (a)ncient (g)reeks worshipped many gods. The people of (e)thiopia fear a civil war. Charleston is a large city (13)

named for an (e)nglish king. The moon was so bright that it illuminated the streets throughout the town. The report of the (l)ewis (15)

and (c)lark expedition is written in all (a)merican history books. Mr. Meyer's collections of (m)exican silverware and (g)erman pottery (19)

are on exhibit in the lobby of the (p)ittsfield (b)uilding. The (c)hinese are members of the (m)ongolian race. They live in the (o)rient. (24)

The *(p)anama (l)imited* is a train that runs between (c)hicago and (n)ew (o)rleans. The churches of the (m)iddle (a)ges and (r)enaissance are (32)

fine examples of (e)uropean architecture. Almost everyone is inspired by the great (f)rench cathedral, (n)otre (d)ame. The movie, *(t)he (37)

(h)unchback of (n)otre (d)ame*, takes place in this church. The story for the movie is from a book by (v)ictor (h)ugo, a (f)rench writer. (43)

In (p)aris we saw the (e)iffel (t)ower. (m)ars, (j)upiter, and the (m)ilky (w)ay are visible on a clear evening. The fifth largest planet of the (50)

solar system is (e)arth. The name of John's airplane is *(s)kyscraper*. Marguerites, a (s)panish exchange student, attended the museum (53)

opening with me last (s)unday. (i) bought this (i)talian cheese at (o)tt's (m)arket on (b)ranning (a)venue. The newly elected mayor is a (60)

(d)emocrat. I believe that Ruth is (j)ewish. Arlene took her (s)cotch collie with her to (p)ortugal. Lindbergh's plane, the *(s)pirit of (s)t. (l)ouis*, (67)

took off from (r)oosevelt (f)ield, (n)ew (y)ork, on (m)ay 20, 1927. He told us that he would arrive early at the airport. (72)

ANSWER SHEET

Practicing Basic Skills in Language Arts • 338

© 2005 Sopris West Educational Services. All rights reserved. Practicing Basic Skills in Language Arts. Purchaser has permission to photocopy this page for classroom use only.

ONE-MINUTE FLUENCY
BUILDER SERIES

SEE TO MARK

	Correct	Error
First Try		
Second Try		

Proper Adjectives and Names of School Subjects

Directions: Mark the letters that should be capitalized.

They all joined in singing a french folk song. The russian immigrant was accused of un-american activities. I like english,

history, and spanish more than science and math. Have you ever seen irish linen? The weightlifter had herculean strength. Who

is your english teacher? We enjoyed the virginian atmosphere of her home. Will you study history or latin? *Numismatics* is a

greek word meaning the collecting of coins and metals. Our english literature class went to a shakespearean play. Each country

has a well-known unit of currency: for example, the british pound, the italian lira, the spanish peseta, the american dollar, and

the french franc. James enjoys civics, german, and biology. Do we use a julian calendar? Dr. Doman has a portuguese accent.

My favorite subjects are geography, algebra I, and spanish. The lawyer testified before the congressional committee. After home

economics, I go to social studies. While on our european tour, we bought several swiss watches. Your texan pride is obvious.

I'd like a pizza with canadian bacon. She is one of the outstanding members of bostonian society. We are studying jacksonian

democracy in american history. Are you in science 101 or science 102? There were many dutch ships on the river. My cousin

is studying nuclear physics. The letter was made official by the presidential seal. Iran is an islamic country. We had tests in

chemistry, english, and european history.

Practicing Basic Skills in Language Arts • 339

© 2005 Sopris West Educational Services. All rights reserved. Practicing Basic Skills in Language Arts. Purchaser has permission to photocopy this page for classroom use only.

ONE-MINUTE FLUENCY
BUILDER SERIES

Proper Adjectives and Names of School Subjects

Directions: Mark the letters that should be capitalized.

	Correct	Error
First Try		
Second Try		

They all joined in singing a ⓕrench folk song. The ⓡussian immigrant was accused of un-ⓐmerican activities. I like ⓔnglish, (4)

history, and ⓢpanish more than science and math. Have you ever seen ⓘrish linen? The weightlifter had ⓗerculean strength. Who (7)

is your ⓔnglish teacher? We enjoyed the ⓥirginian atmosphere of her home. Will you study history or ⓛatin? *Numismatics* is a (10)

ⓖreek word meaning the collecting of coins and metals. Our ⓔnglish literature class went to a ⓢhakespearean play. Each country (13)

has a well-known unit of currency: for example, the ⓑritish pound, the ⓘtalian lira, the ⓢpanish peseta, the ⓐmerican dollar, and (17)

the ⓕrench franc. James enjoys civics, ⓖerman, and biology. Do we use a ⓙulian calendar? Dr. Doman has a ⓟortuguese accent. (21)

My favorite subjects are geography, ⓐlgebra I, and ⓢpanish. The lawyer testified before the ⓒongressional committee. After home (24)

economics, I go to social studies. While on our ⓔuropean tour, we bought several ⓢwiss watches. Your ⓣexan pride is obvious. (27)

I'd like a pizza with ⓒanadian bacon. She is one of the outstanding members of ⓑostonian society. We are studying ⓙacksonian (30)

democracy in ⓐmerican history. Are you in ⓢcience 101 or ⓢcience 102? There were many ⓓutch ships on the river. My cousin (34)

is studying nuclear physics. The letter was made official by the ⓟresidential seal. Iran is an ⓘslamic country. We had tests in (36)

chemistry, ⓔnglish, and ⓔuropean history. (38)

© 2005 Sopris West Educational Services. All rights reserved. Practicing Basic Skills in Language Arts. Purchaser has permission to photocopy this page for classroom use only.

	First Try	Second Try
Correct		
Error		

School Subjects, School Names, and Grades

Directions: Mark the letters that should be capitalized.

I live near south ogden junior high school. Our school offers algebra II as well as general math. Rachel is a sophomore at

bonneville high school. All freshmen at ben lomond high school know they will take at least three years of english and one of

mathematics. Every ninth grader in the local junior high school must have taken general science, utah history, and a foreign

language before entering high school. Since I plan to study acting at weber state college, I'm taking drama I, a speech class, and

theater arts. Joe Lopez is in charge of the ninth grade banquet, which will be held in the home economics area of bell junior

high school. He is taking french, american government, geometry, and computers II. The senior class play will be performed this

week. The high school in Great Falls includes the ninth grade as well as tenth, eleventh, and twelfth grades. Margaret Nusbaum,

president of the eighth grade, is helping to organize the eighth grade dance. Since burch creek elementary school began offering

french and spanish to its sixth graders last year, the school has noticed an improvement in the students' english skills. Besides

science, Jamie is taking physical education, art I, cooking III, german, and world history. My u.s. history teacher emphasized

that the study of history in high school would be more intensified. Marlene's former third grade teacher is now teaching

freshman english at the university of utah. At jefferson school last fall I took advanced math, history, physics, and drama. This

semester, I am taking biology II, advanced reading, girls' chorus, world geography, and earth science I. How many of you have

already taken business english I?

© 2005 Sopris West Educational Services. All rights reserved. Practicing Basic Skills in Language Arts. Purchaser has permission to photocopy this page for classroom use only.

SEE TO MARK

School Subjects, School Names, and Grades

Directions: Mark the letters that should be capitalized.

	Correct	Error
First Try		
Second Try		

I live near south ogden junior high school. Our school offers algebra II as well as general math. Rachel is a sophomore at (6)

bonneville high school. All freshmen at ben lomond high school know they will take at least three years of english and one of (14)

mathematics. Every ninth grader in the local junior high school must have taken general science, utah history, and a foreign (15)

language before entering high school. Since I plan to study acting at weber state college, I'm taking drama I, a speech class, and (19)

theater arts. Joe Lopez is in charge of the ninth grade banquet, which will be held in the home economics area of bell junior (21)

high school. He is taking french, american government, geometry, and computers II. The senior class play will be performed this (26)

week. The high school in Great Falls includes the ninth grade as well as tenth, eleventh, and twelfth grades. Margaret Nusbaum, (26)

president of the eighth grade, is helping to organize the eighth grade dance. Since burch creek elementary school began offering (30)

french and spanish to its sixth graders last year, the school has noticed an improvement in the students' english skills. Besides (33)

science, Jamie is taking physical education, art I, cooking III, german, and world history. My u.s. history teacher emphasized (38)

that the study of history in high school would be more intensified. Marlene's former third grade teacher is now teaching (38)

freshman english at the university of utah. At jefferson school last fall I took advanced math, history, physics, and drama. This (44)

semester, I am taking biology II, advanced reading, girls' chorus, world geography, and earth science I. How many of you have (47)

already taken business english I? (49)

ANSWER SHEET

Practicing Basic Skills in Language Arts • 342

© 2005 Sopris West Educational Services. All rights reserved. Practicing Basic Skills in Language Arts. Purchaser has permission to photocopy this page for classroom use only.

	Correct	Error
First Try		
Second Try		

SEE TO MARK

Titles and Relationships

Directions: Mark the letters that should be capitalized.

Is uncle emmett inviting dad to his camp? The meeting will be addressed by chief of police sandoval and by my father. Have

mother and father met judge krantz? The governors of several states are scheduled to meet with secretary of the interior norton.

Next aunt elena stood up and introduced colonel hawkins. Your father drove us to see grandfather brown. We heard a radio

report of the death of ex-governor lewis. The welcoming party consisted of colonel byrd, lieutenant jack, and my cousin.

Hannah said that mother had gone to a meeting. The author of the book is justice william o. douglas. In the mailbox was a

postcard from cousin ella. Is that your sister? The speaker at the banquet was senator greenwald. Did superintendent hill really

go to school with you, sis? My father is a veteran. Her husband is a colonel in the Marines. What other doctor would you

recommend, dr. king? Does your mother visit aunt loretta often? Last night I met lieutenant franklin. We wondered why dad

was so late. Ex-president ford announced he would not seek re-election. Did you hear president bush's address? I went north

with mother and father last June. Give your report to the doctor in charge. My aunt is acquainted with governor matheson.

Practicing Basic Skills in Language Arts • 343

© 2005 Sopris West Educational Services. All rights reserved. Practicing Basic Skills in Language Arts. Purchaser has permission to photocopy this page for classroom use only.

SEE TO MARK

Titles and Relationships

Directions: Mark the letters that should be capitalized.

	First Try	Second Try
Correct		
Error		

Is uncle emmett inviting dad to his camp? The meeting will be addressed by chief of police sandoval and by my father. Have (6)

mother and father met judge krantz? The governors of several states are scheduled to meet with secretary of the interior norton. (13)

Next aunt ena stood up and introduced colonel hawkins. Your father drove us to see grandfather brown. We heard a radio (19)

report of the death of ex-governor lewis. The welcoming party consisted of colonel byrd, lieutenant jack, and my cousin. (24)

Hannah said that mother had gone to a meeting. The author of the book is justice william o douglas. In the mailbox was a (29)

postcard from cousin ela. Is that your sister? The speaker at the banquet was senator greenwald. Did superintendent hill really (35)

go to school with you, sis? My father is a veteran. Her husband is a colonel in the Marines. What other doctor would you (36)

recommend, dr. king? Does your mother visit aunt loretta often? Last night I met lieutenant franklin. We wondered why dad (43)

was so late. Ex-president ford announced he would not seek re-election. Did you hear president bush's address? I went north (46)

with mother and father last June. Give your report to the doctor in charge. My aunt is acquainted with governor matheson. (50)

Practicing Basic Skills in Language Arts • 344

ANSWER SHEET

© 2005 Sopris West Educational Services. All rights reserved. Practicing Basic Skills in Language Arts. Purchaser has permission to photocopy this page for classroom use only.

ONE-MINUTE FLUENCY
BUILDER SERIES

	Correct	Error
First Try		
Second Try		

Proper Nouns

Directions: Mark the letters that should be capitalized.

My brother and my sister had gone to the circus with uncle vince. mom, coach nelson wants me to help with Little League this

spring. Yesterday dr. anna guthrie moved to Idaho. The date of the prom was announced by miss tyler. My uncle bought mother

and me Mickey Mouse hats at Disneyland. The president of the bonneville High School PTA visited the South. Vernon said, "No,

c.b. burns, m.d. has his office on Washington Boulevard." abe's poem was awarded the prize by principal t.e. carlson. An article

in *Better Homes and Gardens* has made father a better chef. Then sergeant atkins proudly led the parade past queen elizabeth

and prince philip. My uncle todd and father have met the president and the secretary of state. Isabel's painting won president

grover's praise. The secretary of agriculture will report on crop prospects in iowa. Lester b. griffin, our new superintendent of

schools, was born in the Midwest. The president's address was televised by CBS. You should hear captain riley and ed hite, fire

chief, sing "Home on the Range." My uncle has acted in both *Julius Ceasar* and *The King and I.* Have you read of admiral dufek's

work at the South Pole? Did you call, mother? mr. and mrs. darrell z. walker are visiting us. Has anyone seen my father? Does

your uncle george still drive back to Detroit every spring to buy a new car? Have you and dad ever visited Mount Vernon,

mother? She is giving a surprise party for Mrs. Perez, her neighbor. Karl, keith, and ted all received awards at the banquet. I will

ask mother for her permission to go with you.

© 2005 Sopris West Educational Services. All rights reserved. Practicing Basic Skills in Language Arts. Purchaser has permission to photocopy this page for classroom use only.

SEE TO MARK

Proper Nouns

Directions: Mark the letters that should be capitalized.

	Correct	Error
First Try		
Second Try		

My brother and my sister had gone to the circus with (u)ncle (v)ince. (m)om, (c)oach (n)elson wants me to help with Little League this (5)

spring. Yesterday (d)r. (a)nna (g)uthrie moved to Idaho. The date of the prom was announced by (m)iss (t)yler. My uncle bought (m)other (11)

and me Mickey Mouse hats at Disneyland. The president of the (b)onneville High School PTA visited the South. Vernon said, "No, (12)

(c)(b)urns, (m)(d) has his office on Washington Boulevard." (a)be's poem was awarded the prize by (p)rincipal (t)(e) (c)arlson. An article (22)

in *Better Homes and Gardens* has made (f)ather a better chef. Then (s)ergeant (a)tkins proudly led the parade past (q)ueen (e)lizabeth (27)

and (p)rince (p)hilip. My (u)ncle (t)odd and (f)ather have met the president and the secretary of state. Isabel's painting won (p)resident (33)

(g)rover's praise. The secretary of agriculture will report on crop prospects in (i)owa. Lester (b) (g)riffin, our new superintendent of (37)

schools, was born in the Midwest. The president's address was televised by CBS. You should hear (c)aptain (f)iley and (e)l (h)ite, fire (41)

chief, sing "Home on the Range." My uncle has acted in both *Julius Ceasar* and *The King and I*. Have you read of (a)dmiral (d)ufek's (43)

work at the South Pole? Did you call, (m)other? (m)r. and (m)rs. (d)arrell (z) (w)alker are visiting us. Has anyone seen my father? Does (49)

your uncle (g)eorge still drive back to Detroit every spring to buy a new car? Have you and (d)ad ever visited Mount Vernon, (51)

(m)other? She is giving a surprise party for Mrs. Perez, her neighbor. Karl, (k)eith, and (t)ed all received awards at the banquet. I will (54)

ask (m)other for her permission to go with you. (55)

ANSWER SHEET

© 2005 Sopris West Educational Services. All rights reserved. Practicing Basic Skills in Language Arts. Purchaser has permission to photocopy this page for classroom use only.

ONE-MINUTE
FLUENCY
BUILDER SERIES

SEE TO MARK

Capitalization Review

Directions: Mark the letters that should be capitalized.

1. our house needs to be painted.

2. we read a play that was written in 250 b.c.

3. balboa discovered the pacific ocean and claimed it for spain.

4. did i tell you about our recent vacation?

5. dad drove all night on the pennsylvania turnpike.

6. My friend mike martinson moved to arizona.

7. The largest lake in the united states is lake superior.

8. The faces of four presidents are carved in mount rushmore.

9. The professor will be teaching french and german next year.

10. Jenny won a free trip to Disney World in orlando, florida.

11. the woman's hobby was chinese cooking.

12. president bush will visit england, france, and spain.

13. jerusalem is sacred to christianity, judaism, and islam.

14. mary and bill are going to europe next year.

15. my landlady spoke with a southern accent.

16. We lived in the south for several years before moving to the west.

17. The st. louis zoo has a new indian elephant.

18. the colorado river lies west of the mississippi river.

19. Did you watch the dial soap commercial on T.V.?

20. From chicago, helen will fly northeast to toronto, canada.

21. The supervising doctor at community medical center is dr. jones.

22. We voiced our opinion on the bill the senate introduced in congress.

23. My family is planning a reunion at uncle bob's.

24. Charles Dickens is the author of *a tale of two cities*.

25. The pupils from washington high school sang a medley of tunes.

© 2005 Sopris West Educational Services. All rights reserved. Practicing Basic Skills in Language Arts. Purchaser has permission to photocopy this page for classroom use only.

ONE-MINUTE FLUENCY BUILDER SERIES

SEE TO MARK

	Correct	Error
First Try		
Second Try		

Capitalization Review

Directions: Mark the letters that should be capitalized.

1. Our house needs to be painted. (1)

2. We read a play that was written in 250 bc. (4)

3. Balboa discovered the Pacific Ocean and claimed it for Spain. (8)

4. Did I tell you about our recent vacation? (10)

5. Dad drove all night on the Pennsylvania turnpike. (13)

6. My friend Mike Martinson moved to Arizona. (16)

7. The largest lake in the United States is Lake Superior. (20)

8. The faces of four presidents are carved in Mount Rushmore. (22)

9. The professor will be teaching French and German next year. (24)

10. Jenny won a free trip to Disney World in Orlando, Florida. (26)

11. The woman's hobby was Chinese cooking. (28)

12. President Bush will visit England, France, and Spain. (33)

13. Jerusalem is sacred to Christianity, Judaism, and Islam. (37)

14. Mary and Bill are going to Europe next year. (40)

15. My landlady spoke with a Southern accent. (42)

16. We lived in the South for several years before moving to the West. (44)

17. The St. Louis Zoo has a new Indian elephant. (48)

18. The Colorado River lies west of the Mississippi River. (53)

19. Did you watch the Dial soap commercial on T.V.? (54)

20. From Chicago, Helen will fly northeast to Toronto, Canada. (58)

21. The supervising doctor at Community Medical Center is Dr. Jones. (63)

22. We voiced our opinion on the bill the Senate introduced in Congress. (65)

23. My family is planning a reunion at Uncle Bob's. (67)

24. Charles Dickens is the author of A Tale of Two Cities. (71)

25. The pupils from Washington High School sang a medley of tunes. (74)

ANSWER SHEET

Practicing Basic Skills in Language Arts • 348

© 2005 Sopris West Educational Services. All rights reserved. Practicing Basic Skills in Language Arts. Purchaser has permission to photocopy this page for classroom use only.

SEE TO MARK

Capitalization Review

Directions: Mark the letters that should be capitalized.

after breakfast, grandpa took us to the farm. israel is a jewish state. did you study english and history under mr. hong? which

planet has a ring, venus or saturn? kendra and justin nominated ms. adamson for teacher of the year. i shall return sunday,

november 6. the french and indian war lasted seven years. three members of congress graduated from marquette university. did

you eat at burger king last night? is dr. kelly going to lecture in reno, nevada? when queen elizabeth saw that philip II would

crush the netherlands, she sent them aid. are you older or younger than i am? while walking down fourth street with josie, i met

gene. our favorite park is yellowstone national park. we bought our toro power mower at the barclay hardware store. we traveled

on the chesapeake and ohio railroad. the women's relief society will meet at 11:00. in july of 1776, the second continental

congress adopted the declaration of independence. the romantic period began later in american literature. how far is venus from

the earth? in the distance, mother and i could see the jefferson memorial. the *pueblo* was a ship captured by the north koreans. i

hope to enroll in computer skills II and industrial arts. the first conquerors of the english countryside were germanic tribesmen.

was your grandpa in the marines? the president, the secretary of state, a senator, and a governor appeared on television. i lost

my latin and biology books.

© 2005 Sopris West Educational Services. All rights reserved. Practicing Basic Skills in Language Arts. Purchaser has permission to photocopy this page for classroom use only.

SEE TO MARK

Capitalization Review

Directions: Mark the letters that should be capitalized.

	Correct	Error
First Try		
Second Try		

after breakfast, (g)randpa took us to the farm. (i)srael is a (j)ewish state. (d)id you study (e)nglish and (h)istory under (m)r. (h)ong? (w)hich (10)

planet has a ring, (v)enus or (s)aturn? (k)endra and (j)ustin nominated (m)r. (a)damson for (t)eacher of the (y)ear. (i) (s)hall return (s)unday, (20)

(n)ovember 6. (t)he (f)rench and (i)ndian (w)ar lasted seven years. (t)hree members of (c)ongress graduated from (m)arquette (u)niversity. (d)id (30)

you eat at (b)urger (k)ing last night? (i)s (d)r. (k)elly going to lecture in (r)eno, (n)evada? (w)hen (q)ueen (e)lizabeth saw that (p)hilip II would (41)

crush the (n)etherlands, she sent them aid. (a)re you older or younger than (i)am? (w)hile walking down (f)ourth (s)treet with (j)osie, (i) met (49)

(g)ene. (o)ur favorite park is (y)ellowstone (n)ational (p)ark. (w)e bought our (t)oro power mower at the (b)arclay (h)ardware (s)tore. (w)e traveled (60)

on the (c)hesapeake and (o)hio (r)ailroad. (t)he (w)omen's (r)elief (s)ociety will meet at 11:00. (i)n (j)uly of 1776, the (s)econd (c)ontinental (71)

(c)ongress adopted the (d)eclaration of (i)ndependence. (t)he (r)omantic (p)eriod began later in (a)merican literature. (h)ow far is (v)enus from (80)

the earth? (i)n the distance, (m)other and (i) could see the (j)efferson (m)emorial. (t)he (p)ueblo was a ship captured by the (n)orth (k)oreans. (i) (90)

hope to enroll in (c)omputer (s)kills II and industrial arts. (t)he first conquerors of the (e)nglish countryside were (g)ermanic tribesmen. (95)

(w)as your grandpa in the (m)arines? (t)he president, the secretary of state, a senator, and a governor appeared on television. (i) lost (99)

my (l)atin and biology books. (100)

ANSWER SHEET

© 2005 Sopris West Educational Services. All rights reserved. Practicing Basic Skills in Language Arts. Purchaser has permission to photocopy this page for classroom use only.

SEE TO MARK

Capitalization Review

Directions: Mark the letters that should be capitalized.

Their summer cottage in indiana is on the shore of lake michigan. times square is bounded on the south by forty-second street.

Congressman riddle's controversial article was published in the *saturday evening post*. In the autumn, dr. and mrs. rose set off

on their vacation. soon we had left the great plains behind and were flying over the rocky mountains. Leslie has finished the

english homework, but she still has a paper to write for her science class. Ordinarily, the hotels in chicago are not crowded

during july. it has been a long time—oh, perhaps six months—since we have had a letter from jane. memorial day is always a

school holiday. Many of eudora welty's stories are set in the south. Are there camping facilities at arcadia national park? The

glendale cornhusking festival is an event of local interest. The buick convertible got into the parade by mistake. Her souvenirs

from new york city included a gilt model of the statue of liberty and an unused subway token. The industrial revolution began

in europe. A vice president of stevens & company spoke at the banquet. gwendolyn brooks, the famous writer, was born

in kansas. Some of the lava on honshu island is as full of holes as swiss cheese. the northern route is quicker but much less

adventurous. The united states is a member of the north atlantic treaty organization. The highway through canada to alaska was

first called the alcan highway. The town is located just south of the canadian border. My favorite season will always be autumn.

The summer school will offer courses in french, english, algebra, and american history. Mary's father is the director of the local

community fund. Two of my aunts from upstate new york posed with father and me in front of our summer cottage.

Practicing Basic Skills in Language Arts • 351

© 2005 Sopris West Educational Services. All rights reserved. Practicing Basic Skills in Language Arts. Purchaser has permission to photocopy this page for classroom use only.

SEE TO MARK

Capitalization Review

Directions: Mark the letters that should be capitalized.

	Correct	Error
First Try		
Second Try		

(8) Their summer cottage in (i)ndiana is on the shore of (l)ake (m)ichigan. (t)imes (s)quare is bounded on the south by (f)orty-(s)econd (s)treet.

(15) Congressman (r)iddle's controversial article was published in the *(s)aturday (e)vening (p)ost*. In the autumn, (d)r. and (m)rs. (r)ose set off

(20) on their vacation. (s)oon we had left the (g)reat (p)lains behind and were flying over the (r)ocky (m)ountains. Leslie has finished the

(22) (e)nglish homework, but she still has a paper to write for her science class. Ordinarily, the hotels in (c)hicago are not crowded

(27) during (j)uly. (i)t has been a long time—oh, perhaps six months—since we have had a letter from (j)ane. (m)emorial (d)ay is always a

(33) school holiday. Many of (e)udora (w)elty's stories are set in the (s)outh. Are there camping facilities at (a)rcadia (n)ational (p)ark? The

(37) (g)lendale (c)ornhusking (f)estival is an event of local interest. The (b)uick convertible got into the parade by mistake. Her souvenirs

(44) from (n)ew (y)ork (c)ity included a gilt model of the (s)tatue of (l)iberty and an unused subway token. The (i)ndustrial (r)evolution began

(49) in (e)urope. A vice president of (s)tevens & (c)ompany spoke at the banquet. (g)wendolyn (b)rooks, the famous writer, was born

(54) in (k)ansas. Some of the lava on (h)onshu (i)sland is as full of holes as (s)wiss cheese. (t)he northern route is quicker but much less

(62) adventurous. The (u)nited (s)tates is a member of the (n)orth (a)tlantic (t)reaty (o)rganization. The highway through (c)anada to (a)laska was

(65) first called the (a)lcan (h)ighway. The town is located just south of the (c)anadian border. My favorite season will always be autumn.

(68) The summer school will offer courses in (f)rench, (e)nglish, algebra, and (a)merican history. Mary's father is the director of the local

(73) (c)ommunity (f)und. Two of my aunts from upstate (n)ew (y)ork posed with (f)ather and me in front of our summer cottage.

ANSWER SHEET

Practicing Basic Skills in Language Arts • 352

© 2005 Sopris West Educational Services. All rights reserved. Practicing Basic Skills in Language Arts. Purchaser has permission to photocopy this page for classroom use only.

ONE-MINUTE FLUENCY BUILDER SERIES

Ending Punctuation Using . and ?—Primary

Directions: Put the correct punctuation mark at the end of each sentence (. and ?).

	First Try	Second Try
Correct		
Error		

I came to the farm ___

Did the boy have fun ___

Do you want to play ___

The dog is at the farm ___

My doll is in the box ___

The farm is fun ___

Did you find my ball ___

I will eat the duck ___

Do you know my name ___

I want to go home ___

Do you like my hat ___

I like to laugh ___

Father is out at the farm ___

Please find the boy ___

He is on the boat ___

Would you like an apple ___

The baby is in the bed ___

The dog is black ___

The boy is in the house ___

Can you call me ___

I like to look at books ___

Can you run fast ___

The boy is my friend ___

Do you like to fish ___

I saw the bear first ___

Can you see the garden ___

I heard the boat go by ___

© 2005 Sopris West Educational Services. All rights reserved. Practicing Basic Skills in Language Arts. Purchaser has permission to photocopy this page for classroom use only.

ONE-MINUTE FLUENCY
BUILDER SERIES

	First Try	Second Try
Correct		
Error		

SEE TO WRITE

Ending Punctuation Using . and ? —Primary

Directions: Put the correct punctuation mark at the end of each sentence (. and ?).

I came to the farm .

The dog is at the farm .

Did you find my ball ?

I want to go home .

Father is out at the farm .

Would you like an apple ?

The boy is in the house .

Can you run fast ?

I saw the bear first .

Did the boy have fun ?

My doll is in the box .

I will eat the duck .

Do you like my hat ?

Please find the boy .

The baby is in the bed .

Can you call me ?

The boy is my friend .

Can you see the garden ?

Do you want to play ? (3)

The farm is fun . (6)

Do you know my name ? (9)

I like to laugh . (12)

He is on the boat . (15)

The dog is black . (18)

I like to look at books . (21)

Do you like to fish ? (24)

I heard the boat go by . (27)

ANSWER SHEET

Practicing Basic Skills in Language Arts • 354

© 2005 Sopris West Educational Services. All rights reserved. Practicing Basic Skills in Language Arts. Purchaser has permission to photocopy this page for classroom use only.

ONE-MINUTE FLUENCY BUILDER SERIES

Ending Punctuation Using . ? and !—Primary

Directions: Put the correct punctuation mark at the end of each sentence (. ? !).

	First Try	Second Try
Correct		
Error		

Can you open the door ___

We had a great time ___

Mother will tell me a story ___

Did you like the party ___

We walked down the street ___

The basket is full of toys ___

The hills are beautiful ___

Dad will build the house ___

Is she coming with you ___

I go to bed every night ___

Will you give me a penny ___

I have two black shoes ___

The green tree is very tall ___

Do you have any candy ___

I heard the bell ring ___

The wind blew all night ___

Did you ride on the bus ___

Come by my house today ___

I like the other kitten ___

I like to paint pictures ___

Don't close the door ___

Father took me to school ___

I am afraid of the dark ___

We won the game ___

I stopped at the farm ___

Look out for the bee ___

Did you find your dog ___

Practicing Basic Skills in Language Arts • 355

© 2005 Sopris West Educational Services. All rights reserved. Practicing Basic Skills in Language Arts. Purchaser has permission to photocopy this page for classroom use only.

Ending Punctuation Using . ? and !—Primary

Directions: Put the correct punctuation mark at the end of each sentence (. ? !).

		Correct	Error
First Try			
Second Try			

Can you open the door **?**

I go to bed every night **.**

I like the other kitten **.** (3)

We had a great time **!**

Will you give me a penny **?**

I like to paint pictures **.** (6)

Mother will tell me a story **.**

I have two black shoes **.**

Don't close the door **!** (9)

Did you like the party **?**

The green tree is very tall **.**

Father took me to school **.** (12)

We walked down the street **.**

Do you have any candy **?**

I am afraid of the dark **.** (15)

The basket is full of toys **.**

I heard the bell ring **.**

We won the game **!** (18)

The hills are beautiful **.**

The wind blew all night **.**

I stopped at the farm **.** (21)

Dad will build the house **.**

Did you ride on the bus **?**

Look out for the bee **!** (24)

Is she coming with you **?**

Come by my house today **.**

Did you find your dog **?** (27)

ANSWER SHEET

Practicing Basic Skills in Language Arts • 356

© 2005 Sopris West Educational Services. All rights reserved. Practicing Basic Skills in Language Arts. Purchaser has permission to photocopy this page for classroom use only.

	First Try	Second Try
Correct		
Error		

SEE TO WRITE

Ending Punctuation

Directions: Punctuate the sentences below: period (.), question mark (?), exclamation point (!).

Where are you going ___ Stop your talking ___ I am going home ___ The test will be on commas ___ Have you done your

homework ___ Put down that vase ___ Jerry found his books ___ Did Pat bring a tennis racket ___ A man's home is his castle

___ The boys looked worried ___ Our English teacher studied abroad ___ Don't touch that ___ Why do we spend time wishing

___ Congratulations to you ___ When the snow melts, streets get slushy ___ If you want to know, I can't swim ___ We recently

saw that movie ___ What a surprise ___ Who are you ___ For breakfast we had toast and juice ___ May I go with you ___ Go

away, you creep ___ Were many people hurt ___ The game will be held Saturday ___ Hurray ___ We won the championship ___

We will purchase the equipment ___ My father was born in Ohio ___ We had to leave the dog outside ___ Do you think the spot

will show ___ Be quiet, please ___ We read a poem in class ___ Copy each of the sentences ___ No, I can't answer that question

___ Francis made preparations for the trip ___ Is this answer correct ___ Hurry ___ The ship is sinking ___ Molly closed the book

and looked up ___ Don't do that ___ Ouch ___ Where do you live ___

Practicing Basic Skills in Language Arts • 357

© 2005 Sopris West Educational Services. All rights reserved. Practicing Basic Skills in Language Arts. Purchaser has permission to photocopy this page for classroom use only.

ONE MINUTE FLUENCY
BUILDER SERIES

SEE TO WRITE

Ending Punctuation

Directions: Punctuate the sentences below: period (.), question mark (?), exclamation point (!).

	Correct	Error
First Try		
Second Try		

Where are you going **?** Stop your talking **!** I am going home **.** The test will be on commas **.** Have you done your (4)

homework **?** Put down that vase **.** Jerry found his books **.** Did Pat bring a tennis racket **?** A man's home is his castle (8)

. The boys looked worried **.** Our English teacher studied abroad **.** Don't touch that **!** Why do we spend time wishing (12)

? Congratulations to you **!** When the snow melts, streets get slushy **.** If you want to know, I can't swim **.** We recently (16)

saw that movie **.** What a surprise **!** Who are you **?** For breakfast we had toast and juice **.** May I go with you **?** Go (21)

away, you creep **!** Were many people hurt **?** The game will be held Saturday **.** Hurray **!** We won the championship **!** (26)

We will purchase the equipment **.** My father was born in Ohio **.** We had to leave the dog outside **.** Do you think the spot (29)

will show **?** Be quiet, please **.** We read a poem in class **.** Copy each of the sentences **.** No, I can't answer that question (33)

. Francis made preparations for the trip **.** Is this answer correct **?** Hurry **!** The ship is sinking **!** Molly closed the book (38)

and looked up **.** Don't do that **!** Ouch **!** Where do you live **?** (42)

ANSWER SHEET

© 2005 Sopris West Educational Services. All rights reserved. Practicing Basic Skills in Language Arts. Purchaser has permission to photocopy this page for classroom use only.

ONE-MINUTE FLUENCY BUILDER SERIES

SEE TO WRITE

Ending Punctuation

Directions: Write the correct mark (. ? !) at the end of each sentence.

	First Try	Second Try
Correct		
Error		

Why did you leave I saw boats, tanks, and automobiles Don't shoot What a beautiful snowfall Hand me that newspaper,

please The convention was held in Philadelphia Where is it, Freddie Didn't they once live in Galveston When it rains, we

remain indoors Let's win this game Close the door Have you seen my new coat Well, where are you Get out here this instant

What courage the pioneers had They faced many hardships Could you live under such circumstances Here is my new friend

Run for safety These shirts are not for sale May we attend tomorrow's concert In order to get there on time, I arose at six

Where's my ink He answered that he had not seen it Lisa set a new high jump record What a ridiculous costume Leave a

message for Mother You must help me or I'll die That's the winning touchdown We toured Utah last summer Have you ever

done that What fun we had How long did your trip take Send for those books Did you buy that car after all What a deal

you made I hope you'll enjoy it We studied punctuation in English What are you studying Study for at least an hour You will

study or else What a mistake you made Is that your grandmother I saw you at the concert last night Be quiet at once Get off

my property Will you attend the University of Utah Fix dinner tonight, please We won the championship

© 2005 Sopris West Educational Services. All rights reserved. Practicing Basic Skills in Language Arts. Purchaser has permission to photocopy this page for classroom use only.

SEE TO WRITE

Ending Punctuation

Directions: Write the correct mark (. ? !) at the end of each sentence.

	Correct	Error
First Try		
Second Try		

Why did you leave? I saw boats, tanks, and automobiles. Don't shoot! What a beautiful snowfall! Hand me that newspaper, (4)

please. The convention was held in Philadelphia. Where is it, Freddie? Didn't they once live in Galveston? When it rains, we (8)

remain indoors. Let's win this game! Close the door. Have you seen my new coat? Well, where are you? Get out here this instant! (14)

What courage the pioneers had! They faced many hardships. Could you live under such circumstances? Here is my new friend. (18)

Run for safety! These shirts are not for sale. May we attend tomorrow's concert? In order to get there on time, I arose at six. (22)

Where's my ink? He answered that he had not seen it. Lisa set a new high jump record. What a ridiculous costume! Leave a (26)

message for Mother. You must help me or I'll die! That's the winning touchdown! We toured Utah last summer. Have you ever (30)

done that? What fun we had! How long did your trip take? Send for those books. Did you buy that car after all? What a deal (35)

you made! I hope you'll enjoy it. We studied punctuation in English. What are you studying? Study for at least an hour. You will (40)

study or else! What a mistake you made! Is that your grandmother? I saw you at the concert last night. Be quiet at once! Get off (45)

my property! Will you attend the University of Utah? Fix dinner tonight, please. We won the championship! (49)

© 2005 Sopris West Educational Services. All rights reserved. Practicing Basic Skills in Language Arts. Purchaser has permission to photocopy this page for classroom use only.

ONE MINUTE FLUENCY BUILDER SERIES

SEE TO WRITE

Commas—Items in a Series
Directions: Insert commas to separate items in a series.

History geography and spelling have always been easy for me. Books pens pencils and papers have been put away. She had

cereal toast and milk for breakfast. Gerald Kara Bruce and Jamal all received awards at the banquet. We need butter milk

potatoes bread and sugar. The bear came over to the car stood up on his hind legs looked at me through the window and

licked his lips. Have you seen Keiko Sydney or Paige? Pedro opened the door tiptoed in and shut it softly. Among the alloys

are gunmetal bell metal type metal and bronze. You are to bring to the picnic a salad some rolls and a jar of pickles. To get

there you have to take a plane a train and a ship. Dad knows how to cook pancakes bacon and eggs hamburgers hot dogs

and brownies. Men women and children crowded around the limousine to catch a glimpse of the president. Those missing

letters must be in the desk in my purse or under those books. Are you ill preoccupied or just bored? You'll be in charge on

Wednesday Thursday and Friday of this week. Canada Mexico and the United States are in North America. Della's costume

consisted of a beaded dress a plumed hat and high-button shoes. This is a government of the people by the people and for the

people. He spent most of his vacation swimming playing baseball and watching television.

Practicing Basic Skills in Language Arts • 361

© 2005 Sopris West Educational Services. All rights reserved. Practicing Basic Skills in Language Arts. Purchaser has permission to photocopy this page for classroom use only.

SEE TO WRITE

Commas—Items in a Series

Directions: Insert commas to separate items in a series.

History, geography, and spelling have always been easy for me. Books, pens, pencils, and papers have been put away. She had (5)

cereal, toast, and milk for breakfast. Gerald, Kara, Bruce, and Jamal all received awards at the banquet. We need butter, milk, (12)

potatoes, bread, and sugar. The bear came over to the car, stood up on his hind legs, looked at me through the window, and (17)

licked his lips. Have you seen Keiko, Sydney, or Paige? Pedro opened the door, tiptoed in, and shut it softly. Among the alloys (21)

are gunmetal, bell metal, type metal, and bronze. You are to bring to the picnic a salad, some rolls, and a jar of pickles. To get (26)

there you have to take a plane, a train, and a ship. Dad knows how to cook pancakes, bacon and eggs, hamburgers, hot dogs, (32)

and brownies. Men, women, and children crowded around the limousine to catch a glimpse of the president. Those missing (34)

letters must be in the desk, in my purse, or under those books. Are you ill, preoccupied, or just bored? You'll be in charge on (38)

Wednesday, Thursday, and Friday of this week. Canada, Mexico, and the United States are in North America. Della's costume (42)

consisted of a beaded dress, a plumed hat, and high-button shoes. This is a government of the people, by the people, and for the (46)

people. He spent most of his vacation swimming, playing baseball, and watching television. (48)

ANSWER SHEET

Practicing Basic Skills in Language Arts • 362

© 2005 Sopris West Educational Services. All rights reserved. Practicing Basic Skills in Language Arts. Purchaser has permission to photocopy this page for classroom use only.

SEE TO WRITE

Commas to Separate Adjectives

Directions: Insert commas to separate a series of adjectives preceding a noun.

His sharp angry voice disturbed us. It turned out to be a long hot summer. The beach was littered with old rusty tin cans. He

always offers some long involved excuse. The blunt straight-speaking coach was fired. Her smiling happy expression told us

who won. The gruff surly actor hardly seemed a romantic type. The weary anxious faces of the gamblers held our attention.

The engine gave off a loud high-pitched whine. There's a tiny isolated island about three miles east of here. The frothing

heaving waves were terrifying. The tired hungry man was upset. They drove away in a bright shiny expensive sports car. The

little yellow brick house on the corner is for sale. A strong northerly wind swept the snow against the front door. That little

blue TR7 belongs to my uncle. I enjoy eating fresh salty buttery popcorn when I go to the movies. Strong gusty winds blew

across the lake and created a power outage. Red white and blue bunting decorated the speaker's stand. A fluffy tiger-striped cat

was sitting on our back doorstep. A small frightened rabbit scooted across our yard. A long sleek black limousine pulled up in

front of the school.

© 2005 Sopris West Educational Services. All rights reserved. Practicing Basic Skills in Language Arts. Purchaser has permission to photocopy this page for classroom use only.

Commas to Separate Adjectives

Directions: Insert commas to separate a series of adjectives preceding a noun.

	Correct	Error
First Try		
Second Try		

His sharp, angry voice disturbed us. It turned out to be a long, hot summer. The beach was littered with old, rusty tin cans. He (3)

always offers some long, involved excuse. The blunt, straight-speaking coach was fired. Her smiling, happy expression told us (6)

who won. The gruff, surly actor hardly seemed a romantic type. The weary, anxious faces of the gamblers held our attention. (8)

The engine gave off a loud, high-pitched whine. There's a tiny, isolated island about three miles east of here. The frothing, (11)

heaving waves were terrifying. The tired, hungry man was upset. They drove away in a bright, shiny, expensive sports car. The (14)

little, yellow brick house on the corner is for sale. A strong, northerly wind swept the snow against the front door. That little, (17)

blue TR7 belongs to my uncle. I enjoy eating fresh, salty, buttery popcorn when I go to the movies. Strong, gusty winds blew (20)

across the lake and created a power outage. Red, white, and blue bunting decorated the speaker's stand. A fluffy, tiger-striped cat (23)

was sitting on our back doorstep. A small, frightened rabbit scooted across our yard. A long, sleek, black limousine pulled up in (26)

front of the school. (26)

© 2005 Sopris West Educational Services. All rights reserved. Practicing Basic Skills in Language Arts. Purchaser has permission to photocopy this page for classroom use only.

SEE TO WRITE

Commas After Introductory Words

Directions: Insert commas after introductory words.

	Correct	Error
First Try		
Second Try		

Indeed his luck's been very good. Yes I know him. No I haven't forgotten. Yes I have met Professor Strong. Well the first date

of July 15 suits me better than October 24. Oh I haven't decided yet. No the old road that is Highway 29 is not used much

anymore. Yes the garage has been cleaned out. Well the boys will finally meet their new head football coach. No I won't be

able to attend the spring concert next Friday evening. Well did your neighbor win the science fair again? No I do not know

the school nurse. Yes I finally finished the huge batch of dinner dishes. Well the latest weather report has predicted rain for

the weekend. No the mail has not arrived today. Why Mrs. Brown looks much younger with her new hairstyle. No Chuck

is not the new athletic director. Well Ron did say the accident wasn't his fault. Yes the intramural track meet will be held at

Bonneville High School tomorrow. No the church's rummage sale will not be held in April this year. Yes most schools in New

Orleans take a holiday during the Mardi Gras celebration. Yes the *Manchester Guardian* is a British newspaper. Yes I have a

camera. No the heavy snow didn't tie up the morning traffic. Yes I saw the first inning of the game. Indeed his luck's been very

good. Yes I know him. No I haven't forgotten. Yes I have met Professor Strong. Well the first date of July 15 suits me better

than October 24. Oh I haven't decided yet. No the old road which is Highway 29 is not used much anymore. Yes the garage

has been cleaned out. Well the boys will finally meet their new head football coach.

© 2005 Sopris West Educational Services. All rights reserved. Practicing Basic Skills in Language Arts. Purchaser has permission to photocopy this page for classroom use only.

SEE TO WRITE

Commas After Introductory Words

Directions: Insert commas after introductory words.

Indeed, his luck's been very good. Yes, I know him. No, I haven't forgotten. Yes, I have met Professor Strong. Well, the first date (5)

of July 15 suits me better than October 24. Oh, I haven't decided yet. No, the old road that is Highway 29 is not used much (7)

anymore. Yes, the garage has been cleaned out. Well, the boys will finally meet their new head football coach. No, I won't be (10)

able to attend the spring concert next Friday evening. Well, did your neighbor win the science fair again? No, I do not know (12)

the school nurse. Yes, I finally finished the huge batch of dinner dishes. Well, the latest weather report has predicted rain for (14)

the weekend. No, the mail has not arrived today. Why, Mrs. Brown looks much younger with her new hairstyle. No, Chuck (17)

is not the new athletic director. Well, Ron did say the accident wasn't his fault. Yes, the intramural track meet will be held at (19)

Bonneville High School tomorrow. No, the church's rummage sale will not be held in April this year. Yes, most schools in New (21)

Orleans take a holiday during the Mardi Gras celebration. Yes, the *Manchester Guardian* is a British newspaper. Yes, I have a (23)

camera. No, the heavy snow didn't tie up the morning traffic. Yes, I saw the first inning of the game. Indeed, his luck's been very (26)

good. Yes, I know him. No, I haven't forgotten. Yes, I have met Professor Strong. Well, the first date of July 15 suits me better (30)

than October 24. Oh, I haven't decided yet. No, the old road which is Highway 29 is not used much anymore. Yes, the garage (33)

has been cleaned out. Well, the boys will finally meet their new head football coach. (34)

ANSWER SHEET

Practicing Basic Skills in Language Arts • 366

© 2005 Sopris West Educational Services. All rights reserved. Practicing Basic Skills in Language Arts. Purchaser has permission to photocopy this page for classroom use only.

	Correct	Error
First Try		
Second Try		

SEE TO WRITE

Commas for Appositives

Directions: Insert commas to set off appositives.

	Correct	Error
First Try		
Second Try		

The owner Carl Black built that house himself. Jerome my friend will do as I ask. The speaker a famous explorer told

about New Guinea. My youngest brother a fifth grader reads all the same books I do. Paris the capital of France is located

on the Seine River. My new teacher Mrs. Rivera lives only a block away. Mr. Charles my cat thinks he's a member of the

family. The leader the person on horseback moved away. I do not know Dr. Harris the school doctor. I'll meet you at

Martin's the drugstore across from the train station. Did Mr. Sikora your neighbor buy another new car? Ms. Leoni our new

foreign language teacher was born in Italy. John Hancock one of the signers of the Declaration of Independence was from

Massachusetts. Mrs. Laura Bush the First Lady visited our state last weekend. My grandmother a woman in her sixties had

more fun on the camping trip than the rest of us put together. Dr. Torgele my dentist is a ham radio operator. Mrs. Wulf their

neighbor saw the flames and immediately called the fire department. On March 21 the first day of spring the weather is not

always springlike. The guest speaker a former Peace Corps volunteer showed slides of people and places in Brazil. I wonder if

they can win without Cecil Hahn their star player.

© 2005 Sopris West Educational Services. All rights reserved. Practicing Basic Skills in Language Arts. Purchaser has permission to photocopy this page for classroom use only.

	Correct	Error
First Try		
Second Try		

The owner, Carl Black, built that house himself. Jerome, my friend, will do as I ask. The speaker, a famous explorer, told (6)

about New Guinea. My youngest brother, a fifth grader, reads all the same books I do. Paris, the capital of France, is located (10)

on the Seine River. My new teacher, Mrs. Rivera, lives only a block away. Mr. Charles, my cat, thinks he's a member of the (14)

family. The leader, the person on horseback, moved away. I do not know Dr. Harris, the school doctor. I'll meet you at (17)

Martin's, the drugstore across from the train station. Did Mr. Sikora, your neighbor, buy another new car? Ms. Leoni, our new (21)

foreign language teacher, was born in Italy. John Hancock, one of the signers of the Declaration of Independence, was from (24)

Massachusetts. Mrs. Laura Bush, the First Lady, visited our state last weekend. My grandmother, a woman in her sixties, had (28)

more fun on the camping trip than the rest of us put together. Dr. Torgele, my dentist, is a ham radio operator. Mrs. Wulf, their (31)

neighbor, saw the flames and immediately called the fire department. On March 21, the first day of spring, the weather is not (34)

always springlike. The guest speaker, a former Peace Corps volunteer, showed slides of people and places in Brazil. I wonder if (36)

they can win without Cecil Hahn, their star player. (37)

Practicing Basic Skills in Language Arts • 368

© 2005 Sopris West Educational Services. All rights reserved. Practicing Basic Skills in Language Arts. Purchaser has permission to photocopy this page for classroom use only.

ONE-MINUTE
FLUENCY
BUILDER SERIES

	Correct	Error
First Try		
Second Try		

SEE TO WRITE

Commas for Parenthetical Expressions

Directions: Insert commas where needed.

I think if you want my opinion you should go. He didn't however agree with me. Lisa to tell the truth was extremely

pleased with the award. Their house believe it or not is black with pink trim. Later of course things may change. The room

incidentally has a false ceiling. That man by the way is a test pilot. Shaun of course won the prize. This incidentally is my

first job. You go all the way to Twelfth Street and then turn right I think. By the way I forgot to tell you to bring your guitar.

That letter by the way will never get to Spain without more postage. The report however is altogether inaccurate. Mrs. Dean

to tell the truth was quite pleased with our one-act play. This map won't help us I'm afraid until we find out where we are

now. On the other hand I'm afraid that his older brother is just plain lazy. You have to remember of course that in those days

people didn't have telephones. Snoopy after all is a very unusual beagle. The rest of the races however weren't half as exciting

as either of the first two. The Andersons it seems have decided not to move until next September. That disk jockey I admit is

rather annoying. Snoopy is the only dog in the world I suppose who can do imitations.

Practicing Basic Skills in Language Arts • 369

© 2005 Sopris West Educational Services. All rights reserved. Practicing Basic Skills in Language Arts. Purchaser has permission to photocopy this page for classroom use only.

Commas for Parenthetical Expressions

Directions: Insert commas where needed.

	Correct	Error
First Try		
Second Try		

I think, if you want my opinion, you should go. He didn't, however, agree with me. Lisa, to tell the truth, was extremely (6)

pleased with the award. Their house, believe it or not, is black with pink trim. Later, of course, things may change. The room, (11)

incidentally, has a false ceiling. That man, by the way, is a test pilot. Shaun, of course, won the prize. This, incidentally, is my (18)

first job. You go all the way to Twelfth Street and then turn right, I think. By the way, I forgot to tell you to bring your guitar. (20)

That letter, by the way, will never get to Spain without more postage. The report, however, is altogether inaccurate. Mrs. Dean, (25)

to tell the truth, was quite pleased with our one-act play. This map won't help us, I'm afraid, until we find out where we are (28)

now. On the other hand, I'm afraid that his older brother is just plain lazy. You have to remember, of course, that in those days (31)

people didn't have telephones. Snoopy, after all, is a very unusual beagle. The rest of the races, however, weren't half as exciting (35)

as either of the first two. The Andersons, it seems, have decided not to move until next September. That disk jockey, I admit, is (39)

rather annoying. Snoopy is the only dog in the world, I suppose, who can do imitations. (41)

Practicing Basic Skills in Language Arts • 370

© 2005 Sopris West Educational Services. All rights reserved. Practicing Basic Skills in Language Arts. Purchaser has permission to photocopy this page for classroom use only.

SEE TO WRITE

Commas for Nonessential Clauses
Directions: Insert commas to set off nonessential clauses.

Ceilings that are leaking should be repaired. Ms. Cashmore who teaches English must teach in a room with a leaky ceiling.

Her principal trying not to smile has offered to supply all the buckets she needs. Jacelyn Haeg who is my sister will be visiting

me in April. Her Porsche badly damaged in an accident is not working. She and her children who live with her in Seattle

will have to come by plane which is very expensive these days. The school that the children attend is willing to approve their

absence. Miriam enrolled in the advanced chemistry class. Her teacher voted Teacher of the Year last year is the most popular

teacher in the high school. All of the students even those new to the school were excited to be placed in Mr. Field's class.

Advanced chemistry one of the more difficult high school courses gives high school students a good foundation for college

chemistry. The high school choir performed at the community center. The audience mostly senior citizens enjoyed hearing

many of their old favorites. Music often called the universal language can help people recall many happy memories. The choir

students mostly 17 and 18 year olds sang songs from the thirties and forties for the group. The community center provided a

free lunch for all in attendance the senior citizens as well as the high school students.

© 2005 Sopris West Educational Services. All rights reserved. Practicing Basic Skills in Language Arts. Purchaser has permission to photocopy this page for classroom use only.

SEE TO WRITE

ONE-MINUTE FLUENCY
BUILDER SERIES

	Correct	Error
First Try		
Second Try		

Commas for Nonessential Clauses

Directions: Insert commas to set off nonessential clauses.

Ceilings that are leaking should be repaired. Ms. Cashmore, who teaches English, must teach in a room with a leaky ceiling. (2)

Her principal, trying not to smile, has offered to supply all the buckets she needs. Jacelyn Haeg, who is my sister, will be visiting (6)

me in April. Her Porsche, badly damaged in an accident, is not working. She and her children, who live with her in Seattle, (10)

will have to come by plane, which is very expensive these days. The school that the children attend is willing to approve their (11)

absence. Miriam enrolled in the advanced chemistry class. Her teacher, voted Teacher of the Year last year, is the most popular (13)

teacher in the high school. All of the students, even those new to the school, were excited to be placed in Mr. Field's class. (15)

Advanced chemistry, one of the more difficult high school courses, gives high school students a good foundation for college (17)

chemistry. The high school choir performed at the community center. The audience, mostly senior citizens, enjoyed hearing (19)

many of their old favorites. Music, often called the universal language, can help people recall many happy memories. The choir (21)

students, mostly 17 and 18 year olds, sang songs from the thirties and forties for the group. The community center provided a (23)

free lunch for all in attendance, the senior citizens as well as the high school students. (24)

ANSWER SHEET

© 2005 Sopris West Educational Services. All rights reserved. Practicing Basic Skills in Language Arts. Purchaser has permission to photocopy this page for classroom use only.

SEE TO WRITE

Commas for Subordinate Clauses
Directions: Place commas where needed.

	First Try	Second Try
Correct		
Error		

When you go to school don't forget your books. If you leave school early call your mother. Since it is raining I'll take you to school. Because you are my friend I'll give you a Coke. As soon as Calvin gets here we'll go to the movies. When Scott gets here I'll call you. Since tomorrow is your birthday you can have a new dress. Because it is almost winter you will need a new coat and hat. If you don't pass your test you can't go to the party. Since you broke the toy you have to take a nap. If your name is Jana it is your turn to go. When dinner is over the football game will be on. If Walt comes over you can give him some pie. Because I want to go to school it is time to get up. After you get here I can leave. Since my coat is too small may I wear yours? If you want a new car you'll have to get a job. When your homework is finished I'll take you to the store. After school is finished this year we will go on vacation. If you will please take me with you. Whenever it is possible I'll take you with me. Because you are the oldest child it is your responsibility. Since we went yesterday we have to stay home today. After I get back from work you can use my car. As soon as you are old enough you can play football. Because I am older I am the boss. If you want to earn money you have to find a job. When Father gets home he will fix supper. When you go to the football game take your hat with you. If you forget it you will freeze. After Rita leaves for school we can go shopping. When you have enough time you should try making a dress for me. Since you are older it will be easier for you. When the mailman comes early I forget to pick up the mail. If your uncle is bigger don't worry about it. If the picture is bad throw it away. After you do that go to your grandmother's house. Before we got home two inches of snow fell.

Practicing Basic Skills in Language Arts • 373

© 2005 Sopris West Educational Services. All rights reserved. Practicing Basic Skills in Language Arts. Purchaser has permission to photocopy this page for classroom use only.

ONE-MINUTE FLUENCY
BUILDER SERIES

SEE TO WRITE

Commas for Subordinate Clauses
Directions: Place commas where needed.

When you go to school, don't forget your books. If you leave school early, call your mother. Since it is raining, I'll take you to (3)

school. Because you are my friend, I'll give you a Coke. As soon as Calvin gets here, we'll go to the movies. When Scott gets (5)

here, I'll call you. Since tomorrow is your birthday, you can have a new dress. Because it is almost winter, you will need a new (8)

coat and hat. If you don't pass your test, you can't go to the party. Since you broke the toy, you have to take a nap. If your name (10)

is Jana, it is your turn to go. When dinner is over, the football game will be on. If Walt comes over, you can give him some (13)

pie. Because I want to go to school, it is time to get up. After you get here, I can leave. Since my coat is too small, may I wear (16)

yours? If you want a new car, you'll have to get a job. When your homework is finished, I'll take you to the store. After school (18)

is finished this year, we will go on vacation. If you will, please take me with you. Whenever it is possible, I'll take you with me. (21)

Because you are the oldest child, it is your responsibility. Since we went yesterday, we have to stay home today. After I get back (23)

from work, you can use my car. As soon as you are old enough, you can play football. Because I am older, I am the boss. If you (26)

want to earn money, you have to find a job. When Father gets home, he will fix supper. When you go to the football game, take (29)

your hat with you. If you forget it, you will freeze. After Rita leaves for school, we can go shopping. When you have enough (31)

time, you should try making a dress for me. Since you are older, it will be easier for you. When the mailman comes early, I forget (34)

to pick up the mail. If your uncle is bigger, don't worry about it. If the picture is bad, throw it away. After you do that, go to your (37)

grandmother's house. Before we got home, two inches of snow fell. (38)

	Correct	Error
First Try		
Second Try		

ANSWER SHEET

© 2005 Sopris West Educational Services. All rights reserved. Practicing Basic Skills in Language Arts. Purchaser has permission to photocopy this page for classroom use only.

ONE MINUTE FLUENCY BUILDER SERIES

SEE TO MARK

Commas for Independent Clauses

Directions: Place commas before *and, but, or, nor, for,* and *yet* when they join independent clauses.

Byron will help Mother in the kitchen and I will help you in the garage. Keesha washed the dishes and her brother dried them. This model is automatic and that model must be operated by hand. Close the window or I shall surely catch cold. The weather forecast is for rain today but I don't agree. Did you walk home or did you ride your bike? I cannot find the bag that you asked for but here is one just like it. Rockets fly in outer space and jets fly within our atmosphere. Terry and his brother washed and dried the dishes. The batter slammed a liner toward left field but the shortstop caught it. Keiko apologized yet Angie didn't forgive her. The car struck a post but the driver was not injured. Study your English carefully or you will have a difficult time after graduation. I work hard at all my studies but my grades are low. He left a package here for you but I sent it to the office. The cereal is in the cupboard and the fruit and cream are on the table. He asked me to the dance and I accepted happily. I asked Carol to join us but she has other plans. The farmers had planted their crops and the season had been favorable. Most of us are going to the game Friday but we still haven't made arrangements for our transportation. Elena will bring the CDs and Barbara will bring the player. Shelly receives high grades for she studies diligently. This watch is nearly thirty years old but it still keeps good time. Are you still taking notes or are you ready to write your theme? He plays the piano well but he must practice daily. The artist moved his brush quickly and his canvas soon was filled with many colors. Mother decided in our favor for that is what mothers usually do. I have told you the truth but you will not believe me. We hated to see him eat all the food but it was the only way to get him to talk. Gordon is improving in English yet he is failing math. Damon has a good brain and he knows how to use it. Franco studied hard for he wanted to learn. Betty could not find her sweater nor could her sisters find it. The car was nearly full but we piled in. Earl baked three cakes and his friends sold them. The house was small but the grounds were spacious.

© 2005 Sopris West Educational Services. All rights reserved. Practicing Basic Skills in Language Arts. Purchaser has permission to photocopy this page for classroom use only.

ONE-MINUTE FLUENCY
BUILDER SERIES

SEE TO MARK

Commas for Independent Clauses

Directions: Place commas before *and, but, or, nor, for,* and *yet* when they join independent clauses.

	Correct	Error
First Try		
Second Try		

Byron will help Mother in the kitchen, and I will help you in the garage. Keesha washed the dishes, and her brother dried them. (2)

This model is automatic, and that model must be operated by hand. Close the window, or I shall surely catch cold. The weather (4)

forecast is for rain today, but I don't agree. Did you walk home, or did you ride your bike? I cannot find the bag that you asked (6)

for, but here is one just like it. Rockets fly in outer space, and jets fly within our atmosphere. Terry and his brother washed and (8)

dried the dishes. The batter slammed a liner toward left field, but the shortstop caught it. Keiko apologized, yet Angie didn't (10)

forgive her. The car struck a post, but the driver was not injured. Study your English carefully, or you will have a difficult time (12)

after graduation. I work hard at all my studies, but my grades are low. He left a package here for you, but I sent it to the office. (14)

The cereal is in the cupboard, and the fruit and cream are on the table. He asked me to the dance, and I accepted happily. I (16)

asked Carol to join us, but she has other plans. The farmers had planted their crops, and the season had been favorable. Most (18)

of us are going to the game Friday, but we still haven't made arrangements for our transportation. Elena will bring the CDs, and (20)

Barbara will bring the player. Shelly receives high grades, for she studies diligently. This watch is nearly thirty years old, but it (22)

still keeps good time. We voted against the drive, but the majority overruled us. Are you still taking notes, or are you ready to (24)

write your theme? He plays the piano well, but he must practice daily. The artist moved his brush quickly, and his canvas soon (26)

was filled with many colors. Mother decided in our favor, for that is what mothers usually do. I have told you the truth, but (28)

you will not believe me. We hated to see him eat all the food, but it was the only way to get him to talk. Gordon is improving (29)

in English, yet he is failing math. Damon has a good brain, and he knows how to use it. Franco studied hard, for he wanted to (32)

learn. Betty could not find her sweater, nor could her sisters find it. The car was nearly full, but we piled in. Earl baked three (34)

cakes, and his friends sold them. The house was small, but the grounds were spacious. (36)

Practicing Basic Skills in Language Arts • 376

ANSWER SHEET

© 2005 Sopris West Educational Services. All rights reserved. Practicing Basic Skills in Language Arts. Purchaser has permission to photocopy this page for classroom use only.

ONE-MINUTE FLUENCY BUILDER SERIES

SEE TO WRITE

Commas for Introductory Elements and Nouns of Direct Address

Directions: Insert commas where needed.

	Correct	Error
First Try		
Second Try		

No there is no other way out of the valley. As soon as you finish eating call me back. Edith please outline your solution to

the problem. If it rains tomorrow I will wear my new boots. Oh I am sorry to hear that. Since the packages have arrived let's

put them in your room. Playing ball in the street Pat was nearly hit by a truck. After scoring three runs in the first inning the

Yankees relaxed. Come here and help me Tarena. Well Rodney no one was more surprised at the outcome than I. After we had

finished listening to the CDs we played several games. Walking to school I overtook Mr. Moreno. Well what do we do now?

Evan what is your telephone number? At the beginning of the game West High scored two touchdowns. Our game with East

High has been cancelled Charley. Clearing the last hurdle easily the runner sprinted for the finish line. Jack are you here to

pick up the television set? Reaching for a third piece of cake I purposely avoided my dad's eyes. Come here Briana and look

at this strange bug. When he saw the green light flash on he crossed the street. Well only you can make that decision Lee.

Counting on surprise Duke passed on the first down. Yes we make free deliveries. In applying for a position for the summer

months students should make plans early. Dropping their tools the men scampered for safety. While we are waiting for Della to

finish with her interview let's walk through the park. Oh I had planned to go. Watching the sky he saw the tornado approach.

Listen Henrietta while I read the exact words. Locking the gate very carefully the guard left to investigate the noise. At the start

of the campaign Mr. Anson was favored to win. No I cannot go tonight. Riding through the countryside we saw a white calf.

Your plan Ed suits me.

Practicing Basic Skills in Language Arts • 377

© 2005 Sopris West Educational Services. All rights reserved. Practicing Basic Skills in Language Arts. Purchaser has permission to photocopy this page for classroom use only.

SEE TO WRITE

Commas for Introductory Elements and Nouns of Direct Address

Directions: Insert commas where needed.

	First Try	Second Try
Correct		
Error		

No, there is no other way out of the valley. As soon as you finish eating, call me back. Edith, please outline your solution to (3)

the problem. If it rains tomorrow, I will wear my new boots. Oh, I am sorry to hear that. Since the packages have arrived, let's (6)

put them in your room. Playing ball in the street, Pat was nearly hit by a truck. After scoring three runs in the first inning, the (8)

Yankees relaxed. Come here and help me, Tarena. Well, Rodney, no one was more surprised at the outcome than I. After we had (11)

finished listening to the CDs, we played several games. Walking to school, I overtook Mr. Moreno. Well, what do we do now? (14)

Evan, what is your telephone number? At the beginning of the game, West High scored two touchdowns. Our game with East (16)

High has been cancelled, Charley. Clearing the last hurdle easily, the runner sprinted for the finish line. Jack, are you here to (19)

pick up the television set? Reaching for a third piece of cake, I purposely avoided my dad's eyes. Come here, Briana, and look (22)

at this strange bug. When he saw the green light flash on, he crossed the street. Well, only you can make that decision, Lee. (25)

Counting on surprise, Duke passed on the first down. Yes, we make free deliveries. In applying for a position for the summer (27)

months, students should make plans early. Dropping their tools, the men scampered for safety. While we are waiting for Della to (29)

finish with her interview, let's walk through the park. Oh, I had planned to go. Watching the sky, he saw the tornado approach. (32)

Listen, Henrietta, while I read the exact words. Locking the gate very carefully, the guard left to investigate the noise. At the start (35)

of the campaign, Mr. Anson was favored to win. No, I cannot go tonight. Riding through the countryside, we saw a white calf. (38)

Your plan, Ed, suits me. (40)

ANSWER SHEET

© 2005 Sopris West Educational Services. All rights reserved. Practicing Basic Skills in Language Arts. Purchaser has permission to photocopy this page for classroom use only.

SEE TO WRITE

Commas for Appositives and Parenthetical Expressions
Directions: Insert commas where needed.

	First Try	Second Try
Correct		
Error		

The winner a junior received the gold medal. This speech I believe was ill-timed. Some of us on the other hand thought him

guilty. The hours nevertheless went by quickly. Wade Lester the runner-up was given the silver medal. The days moreover

seemed to be jet-propelled. Don my friend will go with us. I mailed the letter to Adele my cousin. Rick Padilla the class

president called the meeting to order. I was as a matter of fact the only one who finished. Jerrold's prize a gold medal with a

blue ribbon was beautiful. Dr. Riegel my new teacher studied in Germany. We succeeded however in finishing our work on

time. Our party was a surprise to Mrs. Listro our English teacher. There were however three others in the race. John Glenn

the astronaut talked about Muskingum College. Mr. Fukai our neighbor is taking us to a movie. I couldn't reach Mr. Eccles

the scoutmaster of our troup before he left the city. Our vice-principal Mr. Hopkins addressed the assembly. Jim the youngest

brother of Wayne Tucker has been asked to represent our school in the district science fair. Two winners Rod and Freda

received equal prizes. Our mascot a little turtle that I bought in Florida goes with us on our automobile trips. He spoke about

gardening his favorite topic.

© 2005 Sopris West Educational Services. All rights reserved. Practicing Basic Skills in Language Arts. Purchaser has permission to photocopy this page for classroom use only.

SEE TO WRITE

Commas for Appositives and Parenthetical Expressions

Directions: Insert commas where needed.

	First Try	Second Try
Correct		
Error		

The winner, a junior, received the gold medal. This speech, I believe, was ill-timed. Some of us, on the other hand, thought him (6)

guilty. The hours, nevertheless, went by quickly. Wade Lester, the runner-up, was given the silver medal. The days, moreover, (11)

seemed to be jet-propelled. Don, my friend, will go with us. I mailed the letter to Adele, my cousin. Rick Padilla, the class (15)

president, called the meeting to order. I was, as a matter of fact, the only one who finished. Jerrold's prize, a gold medal with a (20)

blue ribbon, was beautiful. Dr. Riegel, my new teacher, studied in Germany. We succeeded, however, in finishing our work on (25)

time. Our party was a surprise to Mrs. Listro, our English teacher. There were, however, three others in the race. John Glenn, (29)

the astronaut, talked about Muskingum College. Mr. Fukai, our neighbor, is taking us to a movie. I couldn't reach Mr. Eccles, (33)

the scoutmaster of our troup, before he left the city. Our vice-principal, Mr. Hopkins, addressed the assembly. Jim, the youngest (37)

brother of Wayne Tucker, has been asked to represent our school in the district science fair. Two winners, Rod and Freda, (40)

received equal prizes. Our mascot, a little turtle that I bought in Florida, goes with us on our automobile trips. He spoke about (42)

gardening, his favorite topic. (43)

Practicing Basic Skills in Language Arts • 380

© 2005 Sopris West Educational Services. All rights reserved. Practicing Basic Skills in Language Arts. Purchaser has permission to photocopy this page for classroom use only.

SEE TO WRITE

Commas for Appositives, Parenthetical Expressions, Names, and Titles

Directions: Fill in commas to set off the following:

1. Appositives—interrupters that explain or identify a noun.
2. Parenthetical expressions—a side remark such as *however, in fact, indeed, on the other hand, as a matter of fact, I believe,* etc.
3. Single words like *yes, no, well, indeed, also,* etc.
4. Names or titles of persons spoken to.

Indeed my answer is correct. Listen Henrietta while I read the exact words. Mr. Ellis our neighbor is taking a trip. There were

however three others in the race. Our mascot a little turtle goes with us. No I can see no reason for it. You will remember

dear friend that I wrote to you earlier. As a boy I must admit I was a bit lazy. My how beautiful the sky looks. Mr. Alexander

the baseball coach telephoned him. Of course I forgot all about it. Yvonne why haven't you written? Yes I can understand.

Now however I know better. Polio the dreaded disease has nearly been conquered. Obviously you have taken a wrong turn.

We have ice cream a food everyone likes. I voted for Helen my sister's best friend. Don't let me down Sonja. Tell the truth

Cameron. Roxanne a senior at CMR won the race. Therefore we called a plumber. There were two witnesses Mr. Encinas and

Mr. Sterns. Sweden on the other hand is much colder. Well how did you do it? Nicole you may leave after lunch. The team

as a matter of fact had never played better. However we lost the game. If you insist Dennis you may make your report now.

When the time is right you will know it. The Hardy Boys ace detectives had a T.V. series. Mr. Cho the principal announced

the winners of the speech contest.

Practicing Basic Skills in Language Arts • 381

© 2005 Sopris West Educational Services. All rights reserved. Practicing Basic Skills in Language Arts. Purchaser has permission to photocopy this page for classroom use only.

	First Try	Second Try
Correct		
Error		

	Correct	Error
First Try		
Second Try		

SEE TO WRITE

Commas for Appositives, Parenthetical Expressions, Names, and Titles

Directions: Fill in commas to set off the following:
1. Appositives—interrupters that explain or identify a noun.
2. Parenthetical expressions—a side remark such as *however, in fact, indeed, on the other hand, as a matter of fact, I believe,* etc.
3. Single words like *yes, no, well, indeed, also,* etc.
4. Names or titles of persons spoken to.

Indeed, my answer is correct. Listen, Henrietta, while I read the exact words. Mr. Ellis, our neighbor, is taking a trip. There were, (6)

however, three others in the race. Our mascot, a little turtle, goes with us. No, I can see no reason for it. You will remember, (11)

dear friend, that I wrote to you earlier. As a boy, I must admit, I was a bit lazy. My, how beautiful the sky looks. Mr. Alexander, (16)

the baseball coach, telephoned him. Of course, I forgot all about it. Yvonne, why haven't you written? Yes, I can understand. (20)

Now, however, I know better. Polio, the dreaded disease, has nearly been conquered. Obviously, you have taken a wrong turn. (25)

We have ice cream, a food everyone likes. I voted for Helen, my sister's best friend. Don't let me down, Sonja. Tell the truth, (29)

Cameron. Roxanne, a senior at CMR, won the race. Therefore, we called a plumber. There were two witnesses, Mr. Encinas and (33)

Mr. Sterns. Sweden, on the other hand, is much colder. Well, how did you do it? Nicole, you may leave after lunch. The team, (38)

as a matter of fact, had never played better. However, we lost the game. If you insist, Dennis, you may make your report now. (42)

When the time is right, you will know it. The Hardy Boys, ace detectives, had a T.V. series. Mr. Cho, the principal, announced (47)

the winners of the speech contest. (47)

ANSWER SHEET

Practicing Basic Skills in Language Arts • 382

© 2005 Sopris West Educational Services. All rights reserved. Practicing Basic Skills in Language Arts. Purchaser has permission to photocopy this page for classroom use only.

Commas in Dates and Addresses

Directions: Insert commas to separate dates and addresses.

	Correct	Error
First Try		
Second Try		

Was September 1 2004 a holiday? On August 1 2004 we moved to 2456 Oak Street Ames Ohio. We shall leave for our

vacation on Friday June 14. Our new address is 1509 Moncade Drive Salt Lake City Utah 85056. My uncle has built a new

house at 5892 Sunset Drive Ogden Utah 84403. Who lives at 4587 Lavina Drive Ogden Utah? I was born in Logan Utah on

May 7 1990. Our basketball team has not lost since January 8 2004 but we have had some close calls. He began working here

on September 1 1980 and retired on May 1 2004. The postmark read September 19 2004 but we didn't receive the letter until

last Friday October 7 2004. Forward our mail to 651 Sentinel Drive Provo Utah 86430 where we will be moving next month.

The bombing of Pearl Harbor on December 7 1941 marked the beginning of World War II for the United States. On August 14

1945 Japan surrendered to the Allies. We used to live at 28 Hill Road Columbus Ohio 43213. Thomas Jefferson died on July 4

1826 at the age of eighty-three. The first Transcontinental Railroad was completed on May 10 1869 in Promontory Utah.

© 2005 Sopris West Educational Services. All rights reserved. Practicing Basic Skills in Language Arts. Purchaser has permission to photocopy this page for classroom use only.

ONE-MINUTE FLUENCY
BUILDER SERIES

	Correct	Error
First Try		
Second Try		

Commas in Dates and Addresses

Directions: Insert commas to separate dates and addresses.

Was September 1, 2004, a holiday? On August 1, 2004, we moved to 2456 Oak Street, Ames, Ohio. We shall leave for our (6)

vacation on Friday, June 14. Our new address is 1509 Moncade Drive, Salt Lake City, Utah 85056. My uncle has built a new (9)

house at 5892 Sunset Drive, Ogden, Utah 84403. Who lives at 4587 Lavina Drive, Ogden, Utah? I was born in Logan, Utah, on (15)

May 7, 1990. Our basketball team has not lost since January 8, 2004, but we have had some close calls. He began working here (18)

on September 1, 1980, and retired on May 1, 2004. The postmark read September 19, 2004, but we didn't receive the letter until (23)

last Friday, October 7, 2004. Forward our mail to 651 Sentinel Drive, Provo, Utah 86430, where we will be moving next month. (28)

The bombing of Pearl Harbor on December 7, 1941, marked the beginning of World War II for the United States. On August 14, (31)

1945, Japan surrendered to the Allies. We used to live at 28 Hill Road, Columbus, Ohio 43213. Thomas Jefferson died on July 4, (35)

1826, at the age of eighty-three. The first Transcontinental Railroad was completed on May 10, 1869, in Promontory, Utah. (39)

ANSWER SHEET

© 2005 Sopris West Educational Services. All rights reserved. Practicing Basic Skills in Language Arts. Purchaser has permission to photocopy this page for classroom use only.

SEE TO WRITE

Commas in Series, Dates, and Addresses
Directions: Insert commas where needed.

	First Try	Second Try
Correct		
Error		

Students teachers and parents will enjoy a concert at South Ogden Junior High School 4300 Madison Avenue on Thursday

March 8 2004. We ought to leave on Friday December 22 2004 if not before. From Sunday December 24 2004 to Tuesday

January 7 2005 we will be in beautiful sunny Hawaii. Mr. Avery has taught algebra English and science. Dorothy Sylvia

Alton and Jessie were among his students. But he never taught Lance or Gary or Anetta. He still teaches whatever he must

whenever he must and wherever he must. This is true despite his retirement on May 30 2004. Carol Booker Louise Taft and

Amy Tamaga will give a luncheon for Inez Vargo on Friday April 28 at 3400 South Meadow Lane Apartment 2 South Ogden

Utah 84403. I met her in July 1997 in Oregon. Friday May 12 1999 was our wedding day. John Vogler Joey Porras and Dan

Isgar were ushers at the wedding. Neither my aunt nor my uncle nor my cousins were able to attend. But many of my bride's

relatives and friends came from as far away as Waco Texas. It is generally agreed that Ingrid Sharon and Tonya will be among

the finalists at the exciting beauty contest next Friday. The talent competition may be won by Myra Burke with her clear high

voice. A vain talkative disc jockey will be the host. He can't decide whether to hold the competition at the high school at the

community center or in the local arts theater. The contestants will be honored at a special dinner on Friday May 6 where steak

salad potatoes and pie will be served.

© 2005 Sopris West Educational Services. All rights reserved. Practicing Basic Skills in Language Arts. Purchaser has permission to photocopy this page for classroom use only.

SEE TO WRITE

Commas in Series, Dates, and Addresses

Directions: Insert commas where needed.

	Correct	Error
First Try		
Second Try		

Students, teachers, and parents will enjoy a concert at South Ogden Junior High School, 4300 Madison Avenue, on Thursday, (5)

March 8, 2004. We ought to leave on Friday, December 22, 2004, if not before. From Sunday, December 24, 2004, to Tuesday, (13)

January 7, 2005, we will be in beautiful, sunny Hawaii. Mr. Avery has taught algebra, English, and science. Dorothy, Sylvia, (20)

Alton, and Jessie were among his students. But he never taught Lance or Gary or Anetta. He still teaches whatever he must, (22)

whenever he must, and wherever he must. This is true despite his retirement on May 30, 2004. Carol Booker, Louise Taft, and (26)

Amy Tamaga will give a luncheon for Inez Vargo on Friday, April 28, at 3400 South Meadow Lane, Apartment 2, South Ogden, (31)

Utah 84403. I met her in July 1997, in Oregon. Friday, May 12, 1999, was our wedding day. John Vogler, Joey Porras, and Dan (37)

Isgar were ushers at the wedding. Neither my aunt nor my uncle nor my cousins were able to attend. But many of my bride's (37)

relatives and friends came from as far away as Waco, Texas. It is generally agreed that Ingrid, Sharon, and Tonya will be among (40)

the finalists at the exciting beauty contest next Friday. The talent competition may be won by Myra Burke with her clear, high (41)

voice. A vain, talkative disc jockey will be the host. He can't decide whether to hold the competition at the high school, at the (43)

community center, or in the local arts theater. The contestants will be honored at a special dinner on Friday, May 6, where steak, (47)

salad, potatoes, and pie will be served. (49)

ANSWER SHEET

Practicing Basic Skills in Language Arts • 386

© 2005 Sopris West Educational Services. All rights reserved. Practicing Basic Skills in Language Arts. Purchaser has permission to photocopy this page for classroom use only.

Comma Review

Directions: Insert all missing commas.

	Correct	Error
First Try		
Second Try		

Johnny what is your telephone number? His speech I believe was excellent. Honestly we are not justified in complaining. We reached there on June 14 2004. Reno Nevada lies farther west than Los Angeles California. Footballs helmets and jerseys were stored in the room. Let's give them the best we have team. We visited the Adams Library one of the oldest in America. Your second sentence for example is too long. The center turned jumped and shot. Our neighbor Mr. Jones is taking a trip. Yes I can understand. As a matter of fact I believe you. Obviously you have taken a wrong turn. Tell the truth John. The damage however was less than expected. Lee was born in Evanston Illinois on December 19 1959. Beethoven wrote symphonies quartets concertos and sonatas. Roxanne a senior at Roy High won the race. Well how did you do it? You will remember dear friend that I wrote to you earlier. I saw Mary Joanne Michael and Joe at the store. His new address is 1165 Robin Hood Lane Norman Oklahoma. Therefore the library will be closed on Tuesdays. The plan was simple clear and effective. Our mascot a little turtle goes with us. Now however I know better. There were two witnesses Mr. Nelson and Mr. Anderson. We will meet you in Canton Ohio on Wednesday January 10. John Glenn the astronaut talked about his experiences. Some of us on the other hand thought him guilty. When the tide went out we walked along the sandy beach. Well no one was more surprised than Robbie. Counting on surprise Duke passed on the first down. We drove through sand across plains and up mountains. Of course I forgot all about it. If you insist Dennis you may read. The treaty was signed in Geneva Switzerland on December 15 1906 but was not ratified until March 6 1908. Polio the dreaded disease has nearly been conquered. Sweden on the other hand is much colder. If it rains tomorrow I will wear my new boots. All right class it's time to begin. The letter was addressed to 5064 Hazel Avenue Philadelphia Pennsylvania as you requested. Ladies and gentlemen I leave the decision to you. Three trucks four cars and a trailer were tangled on the icy bridge. As a boy I must admit I was a bit crazy. My how beautiful the sky looks. A flight attendant must be cheerful alert and always pleasant. Mr. Alexander the baseball coach telephoned him.

© 2005 Sopris West Educational Services. All rights reserved. Practicing Basic Skills in Language Arts. Purchaser has permission to photocopy this page for classroom use only.

SEE TO WRITE

Comma Review

Directions: Insert all missing commas.

	Correct	Error
First Try		
Second Try		

Johnny, what is your telephone number? His speech, I believe, was excellent. Honestly, we are not justified in complaining. We (4)
reached there on June 14, 2004. Reno, Nevada, lies farther west than Los Angeles, California. Footballs, helmets, and jerseys were (10)
stored in the room. Let's give them the best we have, team. We visited the Adams Library, one of the oldest in America. Your (12)
second sentence, for example, is too long. The center turned, jumped, and shot. Our neighbor, Mr. Jones, is taking a trip. Yes, (19)
I can understand. As a matter of fact, I believe you. Obviously, you have taken a wrong turn. Tell the truth, John. The damage, (23)
however, was less than expected. Lee was born in Evanston, Illinois, on December 19, 1959. Beethoven wrote symphonies, (28)
quartets, concertos, and sonatas. Roxanne, a senior at Roy High, won the race. Well, how did you do it? You will remember, dear (34)
friend, that I wrote to you earlier. I saw Mary, Joanne, Michael, and Joe at the store. His new address is 1165 Robin Hood Lane, (39)
Norman, Oklahoma. Therefore, the library will be closed on Tuesdays. The plan was simple, clear, and effective. Our mascot, a (44)
little turtle, goes with us. Now, however, I know better. There were two witnesses, Mr. Nelson and Mr. Anderson. We will meet (48)
you in Canton, Ohio, on Wednesday, January 10. John Glenn, the astronaut, talked about his experiences. Some of us, on the (54)
other hand, thought him guilty. When the tide went out, we walked along the sandy beach. Well, no one was more surprised (57)
than Robbie. Counting on surprise, Duke passed on the first down. We drove through sand, across plains, and up mountains. (60)
Of course, I forgot all about it. If you insist, Dennis, you may read. The treaty was signed in Geneva, Switzerland, on December (65)
15, 1906, but was not ratified until March 6, 1908. Polio, the dreaded disease, has nearly been conquered. Sweden, on the other (71)
hand, is much colder. If it rains tomorrow, I will wear my new boots. All right, class, it's time to begin. The letter was addressed (75)
to 5064 Hazel Avenue, Philadelphia, Pennsylvania, as you requested. Ladies and gentlemen, I leave the decision to you. Three (79)
trucks, four cars, and a trailer were tangled on the icy bridge. As a boy, I must admit, I was a bit crazy. My, how beautiful the sky (84)
looks. A flight attendant must be cheerful, alert, and always pleasant. Mr. Alexander, the baseball coach, telephoned him. (88)

ANSWER SHEET

Practicing Basic Skills in Language Arts • 388

© 2005 Sopris West Educational Services. All rights reserved. Practicing Basic Skills in Language Arts. Purchaser has permission to photocopy this page for classroom use only.

Apostrophe to Show Possession

Directions: Insert an apostrophe or apostrophe S to show possession.

	Correct	Error
First Try		
Second Try		

ONE MINUTE FLUENCY BUILDER SERIES

Harolds uncle	someone elses car	tomorrows meeting	ladies hats
Jamess uncle	sailors leave	his keys	boys bikes
daughter-in-laws recipe	a weeks work	anybodys guess	firemens helmets
Poes short story	the twins bike	childrens toys	Charless order
your gloves	Thomass calculator	nobodys paper	teachers lounge
a ladys coat	a moments delay	a dollars worth	her turn
a days end	its collar	three decades history	Ms. Wellss assignment
womens tournament	a months duration	brother-in-laws name	Garys tennis racket
her telephone	3 reporters statements	their locker	six hours time
my cousins picture	thirty cents worth	waitresses hours	somebodys test
our car	one buss schedule	Sues scarf	its water dish
everyones ideas	sister-in-laws house	my records	a mans home
Searss sale	six buses schedules	geeses flight	somebody elses skates
Dickenss novel	my stereo	Mr. Harriss car	Gus Wilsons station
his engine	League of Women Voters office	boys shoes	governors wives
childs room	Miss Joness job	our championship	several birds nests
anothers answer	sheeps wool	an ants view	anyones book
an hours wait	your journal	whose cat	a dogs tail

© 2005 Sopris West Educational Services. All rights reserved. Practicing Basic Skills in Language Arts. Purchaser has permission to photocopy this page for classroom use only.

ONE-MINUTE FLUENCY BUILDER SERIES

SEE TO WRITE

Apostrophe to Show Possession

Directions: Insert an apostrophe or apostrophe S to show possession.

Correct	Error		
First Try			
Second Try			

Harold's uncle	someone else's car	tomorrow's meeting	ladies' hats (4)
James's uncle	sailor's leave	his keys	boy's bikes (7)
daughter-in-law's recipe	a week's work	anybody's guess	firemen's helmets (11)
Poe's short story	the twin's bike	children's toys	Charles's order (15)
your gloves	Thomas's calculator	nobody's paper	teachers' lounge (18)
a lady's coat	a moment's delay	a dollar's worth	her turn (21)
a day's end	its collar	three decades' history	Ms. Wells's assignment (24)
women's tournament	a month's duration	brother-in-law's name	Gary's tennis racket (28)
her telephone	3 reporters' statements	their locker	six hours' time (30)
my cousin's picture	thirty cents' worth	waitresses' hours	somebody's test (34)
our car	one bus's schedule	Sue's scarf	its water dish (36)
everyone's ideas	sister-in-law's house	my records	a man's home (39)
Sears's sale	six buses' schedules	geese's flight	somebody else's skates (43)
Dickens's novel	my stereo	Mr. Harris's car	Gus Wilson's station (46)
his engine	League of Women Voters' office	boy's shoes	governors' wives (49)
child's room	Miss Jones's job	our championship	several birds' nests (52)
another's answer	sheep's wool	an ant's view	anyone's book (56)
an hour's wait	your journal	whose cat	a dog's tail (58)

ANSWER SHEET

© 2005 Sopris West Educational Services. All rights reserved. Practicing Basic Skills in Language Arts. Purchaser has permission to photocopy this page for classroom use only.

One-Minute Fluency Builder Series

Apostrophes to Form Plurals of Letters, Numbers, Signs, and Words

Directions: Insert apostrophes where they are needed.

	First Try	Second Try
Correct		
Error		

That sign has two ms missing.

Can you make 8s on skates?

Your answer to that math problem will have four 6s.

Mr. Prince marked the paper with xs and ss.

The ls and 7s in this ledger are difficult to read.

She used three &s in her composition.

She spells her name with two us.

Avoid using so many ands in your speech.

My name has two is in it.

Spell out your ands; in other words, do not write &s.

No, is do not always come before es.

Do not omit the −s and +s from the math assignment.

Their IQs tested well above average.

Your 3s and 5s look too much alike.

"Mississippi" has four ss, four is, and two ps.

Too many uhs can spoil a good talk.

The whys and wherefores of the situation escaped him.

Are these circled letters ms or ns?

Always cross your ts and dot your is.

Are these 2s or 3s?

The article is full of ands and buts.

How many rs does your name have?

Miss Chadwick told us that the +s indicate good work.

Put −s in front of the numbers.

There are four 7s in his phone number.

Your speech had too many wells.

Practicing Basic Skills in Language Arts • 391

© 2005 Sopris West Educational Services. All rights reserved. Practicing Basic Skills in Language Arts. Purchaser has permission to photocopy this page for classroom use only.

ONE-MINUTE FLUENCY BUILDER SERIES

SEE TO WRITE

Apostrophes to Form Plurals of Letters, Numbers, Signs, and Words

Directions: Insert apostrophes where they are needed.

That sign has two m's missing.

Can you make 8's on skates? (2)

Your answer to that math problem will have four 6's.

Mr. Prince marked the paper with x's and s's. (5)

The 1's and 7's in this ledger are difficult to read.

She used three &'s in her composition. (8)

She spells her name with two u's.

Avoid using so many and's in your speech. (10)

My name has two i's in it.

Spell out your and's; in other words, do not write &'s. (13)

No, i's do not always come before e's.

Do not omit the −'s and +'s from the math assignment. (17)

Their IQ's tested well above average.

Your 3's and 5's look too much alike. (20)

"Mississippi" has four s's, four i's, and two p's.

Too many uh's can spoil a good talk. (24)

The why's and wherefore's of the situation escaped him.

Are these circled letters m's or n's? (28)

Always cross your t's and dot your i's.

Are these 2's or 3's? (32)

The article is full of and's and but's.

How many r's does your name have? (35)

Miss Chadwick told us that the +'s indicate good work.

Put −'s in front of the numbers. (37)

There are four 7's in his phone number.

Your speech had too many well's. (39)

© 2005 Sopris West Educational Services. All rights reserved. Practicing Basic Skills in Language Arts. Purchaser has permission to photocopy this page for classroom use only.

SEE TO WRITE

Apostrophes to Form Plurals of Letters, Numbers, and Signs

Directions: Insert apostrophe S to form plurals.

Your e___ and i___ look alike.

Put +___ or –___ in the blanks.

Don't use t___ and f___; use +___ and o___.

Cursive capital Q___ look strange.

His 3___ and 5___ are never clear.

Make your #___ and &___ clearer.

I had more +___ than –___ last term.

Avoid too many *and*___ in your writing.

Her speech was full of a___.

We sold all the 5___ and 8___.

Make two g___ and four p___.

My little sister knows her ABC___.

You have four *that*___ in your sentence.

You form your 8___ backwards.

Begin the m___ and n___ on the line.

Write the a___ ten times.

Your h___ and k___ look alike.

His u___ look like ie___.

I only had two C___ this year.

All the 4___, 5___, and 6___ were gone.

Capital X___ are strange to write.

Write five 6___ in the right corner.

He had six F___ on his report card.

You need four 7___ in that answer.

Connect the o___ at the mid-line.

Write the O___ twenty times.

B___, 1___, h___, and k___ need to be clear.

Do your a___ look like o___?

My v___ look like u___.

That address has nine 1___ in it.

Now cross out the 7___.

The o___ and a___ look alike.

There are four i___, four s___, and two p___ in Mississippi.

Her small k___ look like capitals.

There are two c___ and two m___ in accommodate.

She can't copy the $___ and ¢___ signs.

© 2005 Sopris West Educational Services. All rights reserved. Practicing Basic Skills in Language Arts. Purchaser has permission to photocopy this page for classroom use only.

	First Try	Second Try
Correct		
Error		

SEE TO WRITE

Apostrophes to Form Plurals of Letters, Numbers, and Signs

Directions: Insert apostrophe S to form plurals.

(1) Your e **'s** and i **'s** look alike.

(3) Put + **'s** or − **'s** in the blanks.

(5) Don't use t **'s** and f **'s** ; use + **'s** and o **'s** .

(7) Cursive capital Q **'s** look strange.

(10) His 3 **'s** and 5 **'s** are never clear.

(12) Make your # **'s** and & **'s** clearer.

(14) I had more + **'s** than − **'s** last term.

(18) Avoid too many *and* **'s** in your writing.

(20) Her speech was full of a **'s** .

(25) We sold all the 5 **'s** and 8 **'s** .

(28) Make two g **'s** and four p **'s** .

(30) My little sister knows her ABC **'s** .

(33) You have four *that* **'s** in your sentence.

(34) You form your 8 **'s** backwards.

(43) Begin the m **'s** and n **'s** on the line.

(44) Write the a **'s** ten times.

(52) Your h **'s** and k **'s** look alike.

(60) His u **'s** look like ie **'s** .

---

(2) I only had two C **'s** this year.

(35) All the 4 **'s** , 5 **'s** , and 6 **'s** were gone.

(36) Capital X **'s** are strange to write.

(37) Write five 6 **'s** in the right corner.

(38) He had six F **'s** on his report card.

(39) You need four 7 **'s** in that answer.

(40) Connect the o **'s** at the mid-line.

(41) Write the O **'s** twenty times.

(45) B **'s** , 1 **'s** , h **'s** , and k **'s** need to be clear.

(47) Do your a **'s** look like o **'s** ?

(49) My v **'s** look like u **'s** .

(50) That address has nine 1 **'s** in it.

(51) Now cross out the 7 **'s** .

(53) The o **'s** and a **'s** look alike.

(56) There are four i **'s** , four s **'s** , and two p **'s** in Mississippi.

(57) Her small k **'s** look like capitals.

(59) There are two c **'s** and two m **'s** in accommodate.

(61) She can't copy the $ **'s** and ¢ **'s** signs.

ANSWER SHEET

© 2005 Sopris West Educational Services. All rights reserved. Practicing Basic Skills in Language Arts. Purchaser has permission to photocopy this page for classroom use only.

Apostrophe Review
Directions: Insert apostrophes where needed.

	First Try	Second Try
Correct		
Error		

Your dogs leash is too short. Wheres the exit? Its been a long time. Your 2s look like 5s. Davids homework is on the table.

Youre going to get a better mark this term. Always cross your ts and dot your is. The girls wont say where theyll be. Doesnt

he know the ABCs? Whos been in my room? Your paper shows great improvement. Its impossible to write that quickly. Theyre

going to be in the next school play. Its right front tire is flat. A pilots life must be exciting. The boys hats are in the clothing

department. Have you seen my mothers hat? She mightve let us know. Several artists paintings are on exhibit. Dont use &s in

place of *ands*. You arent feeling ill, are you? I shouldnt have eaten that extra pie. The cat licked its paw. Get your books; theyre

in the library. Whose books are these? Jill gets all As and Bs on her report card. Dont you know what youre doing? You may

borrow Henrys books. Everything depended on the number of 10s and 20s we had. Lets go watch the baseball game. Thats not

a good idea; its not even logical. Ill receive a months vacation. A freshmans cap was found on the ground. I will help in my

fathers business. Dont you know the answer to Lewiss question? You have too many is in Mississippi. He did a mans work. Ill

see you at Bills house tonight. Its too bad that the dog hurt its foot, isnt it? My cousins watch wasnt lost; it was stolen. Is this

yours, or is it Helens? Wouldnt you like Phils book? The childs hat is lost, isnt it? The teachers book was not in its place.

© 2005 Sopris West Educational Services. All rights reserved. Practicing Basic Skills in Language Arts. Purchaser has permission to photocopy this page for classroom use only.

SEE TO WRITE

Apostrophe Review
Directions: Insert apostrophes where needed.

Your dog's leash is too short. Where's the exit? It's been a long time. Your 2's look like 5's. David's homework is on the table. (6)

You're going to get a better mark this term. Always cross your t's and dot your i's. The girls won't say where they'll be. Doesn't (12)

he know the ABC's? Who's been in my room? Your paper shows great improvement. It's impossible to write that quickly. They're (16)

going to be in the next school play. Its right front tire is flat. A pilot's life must be exciting. The boys' hats are in the clothing (18)

department. Have you seen my mother's hat? She might've let us know. Several artists' paintings are on exhibit. Don't use &'s in (23)

place of *and*'s. You aren't feeling ill, are you? I shouldn't have eaten that extra pie. The cat licked its paw. Get your books; they're (27)

in the library. Whose books are these? Jill gets all A's and B's on her report card. Don't you know what you're doing? You may (31)

borrow Henry's books. Everything depended on the number of 10's and 20's we had. Let's go watch the baseball game. That's not (36)

a good idea; it's not even logical. I'll receive a month's vacation. A freshman's cap was found on the ground. I will help in my (40)

father's business. Don't you know the answer to Lewis's question? You have too many i's in Mississippi. He did a man's work. I'll (46)

see you at Bill's house tonight. It's too bad that the dog hurt its foot, isn't it? My cousin's watch wasn't lost; it was stolen. Is this (51)

yours, or is it Helen's? Wouldn't you like Phil's book? The child's hat is lost, isn't it? The teacher's book was not in its place. (57)

ANSWER SHEET

Practicing Basic Skills in Language Arts • 396

© 2005 Sopris West Educational Services. All rights reserved. Practicing Basic Skills in Language Arts. Purchaser has permission to photocopy this page for classroom use only.

SEE TO WRITE

Apostrophe Review

Directions: Insert apostrophes where needed.

ONE MINUTE FLUENCY
BUILDER SERIES

Its my turn to take care of Yokos cat. Wandas favorite subject in school is math. Some students think its too hard. Its easy

if youve learned how to listen. The girls went to the football game to see Everetts brother play. Hes the best player on the

schools team. Whats your favorite food? Tacos are what Id like to have for dinner. Its almost noon, time for lunch. My

companys coming tomorrow night after Glorias play is over. I want to tell Kendalls mother the good news. The students

studied very hard for the test they missed. The ghost stories werent very scary. He owns Mr. Desalles house. The movie will

begin at 9 oclock. Whatll we do if we miss Janas bus? Its too far to walk. Joses friend wont be able to take us there. After

school, lets go visit Aunt Mai. The childrens toys were all over the house. Roy Feathers house was painted yesterday. It looks

much better. If its not too far, lets walk to the movies. Im sure Nolans mother wont care. If he is careful, it will be all right

with his dad. The notes he plays on his trombone sound good. The teachers get to go home early if it doesnt rain. Tomorrow

is my friends birthday. I cant read the 2s you wrote on the grade card. Devons totals were all wrong. Shell have to do Lamars

report again. Its too bad she cant do it right the first time. His address was changed. The childrens clothes were brand new. Its

time for us to clean Aunt Willas house again. Maybe shell do a good job this time. Its getting dark earlier now. Wouldnt it be

nice if we could see Kennas new car? Diegos brother isnt coming to see us tonight. My sisters husband is a doctor. Wed like to

visit you sometime. Mississippi isnt too far away. His grades are improving every day. Hes going to get all As this time. Id like

for you to take Marlenes mother with you. Shes a lot of fun.

Practicing Basic Skills in Language Arts • 397

© 2005 Sopris West Educational Services. All rights reserved. Practicing Basic Skills in Language Arts. Purchaser has permission to photocopy this page for classroom use only.

ONE-MINUTE FLUENCY
BUILDER SERIES

SEE TO WRITE

Apostrophe Review

Directions: Insert apostrophes where needed.

	First Try	Second Try
Correct		
Error		

It's my turn to take care of Yoko's cat. Wanda's favorite subject in school is math. Some students think it's too hard. It's easy (5)

if you've learned how to listen. The girls went to the football game to see Everett's brother play. He's the best player on the (8)

school's team. What's your favorite food? Tacos are what I'd like to have for dinner. It's almost noon, time for lunch. My (12)

company's coming tomorrow night after Gloria's play is over. I want to tell Kendall's mother the good news. The students (15)

studied very hard for the test they missed. The ghost stories weren't very scary. He owns Mr. Desalle's house. The movie will (17)

begin at 9 o'clock. What'll we do if we miss Jana's bus? It's too far to walk. Jose's friend won't be able to take us there. After (23)

school, let's go visit Aunt Mai. The children's toys were all over the house. Roy Feather's house was painted yesterday. It looks (26)

much better. If it's not too far, let's walk to the movies. I'm sure Nolan's mother won't care. If he is careful, it will be all right (31)

with his dad. The notes he plays on his trombone sound good. The teachers get to go home early if it doesn't rain. Tomorrow (32)

is my friend's birthday. I can't read the 2's you wrote on the grade card. Devon's totals were all wrong. She'll have to do Lamar's (37)

report again. It's too bad she can't do it right the first time. His address was changed. The children's clothes were brand new. It's (41)

time for us to clean Aunt Willa's house again. Maybe she'll do a good job this time. It's getting dark earlier now. Wouldn't it be (45)

nice if we could see Kenna's new car? Diego's brother isn't coming to see us tonight. My sister's husband is a doctor. We'd like to (50)

visit you sometime. Mississippi isn't too far away. His grades are improving every day. He's going to get all A's this time. I'd like (54)

for you to take Marlene's mother with you. She's a lot of fun. (56)

© 2005 Sopris West Educational Services. All rights reserved. Practicing Basic Skills in Language Arts. Purchaser has permission to photocopy this page for classroom use only.

Apostrophe Review

Directions: Insert apostrophes where needed.

Who took Toms coat while we were gone? Sams team just barely lost the game. The little girls doll is very pretty. The birds nest

fell out of the tree. The girls flowers are very pretty. The campers tent was torn by the bear. The childrens toys had to be put

away. The witchs broom was stolen. That coat is yours. The babys toys were all over the room. Johns mother left too early. Its

too late for us to go to school. The coat I had on was hers. The cats were fighting all night. Did you see Anas new car? Marys

coat was torn. Her friends call every night. Whos talking about us? We went to Pedros party yesterday. Jack is here with Bills

sister. We went to the movies. Was Chiens father at the game? Marys friends came home with us. I lost Keeshas dime. How

many letters can you write in a minute? It was the lions turn to roar. That ball belongs to the puppies. It is the puppys ball.

Fathers new car is in the driveway. It is the girls turn to stay home and wash dishes. The ladys dress was torn. Marys brother

ran home faster than the others. My brothers wife called me. Those are Joses new clothes. He left them with his friends. Meis

house looks beautiful. Its our turn to buy Toms lunch. Marias mother went on a long vacation. She wants Susans sister to go

with her. After school we will go to Ebonys house. Its not fair if she cant go. Matts hat fell off and got smashed. That ball is

ours. Do you know if it is yours or not? The nurses work in the hospital. The turtles house isnt very big. The cat ate the dogs

dinner. The ducks waddled to the pond. We left to buy the ducks food. The teachers class was fun all the time. Her students

really enjoyed themselves. It will be fun to see Jims friends. We had a good time at Marios party. It was the teams last chance

to play together. Do you know if that is Rays house? We drove by to see if Jims friends were there. Tonight is Tyrells last game.

Practicing Basic Skills in Language Arts • 399

© 2005 Sopris West Educational Services. All rights reserved. Practicing Basic Skills in Language Arts. Purchaser has permission to photocopy this page for classroom use only.

SEE TO WRITE

Apostrophe Review

Directions: Insert apostrophes where needed.

	Correct	Error
First Try		
Second Try		

Who took Tom's coat while we were gone? Sam's team just barely lost the game. The little girl's doll is very pretty. The bird's nest (4)

fell out of the tree. The girl's flowers are very pretty. The camper's tent was torn by the bear. The children's toys had to be put (7)

away. The witch's broom was stolen. That coat is yours. The baby's toys were all over the room. John's mother left too early. It's (11)

too late for us to go to school. The coat I had on was hers. The cats were fighting all night. Did you see Ana's new car? Mary's (13)

coat was torn. Her friends call every night. Who's talking about us? We went to Pedro's party yesterday. Jack is here with Bill's (16)

sister. We went to the movies. Was Chien's father at the game? Mary's friends came home with us. I lost Keesha's dime. How (19)

many letters can you write in a minute? It was the lion's turn to roar. That ball belongs to the puppies. It is the puppy's ball. (21)

Father's new car is in the driveway. It is the girls' turn to stay home and wash dishes. The lady's dress was torn. Mary's brother (25)

ran home faster than the others. My brother's wife called me. Those are Jose's new clothes. He left them with his friends. Mei's (28)

house looks beautiful. It's our turn to buy Tom's lunch. Maria's mother went on a long vacation. She wants Susan's sister to go (32)

with her. After school we will go to Ebony's house. It's not fair if she can't go. Matt's hat fell off and got smashed. That ball is (35)

ours. Do you know if it is yours or not? The nurses work in the hospital. The turtle's house isn't very big. The cat ate the dog's (38)

dinner. The ducks waddled to the pond. We left to buy the duck's food. The teacher's class was fun all the time. Her students (40)

really enjoyed themselves. It will be fun to see Jim's friends. We had a good time at Mario's party. It was the teams' last chance (43)

to play together. Do you know if that is Ray's house? We drove by to see if Jim's friends were there. Tonight is Tyrell's last game. (46)

ANSWER SHEET

Practicing Basic Skills in Language Arts • 400

© 2005 Sopris West Educational Services. All rights reserved. Practicing Basic Skills in Language Arts. Purchaser has permission to photocopy this page for classroom use only.

ONE-MINUTE FLUENCY BUILDER SERIES

SEE TO WRITE

Apostrophe Review
Directions: Insert apostrophes where needed.

	Correct	Error
First Try		
Second Try		

Our fathers cars are black. The boys ran across the lawn. The teachers are having a meeting today. The pencil is on that boys desk. My teachers name isnt Mrs. Avila. My fathers coat wasnt stolen. The boys played tennis with Austins father. The puppys bowl turned over. The two puppies wagged their tails faster than Ive ever seen. The mens band played loudly. The childrens party ended earlier than Claudes did. The boys ran past Mrs. Bellinos house. This is Jesss book. We put the babies bottles on the floor. This is Dales lunch box. The birds feathers werent red. Antonios best friend was Glendas brother. The girls dresses were shades of blue. Marks car isnt broken down yet. We cant go home today. Isnt that my brothers car? He is using Carolyns pencil. Galens friend wouldnt eat lunch with us. We will have the childrens party today. Lets go to Mr. Quintanas house again tomorrow. Victors class got lost even after wed told them the way to go home. Our neighbors name is Mr. Malcom Chavez. Its 2 oclock and Ive already missed most of school. I let my sisters dog out of her yard. I broke my mothers favorite vase. My mothers going to be mad at me. Its recess time at 3 oclock. Lets go outside with Melissas friends. Its almost time to go to Guss house. Doreenas aunt isnt going home tomorrow. Itll be noon before I can call Annas house. Whatll I tell Guss mother? The schools new name is Central. My teachers name hasnt been changed. Claudettes sister told me to call her mother. Its almost time to go to Adenas house. If itll help, Ill pick you up. Floras new car is beautiful. Whats your friends telephone number? Why dont you write a whole page of ws? If it isnt right, youll have to do it again. After weve gone, please call Rustys mother. The dog hurt itself on the neighbors fence. My new friends name is Amos. Evelyns dog ran through the neighbors yard. It isnt time to leave school yet.

© 2005 Sopris West Educational Services. All rights reserved. Practicing Basic Skills in Language Arts. Purchaser has permission to photocopy this page for classroom use only.

ONE MINUTE FLUENCY
BUILDER SERIES

SEE TO WRITE

Apostrophe Review

Directions: Insert apostrophes where needed.

	First Try	Second Try
Correct		
Error		

Our father's cars are black. The boys ran across the lawn. The teachers are having a meeting today. The pencil is on that boy's (2)

desk. My teacher's name isn't Mrs. Avila. My father's coat wasn't stolen. The boys played tennis with Austin's father. The puppy's (8)

bowl turned over. The two puppies wagged their tails faster than I've ever seen. The men's band played loudly. The children's (11)

party ended earlier than Claude's did. The boys ran past Mrs. Bellino's house. This is Jess's book. We put the babies' bottles on (15)

the floor. This is Dale's lunch box. The bird's feathers weren't red. Antonio's best friend was Glenda's brother. The girls' dresses (21)

were shades of blue. Mark's car isn't broken down yet. We can't go home today. Isn't that my brother's car? He is using Carolyn's (27)

pencil. Galen's friend wouldn't eat lunch with us. We will have the children's party today. Let's go to Mr. Quintana's house (32)

again tomorrow. Victor's class got lost even after we'd told them the way to go home. Our neighbor's name is Mr. Malcom (35)

Chavez. It's 2 o'clock and I've already missed most of school. I let my sister's dog out of her yard. I broke my mother's favorite (40)

vase. My mother's going to be mad at me. It's recess time at 3 o'clock. Let's go outside with Melissa's friends. It's almost time (46)

to go to Gus's house. Doreena's aunt isn't going home tomorrow. It'll be noon before I can call Anna's house. What'll I tell (52)

Gus's mother? The school's new name is Central. My teacher's name hasn't been changed. Claudette's sister told me to call her (57)

mother. It's almost time to go to Adena's house. If it'll help, I'll pick you up. Flora's new car is beautiful. What's your friend's (64)

telephone number? Why don't you write a whole page of w's? If it isn't right, you'll have to do it again. After we've gone, please (69)

call Rusty's mother. The dog hurt itself on the neighbor's fence. My new friend's name is Amos. Evelyn's dog ran through the (73)

neighbor's yard. It isn't time to leave school yet. (75)

ANSWER SHEET

Practicing Basic Skills in Language Arts • 402

© 2005 Sopris West Educational Services. All rights reserved. Practicing Basic Skills in Language Arts. Purchaser has permission to photocopy this page for classroom use only.

Semicolons Between Independent Clauses

Directions: Place semicolons where they are needed in the following sentences.

I must leave now I am expected home. You have worked hard you may have a vacation. The train from Chicago was due at

7:22 it is an hour late. I waited an hour for Ed he did not come. I like potatoes but I prefer rice. Give me the list I'll try to

check the names. I often stay alone I am not afraid. The fire siren blew and I ran to the window. The room grew dark no one

suggested turning on the lights. I prefer quiz shows on television Father likes the mini-series Mother enjoys comedies. Joe

reads only nonfiction, but I prefer fiction. We had to think quickly there was little time. The wind blew fiercely and the rain

spattered against the window. I had a terrible nightmare I dreamed I was in a car accident. Elena is a fine student she has a 3.9

GPA. Jason wrote Uncle Walt a letter he did not answer. Lily had a good report card her father rewarded her. Michael did not

speak clearly no one understood him. The play ended and the audience applauded wildly. Ida understood the lesson but she

could not apply it. I had not done my homework I was not prepared. It is no use crying I cannot help you. You may go now

be careful. The doorbell rang no one answered. The plane crashed its three occupants were all right. I read a dozen short stories

and three novels last week. We returned from the store empty-handed the prices were outrageous. Fred is a junior in high

school and his sister is a freshman in college.

© 2005 Sopris West Educational Services. All rights reserved. Practicing Basic Skills in Language Arts. Purchaser has permission to photocopy this page for classroom use only.

ONE-MINUTE FLUENCY BUILDER SERIES

SEE TO WRITE

Semicolons Between Independent Clauses

Directions: Place semicolons where they are needed in the following sentences.

	Correct	Error
First Try		
Second Try		

I must leave now; I am expected home. You have worked hard; you may have a vacation. The train from Chicago was due at (2)

7:22; it is an hour late. I waited an hour for Ed; he did not come. I like potatoes but I prefer rice. Give me the list; I'll try to (5)

check the names. I often stay alone; I am not afraid. The fire siren blew and I ran to the window. The room grew dark; no one (7)

suggested turning on the lights. I prefer quiz shows on television; Father likes the mini-series; Mother enjoys comedies. Joe (9)

reads only nonfiction, but I prefer fiction. We had to think quickly; there was little time. The wind blew fiercely and the rain (10)

spattered against the window. I had a terrible nightmare; I dreamed I was in a car accident. Elena is a fine student; she has a 3.9 (12)

GPA. Jason wrote Uncle Walt a letter; he did not answer. Lily had a good report card; her father rewarded her. Michael did not (14)

speak clearly; no one understood him. The play ended and the audience applauded wildly. Ida understood the lesson but she (15)

could not apply it. I had not done my homework; I was not prepared. It is no use crying; I cannot help you. You may go now; (18)

be careful. The doorbell rang; no one answered. The plane crashed; its three occupants were all right. I read a dozen short stories (20)

and three novels last week. We returned from the store empty-handed; the prices were outrageous. Fred is a junior in high (21)

school and his sister is a freshman in college. (21)

ANSWER SHEET

Practicing Basic Skills in Language Arts • 404

© 2005 Sopris West Educational Services. All rights reserved. Practicing Basic Skills in Language Arts. Purchaser has permission to photocopy this page for classroom use only.

ONE-MINUTE FLUENCY
BUILDER SERIES

Semicolons Between Independent Clauses Joined by Adverbial Connectives

Directions: Mark semicolons where needed.

	Correct	Error
First Try		
Second Try		

The door was locked however, the windows were open. The weather improved therefore, we changed our plans. I am short of

cash besides, the store is closed. I read the letter that Stan had written. English is required therefore, the student had no choice.

You may go now but be careful. A terrible accident occurred nevertheless, the race went on. The floodwaters were still rising

therefore, the town had to be evacuated. A dog may obey its master however, it also has a mind of its own. I haven't seen her

lately in fact, I saw her last three weeks ago. They knew the road was dangerous furthermore, they were driving an old car.

I went to the party however, I didn't have a good time. We left early nevertheless, we arrived late. Ida has many interesting

hobbies for example, she collects Indian artifacts. It was a windy afternoon otherwise, the garden party would have been a

success. I saw my math teacher and I said hello. Jack never attended class consequently, his grades were terrible. I cannot attend

the convention this weekend moreover, I will not be available next week either. The Pioneers are the best team in the league

that is, they have the best record. An example of a comedy show is *Everybody Loves Raymond*. I did not finish the job because I was

tired besides, it was raining. David attended a private school in New York last semester. We rushed to the box office however, the

concert was sold out. I know Jim well in fact, he is my best friend. The chairman is ill therefore, the meeting is postponed.

© 2005 Sopris West Educational Services. All rights reserved. Practicing Basic Skills in Language Arts. Purchaser has permission to photocopy this page for classroom use only.

SEE TO WRITE

Semicolons Between Independent Clauses Joined by Adverbial Connectives

Directions: Mark semicolons where needed.

	First Try	Second Try
Correct		
Error		

The door was locked; however, the windows were open. The weather improved; therefore, we changed our plans. I am short of (2)

cash; besides, the store is closed. I read the letter that Stan had written. English is required; therefore, the student had no choice. (4)

You may go now but be careful. A terrible accident occurred; nevertheless, the race went on. The floodwaters were still rising; (6)

therefore, the town had to be evacuated. A dog may obey its master; however, it also has a mind of its own. I haven't seen her (7)

lately; in fact, I saw her last three weeks ago. They knew the road was dangerous; furthermore, they were driving an old car. (9)

I went to the party; however, I didn't have a good time. We left early; nevertheless, we arrived late. Ida has many interesting (11)

hobbies; for example, she collects Indian artifacts. It was a windy afternoon; otherwise, the garden party would have been a (13)

success. I saw my math teacher and I said hello. Jack never attended class; consequently, his grades were terrible. I cannot attend (14)

the convention this weekend; moreover, I will not be available next week either. The Pioneers are the best team in the league; (16)

that is, they have the best record. An example of a comedy show is *Everybody Loves Raymond*. I did not finish the job because I was (16)

tired; besides, it was raining. David attended a private school in New York last semester. We rushed to the box office; however, the (18)

concert was sold out. I know Jim well; in fact, he is my best friend. The chairman is ill; therefore, the meeting is postponed. (20)

Practicing Basic Skills in Language Arts • 406

ANSWER SHEET

© 2005 Sopris West Educational Services. All rights reserved. Practicing Basic Skills in Language Arts. Purchaser has permission to photocopy this page for classroom use only.

ONE-MINUTE FLUENCY BUILDER SERIES

SEE TO WRITE

Semicolons in Items in a Series

Directions: Place semicolons where they are needed in the following sentences.

We talked about Frances, my sister Dolly, her friend Rover, her dog and Nip, her cat. Her cats include Martha, a Persian

Lulu, a Siamese and Sam, an alley cat. In the morning, we played tennis, my favorite sport baseball, which I can't stand and

basketball. Three other people were in the car with him: Elinor, his older sister Jim, a cousin from Georgia and Albert, his

best friend. On our trip we visited Denver, Colorado Omaha, Nebraska and Chicago, Illinois. Grandfather ordered roast beef,

potatoes, and vegetables. Three important dates in John's life are September 15, 1949 October 4, 1959 and March 27, 1967.

Alan's family includes his father, a carpenter his mother, a teacher and his two sisters, college students. My favorite colors are

orange, yellow, and brown. I enjoyed dinner because we ate steak, my favorite meat wild rice, an unusual treat and my favorite

vegetable, rutabagas. After the accident they all reported their injuries: Tom, a broken leg Jan, a sprained back and Ellen, a

fractured wrist. Albertson's has stores in Ogden, Utah Rock Springs, Wyoming and Elko, Nevada. My best friends are Emmy, a

student in college Jana, my next door neighbor and Marti, a girl I work with. I read *Tom Sawyer, The Prince and the Pauper,* and

Huckleberry Finn. Tony is baking chocolate cake, cupcakes, and applesauce cookies I am furnishing punch and plates.

Practicing Basic Skills in Language Arts • 407

© 2005 Sopris West Educational Services. All rights reserved. Practicing Basic Skills in Language Arts. Purchaser has permission to photocopy this page for classroom use only.

ONE-MINUTE FLUENCY BUILDER SERIES

	Correct	Error
First Try		
Second Try		

SEE TO WRITE

Semicolons in Items in a Series

Directions: Place semicolons where they are needed in the following sentences.

We talked about Frances, my sister; Dolly, her friend; Rover, her dog; and Nip, her cat. Her cats include Martha, a Persian; (4)

Lulu, a Siamese; and Sam, an alley cat. In the morning, we played tennis, my favorite sport; baseball, which I can't stand; and (7)

basketball. Three other people were in the car with him: Elinor, his older sister; Jim, a cousin from Georgia; and Albert, his (9)

best friend. On our trip we visited Denver, Colorado; Omaha, Nebraska; and Chicago, Illinois. Grandfather ordered roast beef, (11)

potatoes, and vegetables. Three important dates in John's life are September 15, 1949; October 4, 1959; and March 27, 1967. (13)

Alan's family includes his father, a carpenter; his mother, a teacher; and his two sisters, college students. My favorite colors are (15)

orange, yellow, and brown. I enjoyed dinner because we ate steak, my favorite meat; wild rice, an unusual treat; and my favorite (17)

vegetable, rutabagas. After the accident they all reported their injuries: Tom, a broken leg; Jan, a sprained back; and Ellen, a (19)

fractured wrist. Albertson's has stores in Ogden, Utah; Rock Springs, Wyoming; and Elko, Nevada. My best friends are Emmy, a (21)

student in college; Jana, my next door neighbor; and Marti, a girl I work with. I read *Tom Sawyer*, *The Prince and the Pauper*, and (23)

Huckleberry Finn. Tony is baking chocolate cake, cupcakes, and applesauce cookies; I am furnishing punch and plates. (24)

ANSWER SHEET

Practicing Basic Skills in Language Arts • 408

© 2005 Sopris West Educational Services. All rights reserved. Practicing Basic Skills in Language Arts. Purchaser has permission to photocopy this page for classroom use only.

ONE MINUTE FLUENCY
BUILDER SERIES

Correct	Error
First Try	
Second Try	

SEE TO WRITE

Semicolon Review

Directions: Place semicolons where they are needed in the following sentences.

I like guitars electric guitars, however, are another matter. Buy either car, for they are both good cars. My dentist says not to eat so much candy it causes tooth decay. The people we met in St. Croix came from Washington New Paltz, New York and Buenos Aires, Argentina. The moon was a quarter full, and its beams sparkled on the water. Dr. Dawson prefers golf his wife, swimming and his daughters, tennis. Harry has been on the force for twenty years he is almost ready to retire. He is kind he is generous he is wise. I do not play a tuba I do not wish to learn. The river is deep and swift its banks are steep and rocky. For Christmas, I got a radio Keiko, a coat and Marcos, a new suit. Buy either car they are both good. The men at the South Pole rarely got mail, but they could talk to their families by radio. I often stay alone I am not afraid. Lamar is not here, but his brother is. Our opponents had a big lead at halftime we won the game, anyway. We shouted over and over no one answered no one came. Wait for me at the station I'll join you and Pam there. Pablo has no fear, or he would be pacing the floor. Eve was surrounded by notebooks, encyclopedias, and dictionaries but she was reading a letter from Bill. The moon was a quarter full its beams sparkled on the water. I can't go with you ask Tyrell. We have a factory in Salem, Ohio an office in Buffalo, New York and a mill in Andover, Massachusetts. Jay and I will meet you at the train and then drive you to the hotel. Do not eat those apples you will have indigestion. The electricity was off for three hours consequently, everything in the refrigerator was spoiled. Some people enjoy pets others can live without them. At the bottom of the slope, a doctor took care of Mr. Low's sprained ankle his sister, of his skis and his wife, of his hurt feelings. The climate on the island was consistently sunny, dry, and warm, but Kate was afraid it might become monotonous. Kwan is doing very well in fact, she has a B average. Janet did as she was told however, she grumbled ungraciously. She will invite Irene, Lucia, and Enice Graham will ask Nisha and Val. The examinations will be held on Wednesday, June 26 Thursday, June 27 and Friday, June 28. Glenda made a basket just before the final buzzer of the game we won by a score of 78-76.

Practicing Basic Skills in Language Arts • 409

© 2005 Sopris West Educational Services. All rights reserved. Practicing Basic Skills in Language Arts. Purchaser has permission to photocopy this page for classroom use only.

ONE-MINUTE FLUENCY
BUILDER SERIES

SEE TO WRITE

Semicolon Review

Directions: Place semicolons where they are needed in the following sentences.

(1) I like guitars; electric guitars, however, are another matter. Buy either car, for they are both good cars. My dentist says not to eat

(4) so much candy; it causes tooth decay. The people we met in St. Croix came from Washington; New Paltz, New York; and Buenos

(6) Aires, Argentina. The moon was a quarter full, and its beams sparkled on the water. Dr. Dawson prefers golf; his wife, swimming;

(9) and his daughters, tennis. Harry has been on the force for twenty years; he is almost ready to retire. He is kind; he is generous;

(11) he is wise. I do not play a tuba; I do not wish to learn. The river is deep and swift; its banks are steep and rocky. For Christmas,

(14) I got a radio; Keiko, a coat; and Marcos, a new suit. Buy either car; they are both good. The men at the South Pole rarely got

(15) mail, but they could talk to their families by radio. I often stay alone; I am not afraid. Lamar is not here, but his brother is. Our

(18) opponents had a big lead at halftime; we won the game, anyway. We shouted over and over; no one answered; no one came.

(19) Wait for me at the station; I'll join you and Pam there. Pablo has no fear, or he would be pacing the floor. Eve was surrounded

(21) by notebooks, encyclopedias, and dictionaries; but she was reading a letter from Bill. The moon was a quarter full; its beams

(24) sparkled on the water. I can't go with you; ask Tyrell. We have a factory in Salem, Ohio; an office in Buffalo, New York; and a

(25) mill in Andover, Massachusetts. Jay and I will meet you at the train and then drive you to the hotel. Do not eat those apples;

(26) you will have indigestion. The electricity was off for three hours; consequently, everything in the refrigerator was spoiled. Some

(28) people enjoy pets; others can live without them. At the bottom of the slope, a doctor took care of Mr. Low's sprained ankle;

(29) his sister, of his skis; and his wife, of his hurt feelings. The climate on the island was consistently sunny, dry, and warm, but

(31) Kate was afraid it might become monotonous. Kwan is doing very well; in fact, she has a B average. Janet did as she was told;

(32) however, she grumbled ungraciously. She will invite Irene, Lucia, and Enice; Graham will ask Nisha and Val. The examinations

(34) will be held on Wednesday, June 26; Thursday, June 27; and Friday, June 28. Glenda made a basket just before the final buzzer of

(35) the game; we won by a score of 78-76.

© 2005 Sopris West Educational Services. All rights reserved. Practicing Basic Skills in Language Arts. Purchaser has permission to photocopy this page for classroom use only.

SEE TO WRITE

ONE-MINUTE FLUENCY BUILDER SERIES

Colons for Time and Salutations

Directions: Insert a colon in times of day, and after the salutation in a business letter.

	Correct	Error
First Try		
Second Try		

The game will start at 3 30 P.M. Gentlemen The train arrived at 3 45 P.M. Dear Sirs Dear Mr. Cyrus Our guests are arriving on

the 7 15 A.M. flight. Dear Doctor Jennings Dear Madam Come to the party at 6 00 P.M. Dear Mrs. Gomez It was 2 30 when

the minister closed the lesson. Dear Mrs. Wilson From 4 00 until 5 30 I lay awake in my room. To Whom It May Concern Dear

Mr. Casson At the tone the time will be 9 25 A.M. He arrived at the depot with his wife at 6 45 P.M. To the Manager Do not

come any later than 3 00 or you will miss the opening. Dear Department Heads At 11 02 we were on the history lesson and we

wanted to finish geometry by 12 00. There are not many who will make it to school before 7 30 A.M. Dear Miss Kendall Dear

Sir The time was 9 22 when he left for work. We have lunch at our school at 12 05. Dear Ms. Greene At 11 00 we will begin our

lesson. Dear Mayor Tong You must arrive at your destination at 6 00 exactly or you will miss your connection at 6 10. Dear Mrs.

Corning Please begin your talk at 12 00. The swimming lesson will begin at 1 30 P.M. and end at 2 15 P.M. Please do not be late

to the 12 30 appointment as I have another scheduled at 1 20. I will conclude my comments today at 1 30 P.M. The only time

left open for your haircut was 5 15 today. Dear Mr. President To All Department Managers Dear Ms. Kane

© 2005 Sopris West Educational Services. All rights reserved. Practicing Basic Skills in Language Arts. Purchaser has permission to photocopy this page for classroom use only.

SEE TO WRITE

Colons for Time and Salutations

Directions: Insert a colon in times of day, and after the salutation in a business letter.

	First Try	Second Try
Correct		
Error		

The game will start at 3:30 P.M. Gentlemen: The train arrived at 3:45 P.M. Dear Sirs: Dear Mr. Cyrus: Our guests are arriving on (5)

the 7:15 A.M. flight. Dear Doctor Jennings: Dear Madam: Come to the party at 6:00 P.M. Dear Mrs. Gomez: It was 2:30 when (11)

the minister closed the lesson. Dear Mrs. Wilson: From 4:00 until 5:30 I lay awake in my room. To Whom It May Concern: Dear (15)

Mr. Casson: At the tone the time will be 9:25 A.M. He arrived at the depot with his wife at 6:45 P.M. To the Manager: Do not (19)

come any later than 3:00 or you will miss the opening. Dear Department Heads: At 11:02 we were on the history lesson and we (22)

wanted to finish geometry by 12:00. There are not many who will make it to school before 7:30 A.M. Dear Miss Kendall: Dear (25)

Sir: The time was 9:22 when he left for work. We have lunch at our school at 12:05. Dear Ms. Greene: At 11:00 we will begin our (30)

lesson. Dear Mayor Tong: You must arrive at your destination at 6:00 exactly or you will miss your connection at 6:10. Dear Mrs. (33)

Corning: Please begin your talk at 12:00. The swimming lesson will begin at 1:30 P.M. and end at 2:15 P.M. Please do not be late (37)

to the 12:30 appointment as I have another scheduled at 1:20. I will conclude my comments today at 1:30 P.M. The only time (40)

left open for your haircut was 5:15 today. Dear Mr. President: To All Department Managers: Dear Ms. Kane: (44)

ANSWER SHEET

Practicing Basic Skills in Language Arts • 412

© 2005 Sopris West Educational Services. All rights reserved. Practicing Basic Skills in Language Arts. Purchaser has permission to photocopy this page for classroom use only.

ONE-MINUTE FLUENCY
BUILDER SERIES

	First Try	Second Try
Correct		
Error		

Colon Review

Directions: Insert a colon before the lists in the following sentences; omit the colon after a verb or preposition.

Mother needed three things flour, baking soda, and butter. In the truck were these things a stepladder, a can of paint, and a brush. There were three books on the table a history book, a mathematics book, and a dictionary. Get me these books from the shelf the English book, the history book, and the mathematics book. My favorite sports are tennis, jogging, and golf. I have two hobbies that I enjoy stamp collecting and hunting. The equipment you will need for the trip is as follows sleeping bag, food, knife, and water. He had lived in the three largest states Texas, Alaska, and California. The following boys were at the dance Greg, Akira, Malik, and Lee. He was active in many sports football, track, baseball, and basketball. That summer we traveled through Arkansas and Louisiana. On our camping trip we visited the following parks Yosemite, Yellowstone, and Death Valley. I am a hospital volunteer three times per week Tuesday, Wednesday, and Saturday. I have read the following books *Robinson Crusoe*, *Call of the Wild*, and *Treasure Island*. My grocery list included the following milk, butter, eggs, and bread. Our club has four aims to encourage friendship, to entertain, to give experience in acting, and to provide programs for our school. The finalists in the baking contest are Franco, Abby, and Desiree. I usually go fishing with Seth, Ivan, and Mark. For the party we need the following things pretzels, Coke, cheese, and chips. This year we shall cover the units as follows study of the universe, study of the Earth, and study of the life on Earth. That summer we visited Grandmother, Aunt Vivian, and Cousin Erik. We need to keep the following items pencils, papers, ink, and rulers. There were sandwiches, cold drinks, and candy bars in the refrigerator. There are two people in this school that I really respect Mr. Quintana and Mrs. Wolford. We had three kinds of fruit for lunch oranges, apples, and pears.

© 2005 Sopris West Educational Services. All rights reserved. Practicing Basic Skills in Language Arts. Purchaser has permission to photocopy this page for classroom use only.

ONE MINUTE FLUENCY BUILDER SERIES

SEE TO WRITE

Colon Review

Directions: Insert a colon before the lists in the following sentences; omit the colon after a verb or preposition.

	First Try	Second Try
Correct		
Error		

Mother needed three things: flour, baking soda, and butter. In the truck were these things: a stepladder, a can of paint, and a (2)

brush. There were three books on the table: a history book, a mathematics book, and a dictionary. Get me these books from the (3)

shelf: the English book, the history book, and the mathematics book. My favorite sports are tennis, jogging, and golf. I have two (4)

hobbies that I enjoy: stamp collecting and hunting. The equipment you will need for the trip is as follows: sleeping bag, food, (6)

knife, and water. He had lived in the three largest states: Texas, Alaska, and California. The following boys were at the dance: (8)

Greg, Akira, Malik, and Lee. He was active in many sports: football, track, baseball, and basketball. That summer we traveled (9)

through Arkansas and Louisiana. On our camping trip we visited the following parks: Yosemite, Yellowstone, and Death Valley. (10)

I am a hospital volunteer three times per week: Tuesday, Wednesday, and Saturday. I have read the following books: *Robinson* (12)

Crusoe, Call of the Wild, and *Treasure Island.* My grocery list included the following: milk, butter, eggs, and bread. Our club has (13)

four aims: to encourage friendship, to entertain, to give experience in acting, and to provide programs for our school. The (14)

finalists in the baking contest are Franco, Abby, and Desiree. I usually go fishing with Seth, Ivan, and Mark. For the party we (14)

need the following things: pretzels, Coke, cheese, and chips. This year we shall cover the units as follows: study of the universe, (16)

study of the Earth, and study of the life on Earth. That summer we visited Grandmother, Aunt Vivian, and Cousin Erik. We (16)

need to keep the following items: pencils, papers, ink, and rulers. There were sandwiches, cold drinks, and candy bars in the (17)

refrigerator. There are two people in this school that I really respect: Mr. Quintana and Mrs. Wolford. We had three kinds of fruit (18)

for lunch: oranges, apples, and pears. (19)

ANSWER SHEET

Practicing Basic Skills in Language Arts • 414

© 2005 Sopris West Educational Services. All rights reserved. Practicing Basic Skills in Language Arts. Purchaser has permission to photocopy this page for classroom use only.

SEE TO WRITE

Quotation Marks in Conversation

Directions: Insert quotation marks to set off direct conversation.

	First Try	Second Try
Correct		
Error		

You just started that book, I said, and you're already reading the last page. That's how I always read mystery stories,

she said. Why? I asked with interest. It's much more fun reading a mystery when you have some idea of who's guilty, she

explained, and I never can figure it out by myself. If I don't sneak a look at the ending, all through the book I'm under

the strain of trying to guess. When we asked him, he said, There will be no charge. Uncle Jason looked up and said, Stop

behaving like a child. A voice in the dark asked, Where are my boots? Then he shouted, Get off that thin ice! Do you

remember the old man's expression when he said, I never learned to read? I was unable to remember anything after Friends,

Romans, countrymen. Did you hear him shout, What's going on here? With all our hearts let us cry, Justice for all! The

officer said, No one is to leave this room. Have we missed the train? Lester asked. The story is utterly false! shouted

Harry. The imposter even said, You are trespassing in my house! He inquired, Are you hungry? I quickly replied, Yes, I'm

so hungry I could eat dog food. Well, said mother, don't be late for dinner. Play the game fairly, said the coach, and

I'll be proud of you. The child's father asked, What is it, doctor? I think, the doctor answered, that it is not serious. I

will be there as soon as I can, said Ms. Young. The test was hard, said Sue.

Practicing Basic Skills in Language Arts • 415

© 2005 Sopris West Educational Services. All rights reserved. Practicing Basic Skills in Language Arts. Purchaser has permission to photocopy this page for classroom use only.

SEE TO WRITE

Quotation Marks in Conversation

Directions: Insert quotation marks to set off direct conversation.

	First Try	Second Try
Correct		
Error		

"You just started that book," I said, "and you're already reading the last page." "That's how I always read mystery stories," (6)

she said. "Why?" I asked with interest. "It's much more fun reading a mystery when you have some idea of who's guilty," she (10)

explained, "and I never can figure it out by myself. If I don't sneak a look at the ending, all through the book I'm under (11)

the strain of trying to guess." When we asked him, he said, "There will be no charge." Uncle Jason looked up and said, "Stop (15)

behaving like a child." A voice in the dark asked, "Where are my boots?" Then he shouted, "Get off that thin ice!" Do you (20)

remember the old man's expression when he said, "I never learned to read"? I was unable to remember anything after "Friends, (23)

Romans, countrymen." Did you hear him shout, "What's going on here?" With all our hearts let us cry, "Justice for all!" The (28)

officer said, "No one is to leave this room." "Have we missed the train?" Lester asked. "The story is utterly false!" shouted (34)

Harry. The imposter even said, "You are trespassing in my house!" He inquired, "Are you hungry?" I quickly replied, "Yes, I'm (39)

so hungry I could eat dog food." "Well," said mother, "don't be late for dinner." "Play the game fairly," said the coach, "and (47)

I'll be proud of you." The child's father asked, "What is it, doctor?" "I think," the doctor answered, "that it is not serious." "I (55)

will be there as soon as I can," said Ms. Young. "The test was hard," said Sue. (58)

© 2005 Sopris West Educational Services. All rights reserved. Practicing Basic Skills in Language Arts. Purchaser has permission to photocopy this page for classroom use only.

ONE-MINUTE FLUENCY BUILDER SERIES

SEE TO WRITE

Quotation Marks to Enclose Titles

Directions: Insert quotation marks where needed.

Who sang Say It With Music? The essay Self-Reliance is by Emerson. I called my poem Time Out. DaVinci painted *The Last Supper*. The title of Anne's theme is Discounts Can Fool You. For tomorrow Miss Jolly assigned two chapters from *The Scarlet Letter*: The Interview and Hester at Her Needle. The song Seventy-Six Trombones is from *The Music Man*. You can find Frost's Mending Wall in your textbook. Would you call Poe's The Tell-Tale Heart a Gothic mystery story? There is an interesting article entitled The Road to Westport in this months *Digest*. The Scarlet Ibis is one of the first stories we read in the ninth grade. I have just finished reading the chapter Getting Your Driver's License. Last night I read Happy Times in the *Saturday Evening Post*. Alice's magazine has an article entitled The Plight of the Boat People. Billie Jean King wrote an article, Straight Talk, for a magazine. I have just read Bert Harte's short story The Outcasts of Poker Flat. The editorial in tonight's paper is entitled Space Shuttle. Review Chapter 22, Italics and Quotation Marks. After reading Dickens's *A Christmas Carol*, I wrote an essay entitled Scrooge Sees Ghosts.

	Correct	Error
First Try		
Second Try		

© 2005 Sopris West Educational Services. All rights reserved. Practicing Basic Skills in Language Arts. Purchaser has permission to photocopy this page for classroom use only.

SEE TO WRITE

Quotation Marks to Enclose Titles

Directions: Insert quotation marks where needed.

	First Try	Second Try
Correct		
Error		

Who sang "Say It With Music"? The essay "Self-Reliance" is by Emerson. I called my poem "Time Out." DaVinci painted *The* (6)

Last Supper. The title of Anne's theme is "Discounts Can Fool You." For tomorrow Miss Jolly assigned two chapters from *The* (8)

Scarlet Letter: "The Interview" and "Hester at Her Needle." The song "Seventy-Six Trombones" is from *The Music Man.* You can (14)

find Frost's "Mending Wall" in your textbook. Would you call Poe's "The Tell-Tale Heart" a Gothic mystery story? There is an (18)

interesting article entitled "The Road to Westport" in this months *Digest.* "The Scarlet Ibis" is one of the first stories we read in (22)

the ninth grade. I have just finished reading the chapter "Getting Your Driver's License." Last night I read "Happy Times" in the (26)

Saturday Evening Post. Alice's magazine has an article entitled "The Plight of the Boat People." Billie Jean King wrote an article, (28)

"Straight Talk," for a magazine. I have just read Bert Harte's short story "The Outcasts of Poker Flat." The editorial in tonight's (32)

paper is entitled "Space Shuttle." Review Chapter 22, "Italics and Quotation Marks." After reading Dickens's *A Christmas* (36)

Carol, I wrote an essay entitled "Scrooge Sees Ghosts." (38)

ANSWER SHEET

Practicing Basic Skills in Language Arts • 418

 © 2005 Sopris West Educational Services. All rights reserved. Practicing Basic Skills in Language Arts. Purchaser has permission to photocopy this page for classroom use only.

SEE TO WRITE

Quotation Marks Within a Quotation
Directions: Insert correct quotation marks.

	First Try	Second Try
Correct		
Error		

Have you read The Most Dangerous Game? asked Lou. I heard someone say, Is he hungry? stated Andy. I heard him ask,

Why? replied Greg. I could not definitely understand, but I think he shouted. Wow! answered Gina. David said, That

poem by Keats begins A thing of beauty is a joy forever. The Caribbean resort we visited, Kathy said, is called a very private

paradise. Who wrote the short story Murder in the Rue Morgue? Rex asked. Tony replied, I am sure the officer said, Come

ahead! Wee Willie Winkie by Rudyard Kipling is a short story that might interest you, said Mrs. Yost. Sheila said, Ralph ran

in and shouted, They just scored another run! Mrs. Tanner asked, How many have read Chekhov's story The Last Brooch?

Her answer was, Yes, I'll go, said Delores. Do you, asked Sofia, know the tune to The Lonesome Loser? The poem

Now You Know was written by my brother-in-law, said Eva. These new songs don't live long. They are not like Stardust and

Dancing in the Dark, said Mr. Coleman. Mother stated emphatically, You may not wear jeans! replied Jackie. The novel

Ivanhoe is by Sir Walter Scott, corrected Lee, The poem Trees is by Joyce Kilmer. Rosela reported, Phil had trouble saying

There is where their wares are sold. I thought he was saying, Stand aside and let the passengers off, Reuben replied. Roy

exploded, You heard him say, There will be no more free passes.

© 2005 Sopris West Educational Services. All rights reserved. Practicing Basic Skills in Language Arts. Purchaser has permission to photocopy this page for classroom use only.

SEE TO WRITE

Quotation Marks Within a Quotation

Directions: Insert correct quotation marks.

	First Try	Second Try
Correct		
Error		

"Have you read The Most Dangerous Game'?" asked Lou. "I heard him ask, (9)

"I heard someone say, 'Is he hungry?" stated Andy. (17)

"Why?" replied Greg. "I could not definitely understand, but I think he shouted. 'Wow!" answered Gina. David said, "That (24)

poem by Keats begins 'A thing of beauty is a joy forever.'" "The Caribbean resort we visited," Kathy said, "is called 'a very private (32)

paradise.'" "Who wrote the short story 'Murder in the Rue Morgue'?" Rex asked. Tony replied, "I am sure the officer said, 'Come (39)

ahead!'" "'Wee Willie Winkie' by Rudyard Kipling is a short story that might interest you," said Mrs. Yost. Sheila said, "Ralph ran (46)

in and shouted, 'They just scored another run!'" Mrs. Tanner asked, "How many have read Chekhov's story 'The Last Brooch'?" (57)

"Her answer was, 'Yes, I'll go'," said Delores. "Do you," asked Sofia, "know the tune to 'The Lonesome Loser'?" "The poem (63)

'Now You Know' was written by my brother-in-law," said Eva. "These new songs don't live long. They are not like 'Stardust' and (71)

'Dancing in the Dark,'" said Mr. Coleman. "Mother stated emphatically, 'You may not wear jeans!'" replied Jackie. "The novel (77)

Ivanhoe is by Sir Walter Scott," corrected Lee, "The poem 'Trees' is by Joyce Kilmer." Rosela reported, "Phil had trouble saying (84)

"There is where their wares are sold.'" "I thought he was saying, 'Stand aside and let the passengers off,'" Reuben replied. Roy (88)

exploded, "You heard him say, 'There will be no more free passes.'"

© 2005 Sopris West Educational Services. All rights reserved. Practicing Basic Skills in Language Arts. Purchaser has permission to photocopy this page for classroom use only.

	Correct	Error
First Try		
Second Try		

SEE TO WRITE

Quotation Marks and Other Punctuation Marks

Directions: Insert quotation and punctuation marks where needed.

The stoplight is red said the policeman Do not cross now said the man Vance said I won three prizes Mike was the

one exclaimed Denise who fell down the steps Keiko asked Will you please open the door May I please go with you

begged Jan What did you buy at the store asked Franklin A lot of new clothes answered Rita Can you swim very far

asked the lifeguard I hope I can he answered Was your paper turned in late asked his teacher Carmen said Take these

flowers home with you Debbie cried Run or I'll catch you What time does school begin Lou asked My ankle hurts

moaned Juan Don't cry said the nurse I'll help you Tomorrow is a holiday exclaimed the children Do you want hot

dogs for dinner questioned Willa Sure answered Kent Vern and Jasmine are the same size said the lady Is she your

sister Heidi asked Yes answered May I think so Diane did not go to school said her mother Kaur said Look at

that bird fly Tim likes to work puzzles said Henry Heidi please turn the light on said Pearl and shut the door The

children have gone to lunch said Sasha Ramon asked Will you come to the movies with me I can't go tonight answered

her brother The dog has been barking too loudly said Larry Turn the radio off in five minutes said Mother OK said Mia

in a minute Mark are you going asked Yoshi Can we go to the park now asked Ruby Yes said Darnell as soon as

I get ready What is your name asked the boy Jody asked Did you have a good time yesterday Call me when you are

ready said Simon Greg will be home in twenty minutes Joshua said Then we will have a party said Therese It is for his

birthday said Mother I hope we can surprise him she laughed Cole said Let's go out and have a good time That's great

said Keesha Her sister lives with her said Tam Come here said Ray I want to talk to you Just a minute said Hugh

Practicing Basic Skills in Language Arts • 421

© 2005 Sopris West Educational Services. All rights reserved. Practicing Basic Skills in Language Arts. Purchaser has permission to photocopy this page for classroom use only.

	Correct	Error
First Try		
Second Try		

Quotation Marks and Other Punctuation Marks

Directions: Insert quotation and punctuation marks where needed.

"The stoplight is red," said the policeman. "Do not cross now," said the man. Vance said, "I won three prizes." "Mike was the (13)

one," exclaimed Denise, "who fell down the steps!" Keiko asked, "Will you please open the door?" "May I please go with you?" (26)

begged Jan. "What did you buy at the store?" asked Franklin. "A lot of new clothes," answered Rita. "Can you swim very far?" (38)

asked the lifeguard. "I hope I can," he answered. "Was your paper turned in late?" asked his teacher. Carmen said, "Take these (49)

flowers home with you." Debbie cried, "Run or I'll catch you!" "What time does school begin?" Lou asked. "My ankle hurts," (62)

moaned Juan. "Don't cry," said the nurse, "I'll help you." "Tomorrow is a holiday!" exclaimed the children. "Do you want hot (75)

dogs for dinner?" questioned Willa. "Sure," answered Kent. "Vern and Jasmine are the same size," said the lady. "Is she your (87)

sister?" Heidi asked. "Yes," answered May, "I think so." "Diane did not go to school," said her mother. Kaur said, "Look at (103)

that bird fly!" "Tim likes to work puzzles," said Henry. "Heidi, please turn the light on," said Pearl, "and shut the door." "The (117)

children have gone to lunch," said Sasha. Ramon asked, "Will you come to the movies with me?" "I can't go tonight," answered (127)

her brother. "The dog has been barking too loudly," said Larry. "Turn the radio off in five minutes," said Mother. "OK," said Mia, (140)

"in a minute." "Mark, are you going?" asked Yoshi. "Can we go to the park now?" asked Ruby. "Yes," said Darnell, "as soon as (157)

I get ready." "What is your name?" asked the boy. Jody asked, "Did you have a good time yesterday?" "Call me when you are (168)

ready," said Simon. "Greg will be home in twenty minutes," Joshua said. "Then we will have a party," said Therese. "It is for his (180)

birthday," said Mother. "I hope we can surprise him," she laughed. Cole said, "Let's go out and have a good time." "That's great!" (194)

said Keesha. "Her sister lives with her," said Tam. "Come here," said Ray, "I want to talk to you." "Just a minute," said Hugh. (210)

Practicing Basic Skills in Language Arts • 422

© 2005 Sopris West Educational Services. All rights reserved. Practicing Basic Skills in Language Arts. Purchaser has permission to photocopy this page for classroom use only.

ONE-MINUTE FLUENCY BUILDER SERIES

Quotation Marks and Other Punctuation Marks in Conversation

Directions: Insert quotation and punctuation marks where needed.

	First Try	Second Try
Correct		
Error		

Adela said It's cold outside The cat is pretty exclaimed Max Are you coming asked Trina When I went to the store I

spent too much money said Dad It's time to go said Susan The dog is coming in the door exclaimed Yoli Danny said

Look at the two cats running These two animals were sitting said Kia and now they are standing She is a very good

girl said the teacher Did you see the funny clown asked Roman Angie said John put two cats in a box Her son was

washing the floor exclaimed Reed Tammy said Dion drew a picture of a raccoon Today is Sunday said Mel so we don't

have to go to school Did you see the monkey run down the street asked Guy Summer is better than winter said Martha

She has the longest hair in our school said Mehta He is an old man said Flint Math is fun said Joel Cliff said Let

him come to visit us all summer Dave said We have black cows and white sheep on our farm Joyce said The cat's fur felt

soft Here are some pretty pictures for you said Val The little boy and his mother walked to the store said Maria Rose

complained This sack of groceries is too heavy to carry I spoiled my dinner cried Ann because I let it burn The furriest

animal is a cat argued Elana Bea said Two pages in this book are missing When the bird sang I woke up said Joyce The

driver said This is as far as the bus goes Zack said Tim ran to the window to watch the snow The baby cried said Zara

because she was hungry Ruth said Take Vinnie to the dentist He wants to do it himself said Mother The grandfather

clock is very expensive said the salesman We all jumped up quickly said Gabe because we were late for the movies The

weatherman said October was a cool month with little rain The summer was long and hot said Father Can we go to the

movies asked Saul We will be good all day tomorrow

© 2005 Sopris West Educational Services. All rights reserved. Practicing Basic Skills in Language Arts. Purchaser has permission to photocopy this page for classroom use only.

ONE-MINUTE FLUENCY BUILDER SERIES

SEE TO WRITE

Quotation Marks and Other Punctuation Marks in Conversation

Directions: Insert quotation and punctuation marks where needed.

	First Try	Second Try
Correct		
Error		

Adela said, "It's cold outside." "The cat is pretty!" exclaimed Max. "Are you coming?" asked Trina. "When I went to the store, I (14)

spent too much money," said Dad. "It's time to go," said Susan. "The dog is coming in the door!" exclaimed Yoli. Danny said, (26)

"Look at the two cats running." "These two animals were sitting," said Kia, "and now they are standing." "She is a very good (37)

girl," said the teacher. "Did you see the funny clown?" asked Roman. Angie said, "John put two cats in a box." "Her son was (49)

washing the floor!" exclaimed Reed. Tammy said, "Dion drew a picture of a raccoon." "Today is Sunday," said Mel, "so we don't (61)

have to go to school." "Did you see the monkey run down the street?" asked Guy. "Summer is better than winter," said Martha. (71)

"She has the longest hair in our school," said Mehta. "He is an old man," said Flint. "Math is fun," said Joel. Cliff said, "Let (85)

him come to visit us all summer." Dave said, "We have black cows and white sheep on our farm." Joyce said, "The cat's fur felt (93)

soft." "Here are some pretty pictures for you," said Val. "The little boy and his mother walked to the store," said Maria. Rose (103)

complained, "This sack of groceries is too heavy to carry." "I spoiled my dinner," cried Ann, "because I let it burn." "The furriest (115)

animal is a cat," argued Elana. Bea said, "Two pages in this book are missing." "When the bird sang, I woke up," said Joyce. The (127)

driver said, "This is as far as the bus goes." Zack said, "Tim ran to the window to watch the snow." "The baby cried," said Zara, (139)

"because she was hungry." Ruth said, "Take Vinnie to the dentist." "He wants to do it himself," said Mother. "The grandfather (151)

clock is very expensive," said the salesman. "We all jumped up quickly," said Gabe, "because we were late for the movies." The (161)

weatherman said, "October was a cool month with little rain." "The summer was long and hot," said Father. "Can we go to the (170)

movies?" asked Saul. "We will be good all day tomorrow!" (176)

ANSWER SHEET

© 2005 Sopris West Educational Services. All rights reserved. Practicing Basic Skills in Language Arts. Purchaser has permission to photocopy this page for classroom use only.

ONE-MINUTE FLUENCY BUILDER SERIES

Hyphens in Numbers and Fractions

Directions: Write out the following numbers and fractions, using hyphens when necessary.

Scoring: Count 1 point for each answer.

	First Try	Second Try
Correct		
Error		

21 _____ $\frac{1}{2}$ _____ 59 _____

39 _____ 77 _____ 33 _____

$\frac{2}{3}$ _____ 49 _____ $\frac{1}{2}$ _____

55 _____ $\frac{1}{16}$ _____ 25 _____

99 _____ $\frac{1}{5}$ _____ $\frac{1}{10}$ _____

43 _____ $\frac{3}{4}$ _____ $\frac{4}{10}$ _____

$\frac{1}{10}$ _____ $\frac{1}{8}$ _____ 46 _____

$\frac{1}{7}$ _____ $\frac{6}{8}$ _____ 71 _____

87 _____ 95 _____ 89 _____

66 _____ 82 _____ $\frac{1}{16}$ _____

$\frac{5}{8}$ _____ 68 _____ $\frac{1}{6}$ _____

$\frac{1}{4}$ _____ $\frac{1}{4}$ _____ 94 _____

© 2005 Sopris West Educational Services. All rights reserved. Practicing Basic Skills in Language Arts. Purchaser has permission to photocopy this page for classroom use only.

ONE-MINUTE FLUENCY BUILDER SERIES

SEE TO WRITE

Hyphens in Numbers and Fractions

Directions: Write out the following numbers and fractions, using hyphens when necessary.
Scoring: Count 1 point for each answer.

	Correct	Error
First Try		
Second Try		

21	twenty-one	$\frac{1}{2}$	one-half	59	fifty-nine	(3)
39	thirty-nine	77	seventy-seven	33	thirty-three	(6)
$\frac{2}{3}$	two-thirds	49	forty-nine	$\frac{1}{2}$	one-half	(9)
55	fifty-five	$\frac{1}{16}$	one-sixteenth	25	twenty-five	(12)
99	ninety-nine	$\frac{1}{5}$	one-fifth	$\frac{1}{10}$	one-tenth	(15)
43	forty-three	$\frac{3}{4}$	three-fourths	$\frac{4}{10}$	four-tenths	(18)
$\frac{1}{10}$	one-tenth	$\frac{1}{8}$	one-eighth	46	forty-six	(21)
$\frac{1}{7}$	one-seventh	$\frac{6}{8}$	six-eighths	71	seventy-one	(24)
87	eighty-seven	95	ninety-five	89	eighty-nine	(27)
66	sixty-six	82	eighty-two	$\frac{1}{16}$	one-sixteenth	(30)
$\frac{5}{8}$	five-eighths	68	sixty-eight	$\frac{1}{6}$	one-sixth	(33)
$\frac{1}{4}$	one-fourth	$\frac{1}{4}$	one-fourth	94	ninety-four	(36)

ANSWER SHEET

Practicing Basic Skills in Language Arts • 426

© 2005 Sopris West Educational Services. All rights reserved. Practicing Basic Skills in Language Arts. Purchaser has permission to photocopy this page for classroom use only.

	First Try	Second Try
Correct		
Error		

Hyphens and Dashes

Directions: Insert hyphens and dashes in compound numbers, in prefixes, or to indicate an abrupt break in thought.

Can you oh, I see you're busy. Don't lose your self control. The Pan American games will be in Mexico. I thought it was a tongue in cheek remark. We had twenty two different pairs of shoes to choose from. Contrary to popular belief, there were nearly forty five people running for that office. As for that bit of gossip you might as well forget it. My sister in law is coming to visit next week. She will be thirty one on her birthday. He won by a two thirds majority. Your great grandparents will be down on the twenty first of the month. Un American activities have caused a turmoil in the foreign cities. Some of the revolutionaries are said to be pro French. My dog there he goes now meant no harm. Barbara or was it Joan left this book.

That well dressed gentleman is my father. The thin, tired looking dog sat down. Forty three books are left to put away. The cat I don't know whose it is has slept on my porch all day. Crossing the street, the animal looked our way. This is a well lighted room with the ninety one lightbulbs burning. The room was exactly twenty four feet wide. She was just an old fashioned girl in a modern world. The dictator of that country had made sure it was non self governing. This class will improve your skills in the language arts. Fifty two dozen eggs were delivered to my doorstep today. Would you stop yes I see you have. He said I won't tell you what he said. When you come to the library make a sharp right turn for twenty four paces. This is my thirty first year teaching. The court martial started at high noon. The ex champion wanted a rematch right away. His in laws would be there for Thanksgiving. This is an up to date article on the subject. She looked extremely self satisfied. Watch out for the oh, it got you.

The teacher said this was a first rate exercise. She is my ex girlfriend.

© 2005 Sopris West Educational Services. All rights reserved. Practicing Basic Skills in Language Arts. Purchaser has permission to photocopy this page for classroom use only.

ONE-MINUTE FLUENCY BUILDER SERIES

SEE TO WRITE

Hyphens and Dashes

Directions: Insert hyphens and dashes in compound numbers, in prefixes, or to indicate an abrupt break in thought.

	First Try	Second Try
Correct		
Error		

Can you—oh, I see you're busy. Don't lose your self-control. The Pan-American games will be in Mexico. I thought it was a (3)

tongue-in-cheek remark. We had twenty-two different pairs of shoes to choose from. Contrary to popular belief, there were (6)

nearly forty-five people running for that office. As for that bit of gossip— you might as well forget it. My sister-in-law is (10)

coming to visit next week. She will be thirty-one on her birthday. He won by a two-thirds majority. Your great-grandparents (13)

will be down on the twenty-first of the month. Un-American activities have caused a turmoil in the foreign cities. Some of the (15)

revolutionaries are said to be pro-French. My dog—there he goes now—meant no harm. Barbara—or was it Joan—left this book. (20)

That well-dressed gentleman is my father. The thin, tired-looking dog sat down. Forty-three books are left to put away. The cat—I (24)

don't know whose it is—has slept on my porch all day. Crossing the street, the animal looked our way. This is a well-lighted (26)

room with the ninety-one lightbulbs burning. The room was exactly twenty-four feet wide. She was just an old-fashioned girl in (29)

a modern world. The dictator of that country had made sure it was non-self-governing. This class will improve your skills in the (31)

language arts. Fifty-two dozen eggs were delivered to my doorstep today. Would you stop—yes—I see you have. He said—I won't (35)

tell you what he said. When you come to the library make a sharp right turn for twenty-four paces. This is my thirty-first year (37)

teaching. The court-martial started at high noon. The ex-champion wanted a rematch right away. His in-laws would be there for (40)

Thanksgiving. This is an up-to-date article on the subject. She looked extremely self-satisfied. Watch out for the—oh, it got you. (44)

The teacher said this was a first-rate exercise. She is my ex-girlfriend. (46)

ANSWER SHEET

Practicing Basic Skills in Language Arts • 428

© 2005 Sopris West Educational Services. All rights reserved. Practicing Basic Skills in Language Arts. Purchaser has permission to photocopy this page for classroom use only.

ONE-MINUTE FLUENCY BUILDER SERIES

SEE TO WRITE

Hyphen Review
Directions: Insert hyphens where needed.

	First Try	Second Try
Correct		
Error		

John said that eighty five students tried out for the baseball team this year. What kind of accommodations does Snow Bird

have for weekend guests? Greg received a three fourths majority of the vote. The Reiners have spent twenty three years as

missionaries in Africa. You know, of course, that your homework must be done on another sheet of paper. President Kennedy

was forty six at the time of his assassination. In the year 2000, she was sixty nine years old. My uncle, who lives in Salt Lake

City, will be eighty seven years old in April. A three year old child can ask brain puzzling questions. Fifty five percent of the

tickets for Friday's movie have been sold. The bill needs a two thirds majority to pass. Forty five boys entered the contest

sponsored by the *Salt Lake Tribune*. The recreation bill won by a two thirds majority. In twenty years I will be thirty four

years old. When I graduate from college, I will be twenty two years old. One sixth of the student body voted for Chester. My

grandmother will celebrate her ninety first birthday in July. Those mixed up directions took us fifty nine miles on the wrong

road. Twenty five Boy Scouts boarded the *California Zephyr* at the first stop. There were seats for ninety nine delegates, but

only twenty one delegates arrived. The payments are twenty seven dollars a month. About three fourths of the people voted

in the last presidential election. John said that eighty five students tried out for the baseball team this year. What kind of

accommodations does Snow Bird have for weekend guests? Greg received a three fourths majority of the vote. The Reiners have

spent twenty three years as missionaries in Africa. You know, of course, that your homework must be done on another sheet of

paper. President Kennedy was forty six at the time of his assassination.

Practicing Basic Skills in Language Arts • 429

© 2005 Sopris West Educational Services. All rights reserved. Practicing Basic Skills in Language Arts. Purchaser has permission to photocopy this page for classroom use only.

SEE TO WRITE

Hyphen Review

Directions: Insert hyphens where needed.

	First Try	Second Try
Correct		
Error		

(1) John said that eighty-five students tried out for the baseball team this year. What kind of accommodations does Snow Bird

(3) have for weekend guests? Greg received a three-fourths majority of the vote. The Reiners have spent twenty-three years as

(3) missionaries in Africa. You know, of course, that your homework must be done on another sheet of paper. President Kennedy

(5) was forty-six at the time of his assassination. In the year 2000, she was sixty-nine years old. My uncle, who lives in Salt Lake

(10) City, will be eighty-seven years old in April. A three-year-old child can ask brain-puzzling questions. Fifty-five percent of the

(12) tickets for Friday's movie have been sold. The bill needs a two-thirds majority to pass. Forty-five boys entered the contest

(14) sponsored by the *Salt Lake Tribune.* The recreation bill won by a two-thirds majority. In twenty years I will be thirty-four

(16) years old. When I graduate from college, I will be twenty-two years old. One-sixth of the student body voted for Chester. My

(19) grandmother will celebrate her ninety-first birthday in July. Those mixed-up directions took us fifty-nine miles on the wrong

(21) road. Twenty-five Boy Scouts boarded the *California Zephyr* at the first stop. There were seats for ninety-nine delegates, but

(24) only twenty-one delegates arrived. The payments are twenty-seven dollars a month. About three-fourths of the people voted

(25) in the last presidential election. John said that eighty-five students tried out for the baseball team this year. What kind of

(26) accommodations does Snow Bird have for weekend guests? Greg received a three-fourths majority of the vote. The Reiners have

(27) spent twenty-three years as missionaries in Africa. You know, of course, that your homework must be done on another sheet of

(28) paper. President Kennedy was forty-six at the time of his assassination.

ANSWER SHEET

Practicing Basic Skills in Language Arts • 430

© 2005 Sopris West Educational Services. All rights reserved. Practicing Basic Skills in Language Arts. Purchaser has permission to photocopy this page for classroom use only.

ONE-MINUTE FLUENCY BUILDER SERIES

	Correct	Error
First Try		
Second Try		

SEE TO WRITE

Parentheses

Directions: Insert parentheses where needed.

The girl by the way, did you see her? was nearly six feet tall. The high school honor roll was published in the *Franklin News-Herald*. The *Herald* had been taken over by the *News*. He looked up at the clock on the tower. His watch had been stolen.

The *Souls of Black Folk* published in 1903 was written by W.E.B. Du Bois. He said it would be difficult to find *skoff* food. We never spoke. What could we have said? The last quotation page 345 was from Charles Dickens. Carnaby a street in London suddenly became famous. They were talking about William Carlos Williams the American poet. Mr. Meng a friend of the family helped them with money and advice. Did I say Rover never left his master? Perhaps I had better say comrade, for if anyone was the master, it was Rover. I have known seven Prime Ministers, from my grandfather who was Prime Minister in 1846 to Mr. Attlee. The British batteries in Boston and the ships' guns now punished Charlestown with red-hot balls and cartridges or incendiary shells. Arram and his father who were both born on July 27 went to a ball game together on their birthday. Mikala planned to spend the morning with the Silvani girls they are twins and the afternoon with Courtney Ro. Turn left at the first corner do you know Zeevey's drugstore? and then walk to the end of the block. We didn't take all twelve of the cats who would have! with us. There are several poems by Sara Teasdale 1884–1933 in here.

© 2005 Sopris West Educational Services. All rights reserved. Practicing Basic Skills in Language Arts. Purchaser has permission to photocopy this page for classroom use only.

ONE-MINUTE FLUENCY BUILDER SERIES

SEE TO WRITE

Parentheses

Directions: Insert parentheses where needed.

	First Try	Second Try
Correct		
Error		

(2) The girl (by the way, did you see her?) was nearly six feet tall. The high school honor roll was published in the *Franklin News-*

(6) *Herald.* (The *Herald* had been taken over by the *News.*) He looked up at the clock on the tower. (His watch had been stolen.)

(10) The *Souls of Black Folk* (published in 1903) was written by W.E.B. Du Bois. He said it would be difficult to find *skoff* (food). We

(16) never spoke. (What could we have said?) The last quotation (page 345) was from Charles Dickens. Carnaby (a street in London)

(19) suddenly became famous. They were talking about William Carlos Williams (the American poet). Mr. Meng (a friend of the

(21) family) helped them with money and advice. Did I say Rover never left his master? (Perhaps I had better say comrade, for if

(23) anyone was the master, it was Rover.) I have known seven Prime Ministers, from my grandfather (who was Prime Minister

(24) in 1846) to Mr. Attlee. The British batteries in Boston and the ships' guns now punished Charlestown with red-hot balls and

(28) cartridges (or incendiary shells). Arram and his father (who were both born on July 27) went to a ball game together on their

(30) birthday. Mikala planned to spend the morning with the Silvani girls (they are twins) and the afternoon with Courtney Ro. Turn

(32) left at the first corner (do you know Zeevey's drugstore?) and then walk to the end of the block. We didn't take all twelve of the

(36) cats (who would have!) with us. There are several poems by Sara Teasdale (1884–1933) in here.

ANSWER SHEET

Practicing Basic Skills in Language Arts • 432

© 2005 Sopris West Educational Services. All rights reserved. Practicing Basic Skills in Language Arts. Purchaser has permission to photocopy this page for classroom use only.

SEE TO MARK

Underlining Titles of Books, Plays, and Periodicals
Directions: Underline where needed.

	Correct	Error
First Try		
Second Try		

The Pequod is a ship in the book Moby Dick. I read the Salt Lake Tribune. The essay "Self Reliance" is by Emerson. I read The

Chosen for my first book report. For tomorrow, Ms. Cashmore assigned two chapters from Great Expectations. Uncle Vincent

said that he saw the play Little Orphan Annie in Los Angeles. Do you know the tune to "Blueberry Hill"? Kevin keeps all his

copies of the National Geographic magazine. I saw the play The Miracle Worker on television. The title of Sydney's theme is

"Discounts Can Fool You." I'm reading The Pigman for my next book report. Julius Ceasar, Hamlet, A Midsummer Night's

Dream, and Romeo and Juliet are all Shakespearean plays. You should read The Hobbit before you read The Lord of the Rings.

Mike has read The Fellowship of the Ring, The Two Towers, and The Return of the King. Students who are interested in

astronomy will enjoy the magazine Astronomy. Billie Jean King wrote an article called "Straight Talk" for Seventeen magazine.

Shakespeare's comedy plays include The Tempest, Two Gentlemen of Verona, Measure for Measure, The Comedy of Errors, and

Much Ado About Nothing. There is a review of The Other Side of the Mountain in this morning's Salt Lake Tribune. You can

find Frost's poem "Mending Walls" in his Collected Poems.

Practicing Basic Skills in Language Arts • 433

© 2005 Sopris West Educational Services. All rights reserved. Practicing Basic Skills in Language Arts. Purchaser has permission to photocopy this page for classroom use only.

SEE TO MARK

Underlining Titles of Books, Plays, and Periodicals
Directions: Underline where needed.

	First Try	Second Try
Correct		
Error		

The Pequod is a ship in the book Moby Dick. I read the Salt Lake Tribune. The essay "Self Reliance" is by Emerson. I read The (4)

Chosen for my first book report. For tomorrow, Ms. Cashmore assigned two chapters from Great Expectations. Uncle Vincent (5)

said that he saw the play Little Orphan Annie in Los Angeles. Do you know the tune to "Blueberry Hill"? Kevin keeps all his (6)

copies of the National Geographic magazine. I saw the play The Miracle Worker on television. The title of Sydney's theme is (8)

"Discounts Can Fool You." I'm reading The Pigman for my next book report. Julius Ceasar, Hamlet, A Midsummer Night's (12)

Dream, and Romeo and Juliet are all Shakespearean plays. You should read The Hobbit before you read The Lord of the Rings. (15)

Mike has read The Fellowship of the Ring, The Two Towers, and The Return of the King. Students who are interested in (18)

astronomy will enjoy the magazine Astronomy. Billie Jean King wrote an article called "Straight Talk" for Seventeen magazine. (20)

Shakespeare's comedy plays include The Tempest, Two Gentlemen of Verona, Measure for Measure, The Comedy of Errors, and (24)

Much Ado About Nothing. There is a review of The Other Side of the Mountain in this morning's Salt Lake Tribune. You can (27)

find Frost's poem "Mending Walls" in his Collected Poems. (28)

ANSWER SHEET

Practicing Basic Skills in Language Arts • 434

© 2005 Sopris West Educational Services. All rights reserved. Practicing Basic Skills in Language Arts. Purchaser has permission to photocopy this page for classroom use only.

SEE TO MARK

	Correct	Error
First Try		
Second Try		

Underlining Titles of Movies, Works of Art, and Long Musical Compositions

Directions: Underline the proper titles.

Weber State College presents The Nutcracker during the holiday season. The last movie I saw was Superman. Young

Frankenstein, one of the funniest movies I've seen, has returned to the Country Club Theatre. Tchaikovsky named his mournful

sixth symphony Pathetique, meaning pathetic. Its official name is Symphony No. 6 in B Minor, Op. 74. These new songs don't

live long; they are not like "Stardust" and "Dancing in the Dark." Have you seen the original of DaVinci's painting the Mona

Lisa? Art, for many people, includes only such great works of painting and sculpture as Michelangelo's Moses. Walt Disney

produced Snow White and the Seven Dwarfs, which was the first feature-length animated cartoon in color. I just bought a new

CD of "Sail On." Mrs. Dean directed the musical My Fair Lady. The most famous examples of Helenistic sculpture include the

Winged Victory and the Venus de Milo. Mr. Robert Peterson sang "The Last Rose of Summer" from the opera Martha. Greg

has seen Star Wars fifteen times. Bach wrote six concertos for the ruler of Brandenburg, and we call them the Brandenburg

Concertos. The statue The Dance of Siva symbolized the Hindu belief that the god Siva has the power to destroy and re-create

the universe. An early movie, The Life of an American Fireman, had no real plot. The King and I and Titanic are two movies that

you can enjoy seeing many times.

Practicing Basic Skills in Language Arts • 435

© 2005 Sopris West Educational Services. All rights reserved. Practicing Basic Skills in Language Arts. Purchaser has permission to photocopy this page for classroom use only.

SEE TO MARK

	First Try	Second Try
Correct		
Error		

Underlining Titles of Movies, Works of Art, and Long Musical Compositions

Directions: Underline the proper titles.

Weber State College presents The Nutcracker during the holiday season. The last movie I saw was Superman. Young (3)

Frankenstein, one of the funniest movies I've seen, has returned to the Country Club Theatre. Tchaikovsky named his mournful (3)

sixth symphony Pathetique, meaning pathetic. Its official name is Symphony No. 6 in B Minor, Op. 74. These new songs don't (5)

live long; they are not like "Stardust" and "Dancing in the Dark." Have you seen the original of DaVinci's painting the Mona (6)

Lisa? Art, for many people, includes only such great works of painting and sculpture as Michelangelo's Moses. Walt Disney (7)

produced Snow White and the Seven Dwarfs, which was the first feature-length animated cartoon in color. I just bought a new (8)

CD of "Sail On." Mrs. Dean directed the musical My Fair Lady. The most famous examples of Helenistic sculpture include the (9)

Winged Victory and the Venus de Milo. Mr. Robert Peterson sang "The Last Rose of Summer" from the opera Martha. Greg (12)

has seen Star Wars fifteen times. Bach wrote six concertos for the ruler of Brandenburg, and we call them the Brandenburg (14)

Concertos. The statue The Dance of Siva symbolized the Hindu belief that the god Siva has the power to destroy and re-create (15)

the universe. An early movie, The Life of an American Fireman, had no real plot. The King and I and Titanic are two movies that (18)

you can enjoy seeing many times. (18)

ANSWER SHEET

© 2005 Sopris West Educational Services. All rights reserved. Practicing Basic Skills in Language Arts. Purchaser has permission to photocopy this page for classroom use only.

SEE TO MARK

Underlining Titles of Ships, Trains, and Airplanes

Directions: Underline where needed.

	First Try	Second Try
Correct		
Error		

The Titanic sank in 1912. Did you read about the sinking of the Titanic in that old copy of the newspaper? During the war, his

father was the navigator on a plane called Bouncing Betsy. The Pequod is a ship in a novel. The company's plane was called the

Wild Rose. Did you tour the Freedom Train when it came to Ogden? We crossed the ocean on the Arcadia. A six-day luxury trip

aboard the aircraft Imperial 109 turned into a nightmare. Forty-four crates of gold were being loaded aboard the ocean freighter

Sea Dog. The Queen Mary no longer sails the ocean, but is anchored off Long Beach, California. The drone of the clicking tracks

lulled her to sleep as the Metroliner sped across the desert. Pilot Larry McBride gripped the controls of Concorde as it started

to land. The torpedo bomber, the Devastator, had just taken off from the airbase. His new assignment was aboard Atlantis. The

Supermarine docked unnoticed in the dense cove. As she entered the cabin of the Caterina she became frightened. The Flying

Cloud soared high above the heavy storm clouds. Through the window of the Raptor, he saw twenty fighters descending upon

them. The pilot drove the rudder into the floor and peeled the Raptor away. The Archer was still airborne.

Practicing Basic Skills in Language Arts • 437

© 2005 Sopris West Educational Services. All rights reserved. Practicing Basic Skills in Language Arts. Purchaser has permission to photocopy this page for classroom use only.

ONE/MINUTE FLUENCY BUILDER SERIES

Underlining Titles of Ships, Trains, and Airplanes

Directions: Underline where needed.

	First Try	Second Try
Correct		
Error		

The Titanic sank in 1912. Did you read about the sinking of the Titanic in that old copy of the newspaper? During the war, his (2)

father was the navigator on a plane called Bouncing Betsy. The Pequod is a ship in a novel. The company's plane was called the (4)

Wild Rose. Did you tour the Freedom Train when it came to Ogden? We crossed the ocean on the Arcadia. A six-day luxury trip (7)

aboard the aircraft Imperial 109 turned into a nightmare. Forty-four crates of gold were being loaded aboard the ocean freighter (8)

Sea Dog. The Queen Mary no longer sails the ocean, but is anchored off Long Beach, California. The drone of the clicking tracks (10)

lulled her to sleep as the Metroliner sped across the desert. Pilot Larry McBride gripped the controls of Concorde as it started (12)

to land. The torpedo bomber, the Devastator, had just taken off from the airbase. His new assignment was aboard Atlantis. The (14)

Supermarine docked unnoticed in the dense cove. As she entered the cabin of the Caterina she became frightened. The Flying (17)

Cloud soared high above the heavy storm clouds. Through the window of the Raptor, he saw twenty fighters descending upon (18)

them. The pilot drove the rudder into the floor and peeled the Raptor away. The Archer was still airborne. (20)

© 2005 Sopris West Educational Services. All rights reserved. Practicing Basic Skills in Language Arts. Purchaser has permission to photocopy this page for classroom use only.

ONE-MINUTE FLUENCY BUILDER SERIES

SEE TO MARK

Underlining Review
Directions: Underline where needed.

They are naming their new boat the Bumblebee. The Manchester Guardian is a British newspaper. The Bridge of San Luis Rey

is more like a collection of short stories than a novel. He is a conductor on the Santa Fe Chief. Have you read Thomas Hardy's

novel The Return of the Native? The musical My Fair Lady was based on a play by Shaw. Rembrandt stressed action, drama, and

violent contrasts of light and dark in his painting The Night Watch. The Charlie Chaplin movie The Gold Rush and Harold

Lloyd's film Safety Last are two well known silent comedies. He is a photographer for the New York Times. According to today's

Ogden Standard Examiner, the Community Players are going to put on the musical Guys and Dolls next month. Randy just

finished reading The Call of the Wild, and now he's starting The Hobbit. Do you subscribe to Popular Electronics? They are

sailing to Europe on the S.S. Constitution. The ninth graders are reading the play Romeo and Juliet, and they will see the movie

West Side Story at the end of the term. The Zephyr will arrive on track 7 at 10:25 A.M. Teresa gave her book report on The Red

Badge of Courage. The Love Bug is a movie about a Volkswagen. I counted forty-one people waiting for the Shoreline Express.

Practicing Basic Skills in Language Arts • 439

© 2005 Sopris West Educational Services. All rights reserved. Practicing Basic Skills in Language Arts. Purchaser has permission to photocopy this page for classroom use only.

Underlining Review

Directions: Underline where needed.

	First Try	Second Try
Correct		
Error		

They are naming their new boat the Bumblebee. The Manchester Guardian is a British newspaper. The Bridge of San Luis Rey (3)

is more like a collection of short stories than a novel. He is a conductor on the Santa Fe Chief. Have you read Thomas Hardy's (4)

novel The Return of the Native? The musical My Fair Lady was based on a play by Shaw. Rembrandt stressed action, drama, and (6)

violent contrasts of light and dark in his painting The Night Watch. The Charlie Chaplin movie The Gold Rush and Harold (8)

Lloyd's film Safety Last are two well known silent comedies. He is a photographer for the New York Times. According to today's (10)

Ogden Standard Examiner, the Community Players are going to put on the musical Guys and Dolls next month. Randy just (12)

finished reading The Call of the Wild, and now he's starting The Hobbit. Do you subscribe to Popular Electronics? They are (15)

sailing to Europe on the S.S. Constitution. The ninth graders are reading the play Romeo and Juliet, and they will see the movie (17)

West Side Story at the end of the term. The Zephyr will arrive on track 7 at 10:25 A.M. Teresa gave her book report on The Red (20)

Badge of Courage. The Love Bug is a movie about a Volkswagen. I counted forty-one people waiting for the Shoreline Express. (22)

ANSWER SHEET

© 2005 Sopris West Educational Services. All rights reserved. Practicing Basic Skills in Language Arts. Purchaser has permission to photocopy this page for classroom use only.

ONE-MINUTE FLUENCY
BUILDER SERIES

	Correct	Error
First Try		
Second Try		

SEE TO WRITE

Punctuation Combinations

Directions: Properly punctuate the following sentences using . , ? : " " ; – '

Is this the place Mother They said that you were going Lunch hour is from 11 30 AM to 12 30 PM in the Ember Room I ll

help if you say we re both needed Our captain Tom Daly is a senior Thomas Jefferson died on July 4 1826 at the age of eighty

three Watch out yelled the captain Stay away from that rail The team went to the hospital to see Bud he had been hurt

in Sunday s game Paris the capital of France is on the Seine River After the bell rang the room grew quiet Have you read *Gone*

With the Wind This is Dan s key Is Jack s theme called Tom and Becky at School Books pens pencils and papers have been

put away He must be here in five minutes or he will miss the bus I was afraid I would miss the bus however I caught it with a

minute to spare Have you read the poem The Village Blacksmith You of course are welcome Women s coats are in the Ladies

Department Bill completed twenty nine of fifty two passes My brother Bill is taller than I am Is his address 110 Elm Street

Lima Ohio All the readers have liked your story in fact they have praised it Mrs Jenkins asked Have you read Frost s poem

Stopping by Woods on a Snowy Evening I hope Dad that you will like the play We had to think quickly there was little time

Practicing Basic Skills in Language Arts • 441

© 2005 Sopris West Educational Services. All rights reserved. Practicing Basic Skills in Language Arts. Purchaser has permission to photocopy this page for classroom use only.

	Correct	Error
First Try		
Second Try		

SEE TO WRITE

Punctuation Combinations

Directions: Properly punctuate the following sentences using . , ? : " " ; — '

Is this the place, Mother? They said that you were going. Lunch hour is from 11:30 A.M. to 12:30 P.M. in the Ember Room. I'll (11)

help if you say we're both needed. Our captain, Tom Daly, is a senior. Thomas Jefferson died on July 4, 1826, at the age of eighty- (19)

three. "Watch out!" yelled the captain. "Stay away from that rail!" The team went to the hospital to see Bud; he had been hurt (28)

in Sunday's game. Paris, the capital of France, is on the Seine River. After the bell rang, the room grew quiet. Have you read *Gone* (35)

With the Wind? This is Dan's key. Is Jack's theme called "Tom and Becky at School"? Books, pens, pencils, and papers have been (45)

put away. He must be here in five minutes or he will miss the bus. I was afraid I would miss the bus; however, I caught it with a (49)

minute to spare. Have you read the poem "The Village Blacksmith"? You, of course, are welcome. Women's coats are in the Ladies' (58)

Department. Bill completed twenty-nine of fifty-two passes. My brother, Bill, is taller than I am. Is his address 110 Elm Street, (66)

Lima, Ohio? All the readers have liked your story; in fact, they have praised it. Mrs. Jenkins asked, "Have you read Frost's poem (75)

'Stopping by Woods on a Snowy Evening'?" I hope, Dad, that you will like the play. We had to think quickly; there was little time. (84)

ANSWER SHEET

© 2005 Sopris West Educational Services. All rights reserved. Practicing Basic Skills in Language Arts. Purchaser has permission to photocopy this page for classroom use only.

Vocabulary Development

Antonyms 445
Antonyms 447
Synonyms and Antonyms 449
Synonyms and Antonyms 451
Synonyms and Antonyms 453
Homonyms: To, Too, or Two 455
Homonyms: There, Their, They're 457
Homonym Review 459
Homonym Review 461
Homonym Review 463
Homonym Review 465
Prefixes: Pro, En, Re, Im, Dis 467
Prefixes: Mis, Re, Un, Trans, Dis, Con 469
Prefixes: De, Super, Im, Sub, Inter 471
Prefixes: Pre, Manu, Ego, Mono, Sur, Ex 473
Prefixes: Ab, Be, Bi, Co, Com, In, Tri 475
Prefixes: Circum, Com, Con, Dia, Extra, Out,
    Post, Trans, Sym, Syn 477
Prefixes: Mis, Un, Dis, Re, Trans, Con 479
Prefixes: Pre, Mono, Manu, Sur, Ego, Ex 481

ONE-MINUTE FLUENCY BUILDER SERIES

SEE TO WRITE

Antonyms

Directions: Write the opposite for each word.

	First Try	Second Try
Correct		
Error		

fast	full	_____	day
awake	start	_____	ugly
cold	exit	_____	above
tall	alive	_____	dark
sweet	stop	_____	neat
found	laugh	_____	early
pull	closed	_____	rough
true	off	_____	narrow
left	out	_____	dull
happy	down	_____	quiet
short	fat	_____	good
shallow	high	_____	old

Practicing Basic Skills in Language Arts • 445

© 2005 Sopris West Educational Services. All rights reserved. Practicing Basic Skills in Language Arts. Purchaser has permission to photocopy this page for classroom use only.

SEE TO WRITE

Antonyms

Directions: Write the opposite for each word.

				First Try	Second Try
				Correct	Error

fast	**slow**	full	**empty**	day	**night**	(3)
awake	**asleep**	start	**stop**	ugly	**pretty**	(6)
cold	**hot**	exit	**enter**	above	**below**	(9)
tall	**short**	alive	**dead**	dark	**light**	(12)
sweet	**sour**	stop	**go**	neat	**messy**	(15)
found	**lost**	laugh	**cry**	early	**late**	(18)
pull	**push**	closed	**open**	rough	**smooth**	(21)
true	**false**	off	**on**	narrow	**wide**	(24)
left	**right**	out	**in**	dull	**bright**	(27)
happy	**sad**	down	**up**	quiet	**loud**	(30)
short	**tall**	fat	**thin**	good	**bad**	(33)
shallow	**deep**	high	**low**	old	**new**	(36)

© 2005 Sopris West Educational Services. All rights reserved. Practicing Basic Skills in Language Arts. Purchaser has permission to photocopy this page for classroom use only.

ONE-MINUTE FLUENCY BUILDER SERIES

SEE TO WRITE

Antonyms
Directions: Write the opposite for each word.

different	out	_____	_____	went
came	down	_____	_____	different
give	day	_____	_____	take
up	old	_____	_____	same
no	right	_____	_____	hot
here	pretty	_____	_____	begin
strong	went	_____	_____	here
there	end	_____	_____	near
take	ugly	_____	_____	weak
out	night	_____	_____	over
under	in	_____	_____	take
yes	pretty	_____	_____	play

Practicing Basic Skills in Language Arts • 447

© 2005 Sopris West Educational Services. All rights reserved. Practicing Basic Skills in Language Arts. Purchaser has permission to photocopy this page for classroom use only.

ONE-MINUTE FLUENCY BUILDER SERIES

SEE TO WRITE

Antonyms

Directions: Write the opposite for each word.

	First Try		Correct	Error
	Second Try			

different	_____	same	_____	went	**came**	(3)
came	_____	went	_____	different	**same**	(6)
give	_____	take	_____	take	**give**	(9)
up	_____	down	_____	same	**different**	(12)
no	_____	yes	_____	hot	**cold**	(15)
here	_____	there	_____	begin	**end**	(18)
strong	_____	weak	_____	here	**there**	(21)
there	_____	here	_____	near	**far**	(24)
take	_____	give	_____	weak	**strong**	(27)
out	_____	in	_____	over	**under**	(30)
under	_____	over	_____	take	**give**	(33)
yes	_____	no	_____	play	**work**	(36)

out	**in**
down	**up**
day	**night**
old	**new**
right	**wrong**
pretty	**ugly**
went	**came**
end	**begin**
ugly	**pretty**
night	**day**
in	**out**
pretty	**ugly**

ANSWER SHEET

Practicing Basic Skills in Language Arts • 448

© 2005 Sopris West Educational Services. All rights reserved. Practicing Basic Skills in Language Arts. Purchaser has permission to photocopy this page for classroom use only.

	Correct	Error
First Try		
Second Try		

SEE TO WRITE

Synonyms and Antonyms

Directions: Write different (D), same (S), or opposite (O).

first - last	shout - yell	swift - quick
small - little	bottom - top	sick - weak
tall - thin	thunder - lightning	good - bad
young - old	gift - present	wait - sit
full - empty	all - some	present - here
car - truck	dry - wet	cold - hot
same - alike	question - ask	push - pull
deep - long	reply - answer	run - hop
laugh - cry	teeth - mouth	go - depart
skip - walk	hard - soft	open - close
begin - start	warm - dry	sour - salty
water - wet	new - old	ride - car

Practicing Basic Skills in Language Arts • 449

© 2005 Sopris West Educational Services. All rights reserved. Practicing Basic Skills in Language Arts. Purchaser has permission to photocopy this page for classroom use only.

ONE-MINUTE FLUENCY
BUILDER SERIES

SEE TO WRITE

Synonyms and Antonyms

Directions: Write different (D), same (S), or opposite (O).

	Word Pair		Word Pair		Word Pair		Word Pair	
O	first - last	S	shout - yell	S	white - black	S	swift - quick	(4)
S	small - little	O	bottom - top	O	day - sun	D	sick - weak	(8)
D	tall - thin	D	thunder - lightning	D	candy - sweet	O	good - bad	(12)
O	young - old	S	gift - present	S	skinny - thin	D	wait - sit	(16)
O	full - empty	D	all - some	D	frown - sad	D	present - here	(20)
D	car - truck	O	dry - wet	O	yes - no	O	cold - hot	(24)
S	same - alike	D	question - ask	D	angry - mad	O	push - pull	(28)
D	deep - long	S	reply - answer	S	morning - noon	D	run - hop	(32)
O	laugh - cry	D	teeth - mouth	D	dark - light	S	go - depart	(36)
D	skip - walk	O	hard - soft	O	funny - serious	O	open - close	(40)
S	begin - start	D	warm - dry	D	food - eat	D	sour - salty	(44)
D	water - wet	O	new - old	O	wealthy - rich	D	ride - car	(48)

	Correct	Error
First Try		
Second Try		

Practicing Basic Skills in Language Arts • 450

ANSWER SHEET

© 2005 Sopris West Educational Services. All rights reserved. Practicing Basic Skills in Language Arts. Purchaser has permission to photocopy this page for classroom use only.

SEE TO WRITE

Synonyms and Antonyms

Directions: Write different (D), same (S), or opposite (O).

near - close	bees - spiders	wrong - incorrect
rowboat - sailboat	glad - happy	hill - valley
high - low	tape - glue	fast - slow
true - false	big - little	liquid - water
book - magazine	poor - poverty	giggle - laugh
gigantic - huge	whisper - talk	hire - pay
cup - glass	throw - catch	warm - cool
polite - rude	float - sink	floor - ceiling
candy - cake	yell - whisper	shiny - bright
stop - end	boy - girl	sour - sweet
hungry - fat	fire - smoke	rich - poor	entrance - exit
play - work	woman - lady	pen - pencil	early - late

© 2005 Sopris West Educational Services. All rights reserved. Practicing Basic Skills in Language Arts. Purchaser has permission to photocopy this page for classroom use only.

ONE MINUTE FLUENCY BUILDER SERIES

SEE TO WRITE

Synonyms and Antonyms

Directions: Write different (D), same (S), or opposite (O).

	Correct	Error
First Try		
Second Try		

near - close	S	bees - spiders	D	outside - inside	O	wrong - incorrect	S (4)
rowboat - sailboat	D	glad - happy	S	late - tardy	S	hill - valley	O (8)
high - low	O	tape - glue	D	bird - plane	D	fast - slow	O (12)
true - false	O	big - little	O	thin - thick	O	liquid - water	D (16)
book - magazine	D	poor - poverty	D	read - write	D	giggle - laugh	D (20)
gigantic - huge	S	whisper - talk	D	girl - female	D	hire - pay	D (24)
cup - glass	D	throw - catch	D	lamp - candle	O	warm - cool	O (28)
polite - rude	O	float - sink	O	mad - glad	O	floor - ceiling	O (32)
candy - cake	D	yell - whisper	O	middle - east	O	shiny - bright	S (36)
stop - end	S	boy - girl	O	dirty - filthy	O	sour - sweet	O (40)
hungry - fat	D	fire - smoke	D	rich - poor	D	entrance - exit	O (44)
play - work	O	woman - lady	S	pen - pencil	D	early - late	O (48)

ANSWER SHEET

© 2005 Sopris West Educational Services. All rights reserved. Practicing Basic Skills in Language Arts. Purchaser has permission to photocopy this page for classroom use only.

	First Try	Second Try
Correct		
Error		

SEE TO WRITE

Synonyms and Antonyms
Directions: Write different (D), same (S), or opposite (O).

_____ gone - absent _____ white - yellow _____ smooth - rough _____ buy - sell

_____ over - on _____ bad - wicked _____ inside - beside _____ tight - loose

_____ raise - lower _____ strong - muscles _____ distant - far _____ tame - tied

_____ win - play _____ day - night _____ right - write _____ spotless - clean

_____ straight - crooked _____ dead - alive _____ left - right _____ eat - drink

_____ city - country _____ answer - write _____ tidy - neat _____ wild - tame

_____ young - child _____ correct - right _____ cold - wet _____ night - moon

_____ beautiful - pretty _____ new - first _____ before - after _____ arrive - come

_____ ugly - fat _____ shiny - dull _____ love - hate _____ chair - sofa

_____ noisy - loud _____ finish - win _____ feeble - weak _____ asleep - awake

_____ mean - tired _____ gentleman - man _____ knife - fork _____ mad - sad

_____ odd - even _____ frown - smile _____ male - boy _____ leave - going

Practicing Basic Skills in Language Arts • 453

© 2005 Sopris West Educational Services. All rights reserved. Practicing Basic Skills in Language Arts. Purchaser has permission to photocopy this page for classroom use only.

SEE TO WRITE

Synonyms and Antonyms

Directions: Write different (D), same (S), or opposite (O).

gone - absent	**S**	white - yellow	**D**	smooth - rough	**O**	buy - sell (4)
over - on	**D**	bad - wicked	**S**	inside - beside	**D**	tight - loose (8)
raise - lower	**O**	strong - muscles	**D**	distant - far	**S**	tame - tied (12)
win - play	**D**	day - night	**O**	right - write	**D**	spotless - clean (16)
straight - crooked	**O**	dead - alive	**O**	left - right	**O**	eat - drink (20)
city - country	**D**	answer - write	**D**	tidy - neat	**S**	wild - tame (24)
young - child	**D**	correct - right	**S**	cold - wet	**D**	night - moon (28)
beautiful - pretty	**S**	new - first	**D**	before - after	**O**	arrive - come (32)
ugly - fat	**D**	shiny - dull	**O**	love - hate	**O**	chair - sofa (36)
noisy - loud	**S**	finish - win	**D**	feeble - weak	**S**	asleep - awake (40)
mean - tired	**D**	gentleman - man	**S**	knife - fork	**D**	mad - sad (44)
odd - even	**O**	frown - smile	**O**	male - boy	**S**	leave - going (48)

ANSWER SHEET

Practicing Basic Skills in Language Arts • 454

© 2005 Sopris West Educational Services. All rights reserved. Practicing Basic Skills in Language Arts. Purchaser has permission to photocopy this page for classroom use only.

ONE-MINUTE FLUENCY
BUILDER SERIES

	Correct	Error
First Try		
Second Try		

Homonyms: To, Too, or Two
Directions: Fill in each blank with to, too, two.

1. She is going _____ the new movie.

3. It is _____ rainy for a picnic.

5. We want to go _____.

7. The family drove _____ Denver and back?

9. What are you going _____ do today?

11. Do you remember when you were _____ years old?

13. John is going _____ run in the 25 mile race.

15. The box was _____ heavy.

17. Do you want some ice cream _____?

19. It takes twelve things _____ make one dozen.

21. Janet has _____ sisters.

23. Sue was _____ tired for a party last night.

25. Mary ate _____ much cake.

27. Which assignment do we have _____ finish tonight?

29. Mother needs a rest, _____.

2. Jan and her family went _____ Canada last year.

4. Are you going _____ have a fun summer?

6. Janet would like a new bike _____.

8. Fanny ate _____ hamburgers.

10. It is _____ hot for tennis.

12. There are _____ many people here.

14. Is it going _____ snow soon?

16. Are you _____ ill today?

18. There are _____ cars in the neighbor's garage.

20. What time do you have _____ leave for school?

22. Do you want _____ go with me next week?

24. Joe has _____ finish his homework before going out.

26. Dan went _____ the zoo yesterday.

28. Betty owns _____ dogs.

30. It is _____ bad that your grandfather is sick.

© 2005 Sopris West Educational Services. All rights reserved. Practicing Basic Skills in Language Arts. Purchaser has permission to photocopy this page for classroom use only.

ONE-MINUTE FLUENCY
BUILDER SERIES

SEE TO WRITE

Homonyms: To, Too, or Two

Directions: Fill in each blank with *to*, *too*, *two*.

	First Try	Second Try
Correct		
Error		

1. She is going **to** the new movie.

2. Jan and her family went **to** Canada last year. (2)

3. It is **too** rainy for a picnic.

4. Are you going **to** have a fun summer? (4)

5. We want to go **too** .

6. Janet would like a new bike **too** . (6)

7. The family drove **to** Denver and back?

8. Fanny ate **two** hamburgers. (8)

9. What are you going **to** do today?

10. It is **too** hot for tennis. (10)

11. Do you remember when you were **two** years old?

12. There are _____ many people here. (12)

13. John is going **to** run in the 25 mile race.

14. Is it going **to** snow soon? (14)

15. The box was **too** heavy.

16. Are you **too** ill today? (16)

17. Do you want some ice cream **too** ?

18. There are **two** cars in the neighbor's garage. (18)

19. It takes twelve things **to** make one dozen.

20. What time do you have **to** leave for school? (20)

21. Janet has **two** sisters.

22. Do you want **to** go with me next week? (22)

23. Sue was _____ tired for a party last night.

24. Joe has **to** finish his homework before going out. (24)

25. Mary ate **too** much cake.

26. Dan went **to** the zoo yesterday. (26)

27. Which assignment do we have **to** finish tonight?

28. Betty owns **two** dogs. (28)

29. Mother needs a rest, **too** .

30. It is **too** bad that your grandfather is sick. (30)

ANSWER SHEET

© 2005 Sopris West Educational Services. All rights reserved. Practicing Basic Skills in Language Arts. Purchaser has permission to photocopy this page for classroom use only.

	Correct	Error
First Try		
Second Try		

ONE-MINUTE FLUENCY
BUILDER SERIES

SEE TO WRITE

Homonyms: There, Their, They're

Directions: Fill in each blank with *there, their, they're*.

1. If you give them _____ food they will quit barking.

2. Sit over _____ on the blue chair.

3. Call them and see if _____ going to the party.

4. If we leave tomorrow, _____ going with us.

5. Look over _____!

6. How many students are _____ in the class?

7. Is _____ going to be an assembly today?

8. _____ happy about his new job.

9. Have you seen _____ new car?

10. We are glad _____ home.

11. Are _____ any cookies left in the box?

12. We will be _____ at three o'clock.

13. _____ having a party tonight.

14. Are you going _____ tomorrow?

15. Are you sure that _____ not home?

16. They invited us to _____ cabin.

17. Put the book _____ on the table.

18. If you see _____ child let them know.

19. _____ is a motorcycle outside.

20. There are six cars in _____ garage.

21. _____ are ten people in my family.

22. When we go _____ going to watch Jim.

23. Have you seen _____ new twins?

24. _____ has been a lot of snow this year.

25. _____ children are crying because they are lost.

Practicing Basic Skills in Language Arts • 457

© 2005 Sopris West Educational Services. All rights reserved. Practicing Basic Skills in Language Arts. Purchaser has permission to photocopy this page for classroom use only.

ONE-MINUTE FLUENCY BUILDER SERIES

SEE TO WRITE

Homonyms: There, Their, They're

Directions: Fill in each blank with *there, their, they're.*

	First Try	Second Try
Correct		
Error		

1. If you give them **their** food they will quit barking.

2. Sit over **there** on the blue chair. (2)

3. Call them and see if **they're** going to the party.

4. If we leave tomorrow, **they're** going with us. (4)

5. Look over **there** !

6. How many students are **there** in the class? (6)

7. Is **there** going to be an assembly today?

8. **They're** happy about his new job. (8)

9. Have you seen **their** new car?

10. We are glad **they're** home. (10)

11. Are **there** any cookies left in the box?

12. We will be **there** at three o'clock. (12)

13. **They're** having a party tonight.

14. Are you going **there** tomorrow? (14)

15. Are you sure that **they're** not home?

16. They invited us to **their** cabin. (16)

17. Put the book **there** on the table.

18. If you see **their** child let them know. (18)

19. **There** is a motorcycle outside.

20. There are six cars in **their** garage. (20)

21. **There** are ten people in my family.

22. When we go **they're** going to watch Jim. (22)

23. Have you seen **their** new twins?

24. **There** has been a lot of snow this year. (24)

25. **Their** children are crying because they are lost. (25)

ANSWER SHEET

© 2005 Sopris West Educational Services. All rights reserved. Practicing Basic Skills in Language Arts. Purchaser has permission to photocopy this page for classroom use only.

SEE TO MARK

	Correct	Error
First Try		
Second Try		

ONE-MINUTE FLUENCY
BUILDER SERIES

Homonym Review

Directions: Underline the word that will make a correct sentence.

1. (Who's, Whose) coat are you wearing?   2. That snow (scene, seen) was beautiful.   3. We will burn a lot of (wood, would) in our fireplace.   4. All the work we did was in (vein, vane, vain).   5. The bus (fair, fare) wasn't very much.   6. I got the (right, write) telephone number the first time I called.   7. Would you give me a big (peace, piece) of cake?   8. The (capital, capitol) of Kansas is Topeka.   9. It is (to, two, too) late for John to come over.   10. It is midnight (all ready, already).   11. Mary drank the (whole, hole) bottle of Coke.   12. He is going to (steel, steal) third base.   13. Tom was the (forth, fourth) person in line.   14. (Their, There) goes that bunch of dogs again.   15. We walked briskly (threw, through) the forest.   16. Her hair is very (coarse, course).   17. Mary's boyfriend is very (weak, week).   18. Our (principle, principal) isn't very old.   19. (It's, Its) not cold enough to wear your winter coat.   20. It is (altogether, all together) too late to walk home alone.   21. She is going to (wear, where) her new jeans.   22. (Here, Hear) comes my mother right now.   23. The (weather, whether) is very changeable this time of the year.   24. Are your muscles (sore, soar)?   25. The (soul, sole) of his shoe had a hole in it.   26. The (sails, sales) of his boat were torn.   27. The state (fair, fare) begins next (week, weak).   28. Her (waste, waist) is very tiny.   29. I (would, wood) like to have something (sweet, suite) to eat.   30. Have you (seen, scene) Jimmy's new (pear, pare, pair) of shoes?   31. The truck had to (tow, toe) us to the garage.   32. She fell in the big (hole, whole).   33. It was (there, their) turn to fix dinner.   34. She took (to, too, two) friends with her.   35. We aren't sure (whether, weather) we should stay home or not.   36. The band (lead, led) the parade.

Practicing Basic Skills in Language Arts • 459

© 2005 Sopris West Educational Services. All rights reserved. Practicing Basic Skills in Language Arts. Purchaser has permission to photocopy this page for classroom use only.

ONE-MINUTE FLUENCY
BUILDER SERIES

SEE TO MARK

Homonym Review

Directions: Underline the word that will make a correct sentence.

	Correct	Error
First Try		
Second Try		

1. (Who's, Whose) coat are you wearing?   2. That snow (scene, seen) was beautiful.   3. We will burn a lot of (wood, would) in   (3)

our fireplace.   4. All the work we did was in (vein, vane, vain).   5. The bus (fair, fare) wasn't very much.   6. I got the (right,   (6)

write) telephone number the first time I called.   7. Would you give me a big (peace, piece) of cake?   8. The (capital, capitol)   (8)

of Kansas is Topeka.   9. It is (to, two, too) late for John to come over.   10. It is midnight (all ready, already).   11. Mary   (10)

drank the (whole, hole) bottle of Coke.   12. He is going to (steel, steal) third base.   13. Tom was the (forth, fourth) person in   (13)

line.   14. (Their, There) goes that bunch of dogs again.   15. We walked briskly (threw, through) the forest.   16. Her hair is   (15)

very (coarse, course).   17. Mary's boyfriend is very (weak, week).   18. Our (principle, principal) isn't very old.   19. (It's, Its)   (19)

not cold enough to wear your winter coat.   20. It is (altogether, all together) too late to walk home alone.   21. She is going to   (20)

(wear, where) her new jeans.   22. (Here, Hear) comes my mother right now.   23. The (weather, whether) is very changeable   (23)

this time of the year.   24. Are your muscles (sore, soar)?   25. The (soul, sole) of his shoe had a hole in it.   26. The (sails,   (26)

sales) of his boat were torn.   27. The state (fair, fare) begins next (week, weak).   28. Her (waste, waist) is very tiny.   29. I   (29)

(would, wood) like to have something (sweet, suite) to eat.   30. Have you (seen, scene) Jimmy's new (pear, pare, pair) of   (33)

shoes?   31. The truck had to (tow, toe) us to the garage.   32. She fell in the big (hole, whole).   33. It was (there, their) turn   (36)

to fix dinner.   34. She took (to, too, two) friends with her.   35. We aren't sure (whether, weather) we should stay home or   (38)

not.   36. The band (lead, led) the parade.   (39)

© 2005 Sopris West Educational Services. All rights reserved. Practicing Basic Skills in Language Arts. Purchaser has permission to photocopy this page for classroom use only.

	Correct	Error
First Try		
Second Try		

ONE-MINUTE FLUENCY BUILDER SERIES

Homonym Review

Directions: Underline the word that will make a correct sentence.

1. This is the first (week, weak) of December.   2. (Where, Wear) should I put these envelopes?   3. I (would, wood) like to stay home tonight.   4. Mary is my (forth, fourth) cousin.   5. Mr. Jones (lead, led) the band.   6. (It's, Its) my turn to babysit.   7. The bus (fair, fare) cost too much.   8. Jimmy ate the (whole, hole) cake.   9. Jane broke her big (tow, toe).   10. He is too (weak, week) to lift the box.   11. The candy bar was so (sweet, suite) it gave me a toothache.   12. The (principal, principle) of our school is a woman.   13. We are going to cut (wood, would) tomorrow.   14. Susan fell in a big (hole, whole).   15. John has a new (pare, pair) of shoes.   16. His shoe (sole, soul) was torn.   17. The holiday (sails, sales) are doing well.   18. His leg is made of (steal, steel).   19. Mary is going to (write, right) Jimmy a long letter.   20. Is it (too, to, two) late to go out for dinner?   21. The pencil (led, lead) broke.   22. Are you (all ready, already) to go?   23. She has (scene, seen) our new house.   24. (Who's, Whose) house are you going to visit?   25. The county (fair, fare) is almost over.   26. Ed has a (sore, soar) back.   27 My friend has a new (sail, sale) boat.   28. (Wood, Would) you show me how to make the dress?   29. She is going to (where, wear) jeans to the party.   30. He bought a weather (vain, vane) for the barn.   31. The (vain, vein, vane) in her leg is blue.   32. The new year is a time of (peace, piece).   33. Can I have another (peace, piece) of cake?   34. It is just the (principal, principle) of the matter.   35. Tom (threw, through) the ball clear across the field.   36. I like to eat (pares, pears, pairs) better than apples.   37. Did you (waste, waist) all of your food?

© 2005 Sopris West Educational Services. All rights reserved. Practicing Basic Skills in Language Arts. Purchaser has permission to photocopy this page for classroom use only.

ONE MINUTE FLUENCY BUILDER SERIES

SEE TO MARK

Homonym Review

Directions: Underline the word that will make a correct sentence.

	Correct	Error
First Try		
Second Try		

1. This is the first (week, weak) of December.   2. (Where, Wear) should I put these envelopes?   3. I (would, wood) like (3)

to stay home tonight.   4. Mary is my (forth, fourth) cousin.   5. Mr. Jones (lead, led) the band.   6. (It's, Its) my turn to (6)

babysit.   7. The bus (fair, fare) cost too much.   8. Jimmy ate the (whole, hole) cake.   9. Jane broke her big (tow, toe).   10. He (9)

is too (weak, week) to lift the box.   11. The candy bar was so (sweet, suite) it gave me a toothache.   12. The (principal, (12)

principle) of our school is a woman.   13. We are going to cut (wood, would) tomorrow.   14. Susan fell in a big (hole, (14)

whole).   15. John has a new (pare, pair) of shoes.   16. His shoe (sole, soul) was torn.   17. The holiday (sails, sales) are doing (17)

well.   18. His leg is made of (steal, steel).   19. Mary is going to (write, right) Jimmy a long letter.   20. Is it (too, to, two) late (20)

to go out for dinner?   21. The pencil (led, lead) broke.   22. Are you (all ready, already) to go?   23. She has (scene, seen) our (23)

new house.   24. (Who's, Whose) house are you going to visit?   25. The county (fair, fare) is almost over.   26. Ed has a (sore, (26)

soar) back. 27 My friend has a new (sail, sale) boat.   28. (Wood, Would) you show me how to make the dress?   29. She is going (28)

to (where, wear) jeans to the party.   30. He bought a weather (vain, vane) for the barn.   31. The (vain, vein, vane) in her leg is (31)

blue.   32. The new year is a time of (peace, piece).   33. Can I have another (peace, piece) of cake?   34. It is just the (principal, (33)

principle) of the matter.   35. Tom (threw, through) the ball clear across the field.   36. I like to eat (pares, pears, pairs) better (36)

than apples.   37. Did you (waste, waist) all of your food? (37)

ANSWER SHEET

© 2005 Sopris West Educational Services. All rights reserved. Practicing Basic Skills in Language Arts. Purchaser has permission to photocopy this page for classroom use only.

SEE TO MARK

Homonym Review

Directions: Underline the word that will make a correct sentence.

	Correct	Error
First Try		
Second Try		

1. (Its, It's) a long way to drive for one day.   2. That car was made out of (lead, led).   3. She left (they're, there, their) clothes

in the old car.   4. We went (to, too, two) the (fair, fare) with Mary's (two, to, too) brothers.   5. The tractor had to (tow, toe)

him out of the ditch.   6. Don drove into the (whole, hole) load of hay.   7. Her hotel (sweet, suite) was fabulous.   8. She

was too (weak, week) to visit with us.   9. (Wear, Where) did you get your new (pair, pare, pear) of pants?   10. The school

(principle, principal) came to the meeting.   11. Did you (here, hear) about the new teacher?   12. She likes to (soar, sore)

in airplanes.   13. We drove right (through, threw) the mud puddle.   14. I want to go home (write, right) now.   15. Don't

(steal, steel) or you will be punished.   16. (Write, right) this address in your book.   17. Mary has a (whole, hole) in her

dress.   18. (Where, Wear) are you going on your vacation?   19. I don't know (weather, whether) I should go or not.   20. That

material feels very (coarse, course).   21. What is your state (capital, capitol)?   22. The picture was of a winter (scene,

seen).   23. Her (hair, hare) was so long it touched the floor.   24. Will you please (wear, where) a dress to school?   25. (Here,

Hear) is the coat I promised you.   26. (Their, There) new house is a mess.   27. (There, Their) goes that fancy car

again.   28. Did you (see, sea) that new girl?   29. The (air, heir) in here is suffocating.   30. The (sun, son) is not shining again

today.   31. My (sun, son) is going to college.   32. Mary was the (forth, fourth) person to call me.   33. Mike is (air, heir) to a

large fortune.   34. (Where, Wear) are you going Saturday night?   35. Don't (waist, waste) any more time on that mess.

Practicing Basic Skills in Language Arts • 463

ONE MINUTE FLUENCY
BUILDER SERIES

© 2005 Sopris West Educational Services. All rights reserved. Practicing Basic Skills in Language Arts. Purchaser has permission to photocopy this page for classroom use only.

	Correct	Error
First Try		
Second Try		

Homonym Review

Directions: Underline the word that will make a correct sentence.

1. (Its, It's) a long way to drive for one day. 2. That car was made out of (lead, led). 3. She left (they're, there, their) clothes (3)

in the old car. 4. We went (to, too, two) the (fair, fare) with Mary's (two, to, too) brothers. 5. The tractor had to (tow, toe) (7)

him out of the ditch. 6. Don drove into the (whole, hole) load of hay. 7. Her hotel (sweet, suite) was fabulous. 8. She (9)

was too (weak, week) to visit with us. 9. (Wear, Where) did you get your new (pair, pare, pear) of pants? 10. The school (12)

(principle, principal) came to the meeting. 11. Did you (here, hear) about the new teacher? 12. She likes to (soar, sore) (15)

in airplanes. 13. We drove right (through, threw) the mud puddle. 14. I want to go home (write, right) now. 15. Don't (17)

(steal, steel) or you will be punished. 16. (Write, right) this address in your book. 17. Mary has a (whole, hole) in her (20)

dress. 18. (Where, Wear) are you going on your vacation? 19. I don't know (weather, whether) I should go or not. 20. That (22)

material feels very (coarse, course). 21. What is your state (capital, capitol)? 22. The picture was of a winter (scene, (25)

seen). 23. Her (hair, hare) was so long it touched the floor. 24. Will you please (wear, where) a dress to school? 25. (Here, (28)

Hear) is the coat I promised you. 26. (Their, There) new house is a mess. 27. (There, Their) goes that fancy car (30)

again. 28. Did you (see, sea) that new girl? 29. The (air, heir) in here is suffocating. 30. The (sun, son) is not shining again (33)

today. 31. My (sun, son) is going to college. 32. Mary was the (forth, fourth) person to call me. 33. Mike is (air, heir) to a (36)

large fortune. 34. (Where, Wear) are you going Saturday night? 35. Don't (waist, waste) any more time on that mess. (38)

ANSWER SHEET

© 2005 Sopris West Educational Services. All rights reserved. Practicing Basic Skills in Language Arts. Purchaser has permission to photocopy this page for classroom use only.

	Correct	Error
First Try		
Second Try		

SEE TO MARK

ONE MINUTE FLUENCY
BUILDER SERIES

Homonym Review
Directions: Underline the word that will make a correct sentence.

1. The (to, two, too) men were (to, two, too) tired to (lode, load) the metal pipes back on (they're, there, their) truck.   2. After working all day in the (rein, rain) we looked forward to a fire in the (great, grate), a great (dessert, desert) after dinner, and an evening of (peace, piece) and quiet.   3. The defense (council, counsel) questioned him about the psychology (course, coarse) he had taken.   4. Above the (mantel, mantle) was a painting of Lady Ellen wearing a red velvet (mantle, mantel).   5. Then a second voice, (hoarse, horse) with fatigue, announced that the (missile, missal) had hit its mark.   6. A (canvass, canvas) of the staff showed that no (one, won) in the diplomatic (corps, core) was ever idle, whether the weather was (fair, fare) or (foul, fowl).   7. Even a second-rate (prophet, profit) could have told him that selling (led, lead) tokens for bus (fares, fairs) (would, wood) bring very little profit.   8. (Whose, Who's) the movie (idle, idol) (whose, who's) picture is on every magazine cover these days?   9. (It's, Its) part of his plan to see that (there, they're, their) caught with (there, they're, their) hands in the till.   10. As they walked along the (key, quay), Jane dropped her (quay, key) and it fell (through, threw) a crack.   11. Mrs. Smith took her coat to the tailor, requesting that she (alter, altar) it to fit her better.   12. John was (baring, bearing) his teeth while (bearing, baring) a heavy burden on his shoulders.   13. The porter reserved an upper (birth, berth) for us on the train.   14. The boys built a treehouse on the (bow, bough) of a tree.   15. The truck driver forgot to release the (break, brake) before moving out of the parking spot.   16. The horses trotted in single file along the (bridal, bridle) path through the woods.   17. The campaign workers went in a house-to-house (canvass, canvas) to solicit notes for (their, they're, there) candidate.

© 2005 Sopris West Educational Services. All rights reserved. Practicing Basic Skills in Language Arts. Purchaser has permission to photocopy this page for classroom use only.

SEE TO MARK

	First Try	Second Try
Correct		
Error		

Homonym Review

Directions: Underline the word that will make a correct sentence.

1. The (to, two, too) men were (to, two, too) tired to (lode, load) the metal pipes back on (they're, there, their) truck.   2.   After (4)

working all day in the (rein, rain) we looked forward to a fire in the (great, grate), a great (dessert, desert) after dinner, and an (7)

evening of (peace, piece) and quiet.   3.   The defense (council, counsel) questioned him about the psychology (course, coarse) (10)

he had taken.   4.   Above the (mantel, mantle) was a painting of Lady Ellen wearing a red velvet (mantle, mantel).   5.   Then (12)

a second voice, (hoarse, horse) with fatigue, announced that the (missile, missal) had hit its mark.   6.   A (canvass, canvas) of (15)

the staff showed that no (one, won) in the diplomatic (corps, core) was ever idle, whether the weather was (fair, fare) or (foul, (19)

fowl).   7.   Even a second-rate (prophet, profit) could have told him that selling (led, lead) tokens for bus (fares, fairs) (would, (23)

wood) bring very little profit.   8.   (Whose, Who's) the movie (idle, idol) (whose, who's) picture is on every magazine cover these (26)

days?   9.   (It's, Its) part of his plan to see that (there, they're, their) caught with (there, they're, their) hands in the till.   10.   As (29)

they walked along the (key, quay), Jane dropped her (quay, key) and it fell (through, threw) a crack.   11.   Mrs. Smith took her (32)

coat to the tailor, requesting that she (alter, altar) it to fit her better.   12.   John was (baring, bearing) his teeth while (bearing, (35)

baring) a heavy burden on his shoulders.   13.   The porter reserved an upper (birth, berth) for us on the train.   14.   The boys (36)

built a treehouse on the (bow, bough) of a tree.   15.   The truck driver forgot to release the (break, brake) before moving out of (38)

the parking spot.   16.   The horses trotted in single file along the (bridal, bridle) path through the woods.   17.   The campaign (39)

workers went in a house-to-house (canvass, canvas) to solicit notes for (their, they're, there) candidate. (41)

ANSWER SHEET   Practicing Basic Skills in Language Arts • 466

© 2005 Sopris West Educational Services. All rights reserved. Practicing Basic Skills in Language Arts. Purchaser has permission to photocopy this page for classroom use only.

SEE TO WRITE

Prefixes: Pro, En, Re, Im, Dis

Directions: Write in the meaning of the prefix.

KEY: pro—for; en—make; re—back, again; im—not, in, within, into; dis—down, from, away

	First Try	Second Try
Correct		
Error		

pro _____	re _____	im _____
re _____	en _____	en _____
dis _____	im _____	pro _____
en _____	re _____	dis _____
pro _____	en _____	im _____
im _____	pro _____	en _____
dis _____	im _____	pro _____
pro _____	en _____	en _____

© 2005 Sopris West Educational Services. All rights reserved. Practicing Basic Skills in Language Arts. Purchaser has permission to photocopy this page for classroom use only.

ONE-MINUTE FLUENCY BUILDER SERIES

SEE TO WRITE

Prefixes: Pro, En, Re, Im, Dis

Directions: Write in the meaning of the prefix.

KEY: pro—for; en—make; re—back, again; im—not, in, within, into; dis—down, from, away

	Correct	Error
First Try		
Second Try		

pro — for	re — back, again	en — make	im — not, in, within, into	(4)
re — back, again	en — make	dis — down, from, away	en — make	(8)
dis — down, from, away	im — not, in, within, into	en — make	pro — for	(12)
en — make	re — back, again	pro — for	dis — down, from, away	(16)
pro — for	en — make	dis — down, from, away	im — not, in, within, into	(20)
im — not, in, within, into	pro — for	dis — down, from, away	en — make	(24)
dis — down, from, away	im — not, in, within, into	dis — down, from, away	pro — for	(28)
pro — for	en — make	dis — down, from, away	en — make	(32)

ANSWER SHEET

Practicing Basic Skills in Language Arts • 468

© 2005 Sopris West Educational Services. All rights reserved. Practicing Basic Skills in Language Arts. Purchaser has permission to photocopy this page for classroom use only.

ONE MINUTE FLUENCY BUILDER SERIES

SEE TO WRITE

Prefixes: Mis, Re, Un, Trans, Dis, Con

Directions: Write in the meaning of the prefix.
KEY: mis—wrongly; re—again; un—not; trans—across; dis—opposite of; con—together

	Correct	Error
First Try		
Second Try		

un _____	dis _____	mis _____	re _____
con _____	mis _____	re _____	un _____
trans _____	re _____	mis _____	re _____
un _____	con _____	dis _____	un _____
dis _____	re _____	con _____	trans _____
re _____	dis _____	mis _____	con _____
trans _____	mis _____	re _____	un _____
dis _____	con _____	re _____	mis _____

© 2005 Sopris West Educational Services. All rights reserved. Practicing Basic Skills in Language Arts. Purchaser has permission to photocopy this page for classroom use only.

ONE-MINUTE FLUENCY BUILDER SERIES

SEE TO WRITE

Prefixes: Mis, Re, Un, Trans, Dis, Con

Directions: Write in the meaning of the prefix.
KEY: mis—wrongly; re—again; un—not; trans—across; dis—opposite of; con—together

	Correct	Error
First Try		
Second Try		

un __ **not**	dis __ **opposite of**	mis __ **wrongly**	re __ **again**	(4)
con __ **together**	mis __ **wrongly**	re __ **again**	un __ **not**	(8)
trans __ **across**	re __ **again**	mis __ **wrongly**	re __ **again**	(12)
un __ **not**	con __ **together**	dis __ **opposite of**	un __ **not**	(16)
dis __ **opposite of**	re __ **again**	con __ **together**	trans __ **across**	(20)
re __ **again**	dis __ **opposite of**	mis __ **wrongly**	con __ **together**	(24)
trans __ **across**	mis __ **wrongly**	re __ **again**	un __ **not**	(28)
dis __ **opposite of**	con __ **together**	re __ **again**	mis __ **wrongly**	(32)

ANSWER SHEET

Practicing Basic Skills in Language Arts • 470

© 2005 Sopris West Educational Services. All rights reserved. Practicing Basic Skills in Language Arts. Purchaser has permission to photocopy this page for classroom use only.

	First Try	Second Try
Correct		
Error		

SEE TO WRITE

Prefixes: De, Super, Im, Sub, Inter

Directions: Write in the meaning of the prefix.
KEY: de—down, from, away; super—over, above; im—not, in, within, into;
sub—under, below, lower; inter—between, among

de _____	sub _____	super _____	inter _____
sub _____	inter _____	im _____	super _____
im _____	de _____	sub _____	inter _____
sub _____	super _____	im _____	de _____
super _____	de _____	inter _____	sub _____
de _____	inter _____	im _____	super _____
sub _____	inter _____	de _____	inter _____
de _____	sub _____	super _____	im _____

Practicing Basic Skills in Language Arts • 471

© 2005 Sopris West Educational Services. All rights reserved. Practicing Basic Skills in Language Arts. Purchaser has permission to photocopy this page for classroom use only.

ONE MINUTE FLUENCY
BUILDER SERIES

	First Try	Second Try
Correct		
Error		

SEE TO WRITE

Prefixes: De, Super, Im, Sub, Inter

Directions: Write in the meaning of the prefix.

KEY: de—down, from, away; super—over, above; im—not, in, within, into;
sub—under, below, lower; inter—between, among

							#
de — down, from, away	sub — under, below, lower	super — over, above	inter — between, among	(4)
sub — under, below, lower	inter — between, among	im — not, in, within, into	super — over, above	(8)
im — not, in, within, into	de — down, from, away	sub — under, below, lower	inter — between, among	(12)
sub — under, below, lower	super — over, above	im — not, in, within, into	de — down, from, away	(16)
super — over, above	de — down, from, away	inter — between, among	sub — under, below, lower	(20)
de — down, from, away	inter — between, among	im — not, in, within, into	super — over, above	(24)
sub — below, under, lower	inter — between, among	de — down, from, away	inter — between, among	(28)
de — down, from, away	sub — under, below, lower	super — over, above	im — not, in, within, into	(32)

ANSWER SHEET

Practicing Basic Skills in Language Arts • 472

© 2005 Sopris West Educational Services. All rights reserved. Practicing Basic Skills in Language Arts. Purchaser has permission to photocopy this page for classroom use only.

	Correct	Error
First Try		
Second Try		

SEE TO WRITE

ONE MINUTE FLUENCY BUILDER SERIES

Prefixes: Pre, Manu, Ego, Mono, Sur, Ex

Directions: Write in the meaning of the prefix.
KEY: pre—before; manu(i)—hand; ego—I, self; mono—one; sur—over; ex—out

pre _____	mono _____	manu(i) _____	sur _____
ex _____	manu(i) _____	ego _____	mono _____
ego _____	mono _____	manu(i) _____	sur _____
pre _____	ex _____	mono _____	ego _____
sur _____	pre _____	ex _____	mono _____
pre _____	sur _____	manu(i) _____	sur _____
manu(i) _____	pre _____	sur _____	ex _____
sur _____	pre _____	mono _____	ego _____

© 2005 Sopris West Educational Services. All rights reserved. Practicing Basic Skills in Language Arts. Purchaser has permission to photocopy this page for classroom use only.

SEE TO WRITE

Prefixes: Pre, Manu, Ego, Mono, Sur, Ex

Directions: Write in the meaning of the prefix.

KEY: pre—before; manu(i)—hand; ego—I, self; mono—one; sur—over; ex—out

	Correct	Error
First Try		
Second Try		

Prefix	Meaning	Prefix	Meaning	Prefix	Meaning	Prefix	Meaning	#
pre	before	mono	one	manu(i)	hand	sur	over	(4)
ex	out	manu(i)	hand	ego	I, self	mono	one	(8)
ego	I, self	mono	one	manu(i)	hand	sur	over	(12)
pre	before	ex	out	mono	one	ego	I, self	(16)
sur	over	sur	over	ex	out	mono	one	(20)
pre	before	pre	before	manu(i)	hand	sur	over	(24)
manu(i)	hand	pre	before	sur	over	ex	out	(28)
sur	over	pre	before	mono	one	ego	I, self	(32)

© 2005 Sopris West Educational Services. All rights reserved. Practicing Basic Skills in Language Arts. Purchaser has permission to photocopy this page for classroom use only.

ONE-MINUTE FLUENCY BUILDER SERIES

SEE TO WRITE

Prefixes: Ab, Be, Bi, Co, Com, In, Tri

Directions: Write in the meaning of the prefix.

KEY: ab—from, away; be—on, around, over; bi—two; co—with, together, jointly; com—with, together, jointly; in—not, in, within, into; tri—three

ab	be	bi	co
in	tri	be	ab
tri	co	com	bi
in	bi	ab	com
co	tri	in	bi
ab	be	bi	co
com	tri	bi	be
be	ab	co	com

© 2005 Sopris West Educational Services. All rights reserved. Practicing Basic Skills in Language Arts. Purchaser has permission to photocopy this page for classroom use only.

ONE-MINUTE FLUENCY BUILDER SERIES

	Correct	Error
First Try		
Second Try		

SEE TO WRITE

Prefixes: Ab, Be, Bi, Co, Com, In, Tri

Directions: Write in the meaning of the prefix.

KEY: ab—from, away; be—on, around, over; bi—two; co—with, together, jointly; com—with, together, jointly; in—not, within, into; tri—three

ab — from, away	be — on, around, over	bi — two	co — with, together, jointly	(4)
in — not, in, within, into	tri — three	be — on, around, over	ab — from, away	(8)
tri — three	co — with, together, jointly	com — with, together, jointly	bi — two	(12)
in — not, in, within, into	bi — two	ab — from, away	com — with, together, jointly	(16)
co — with, together, jointly	tri — three	in — not, in, within, into	bi — two	(20)
ab — from, away	be — on, around, over	bi — two	co — with, together, jointly	(24)
com — with, together, jointly	tri — three	bi — two	be — on, around, over	(28)
be — on, around, over	ab — from, away	co — with, together, jointly	com — with, together, jointly	(32)

Practicing Basic Skills in Language Arts • 476

ANSWER SHEET

© 2005 Sopris West Educational Services. All rights reserved. Practicing Basic Skills in Language Arts. Purchaser has permission to photocopy this page for classroom use only.

ONE MINUTE FLUENCY
BUILDER SERIES

Prefixes: Circum, Com, Con, Dia, Extra, Out, Post, Trans, Sym, Syn

Directions: Write in the meaning of the prefix.

KEY: circum—around; com, con—with, together; dia—across, through; extra—beyond; out—out, beyond; post—after; trans—across; sym, syn—with, together

	First Try	Second Try
Correct		
Error		

circum	dia	out	post
com, con	extra	trans	sym, syn
dia	circum	post	out
com, con	trans	extra	sym, syn
post	sym, syn	out	circum
dia	post	dia	post
com, con	circum	extra	out
trans	extra	dia	trans

© 2005 Sopris West Educational Services. All rights reserved. Practicing Basic Skills in Language Arts. Purchaser has permission to photocopy this page for classroom use only.

ONE MINUTE FLUENCY BUILDER SERIES

SEE TO WRITE

Prefixes: Circum, Com, Con, Dia, Extra, Out, Post, Trans, Sym, Syn

Directions: Write in the meaning of the prefix.

KEY: circum—around; com, con—with, together; dia—across, through; extra—beyond; out—out, beyond; post—after; trans—across; sym, syn—with, together

circum	around	dia	across, through	out	out, beyond	post	after	(4)
com, con	with, together	extra	beyond	trans	across	sym, syn	with, together	(8)
dia	across, through	circum	around	post	after	out	out, beyond	(12)
com, con	with, together	trans	across	extra	beyond	sym, syn	with, together	(16)
post	after	sym, syn	with, together	out	out, beyond	circum	around	(20)
dia	across, through	post	after	dia	across, through	post	after	(24)
com, con	with, together	circum	around	extra	beyond	out	out, beyond	(28)
trans	across	extra	beyond	dia	across, through	trans	across	(32)

	Correct	Error
First Try		
Second Try		

ANSWER SHEET

Practicing Basic Skills in Language Arts • 478

© 2005 Sopris West Educational Services. All rights reserved. Practicing Basic Skills in Language Arts. Purchaser has permission to photocopy this page for classroom use only.

ONE MINUTE FLUENCY BUILDER SERIES

SEE TO WRITE

Prefixes: Mis, Un, Dis, Re, Trans, Con

Directions: Write in the prefix that completes the word.

KEY: mis—wrongly; un—not; dis—opposite of; re—again; trans—across; con—together

	Correct	Error
First Try		
Second Try		

I always _____ spell that word. It is messy so I will _____ write it. For an A, you can't leave homework _____ done. We will _____ connect the radio before _____ port our furniture to the new house.

repairing it. Things packed together are _____ centrated. When I think of something again, I _____ member. You look sad. Are you _____ happy? If you do not understand, you _____ understand. Things _____ tainer. My dad moved across the state when he was _____ ferred. If it is not _____ are held together in a _____ allowed. When people agree together they have _____ cord. Ed read it wrong and _____ allowed, it is _____ take. If you do not have luck, you are _____ lucky. When I move plants across the yard, I _____ made a _____ plant them. When you lose courage, you are _____ couraged. If she comes back, she _____ turns. If you lay it in the wrong place, you _____ lay it. If he sells it again, he _____ sells it. A flight across the ocean is a _____ Atlantic flight. If you do not have health, you are _____ healthy. Joe's war wounds _____ abled him. Southern states joined together in the _____ federacy. If they get it again, they _____ gain it. If it is not likely to be, it is _____ likely. If he judges wrongly, he _____ judges. When they talk together, they _____ verse. If it is not at all agreeable, it is _____ agreeable. Sally was not friendly. In fact, she was quite _____ friendly. To get the German message across, Hans _____ lated it into English. When people do not agree they have _____ cord. If he sells it again, he _____ sells it. Ed read it wrong and made a _____ take. Are you _____ happy?

© 2005 Sopris West Educational Services. All rights reserved. Practicing Basic Skills in Language Arts. Purchaser has permission to photocopy this page for classroom use only.

SEE TO WRITE

Prefixes: Mis, Un, Dis, Re, Trans, Con

Directions: Write in the prefix that completes the word.

KEY: mis—wrongly; un—not; dis—opposite of; re—again; trans—across; con—together

ONE MINUTE FLUENCY BUILDER SERIES

	Correct	Error
First Try		
Second Try		

I always **mis** spell that word. It is messy so I will **re** write it. For an A, you can't leave homework (2)

un done. We will **trans** port our furniture to the new house. **Dis** connect the radio before (5)

repairing it. Things packed together are **con** centrated. When I think of something again, I **re** (7)

member. You look sad. Are you **un** happy? If you do not understand, you **mis** understand. Things (9)

are held together in a **con** tainer. My dad moved across the state when he was **trans** ferred. If it is not (11)

allowed, it is **dis** allowed. When people agree together they have **con** cord. Ed read it wrong and (13)

made a **mis** take. If you do not have luck, you are **un** lucky. When I move plants across the yard, I (15)

trans plant them. When you lose courage, you are **dis** couraged. If she comes back, she **re** (18)

turns. If you lay it in the wrong place, you **mis** lay it. If he sells it again, he **re** sells it. A flight (20)

across the ocean is a **trans** Atlantic flight. If you do not have health, you are **un** healthy. Joe's war (22)

wounds **dis** abled him. Southern states joined together in the **con** federacy. If they get it again, they (24)

re gain it. If it is not likely to be, it is **un** likely. If he judges wrongly, he **mis** judges. When (27)

they talk together, they **con** verse. If it is not at all agreeable, it is **dis** agreeable. Sally was not friendly. (29)

In fact, she was quite **un** friendly. To get the German message across, Hans **trans** lated it into English. (31)

When people do not agree they have **dis** cord. If he sells it again, he **re** sells it. Ed read it wrong and (33)

made a **mis** take. Are you **un** happy? (35)

ANSWER SHEET

Practicing Basic Skills in Language Arts • 480

© 2005 Sopris West Educational Services. All rights reserved. Practicing Basic Skills in Language Arts. Purchaser has permission to photocopy this page for classroom use only.

SEE TO WRITE

Prefixes: Pre, Mono, Manu, Sur, Ego, Ex

Directions: Write in the prefix that completes the word.

KEY: pre—before; mono—one; manu(i)—hand; sur—over; ego—I, self; ex—out

	First Try	Second Try
Correct		
Error		

1. The top of a table is a _____ face.

2. To spread out a room, you _____ pand it.

3. A part taken out of a book is an _____ cerpt.

4. He _____ passed at English by getting grades over the other students.

5. Mike is _____ tistical because he thinks of himself as so important.

6. You _____ dict something if you say it before it happens.

7. " _____ meditated" murder means "planned beforehand."

8. We rode the _____ rail, a one-rail train.

9. My son is not in school yet; he is a _____ schooler.

10. You _____ pay when you pay beforehand.

11. He spoke in a _____ tone when he spoke in one tone.

12. We _____ pared the lesson when we did it beforehand.

13. If you are not included, you are _____ cluded.

14. A baby is _____ centric because his world is centered around himself.

15. I had a _____ cure when I treated my hands.

16. The boys did _____ al labor when they worked with their hands.

17. A handwritten book is a _____ script.

18. His hard work was _____ fest, because it showed up at every hand.

19. If you _____ claim, you cry out.

20. Glen is an _____ maniac because he thinks only of himself.

21. A one-winged plane is a _____ plane.

22. We paid a _____ tax, which is a tax over another tax.

23. A _____ chrome picture has only one color.

24. Mr. Smith paid a charge over the price, called a _____ charge.

25. If you outdo the speed limit, you _____ ceed it.

26. You take an _____ trip when you have been thinking well of yourself.

© 2005 Sopris West Educational Services. All rights reserved. Practicing Basic Skills in Language Arts. Purchaser has permission to photocopy this page for classroom use only.

ONE-MINUTE FLUENCY
BUILDER SERIES

SEE TO WRITE

Prefixes: Pre, Mono, Manu, Sur, Ego, Ex

Directions: Write in the prefix that completes the word.
KEY: pre—before; mono—one; manu(i)—hand; sur—over; ego—I, self; ex—out

	First Try	Second Try
Correct		
Error		

1. The top of a table is a **sur** _____ face.

2. To spread out a room, you **ex** _____ pand it. (2)

3. A part taken out of a book is an **ex** _____ cerpt.

4. He **sur** _____ passed at English by getting grades over the other students. (4)

5. Mike is **ego** _____ tistical because he thinks of himself as so important.

6. You **pre** _____ dict something if you say it before it happens. (6)

7. " **Pre** _____ meditated" murder means "planned beforehand."

8. We rode the **mono** _____ rail, a one-rail train. (8)

9. My son is not in school yet; he is a **pre** _____ schooler.

10. You **pre** _____ pay when you pay beforehand. (10)

11. He spoke in a **mono** _____ tone when he spoke in one tone.

12. We **pre** _____ pared the lesson when we did it beforehand. (12)

13. If you are not included, you are **ex** _____ cluded.

14. A baby is **ego** _____ centric because his world is centered around himself. (14)

15. I had a **mani** _____ cure when I treated my hands.

16. The boys did **manu** _____ al labor when they worked with their hands. (16)

17. A handwritten book is a **manu** _____ script.

18. His hard work was **mani** _____ fest, because it showed up at every hand. (18)

19. If you **ex** _____ claim, you cry out.

20. Glen is an **ego** _____ maniac because he thinks only of himself. (20)

21. A one-winged plane is a **mono** _____ plane.

22. We paid a **sur** _____ tax, which is a tax over another tax. (22)

23. A **mono** _____ chrome picture has only one color.

24. Mr. Smith paid a charge over the price, called a **sur** _____ charge. (24)

25. If you outdo the speed limit, you **ex** _____ ceed it.

26. You take an **ego** _____ trip when you have been thinking well of yourself. (26)

ANSWER SHEET

Practicing Basic Skills in Language Arts • 482

© 2005 Sopris West Educational Services. All rights reserved. Practicing Basic Skills in Language Arts. Purchaser has permission to photocopy this page for classroom use only.

Dictionary Skills

Alphabet: Beginning, Middle, End of
Alphabet... 485

Alphabet: Beginning, Middle, End of
Alphabet... 487

Alphabet: Two Letters That Follow a
Letter 489

Alphabet: Two Letters That Come Before
a Letter.. 491

Alphabet: Two Letters That Come Before
and After a Letter 493

Alphabet: Two Letters That Come Before
and After a Letter 495

Alphabetical Order: Before or After Guide
Word.. 497

Alphabetical Order: Before or After Guide
Word.. 499

Alphabetical Order: Before or After Guide
Word.. 501

Alphabetical Order: Before or After Guide
Word.. 503

Alphabetical Order: Before, After, or
Between Guide Words.............................. 505

Alphabetical Order: Before, After, or
Between Guide Words.............................. 507

Alphabetical Order: Found on Which
Page?... 509

Alphabetical Order: Placing 4 Words in
Alphabetical Order 511

Alphabetical Order: Placing 4 Words in
Alphabetical Order 513

Alphabetical Order: Placing 5 Words in
Alphabetical Order 515

Alphabetical Order: Placing 5 Words in
Alphabetical Order 517

Alphabetical Order: Placing 5 Words in
Alphabetical Order 519

Alphabetical Order: Placing 5 Words in
Alphabetical Order 521

Alphabetical Order: Placing 5 Words in
Alphabetical Order 523

Alphabetical Order: Placing 5 Words in
Alphabetical Order 525

Alphabetical Order: Choose Words
Falling Between Two Guide Words 527

Alphabetical Order: Choose Words
Falling Between Two Guide Words 529

Alphabetical Order: Choose Words
Falling Between Two Guide Words 531

Alphabetical Order: Choose Words
Falling Between Two Guide Words 533

Alphabetical Order: Choose Words
Falling Between Two Guide Words 535

Alphabetical Order: Choose Words
Falling Between Two Guide Words 537

Guide Words: Before Page, Same Page,
After Page 539

Guide Words: Before Page, Same Page,
After Page 541

Guide Words: Before Page, Same Page,
After Page 543

Guide Words: Before Page, Same Page,
After Page 545

Guide Words: Find Page in Dictionary
for Each Word 547

SEE TO WRITE OR SEE TO SAY

	Correct	Error
First Try		
Second Try		

Alphabet: Beginning, Middle, End of Alphabet

Directions: Indicate whether each letter comes at the beginning (B), middle, (M), or end (E) of the alphabet.

Beginning (B) ABCDEFG Middle (M) HIJKLMNOPQ End (E) RSTUVWXYZ

y ___	e ___	r ___	p ___	o ___	p ___	r ___	e ___	q ___
a ___	k ___	l ___	s ___	j ___	l ___	s ___	a ___	g ___
z ___	x ___	m ___	n ___	x ___	b ___	n ___	m ___	x ___
q ___	e ___	r ___	t ___	p ___	w ___	m ___	d ___	s ___
x ___	c ___	f ___	k ___	l ___	i ___	o ___	o ___	p ___
i ___	y ___	e ___	x ___	c ___	w ___	o ___	i ___	p ___
j ___	m ___	n ___	o ___	p ___	e ___	h ___	k ___	p ___
f ___	o ___	e ___	j ___	s ___	m ___	b ___	i ___	s ___
i ___	u ___	y ___	c ___	o ___	p ___	a ___	c ___	x ___
j ___	k ___	s ___	m ___	n ___	s ___	r ___	r ___	s ___
j ___	d ___	e ___	s ___	c ___	b ___	e ___	r ___	s ___
r ___	j ___	s ___	s ___	o ___	l ___	r ___	s ___	s ___
u ___	o ___	o ___	b ___	v ___	w ___	t ___	u ___	u ___
m ___	o ___	w ___	s ___	h ___	c ___	x ___	y ___	y ___
j ___	k ___	s ___	u ___	i ___	w ___	x ___	o ___	b ___

© 2005 Sopris West Educational Services. All rights reserved. Practicing Basic Skills in Language Arts. Purchaser has permission to photocopy this page for classroom use only.

ONE-MINUTE FLUENCY — BUILDER SERIES

SEE TO WRITE OR SEE TO SAY

Alphabet: Beginning, Middle, End of Alphabet

Directions: Indicate whether each letter comes at the beginning (B), middle, (M), or end (E) of the alphabet.

Beginning (B) ABCDEFG

Middle (M) HIJKLMNOPQ

End (E) RSTUVWXYZ

	Correct	Error
First Try		
Second Try		

y **E**	e **B**	o **M**	r **E**	e **B**	p **M**	o **M**	r **E**	e **B**	e **B**	q **M**	(11)
a **B**	k **M**	l **M**	j **M**	s **E**	n **M**	i **M**	s **E**	a **B**	a **B**	g **B**	(22)
z **E**	x **E**	c **B**	m **M**	n **M**	i **M**	n **M**	n **M**	m **M**	m **M**	x **E**	(33)
q **M**	e **B**	i **M**	r **E**	t **E**	r **E**	m **M**	m **M**	d **B**	d **B**	s **E**	(44)
x **E**	c **B**	j **M**	e **B**	k **M**	l **M**	o **M**	o **M**	o **M**	o **M**	p **M**	(55)
i **M**	y **E**	r **E**	b **B**	x **E**	c **B**	o **M**	o **M**	i **M**	i **M**	p **M**	(66)
j **M**	m **M**	x **E**	e **B**	o **M**	p **M**	p **M**	h **M**	k **M**	k **M**	p **M**	(77)
f **B**	o **M**	i **M**	n **M**	j **M**	r **E**	r **E**	b **B**	i **M**	i **M**	s **E**	(88)
i **M**	u **E**	e **B**	e **B**	c **B**	w **E**	d **B**	i **M**	b **B**	b **B**	x **E**	(99)
j **M**	k **M**	l **M**	y **E**	m **M**	e **B**	s **E**	b **B**	r **E**	r **E**	s **E**	(110)
j **M**	d **B**	o **M**	s **E**	s **E**	m **M**	o **M**	a **B**	r **E**	r **E**	s **E**	(121)
r **E**	j **M**	k **M**	e **B**	o **M**	j **M**	p **M**	p **M**	s **E**	s **E**	m **M**	(132)
u **E**	o **M**	h **M**	w **E**	v **E**	b **B**	s **E**	e **B**	y **E**	y **E**	y **E**	(143)
m **M**	o **M**	r **E**	s **E**	h **M**	r **E**	s **E**	x **E**	o **M**	o **M**	o **M**	(154)
j **M**	k **M**	s **E**	r **E**	i **M**	u **E**	o **M**	x **E**	w **E**	w **E**	b **B**	(165)

ANSWER SHEET

© 2005 Sopris West Educational Services. All rights reserved. Practicing Basic Skills in Language Arts. Purchaser has permission to photocopy this page for classroom use only.

SEE TO WRITE OR SEE TO SAY

	Correct	Error
First Try		
Second Try		

Alphabet: Beginning, Middle, End of Alphabet

Directions: Indicate whether each letter comes at the beginning (B), middle (M), or end (E) of the alphabet.

Beginning (B) ABCDEFG Middle (M) HIJKLMNOPQ End (E) RSTUVWXYZ

f	o	s	j	l	q	g	n	g	a
a	h	j	a	n	e	h	e	l	g
m	w	f	x	q	i	j	c	z	g
x	a	a	e	v	d	f	a	w	v
u	w	j	b	k	s	x	b	r	e
e	p	i	q	r	c	s	d	i	h
s	v	n	y	l	b	f	p	i	j
b	x	r	q	p	f	c	h	v	w
d	f	u	d	h	k	g	j	d	w
i	l	z	n	i	u	v	l	n	t
o	k	w	v	d	l	l	n	w	y
y	f	s	r	b	n	i	p	y	f
c	b	f	p	s	v	a	q	b	r
w	c	v	i	e	p	u	o	i	s
d	s	i	f	u	w	b	m	e	p
n	p	b	u	z	h	w	i	j	i
q	e	c	s	f	o	n	r	a	j

Practicing Basic Skills in Language Arts • 487

© 2005 Sopris West Educational Services. All rights reserved. Practicing Basic Skills in Language Arts. Purchaser has permission to photocopy this page for classroom use only.

ONE-MINUTE FLUENCY — BUILDER SERIES

SEE TO WRITE OR SEE TO SAY

Alphabet: Beginning, Middle, End of Alphabet

Directions: Indicate whether each letter comes at the beginning (B), middle (M), or end (E) of the alphabet.

Beginning (B) ABCDEFG
Middle (M) HIJKLMNOPQ
End (E) RSTUVWXYZ

	Correct	Error
First Try		
Second Try		

Answer grid (each cell shows the prompt letter followed by the keyed response B / M / E):

Row	1	2	3	4	5	6	7	8	9	10	11	#
1	f B	o M	s E	j M	l M	q M	g B	n M	g B	a B	a B	(11)
2	a B	h M	j M	a B	n M	e M	h M	e B	l M	e B	g B	(22)
3	m M	g B	w E	f M	q M	i B	j M	c B	z E	c B	g B	(33)
4	x E	v E	a B	e B	v E	d B	f E	a B	w E	i B	v E	(44)
5	u E	w B	e B	b B	k M	s B	x E	b B	r E	a B	e B	(55)
6	e B	h M	j M	i M	r E	c B	s M	d B	i M	b M	h M	(66)
7	s E	p M	i M	q M	l M	b B	f B	p M	i M	s M	j M	(77)
8	b B	v E	q M	n M	p M	f B	c B	b B	v E	f B	w E	(88)
9	d B	f B	u E	d B	h M	k M	g B	j B	d B	c B	w E	(99)
10	i M	w E	d B	v E	i M	u E	v E	h M	n M	d B	t E	(110)
11	o M	t E	n M	w E	d B	l M	l M	i M	w E	n M	w E	(121)
12	y E	y E	v E	r E	n M	n M	b B	d B	y E	p M	y E	(132)
13	c B	w B	r E	s E	b B	p M	i B	b B	b B	q B	f B	(143)
14	w E	f B	p M	f B	q B	v M	a B	o M	i E	a B	r B	(154)
15	d B	b B	i E	v E	o E	p M	u E	m M	e B	b B	s E	(165)
16	n M	s E	f B	b B	e B	h M	b B	i M	j M	j M	p M	(176)
17	q M	c B	o M	s B	f B	o M	n B	r E	a B	n M	j M	(187)

© 2005 Sopris West Educational Services. All rights reserved. Practicing Basic Skills in Language Arts. Purchaser has permission to photocopy this page for classroom use only.

ANSWER SHEET

SEE TO WRITE

ONE MINUTE FLUENCY BUILDER SERIES

First Try / Second Try / Correct / Error

Alphabet: Two Letters That Follow a Letter

Alphabet: a b c d e f g h i j k l m n o p q r s t u v w x y z

Directions: Write the two letters that follow each given letter.

n	o	f	a	j	l	h
m	u	a	a	u	b	x
w	x	s	o	e	r	w
b	i	p	o	n	i	p
v	c	k	y	n	d	p
w	d	l	n	j	r	n
u	q	f	v	w	k	k
y	f	j	b	q	b	a
y	n	i	c	x	l	d
e	s	e	h	c	x	d
b	j	o	j	i	y	f
d	a	e	i	x	s	h
q	w	s	u	g	r	l
m	l	y	v	c	f	k
b	d	g	i	v	x	n
y	p	s	p	l	n	g
w	l	i	d	m	p	q

© 2005 Sopris West Educational Services. All rights reserved. Practicing Basic Skills in Language Arts. Purchaser has permission to photocopy this page for classroom use only.

ONE-MINUTE FLUENCY BUILDER SERIES

SEE TO WRITE

	Correct	Error
First Try		
Second Try		

Alphabet: Two Letters That Follow a Letter

Alphabet: a b c d e f g h i j k l m n o p q r s t u v w x y z

Directions: Write the two letters that follow each given letter.

n **o** **p**	o **p** **q**	f **g** **h**	a **b** **c**	j **k** **l**	l **m** **n**	h **i** **j**	(14)
m **n** **o**	u **v** **w**	a **b** **c**	a **b** **c**	u **v** **w**	b **c** **d**	x **y** **z**	(28)
w **x** **y**	x **y** **z**	s **t** **u**	o **p** **q**	e **f** **g**	r **s** **t**	w **x** **y**	(42)
b **c** **d**	i **j** **k**	p **q** **r**	o **p** **q**	n **o** **p**	i **j** **k**	p **q** **r**	(56)
v **w** **x**	c **d** **e**	k **l** **m**	y **z** **-**	n **o** **p**	d **e** **f**	p **q** **r**	(70)
w **x** **y**	d **e** **f**	l **m** **n**	n **o** **p**	j **k** **l**	r **s** **t**	n **o** **p**	(84)
u **v** **w**	q **r** **s**	f **g** **h**	v **w** **x**	w **x** **y**	k **l** **m**	k **l** **m**	(98)
y **z** **-**	f **g** **h**	j **k** **l**	b **c** **d**	q **r** **s**	b **c** **d**	a **b** **c**	(112)
y **z** **-**	n **o** **p**	i **j** **k**	c **d** **e**	x **y** **z**	l **m** **n**	d **e** **f**	(126)
e **f** **g**	s **t** **u**	e **f** **g**	h **i** **j**	c **d** **e**	x **y** **z**	d **e** **f**	(140)
b **c** **d**	j **k** **l**	o **p** **q**	j **k** **l**	i **j** **k**	y **z** **-**	f **g** **h**	(154)
d **e** **f**	a **b** **c**	e **f** **g**	i **j** **k**	x **y** **z**	s **t** **u**	h **i** **j**	(168)
q **r** **s**	w **x** **y**	s **t** **u**	u **v** **w**	g **h** **i**	r **s** **t**	l **m** **n**	(182)
m **n** **o**	l **m** **n**	y **z** **-**	v **w** **x**	c **d** **e**	f **g** **h**	k **l** **m**	(196)
b **c** **d**	d **e** **f**	g **h** **i**	i **j** **k**	v **w** **x**	x **y** **z**	n **o** **p**	(210)
y **z** **-**	p **q** **r**	s **t** **u**	p **q** **r**	l **m** **n**	n **o** **p**	g **h** **i**	(224)
w **x** **y**	l **m** **n**	i **j** **k**	d **e** **f**	m **n** **o**	p **q** **r**	q **r** **s**	(238)

© 2005 Sopris West Educational Services. All rights reserved. Practicing Basic Skills in Language Arts. Purchaser has permission to photocopy this page for classroom use only.

ONE-MINUTE FLUENCY BUILDER SERIES

SEE TO WRITE

Alphabet: Two Letters That Come Before a Letter

Alphabet: a b c d e f g h i j k l m n o p q r s t u v w x y z

Directions: Write the two letters that come before each given letter.

___ ___ q	___ ___ w	___ ___ e	___ ___ r	___ ___ t	___ ___ u
___ ___ i	___ ___ o	___ ___ p	___ ___ a	___ ___ s	___ ___ f
___ ___ g	___ ___ h	___ ___ j	___ ___ k	___ ___ l	___ ___ x
___ ___ c	___ ___ v	___ ___ b	___ ___ n	___ ___ m	___ ___ w
___ ___ e	___ ___ r	___ ___ t	___ ___ y	___ ___ u	___ ___ o
___ ___ p	___ ___ a	___ ___ s	___ ___ d	___ ___ f	___ ___ h
___ ___ i	___ ___ j	___ ___ k	___ ___ j	___ ___ k	___ ___ z
___ ___ x	___ ___ c	___ ___ v	___ ___ b	___ ___ n	___ ___ q
___ ___ w	___ ___ e	___ ___ r	___ ___ t	___ ___ y	___ ___ i
___ ___ o	___ ___ p	___ ___ a	___ ___ s	___ ___ d	___ ___ h
___ ___ j	___ ___ k	___ ___ l	___ ___ z	___ ___ x	___ ___ v
___ ___ b	___ ___ n	___ ___ m	___ ___ q	___ ___ w	___ ___ r
___ ___ t	___ ___ y	___ ___ u	___ ___ i	___ ___ o	___ ___ a
___ ___ s	___ ___ d	___ ___ f	___ ___ g	___ ___ h	___ ___ k
___ ___ l	___ ___ z	___ ___ c	___ ___ c	___ ___ v	___ ___ n
___ ___ m	___ ___ q	___ ___ e	___ ___ e	___ ___ r	___ ___ y
___ ___ u	___ ___ i	___ ___ p	___ ___ p	___ ___ a	___ ___ d

Practicing Basic Skills in Language Arts • 491

© 2005 Sopris West Educational Services. All rights reserved. Practicing Basic Skills in Language Arts. Purchaser has permission to photocopy this page for classroom use only.

SEE TO WRITE

Alphabet: Two Letters That Come Before a Letter

Alphabet: a b c d e f g h i j k l m n o p q r s t u v w x y z

Directions: Write the two letters that come before each given letter.

	First Try	Second Try
Correct		
Error		

o p **q**	u v **w**	c d **e**	p q **r**	r s **t**	w x **y**	s t **u**	(14)
g h **i**	m n **o**	d e **f**	- a **b**	q r **s**	x y **z**	r s **t**	(28)
e f **g**	f g **h**	h i **j**	i j **k**	k l **l**	c d **d**	k l **f**	(42)
a b **c**	b c **d**	- a **b**	k l **l**	i j **k**	d e **z**	i j **x**	(56)
c d **e**	d e **f**	r s **s**	w x **w**	s t **t**	e f **q**	m n **o**	(70)
n o **p**	o p **q**	b c **b**	b c **c**	d e **d**	n o **o**	g h **h**	(84)
g h **i**	h i **i**	h i **h**	h i **h**	e f **e**	g h **g**	g h **g**	(98)
v w **x**	w x **x**	- a **-**	- a **-**	i j **i**	h i **h**	- a **z**	(112)
u v **v**	v w **w**	t u **u**	r s **r**	s t **s**	u v **u**	s t **i**	(126)
m n **n**	n o **o**	d e **d**	q r **q**	r s **r**	v w **v**	r s **h**	(140)
h i **i**	i j **j**	v w **w**	s t **t**	- - **s**	o p **p**	- - **u**	(154)
- a **-**	l m **m**	u v **u**	r s **r**	- - **w**	h i **h**	- - **v**	(168)
r s **s**	w x **x**	i j **i**	q r **q**	c d **o**	f g **g**	i j **r**	(182)
q r **r**	b c **b**	k l **k**	o p **o**	d e **h**	e f **f**	m n **s**	(196)
i j **j**	x y **y**	s t **s**	- a **-**	e f **i**	c d **j**	n o **i**	(210)
k l **l**	c d **d**	d e **d**	i j **i**	f g **m**	d e **b**	x y **n**	(224)
s t **t**	- a **-**	v w **w**	m n **l**	- - **a**	e f **c**	b c **d**	(238)

Practicing Basic Skills in Language Arts • 492

ANSWER SHEET

ONE-MINUTE FLUENCY BUILDER SERIES

© 2005 Sopris West Educational Services. All rights reserved. Practicing Basic Skills in Language Arts. Purchaser has permission to photocopy this page for classroom use only.

	Correct	Error
First Try		
Second Try		

ONE-MINUTE FLUENCY
BUILDER SERIES

Alphabet: Two Letters That Come Before and After a Letter

Alphabet: a b c d e f g h i j k l m n o p q r s t u v w x y z
Directions: Write the letters that come before and after the given letter.

___ a ___	___ s ___	___ d ___	___ f ___	___ g ___	___ h ___
___ k ___	___ l ___	___ q ___	___ w ___	___ e ___	___ r ___
___ y ___	___ u ___	___ i ___	___ o ___	___ p ___	___ a ___
___ d ___	___ f ___	___ g ___	___ h ___	___ j ___	___ j ___
___ l ___	___ z ___	___ x ___	___ c ___	___ v ___	___ b ___
___ m ___	___ q ___	___ w ___	___ e ___	___ r ___	___ t ___
___ u ___	___ i ___	___ o ___	___ p ___	___ a ___	___ s ___
___ f ___	___ f ___	___ g ___	___ h ___	___ j ___	___ k ___
___ z ___	___ x ___	___ c ___	___ v ___	___ b ___	___ n ___
___ q ___	___ w ___	___ e ___	___ r ___	___ t ___	___ y ___
___ i ___	___ o ___	___ p ___	___ a ___	___ s ___	___ d ___
___ g ___	___ h ___	___ j ___	___ k ___	___ k ___	___ l ___
___ x ___	___ c ___	___ v ___	___ b ___	___ n ___	___ m ___
___ w ___	___ e ___	___ r ___	___ t ___	___ y ___	___ u ___
___ o ___	___ p ___	___ a ___	___ s ___	___ d ___	___ f ___
___ h ___	___ h ___	___ j ___	___ k ___	___ l ___	___ z ___
___ x ___	___ c ___	___ v ___	___ b ___	___ n ___	___ q ___

© 2005 Sopris West Educational Services. All rights reserved. Practicing Basic Skills in Language Arts. Purchaser has permission to photocopy this page for classroom use only.

ONE-MINUTE FLUENCY BUILDER SERIES

SEE TO WRITE

Alphabet: Two Letters That Come Before and After a Letter

Alphabet: a b c d e f g h i j k l m n o p q r s t u v w x y z

Directions: Write the letters that come before and after the given letter.

	Correct	Error
First Try		
Second Try		

– a b	r s t	c d e	e f g	f g h	g h i	i j k	(14)
j k l	k l m	t u v	p q r	d e f	h i j	s t u	(28)
x y z	t u v	d e f	q r s	o p q	r s t	r s t	(42)
c d e	d e f	g h i	h i j	n o p	a b c	k l m	(56)
k l m	e f g	f g h	g h i	h i j	i j k	h i j	(70)
l m n	x y z	w x y	v w x	b c d	a b c	m n o	(84)
t u v	m n o	u v w	d e f	c d e	s t u	x y z	(98)
e f g	t u v	e f g	f g h	e f g	r s t	c d e	(112)
y z –	g h i	f g h	q r s	p q r	a b c	k l m	(126)
p q r	h i j	o p q	– a b	q r s	r s t	l m n	(140)
h i j	u v w	g h i	h i j	– a b	i j k	t u v	(154)
f g h	e f g	f g h	b c d	j k l	k l m	e f g	(168)
w x y	f g h	u v w	c d e	l m n	m n o	q r s	(182)
v w x	x y z	d e f	d e f	a b c	u v w	h i j	(196)
n o p	w x y	n o p	o p q	s t u	t u v	f g h	(210)
g h i	x y z	f g h	h i j	c d e	e f g	y z –	(224)
w x y	b c d	u v w	a b c	l m n	l m n	q r s	(238)

ANSWER SHEET

© 2005 Sopris West Educational Services. All rights reserved. Practicing Basic Skills in Language Arts. Purchaser has permission to photocopy this page for classroom use only.

ONE-MINUTE FLUENCY
BUILDER SERIES

SEE TO WRITE

Alphabet: Two Letters That Come Before and After a Letter

Directions: Write the letters that come before and after the given letter.

First Try	Correct	Error
Second Try		

q	w	e	r	t	y	u
i	o	o	p	a	s	d
f	g	h	j	k	l	z
x	c	v	b	n	m	q
e	w	r	t	y	u	i
o	p	a	s	d	f	g
h	j	k	l	z	x	c
v	b	n	m	q	w	e
r	t	y	u	i	o	p
a	s	d	f	g	h	j
k	l	z	x	c	v	b
n	m	q	w	e	r	t
y	u	i	o	p	a	s
d	f	g	h	j	k	l
z	c	v	b	n	m	q
w	e	r	t	y	u	i
o	p	a	s	d	f	g

© 2005 Sopris West Educational Services. All rights reserved. Practicing Basic Skills in Language Arts. Purchaser has permission to photocopy this page for classroom use only.

ONE-MINUTE FLUENCY
BUILDER SERIES

SEE TO WRITE

Alphabet: Two Letters That Come Before and After a Letter
Directions: Write the letters that come before and after the given letter.

	Correct	Error
First Try		
Second Try		

Item 1	Item 2	Item 3	Item 4	Item 5	Item 6	Item 7	
p **q** r	v **w** x	d **e** f	q **r** s	s **t** u	x **y** z	t **u** v	(14)
h **i** j	n **o** p	n **o** p	o **p** q	- **a** b	r **s** t	c **d** e	(28)
e **f** g	f **g** h	g **h** i	i **j** k	i **j** k	k **l** m	y **z** -	(42)
w **x** y	b **c** d	u **v** w	a **b** c	k **l** m	l **m** n	p **q** r	(56)
d **e** f	v **w** x	q **r** s	s **t** u	m **n** o	m **n** o	h **i** j	(70)
n **o** p	o **p** q	- **a** b	r **s** t	x **y** z	u **v** w	g **h** i	(84)
g **h** i	i **j** k	i **j** k	k **l** m	- **a** b	w **x** y	b **c** d	(98)
u **v** w	a **b** c	m **n** o	- **a** b	k **l** m	v **w** x	d **e** f	(112)
q **r** s	s **t** u	x **y** z	t **u** v	t **u** v	n **o** p	o **p** q	(126)
- **a** b	r **s** t	c **d** e	e **f** g	h **i** j	g **h** i	i **j** k	(140)
i **j** k	k **l** m	y **z** -	w **x** y	f **g** h	h **i** j	a **b** c	(154)
k **l** m	l **m** n	m **n** o	v **w** x	w **x** y	r **s** t	s **t** u	(168)
x **y** z	t **u** v	r **s** t	r **s** t	g **h** i	s **t** u	r **s** t	(182)
c **d** e	e **f** g	g **h** i	f **g** h	a **b** c	a **b** c	k **l** m	(196)
y **z** -	b **c** d	u **v** w	d **e** f	s **t** u	m **n** o	p **q** r	(210)
v **w** x	d **e** f	q **r** s	q **r** s	t **u** v	h **i** j	h **i** j	(224)
n **o** p	o **p** q	- **a** b	- **a** b	c **d** e	f **g** h	f **g** h	(238)

ANSWER SHEET

Practicing Basic Skills in Language Arts • 496

© 2005 Sopris West Educational Services. All rights reserved. Practicing Basic Skills in Language Arts. Purchaser has permission to photocopy this page for classroom use only.

ONE-MINUTE FLUENCY BUILDER SERIES

SEE TO WRITE

	Correct	Error
First Try		
Second Try		

Alphabetical Order: Before or After Guide Word

Directions: Alphabetically, does the word come before or after the guide word to its right? Put a check in the appropriate blank.

A B C D E F G

word		guide
fun	—	desk
stole	—	desk
happy	—	desk
pony	—	desk
cat	—	desk
ask	—	box
cow	—	box
am	—	box
eat	—	box
dust	—	box
rat	—	pan
open	—	pan
nose	—	pan
map	—	pan
quit	—	pan

H I J K L M N O P Q

word		guide
pop	—	off
not	—	off
men	—	off
rat	—	off
queen	—	off
luck	—	time
sun	—	time
up	—	time
zip	—	time
run	—	time
zoo	—	kick
come	—	kick
stop	—	kick
gum	—	kick
lost	—	kick

R S T U V W X Y Z

word		guide
good	—	food
elf	—	food
ham	—	food
dot	—	food
jot	—	food
top	—	want
you	—	want
zoo	—	want
ugly	—	want
van	—	want
king	—	go
happy	—	go
food	—	go
it	—	go
jump	—	go

word		guide
new	—	many
love	—	many
on	—	many
toy	—	many
pat	—	many
rip	—	sit
pet	—	sit
toy	—	sit
up	—	sit
quit	—	sit
fix	—	eye
dog	—	eye
gum	—	eye
can't	—	eye
hum	—	eye

© 2005 Sopris West Educational Services. All rights reserved. Practicing Basic Skills in Language Arts. Purchaser has permission to photocopy this page for classroom use only.

SEE TO WRITE

Alphabetical Order: Before or After Guide Word

Directions: Alphabetically, does the word come before or after the guide word to its right? Put a check in the appropriate blank.

First Try		
Second Try		

	Correct	Error

A B C D E F G

Word	Before	Guide Word	After	
fun		desk	X	
stole		desk	X	
happy		desk	X	
pony		desk	X	
cat	X	desk		(5)
ask	X	box		
cow		box	X	
am	X	box		
eat		box	X	
dust		box	X	(10)
rat		pan	X	
open	X	pan		
nose	X	pan		
map	X	pan		
quit		pan	X	(15)

H I J K L M N O P Q

Word	Before	Guide Word	After	
pop		off	X	
not	X	off		
men	X	off		
rat		off	X	
queen		off	X	(20)
luck	X	time		
sun	X	time		
up		time	X	
zip		time	X	
run	X	time		(25)
zoo		kick	X	
come	X	kick		
stop		kick	X	
gum	X	kick		
lost		kick	X	(30)

R S T U V W X Y Z

Word	Before	Guide Word	After	
good		food	X	
elf	X	food		
ham		food	X	
dot	X	food		
jot		food	X	(35)
top	X	want		
you		want	X	
zoo		want	X	
ugly	X	want		
van		want	X	(40)
king		go	X	
happy		go	X	
food	X	go		
it		go	X	
jump		go	X	(45)

Word	Before	Guide Word	After	
new		many	X	
love	X	many		
on		many	X	
toy		many	X	
pat		many	X	(50)
rip	X	sit		
pet	X	sit		
toy		sit	X	
up		sit	X	
quit	X	sit		(55)
fix		eye	X	
dog	X	eye		
gum		eye	X	
can't	X	eye		
hum		eye	X	(60)

ANSWER SHEET

Practicing Basic Skills in Language Arts • 498

ONE-MINUTE FLUENCY BUILDER SERIES

ONE MINUTE FLUENCY BUILDER SERIES

SEE TO WRITE

	First Try	Second Try
Correct		
Error		

Alphabetical Order: Before or After Guide Word

Directions: Alphabetically, does the word come before or after the guide word to its right? Put a check in the appropriate blank.

A B C D E F G

dip	___	desk	___
day	___	desk	___
duck	___	desk	___
dam	___	desk	___
dock	___	desk	___
paper	___	pick	___
pack	___	pick	___
pretty	___	pick	___
play	___	pick	___
pen	___	pick	___
base	___	black	___
boat	___	black	___
brat	___	black	___
bet	___	black	___
bike	___	black	___

H I J K L M N O P Q

met	___	many	___
mop	___	many	___
mitt	___	many	___
much	___	many	___
men	___	many	___
it	___	if	___
is	___	if	___
ice	___	if	___
in	___	if	___
idea	___	if	___
clap	___	come	___
cut	___	come	___
cry	___	come	___
chop	___	come	___
cap	___	come	___

R S T U V W X Y Z

glad	___	gone	___
grow	___	gone	___
game	___	gone	___
ghost	___	gone	___
get	___	gone	___
fat	___	food	___
flag	___	food	___
from	___	food	___
fell	___	food	___
fix	___	food	___
have	___	help	___
not	___	help	___
hum	___	help	___
him	___	help	___
ham	___	help	___

at	___	all	___
ask	___	all	___
am	___	all	___
add	___	all	___
aim	___	all	___
sip	___	stop	___
slam	___	stop	___
soap	___	stop	___
seal	___	stop	___
smell	___	stop	___
out	___	off	___
over	___	off	___
oak	___	off	___
odd	___	off	___
oh	___	off	___

© 2005 Sopris West Educational Services. All rights reserved. Practicing Basic Skills in Language Arts. Purchaser has permission to photocopy this page for classroom use only.

ONE MINUTE FLUENCY BUILDER SERIES

SEE TO WRITE

	Correct	Error
First Try		
Second Try		

Alphabetical Order: Before or After Guide Word

Directions: Alphabetically, does the word come before or after the guide word to its right? Put a check in the appropriate blank.

A B C D E F G

#	Word	before	after	Guide Word
1	dip	—	X	desk
2	day	X	—	desk
3	duck	—	X	desk
4	dam	X	—	desk
5	dock	—	X	desk
6	paper	X	—	pick
7	pack	X	—	pick
8	pretty	—	X	pick
9	play	—	X	pick
10	pen	X	—	pick
11	base	X	—	black
12	boat	—	X	black
13	brat	—	X	black
14	bet	X	—	black
15	bike	X	—	black

H I J K L M N O P Q

#	Word	before	after	Guide Word
16	met	—	X	many
17	mop	—	X	many
18	mitt	—	X	many
19	much	—	X	many
20	men	—	X	many
21	it	—	X	if
22	is	—	X	if
23	ice	X	—	if
24	in	—	X	if
25	idea	X	—	if
26	clap	—	X	come
27	cut	—	X	come
28	cry	—	X	come
29	chop	X	—	come
30	cap	X	—	come

R S T U V W X Y Z

#	Word	before	after	Guide Word
31	glad	X	—	gone
32	grow	—	X	gone
33	game	X	—	gone
34	ghost	X	—	gone
35	get	X	—	gone
36	fat	X	—	food
37	flag	X	—	food
38	from	—	X	food
39	fell	X	—	food
40	fix	X	—	food
41	have	X	—	help
42	not	—	X	help
43	hum	—	X	help
44	him	—	X	help
45	ham	X	—	help

(all / stop / off)

#	Word	before	after	Guide Word
46	at	—	X	all
47	ask	—	X	all
48	am	—	X	all
49	add	X	—	all
50	aim	X	—	all
51	sip	X	—	stop
52	slam	X	—	stop
53	soap	X	—	stop
54	seal	X	—	stop
55	smell	X	—	stop
56	out	—	X	off
57	over	—	X	off
58	oak	X	—	off
59	odd	X	—	off
60	oh	—	X	off

ANSWER SHEET

© 2005 Sopris West Educational Services. All rights reserved. Practicing Basic Skills in Language Arts. Purchaser has permission to photocopy this page for classroom use only.

SEE TO WRITE

Alphabetical Order: Before or After Guide Word

Directions: Alphabetically, does the word come before or after the guide word to its right? Put a check in the appropriate blank.

First Try	Second Try
Correct	
Error	

ABCDEFG

Word		Guide Word
travel	_	truck _
try	_	truck _
trick	_	truck _
tree	_	truck _
trot	_	truck _
pale	_	pain _
paste	_	pain _
pace	_	pain _
page	_	pain _
pan	_	pain _
clock	_	clean _
claim	_	clean _
clue	_	clean _
cloud	_	clean _
clam	_	clean _

HIJKLMNOPQ

Word		Guide Word
brick	_	break _
beat	_	break _
broke	_	break _
brush	_	break _
brain	_	break _
inch	_	into _
invent	_	into _
index	_	into _
infect	_	into _
invite	_	into _
glad	_	glide _
glue	_	glide _
glee	_	glide _
gloom	_	glide _
glass	_	glide _

RSTUVWXYZ

Word		Guide Word
flu	_	flag _
flip	_	flag _
fleet	_	flag _
fly	_	flag _
floor	_	flag _
diaper	_	diet _
differ	_	diet _
dig	_	diet _
dial	_	diet _
dipper	_	diet _
queen	_	quick _
quake	_	quick _
quart	_	quick _
quiet	_	quick _
question	_	quick _

Word		Guide Word
make	_	man _
made	_	man _
mark	_	man _
magic	_	man _
ma	_	man _
relate	_	replace _
renew	_	replace _
real	_	replace _
refuse	_	replace _
retain	_	replace _
rain	_	race _
rake	_	race _
rabbit	_	race _
rag	_	race _
radar	_	race _

ONE-MINUTE FLUENCY BUILDER SERIES

Practicing Basic Skills in Language Arts • 501

© 2005 Sopris West Educational Services. All rights reserved. Practicing Basic Skills in Language Arts. Purchaser has permission to photocopy this page for classroom use only.

ONE-MINUTE FLUENCY — BUILDER SERIES

SEE TO WRITE

Alphabetical Order: Before or After Guide Word

Directions: Alphabetically, does the word come before or after the guide word to its right? Put a check in the appropriate blank.

	First Try	Second Try
Correct		
Error		

A B C D E F G

Word	before	guide	after
travel	X	truck	—
try	—	truck	X
trick	X	truck	—
tree	X	truck	—
trot	X	truck	— (5)
pale	—	pain	X
paste	—	pain	X
pace	X	pain	—
page	X	pain	—
pan	—	pain	X (10)
clock	—	clean	X
claim	X	clean	—
clue	—	clean	X
cloud	—	clean	X
clam	X	clean	— (15)

H I J K L M N O P Q

Word	before	guide	after
brick	—	break	X
beat	X	break	—
broke	—	break	X
brush	—	break	X
brain	X	break	— (20)
inch	X	into	—
invent	—	into	X
index	X	into	—
infect	X	into	—
invite	—	into	X (25)
glad	X	glide	—
glue	—	glide	X
glee	X	glide	—
gloom	—	glide	X
glass	X	glide	— (30)

R S T U V W X Y Z

Word	before	guide	after
flu	—	flag	X
flip	—	flag	X
fleet	—	flag	X
fly	—	flag	X
floor	—	flag	X (35)
diaper	X	diet	—
differ	—	diet	X
dig	—	diet	X
dial	X	diet	—
dipper	—	diet	X (40)
queen	X	quick	—
quake	X	quick	—
quart	X	quick	—
quiet	—	quick	X
question	X	quick	— (45)

Word	before	guide	after
make	X	man	—
made	X	man	—
mark	—	man	X
magic	X	man	—
ma	X	man	— (50)
relate	X	replace	—
renew	X	replace	—
real	X	replace	—
refuse	X	replace	—
retain	—	replace	X (55)
rain	—	race	X
rake	—	race	X
rabbit	X	race	—
rag	—	race	X
radar	—	race	X (60)

ANSWER SHEET

Practicing Basic Skills in Language Arts • 502

© 2005 Sopris West Educational Services. All rights reserved. Practicing Basic Skills in Language Arts. Purchaser has permission to photocopy this page for classroom use only.

ONE-MINUTE FLUENCY BUILDER SERIES

SEE TO WRITE

Alphabetical Order: Before or After Guide Word

Directions: Alphabetically, does the word come before or after the guide word to its right? Put a check in the appropriate blank.

	First Try	Second Try
Correct		
Error		

A B C D E F G

Word			Guide Word
pain	__	__	pair
pail	__	__	pair
paid	__	__	pair
glove	__	__	gloom
gloat	__	__	gloom
gloss	__	__	gloom
early	__	__	earth
earn	__	__	earth
earache	__	__	earth
grim	__	__	grip
grin	__	__	grip
grief	__	__	grip

H I J K L M N O P Q

Word			Guide Word
black	__	__	blade
blank	__	__	blade
blab	__	__	blade
faint	__	__	fair
fail	__	__	fair
faith	__	__	fair
father	__	__	fate
fatal	__	__	fate
fatty	__	__	fate
pear	__	__	person
peel	__	__	person
pen	__	__	person

R S T U V W X Y Z

Word			Guide Word
boot	__	__	book
boom	__	__	book
boost	__	__	book
explain	__	__	expert
expect	__	__	expert
explore	__	__	expert
forbid	__	__	force
fork	__	__	force
form	__	__	force
mail	__	__	man
match	__	__	man
main	__	__	man

Word			Guide Word
bother	__	__	both
bottle	__	__	both
bottom	__	__	both
direct	__	__	dirt
dirty	__	__	dirt
dire	__	__	dirt
good	__	__	goose
goof	__	__	goose
goods	__	__	goose
sad	__	__	sack
sail	__	__	sack
sale	__	__	sack

© 2005 Sopris West Educational Services. All rights reserved. Practicing Basic Skills in Language Arts. Purchaser has permission to photocopy this page for classroom use only.

ONE-MINUTE FLUENCY BUILDER SERIES

	First Try	Second Try
Correct		
Error		

Alphabetical Order: Before or After Guide Word

Directions: Alphabetically, does the word come before or after the guide word to its right? Put a check in the appropriate blank.

A B C D E F G

Word	Before	After	Guide Word
pain	X	—	pair
pail	X	—	pair
paid	X	—	pair
glove	—	X	gloom (4)
gloat	X	—	gloom
gloss	—	X	gloom
early	X	—	earth
earn	X	—	earth (8)
earache	X	—	earth
grim	X	—	grip
grin	X	—	grip
grief	X	—	grip (12)

H I J K L M N O P Q

Word	Before	After	Guide Word
black	X	—	blade
blank	—	X	blade
blab	X	—	blade (16)
faint	X	—	fair
fail	X	—	fair
faith	—	X	fair
father	—	X	fate
fatal	X	—	fate (20)
fatty	—	X	fate
pear	X	—	person
peel	X	—	person
pen	X	—	person (24)

R S T U V W X Y Z

Word	Before	After	Guide Word
boot	—	X	book
boom	—	X	book
boost	—	X	book (28)
explain	—	X	expert
expect	X	—	expert
explore	—	X	expert
forbid	X	—	force
fork	—	X	force (32)
form	—	X	force
mail	X	—	man
match	X	—	man
main	X	—	man (36)

Word	Before	After	Guide Word
bother	—	X	both
bottle	—	X	both
bottom	—	X	both (40)
direct	X	—	dirt
dirty	—	X	dirt
dire	X	—	dirt
good	X	—	goose
goof	X	—	goose (44)
goods	X	—	goose
sad	X	—	sack
sail	—	X	sack
sale	—	X	sack (48)

ANSWER SHEET

© 2005 Sopris West Educational Services. All rights reserved. Practicing Basic Skills in Language Arts. Purchaser has permission to photocopy this page for classroom use only.

SEE TO WRITE

ONE-MINUTE FLUENCY
BUILDER SERIES

Alphabetical Order: Before, After, or Between Guide Words

Directions: Alphabetically, does the word come before, after, or between the guide words? Put a check in the appropriate blank.

	First Try	Second Try
Correct		
Error		

Column 1 — A B C D E F G

Guide words: deer ___ doll

dust	deer ___	doll ___
dart	deer ___	doll ___
diet	deer ___	doll ___
dye	deer ___	doll ___
date	deer ___	doll ___
dish	deer ___	doll ___
dump	deer ___	doll ___
dance	deer ___	doll ___
dull	deer ___	doll ___
drop	deer ___	doll ___

Guide words: photo ___ pop

prefer	photo ___	pop ___
pay	photo ___	pop ___
pie	photo ___	pop ___
pest	photo ___	pop ___
play	photo ___	pop ___
pull	photo ___	pop ___
pick	photo ___	pop ___
pry	photo ___	pop ___
peck	photo ___	pop ___
place	photo ___	pop ___

Column 2 — H I J K L M N O P Q

Guide words: mess ___ more

mix	mess ___	more ___
mug	mess ___	more ___
mile	mess ___	more ___
make	mess ___	more ___
mail	mess ___	more ___
music	mess ___	more ___
mind	mess ___	more ___
mist	mess ___	more ___
my	mess ___	more ___
mash	mess ___	more ___

Guide words: bid ___ boat

blue	bid ___	boat ___
base	bid ___	boat ___
by	bid ___	boat ___
but	bid ___	boat ___
black	bid ___	boat ___
brain	bid ___	boat ___
band	bid ___	boat ___
blind	bid ___	boat ___
bump	bid ___	boat ___
bear	bid ___	boat ___

Column 3 — R S T U V W X Y Z

Guide words: chair ___ creep

clean	chair ___	creep ___
cave	chair ___	creep ___
cent	chair ___	creep ___
curt	chair ___	creep ___
class	chair ___	creep ___
cycle	chair ___	creep ___
cool	chair ___	creep ___
circus	chair ___	creep ___
car	chair ___	creep ___
cub	chair ___	creep ___

Guide words: if ___ is

in	if ___	is ___
ice	if ___	is ___
iron	if ___	is ___
Italy	if ___	is ___
ill	if ___	is ___
igloo	if ___	is ___
itch	if ___	is ___
idiot	if ___	is ___
it	if ___	is ___
ivy	if ___	is ___

Practicing Basic Skills in Language Arts • 505

© 2005 Sopris West Educational Services. All rights reserved. Practicing Basic Skills in Language Arts. Purchaser has permission to photocopy this page for classroom use only.

SEE TO WRITE

Alphabetical Order: Before, After, or Between Guide Words

Directions: Alphabetically, does the word come before, after, or between the guide words? Put a check in the appropriate blank.

	First Try	Second Try
Correct		
Error		

A B C D E F G

Guide words: **deer** | **doll**

Word	before	between	after
dust			X
dart	X		
diet		X	
dye			X
date (5)	X		
dish		X	
dump			X
dance	X		
dull			X
drop (10)		X	

Guide words: **photo** | **pop**

Word	before	between	after
prefer			X
pay	X		
pie		X	
pest	X		
play (15)		X	
pull			X
pick		X	
pry			X
peck	X		
place (20)		X	

H I J K L M N O P Q

Guide words: **mess** | **more**

Word	before	between	after
mix		X	
mug			X
mile		X	
make	X		
mail (25)	X		
music			X
mind		X	
mist		X	
my			X
mash (30)	X		

Guide words: **bid** | **boat**

Word	before	between	after
blue		X	
base	X		
by			X
but			X
black (35)		X	
brain		X	
band	X		
blind		X	
bump			X
bear (40)	X		

R S T U V W X Y Z

Guide words: **chair** | **creep**

Word	before	between	after
clean		X	
cave	X		
cent	X		
curt			X
class (45)		X	
cycle			X
cool		X	
circus		X	
car	X		
cub (50)			X

Guide words: **if** | **is**

Word	before	between	after
in		X	
ice	X		
iron		X	
Italy			X
ill (55)		X	
igloo		X	
itch			X
idiot	X		
it			X
ivy (60)			X

ANSWER SHEET

Practicing Basic Skills in Language Arts • 506

© 2005 Sopris West Educational Services. All rights reserved. Practicing Basic Skills in Language Arts. Purchaser has permission to photocopy this page for classroom use only.

ONE-MINUTE FLUENCY BUILDER SERIES

	Correct	Error
First Try		
Second Try		

SEE TO WRITE

Alphabetical Order: Before, After, or Between Guide Words

Directions: Alphabetically, does the word come before, after, or between the guide words? Put a check in the appropriate blank.

A B C D E F G — guide words: head ___ hold ___

Word	head	hold
bag	___	___
van	___	___
hear	___	___
go	___	___
it	___	___
stop	___	___
hide	___	___
eat	___	___
him	___	___
jug	___	___

keep ___ king ___

Word	keep	king
kid	___	___
long	___	___
jam	___	___
key	___	___
foot	___	___
kiss	___	___
man	___	___
girl	___	___
kill	___	___
fun	___	___

H I J K L M N O P Q — guide words: take ___ to ___

Word	take	to
time	___	___
up	___	___
sun	___	___
ran	___	___
the	___	___
ten	___	___
coat	___	___
job	___	___
under	___	___
song	___	___

eat ___ even ___

Word	eat	even
enter	___	___
cone	___	___
hello	___	___
egg	___	___
fix	___	___
edit	___	___
deck	___	___
gone	___	___
elf	___	___
boy	___	___

R S T U V W X Y Z — guide words: want ___ will ___

Word	want	will
van	___	___
when	___	___
uncle	___	___
x-ray	___	___
you	___	___
top	___	___
way	___	___
we	___	___
bad	___	___
wide	___	___

name ___ nun ___

Word	name	nun
make	___	___
near	___	___
off	___	___
night	___	___
play	___	___
love	___	___
nose	___	___
moon	___	___
now	___	___
open	___	___

© 2005 Sopris West Educational Services. All rights reserved. Practicing Basic Skills in Language Arts. Purchaser has permission to photocopy this page for classroom use only.

ONE-MINUTE FLUENCY BUILDER SERIES

SEE TO WRITE

Alphabetical Order: Before, After, or Between Guide Words

Directions: Alphabetically, does the word come before, after, or between the guide words? Put a check in the appropriate blank.

	Correct	Error
First Try		
Second Try		

A B C D E F G
(Guide words: head / hold for 1–10; keep / king for 11–20)

#	Word	before	between	after
1	bag	X		
2	van			X
3	hear		X	
4	go	X		
5	it			X
6	stop			X
7	hide		X	
8	eat	X		
9	him		X	
10	jug			X
11	kid		X	
12	long			X
13	jam	X		
14	key		X	
15	foot	X		
16	kiss			X
17	man			X
18	girl	X		
19	kill		X	
20	fun	X		

H I J K L M N O P Q
(Guide words: take / to for 21–30; eat / even for 31–40)

#	Word	before	between	after
21	time		X	
22	up			X
23	sun	X		
24	ran	X		
25	the		X	
26	ten		X	
27	coat	X		
28	job	X		
29	under			X
30	song	X		
31	enter		X	
32	cone	X		
33	hello			X
34	egg		X	
35	fix			X
36	edit		X	
37	deck	X		
38	gone			X
39	elf		X	
40	boy	X		

R S T U V W X Y Z
(Guide words: want / will for 41–50; name / nun for 51–60)

#	Word	before	between	after
41	van	X		
42	when		X	
43	uncle	X		
44	x-ray			X
45	you			X
46	top	X		
47	way		X	
48	we		X	
49	bad	X		
50	wide		X	
51	make	X		
52	near		X	
53	off			X
54	night		X	
55	play			X
56	love	X		
57	nose		X	
58	moon	X		
59	now		X	
60	open			X

ANSWER SHEET

© 2005 Sopris West Educational Services. All rights reserved. Practicing Basic Skills in Language Arts. Purchaser has permission to photocopy this page for classroom use only.

ONE MINUTE FLUENCY
BUILDER SERIES

THINK TO WRITE

Alphabetical Order: Found on Which Page?

Directions: Does the word come on page A, page B, page C, or none of the pages listed (D)?

GUIDE WORDS:	A	B	C	D
	belt – bit	black – boat	book – bride	(none)

board		before		blow
brace		bookmark		bet
boil		bribe		birthday
blackout		bow		blush
bubble		bill		boast
blot		bottom		blade
build		bread		bench
bleach		boot		bomb
big		bo		blue
bird		broke		bloom
bend		bud		branch
boom		bottle		boathouse
batch		bike		blank
block		bitter		brain

	Correct	Error
First Try		
Second Try		

© 2005 Sopris West Educational Services. All rights reserved. Practicing Basic Skills in Language Arts. Purchaser has permission to photocopy this page for classroom use only.

THINK TO WRITE

Alphabetical Order: Found on Which Page?

Directions: Does the word come on page A, page B, page C, or none of the pages listed (D)?

GUIDE WORDS:

	A	B	C	D
	belt – bit	black – boat	book – bride	(none)	

board	**B**		before	**D**	blow	**B**	(3)
brace	**C**		bookmark	**C**	bet	**A**	(6)
boil	**D**		bribe	**C**	birthday	**A**	(9)
blackout	**B**		bow	**C**	blush	**B**	(12)
bubble	**D**		bill	**A**	boast	**B**	(15)
blot	**B**		bottom	**C**	blade	**B**	(18)
build	**D**		bread	**C**	bench	**A**	(21)
bleach	**B**		boot	**C**	bomb	**D**	(24)
big	**A**		bo	**B**	blue	**B**	(27)
bird	**A**		broke	**D**	bloom	**B**	(30)
bend	**A**		bud	**D**	branch	**C**	(33)
boom	**C**		bottle	**C**	boathouse	**D**	(36)
batch	**D**		bike	**A**	blank	**B**	(39)
block	**B**		bitter	**D**	brain	**C**	(42)

	First Try	Second Try
Correct		
Error		

ANSWER SHEET

Practicing Basic Skills in Language Arts • 510

© 2005 Sopris West Educational Services. All rights reserved. Practicing Basic Skills in Language Arts. Purchaser has permission to photocopy this page for classroom use only.

Alphabetical Order: Placing 4 Words in Alphabetical Order

Directions: Number each group of words in alphabetical order from 1 to 4.

First Try		
Second Try		
	Correct	Error

ONE-MINUTE FLUENCY BUILDER SERIES

____ green

____ floor

____ claw

____ says

____ through

____ chair

____ size

____ rewards

____ field

____ ax

____ screamed

____ alarm

____ drum

____ grumpy

____ pray

____ froze

____ know

____ hidden

____ give

____ fall

____ sea

____ feathers

____ weather

____ beach

____ beans

____ spread

____ meal

____ deaf

____ pile

____ stain

____ loan

____ cuff

____ trick

____ seed

____ gruff

____ cross

© 2005 Sopris West Educational Services. All rights reserved. Practicing Basic Skills in Language Arts. Purchaser has permission to photocopy this page for classroom use only.

	Correct	Error
First Try		
Second Try		

THINK TO WRITE

Alphabetical Order: Placing 4 Words in Alphabetical Order

Directions: Number each group of words in alphabetical order from 1 to 4.

ONE-MINUTE FLUENCY BUILDER SERIES

(4)

3 ___ green
2 ___ floor
1 ___ claw
4 ___ says

(8)

1 ___ drum
3 ___ grumpy
4 ___ pray
2 ___ froze

(12)

1 ___ beans
4 ___ spread
3 ___ meal
2 ___ deaf

(16)

4 ___ through
1 ___ chair
3 ___ size
2 ___ rewards

(20)

4 ___ know
3 ___ hidden
2 ___ give
1 ___ fall

(24)

3 ___ pile
4 ___ stain
2 ___ loan
1 ___ cuff

(28)

3 ___ field
2 ___ ax
4 ___ screamed
1 ___ alarm

(32)

3 ___ sea
2 ___ feathers
4 ___ weather
1 ___ beach

(36)

4 ___ trick
3 ___ seed
2 ___ gruff
1 ___ cross

ANSWER SHEET

© 2005 Sopris West Educational Services. All rights reserved. Practicing Basic Skills in Language Arts. Purchaser has permission to photocopy this page for classroom use only.

Alphabetical Order: Placing 4 Words in Alphabetical Order

Directions: Number each group of words in alphabetical order from 1 to 4.

	First Try	Second Try
Correct		
Error		

table ____	carry ____	follow ____
zebra ____	glove ____	slowly ____
cookie ____	among ____	gone ____
yet ____	feet ____	bulb ____

two ____	fly ____	change ____
feet ____	magnify ____	berry ____
heavy ____	prince ____	mind ____
zebra ____	either ____	air ____

beans ____	bell ____	believe ____
spread ____	easy ____	direction ____
meal ____	attic ____	moth ____
deaf ____	reached ____	syllable ____

ONE MINUTE FLUENCY
BUILDER SERIES

© 2005 Sopris West Educational Services. All rights reserved. Practicing Basic Skills in Language Arts. Purchaser has permission to photocopy this page for classroom use only.

ONE-MINUTE FLUENCY
BUILDER SERIES

	First Try	Second Try
Correct		
Error		

Alphabetical Order: Placing 4 Words in Alphabetical Order

Directions: Number each group of words in alphabetical order from 1 to 4.

(4)

2 _____ table
4 _____ zebra
1 _____ cookie
3 _____ yet

(16)

2 _____ carry
4 _____ glove
1 _____ among
3 _____ feet

(28)

2 _____ follow
4 _____ slowly
3 _____ gone
1 _____ bulb

(8)

3 _____ two
1 _____ feet
2 _____ heavy
4 _____ zebra

(20)

2 _____ fly
3 _____ magnify
4 _____ prince
1 _____ either

(32)

3 _____ change
2 _____ berry
4 _____ mind
1 _____ air

(12)

1 _____ beans
4 _____ spread
3 _____ meal
2 _____ deaf

(24)

2 _____ bell
3 _____ easy
1 _____ attic
4 _____ reached

(36)

1 _____ believe
2 _____ direction
3 _____ moth
4 _____ syllable

© 2005 Sopris West Educational Services. All rights reserved. Practicing Basic Skills in Language Arts. Purchaser has permission to photocopy this page for classroom use only.

ANSWER SHEET

ONE-MINUTE FLUENCY BUILDER SERIES

Alphabetical Order: Placing 5 Words in Alphabetical Order

Directions: Number each group of words in alphabetical order from 1 to 5.

	First Try	Second Try
Correct		
Error		

slept
_____

sold
_____

sighed
_____

stars
_____

steps
_____

chief
_____

charm
_____

castle
_____

bury
_____

busy
_____

double
_____

helicopter
_____

dance
_____

handle
_____

quickly
_____

chief
_____

church
_____

check
_____

choose
_____

chain
_____

business
_____

burn
_____

busy
_____

bury
_____

bush
_____

safely
_____

stubby
_____

spread
_____

sorry
_____

slow
_____

pair
_____

pack
_____

patch
_____

pass
_____

penny
_____

have
_____

bunch
_____

son
_____

hung
_____

save
_____

noise
_____

toy
_____

tail
_____

nice
_____

tray
_____

© 2005 Sopris West Educational Services. All rights reserved. Practicing Basic Skills in Language Arts. Purchaser has permission to photocopy this page for classroom use only.

THINK TO WRITE

ONE-MINUTE FLUENCY BUILDER SERIES

	Correct	Error
First Try		
Second Try		

Alphabetical Order: Placing 5 Words in Alphabetical Order

Directions: Number each group of words in alphabetical order from 1 to 5.

(5)
- 2 slept
- 3 sold
- 1 sighed
- 4 stars
- 5 steps

(10)
- 3 chief
- 5 church
- 2 check
- 4 choose
- 1 chain

(15)
- 2 pair
- 1 pack
- 4 patch
- 3 pass
- 5 penny

(20)
- 5 chief
- 4 charm
- 3 castle
- 1 bury
- 2 busy

(25)
- 4 business
- 1 burn
- 5 busy
- 2 bury
- 3 bush

(30)
- 2 have
- 1 bunch
- 5 son
- 3 hung
- 4 save

(35)
- 2 double
- 4 helicopter
- 1 dance
- 3 handle
- 5 quickly

(40)
- 1 safely
- 5 stubby
- 4 spread
- 3 sorry
- 2 slow

(45)
- 2 noise
- 4 toy
- 3 tail
- 1 nice
- 5 tray

ANSWER SHEET

© 2005 Sopris West Educational Services. All rights reserved. Practicing Basic Skills in Language Arts. Purchaser has permission to photocopy this page for classroom use only.

ONE-MINUTE FLUENCY BUILDER SERIES

THINK TO WRITE

Alphabetical Order: Placing 5 Words in Alphabetical Order

Directions: Number each group of words in alphabetical order from 1 to 5.

	First Try	Second Try
Correct		
Error		

learn _____
lady _____
loud _____
life _____
list _____

thin _____
trip _____
toward _____
tiniest _____
trouble _____

seven _____
sank _____
many _____
snake _____
merry _____

center _____
cabbage _____
clumsy _____
crabs _____
costume _____

threat _____
third _____
thread _____
thief _____
true _____

bottom _____
buy _____
break _____
between _____
because _____

chase _____
check _____
church _____
choice _____
cave _____

dee _____
bend _____
beans _____
bread _____
dog _____

sight _____
sky _____
cried _____
fist _____
cold _____

Practicing Basic Skills in Language Arts • 517

© 2005 Sopris West Educational Services. All rights reserved. Practicing Basic Skills in Language Arts. Purchaser has permission to photocopy this page for classroom use only.

ONE-MINUTE FLUENCY BUILDER SERIES

THINK TO WRITE

	Correct	Error
First Try		
Second Try		

Alphabetical Order: Placing 5 Words in Alphabetical Order

Directions: Number each group of words in alphabetical order from 1 to 5.

(5)
2	learn
1	lady
5	loud
3	life
4	list

(10)
2	center
1	cabbage
3	clumsy
5	crabs
4	costume

(15)
2	chase
3	check
5	church
4	choice
1	cave

(20)
1	thin
4	trip
3	toward
2	tiniest
5	trouble

(25)
4	threat
2	third
3	thread
1	thief
5	true

(30)
4	dee
2	bend
1	beans
3	bread
5	dog

(35)
4	seven
3	sank
1	many
5	snake
2	merry

(40)
3	bottom
5	buy
4	break
2	between
1	because

(45)
4	sight
5	sky
2	cried
3	fist
1	cold

ANSWER SHEET

Practicing Basic Skills in Language Arts • 518

© 2005 Sopris West Educational Services. All rights reserved. Practicing Basic Skills in Language Arts. Purchaser has permission to photocopy this page for classroom use only.

ONE MINUTE FLUENCY BUILDER SERIES

THINK TO WRITE

	First Try	Second Try
Correct		
Error		

Alphabetical Order: Placing 5 Words in Alphabetical Order

Directions: Number each group of words in alphabetical order from 1 to 5.

Group 1
- firm
- present
- fellow
- pain
- perhaps

Group 2
- explain
- exchange
- example
- exactly
- extra

Group 3
- insist
- insect
- instead
- in
- into

Group 4
- paid
- pain
- pajamas
- palm
- paragraph

Group 5
- muffle
- pause
- ordinary
- mumble
- orchard

Group 6
- spare
- wiggle
- wriggle
- thick
- thicket

Group 7
- polite
- mention
- absolute
- violin
- glance

Group 8
- model
- motor
- mesa
- microscope
- muffle

Group 9
- season
- service
- several
- soldier
- square

Practicing Basic Skills in Language Arts • 519

© 2005 Sopris West Educational Services. All rights reserved. Practicing Basic Skills in Language Arts. Purchaser has permission to photocopy this page for classroom use only.

THINK TO WRITE

	Correct	Error
First Try		
Second Try		

Alphabetical Order: Placing 5 Words in Alphabetical Order

Directions: Number each group of words in alphabetical order from 1 to 5.

(5)

2	firm
5	present
1	fellow
3	pain
4	perhaps

(10)

1	paid
2	pain
3	pajamas
4	palm
5	paragraph

(15)

4	polite
3	mention
1	absolute
5	violin
2	glance

(20)

4	explain
3	exchange
2	example
1	exactly
5	extra

(25)

1	muffle
5	pause
4	ordinary
2	mumble
3	orchard

(30)

3	model
4	motor
1	mesa
2	microscope
5	muffle

(35)

3	insist
2	insect
4	instead
1	in
5	into

(40)

1	spare
4	wiggle
5	wriggle
2	thick
3	thicket

(45)

1	season
2	service
3	several
4	soldier
5	square

ANSWER SHEET

Practicing Basic Skills in Language Arts • 520

© 2005 Sopris West Educational Services. All rights reserved. Practicing Basic Skills in Language Arts. Purchaser has permission to photocopy this page for classroom use only.

First Try | | |
Second Try | | |
Correct | Error

THINK TO WRITE

Alphabetical Order: Placing 5 Words in Alphabetical Order

Directions: Number each group of words in alphabetical order from 1 to 5.

company	usual	thousand
drive	under	press
case	weigh	tale
doubt	wheat	rose
central	voice	shade

none	bean	perhaps
nephew	age	microscope
notebook	agree	sprinkle
naturally	kite	perfect
neighbor	fire	percent

deal	spent	thick
dollar	beyond	thirty
directory	bar	tale
dictionary	send	tamarind
dentist	honor	thump

Practicing Basic Skills in Language Arts • 521

© 2005 Sopris West Educational Services. All rights reserved. Practicing Basic Skills in Language Arts. Purchaser has permission to photocopy this page for classroom use only.

	Correct	Error
First Try		
Second Try		

ONE-MINUTE FLUENCY
BUILDER SERIES

Alphabetical Order: Placing 5 Words in Alphabetical Order
Directions: Number each group of words in alphabetical order from 1 to 5.

(5)

3	company
5	drive
1	case
4	doubt
2	central

(10)

4	none
3	nephew
5	notebook
1	naturally
2	neighbor

(15)

1	deal
5	dollar
4	directory
3	dictionary
2	dentist

(20)

2	usual
1	under
4	weigh
5	wheat
3	voice

(25)

3	bean
1	age
2	agree
5	kite
4	fire

(30)

5	spent
2	beyond
1	bar
4	send
3	honor

(35)

5	thousand
1	press
4	tale
2	rose
3	shade

(40)

4	perhaps
1	microscope
5	sprinkle
3	perfect
2	percent

(45)

3	thick
4	thirty
1	tale
2	tamarind
5	thump

ANSWER SHEET

Practicing Basic Skills in Language Arts • 522

© 2005 Sopris West Educational Services. All rights reserved. Practicing Basic Skills in Language Arts. Purchaser has permission to photocopy this page for classroom use only.

ONE-MINUTE FLUENCY
BUILDER SERIES

THINK TO WRITE

Alphabetical Order: Placing 5 Words in Alphabetical Order

Directions: Number each group of words in alphabetical order from 1 to 5.

____ simple	____ reply	____ lizard
____ certain	____ shoulder	____ lemon
____ healthy	____ practice	____ librarian
____ offer	____ special	____ license
____ train	____ swarm	____ least

____ whether	____ shinny	____ knee
____ block	____ sheath	____ jacket
____ mistake	____ whisper	____ kept
____ fold	____ whistle	____ knock
____ thicket	____ whole	____ jungle

____ twist	____ nature	____ arrive
____ lemon	____ license	____ appear
____ loft	____ orchard	____ article
____ librarian	____ pitch	____ agree
____ loaf	____ possible	____ amaze

Practicing Basic Skills in Language Arts • 523

© 2005 Sopris West Educational Services. All rights reserved. Practicing Basic Skills in Language Arts. Purchaser has permission to photocopy this page for classroom use only.

ONE-MINUTE
FLUENCY
BUILDER SERIES

THINK TO WRITE

	Correct	Error
First Try		
Second Try		

Alphabetical Order: Placing 5 Words in Alphabetical Order

Directions: Number each group of words in alphabetical order from 1 to 5.

(5)

4	simple
1	certain
2	healthy
3	offer
5	train

(10)

5	whether
1	block
3	mistake
2	fold
4	thicket

(15)

5	twist
1	lemon
4	loft
2	librarian
3	loaf

(20)

2	reply
3	shoulder
1	practice
4	special
5	swarm

(25)

2	shinny
1	sheath
3	whisper
4	whistle
5	whole

(30)

2	nature
1	license
3	orchard
4	pitch
5	possible

(35)

5	lizard
2	lemon
3	librarian
4	license
1	least

(40)

4	knee
1	jacket
3	kept
5	knock
2	jungle

(45)

4	arrive
3	appear
5	article
1	agree
2	amaze

ANSWER SHEET

Practicing Basic Skills in Language Arts • 524

© 2005 Sopris West Educational Services. All rights reserved. Practicing Basic Skills in Language Arts. Purchaser has permission to photocopy this page for classroom use only.

ONE-MINUTE FLUENCY
BUILDER SERIES

THINK TO WRITE

Alphabetical Order: Placing 5 Words in Alphabetical Order

Directions: Number each group of words in alphabetical order from 1 to 5.

First Try	Correct	Error
Second Try		

_____ wound
_____ wreck
_____ village
_____ wheat
_____ vacation

_____ condition
_____ giant
_____ dangerous
_____ circle
_____ cover

_____ adjust
_____ amuse
_____ applause
_____ aunt
_____ adventure

_____ shove
_____ tale
_____ soda
_____ thick
_____ tease

_____ obey
_____ nervous
_____ private
_____ pretend
_____ orbit

_____ decoy
_____ cotton
_____ argue
_____ bore
_____ eager

_____ mumble
_____ length
_____ obey
_____ picnic
_____ nature

_____ lemon
_____ initial
_____ knock
_____ huddle
_____ joy

_____ click
_____ celebrate
_____ cough
_____ confuse
_____ claim

© 2005 Sopris West Educational Services. All rights reserved. Practicing Basic Skills in Language Arts. Purchaser has permission to photocopy this page for classroom use only.

ONE-MINUTE FLUENCY
BUILDER SERIES

THINK TO WRITE

Alphabetical Order: Placing 5 Words in Alphabetical Order

Directions: Number each group of words in alphabetical order from 1 to 5.

First Try		Correct	Error
Second Try			

(5)

4	wound
5	wreck
2	village
3	wheat
1	vacation

(10)

2	condition
5	giant
4	dangerous
1	circle
3	cover

(15)

1	adjust
3	amuse
4	applause
5	aunt
2	adventure

(20)

1	shove
3	tale
2	soda
5	thick
4	tease

(25)

2	obey
1	nervous
5	private
4	pretend
3	orbit

(30)

4	decoy
3	cotton
1	argue
2	bore
5	eager

(35)

2	mumble
1	length
4	obey
5	picnic
3	nature

(40)

5	lemon
2	initial
4	knock
1	huddle
3	joy

(45)

3	click
1	celebrate
5	cough
4	confuse
2	claim

ANSWER SHEET

Practicing Basic Skills in Language Arts • 526

© 2005 Sopris West Educational Services. All rights reserved. Practicing Basic Skills in Language Arts. Purchaser has permission to photocopy this page for classroom use only.

ONE-MINUTE FLUENCY BUILDER SERIES

	Correct	Error
First Try		
Second Try		

Alphabetical Order: Choose Words Falling Between Two Guide Words

Directions: Mark an X before each word that comes between the guide words.

bite   move
___ apple
___ guess
___ party

matter   winter
___ lad
___ shall
___ clock

depend   island
___ juice
___ caught
___ king

airport   forest
___ tank
___ dress
___ colors

sea   zebra
___ talk
___ paper
___ unicorn

grain   toast
___ fair
___ prince
___ shall

bark   heart
___ apple
___ gift
___ kind

cleaning   people
___ move
___ noise
___ great

book   house
___ apple
___ kite
___ gift

© 2005 Sopris West Educational Services. All rights reserved. Practicing Basic Skills in Language Arts. Purchaser has permission to photocopy this page for classroom use only.

ONE-MINUTE FLUENCY BUILDER SERIES

	Correct	Error
First Try		
Second Try		

Alphabetical Order: Choose Words Falling Between Two Guide Words

Directions: Mark an X before each word that comes between the guide words.

bite   move
____ apple
X guess
____ party

matter   winter
____ lad
X shall
____ clock

depend   island
____ juice
____ caught
____ king   (2)

airport   forest
____ tank
X dress
X colors

sea   zebra
X talk
____ paper
X unicorn

grain   toast
____ fair
X prince
X shall   (8)

bark   heart
X apple
____ gift
X kind

cleaning   people
X move
X noise
X great

book   house
____ apple
____ kite
X gift   (13)

© 2005 Sopris West Educational Services. All rights reserved. Practicing Basic Skills in Language Arts. Purchaser has permission to photocopy this page for classroom use only.

	First Try	Second Try
Correct		
Error		

Alphabetical Order: Choose Words Falling Between Two Guide Words

Directions: Mark an X before each word that comes between the guide words.

chief   judge

___ bend

___ sky

___ hung

mean   spread

___ queen

___ live

___ toast

choice   hide

___ sky

___ kind

___ drive

heat   many

___ jungle

___ knife

___ learn

pie   time

___ choice

___ sight

___ read

live   wrist

___ give

___ might

___ round

noise   voice

___ toy

___ fool

___ wrist

moon   would

___ hungry

___ bunch

___ show

prince   toad

___ mouse

___ road

___ south

Practicing Basic Skills in Language Arts • 529

© 2005 Sopris West Educational Services. All rights reserved. Practicing Basic Skills in Language Arts. Purchaser has permission to photocopy this page for classroom use only.

SEE TO MARK

ONE-MINUTE FLUENCY
BUILDER SERIES

	Correct	Error
First Try		
Second Try		

Alphabetical Order: Choose Words Falling Between Two Guide Words

Directions: Mark an X before each word that comes between the guide words.

chief   judge

        bend

X   sky

X   hung

mean   spread

X   queen

        live

        toast

choice   hide

        sky

        kind

X   drive

(3)

heat   many

X   jungle

X   knife

X   learn

pie   time

        choice

X   sight

X   read

live   wrist

        give

X   might

X   round

(10)

noise   voice

X   toy

        fool

        wrist

moon   would

        hungry

        bunch

X   show

prince   toad

        mouse

X   road

X   south

(14)

ANSWER SHEET

© 2005 Sopris West Educational Services. All rights reserved. Practicing Basic Skills in Language Arts. Purchaser has permission to photocopy this page for classroom use only.

SEE TO MARK

	Correct	Error
First Try		
Second Try		

ONE-MINUTE FLUENCY
BUILDER SERIES

Alphabetical Order: Choose Words Falling Between Two Guide Words

Directions: Mark an X before each word that comes between the guide words.

baboon   barefoot

_____ band

_____ because

_____ brown

spray   sway

_____ stray

_____ sorry

_____ sing

gown   grown

_____ gave

_____ greet

_____ gift

pack   patch

_____ people

_____ pair

_____ pay

pocket   pour

_____ paper

_____ pond

_____ play

bird   burn

_____ because

_____ brought

_____ blot

straw   string

_____ stray

_____ street

_____ strong

chase   church

_____ choice

_____ check

_____ case

match   mouse

_____ money

_____ mug

_____ mist

Practicing Basic Skills in Language Arts • 531

© 2005 Sopris West Educational Services. All rights reserved. Practicing Basic Skills in Language Arts. Purchaser has permission to photocopy this page for classroom use only.

ONE MINUTE FLUENCY BUILDER SERIES

	First Try	Second Try
Correct		
Error		

Alphabetical Order: Choose Words Falling Between Two Guide Words

Directions: Mark an X before each word that comes between the guide words.

baboon   barefoot

X band

___ because

___ brown

spray   sway

X stray

___ sorry

___ sing

gown   grown

___ gave

X greet

___ gift   (3)

pack   patch

X people

X pair

___ pay

pocket   pour

___ paper

X pond

X play

bird   burn

___ because

X brought

X blot   (7)

straw   string

X stray

X street

___ strong

chase   church

X choice

X check

___ case

match   mouse

X money

___ mug

X mist   (13)

ANSWER SHEET

© 2005 Sopris West Educational Services. All rights reserved. Practicing Basic Skills in Language Arts. Purchaser has permission to photocopy this page for classroom use only.

Alphabetical Order: Choose Words Falling Between Two Guide Words

Directions: Mark an X before each word that comes between the guide words.

	First Try	Second Try
Correct		
Error		

public puff

___ resume

___ nimble

___ pudgy

blind compound

___ candy

___ build

___ because

aid any

___ anywhere

___ abode

___ agate

acre anxious

___ ambush

___ viper

___ annex

temple tower

___ tempt

___ tektite

___ tension

measure obey

___ motor

___ over

___ meet

town tube

___ toxic

___ tiller

___ tidbit

please puddle

___ prose

___ qualm

___ nimble

mouse muddy

___ meat

___ motor

___ neat

© 2005 Sopris West Educational Services. All rights reserved. Practicing Basic Skills in Language Arts. Purchaser has permission to photocopy this page for classroom use only.

ONE-MINUTE FLUENCY BUILDER SERIES

	Correct	Error
First Try		
Second Try		

Alphabetical Order: Choose Words Falling Between Two Guide Words

Directions: Mark an X before each word that comes between the guide words.

public   puff

___ resume

___ nimble

X pudgy

acre   anxious

X ambush

___ viper

X annex

town   tube

X toxic

___ tiller

___ tidbit

blind   compound

X candy

X build

___ because

temple   tower

X tempt

___ tektite

X tension

please   puddle

X prose

___ qualm

___ nimble

aid   any

___ anywhere

___ abode

___ agate   (3)

measure   obey

X motor

___ over

X meet   (9)

mouse   muddy

X meat

___ motor

___ neat   (11)

© 2005 Sopris West Educational Services. All rights reserved. Practicing Basic Skills in Language Arts. Purchaser has permission to photocopy this page for classroom use only.

SEE TO MARK

ONE-MINUTE
FLUENCY
BUILDER SERIES

	First Try	Second Try
Correct		
Error		

Alphabetical Order: Choose Words Falling Between Two Guide Words

Directions: Mark an X before each word that comes between the guide words.

marble   mention

_____ march

_____ meat

_____ mice

several   stall

_____ station

_____ steel

_____ seven

main   motor

_____ medicine

_____ many

_____ muddy

fact   firm

_____ fear

_____ fish

_____ fancy

chocolate   copy

_____ center

_____ cold

_____ chicken

block   broad

_____ blur

_____ because

_____ broad

gram   horrible

_____ improve

_____ grace

_____ handy

promise   purpose

_____ program

_____ project

_____ puppy

safety   sweater

_____ swimming

_____ silly

_____ school

Practicing Basic Skills in Language Arts • 535

© 2005 Sopris West Educational Services. All rights reserved. Practicing Basic Skills in Language Arts. Purchaser has permission to photocopy this page for classroom use only.

ONE-MINUTE FLUENCY
BUILDER SERIES

	Correct	Error
First Try		
Second Try		

Alphabetical Order: Choose Words Falling Between Two Guide Words

Directions: Mark an X before each word that comes between the guide words.

marble   mention

X	march			station
X	meat			steel
X	mice			seven	(4)

main   motor

X	medicine
X	many
X	muddy

fact   firm

X	fear			center
	fish	X		cold
X	fancy			chicken	(9)

chocolate   copy

X	blur
	because
X	broad

gram   horrible

	improve			program
	grace			project
X	handy	X		puppy	(13)

promise   purpose

safety   sweater

	swimming
X	silly
X	school

© 2005 Sopris West Educational Services. All rights reserved. Practicing Basic Skills in Language Arts. Purchaser has permission to photocopy this page for classroom use only.

ONE-MINUTE FLUENCY BUILDER SERIES

SEE TO MARK

Alphabetical Order: Choose Words Falling Between Two Guide Words

Directions: Mark an X before each word that comes between the guide words.

send   square

_____ slight

_____ seven

_____ squeeze

dandelion   direction

_____ directory

_____ division

_____ dance

range   rope

_____ rose

_____ river

_____ rapid

neighbor   nurse

_____ notebook

_____ near

_____ night

assure   battle

_____ allow

_____ baby

_____ band

nap   notice

_____ normal

_____ nail

_____ never

insist   island

_____ imagination

_____ Indian

_____ ivory

earth   fear

_____ example

_____ easy

_____ find

picnic   pony

_____ payment

_____ polite

_____ pretty

© 2005 Sopris West Educational Services. All rights reserved. Practicing Basic Skills in Language Arts. Purchaser has permission to photocopy this page for classroom use only.

	First Try	Second Try
Correct		
Error		

Alphabetical Order: Choose Words Falling Between Two Guide Words

Directions: Mark an X before each word that comes between the guide words.

send square

X _____ slight _____ directory _____ notebook

range rope

X _____ seven _____ division _____ rose

X _____ squeeze _____ dance _____ river

X _____ rapid (4)

neighbor nurse

X _____ notebook _____ allow _____ normal

nap notice

X _____ near _____ baby _____ nail

X _____ night _____ band _____ never (10)

insist island

X _____ imagination _____ example _____ payment

picnic pony

X _____ Indian _____ easy _____ polite

_____ ivory _____ find _____ pretty (13)

© 2005 Sopris West Educational Services. All rights reserved. Practicing Basic Skills in Language Arts. Purchaser has permission to photocopy this page for classroom use only.

ONE-MINUTE FLUENCY BUILDER SERIES

Guide Words: Before Page, Same Page, After Page

Directions: In front of each of these words, put a B if it is before the guide word, S if it is on the same page, and A if it is after the page.

	First Try	Second Try
Correct		
Error		

importunate   improbable

_____ indigo	_____ improve
_____ inadequacy	_____ imperfection
_____ impolite	_____ impose
_____ impression	_____ impound
_____ implement	_____ imprison
_____ inability	_____ impeach

bruise   buckle

_____ budge	_____ buffoon
_____ bubble	_____ broadcast
_____ browse	_____ bronze
_____ bucket	_____ bud
_____ brush	_____ buckskin
_____ brutal	_____ broil

breathe   bridle

_____ bribe	_____ brevity
_____ bronco	_____ breather
_____ brazen	_____ broken
_____ bring	_____ bramble
_____ bracket	_____ brief
_____ bridge	_____ breath

ape   apology

_____ aphid	_____ apiary
_____ appearance	_____ apoplexy
_____ antler	_____ arbitrary
_____ apologetics	_____ anybody
_____ apathy	_____ arcade
_____ aperture	_____ apartment

Practicing Basic Skills in Language Arts • 539

© 2005 Sopris West Educational Services. All rights reserved. Practicing Basic Skills in Language Arts. Purchaser has permission to photocopy this page for classroom use only.

ONE MINUTE FLUENCY BUILDER SERIES

	Correct	Error
First Try		
Second Try		

SEE TO WRITE

Guide Words: Before Page, Same Page, After Page

Directions: In front of each of these words, put a B if it is before the guide word, S if it is on the same page, and A if it is after the page.

importunate   improbable

A	indigo	A	improve
A	inadequacy	B	imperfection
B	impolite	S	impose
S	impression	S	impound
B	implement	S	imprison
A	inability	B	impeach (12)

bruise   buckle

A	budge	A	buffoon
S	bubble	B	broadcast
B	browse	B	bronze
S	bucket	A	bud
S	brush	A	buckskin
S	brutal	B	broil (24)

breathe   bridle

S	bribe	S	brevity
A	bronco	S	breather
B	brazen	A	broken
A	bring	B	bramble
B	bracket	A	brief
S	bridge	B	breath (36)

ape   apology

S	aphid	S	apiary
A	appearance	A	apoplexy
B	antler	A	arbitrary
S	apologetics	B	anybody
B	apathy	A	arcade
S	aperture	B	apartment (48)

ANSWER SHEET

Practicing Basic Skills in Language Arts • 540

© 2005 Sopris West Educational Services. All rights reserved. Practicing Basic Skills in Language Arts. Purchaser has permission to photocopy this page for classroom use only.

	Correct	Error
First Try		
Second Try		

Guide Words: Before Page, Same Page, After Page

Directions: In front of each of these words, put a B if it is before the guide word, S if it is on the same page, and A if it is after the page.

ONE MINUTE FLUENCY BUILDER SERIES

preacher   precisionist

___ preamble   ___ precedent
___ prescribe   ___ precipitation
___ prairie   ___ pragmatics
___ pow-wow   ___ precinct
___ preeminent   ___ predecessor
___ poverty   ___ presage

other   outclass

___ oven   ___ ought
___ otherwise   ___ ottoman
___ oriental   ___ ourselves
___ orifice   ___ organ
___ original   ___ outlaw
___ outrage   ___ outdoors

lording   louse

___ lubricant   ___ love
___ lord   ___ lounge
___ lost   ___ loot
___ longitudinal   ___ lose
___ lottery   ___ loosen
___ lousy   ___ lozenge

honor   hopscotch

___ hitch   ___ hooligan
___ Hopi   ___ hood
___ hornet   ___ humanity
___ holiday   ___ horizon
___ hopper   ___ homage
___ hollandaise   ___ horror

© 2005 Sopris West Educational Services. All rights reserved. Practicing Basic Skills in Language Arts. Purchaser has permission to photocopy this page for classroom use only.

ONE-MINUTE FLUENCY BUILDER SERIES

SEE TO WRITE

Guide Words: Before Page, Same Page, After Page

Directions: In front of each of these words, put a B if it is before the guide word, S if it is on the same page, and A if it is after the page.

	Correct	Error
First Try		
Second Try		

---

preacher   precisionist

S	preamble	S	precedent
A	prescribe	S	precipitation
B	prairie	B	pragmatics
B	pow-wow	S	precinct
A	preeminent	A	predecessor
B	poverty	A	presage (12)

other   outclass

A	oven	S	ought
S	otherwise	S	ottoman
B	oriental	S	ourselves
B	orifice	B	organ
B	original	A	outlaw
A	outrage	A	outdoors (24)

---

lording   louse

A	lubricant	A	love
B	lord	S	lounge
S	lost	B	loot
B	longitudinal	S	lose
S	lottery	B	loosen
A	lousy	A	lozenge (36)

honor   hopscotch

B	hitch	S	hooligan
S	Hopi	S	hood
A	hornet	A	humanity
B	holiday	A	horizon
S	hopper	B	homage
B	hollandaise	A	horror (48)

ANSWER SHEET

© 2005 Sopris West Educational Services. All rights reserved. Practicing Basic Skills in Language Arts. Purchaser has permission to photocopy this page for classroom use only.

SEE TO WRITE

	Correct	Error
First Try		
Second Try		

Guide Words: Before Page, Same Page, After Page

Directions: In front of each of these words, put a B if it is before the guide word, S if it is on the same page, and A if it is after the page.

describable   despicable

_____ designation	_____ despite
_____ decoy	_____ desertion
_____ describe	_____ destroyer
_____ detachment	_____ desperation
_____ decompress	_____ deface
_____ detain	_____ dedicate

ruby   ruler

_____ robin	_____ ribber
_____ rubicund	_____ ruffle
_____ rugged	_____ rumble
_____ rodent	_____ rude
_____ ruckus	_____ rumor
_____ ruminate	_____ rummage

barren   basil

_____ barrette	_____ banal
_____ bare	_____ basify
_____ bassoon	_____ barnyard
_____ basilica	_____ batch
_____ bewitch	_____ basement
_____ basalt	_____ barrage

trade   train

_____ tramp	_____ trance
_____ tractable	_____ traceable
_____ trademark	_____ trail
_____ transcribe	_____ tramway
_____ tractor	_____ tourney
_____ tragedy	_____ traffic

© 2005 Sopris West Educational Services. All rights reserved. Practicing Basic Skills in Language Arts. Purchaser has permission to photocopy this page for classroom use only.

	Correct	Error
First Try		
Second Try		

ONE-MINUTE FLUENCY BUILDER SERIES

Guide Words: Before Page, Same Page, After Page

Directions: In front of each of these words, put a B if it is before the guide word, S if it is on the same page, and A if it is after the page.

describable despicable

S	designation	**A**	despite	
B	decoy	**S**	desertion	
S	describe	**A**	destroyer	
A	detachment	**S**	desperation	
B	decompress	**B**	deface	
A	detain	**B**	dedicate	(12)

ruby ruler

B	robin	**B**	ribber	
B	rubicund	**S**	ruffle	
S	rugged	**A**	rumble	
B	rodent	**S**	rude	
S	ruckus	**A**	rumor	
A	ruminate	**A**	rummage	(24)

barren basil

S	barrette	**B**	banal	
B	bare	**S**	basify	
A	bassoon	**B**	barnyard	
A	basilica	**A**	batch	
A	bewitch	**S**	basement	
S	basalt	**B**	barrage	(36)

trade train

A	tramp	**A**	trance	
B	tractable	**B**	traceable	
S	trademark	**S**	trail	
A	transcribe	**A**	tramway	
B	tractor	**B**	tourney	
S	tragedy	**S**	traffic	(48)

© 2005 Sopris West Educational Services. All rights reserved. Practicing Basic Skills in Language Arts. Purchaser has permission to photocopy this page for classroom use only.

ONE-MINUTE FLUENCY
BUILDER SERIES

	Correct	Error
First Try		
Second Try		

Guide Words: Before Page, Same Page, After Page

Directions: In front of each of these words, put a B if it is before the guide word, S if it is on the same page, and A if it is after the page.

most   moulage

	mother	____	mud
____	motif	____	much
____	moon	____	mop
____	motive	____	mouse
____	mortar	____	mosquito
____	move	____	motor

pancake   pant

	pear	____	paper
____	panther	____	panic
____	palm	____	pamper
____	pan	____	panda
____	pane	____	pang
____	pantry	____	pale

describe   desperation

	detail	____	denote
____	desire	____	demonstrate
____	detach	____	demon
____	deserve	____	deny
____	desk	____	desert
____	date	____	dentist

shelf   shifter

	shiftless	____	shatter
____	sheaf	____	sheared
____	shield	____	shekel
____	shirt	____	shocker
____	shepherd	____	sherbet
____	shelter	____	shining

© 2005 Sopris West Educational Services. All rights reserved. Practicing Basic Skills in Language Arts. Purchaser has permission to photocopy this page for classroom use only.

ONE-MINUTE FLUENCY BUILDER SERIES

	Correct	Error
First Try		
Second Try		

SEE TO WRITE

Guide Words: Before Page, Same Page, After Page

Directions: In front of each of these words, put a B if it is before the guide word, S if it is on the same page, and A if it is after the page.

most   moulage

S	mother	A	mud
S	motif	A	much
B	moon	B	mop
S	motive	A	mouse
B	mortar	B	mosquito
A	move	S	motor

(12)

pancake   pant

A	pear	A	paper
A	panther	S	panic
B	palm	B	pamper
B	pan	S	panda
S	pane	S	pang
A	pantry	B	pale

(24)

describe   desperation

A	detail	B	denote
S	desire	B	demonstrate
A	detach	B	demon
S	deserve	B	deny
S	desk	S	desert
B	date	B	dentist

(36)

shelf   shifter

A	shiftless	B	shatter
B	sheaf	B	sheared
S	shield	B	shekel
A	shirt	A	shocker
S	shepherd	S	sherbet
S	shelter	A	shining

(48)

© 2005 Sopris West Educational Services. All rights reserved. Practicing Basic Skills in Language Arts. Purchaser has permission to photocopy this page for classroom use only.

ONE-MINUTE FLUENCY BUILDER SERIES

SEE TO WRITE

	First Try	Second Try
Correct		
Error		

Guide Words: Find Page in Dictionary for Each Word

Directions: Using a dictionary, write the page number on which the word appears.

crocodile	unit	_____	arrow
academy	pitcher	_____	gem
accent	instrument	_____	clout
boxer	juvenile	_____	walrus
flamingo	lasso	_____	zebra
iceberg	lad	_____	wreath
lens	mallard	_____	aquarium
television	penguin	_____	clog
stag	English sparrow	_____	jellyfish
rudder	enclosure	_____	onion
ransom	footstool	_____	olive branch
pot	handspring	_____	American
megaphone	occasion	_____	occupant
tonsil	understanding	_____	uniform
chart	appendix	_____	porch
future	teapot	_____	dictionary
trout	skydiving	_____	planet

Practicing Basic Skills in Language Arts • 547

© 2005 Sopris West Educational Services. All rights reserved. Practicing Basic Skills in Language Arts. Purchaser has permission to photocopy this page for classroom use only.

ONE-MINUTE FLUENCY BUILDER SERIES

Guide Words: Find Page in Dictionary for Each Word

Directions: Using a dictionary, write the page number on which the word appears.

crocodile	unit	arrow	(3)
academy	pitcher	gem	(6)
accent	instrument	clout	(9)
boxer	juvenile	walrus	(12)
flamingo	lasso	zebra	(15)
iceberg	lad	wreath	(18)
lens	mallard	aquarium	(21)
television	penguin	clog	(24)
stag	English sparrow	jellyfish	(27)
rudder	enclosure	onion	(30)
ransom	footstool	olive branch	(33)
pot	handspring	American	(36)
megaphone	occasion	occupant	(39)
tonsil	understanding	uniform	(42)
chart	appendix	porch	(45)
future	teapot	dictionary	(48)
trout	skydiving	planet	(51)

ANSWERS MAY VARY

ANSWER SHEET

Practicing Basic Skills in Language Arts • 548

© 2005 Sopris West Educational Services. All rights reserved. Practicing Basic Skills in Language Arts. Purchaser has permission to photocopy this page for classroom use only.

Appendix

Student _____ Grade _____ Academic Year _____ Skill _____

Equal Interval Graph

Count per Minute

300 290 280 270 260 250 240 230 220 210 200 190 180 170 160 150 140 130 120 110 100 90 80 70 60 50 40 30 20 10 0

1 2 3 4 5 6 7 8 9 10 11 12 13 14 15 16 17 18 19 20 21 22 23 24 25 26 27 28 29 30 31 32 33 34 35 36 37 38 39 40 41 42 43 44 45

Days

Date | M | T | W | Th | F | Date | M | T | W | Th | F | Date | M | T | W | Th | F

Date | M | T | W | Th | F | Date | M | T | W | Th | F | Date | M | T | W | Th | F

Date | M | T | W | Th | F | Date | M | T | W | Th | F | Date | M | T | W | Th | F

Copyright 2004 Sopris West Educational Services. Practicing Basic Skills in Language Arts. This page may be photocopied.

Academic Chart

Student _____ **Grade** _____ **Academic Year** _____ **Skill** _____

Weeks

	1	2	3	4	5	6	7	8	9	10

Count per Minute: 300, 200, 100, 90, 80, 70, 60, 50, 40, 30, 20, 10, 9, 8, 7, 6, 5, 4, 3, 2, 1

M W F | M W F | M W F | M W F | M W F | M W F | M W F | M W F | M W F | M W F

Days

0 — 10 — 20 — 30 — 40 — 50 — 60 — 70

Date | M T W Th F | Date | M T W Th F
Date | M T W Th F | Date | M T W Th F
Date | M T W Th F | Date | M T W Th F

Copyright 2004 Sopris West Educational Services. Practicing Basic Skills in Language Arts. This page may be photocopied.